MySQL Cluster 7.5

inside and out

Mikael Ronström

February 9, 2018

February 2018: First edition
Revision History for First edition:
2 feb 2018 First release

Förlag: BoD - Books on Demand, Stockholm, Sverige
Tryck: BoD - Books on Demand, Norderstedt, Tyskland
ISBN: 978-91-7699-814-4

Contents

ABOUT MySQL CLUSTER 7.5   XVII
    0.1   About the author Mikael Ronström xviii
    0.2   Purpose of the book xix

I   WHEN TO USE MySQL CLUSTER   1

1   WHAT IS SPECIAL WITH MySQL CLUSTER   2
    1.1   AlwaysOn for reads and writes 3
    1.2   Global solution for replication 4
    1.3   Consistency of data in large clusters 6
    1.4   High read and write Scalability 8
    1.5   Predictable response time 10
    1.6   Base platform for data storage 11
    1.7   Multi-dimensional scaling 12
    1.8   Non-blocking 2PC transaction protocol 12
    1.9   Global checkpoints 13
    1.10 Automatically Parallelised and Distributed Queries 13

2   RATIONALE FOR MySQL CLUSTER   14
    2.1   Separation of Data Server and Query Server 14
    2.2   Predictable response time requirements 21
    2.3   MySQL Cluster and multi-core architectures 27
    2.4   Shared nothing architecture 28
    2.5   MySQL Cluster and the CAP theorem 29
    2.6   OLTP, OLAP and relational models 30
    2.7   Data storage requirements 31

3   USE CASES FOR MySQL CLUSTER   33
    3.1   Networking applications 34
    3.2   Telecom servers 36
    3.3   Gaming systems 41
    3.4   Financial applications 43

3.5   Fraud Detection   44

3.6   Web applications   44

3.7   Soft real-time applications   45

3.8   Oracle OpenStack   45

3.9   GE   46

3.10   Hadoop File Server   49

3.11   LDAP Server   51

3.12   NoSQL Applications   51

3.13   Conclusion   52

4   NDB AND INNODB   53

4.1   Differences between NDB and InnoDB   53

4.2   Consistency Model differences   57

4.3   Foreign Key differences   58

4.4   Differences in Online Change   58

4.5   Challenges in replacing InnoDB   58

5   MYSQL CLUSTER AND INNODB CLUSTER   59

5.1   Comparison to Galera Cluster   59

5.2   Group Replication   59

5.3   Differences between MySQL clustering solutions   60

5.4   Differences in query execution   63

5.5   Differences in recovery   63

5.6   Differences in handling node failures   64

5.7   Sharding differences   65

5.8   Multi-master differences   65

5.9   Detailed differences   66

5.10   What clustering solution to select   67

II   INTRODUCTION TO DATABASE CONCEPTS   70

6   RELATION MODEL   71

6.1   Basic concepts   71

6.2   Distributed Relational Model   73

6.3   Replicated Relational Model   74

6.4   Hashmaps   75

6.5   Read backup replica tables   76

6.6   Fully replicated tables   76

7   TRANSACTIONAL MODEL   77

7.1   Basic transaction theory   77

7.2   Locking theory   79

7.3 Distributed transactions 82

8 COMPUTER MODEL 85

8.1 CPU Core 85

8.2 CPU Socket 89

8.3 Computer 90

8.4 Computer network 91

8.5 Distributed Data Centers 91

III INTRODUCTION TO MySQL CLUSTER 92

9 MySQL CLUSTER ARCHITECTURE 93

9.1 Node group concept (Shards) 95

9.2 Program types 96

10 MySQL CLUSTER APIs 100

10.1 MySQL APIs 102

10.2 Direct NDB APIs 102

10.3 memcached 103

10.4 OpenLDAP 103

IV GETTING STARTED 104

11 GETTING STARTED FOR DEVELOPERS 106

11.1 Getting Started on Mac OS X 106

11.2 Getting Started on Windows 120

11.3 Using MySQL Cluster Configurator for development 121

12 INSTALLING MySQL CLUSTER 122

12.1 Installing using *yum* 122

12.2 Installing using *apt* 125

12.3 Installing using *Zypper* on Suse 126

12.4 MySQL Cluster packages 126

12.5 Install using an RPM package 128

12.6 Installing on Debian 128

12.7 Installing tarballs on Linux 129

12.8 Installing on Solaris 129

12.9 Preparing to run MySQL Cluster on Linux 129

12.10 Installing on FreeBSD 132

13 STARTING PROGRAMS 133

13.1 Order of starting 133

13.2 Starting *ndb_mgmd* 135

13.3 Starting *ndbmtd* 138

13.4 Starting a MySQL Server (*mysqld*) 141

13.5 Starting *ndb_mgm* 142

13.6 Starting *mcmd* 143

14 MySQL Cluster configuration files   144

14.1 General rules for MySQL configuration files 144

14.2 Cluster configuration file 145

14.3 MySQL configuration file 147

15 MySQL Cluster and Docker   149

15.1 Using Docker to avoid installation problems 150

15.2 Using Docker on a single host 152

15.3 Using Docker overlay network 152

15.4 Using Docker Swarm 153

15.5 Setting the password on MySQL Server container 153

15.6 Running the NDB management client 153

15.7 Using Docker to limit memory resources 153

15.8 Using Docker to limit CPU resources 154

15.9 Using Docker and cgroups to control CPU and memory 155

16 Building MySQL Cluster   156

16.1 Linux 157

16.2 Solaris 158

16.3 FreeBSD 158

16.4 Mac OS X 158

16.5 Windows 158

17 HW setups for MySQL Cluster   159

17.1 Single host setup 159

17.2 NDB as an In-memory storage engine for MySQL 160

17.3 Minimum configuration for AlwaysOn 160

17.4 Setting up MySQL Cluster for secure operation 162

17.5 Scaling out from the simple HA setup 163

17.6 Set up of MySQL Cluster for multi-cluster apps 166

V   MySQL Cluster as a SQL engine   168

18 Basic SQL statements   170

18.1 Create a table 170

18.2 Altering a table 172

18.3 Querying a table   174

18.4 Writing to a table   176

18.5 Transactions   176

18.6 Drop/Truncate Table   176

18.7 Indexes   176

18.8 Foreign Keys   180

18.9 Optimize/Analyze Table   180

18.10 BLOBs   180

18.11 Row format of NDB tables   180

18.12 Disk Data Columns   180

18.13 MySQL Replication of NDB tables   180

19 NDB ROW DATA STRUCTURE   181

19.1 Row format   181

19.2 Fixed row format   185

19.3 Dynamic row format   186

20 FOREIGN KEY HANDLING   187

20.1 Foreign key considerations   190

21 BLOB HANDLING   191

22 DISK COLUMNS   193

22.1 Row format for disk columns   194

22.2 Tablespaces   194

22.3 UNDO log   195

22.4 Syntax for disk data   195

22.5 Page Manager   197

22.6 Considerations for disk data tables   198

23 TABLE OPTIONS   200

23.1 Read Backup feature   200

23.2 Fully replicated tables   201

23.3 Partitioning of tables   202

23.4 Considerations for selecting number of partitions   204

23.5 Partition Balance   205

23.6 Setting explicit number of partitions   207

23.7 No REDO logging   207

23.8 Schema Considerations   208

24 MySQL CONCEPTS IN NDB STORAGE ENGINE   209

24.1 MySQL Queries   209

24.2 MySQL Databases   209

24.3 MySQL Triggers 209

24.4 MySQL Views 210

24.5 MySQL Events 210

24.6 MySQL Stored Procedures 210

24.7 MySQL Functions 211

24.8 MySQL User Management 211

24.9 MySQL Transactions 211

24.10 Savepoints 211

24.11 MySQL Prepared Statements 211

24.12 MySQL Explain statements 211

24.13 Table locks 212

24.14 XA support 212

25 ALTERING A TABLE   213

25.1 Online meta data operations 213

25.2 Online Add Column 215

25.3 Online Create Tablespace 216

25.4 Online Create Logfile group 216

25.5 Online Add Node 217

25.6 Optimize Table 218

25.7 Reorganise Table 219

25.8 Offline meta data operations 219

VI   CONCEPTS IN MySQL CLUSTER   221

26 NON-BLOCKING 2PC   223

26.1 Idea behind new two-phase commit protocol 224

26.2 Achieving a non-blocking commit protocol 226

26.3 Global checkpoint protocol 227

26.4 Handling cluster crash 229

26.5 Impact of Read Backup feature 230

26.6 Conclusions 230

27 ROUTING OF READS AND WRITES   231

27.1 Choosing the MySQL Server 231

27.2 Choosing the node of the transaction coordinator 232

27.3 Choosing the tc thread 233

27.4 Choosing the data node for reading 233

27.5 Choosing the ldm thread 233

27.6 Choosing the data nodes for writing 233

28 CONCURRENCY CONTROL   234

28.1 Row locking 235

28.2 Consistency Models 236

28.3 Read Committed mode 237

28.4 Locking and Unique indexes 237

28.5 Locking and BLOB tables 238

29 PARALLEL QUERY 239

29.1 Full table scan in NDB 239

29.2 Range scan in NDB 239

29.3 Partition pruned range scans 240

29.4 Pushdown joins 240

29.5 Condition pushdown 242

30 SPECIALISED MySQL SERVERS 243

VII TOOLS TO IMPORT AND EXPORT DATA 244

31 IMPORT DATA 246

31.1 *ndb_restore* using Backups 247

31.2 Importing from mysqldump files 247

31.3 Alter Table 247

31.4 *mysqlimport* 247

32 EXPORT DATA 248

32.1 *mysqldump* 248

32.2 SELECT INTO OUTFILE 249

33 BACKUP 250

33.1 Backup algorithm 250

33.2 The START BACKUP command 251

33.3 Aborting a backup 251

33.4 Backup file placement 251

33.5 Backup configuration 252

33.6 Backup file management 252

33.7 Backing up metadata in MySQL Cluster 252

34 RESTORE 254

34.1 Restoring metadata 256

34.2 Partial restore 256

34.3 Restore for upgrade 257

34.4 Restore as part of MySQL Cluster Replication 258

34.5 Restoring Distributed Privileges 259

34.6 Various other use cases for *ndb_restore* 259

34.7 Special parameters for *ndb_restore* 259

VIII MYSQL CLUSTER APIS   260

35 C++ NDB API   262
    35.1 Meta data operations 263
    35.2 Initialising the NDB API and MySQL client API 263
    35.3 Concurrency in the NDB API 263
    35.4 Ndb cluster connection 264
    35.5 Ndb object 266
    35.6 Setting up a row 267
    35.7 Transactions 269
    35.8 Key operations 272
    35.9 Scan operations 273
    35.10 Options 275
    35.11 Scan partitioning info 276
    35.12 Interpreter commands as part of NDB API operations 283
    35.13 Scan example 284
    35.14 NDB Event API 285
    35.15 Pushdown Join 288
    35.16 Asynchronous API 289
    35.17 *flexAsynch* Architecture 289

36 CLUSTERJ, API FOR JAVA AND SCALA   290
    36.1 Installing ClusterJ 290
    36.2 Compiling ClusterJ applications 291
    36.3 Executing a ClusterJ application 291
    36.4 ClusterJ annotations 295
    36.5 Startup example code 297
    36.6 Session Object 298
    36.7 Transactions 301
    36.8 Creating a query 302
    36.9 Column type mappings 305
    36.10 ClusterJ reconnect 306
    36.11 Dynamic mapping of rows 306

37 NODE.JS API   307
    37.1 Installing Database Jones 307
    37.2 Installing *ndb* adapter 308
    37.3 The Tweet sample application 309
    37.4 ConnectionProperties 310

37.5 Cluster connection object 312

37.6 Startup example 314

37.7 Session operations 315

37.8 Final comments 319

IX GLOBAL REPLICATION   320

38 INTERNALS OF MYSQL CLUSTER REPLICATION   321

38.1 Data node triggers 321

38.2 Epochs 322

38.3 Epoch Buffers 322

38.4 Send buffers 324

38.5 MySQL replication server internals 324

38.6 Limitations of MySQL Cluster Replication 324

39 MULTI-SITE MYSQL CLUSTER   327

39.1 MySQL Replication 328

39.2 Architecture of MySQL Cluster Replication 329

39.3 Tables used by MySQL Cluster Replication 331

39.4 Epochs 336

39.5 Setting up a replication channel between two clusters 337

39.6 Point-in-Time backups 341

39.7 Read Slave Clusters 341

39.8 Characteristics of slave applier for NDB 342

39.9 Purging MySQL Replication files 342

40 GLOBAL FAIL-OVER ARCHITECTURE   344

40.1 Setup for fail-over scenario 344

40.2 Discovering failure of a replication channel 344

40.3 Discover failure of a cluster 348

40.4 Cluster fail over 350

41 GLOBALLY DISTRIBUTED MYSQL CLUSTER   351

41.1 NDB$MAX_DELETE_WIN(column_name) 351

41.2 NDB$OLD(column_name) 352

41.3 NDB$EPOCH2 353

41.4 Conflict detection tables 353

41.5 Setup for circular replication 355

41.6 ndb-log update-as-minimal 358

41.7 Insert-Insert conflicts 358

42 EXTREMELY AVAILABLE SOLUTIONS   359

42.1 Setting up transaction-based conflict detection 360

42.2 Characteristics of this solution 362

42.3 Conflict handling 362

42.4 More comments 363

X   MANAGEMENT OF MYSQL CLUSTER   364

43 NDBINFO TABLES   366

43.1 Reasons to use *ndbinfo* 366

43.2 How ndbinfo works 367

43.3 Metadata tables 369

43.4 Connection information 370

43.5 Configuration information 371

43.6 Transaction information 371

43.7 Live transaction information 373

43.8 Memory information 374

43.9 Thread statistics 376

43.10 Node information 378

43.11 Restart information 379

43.12 Local checkpoint information 381

43.13 Disk page cache information 382

43.14 Communication information 383

43.15 Status of REDO and UNDO logs 383

43.16 Fragment statistics 384

43.17 Error messages 385

43.18 Summary of *ndbinfo* information 385

44 NDB MANAGEMENT CLIENT *ndb_mgm*   386

44.1 SHOW command 386

44.2 START/STOP commands 387

44.3 REPORT command 389

44.4 STATUS command 389

44.5 PROMPT command 390

44.6 ENTER SINGLE USER MODE command 390

44.7 CLUSTERLOG command 391

44.8 DUMP command 391

44.9 EXIT/QUIT command 391

44.10 CONNECT command 391

44.11 PURGE STALE SESSIONS 392

45 CLUSTER LOG AND NODE LOGS   393

45.1 The Cluster log 393

45.2 Management server node log 397

45.3 Data node logs 397

45.4 Summary of logs 404

46 TROUBLESHOOTING NDB   405

46.1 Data node crash output 406

46.2 Debugging MySQL Cluster 409

47 ONLINE CHANGES OF CONFIGURATION   411

47.1 Cluster configuration 411

47.2 Adding nodes to the cluster 411

47.3 Managing the configuration database 412

47.4 Procedure to perform online config changes 418

47.5 Online changes of MySQL Server configuration 419

47.6 Online add MySQL Server 419

47.7 Online change of data node configuration 419

47.8 Online add data node 420

XI   RECOVERY IN MySQL CLUSTER   422

48 CRASH HANDLING   424

48.1 Replication inside a cluster 424

48.2 Failures supported from a fully functional cluster 425

48.3 Arbitrator 426

48.4 External Arbitrator 426

48.5 Handling startup and network partitioning 426

49 NDB RECOVERY ARCHITECTURE   428

49.1 Transaction protocol 430

49.2 Transaction coordinator failure protocol 432

49.3 Global Checkpoint protocol 432

49.4 Local checkpoint protocol 434

49.5 Schema transaction protocol 436

49.6 Node registration protocol 436

49.7 Heartbeat protocol 437

49.8 Node failure protocol 437

49.9 Graceful shutdown protocol 437

49.10 Watchdog handling 438

49.11 Node restart activities 438

49.12 Initial node restart activities 439

50 Optimising restart times   440
    50.1 Early phases 440
    50.2 Load data phase 441
    50.3 UNDO log execution 441
    50.4 REDO log execution 442
    50.5 Rebuild ordered indexes 442
    50.6 Rebuild unique indexes 442
    50.7 Copy fragment phase 442
    50.8 Local checkpoint phase 443
    50.9 Initial node restart 443
    50.10 Handling MySQL Replication Servers 444
    50.11 Final words 444

51 NDB startup   445
    51.1 Initial start 445
    51.2 Node restart 445
    51.3 System restart 446
    51.4 Initial node restart 446
    51.5 NDB start phases 447

XII Internals of NDB Cluster   449

52 Data Node Architecture   451
    52.1 Block and Signal Architecture 451
    52.2 Receive handling in Data Node 454
    52.3 Send handling in Data Node 454
    52.4 NDB connection setup protocol 455
    52.5 NDB signal header definition 456

53 API Node Architecture   458
    53.1 Cluster connection 458
    53.2 User threads 459
    53.3 NDB API send threads 459
    53.4 NDB API receive threads 459
    53.5 NDB API cluster manager threads 460
    53.6 Blocks in API nodes 460

54 Blocks in a Data Node   461
    54.1 LDM Blocks 461
    54.2 TC blocks 463
    54.3 Main thread blocks 463
    54.4 Rep blocks 466

54.5   THRMAN   467

54.6   TRPMAN   467

55 VIRTUAL MACHINE IN DATA NODES   468

55.1   Thread types in *ndbmtd*   468

55.2   Communication between threads in *ndbmtd*   470

55.3   Scheduler in *ndbmtd*   470

55.4   Single-threaded Data Nodes, *ndbd*   470

56 DETAILED NDB INTERNALS   472

56.1   Internal triggers in MySQL Cluster   472

56.2   Transporter Model   472

56.3   Memory Allocation principles   473

56.4   Angel process   473

57 SIGNAL FLOWS IN NDB   474

57.1   Key operations   474

57.2   Table scan operations   480

57.3   Pushdown joins   482

57.4   Foreign Keys   483

57.5   Table Reorganisation   483

57.6   Meta data operations   483

57.7   Cluster Manager operations   483

57.8   Local checkpoint protocol   483

XIII   CONFIGURING MYSQL CLUSTER   486

58 PROCEDURE TO DEFINE CONFIGURATION   488

58.1   Setting *NoOfReplicas* and *NoOfFragmentLogParts*   488

58.2   Setting up nodes   489

58.3   Example *config.ini*   491

59 CONFIGURING DATA NODES   492

59.1   Configuring memory resources   492

59.2   Configuring Transaction resources   493

59.3   Configuring Schema resources   497

59.4   Event configuration   500

59.5   Basic thread configurations   501

59.6   Restart configuration   502

59.7   Configuring Deadlock Detection   506

59.8   Configuring logging   507

59.9   Diskless configuration   507

59.10 Watchdog checks 507

59.11 Configuring index statistics 508

59.12 Specialized configuration options 510

59.13 Example *config.ini* 513

60 CONFIGURATION OF API AND MGM NODES   **514**

60.1 Configuring send buffers 514

60.2 Configuring arbitration 514

60.3 Configuring scan batching 514

60.4 Connect configuration 515

60.5 *HeartbeatThreadPriority* 516

60.6 *DefaultOperationRedoProblemAction* 516

60.7 *DefaultHashmapSize* 516

60.8 *ApiVerbose* 517

60.9 Management server nodes 517

60.10 Example configuration 518

61 COMMUNICATION CONFIGURATION   **519**

61.1 Configuring send buffers 519

61.2 *Group* 520

61.3 *SendSignalId* 520

61.4 *Checksum* 520

61.5 *OverloadLimit* 520

61.6 *ReceiveBufferMemory* 520

61.7 Configuring OS properties 521

62 CONFIGURING MySQL CLUSTER FILE SYSTEMS   **522**

62.1 Directory placement 522

62.2 Compressed files 524

62.3 Configuring the REDO log files and local checkpoints 524

62.4 Configuring backups 529

62.5 Configuring global checkpoints 529

62.6 Memory Buffers for disk columns 530

62.7 New tablespace and undo log files 530

62.8 File system configurations 530

62.9 Final words 531

63 CONFIGURING THE MySQL SERVER   **533**

63.1 Basic MySQL server options 533

63.2 Connection options 535

63.3 Defaults for table creation 536

63.4 Alter table options 537

63.5   Execution options 537
63.6   Optimizer options 541
63.7   Receive thread configuration 542
63.8   MySQL Cluster replication setup 542
63.9   *--ndb-show-foreign-key-mock-tables* 545
63.10 Version information 545
63.11 *--core-file* 545
63.12 MySQL Server Status variables 545

64 ANALYSIS OF HYPERTHREADING PERFORMANCE   546
64.1   *x86* servers 546
64.2   SPARC servers 548

65 ADVANCED THREAD CONFIGURATIONS   550
65.1   Setting up ndbd for real-time operation 550
65.2   Setting up ndbtmd for real-time operations 552

66 LINUX CONFIGURATION   559
66.1   Linux infrastructure 559
66.2   Linux receive interrupt handling 560
66.3   Transmit Packet Steering (XPS) 563
66.4   Linux CPU isolation 564
66.5   Conclusion 564
66.6   Example CPU budget 565

67 BASIC CONFIGURATION SETUP   567

XIV VARIOUS TOPICS   571

68 PLATFORM SUPPORT   572
68.1   MySQL Cluster on x86 572
68.2   MySQL Cluster on Linux 572
68.3   MySQL Cluster on Windows 572
68.4   MySQL Cluster on Solaris 572
68.5   MySQL Cluster on Mac OS X 572
68.6   MySQL Cluster on Intel NUC 573
68.7   MySQL Cluster on FreeBSD 573
68.8   MySQL Cluster on ARM 573
68.9   MySQL Cluster on Power 573

69 MYSQL CLUSTER IN THE CLOUD   574
69.1   General considerations 574
69.2   Cloud Architectures 575

69.3 Cloud instances for MySQL Cluster 576

69.4 Size of MySQL Servers in the Cloud 580

69.5 Availability Domains/Zones 581

69.6 Azure cloud 582

70 TEST FRAMEWORK   583

70.1 MTR 583

70.2 Autotest 584

70.3 Hugo 584

70.4 Battery of tests 585

70.5 Unit tests 585

70.6 Manual tests 585

71 DBT2-0.37.50 BENCHMARK SCRIPTS   586

71.1 How to setup benchmarks on Linux/Solaris/Mac OS X 586

71.2 Sysbench benchmark 590

71.3 DBT2 benchmark 594

71.4 flexAsynch benchmark 598

71.5 Restart tests 602

71.6 Advanced configurations 602

72 HISTORY OF MySQL CLUSTER   610

73 MySQL CLUSTER VERSIONS   614

73.1 MySQL Cluster 7.5 614

73.2 MySQL Cluster 7.4 615

73.3 MySQL Cluster 7.3 615

73.4 MySQL Cluster 7.2 615

73.5 MySQL Cluster 6.3 615

ABOUT MySQL CLUSTER 7.5

MySQL Cluster is a combination of the MySQL Server and the NDB storage engine. NDB is a distributed data server supporting tables with in-memory rows and indexes and non-indexed data stored on disk. MySQL is a query server that can use multiple storage engines beneath. MySQL has a wide variety of interfaces from all possible languages. Being a part of MySQL, NDB has access to all of those interfaces. In addition NDB can be accessed from many other direct interfaces to its data services. Thus MySQL Cluster have a large breadth in how it can be used together with the possibility to have optimised access paths for applications requiring this. We will use the terms MySQL Cluster, NDB Cluster and NDB interchangably in the book.

NDB always uses transactions to change the database content. At any point in time the data is recoverable. One of the key concepts in MySQL Cluster is to support all sorts of management changes while still being fully operational and the database content is available for both read and write.

NDB was designed with telecom databases in mind. Thus both high availability and high performance and predictable response times are very important. The development of HW has led to a tremendous increase in what can be supported by an in-memory database. In addition the disk parts in NDB can be used to build file systems and other storage systems with many petabytes of data in them. HopsFS is an example of such a file system implementing Hadoop HDFS on top of NDB, using NDB for the Name Nodes of HDFS.

The MySQL Cluster 7.5 software have been designed to handle these new computers with a special focus on real-time applications with ALWAYS ON as a keyword. It can support large database sizes with up to a few terabytes per cluster and using disk columns this can increase another tenfold.

MySQL Cluster 7.5 offers a much greater ability to use NDB for web applications that require read scalability more than write scalability. Thus 7.5 has greatly expanded the number of use cases where NDB is a good fit. We hope to expand even further in upcoming versions of MySQL Cluster. MySQL Cluster 7.4 improved restart performance and made a major quality improvement.

We expect that the most important selector for using MySQL Cluster is its very high availability. It is used in applications with billions of users relying on it to always be up and running to use their phones, smart phones, games of all sorts, financial services and even as part of very large storage systems. Most importantly NDB can handle writes when upgrading software, when scaling out the system, when adding new columns to tables, when adding new indexes to tables, when taking backups, when performing various checkpoints.

Applications that require predictable response times is another target category for MySQL Cluster usage. NDB have many parts that are developed in order to be able to deliver a real-time experience although being built on top of standard operating systems such as Linux, Solaris, Windows and Mac OS X. NDB can deliver predictable response times per query down to round about 100 microseconds even in a loaded cluster.

Write intensive applications is a key category of MySQL Cluster. NDB is designed to always support writes through all management operations. All algorithms are designed to handle as much write throughput as read throughput. Applications that do massive amounts of updates is an important use case for MySQL Cluster.

NDB is designed for scalable applications where all application servers always can see the latest view on data, even when running with hundreds of application servers. This is a notable difference to other MySQL clustering solutions that require the application to divide the application into shards that are more or less standalone parts and even within the same shard it is necessary to route write transactions and read transactions differently.

MySQL Cluster is a true distributed database, all applications see the same view of data, independent of which replica and which shard they access and independent of which MySQL Server or API node they use to access the cluster.

Performance is something that NDB shines in as well.

NDB have shown how to handle 200 million reads per second in one cluster already a few years ago. SICS have showed that a Hadoop File Server (HopsFS) can handle more than 1 million file operations even with just 12 data nodes showing scalability going from 2 to 12 data nodes and going from 2 to 60 HDFS name nodes.

For writes NDB have been shown to handle a billion updates per minute in benchmarks. There are users that perform a million updating transactions per second in normal operation.

MySQL Cluster has a number of auto-parallelisation features such that SQL queries can be parallelised automatically by the MySQL Server and the NDB Data servers.

0.1   About the author Mikael Ronström

Mikael Ronström has been working on NDB since he started performing his Ph.D research on databases and mathematics in the early 1990s while working in the Ericsson systems department.

The first demo version of NDB was version 0.3 that was demoed for the swedish telco operator Telia in 1998 where an AXE switch queried NDB for number translations where NDB was running on a pair of Sun SPARC computers interconnected with Dolphin SCI cards and interconnected to the AXE switch using Ethernet. The response time requirement was an essential initial requirement together with the ability to manage switch data from a database API external to the AXE switch. The demo showed off response times in the order of 4 milliseconds from the request made in the CPU of the AXE, transferred over a local network in the AXE to a regional processor that implemented the Ethernet, over Ethernet and TCP/IP over to one of the SPARC computers, from there it requested the data in any of the two SPARC computers over SCI and it was passed the same way back. The telco industry in the 1980s and 1990s was driven by a need to move the data of the telco network into computers that were accessible through standardised interfaces such as SQL, CORBA and many other standard interfaces. At the same time this data needed to be accessible in predictable times which led to requirements of accessing data in milliseconds and performing fairly complex data interactions in this time. The predictable response time requirement led to requirements on a main-memory DBMS. Telco databases will get requests for its data around the clock since there is always someone making a phone call or using some other telecom service. This led to requirements of a highly available DBMS.

Since then the author has been busy continuing this development. From 1999 to 2003 this development happened inside Ericsson Business Innovation, since 2003 this development has been a part of MySQL. Mikael Ronström has also developed many other areas of the MySQL Server such as MySQL Partitioning, the MySQL Thread pool and he led the development to scale the MySQL Server from 4 CPUs to 64 CPUs during 2008 to 2012. He has been involved in early phases of the MySQL Fabric development, assisted the MySQL replication team to scale MySQL replication better. His current assignment at Oracle is as Senior MySQL Architect.

In 2006 he worked as an independent consultant on MySQL matters in MySQL, Dolphin and local swedish companies.

In addition during his days as a consultant he started the development of the benchmark suite that MySQL now releases as dbt2-0.37.50.15. This benchmark tool is presented in this book.

0.2 PURPOSE OF THE BOOK

I have been busy researching and developing NDB for the past 25 years. The last 10 years I have considered writing a book about MySQL Cluster. Until now I always concluded that it was more important to spend my time on developing yet one more feature or improving the performance or fixing some bug.

In 2015 I felt that the time had come to write a book on what has been developed in MySQL Cluster. This insight comes from a number of factors. First the product is becoming more and more general purpose and thus can be used by more and more people. Early users of NDB were advanced users that were willing to spend a considerable effort to understand and make use of the unique characteristics of it.

Another reason is that the product has so many interesting features that is hard to fully grasp unless you describe how the product can be used. The MySQL manual is a good tool to understand details in how MySQL Cluster works, how to set it up, how to configure it and so forth. But this book is intended to explain when it is feasible to use NDB and understand also why all the configuration options exists. It ensures that all concepts are fully explained such that it is possible for students to understand the description of how it works.

This book explains a lot more details on some advanced configuration options that I personally use a lot when setting up MySQL Cluster. It describes use cases for various ways of managing it. It goes to some effort in describing what hardware or cloud configurations that can be efficiently used to run NDB on.

Another reason is simply that it fills a gap, there is no such book describing describing both internals and use of MySQL Cluster.

The purpose is to further the understanding of what MySQL Cluster can do in a world where scalable real-time data servers is becoming more and more important. It has matured in an environment with very high requirements on availability. It has been shown in 15 years to deliver not only 5 9's of availability but even 6 9's of availability. This means that in production it has been shown to have less than 30 seconds of downtime per year with a large set of servers making up the statistical population.

If you build infrastructure that depends on high availability data you should read this book about MySQL Cluster 7.5 to see what it can do for you.

The book is targeted towards the specific MySQL Cluster version 7.5, this version is based on the MySQL 5.7 version together with many important improvements of the NDB storage engine. Most of the book is applicable to older versions of NDB. We will provide some information about what has been added in 7.3, 7.4, 7.5.

It is not a book about MySQL InnoDB Cluster. It provides a comparison of MySQL clustering based on NDB compared to MySQL InnoDB Cluster and other similar MySQL clustering solutions, to aid a user in understanding what solution to use. This book is about MySQL clustering based on NDB.

It is not a book about SQL, although some mentioning of SQL statements will be presented, there are other books describing how to use SQL in a much better way. It will primarily mention if there are special things in SQL required to use MySQL Cluster in an efficient manner.

Part I

When to use MySQL Cluster

Chapter 1

What is special with MySQL Cluster

MySQL Cluster is a DBMS (DataBase Management System) that is designed for the most demanding mission-critical applications in the telecom network, in internet infrastructure applications, in financial applications, in storage infrastructure applications, in web applications, in mobile apps and many other applications such as gaming, train control, vehicle control and a lot more you probably can come up with better than me.

It is probably the DBMS with the highest availability statistics surpassing most competitors by more than a magnitude higher availability.

When a transaction in NDB has completed, all replicas have been updated and you will always be able to see your own updates. This is an important feature that makes application development a lot easier compared to when using eventual consistency.

The requirements from the telecom network was that complex transactions have to be completed in ten milliseconds. NDB supports this requirement and this makes NDB useful also in financial applications and many other application categories that require bounded latency on the queries.

It is also known by the names NDB, NDB Cluster and MySQL NDB Cluster where NDB stands for Network DataBase.

It is designed with the following features in mind:

1. Class 6 Availability (less than 30 seconds downtime per year)

2. Data consistency in large clusters

3. High Write Scalability and Read Scalability

4. Predictable response time

5. Available with MySQL interface, LDAP interface, file system interfaces

6. Available with APIs from all modern languages

To reach Class 6 NDB supports online software changes, online schema changes, online add node, global solutions with highly available fail-over cases. It is designed with two levels of replication where the first level is local replication to protect against HW and SW failures. The second level is a global replication level that protects against outages due to conflicts, power issues, earthquakes and so forth. The global replication can also be used to perform more complex changes compared to the local replication level.

In both the local replication and in the global replication level NDB is designed to support multi-master solutions. In the local replication this is completely transparent to the user.

MySQL Cluster was developed in response to the development of Network Databases in the telecom world in the 1980s and 1990s. It was originally developed at Ericsson where I spent 13 years learning telecom and databases and developing real-time systems for switches and databases. It has been a part of MySQL since 2003 and it has been in production at many different mission-critical applications across the world since then.

At the moment there are at least several tens of thousands of clusters running in production and probably a lot more. NDB has proven itself in all the above listed areas and have added a few more unique selling points over time such as a parallel query feature and good read scalability as well as scalable writes that has been there from day one.

Experience have shown that NDB meet Class 6 availability (less than 30 seconds of downtime per year) and for extended periods even Class 8 availability (less than 0.3 seconds of downtime per year).

To get a quick idea if MySQL Cluster is something for your application I will list the unique selling points (USPs) of MySQL Cluster.

1.1 ALWAYSON FOR READS AND WRITES

I use the term AlwaysOn here to mean a DBMS that is essentially never down. MySQL Cluster makes it possible to solve most online changes with its set of features.

This includes the following points:

1. Can survive multiple node crashes in one cluster

2. Can handle Add Column while writes happen

3. Can Add/Drop indexes while writes happen

4. Can Add/Drop foreign keys while writes happen

5. Can Add new shards while writing

6. Can reorganise data to use new shards while writing

7. Can perform software upgrade while writing (multiple version steps)

8. Automated node failure detection and handling

9. Automated recovery after node failure

10. Transactional node failures => Can survive multiple node failures per node group while writes happens

11. Schema changes are transactional

12. Support global failover for the most demanding changes

13. Support global online switch over between clusters in different geographies

One of the base requirement for NDB was to always support both reads and writes. The only acceptable downtime is for a short time when a node fails. It can take up to a few seconds to discover that the node has failed (the time is dependent on the responsiveness of the operating system used). As soon as the failure have been discovered, data is immediately available for reads and writes, the reconfiguration time is measured in microseconds.

There are many other solutions that build on a federation of databases. This means stand-alone DBMSs that replicate to each other at commit time. Given that they are built as stand-alone DBMSs they are not designed to communicate with other systems until it is time to commit the transactions. Thus with large transactions the whole transaction has to applied on the backup replicas before commit if immediate failover has to happen. This technique would in turn stop all other commits since the current replication techniques uses some form of token that is passed around and thus large transactions would block the entire system in that case.

Thus these systems can never provide synchronous replication AND at the same time providing this immediate failover and predictable response time independent of transaction sizes. NDB can deliver this since it is designed as a distributed DBMS where all replicas are involved before committing the transaction. Thus large transactions will block all rows they touch, but all other rows are available for other transactions to concurrently read and write.

NDB was designed from the start to handle as many failures as possible. It is possible e.g. to start with 4 replicas and see one failure at a time and end up with only 1 replica alive and we can still continue to both read and write the database.

Many management operations are possible to perform while the system continues to both read and write. This is a unique feature where NDB is at the forefront. It is possible to add/drop indexes, add columns, add/drop foreign keys, upgrade software, add new data nodes and reorganise data to use those new nodes. All failure handling is automated, both failure detection, failure handling and recovery of the nodes involved.

Schema changes are transactional, such that if they fail they can be rolled back. Schema transactions and user transactions cannot be combined in one transaction.

1.2   GLOBAL SOLUTION FOR REPLICATION

This includes the following points:

1. Synchronous replication inside one cluster

2. Asynchronous replication between clusters

3. Conflict detection when using multiple master clusters

4. Replication architecture designed for real-world physics

MySQL Cluster has a unique feature in that it supports multiple levels of replication. The base replication is the replication inside the cluster. This replication is synchronous and as soon as you have updated an object you will see the update in all other parts of the cluster.

The next level of replication is asynchronous replication between clusters. This replication takes a set of transactions for the last 100 millisecond period or so and replicates it to the other cluster. Thus the other cluster will see the updates from the updated cluster with a small delay.

These replication modes are independent of each other. It is possible to replicate to/from InnoDB using this approach.

The asynchronous replication supports multiple master clusters. This requires conflict detection handling and NDB provides APIs to handle conflicts when conflicting updates occur. Several different conflict detection mechanisms are supported. It is possible to create complex replication architecture with things such as circular replication as well.

The replication architecture is designed to handle real-world physics. The default synchronous replication is designed for communication inside a data center where latency is less than 100 microseconds to communicate between nodes and communication paths are wide (nowadays often 10G Ethernet, but normally at least gigabit ethernet). With the development of clouds we have a new level which is availability domains/zones, these normally communicate between each other in less than a millisecond and down to 400 microseconds. Local replication can be used between availability domains.

When communicating between data centers in different regions the latency is normally at least 10 milliseconds and can reach 100 milliseconds if they are very far apart. In this case we provide the asynchronous replication option.

This means that wherever you placed your data in the world, there is a replication solution for that inside MySQL Cluster.

The global replication solution enables continued operation in the presence of earthquakes and other major disturbances. It makes it possible to perform the most demanding changes with small disturbances. There is methods to ensure that switching over applications from one cluster to another can be performed in a completely online fashion using transactional update anywhere logic.

Thus if users want to follow the trends and move their data in MySQL Cluster from on-premise to the cloud, this can be made without any downtime at all.

1.2.1 HARDENED HIGH AVAILABILITY

MySQL Cluster was originally designed for latency in the order of a few milliseconds. It was designed for Class 5 availability (less than 5 minutes of downtime per year). It turns out that we have achieved Class 6 availability in reality (less than 30 seconds of downtime per year).

MySQL Cluster was first put into production in a high availability environment in 2004 using version 3.4 of the product. This user is still operating this cluster and now using a 7.x version.

Thousands and thousands of clusters have since been put into production usage.

With modern hardware we are now able to deliver response time on the order of 100 microseconds and even faster using specialised communication HW. At the same time the applications creates larger transactions. Thus we still maintain latency of transactions on the order of a few milliseconds.

1.3   Consistency of data in large clusters

This includes the following points:

1. Fully synchronous transactions with non-blocking two-phase-commit protocol

2. Data immediately seen after commit from any node in the cluster

3. Can always read your own updates

4. Cross-shard transactions and queries

In the MySQL world as well as in the NoSQL world there is a great debate about how to replicate for highest availability. Our design uses fully synchronous transactions.

Most designs have moved towards complex replication protocols since the simple two-phase commit protocol is a blocking protocol. Instead of moving to a complex replication protocol we solved the blocking part. Our two-phase commit protocol is non-blocking since we can rebuild the transaction state after a crash in a new node. Thus independent of how many crashes we experience we will always be able to find a new node to take over the transactions from the failed node (as long as the cluster is still operational, a failed cluster will always require a recovery action, independent of replication protocol).

During this node failure takeover the rows that were involved in the transactions that lost their transaction coordinator remains locked. The remainder of the rows are unaffected, they can immediately be used in new transactions from any alive transaction coordinator. The locked rows will remain locked until we have rebuilt the transaction states and decided the outcome of the transactions that lost their transaction coordinator.

When a transaction have completed, NDB have replicated not only the logs of the changes. NDB have also updated the data in each replica. Thus independent of which replica is read, it will always see the latest changes.

Thus we can handle cross-shard transactions and queries, it means that we make the data available for reads immediately after committing the data.

The requirement to always be able to read your own updates we solve either by always sending reads to the primary replica or through a setting on the table to use the read backup feature in which case the commit acknowledged is delayed shortly to ensure that we can immediately read the backup replicas and see our own update.

1.3.1   Cluster within one data center

NDB was originally designed for clusters that resided within one data center. The latency to send messages within one data center can be anywhere between a few microseconds to below one hundred microseconds for very large data centers. This means that we can complete a transaction within less than a millisecond and that complex transactions with tens of changes can be completed within ten milliseconds.

Using low latency HW the latency in this case can be brought down even further. Dolphin ICS in Norway is a company that have specialised in low latency interconnect technology. Using their SuperSocket drivers it is possible to bring down latency in sending a message from

Cluster in one data center

one node to another to less than one microsecond. Actually the first communication technology that worked with NDB was based on Dolphin HW already in the 1990s.

Using SuperSocket HW is equivalent in speed to using RDMA protocols. NDB have supported specialised HW interconnects in the past from OSE Delta and from Dolphin and there has been experimental work on Infiniband transporters. But using SuperSocket driver technology removed the need for specialised transporter technology.

It is possible to use Infiniband technology with NDB using IPoIB (IP over Infiniband). This has great bandwidth, but not any other significant advantages compared to using Ethernet technologies.

1.3.2 CLUSTER WITHIN ONE REGION

In a cloud provider it is customary to bring down entire data centers from time to time. To build a highly available solution in a cloud often requires the use of several data centers in the same region. Most cloud providers have three data centers per region. Most cloud providers promise latency of 1-2 milliseconds between data centers whereas the Oracle cloud provides latency below half a millisecond. Inside a cloud data center the latency is below 100 microseconds.

This setup works fine with NDB and will be covered in more detail in the chapter on MySQL Cluster in the cloud. The main difference is that the latency to communicate is a magnitude higher in this case. Thus not all applications will be a fit for this setup.

1.3.3 SEVERAL CLUSTERS IN DIFFERENT REGIONS

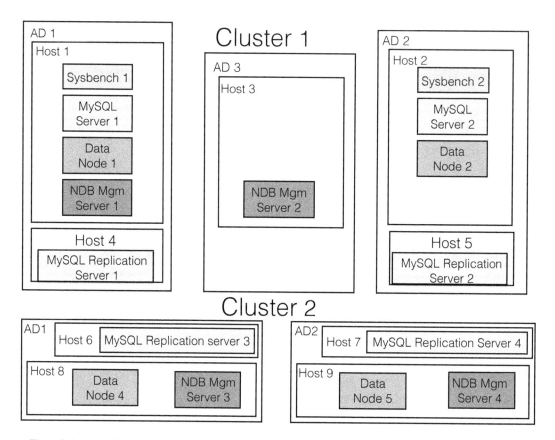

For global replication we use an asynchronous replication protocol that is able to handle many clusters doing updates at the same time and providing conflict detection protocols (more on that below). Thus we use two levels of replication for the highest availability. MySQL Cluster is safe for earthquakes, data center failures and the most complex software and hardware upgrades.

NDB is unique in bringing both the best possible behaviour in a local cluster while at the same time providing support of global replication.

The figure below shows a complex setup that uses two clusters in different regions and each cluster resides in several availability domains (ADs) within one region. MySQL Cluster Replication is used to ensure that an NDB setup with global replication will survive in the presence of an entire region being down.

We will cover this setup in greater detail in the part on Global Replication.

1.4 HIGH READ AND WRITE SCALABILITY

MySQL Cluster can scale to 48 data nodes and around 200 MySQL Servers. NDB have shown in benchmarks that it can scale up to 20 million write transactions per second and more than

200 million reads per second.

To achieve the optimal scaling the following points are important:

1. Partition pruned index scans (optimised routing and pruning of queries)

2. Distribution-aware transaction routing (semi-automatic)

3. Partitioning schemes

NDB is designed to scale both for reads and writes. NDB implements sharding transparent to the user. It can include up to 24 node groups where data is stored. It is also possible to fully replicate tables within all node groups. The data nodes can be accessed from more than 200 MySQL Servers that all see the same view of the data. This makes it possible to issue tens of millions of SQL queries per second against the same data set using local access thus providing perfect read scalability.

To provide optimal scaling in a distributed system it is still important to provide hints and write code taking account of the partitioning scheme used.

Costs of sending have been and continuos to be one of the main costs in a distributed system. In order to optimise the sending it is a good idea to start the transaction at the node where the data resides. We call this Distribution-aware transaction routing.

When using the NDB API it is possible to explicitly state which node to start the transaction at. For the most part it is easier for the application to state that the transaction should start at the node where the primary replica of a certain record resides.

When using SQL the default mechanism is to place the transaction at the node that the first query is using. If the first query is

```
mysql> SELECT * from table where pk = 1;
```

then the transaction will be started at the node where the record with primary key column pk equal to 1 is stored. This can be found by using the hash on the primary key (or distribution key if only a part of the primary key is used to distribute the records).

The next problem in a shared nothing database is that the number of partitions grows with the number of nodes and in NDB also with the number of threads used. When scanning the table using some ordered index it is necessary to scan all partitions unless the partition key is fully provided.Thus the cost of scanning using ordered index grows with a growing cluster.

To counter this it is important to use partition pruned index scans as much as possible. A partition pruned index scan is an index scan where the full partition key is provided as part of the index scan. Since the partition key is provided we can limit the search to the partition that the rows with this partition key are stored.

In TPC C for example it is a good idea to use warehouse id as the distribution key for all tables. This means that any query that accesses only one warehouse only need to be routed to one partition. Thus there is no negative scaling effect.

If it isn't possible to use partition pruned index scans there is one more method to decrease cost of ordered index scans. By default tables are distributed over all nodes and all *ldm* threads (ldm stands for Local Database Manager and contains the record storage, hash indexes and ordered indexes and the local recovery logic). It is possible to specify when creating the table to use less partitions in the table. The minimum is to have one partition per node group by using standard partitioning schemes. It is possible to specify the exact number of partitions, but when specifying an exact number of partitions the data will not be evenly spread over the nodes, this requires more understanding of the system and its behaviour. Therefore we have designed options that use less partitions in a balanced manner.

By using these schemes in an efficient manner it is possible to develop scalable applications that can do many millions of complex transactions per second. A good example of an application that have been successful in this is HopsFS. They have developed the meta data layer of Hadoop HDFS using NDB. They use the id of the parent directory as distribution key which gives good use of partitioned pruned index scans for almost all file operations. They have shown that this scaled to at least 12 data nodes and 60 application nodes (they ran out of lab resources to show any bigger clusters).

A presentation of these results in a research paper at the 17th IEEE/ACM International Symposium on Cluster, Cloud and Grid Computing won the IEEE Scale Challenge Award in 2017.

1.5   PREDICTABLE RESPONSE TIME

This includes the following points:

1. Main memory storage for predictable response time

2. Durable by committing on multiple computers in memory (Network Durable)

3. CPU cache optimised distributed hash algorithm

4. CPU cache optimised T-tree index (ordered index)

5. Application defined partitioning (primary key partitioning by default)

6. Batched key lookup access

7. Several levels of piggybacking in network protocols

8. Maintaining predictable response time while improving throughput

Piggybacking happens in several levels, one level is that we pack many commit messages and some other messages together in special PACKED_SIGNAL messages. The other is that we use one socket for communication between nodes. Given that our internal architecture uses an asynchronous programming model means that we automatically can batch a lot of messages together in one TCP/IP message. We execute a set of messages and collect the responses from these messages in internal buffers until we're done executing and only then do we send the messages. Finally we execute in many threads in parallel such that when sending we can collect messages from many threads.

The telecom applications, financial applications and gaming applications have strict requirements on the time one is allowed to take before one responds to the set of queries in a transaction. We have demanding users that require complex transactions with tens of interactions with hundreds of rows to complete within a few milliseconds in a system that is loaded to 90% of its capacity.

This is an area where one would probably not expect to find an open source DBMS such as MySQL at the forefront. But in this application area MySQL Cluster comes out at the top. The vendors selecting MySQL Cluster have often tough requirements, up to more than millions of transactions per second, Class 6 availability and at the same time providing 24x7 services and being available to work with users when they have issues.

The data structures used in NDB have been engineered with a lot of thought on how to make them use CPU caches in the best possible manner. As a testament to this we have shown that the threads handling the indexes and the data have an IPC of 1.27 (IPC = Instruction Per Cycle). Normal DBMS usually report an IPC of around 0.25.

1.6 BASE PLATFORM FOR DATA STORAGE

This includes the following points:

1. MySQL storage engine for SQL access

2. OpenLDAP backend for LDAP access

3. HopsFS metadata backend for Hadoop HDFS (100s of PByte data storage)

4. Prototypes of distributed disk block devices

5. Integrated into Oracle OpenStack

MySQL Cluster can be used as a base platform for many different types of data. A popular use is SQL access using MySQL. Another popular approach is to use NDB as the backend in an LDAP server. OpenLDAP have a backend storage engine that can use NDB. Some users have developed their own proprietary LDAP servers based on top of NDB (e.g. Juniper).

SICS, a research lab connected to KTH in Stockholm, Sweden, have developed HopsFS, this is a metadata backend to Hadoop HDFS for storing many, many petabytes of data into HDFS and enabling HDFS to handle many millions of file operations per second. HopsFS uses disk data in NDB to store small files that are not efficient to store in HDFS itself.

Personally I have worked on a hobby project, iClaustron, to develop a file system on top of NDB that uses the FUSE API to provide a distributed file system.

Prototypes have been built successfully where NDB was used to store disk blocks to implement a distributed block device.

NDB have been integrated into Oracle OpenStack and a number of other Oracle products.

The list of use cases where it is possible to build advanced data services on top of NDB is long and will hopefully grow longer over the years in the future. One of the main reasons for this is that NDB separates the data server functionality from the query server functionality.

1.7 MULTI-DIMENSIONAL SCALING

This includes the following points:

1. Scaling inside a thread

2. Scaling with many threads

3. Scaling with many nodes

4. Scaling with many MySQL Servers

5. Scaling with many clusters

6. Built-in Load balancing in NDB API (even in presence of node failures)

MySQL Cluster have always been built for numerous levels of scaling. From the beginning it scaled to a number of different nodes. The user can always scale by using many clusters (some of our users use this approach). Since MySQL Cluster 7.0 there is a multithreaded data node, each successive new version after that have improved our support for multithreading in the data node and in the API nodes. The MySQL Server scales to a significant number of threads. A data node together with a MySQL Server scales to use the largest dual socket x86 servers.

MySQL Cluster have designed a scalable architecture inside each thread that makes good use of the CPU resources inside a node. This architecture has the benefit that the more load the system gets, the more efficient it executes. Thus we get an automatic overload protection.

In the NDB API we have an automatic load balancer built in. This load balancer will automatically pick the most suitable data node to perform the task specified by the application in the NDB API.

1.8 NON-BLOCKING 2PC TRANSACTION PROTOCOL

MySQL Cluster uses a two-phase commit protocol. The research literature talks about this protocol as a blocking protocol. Our variant of this protocol is non-blocking. The problem is that a transaction has a coordinator role. The problem is what to do at crashes of the coordinator role.

NDB have a protocol to take over the transaction coordinator role for a crashed node. The state of the transaction coordinator is rebuilt in the new transaction coordinator by asking the transaction participants about the state of all ongoing transactions. We use this take over protocol to decide on either abort or commit of each transaction that belonged to the crashed node. Thus there is no need to wait for the crashed node to come back.

The protocol is recursive such that the transaction coordinator role can handle multiple node failures until the entire cluster fails.

Thus there are no blocking states in our two-phase commit protocol. Normally a node failure is handled within a second or two or less than this unless large transactions was ongoing at crash time.

1.9 GLOBAL CHECKPOINTS

NDB uses a method called Network Durable transactions, this means that when a transaction is acknowledged towards the API we know that the transaction is safe on several computers. It is however not yet safe on durable media (e.g. hard drive, SSD, NVMe or persistent memory).

In order to ensure that we recover a consistent point after a cluster crash we create regular consistent commit points. We call those global checkpoints. We actually create two types of global checkpoints. One of them are used for MySQL Cluster Replication. These are created around once per 100 milliseconds. These are called epochs in MySQL Cluster Replication. The epochs are not durable on disk. Each second or two we create a global checkpoint that is durable. When we recover after a complete cluster crash we recover to one of those global checkpoints.

The NDB API provides the global checkpoint identifier of the transaction committed, this makes it possible to wait for this global checkpoint to be durable on disk if this is necessary.

The global checkpoint identifier is heavily used in our recovery protocols. It is a very important building block of NDB.

1.10 AUTOMATICALLY PARALLELISED AND DISTRIBUTED QUERIES

Any range scan that is scanning more than one partition will be automatically parallelised. As an example we have 4 range scans in the Sysbench OLTP benchmark. Using data nodes with 8 partitions per table will execute those scan queries twice as fast compared to tables with only one partition. This is a case without any filtering in the data nodes. With filtering the improvement will be bigger.

In MySQL Cluster 7.2 a method to execute complex SQL queries was added. This method uses a framework where a multi-table join can be sent as one query to the data nodes. The manner it executes is that it reads one table at a time, each table reads a set of rows and sends the data of these rows back to the API node. At the same time it sends key information onwards to the second table together with information sent in the original request. This query execution is automatically parallelised in the data nodes.

There is still a bottleneck in that only one thread in the MySQL Server will be used to process the query results. Queries where lots of filtering are pushed to the data nodes can be highly parallelised.

There is a number of limitations on this support, the EXPLAIN command in MySQL will give a good idea about what will be used and some reasons why the pushdown of the joins to the data nodes doesn't work (pushing down joins to data nodes enables the query to be automatically parallelised).

Interestingly the MySQL Server can divide a large join into several parts where one part is pushed to the data node and another part is executed from the MySQL Server using normal single-table reads.

CHAPTER 2

RATIONALE FOR MySQL CLUSTER

The idea to build NDB Cluster that later was merged into the MySQL framework and became MySQL Cluster came from the analysis I did as part of my Ph.D studies. I was working at Ericsson and participated in a study about the new UMTS mobile system developed in Europe that later turned into 3G. As part of this study we did a lot of work on understanding the requirements of network databases for the UMTS system. In addition I studied a number of related areas like Number Portability, Universal Personal Telephony, Routing Servers, Name Servers (e.g. DNS Servers), Intelligent Network Servers. Other application areas I studied was News-on-demand, multimedia email services, event data services and finally I studied data requirements for a pet appplication of mine which is genealogy.

Areas of study was requirements on response times, transaction rates and availability and a few more aspects.

These studies led to a few conclusions:

1. Predictable response time requirements required a main memory database

2. Predictable response time requirements required using a real-time scheduler

3. Throughput requirements required a main memory database

4. Throughput requirements required building a scalable database

5. Availability requirements required using replicated data

6. Availability requirements required using a Shared-Nothing Architecture

7. Availability requirements means that applications should not execute inside the DBMS unless in a protected manner

8. Certain applications needs to store large objects on disk inside the DBMS

9. The most common operation is key lookup

10. Most applications studied were write intensive

2.1 SEPARATION OF DATA SERVER AND QUERY SERVER

In MySQL there is a separation of the Query Server and the Data Server functionality. The Query Server is what takes care of handling the SQL queries and maps those to lower layers call into the Data Server. The API to the Data Server in MySQL is the storage engine API.

Almost all DBMS have a similar separation between Data Server and Query Server. However there are many differences in how to locate the interfaces between Data Server and Query Server and Query Server and the application.

2.1.1 FULLY INTEGRATED MODEL

The figure below shows a fully integrated model where the application is running in the same binary as the DBMS. This gives very low latency. The first database product I worked on was called DBS and was a database subsystem in AXE that generated PLEX code (PLEX was the programming language used in AXE) from SQL statements. This is probably the most efficient SQL queries that exists, a select query that read one column using a primary key took 2 assembler instructions in the AXE CPU (APZ).

There was methods to query and update the data through external interfaces, but those were a lot slower compared to internal access.

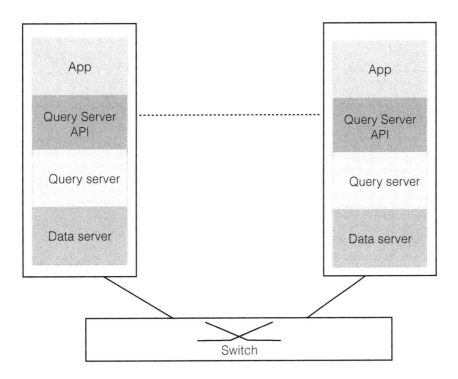

This model is not flexible, it's great in some applications, but the applications have to be developed with the same care as the DBMS since it is running in the same memory. It is not a model that works well to get the absolutely best availability. It doesn't provide the benefits of scaling the DBMS in many different directions.

The main reason for avoiding this approach is the high availability requirement. If the application gets a wrong pointer and writes some data out of place, it can change the data inside the DBMS. Another problem with this approach is that it becomes difficult to manage in a shared nothing architecture since the application will have to be colocated with its data for the benefits to be of any value.

2.1.2 COLOCATED QUERY SERVER AND DATA SERVER

The next step that one would take is to separate the Query Server from the API, but still colocating the Query Server and the Data Server as shown in the figure.

This is the model used by most DBMSs. This makes the DBMS highly specialised, if the external API is using SQL, every access to the Data Server have to go through SQL. If the external API is LDAP, all access have to use LDAP to get access to the data.

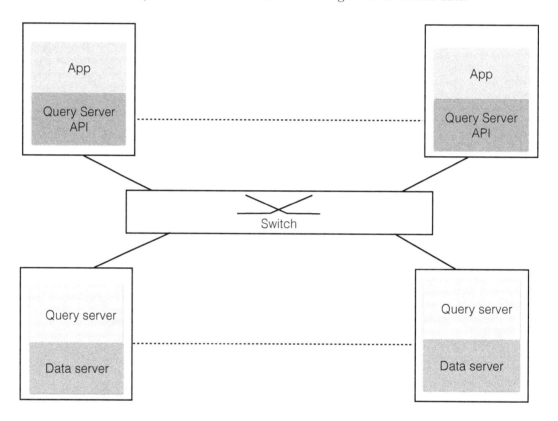

Some examples of this model is Oracle, IBM DB2, MySQL/InnoDB and various LDAP server solutions. Its drawback is that it isn't good to handle mixed workloads that use both complex queries where a language like SQL is suitable and many simple queries that are the bulk of the application.

The Query Server functionality requires a lot of code to manage all sorts of complex queries, it requires a flexible memory model that can handle many concurrent memory allocations from many different threads.

The Data Server is much more specialised software, it has a few rather simple queries that it can handle, the code to handle those are much smaller compared to the Query Server functionality.

Thus even in this model the argument for separating the Query Server and the Data Server due to availability requirements is a strong argument. Separating them means that there is no risk for flaws in the Query Server code to cause corruption of the data. The high availability requirements of NDB led us to choose a model where we wanted to minimise the amount of code that had direct access to the data.

Most DBMSs uses SQL or some other high-level language to access it. The translation from SQL to low-level primitives gives a fairly high overhead. The requirements on high throughput of primary key operations for NDB meant that it was important to provide an access path to data which didn't require the access to go through a layer like SQL.

These two arguments were strong advocates for separation of the query server and Data Server functionality.

2.1.3 NDB MODEL

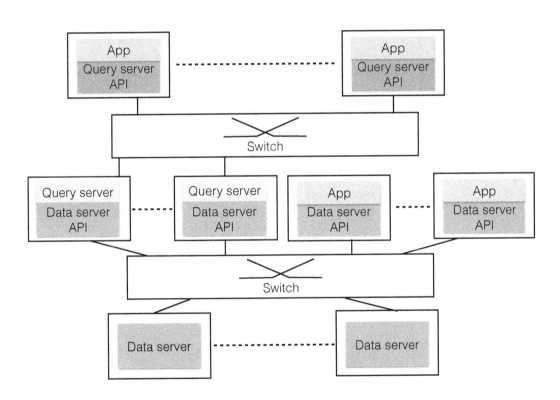

The above reasoning led to the conclusion to separate the Query Server facilities from the Data Server facility. The Data Server provides a low-level API where it is possible to access rows directly through a primary key or unique key and it is possible to scan a table using a full table scan or an index scan on an ordered index. It is possible to create and alter meta data objects. It is possible to create asynchronous event streams that provide information about any changes to the data in the Data Server. The Data Server will handle the recovery of data, it will handle the data consistency and replication of data.

This ensures that the development of the Data Server can be focused and there is very little interaction with the development of the Query Server parts. It does not have to handle SQL, LDAP, query optimisation, file system APIs or any other higher level functionality required to support the Query Server functionality. This greatly diminishes the complexity of the Data Server.

Later on we have added capabilities to perform a bit more complex query executions to handle complex join operations.

BENEFITS OF NDB MODEL

The figure of the NDB model above shows how a network API between the Data Server and the Query Server it is possible to both use it with SQL as the API, to access the Data Server API directly and to use the LDAP API to the same Data Servers that supports SQL and applications using the Data Server API directly and file system services on top of NDB. Thus providing a flexible application development.

The nice thing with development of computers is that they develop to get more and more bandwidth for networking. In addition it is possible to colocate the Query Server process and the Data Server process on the same machine. In this context the integration of the Query Server and the Data Server is almost at the same level as the integration when they are part of the same process. Some DBMSs use the colocated model, but still use multiple processes to implement the DBMS.

This separation of the Data Server and the Query Server have been essential for NDB. It means that one can use NDB to build an SQL server, it means that you can use NDB to build an LDAP server, you can use it to build various networking servers, meta data servers for scalable file systems and it means that you can use NDB to build a file server and you can even use it to build a distributed block device to handle petabytes of data. We will discuss all those use cases and a few more later on in this book.

DRAWBACKS OF NDB MODEL

There is a drawback to the separation of Query Server and the Data Server. To query the data we have to pass through several threads to access the data. This increases the latency of accessing the data when you use SQL access. Writing a combined Query Server and Data Server to implement a SQL engine is always faster for a single DBMS server. NDB is however designed for a distributed environment with replication and sharding from the ground up.

We have worked hard to optimise SQL access in the single server case, and we're continuing this work. The performance is now almost at par with the performance one can achieve with a combined Query Server and Data Server.

UNDERSTANDING THE NDB MODEL

When I performed my research work an important part of the research was to understand the impact of the separation of the Data Server and the Query Server.

Choosing a network-based protocol as the Data Server API was a choice to ensure the highest level of reliability of the DBMS and its applications. We have a clear place where we can check the correctness of the API calls and only through this API can the application change the data in the Data Server.

Another reason that made it natural to choose a network protocol as API was that the development of technologies for low-latency and high bandwidth had started already in the 1990s. The first versions of NDB Cluster had an SCI transporter as its main transporter which ensured that communication between computers could happen in microseconds. TCP/IP sockets have since replaced it since SCI and Infiniband now have support for TCP/IP sockets that is more or less as fast as direct use of SCI and Infiniband.

One more reason for using a network protocol as API is that it enables us to build scalable Data Servers.

As part of the research we looked deeply into the next generation mobile networks and their use of network databases. From these studies it was obvious that the traffic part of the applications almost always made simple queries, mostly key lookups and in some cases slightly more complex queries were used.

At the same time there are management applications in the telecom network, these applications will often use more complex queries and will almost always use some sort of standard access method such as SQL.

Normally the traffic queries have strict requirements on response times whereas the management applications have less strict requirements on response times.

It was clear that there was a need for both a fast path to the data as well as standard APIs used for more complex queries and for data provisioning.

From this it was clear that it was desirable to have a clearly defined Data Server API in a telecom DBMS to handle most of the traffic queries. Thus we can develop the Data Server to handle real-time applications while at the same time supporting applications that focus more on complex queries and analysing the data. Applications requiring real-time access can use the same cluster as applications with less requirements on real-time access but with needs to analyse the data.

2.1.4 HOW WE DID IT

To make it easier to program applications we developed the C++ NDB API that is used to access the NDB Data Server protocol.

The marriage between MySQL and NDB Cluster was a natural one since NDB Cluster had mainly focused on the Data Server parts and by connecting to the MySQL Server we had a natural implementation of the Query Server functionality.

The requirements on fast failover times in telecom DBMSs made it necessary to implement NDB Cluster as a shared nothing DBMS. The Data Server API has support for storing relational tables in a shared nothing architecture. The methods available in the NDB Data Server API are methods for key-value access for read and write, scan access using full table scan and ordered index scans. In 7.2 we added some functionality to pushdown join execution into the Data Server API. There is a set of interfaces to create tables, drop tables, create foreign keys, drop foreign keys, alter a table, adding and dropping columns, adding and dropping indexes and so forth. There is also an event API to track data changes in NDB.

To decrease the amount of interaction we added an interpreter to the NDB Data Server, this can be used for simple pushdown of filters, it can be used to perform simple update operations (such as increment a value) and it can handle LIKE filters.

2.1.5   ADVANTAGES AND DISADVANTAGES

What have the benefits and disadvantages of these architecturial choices been over the 15 years NDB have been in production usage?

One advantage is that MySQL Cluster can be used for many different things.

One important use case is what it was designed for. There are many good examples of applications written against any of the direct NDB APIs to serve telecom applications, financial applications and web applications while still being able to access the same data through an SQL interface in the MySQL Server. These applications uses the performance advantage that makes it possible to scale applications to as much as hundreds of millions of operations per second.

Another category in poular use with MySQL Cluster is to implement an LDAP server as a Query Server on top of the NDB Data Server (usually based on OpenLDAP). This would have been difficult using a Query Server API since the Query Server adds a significant overhead to simple requests.

The latest example of use cases is to use the Data Server to implement a scalable file system. This has been implemented by HopsFS in replacing the Name Server in Hadoop HDFS with a set of Name Servers that use a set of NDB Data Servers to store the actual metadata. Most people that hear about such an architecture being built on something with MySQL in the name will immediately think of the overhead in using SQL interface to implement a file system. But it isn't the SQL interface which is used, it is implemented directly on top of the Java implementation of the NDB API, ClusterJ.

The final category is using MySQL Cluster with the SQL interface. There are many applications that want to get the high availability of NDB but still want to use the SQL interface. There are many pure SQL applications that see the benefit of the data consistency of MySQL Servers using NDB and the availability and scalability of NDB.

The disadvantages is that DBMSs that have a more direct API between the Query Server and the Data Server will get benefits in that they don't have to go over a network API to access its data. With NDB Cluster you pay this extra cost to get higher availability, more flexible access to your data and higher scalability and more predictable response times.

This cost was a surprise to many early users of NDB. We have worked hard since the inception of NDB Cluster into MySQL to ensure that the performance of SQL queries is as close as possible to the colocated Query Server and Data Server APIs. We've gotten close and we are continously working on getting closer. Early versions lacked many optimisations using batching, and many more important optimisations that have been added over the years.

Performance of MySQL Cluster is today close to the performance of MySQL/InnoDB for SQL applications and as soon as some of the parallelisation abilities of MySQL Cluster is made use of, the performance is better.

By separating the Data Server and the Query Server we have made it possible to work on parallelising some queries in an easy manner. This makes the gap much smaller and for many complex queries NDB will outperform local storage engines.

2.2 PREDICTABLE RESPONSE TIME REQUIREMENTS

As part of my Ph.D thesis I studied databases in general and looked at what issues DBMSs had when executing in an OS. What I discovered was that the DBMS is spending most of its time in handling context switches, waiting for disks and in various networking operations. Thus I wanted a solution that avoided the overhead of context switches between different tasks in the DBMS while at the same time integrating networking close to the operations of the DBMS.

When analysing the requirements for predictable response times in NDB Cluster based on its usage in telecom databases two things were important. The first requirement is that we need to be able to respond to queries within a few milliseconds (today down to tens of microseconds). The second requirement is that we need to do this while at the same time supporting a mix of simple traffic queries combined with a number of more complex queries.

The first requirement was the main requirement that led to NDB Cluster using a main memory storage model with durability on disk using a REDO log and various checkpoints.

The second requirement is a bit harder to handle. To solve the second requirement in a large environment with many CPUs can be done by allowing the traffic queries and management queries to run on different CPUs. This model will not work at all in a confined environment with only 1-2 CPUs and it will be hard to get it to work in a large environment since the usage of the management queries will come and go quickly.

The next potential solution is to simply leave the problem to the OS. Modern OSs of today use a time-sharing model. However each time quanta is fairly long compared to our requirement of responding within parts of a millisecond.

Another solution would be to use a real-time operating system, but this would make the product too limited. Even in the telecom application space real-time operating systems is mostly used in the access network.

There could be simple transactions with only a single key lookup. Number translation isn't much more than this simple key lookup query. At the same time most realistic transactions are looking more like the one below where there is a number of lookup's and a number of index scan's as part of the transaction and some of those lookup's do updates.

There are complex queries that analyse data (these are mostly read-only transactions) and these could do thousands or more of these lookup's and scans and they could all execute as part of one single query. It would be hard to handle predictability of response times if these were mixed using normal threads using time-sharing in the OS.

Most DBMS today use the OS to handle the requirements on reponse times. As an example if one uses MySQL/InnoDB and send various queries to the MySQL Server, some traffic queries and some management queries, MySQL will use different threads for each query. MySQL will deliver good throughput in the context of varying workloads since the OS will use time-sharing to fairly split the CPU usage amongst the various threads. It will not be able to handle response time requirements of parts of a millisecond with a mixed load of simple and complex queries.

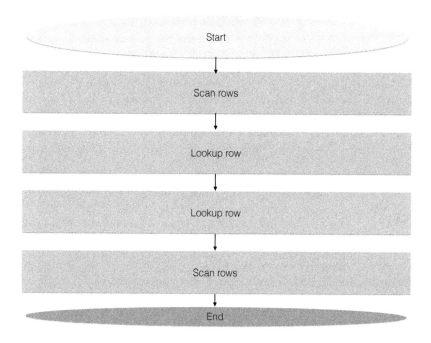

2.2.1   AXE VM

When designing NDB Cluster we wanted to avoid this problem. NDB was initially designed within Ericsson. In Ericsson a real-time telecom switch had been developed in the 70s, the AXE. The AXE is still in popular use today and new versions of it is still developed. AXE had a solution to this problem which was built around a message passing machine.

AXE had its own operating system and at the time its own CPUs. The computer architecture of an AXE was very efficient and the reason behind this was exactly that the cost of switching between threads was almost zero. It got this by using asynchronous programming using modules called blocks and messages called signals.

I spent a good deal of the 90s developing a virtual machine for AXE called AXE VM that inspired the development of a real product called APZ VM (APZ is the name of the CPU subsystem in the AXE). This virtual machine was able to execute on any computer.

The AXE VM used a model where execution was handled as execution of signals. A signal is simply a message, this message contains an address label, it contains a signal number and it contains data of various sizes. A signal is executed inside a block, a block is a module that is self-contained, it owns all its data and the only manner to get to the data in the block is through sending a signal to the block.

The AXE VM implemented a real-time operating system inside a normal operating system such as Windows, Linux, Solaris or Mac OS X. This solves the problem with predictable response time, it gives low overhead for context switching between execution of different queries and it makes it possible to integrate networking close to the execution of signals.

The implementation of NDB borrowed ideas from the AXE architecture and implemented an architecture with a number of blocks and signals sent between those blocks. A nice side effect of this was that the code is using a message passing oriented implementation. This is nice when implementing a distributed database engine.

The first figure shows how NDB uses blocks with its own data and signals passed between blocks to handle things. This was the initial architecture of NDB Cluster and is still the architecture used in data nodes uses the *ndbd* binary.

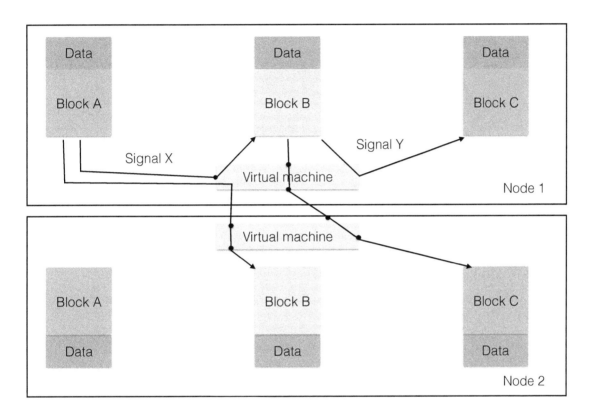

The figure below shows how the full NDB architecture looks like in the data nodes that uses the *ndbmtd* binary. It shows how it uses the AXE architecture to implement a distributed message passing system using blocks and a VM (virtual machine) that implements message passing between blocks in the same thread, message passing between blocks in the same process and message passing between blocks in different processes, it can handle different transporters of the messages between processes (currently only TCP/IP sockets), scheduling of signal execution and interfacing the OS with CPU locking, thread priorities and various other things.

In MySQL Cluster 7.0 we introduced multiple block threads in the architecture. We have further advanced this such that the performance of a data node is now much higher and can nicely fill up a 16-core machine and a 32-core machine and with some drop of scalability even a 48-core machine. The second figure shows the full model used in MySQL Cluster 7.5.

A signal can be local to the thread in which case the virtual machine will discover this and put it into the scheduler queue of the own thread. It could be a message to another block in

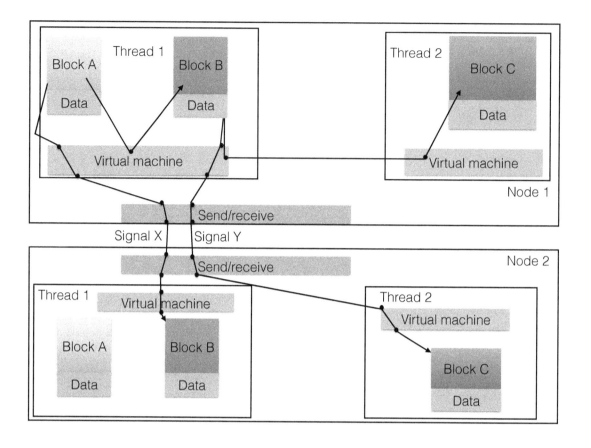

the same node but in a different thread. In this case we have highly optimised non-locking code to transfer the message using memory barriers to the other thread and place it into the scheduler queue of this thread. A message could be targeted for another node, in this case we use the send mechanism to send it over the network using a TCP/IP socket.

The target node could be another data node, it could be a management server or a MySQL Server. The management server and MySQL Server uses a different model where each thread is its own block. The addressing label contains a block number and a thread id, but this label is interpreted by the receiver, only the node id is used at the send side to determine where to send the message. In the data node a receiver thread will receive the message and will transport it to the correct block using the same mechanism used for messages to other threads.

Another positive side effect of basing the architecture on the AXE was that we inherited an easy model for tracing crashes. Signals go through so called job buffers. Thus we have access to a few thousand of the last executed signals in each thread and the data of the signals. This trace comes for free. In addition we borrowed another concept called Jump Address Memory (JAM), this shows the last jumps that the thread did just before the crash. This is implemented through a set of macros that we use in a great number of places in the code. This has some overhead, but the payback is huge in terms of fixing crashes. It means that we can get informative crash traces from the users that consume much less disk space than a core file would consume and still it delivers more real information than the core files would do.

The overhead of generating those jump addresses is on the order of 10-20% in the data node threads. This overhead has paid off in making it a lot easier to support the product.

The AXE VM had a lot of handling of the language used in AXE called PLEX. This is no longer present in NDB. But NDB still is implemented using signals and blocks. The blocks are implemented in C++ and in AXE VM it was possible to have such blocks, they were called simulated blocks. In NDB all blocks are nowadays simulated blocks.

2.2.2 HOW DOES IT WORK

How does this model enable response times of down to parts of a millisecond in a highly loaded system?

First of all it is important to state that NDB handles this. There are demanding users in the telecom, networking and in financial sectors and lately in the storage world that expects to run complex transactions involving tens of different key lookups and scan queries and that expects these transactions to complete within a few milliseconds at 90-95% load in the system.

For example in the financial sector missing the deadline might mean that you miss the opportunity to buy or sell some stock equity in real-time trading. In the telecom sector your telephone call setup and other telco services depends on immediate responses to complex transactions.

At the same time these systems need to ensure that they can analyse the data in real-time, these queries have less demanding response time requirements, running those queries isn't allowed to impact the response time of the traffic queries.

The virtual machine model implements this by using a design technique where each signal is only allowed to execute for a few microseconds. A typical key lookup query in modern CPUs takes less than two microseconds to execute. Scanning a table is divided up into scanning a few rows at a time where each such scan takes less than ten microseconds. All other maintenance work to handle restarts, node failures, aborts, creating new tables and so forth is similarly implemented with the same requirements on signal execution.

Thus a typical traffic transaction is normally handled by one key lookup or a short scan query and the response is sent back to the API node. A transaction consists of a number of such interactions normally in the order of tens of such queries. Thus each interaction needs to complete within 100-200 microseconds in order to handle response times of a few millseconds.

NDB can handle this response time requirement even when 20-30 messages are queued up before the message given that each message will only take on the order of 1-2 microseconds to execute. Thus most of the time is still spent in the transporter layer sending the message and receiving the message.

A complex query will execute in this model by being split into many small signal executions. Each time a signal is completed it will put itself back into the queue of signals and wait for its next turn.

Traffic queries will always have the ability to meet strict requirements on response time. Another nice thing with this model is that it will adapt to varying workloads within a few microseconds. If there is currently no traffic queries to execute, the complex query will get the CPU to itself since the next signal will execute immediately after being put on the queue.

In the figure below we have shown an example of how the execution of a primary key read operation might be affected by delays in the various steps it handles as part of the lookup. In this example case (the execution times are rough estimates of an example installation) the total latency to execute the primary key lookup query is 19.7 microseconds plus the time for a few thread wakeups. The example case represents a case where load is around 80%. We will go through in detail later in this book what happens during the execution of a transaction.

The figure clearly shows the benefits of avoiding the wakeups. Most of the threads in the NDB data nodes have the possibility to spin before going back to sleep. By spinning for a few hundred microseconds in the data nodes the latency of requests will go down since most of the wakeup times disappear. Decreasing the wakeup times also benefits query execution time positively since the CPU caches are warmer when we come back to continue executing a transaction.

In a benchmark we often see that performance scales better than linearly going from one to four threads. The reason is that with a few more active transactions the chance of finding threads already awake increases and thus the latency incurred by wakeups decreases as load increases.

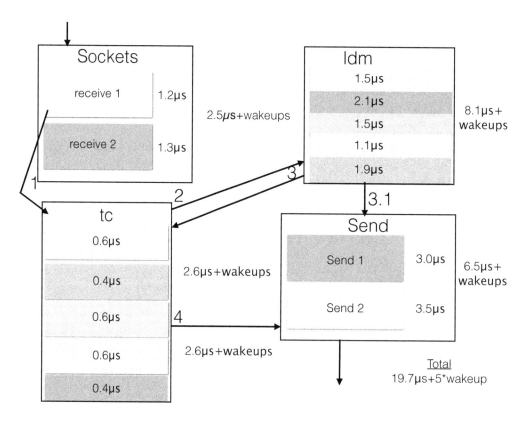

We opted for a functional division of the threads. We could have put all parts into one thread type that handles everything. This would decrease the amount of wakeups needed to execute one lookup. It would decrease the scalability at the same time. It is likely that we will make this more configurable in future versions of NDB.

There is one more important aspect of this model. As load increases two things happens.

First we execute more and more signals every time we have received a set of signals. This means that the overhead to collect each signal decreases. Second executing larger and larger sets of signals means that we send larger and larger packets. Thus the cost per packet decreases. Thus NDB data nodes executes more and more efficiently as load increases. This is an important characteristic that avoids many overload problems.

This means in the above example that as load increases the amount of wakeups decrease, we spend more time in queues, but at the same time we spend less time in waiting for wakeups. Thus the response time is kept almost stable until we reach a high load. The latency of requests starts to dramatically increase around 90-95% load. Up until 90% load the latency is stable and you can get very stable response times.

The functional division of threads makes NDB data nodes behave better compared to if everything was implemented as one single thread type. If the extra latency for wakeups one can use the spinning feature discussed above. This have the effect that we can get very low response times in the case of a lightly loaded cluster. Thus we could get response times down to below 30 microseconds for most operation types. Updating transactions will take a bit longer since they have to visit each node several times before the transaction is complete, a minimum of 5 times for a simple update transaction and a minimum of 7 times for a simple update transaction on a table that uses the read backup feature (explained in a later chapter).

The separation of Data Server and Query Server functionality makes it possible to use different Query Server for traffic queries to the ones used for complex queries. In the MySQL Cluster model this means that you can use a set of MySQL Servers in the cluster to handle short real-time queries. You can use a different set of MySQL Servers to handle complex queries. Thus MySQL Cluster can handle real-time requirements in a proper configuration of the cluster when executing SQL queries.

The separation of Data Server and Query Server functionality might mean that MySQL Cluster have slightly longer minimum response time compared to a local storage engine in MySQL, but MySQL Cluster will continue to deliver low and predictable response times using varying workloads and executing at high loads.

One experiment that was done when developing pushdown join functionality showed that the latency of pushed down joins was the same when executing in an idle cluster compared to a cluster that performed 50.000 update queries per second concurrently with the join queries.

2.3 MYSQL CLUSTER AND MULTI-CORE ARCHITECTURES

In 2008 the MySQL team started working hard on solving the challenge that modern processors have more CPUs and CPU cores. Before that the normal server computer had 2 CPUs and some times even 4 CPUs. MySQL scaled well to those types of computers. However when the single threaded performance was harder and harder to further develop the processor manufacturers started developing processors with a lot more CPUs and CPU cores. Lately we've seen the introduction of various server processors from AMD, Intel and Oracle that have 32 CPU cores per processor and each CPU core can have 2-8 CPUs dependent on the CPU architecture (2 for x86 and 8 for SPARC and Power).

MySQL have now developed such that each MySQL Server can scale beyond 64 CPUs and each NDB data node can scale to around 64 CPUs as well. Modern standard dual socket servers come equipped with up to 128 CPUs for x86s and up to 512 CPUs for SPARC computers.

The development of more and more CPUs per generation have slowed down now compared to a few years ago. But both MySQL Server and NDB data nodes are developed in such a fashion that we try to keep up with the further development of scalability in modern computers.

Both NDB data nodes and MySQL Server nodes can scale to at least a large processor with 32 CPU cores for x86. The MySQL Cluster architecture still makes it possible to have more than one node per computer. Thus the MySQL Cluster architecture will work nicely for all types of computers, even with the largest computers. NDB is tested with computers that have up to 120 CPUs for x86 and up to 1024 CPUs with SPARC machines.

2.4   SHARED NOTHING ARCHITECTURE

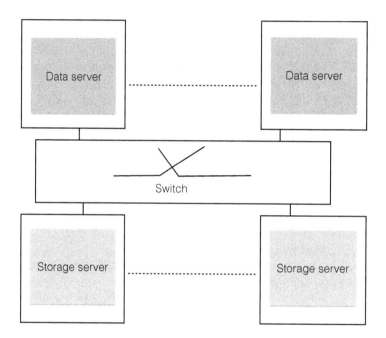

Most traditional DBMSs used in high-availability setups are using a shared disk approach as shown by the figure above. Shared disk architecture means that the disks are shared by all nodes in the cluster. In reality the shared disk is a set of storage servers, implemented either by software or a combination of hardware and software. Modern shared disk DBMS mostly rely on pure software solutions for the storage server part.

Shared disk have advantages for query throughput in that all data is accessible from each server. This means that it reads data from the storage server to perform its queries. This approach has limited scalability but each server can be huge. In most cases the unit transported between Storage Server and Data Server is pages of some standard size such as 8 kByte.

It is very hard to get fast failover cases in a shared disk architecture since it is necessary to replay the global REDO log as part of failover handling. Only after this replay can pages that was owned by a failed node be read or written again.

This is the reason why all telecom databases use the shared nothing approach instead as shown in the figure below. With shared nothing the surviving node can instantly take over, the only delay in taking over is the time it takes to discover that the node has failed. The time it takes to discover this is mostly dependent on the operating system and a shared nothing database can handle discovery and take over in sub-seconds if the OS supports it.

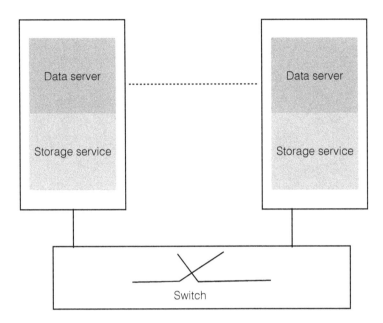

An interesting note is that shared disk implementations depends on a high-availability file system that is connected to all nodes. The normal implementation of such a high-availability storage system is to use a shared nothing approach. Interestingly NDB could be used to implement such a high-availability storage system. It is an intriguing fact that you can build a highly available shared disk DBMS on top of a storage subsystem that is implemented on top of NDB.

2.5 MySQL Cluster and the CAP theorem

The CAP theorem says that one has to focus on a maximum of two of the three properties Consistency, Availability and Partitioning where partitioning refers to network partitioning. NDB focus on consistency and availability. If the cluster becomes partitioned we don't allow both partitions to continue, this would create consistency problems. We try to achieve the maximum availability without sacrificing consistency.

We go a long way to ensure that we will survive as many partitioning scenarios as possible without violating consistency. We will describe this in a later chapter on handling crashes in MySQL Cluster.

However there is more to the CAP theorem and MySQL Cluster. We support replicating from one cluster to another cluster in another part of the world. This replication is asynchronous. For replication between clusters we sacrifice consistency to improve availability in the presence of Partitioning (network partitioning). The figure below shows an architecture for replication between two clusters. As can be seen here it is possible to have two replication channels. Global replication is implemented using standard MySQL Replication where the replication happens in steps of a group of transactions (epochs).

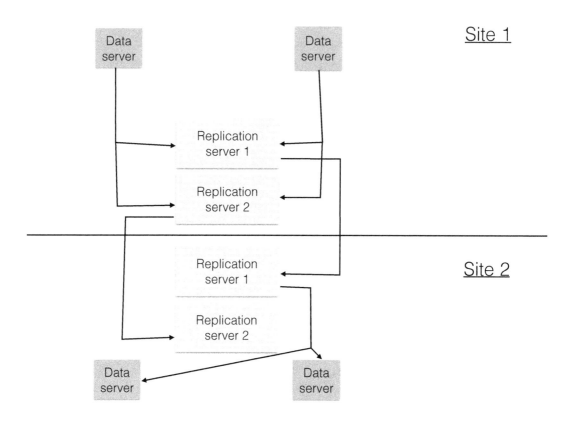

If the network is partitioned between the two clusters (or more than two clusters) then each cluster will continue to operate. How failures are handled here is manually handled (implemented as a set of automated scripts that might have some manual interaction points).

MySQL Cluster gives the possibility to focus on consistency in each individual local cluster but still providing the extra level of availability by handling partitioned networks and disasters hitting a complete region of the world. Global replication is implemented and used by many users using this in critical applications.

The replication between clusters can support writing in all clusters with conflict resolution. More on this in the chapter on MySQL Cluster Replication.

2.6   OLTP, OLAP AND RELATIONAL MODELS

There are many DBMSs implemented in this world. They all strive to do similar things. They take data and place it in some data structure for efficient access. DBMSs can be divided into

OLTP (On-line Transaction Processing) and OLAP (On-line Analytical Processing). There are databases focused on special data sets such as hierarchical data referred to as graph databases, other types are specialised DBMSs for geographical data (GIS). There is a set of DBMSs focused on time-series data.

The most commonly used DBMSs are based on the relational model. Lately we have seen a development of numerous Big Data solutions. These data solutions focus on massive data sets that require scaling into thousands of computers and more. MySQL Cluster will scale to hundreds of computers, but will do so while maintaining consistency inside the cluster. It will provide predictable response times even in large clusters.

MySQL Cluster is a DBMS focused on OLTP, one of the most unique points of NDB is that 1 transaction with 10 operations takes similar time to 10 transactions with 1 operation each. An OLTP DBMS always focus on row-based storage and so does MySQL Cluster. An OLAP DBMS will often focus on columnar data storage since it makes scanning data in modern processors much faster. At the same time the columnar storage increases the overhead in changing the data. MySQL Cluster use row storage.

2.7 DATA STORAGE REQUIREMENTS

In the past almost all DBMSs focused on storing data on disk with a page cache. In the 1990s the size of main memory grew to a point where it was sometimes interesting to use data which always resides in memory. Nowadays most major DBMS have a main memory options, many of those are used for efficient analytics, but some also use it for higher transaction throughput and best possible response time.

NDB chose to store data in main memory mainly to provide predictable response time. At the same time we have developed an option for tables to store some columns on disk with a page cache. This can be used to provide a much larger data set stored in NDB using SSD storage. Disk data is primarily intended for use with SSDs since most current MySQL Cluster applications have stringent requirements on response time.

2.7.1 MySQL Cluster and Big Data

MySQL Cluster was designed long before Big Data solutions came around, but the design of NDB fits well into the Big Data world. It has automatic sharding of the data, queries can get data from all shards in the cluster. NDB is easy to work with since it uses transactions to change data which means that the application won't have to consider how to solve data inconsistencies.

The data structures in NDB is designed for main memory. The hash index is designed to avoid CPU cache misses and so is the access to the row storage. The ordered index is using a T-tree data structure specifically designed for main memory. The page cache uses a modern caching algorithm which takes into account both data in the page cache as well as data that have since long been evoked from the page cache when making decisions of the heat level of a page.

Thus the basic data structure components in NDB are all of top notch quality which gives us the ability to deliver benchmarks with 200 million reads per second and beyond.

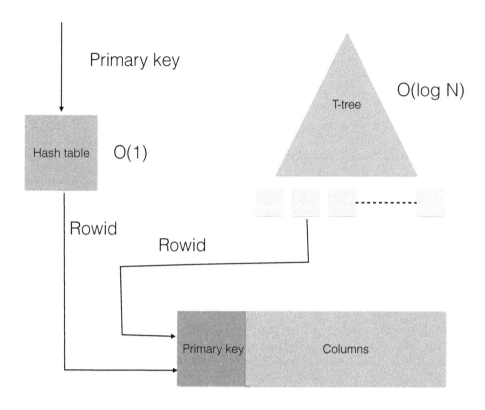

2.7.2 UNIQUE SELLING POINT OF MYSQL CLUSTER

The most important unique selling points for MySQL Cluster comes from our ability to failover instantly, to be able to add indexes, drop indexes, add columns, add tables, drop tables, add node groups and reorganise data to use those new node groups, change software in one node at a time or multiple at a time, add tablespaces, add files to tablespaces. All of these changes and more can all be done while the DBMS is up and running and all data can still be both updated and read, including the tables that are currently changed. All of this can happen even with nodes in the cluster leaving and joining. The most unique feature of MySQL Cluster I call AlwaysOn. It is designed to never go down, only bugs in the software or very complex changes can bring down the system and even that can be handled most of the time by using MySQL replication to a backup cluster.

There are many thousands of NDB clusters up and running that have met tough requirements on availability. Important to remember here is that to reach such high availability requires a skilled operational team and processes to handle all types of problems that can occur and of course 24x7 support.

CHAPTER 3

USE CASES FOR MySQL CLUSTER

You might wonder how many people are using MySQL Cluster. In reality billions of people on the earth is using NDB indirectly. You might be using NDB when doing any of of the following: placing a phone call (HLR), starting your computer (DHCP), opening up a web page (DNS, Web Server, ..), logging into an on-line computer game, playing an on-line computer game, placing a stock order, watching some video service, paying for a service on the internet, shopping in a store, placing a bet in an online betting service, handling documents on the internet, reading online news, anything related to phone call services.

The list of things that could invoke usage of MySQL Cluster is long. In this chapter we will describe a few of the use cases and what characteristics of NDB that makes developers select it as their data management solution.

NDB was originally developed at Ericsson for telecom database requirements, these requirements included Class 5 availability, high update rates and low latency operations in a distributed system.

Class 5 availability means that it is available 99.999% of the time, available means that both reads and writes are possible. This means no more than 5 minutes downtime per year. To reach this requirement the database must be both readable and writeable during all normal management actions. This includes during software upgrade, computer upgrades, application upgrades, and most common schema changes.

The only downtime allowed is when the entire cluster fails. To reach the highest availability one needs to combine MySQL Cluster in two data centers with MySQL Cluster Replication between the data centers. Using this setup it is possible to reach Class 6 availability (less than 30 seconds downtime per year) and higher.

In the IT world a system that can reach Class 4 availability (no more than 50 minutes downtime per year) is considered a high availability system. Most cloud vendors doesn't promise more than 99.95% availability even when using replication in several availability zones (thus an application in the cloud will have to live with up to 260 minutes of downtime per year for the cloud itself).

Given that most applications would define their system as an HA application (HA = high availability) already when reaching Class 4 availability (almost an hour downtime per year), I use a new term for MySQL Cluster, the term is AlwaysOn, this is the most important unique selling point of MySQL Cluster. Thus to be an AlwaysOn system requires reaching Class 6 availability. This can only be reached by combining very high availability inside one cluster combined with replication to other regions of the world.

Quite a few database management systems can handle millions of reads per second. There are very few systems that can reach millions of writes per second. NDB has demonstrated

205 million reads per second and around 20 million writes per second. This benchmarks was performed almost five years ago.

MySQL Cluster can perform distributed transactions involving hundreds of rows being read and written in a few millisecond and a single simple transaction can complete in much less than 100 microseconds.

Finally some words on use cases where MySQL Cluster normally would not fit. If your application doesn't require high availability and simply requires low latency and high throughput and the database fits in one machine. In this case it is difficult for NDB to compete since a database that runs everything in memory with no context switches is difficult to beat with an architecture designed for a distributed system.

Even in such scenarios NDB have decent performance and latency. We have worked hard in every version to minimise the latency and maximise the throughput while at the same time allowing the architecture to scale towards extreme transaction rates.

MySQL Cluster is mainly intended for OLTP applications that does a bit of analytical queries. The performance of complex queries depends a bit on how well the query integrates with the NDB architecture.

As soon as some sort of replication comes into play MySQL Cluster have a large advantage with its efficient replication solution. Traditionally NDB have been a perfect fit for use cases with high update rates. With the introduction of the possibility to read any replica in MySQL Cluster 7.5 there is a much better fit for use cases with high read rates.

The new feature introduced in MySQL Cluster 7.5 to have tables that are replicated in all data nodes in the cluster means that you can build cluster scenarios where we use NDB for read scaling of one data set with up to 48 machines that can handle tens of millions of SQL queries for one data set of sizes up to a terabyte.

3.1   NETWORKING APPLICATIONS

Networking applications was the first category where MySQL Cluster found market success. The first user that put NDB into production was the company Bredbandsbolaget in Sweden. They used (and still do as far as I know) NDB for a networking application to support their Internet access service. NDB was used as the data layer in a DNS and DHCP infrastructure. Interestingly I used this service myself personally for about 10 years. The service is still operational and have used MySQL Cluster from version 3.4 and up.

Networking infrastructure requires a number of services to map names to numbers, lease addresses and various authorization and authentication services.

All of those are fairly mild in their requirements on throughput and scalability, but they have tough requirements on availability and predictable response times. It is a natural fit for MySQL Cluster.

3.1.1   DNS SERVER

We start by showing the simplest possible application which is a DNS Server. The DNS server performs translation from web addresses to IP numbers. As an example one might come in with www.dn.se and get back 169.123.124.55 (not any real IP address). Thus the web server (or some more local DNS server) does a DNS lookup to the DNS server. This arrives at the DNS Server that looks it up using some kind of database query (most likely a simple primary key lookup in this case) using the web address as key and retrieving one or more IP addresses. The DNS server will then package a response package to the requester.

In the figure we have only shown the DNS Server computers and the data nodes. Most likely there are computers handling management queries, a computer handling one or more NDB management servers. There could be more than 2 DNS server computers, and there could be more than 2 data nodes. There could be other applications running in the same cluster to handle other service types.

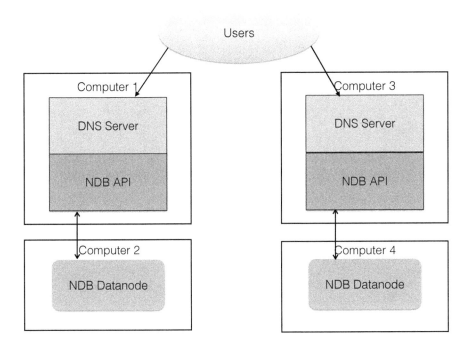

A DNS server is a fit for NDB and was actually one of the first applications where MySQL Cluster was brought into production usage. The benefit that MySQL Cluster provides is the high availability story. A DNS server that is down will be quickly noted by the customers of the ISP. DNS Servers higher up in the DNS caching chain will have even more impact. It is essential that DNS servers are developed with high availability in mind.

The DNS server application is mostly about reading the data. This means that we could make use of the feature to fully replicate the data and thus have the DNS server scale to 48 data nodes and in this case it makes sense to colocate the DNS servers and the data nodes such that the DNS server only reads from its local data node.

In the figure we have shown a case where the DNS server and the data nodes are placed on separate machines. This is probably easier to manage since one can upgrade the DNS server more independently of the NDB data nodes, MySQL Servers and NDB management servers.

3.1.2   DHCP Server

The figure above for how to handle a DNS server using NDB works for a a DHCP server as well. A DHCP server handles short term leases of IPv4 addresses. A computer that starts up (or a router even more likely) will send a request for a lease of an IPv4 address. The DHCP server will look for a free IP address and return an IP address that the requester can use.

One major difference is that this application will make updates to its data on most requests. This makes it even more important to handle high availability. A DNS server could possibly get away with a short read-only mode. But for a DHCP server a read-only mode or server being down is the same thing since a DHCP server needs to write data as part of most user requests.

A DHCP server is a good example of an application that can use MySQL Cluster and was part of the first use cases in production for NDB.

An open source DHCP Server called Kea have tested and verified all sorts of failure scenarios with multiple DHCP servers working together in a cluster using MySQL Cluster. To find descriptions of these and documentation on how to set it up for use with Kea simply google with key words MySQL+Cluster+Kea.

3.1.3   RADIUS Server

Another common service used in both IT environments as well as telecom environments is AAA servers (Triple A). This stands for Authentication, Authorization and Accounting.

RADIUS is a protocol that implements the requests for AAA services.

A RADIUS server uses a database in most cases to provide its services and it is important that this database is highly available since otherwise it is not possible to authenticate and authorize the users.

Thus it is a similar service to DNS server and DHCP server where there is both a read part and an update part and the service need to be AlwaysOn.

An example of a product in this category using MySQL Cluster is the Juniper product SBR Carrier. It makes use of all the benefits of NDB by providing a set of applications that directly access the data through the NDB API, they have LDAP access using an LDAP server, storing data in NDB accessed through the NDB API, they can also access data through SQL and the MySQL Servers.

3.2   Telecom servers

DNS and DHCP servers are good examples coming from the IT world. There are many examples coming from the telecom world as well. Most of the original requirements on MySQL Cluster came from this application category. Thus there is an obvious fit for many telecom applications.

The decision process to bring in a new product into a telecom network is a bit longer than in the networking area, but the market success for MySQL Cluster in the telecom sector have been excellent and in a number of categories NDB is the market leader.

The name NDB originally came from Network DataBase. Network databases started appearing as separate telecom nodes in the 1980s beginning with the introduction of 800-numbers in the US. 800-numbers was numbers where the receiver of the call always paid for the call. These numbers were popular for companies since they made it easy to get in touch with its customers for all sorts of reasons.

When 800-numbers was introduced there was a need to make an intelligent translation of this 800-number to a real phone number. It was possible to use time of day, originator of the call and many other aspects to calculate the number.

What happened was that the telecom operator had to handle a large database with number translation information. The first network databases were written as applications bundled with the data. This meant that the application was harder to manage than necessary. Thus it was desirable to put the data into a real database and thus make it possible to manage its data using standard interfaces such as SQL queries.

Traditional databases didn't qualify for this task since availability requirements was higher than what could be provided by the traditional DBMS vendors.

This led to the development of a new category of DBMSs that all originated from telecom vendors and from telecom operators. NDB was one of those DBMSs developed, but there were many other competing implementations, in Ericsson alone there were a number of competing solutions.

The combination of the characteristics of NDB and the characteristics of MySQL and the market success of MySQL made MySQL Cluster the market winner in this application category.

Thus many other applications can ride on the benefits of this development in the telecom industry to develop many other applications. The first benefactor was the IT sector that got a number of network applications that made good use of the high availability features of NDB.

There are many different types of network databases using NDB in use today in all sorts of telecom networks using many thousands of servers.

The newest development in the telecom industry that happened in the first years of the new millenium is that the telecom vendors realised that it was time to ensure that many of those telecom applications should use a common database.

The availability requirements on this common database is even higher than the individual applications. This was a good fit for MySQL Cluster. It was an early market success for NDB.

The variety of applications and how they are implemented in the telecom network is simply to great to put into one picture. There are examples using only SQL for the entire application, there are examples using the NDB API for most of traffic use cases and SQL for management use cases and there are use cases involving Java APIs and LDAP APIs.

I will provide a few example applications from the telecom sector. A few examples can also be found at the MySQL home page, such as the Myriad use case of MySQL Cluster.

3.2.1 NUMBER PORTABILITY DEMO

The origin of MySQL Cluster is an Ericsson project that started in 1997 (thoughts on NDB started already in 1991 see chapter on history of MySQL Cluster). The original aim of this project was to develop a prototype of Number Portability for a telecom vendor.

At the time most phones were still fixed phones and the numbers were connected to the telecom switches. The first few numbers in the telephone number assisted in deciding where to connect the call. This prevented telephone users from keeping the same telephone number when they moved to a new region of their country. In a similar fashion to mobile phones there was a need to develop a more flexible numbering scheme. The idea here was to use a database to translate from the users telephone number to the physical telephone number, the physical telephone number still pointed out which switches to use in the connection setup.

Number Portability Demo

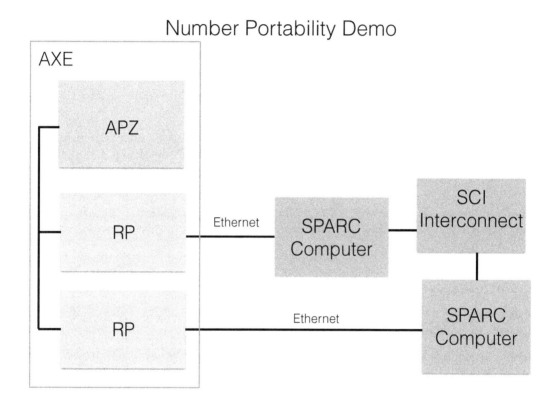

NDB was developed to provide this number translation through a database table. By making this database table external to the telecom switch and by providing a database interface the management of the number portability application became much easier compared to executing proprietary commands towards the telecom switches.

The prototype was built using the telecom switch from Ericsson called AXE. The AXE had a central processor called APZ and many assisting regional processors (RPs). Some of those regional processors had the ability to connect via Ethernet and TCP/IP.

The first prototype of NDB connected two regional processors in AXE to two SPARC machines that contained the database as seen in the figure above. As part of a call setup a message was sent from the APZ to one of the RPs connecting to a SPARC server over Ethernet. Next the message was sent over Ethernet to the SPARC and there an application program accessed one of the database servers over SCI using an early version of the NDB API. Finally the message was delivered back to the APZ in the same fashion to enable the use of portable telephone numbers.

Updates of the data in this application was done only when people moved, so it was a management procedure that happened outside of the telecom switch. There was a lot of work done in the 1990s to standardize management of telecom switches and the introduction of network databases was one such trend that is nowadays a standard part of any telecom network.

The project as such was a success and we managed to prove that one could access an external DBMS within 4 milliseconds as part of setting up a connection. The success of NDB came much later since there was intense competition at this time at Ericssson in this area. Another popular open source database Mnesia (part of Erlang) also originated from Ericsson in those days and also two other internal database projects within Ericsson.

Availability and response time were the two main requirements on the database product used in those cases. To provide response time we used Dolphin SCI cards to connect the nodes in the cluster. At this time the TCP/IP interface was only a debugging interface used in development whereas the Dolphin SCI cards provided the communication between ths SPARC servers in this Number Portability Demo.

The software architecture of NDB internally borrowed a lot of ideas from the AXE and this is a major reason why we have been able to build a DBMS that can handle hundreds of millions of reads per second.

3.2.2   JUNIPER SBR CARRIER DATABASE

Juniper offers a solution for various needs in telecom networks. The product has extensive documentation freely available.

This product implements among other things a RADIUS server, a DIAMETER server, access directly from MySQL Server using SQL, an HLR and many other telco services. NDB serves all these applications with a highly available data service with many different APIs.

NDB is here used in another important application category for MySQL Cluster. It is used as a high availability session store. This was a first use of NDB in web applications.

The large variety of ways to access to MySQL Cluster was an important reason for developing NDB. The management of telecom networks are using a flurry of standard interfaces. The ability to combine access using standard interfaces such as SQL and LDAP combined with low level APIs that can be used for traffic parts of the application is an important combination that solves a real problem in telecom networks.

The management applications are often costly to develop and requires the use of standard interfaces to make it easy to use various 3rd party tools as part of the application development.

At the same time the traffic applications have stringent needs on predictable latency, high throughput and very high availability. Here the use of a low level API can be used to squeeze out a lot more performance from small servers.

This combination was an integral part of the thoughts that led to the development of MySQL Cluster.

The database can here be accessed using various means, through an LDAP interface, there

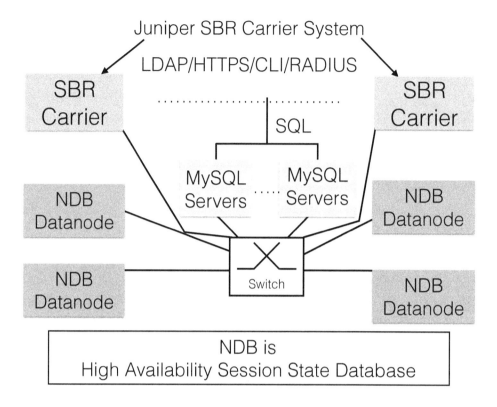

is the traditional MySQL interface that carries SQL, there is application programs that uses NDB API to implement the RADIUS server parts, the DIAMETER server and the HLR parts and many other parts.

This service is an integral part of a telecom network that provides authentication and authorization of users entering a private network.

It is implemented in hundreds of networks world-wide at places like airports in large parts of the world.

Most applications of MySQL Cluster have an international presence since it is possible to have high availability of the cluster combined with geographical replication to other sites as well.

3.2.3 UNIVERSAL DATABASE

This is a product that has different names from different vendors. It makes it possible to store data about users and their services in a stand-alone system that all other systems can use (HLR, AAA, Number Translation) and so forth. It is a system that has the absolutely highest availability requirements and MySQL Cluster is a fit for these systems and is heavily used in this category by major telco vendors such as Alcatel (nowadays Nokia).

3.2.4 HLR

An HLR (Home Location Register) is used in a call setup to find out where a mobile is currently located. Thus each time the mobile is changing location area the HLR needs to update the location information of the mobile. The HLR also keeps track of various telecom services of the mobile subscription.

This is a important and key part of the mobile telecom network and requires the outmost availability. Many operators implement their own services using MySQL Cluster such as Italtel.

3.2.5 VIDEO SERVICES

A more recent example in the telecom industry is using MySQL Cluster for various video on demand (VoD) services.

3.2.6 OTHER TELCO SERVICES

Here is a list of a few other telecom services that benefits from using MySQL Cluster.

1. Service Delivery Applications

2. Mobile Content Apps

3. Online mobile portals

4. Payment Gateways

5. Software Defined Networking (SDN)

6. Network Function Virtualization (NFV)

7. Voice over IP applications

3.3 GAMING SYSTEMS

One category of applications that have found a fit with MySQL Cluster is gaming applications. I often used this example to describe my work for my kids when they were small since they played a lot of the games that was supported in various ways by MySQL Cluster.

The developers of gaming applications differ quite a lot from the telecom developers. Telecom developers are used to developing applications at a low level and they are used to long development cycles with extensive testing. This means that they are often more willing to commit to developing on a lower level where they can get gains of up to 10x better performance by doing more development work.

The gaming industry requires more online development and much faster reaction to the needs of the gamers. Thus this category of developers often use more hardware and larger clusters than the telecom sectors. They are much more inclined to use the MySQL Servers as front-ends to the NDB data nodes rather than an NDB API application or the Java API towards NDB.

The figure above shows the three levels of servers involved in the gaming applications. First we have the gaming apps themselves, second we have a set of MySQL Servers and lastly we have a set of NDB data nodes.

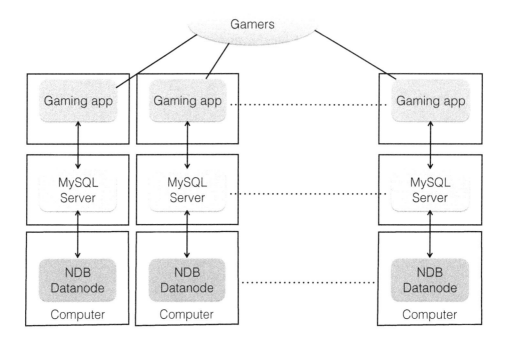

The application parts that makes use of MySQL Cluster differs wildly. One example could be to handle the gamer profiles when the gamer logs into the application. Another use case could be maintaining various statistics about the game and another use case could keep the real-time status of the ongoing games in the database.

Gaming applications make a lot of updates as part of all those parts of the applications. There is a great variety of complex read queries originating from this type of applications. Thus our pushdown of join queries into the data nodes is an important feature for this type of applications.

A gaming company will receive lots of bad marketing if the gaming applications are not working properly due to some type of outage. In this application the high availability is a key differentiator to make use of MySQL Cluster, but also its write scalability as well as its ability to run many parallel complex queries on the data.

NDB makes it easy to scale the application since the application layer, the MySQL Server layer and the data node layer can be scaled independently of each other.

Gaming applications is one of the most demanding applications on the scalability of MySQL Cluster. A case study of how BigFish, a gaming company, uses MySQL Cluster is available on the MySQL web site.

3.4 FINANCIAL APPLICATIONS

Financial applications was the first focus areas for MySQL Cluster around the years 2000-2002. We actually delivered a working solution to a customer in this area using version 1.1 of NDB. The focus at the time was mostly on being able to handle the throughput requirements of the combination of a busy stock feed and the many queries in real-time to find out what stocks are available for buying. To meet those requirements was hard at the time.

The IT crash delayed our entry into this area considerably. The applications in this category have requirements that make MySQL Cluster a very good fit in some cases.

The figure below shows how this application can make use also of the ClusterJ interface. The ClusterJ is an interface that uses Java and object-mapping to work with NDB. This makes it easy to develop applications using this interface that have very good performance.

It is possible of course to replace ClusterJ by JDBC and a MySQL server if it is desirable to use SQL for queries.

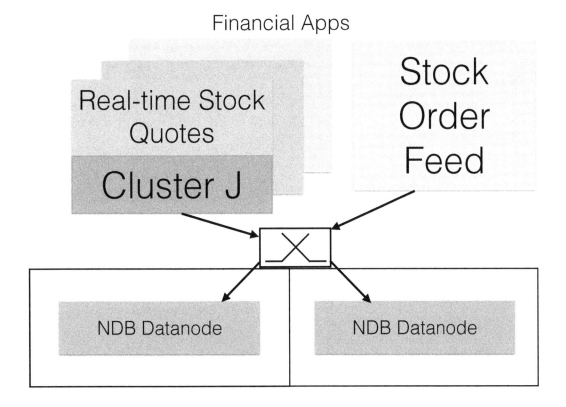

There are many potential use cases around payment services. One could use MySQL Cluster for whitelists and blacklists, one could use NDB to handle various micro payment services.

In this category many applications are developed using Java and ClusterJ, our Java NDB API, that gives direct access to cluster data is an important part of use cases in this category.

3.4.1 TRADING APPLICATION

In a trading application as shown above, there is a stream of updates coming from each new stock order. These updates have to be applied at a high speed with low delay. At the same time it is important to deliver reads of this data as well with predictable response time.

This application requires high availability during the time the stock exchange is open, but when the stock exchange shuts down the system can be stopped. NDB have been shown to handle a million transactions per second while at the same providing room for other types of analytical queries as well in use cases like this one.

The reason to choose MySQL Cluster for this application is its ability to deliver predictable response time. We had a user some years ago that used all real-time options of MySQL Cluster and real-time options on the applications side. They were able to perform 100% of the read operations returning in a few hundred microseconds or less. MySQL Cluster can handle millions of transactions per second which is a requirement in a busy stock exchange that could have large peak loads.

3.4.2 PAYMENT SERVICES

There are many parts of a payment service where MySQL Cluster can be used in an efficient manner. Examples are handling micro payments and fraud detection. Any payment services of eCommerce on the internet is required to have high availability since a payment service being down leads to lost revenue quickly.

At MySQL Connect 2012 PayPal gave a keynote presentation about their reasons for choosing MySQL Cluster for a global fraud detection service. This application category has quite a few use cases for NDB.

3.4.3 ONLINE BANKING SERVICES

A current trend in banking is to provide online banking services without having any physical offices of the bank to visit. Many such banking services rely on a high availability data store and we have a number of examples of such users using MySQL Cluster.

3.5 FRAUD DETECTION

A white paper on MySQLs home page shows how Anura.io use MySQL Cluster for fraud detection.

3.6 WEB APPLICATIONS

MySQL has been traditionally used for all sorts of web applications. This hasn't been an area where MySQL Cluster had a lot of impact in the past. Our initial success in this category was where NDB was used as a session database for e-commerce applications and in various other parts of the e-commerce applications.

Interestingly the first prototype application in this category was developed already in 1999, it was a web cache server based on an old implementation of the NDB API in Java. This development was important since it brought NDB into the presence of Ericsson Business Innovation where NDB matured from an innovation into a product ready for market launch.

With the changes in MySQL Cluster 7.5, it is easy to setup a set of computers that all acts as masters where you can read all data locally. This is a good fit for many web applications where MySQL is traditionally used with MySQL replication. The benefits of using MySQL Cluster in those cases comes from the ease in setting up replication and that data changes are synchronous so there is never any need to worry about replication lags, there will never be any lag.

In the past most people that tried to use MySQL Cluster with Wordpress had performance issues since most of the complex queries had to go over the network. Now by using a setup with full replication combined with colocating each data node with a MySQL Server means that all reads will be local and will not require to use the network. At the same time any update is immediately seen by all MySQL Servers at once. With this setup in 7.5 and later MySQL Cluster versions it should be possible to get good scalability using MySQL Cluster.

The benefits of using NDB here is that all MySQL Servers see the updates immediately, it is easy to continue scaling the cluster by simply adding more data nodes and MySQL Servers. One could easily start with e.g. 3 replicas of the data and continue in steps of 3 servers at the time to grow the number of servers up to 48 servers. No downtime is needed during this scaling process, only a number of rolling restarts where the cluster is still fully operational and with 3 replicas it will be replicated during the rolling restarts (e.g. by restarting 1/3 of the servers at a time).

Examples of web applications that would benefit from using MySQL Cluster:

1. eCommerce Applications

2. Session Databases

3. Enterprise Application Servers

4. User Profile Management

5. Highly available Web sites

6. Online Gaming State

7. Virtual Reality Worlds

3.7 SOFT REAL-TIME APPLICATIONS

The development of various control applications requires a real-time database with very high availability. MySQL Cluster have a good fit thus for controlling trains, cars and many other vehicles. Predictable response time with very high availability of the service is again a key factor in choosing NDB here.

This is a new category of applications that is still in its infancy and will continue to develop over the coming years.

3.8 ORACLE OPENSTACK

OpenStack is a framework developed by a large number of corporations to develop applications for various cloud environments, both private and public.

Part of the OpenStack framework is a database that contains various configuration data and other information. The various components of OpenStack all make use of this database.

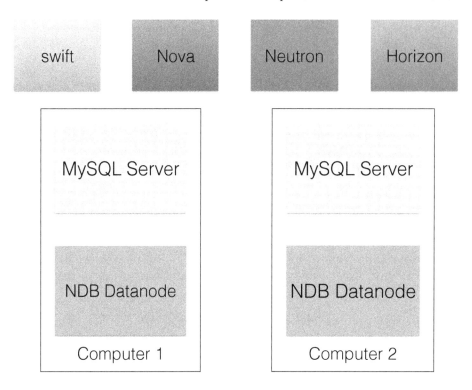

In the Oracle solution for OpenStack there is a high availability configuration where MySQL Cluster is used for this database. The reason for MySQL Cluster is the simplicity in setting up a highly available environment where all MySQL servers can be used for both updating and reading. There is no need to specifically handle master and slave roles of the MySQL Server since the MySQL Cluster data is updated using transactions and thus all MySQL Servers acts as masters.

The same database can also be used for application data of the OpenStack installation.

3.9   GE

General Electric presented a number of templates for how GE applications should setup data services as part of the keynote session on MySQL Central, a recent MySQL Conference held in conjunction with Oracle Open World 2015. They all included using MySQL Cluster. They used synchronous replication inside each cluster, but they also used MySQL Cluster replication between the clusters and made use of multi-master support for MySQL replication using NDB.

In the selection of DBMS to use the following requirements was placed on the DBMS:

1. Available across regions

2. Scalable Data Store

3. Class 5 availability (less than 5 minutes downtime per year)

4. Quick deployment and ease of use

5. Performance and Productivity

6. Time to market and cost

Many different solutions was tested ranging from SQL databases, NoSQL databases, MySQL with replication and MySQL Cluster. MySQL Cluster was selected among other things for its solutions for redundancy, ACID compliant and its auto-sharding features.

GE developed a number of templates for how to use MySQL Cluster in GE applications.

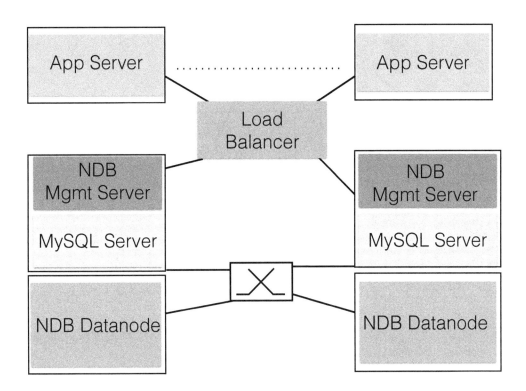

The first template shows how to setup a local cluster. It uses a standard HA setup for MySQL Cluster where two computers are used for the data nodes and two computers for the MySQL Servers. NDB management servers are placed on the MySQL Server computers. This architecture can survive all single failures of one computer. It is easy to scale up both the MySQL layer (no need for extra NDB management servers though when adding more MySQL Servers) and the Data node layer.

On top of this local cluster the applications access a load balancer that will balance requests between the MySQL Servers. The NDB API contains similar functionality to ensure that data nodes are used in a balanced manner.

Takeways that GE had was to not colocate data nodes and NDB management servers. They saw the need to organize nodes correctly and to consider carefully the size of RAM to avoid running out of memory in the database.

They used MySQL Enterprise Monitor (MEM) to monitor the MySQL Server. MEM 4.0 have been extended to now also monitor the MySQL Cluster components, it is now more valuable to use MEM in combination with NDB. MEM provides graphical interfaces to information derived from the ndbinfo database that provides information about various statistics and states of internal operations of the MySQL Cluster.

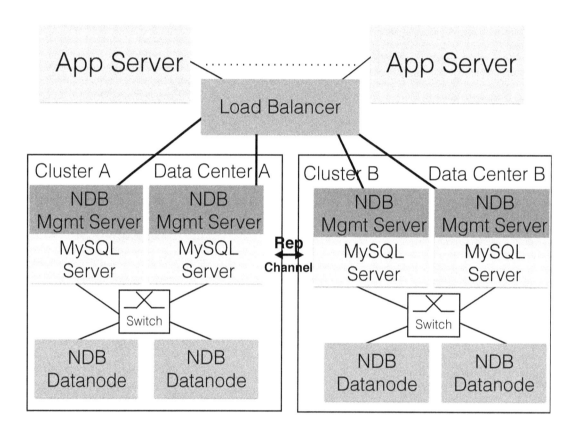

The next template uses MySQL replication combined with MySQL Cluster to provide availability across regions of the world. In this case both MySQL Servers have a replication channel to the other cluster and these can be used to fail over to another replication channel in case of failure of a MySQL Server.

The MySQL replication can be extended in MySQL Cluster to handle multi-site replication with more than two sites. It can handle updates coming from any of those sites. In this case there are conflict detection mechanisms available to select which transaction that should survive in case of conflicts. A number of different methods exist here that will be presented in the part on Global Replication.

3.10 HADOOP FILE SERVER

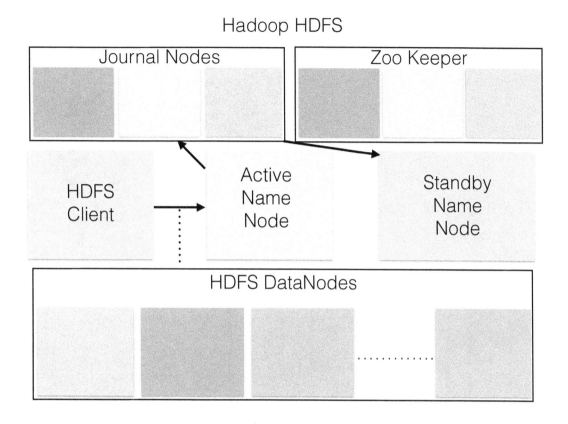

An interesting use case for MySQL Cluster is to implement a file system upon NDB. This is an idea I pursued myself in a hobby project of mine, iClaustron. Another example is HopsFS which is an implementation of a Hadoop File Server where the metadata servers are using MySQL Cluster to store the metadata of the file system. Another prototype have been built where NDB is used as a block device, this used the disk data parts of NDB.

NDB fits very well to implement a transactional file system. NDB can handle millions of updates per second, it can use the disk data implementation to handle parts residing on disk. The low level APIs ensure that the overhead of SQL isn't bothering the implementation. It solves the problem of redundancy internally in NDB, file system implementors can focus on the interface issues and solving problems with a relational database to implement a hierarchical file system. The main problem here comes when moving entire parts of the file system from one place to another.

In a traditional implementation of Hadoop HDFS there is only one active Name Node handling the metadata of HDFS. Thus the file system cannot sustain more than about 75k file operations per second and the total metadata size can only grow to around 100 GBytes.

The single name node makes use of three journal nodes to replicate the changes to a stand-by name node. In addition three Zone-keeper nodes are used for heartbeating. A total of 8 nodes are needed to provide high availability of the meta data in Hadoop HDFS. This provides no scalability, only availability.

Another problem is that a large part of the files used are small files that are only a few kBytes in size. To access those through the name nodes and HDFS data nodes introduces a lot of extra latency in their access.

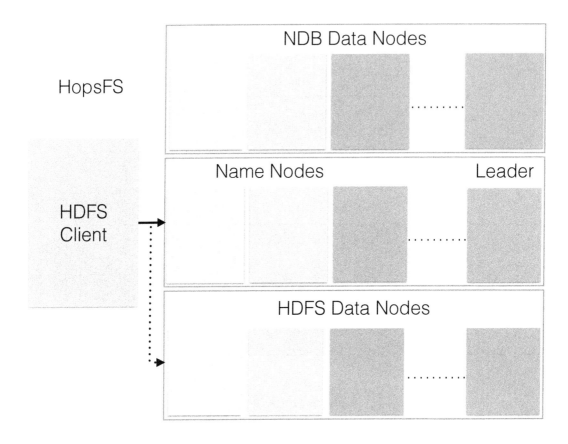

With HopsFS using the MySQL Cluster 7.5 the file system can scale to at least 1.4M file operations per second and given enough machines it is likely that it can scale to about 5M file operations per second. The total metadata size can scale to many tens of terabytes and it is possible to store a part of the files in MySQL Cluster. The remainder of the larger files are stored in the Hadoop Data Nodes.

SICS, a research institute have developed HopsFS and it was presented at USENIX in early 2017. It has been proven to scale to 60 Name Nodes with 12 NDB data nodes used to store the actual data.

HopsFS is implemented in Java and uses the ClusterJ, the direct NDB API accessible from Java.

HopsFS won the IEEE Scale Challenge Award in 2017 and was presented at Usenix the same year.

Using MySQL Cluster provides better scalability compared to a centralised metadata server, it provides better availability compared to a replicated centralised meta data server.

In iClaustron the idea is to store both metadata and file data in MySQL Cluster.

3.10.1 HopsYARN

Another part of the Hops infrastructure that uses MySQL Cluster is HopsYARN. It implements scheduling and resource handling services in the Hadoop framework.

Again the simplicity of getting high availability together with predictable response time is the key factor in choosing MySQL Cluster.

3.11 LDAP SERVER

It is possible to implement an LDAP server on top of MySQL Cluster. Some users implement their own LDAP servers, but there is also a back end interface to MySQL Cluster for the OpenLDAP server that works. Using LDAP on top of MySQL Cluster provides highly available solutions for various security services.

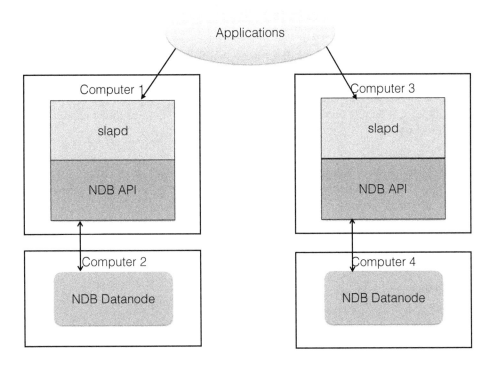

3.12 NoSQL APPLICATIONS

Using NDB as a key-value store by using the asynchronous API of the NDB API provides a clustered key-value store that can handle hundreds of millions of key-value lookups per second.

There are many other NoSQL applications where NDB will be a good fit as well. It was designed for scalable and networked applications.

3.13   CONCLUSION

MySQL Cluster is used in a lot of applications that requires having data always available. Most of those applications require response time to be predictable. Most of them fit into sizes of memory in modern servers.

The range of applications is very wide showing that MySQL Cluster is now a mature product that have been applied in so different application types as telecom applications, networking applications, gaming, betting, file services, LDAP servers, web sessions, web applications, real-time financial applications, medical applications and much more.

The most common reasons for not selecting MySQL Cluster is requiring bigger data sizes, or simply not being able to afford memory as data storage. MySQL Cluster have an option that one can store non-indexed attributes on disk using a page cache. This option makes it possible to store bigger data sets in MySQL Cluster. The other nice thing for MySQL Cluster is that memory is getting more and more affordable and the development of new memory types such as the new 3D XPoint by Intel promises to deliver almost 10x more memory for the same price with only slightly worse performance. Thus as technology develops, more and more applications will be able to use MySQL Cluster.

It is important to remember that MySQL Cluster is a fully recoverable DBMS. This means that a consistent database is restored in cases of a full cluster crash.

As a conclusion we can see that the decision in NDB Cluster to divide the Data Server from the Query Server is an important choice that allows NDB to be used in many other areas other than as an SQL database.

We can build an SQL Server on top of the Data Server as has been shown in NDB. We can similarly build a file server on top of NDB as has been shown by HopsFS in developing a Hadoop File Server based on NDB. Similarly we can build an LDAP Server on top of NDB as has been shown in OpenLDAP and by numerous telco users of MySQL Cluster.

Thus the architecture of NDB makes MySQL Cluster useful for many types of data services requiring high scalability, high performance and high availability.

Personally I am looking forward to seeing MySQL Cluster used to implement various genealogical databases.

CHAPTER 4

NDB AND INNODB

One place where one could consider using MySQL Cluster is to replace use cases where MySQL/InnoDB is currently used. There are cases when this is a good idea to do and there are cases when such a switch is not a good idea.

This chapter we will try to give some descriptions of the differences between MySQL/InnoDB and MySQL Cluster to assist in understanding if a switch to NDB makes sense.

We will use the term NDB in this chapter for MySQL Cluster since MySQL Cluster is a MySQL Server using the NDB storage engine, this comparison is a comparison of the InnoDB storage engine and the NDB storage engine. They both use the same MySQL Server code.

4.1 DIFFERENCES BETWEEN NDB AND INNODB

The differences can be categorized as performance differences, feature differences, availability differences, differences in how consistency is handled and there are some minor differences in how features are implemented.

4.1.1 PERFORMANCE DIFFERENCES

The first thing to consider is whether the performance will be improved or if it will be worse using NDB. The answer is very much "it depends".

First of all it is important that we are here considering whether to use NDB or InnoDB as a storage engine. The most important difference here is that InnoDB is a local storage engine, thus each call from the MySQL Server code into the storage engine is a local call and will never leave the MySQL Server process. Each call will in most cases be evaluated in the same thread as the MySQL Server process.

This has advantages in that very few context switches are required to execute a short query. It has disadvantages in that it makes it difficult to make use of several threads and even more so using several computers to execute a query.

When calls are made into the NDB storage engine it will frequently have to traverse a transporter (a socket) and return again as part of the storage engine call. To handle this the NDB storage engine has done a lot of optimisations to perform those calls in a batching mode. But many queries are still going to involve frequent communication with the data node.

There are a few dimensions where NDB and InnoDB differs. The first as mentioned is that NDB is a distributed storage engine whereas InnoDB is a local storage engine. The second dimension is that NDB stores most of the data in memory and InnoDB stores things on disk using a page cache. The third dimension that NDB and InnoDB differs in is the threading model. NDB consists of multiple data nodes and each data node consists of multiple threads that need to communicate. InnoDB makes accesses to data from the MySQL Server thread and uses various mutexes, condition variables and other ways of handling concurrent threads accessing the same data.

So what does this mean for performance? It means that the performance story is mixed. There are many cases where InnoDB is faster when access is made through the MySQL Server, but there are also cases where NDB is faster and there are lots of cases where performance is similar.

As an example from Sysbench InnoDB has advantages in that there is no context switches to handle during execution of a simple SQL query. At the same time a query that performs an ordered index scan searching for 100 rows (a common query in Sysbench) can automatically parallelise this search in NDB. Since InnoDB uses lots of mutexes to protect shared data structures it will suffer contention for write-intensive application. NDB divides data into separate threads and can thus scale very well for write-intensive applications. Each data node can handle millions of updates per second.

Performance has two components, latency and throughput. Latency is affected by both the distributed nature, the threading model and whether data is resident in memory or not. If InnoDB has the requested data in memory InnoDB will almost always return data faster than NDB unless it is a complex query that contains parts that can be parallelised. As an example in the Sysbench benchmark there is a number of queries that read 100 rows from an index. In InnoDB these 100 rows will be scanned using a secondary index in InnoDB from one thread. In NDB this access will be automatically parallelised to access all partitions of the table. This means that those queries will return their data to the MySQL Server quite quickly. If these queries contain a filter that is applied to the rows before returning them as results the NDB engine have even bigger advantages since these condition filters will be executed in parallel on all partitions. Thus NDB have a lot of automatic parallelisation of the queries since data is spread on many different partitions.

InnoDB will perform its request in one thread and will stay in this thread, this means no extra delays to perform thread switching and sending over sockets or other communication media. It means of course that no automatic parallelisation will occur.

The most similar comparison of the NDB storage engine and the InnoDB storage engine is when NDB is using 1 replica. There should only be 1 data node to ensure that all communication is with the local NDB data node. In this case NDB will not perform any distributed message that could potentially be limited by the bandwidth of e.g. Gigabit Ethernet or some other media used. NDB will still use a more complex threading model, but in this setup the latency of NDB is as small as is possible.

The above model isn't practical for NDB, in order to make a more realistic comparison we should use two data nodes on different machines and there should be a MySQL Server on each of those machines colocated with the data node.

If we use this setup and ensure that all tables are created with the *ndb-read-backup* configuration variable set and the *ndb-data-node-neighbour* set to point to the node id of the local data node of the MySQL Server (this will happen automatically if the data node and the MySQL Server is in the same OS such that they can both access the hostname of the data node). In this case all normal SELECT statements will be made locally. Only updates and SELECTs using a special LOCK mode (e.g. LOCK IN SHARED MODE) will be distributed.

The above manner to setup NDB is the proper one to use if the aim is to replace InnoDB with NDB. With this configuration setup we have a good chance that performance of the application will be on par with the InnoDB application and sometimes better. With NDB as a storage engine the replication is automatically in place and all replicas are always kept in synch with each other.

So far we have mainly discussed the latency. Throughput performance is a bit more complex to analyse. When using many concurrent threads the performance of InnoDB scales fairly linearly to start with, after adding more and more threads InnoDB will start to get diminishing return from adding more threads and at some point a maximum performance is achieved. The throughput in InnoDB is dependent on whether the queries are SELECT queries or if they are updating queries. InnoDB has good scalability for SELECT queries, but for updating queries the scalability is a bit more limited.

NDB scales almost perfectly linear in number of concurrent threads. After reaching the number of threads equal to the number of CPU cores the throughput increases with a different steps per thread but still fairly linear. After using more threads than the number of CPUs available the performance continues to increase but slower. For InnoDB the maximum performance is usually reached around 100 threads. For NDB one can usually scale to around 200-300 threads and with more cluster connections it might scale to 500-600 threads (these numbers reflect common benchmarks used, could be different for other applications).

Interestingly the latency of requests goes down with a small number of threads. The reason is that one thread will start up a number of threads, the other thread might therefore get access to those threads without having to wake them up and this might speed up things. One can improve latency in NDB by using a special configuration parameter that makes threads in the data node spin for a while before going to sleep.

NDB scalability is the same for SELECT queries and updating queries. This is an important benefit for NDB that it has excellent scalability for writes as well as for SELECTs. In addition several MySQL Servers can access the data simultaneously such that a cluster could handle at least tens of millions of SQL queries per second.

The main reason to choose NDB would normally be high availability coupled with a simpler consistency model for a cluster setup and predictable latency.

PARALLELISING QUERY EXECUTION

One important thing that makes the comparison between InnoDB and NDB even harder to describe is that NDB sometimes will parallelise query execution in the data nodes. E.g. when one makes a SELECT with a condition the condition will be pushed down to the NDB data node threads. If the NDB data node uses e.g. 8 LDM threads in a two-node setup this means that all 8 LDM threads in both nodes can scan the table in parallel and perform the condition evaluation.

NDB can parallelise join queries automatically in the same fashion. If the first table have a condition to evaluate this can be evaluated in parallel in all eight threads. Next each row that is found in first table is sent for read of e.g. the primary key in the second table. In this case the join is to a great extent parallelised for execution in the data nodes.

The execution of resulting rows in the MySQL Server is still performed in only one thread, but this can still result in considerable speedups of query execution since all fetching of data is parallelised. The best case for NDB is when filters are pushed to the data nodes. If only a small percentage of the rows are sent back to the MySQL server and we are performing a join operation, the query will be heavily parallelised. If most rows need to be transported back to the single MySQL server thread there will still be a parallelisation of fetching rows, but no parallelisation of filter execution.

The MySQL Server can decide to push down only a subset of the joins and several subsets of the join query. More on pushdown of joins into the data nodes in a later chapter.

A number of users have made good use of this feature and combined with the Read Backup replica feature and the Fully Replicated table feature it can make some queries go magnitudes faster.

All query execution in InnoDB is currently serialised in one thread. Thus there is no comparative analysis for InnoDB and parallelisation.

4.1.2 AVAILABILITY DIFFERENCES

The most important difference between NDB and InnoDB is the availability story. NDB was designed for subsecond failover and the ability to perform any management changes online. This is the most common reason for choosing NDB instead of InnoDB. It's not that common to choose NDB purely from a performance point of view for SQL applications. The story is different when comparing an NDB API application towards an SQL application. If the user will use a combination of NDB API applications and SQL applications the performance story is quite different.

One of the advantages of NDB is that it supports synchronous replication out of the box, it supports multi-master replication inside the cluster. It supports replication between clusters where all clusters can update the data and one uses conflict detection and resolution to handle any conflicting updates. Thus when replicating between clusters, updates can occur in all clusters at the same time and conflict detection will decide what update that will survive.

These are all unique features of NDB.

4.1.3 CAPABILITY DIFFERENCES

As a storage engine NDB has more limited capabilities compared to InnoDB. New features in the MySQL Server are usually designed for InnoDB first and then implemented in NDB. Thus some features of InnoDB doesn't exist in NDB or are not as well integrated into NDB yet.

NDB doesn't support fulltext indexes. It does support the GIS feature, it has no special GIS index support. JSON support exists in NDB as well, NDB can index stored generated columns, it cannot index virtual generated columns.

NDB support up to 512 columns with a maximum row size of 14 kBytes, NDB don't support indexes on prefixes of BLOBs and NDB doesn't support savepoints.

When analysing whether NDB can replace InnoDB in an application one has to check if NDB has the necessary features to support the application.

4.2 CONSISTENCY MODEL DIFFERENCES

All database engines have different ways of supporting concurrent access to data. A few database engines such as Oracle, MySQL/InnoDB use a model where one can query the data as if the time has stopped. This means that the query results is consistent, but the result is as old as the query is. Thus if a query takes one minute to execute, all the data used in calculating the result was up to one minute old when the query completed.

Other database engines such as IBM DB2, Microsoft SQL Server (can support both models) and NDB use a model where you read the latest committed data instead.

In this model the query results are always based on the latest data, but at the same time the query result doesn't show a consistent model of the data at any specific point in time.

When running large and complex queries it isn't really possible to get both an up-to-date as well as a consistent view of the data. This is only if possible if all updates to the database are stopped.

This is another difference between InnoDB and NDB. NDB and InnoDB both use row locks to implement concurrency control, but InnoDB also keeps old records around to ensure that all currently running transactions can acquire an old but consistent view of the data. This increases the memory requirements as well when there are lots of updates in parallel with long-running queries.

Given that NDB is targeted for real-time applications with high requirements on write scalability we have opted at the moment to not support old but consistent views in NDB (called Repeatable Read in MySQL terminology). To support this is possible in NDB but would require overhead in each row of the table as well as keeping rows around for longer and increase processing overhead. Thus less memory would be used to store application data to support repeatable read.

InnoDB have the ability to lock ranges which isn't possible in NDB, NDB only supports row locks and no range locks. The reason is that NDB supports transparent sharding that makes it very hard to lock a range since the range is distributed over many servers.

For the most part these differences is mostly a philosophical difference. Some applications will benefit from the old but consistent view and some will benefit more from reading the latest committed rows and for some applications it doesn't really matter.

We can use a metaphor to explain the difference. Assume that we have a train in a station where we need to count some characteristic of the train. In the consistent view we freeze time and perform the analysis on the train as it was at the we started the analysis. When the query is done and we plan to take some action based on the analysis the train might already have left the station and now have different characteristics.

The model where one reads the latest data will not freeze time, it will start the analysis while the train is still in the station and will continue the analysis when the train is moving and will thus arrive at an analysis which is more up-to-date, but still none of the variants will deliver a perfect view of the world. The problem is simply that the world is moving when we are analysing it. The question is whether we want to analyse the most recent or an old historical view.

4.3 FOREIGN KEY DIFFERENCES

Both InnoDB and NDB support foreign keys. The NDB foreign keys were designed to be as close to InnoDB foreign keys as possible, it was not possible to make them exactly the same since NDB is a distributed engine.

4.4 DIFFERENCES IN ONLINE CHANGE

NDB is designed for the highest possible availability. Thus you can add and drop indexes while data can be read and written. InnoDB doesn't support writes while adding an index. NDB can add a column with a quick online operation.

Another major difference is that NDB development focus quite a lot on supporting online software upgrades and online software downgrade. This is necessary to support the demanding telecom database requirements.

NDB supports online repartitioning of a table, InnoDB cannot handle writes during such a change.

4.5 CHALLENGES IN REPLACING INNODB

As can be seen from the above description it can sometimes be tough to move an application from InnoDB storage engine to the NDB storage engine. This is true for any move from one database engine to another.

The easiest is always to write your application against NDB at once, but it is possible to move it from MySQL/InnoDB and from many other database engines. It is though some work involved in moving towards a new database engine.

A successful example of such a move is in supporting the OpenStack database. The database in OpenStack supports a number of parts of the OpenStack architecture such as Nova, Neutron and so forth. In the Oracle OpenStack solution for Linux and Solaris it is possible to replace the MySQL/InnoDB with a high availability option using MySQL Cluster.

CHAPTER 5

MySQL Cluster and InnoDB Cluster

At the end of 2016 MySQL introduced a new clustering option based on the new group replication feature. Important note here is that this book is NOT about MySQL InnoDB Cluster or Galera Cluster. We only introduce it here to assist the user in understanding when to choose clustering based on group replication and when to choose clustering based on NDB.

5.1 Comparison to Galera Cluster

The comparison in this chapter will to a great extent carry over to any other clustering solutions, such as Galera Cluster, provided in the MySQL community.

5.2 Group Replication

The traditional MySQL replication is an asynchronous replication. The transaction is committed on the master first, the transaction is logged in the replication log and the reply to the requester is sent. At this time the slaves can retrieve the log and apply it. Traditional MySQL replication is based on a pull model where the participants pull the changes in when they are ready for it. Thus in a crash situation where the master fails, transactions will be lost since there will always be a set of transactions that wasn't pulled in by any slave yet.

The group replication is based on push replication instead. It uses a PAXOS protocol to ensure that the participants arrive at the same commit order. Thus there is a huge difference at commit time in traditional MySQL replication and in MySQL group replication. In MySQL group replication the committer has to wait until a majority of the participants in the group has received the transaction and a couple of rounds to ensure that all nodes comes to the same commit decision. Normally a group consists of 3 participants, a majority of the 3 participants is 2 and the committer is one of those.

It will normally wait for a response from at least one other participant before the commit is completed. There is more than one phase involved in the PAXOS protocol. Normally three phases are needed to come to a conclusion of the transaction protocol.

This means that MySQL group replication can be used to build a high availability solution.

Both InnoDB clustering using group replication and NDB is designed for local area network installations. Both of them can be used also in wide area networks, but it will have an impact on performance. Both NDB and InnoDB clustering can be combined with asynchronous replication between data centers. NDB can support multi-master functionality in this case and handle conflict detection in an advanced manner. This is not supported with group replication.

5.3 Differences between MySQL clustering solutions

One difference is that MySQL Cluster is a tightly integrated clustering solutions whereas MySQL InnoDB Cluster is a loosely integrated clustering solution. What this means is that NDB was built as a clustering solution from ground up. It doesn't have a non-clustering mode.

MySQL InnoDB Cluster is built from a set of MySQL Servers that communicate at commit time. Another important difference is that MySQL Cluster was designed for predictable response time.

This leads to some differences. In MySQL Cluster the ordering of transactions are based on row locks that are taken in the prepare phase. Thus there is more communication messages in an NDB transaction, at the same time communication is tightly integrated in NDB with several levels of piggybacking of communication happening.

In MySQL InnoDB Cluster the transaction is executed in its entirety inside one MySQL Server before commit time. This means that there are no distributed transactions possible.

Thus MySQL Cluster can execute cross-shard transactions, it also supports cross-shard joins. MySQL InnoDB Cluster cannot execute cross-shard transactions and cannot execute cross-shard joins.

MySQL InnoDB Cluster doesn't scale for writes beyond what one MySQL Server can handle. MySQL Cluster can scale to 48 data nodes and 200 MySQL Servers simultaneously changing the data.

MySQL InnoDB Cluster can scale up to 9 replicas for read scaling. NDB can scale to 48 replicas using fully replicated tables accessed from 200 MySQL Servers.

As mentioned in the previous chapter NDB has a lot more capabilities for online changes compared to InnoDB and this is true also when comparing NDB to MySQL InnoDB Cluster.

5.3.1 Architecture of MySQL InnoDB Cluster

To show the difference on a setup of MySQL InnoDB Cluster and MySQL Cluster the figure below shows the setup of MySQL InnoDB Cluster.

As can be seen one InnoDB Cluster consists of one master server and two or more participant servers. It can have a set of read slaves. All write transactions have to be routed to the Master server. Read transactions can go to either to one of the participant servers or one of the read slaves. It can go to the master server if it needs to be sure to read the latest view of the data. In order to handle this the architecture needs the MySQL Router to decide which MySQL Server to route a transaction to.

The MySQL Router is an important tool to ensure that MySQL InnoDB Cluster applications can scale well. It requires that the application distinguish read transactions from write transactions and it means that an application can only be guaranteed to see its own updates if it uses the same master MySQL Server all the time. This is a solution that mainly is designed for applications that does a lot more reads than writes. The design is mainly targeted for web applications where there is a background activity to update the database in special updating transactions and most web requests are pure read-only transactions and for those it is mostly ok to see an old view of the data. However e-commerce applications, telecom applications, financial applications will benefit from the MySQL Cluster model where all MySQL Servers

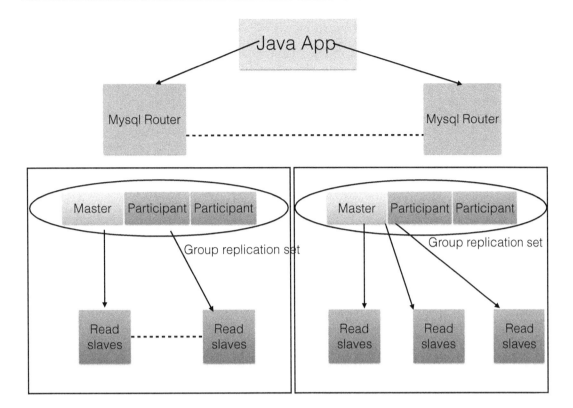

can see the updates made by a previous transaction and all MySQL Servers always see the most current view of the data.

If it is necessary to scale the application to more than one group replication set sharding is the only manner. This means that all transactions have to execute in its entirety in one group replication set. Thus the application needs to split up data in some dimension. The current GA solution for MySQL InnoDB Cluster has no support for sharding, this has to be implemented by the users of MySQL InnoDB Cluster.

5.3.2 ARCHITECTURE OF NDB IN COMPARISON

MySQL clustering based on NDB is a lot easier to setup and handle. One sets up a number of MySQL Servers and a number of NDB data nodes. Not only is it easier to setup a cluster using MySQL Cluster, the latency is lower compared to MySQL InnoDB Cluster.

In a single node setup InnoDB had the advantage of being able to execute the query directly in the MySQL Server. With MySQL InnoDB Cluster two more delays are introduced. The first one is the introduction of the MySQL Router. This introduces one more network jump before reaching the MySQL Server. The second is group replication that gets involved in updating transactions. For updating transactions the latency is longer since 3 replicas have to be involved in a transaction protocol with three phases. NDB has the same latency as it had when compared to a single node MySQL/InnoDB. Given that NDB was close to MySQL/InnoDB already in the single node case, it is obvious that NDB have a clear advantage in both throughput and latency when comparing MySQL InnoDB Cluster and MySQL Cluster.

The throughput advantage comes from the fact that all MySQL Servers can be used for both reads and writes. This means that in write intensive workloads the throughput scales with more MySQL Servers added to the cluster. For MySQL InnoDB Cluster the scalability is limited to what one MySQL Server can handle since all writes will go through one master MySQL Server.

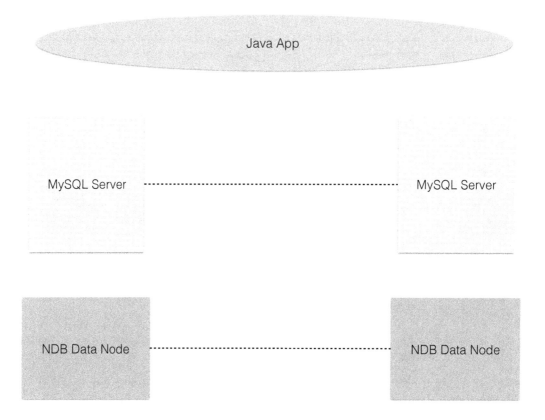

As the figure shows there is no need to use a MySQL Router for MySQL Cluster although it is possible. In the case of using Java, the JDBC driver for MySQL supports round-robin selection of a MySQL Server from the client without using any router. For MySQL connectors that don't support round-robin routing a MySQL Router is still required to distribute the load amongst the MySQL Servers in the cluster.

One important difference is that with MySQL Cluster all MySQL Servers see the same data, thus you can send the query to any MySQL Server connected to the cluster, there can be hundreds of those MySQL Servers. Each MySQL Server can read and update data in the entire cluster.

With MySQL InnoDB Cluster you must connect to the master MySQL Server in one group to update data, and you can only read and update the data in this group. With a sharded solution the application will have to handle all queries against all shards whereas in MySQL Cluster all data in all shards (node groups) are available for querying. It is possible to perform both queries and updating transactions that span multiple shards in MySQL Cluster.

In order to read data in MySQL InnoDB Cluster you can connect to any MySQL Server in the group. If you connect to a non-master MySQL Server you might see an older version of the data. The commit phase only ships the logs to all other MySQL Servers in the group, the logs have not been executed at commit time. Non-master MySQL Servers will show data up to the point the replication logs have been executed.

In order to do cross-shard queries, the application will have to do the work of sending the queries and collecting the data together.

The MySQL InnoDB Cluster solution is aimed at building highly available solutions with read scaling.

MySQL Cluster is designed to build scalable applications for both read and write at very high availability and is targeting applications that require predictable response times.

The fact that any MySQL Server can be used for both updates and reads makes it easier to develop a scalable application using MySQL Cluster whereas MySQL InnoDB Cluster have the advantages coming from the fact that InnoDB storage engine is supporting more features.

5.4 DIFFERENCES IN QUERY EXECUTION

InnoDB will execute each query in a single thread in one MySQL Server.

NDB will control execution of the query from a single thread in one MySQL Server. NDB can push down query condition evaluation to data nodes. These are evaluated in parallel if scans are sent to multiple partitions. In addition NDB can push down joins to the NDB data nodes. Thus NDB can achieve substantial parallelism in the execution of a single query.

5.5 DIFFERENCES IN RECOVERY

Since MySQL InnoDB Cluster is a set of MySQL Server that have been configured to work together it means that when they restart they first restart locally, then they take contact with the other servers and start the distributed recovery. In MySQL Cluster the restart of a node is tightly integrated, the node becomes part of the cluster early on and must respect the heartbeat protocol all through the restart.

As an example in MySQL Cluster already in the first phase of cluster recovery we will decide which nodes are capable to restore to the recovery point for the cluster. Those nodes that cannot do that will have to wait until the first set of nodes have completed their recovery. After they have completed the cluster recovery the remaining nodes will startup using the live cluster nodes to get the node up to the most recent version of all data.

There is a difference in how synchronisation of a starting node happens. In both clustering solutions a local recovery is the first step. This step recovers the existing transactions the local node saw before it stopped. The synchronisation phase differs significantly. In MySQL Cluster the starting node start participating in the distributed transactions at a synchronisation point for each table partition. Then one row at a time (with a certain level of parallelism) is synchronised where each node is using a live node to synch up. The live node knows if the row needs to be sent to the starting node based on a commit timestamp in the row. Thus the algorithm is certain to progress towards completion even if the system executes at a high update rate and even if the database is large.

The MySQL InnoDB Cluster instead relies on that the starting node plays catch up with the live node(s). In order to catch up the starting node must apply the logs faster than new ones are generated. It needs to have sufficient space to store all the new logs generated while applying the log from the live nodes. There is no guarantee that the algorithm will be able to complete when a high update rate happens while recovering. The biggest challenge is to bring up a new node from scratch with a large database that have heavy update activity. MySQL Cluster is designed to be recoverable even when millions of updates per second are occuring while recovering data nodes.

When the new node have come close enough to the live nodes it will be declared as up, at this point it can do updates. The risk that a MySQL Server in MySQL InnoDB Cluster isn't recoverable increases when the data set is large and when the update rate is high. For web applications the recovery in MySQL InnoDB Cluster will work just fine. But for large applications with large data sets and heavy writing the availability is much better with MySQL Cluster given that its recovery algorithm guarantees success.

In the Ph.D thesis by Mikael Ronström these algorithms were both analysed for the telecom data server market. The NDB solution was selected since it has a certain progress, there is no reliance on that the starting node can catch up with the live node and there is no moment where all commits have to stop while the new node enters again. The MySQL Cluster algorithm is certain to complete which is important to reach the highest availability level.

Since MySQL Cluster is a tightly integrated cluster it is designed for automatic recovery. The data nodes will start recovery automatically after a failure and if the machine stops it is desirable to ensure that the data nodes starts up again from the OS startup scripts. MySQL InnoDB Cluster is a loosely integrated cluster and thus requires either manual intervention or that one has written scripts to automate recovery. One can say that they are designed with slightly different design philosophies.

5.6 Differences in handling node failures

The next difference is how the cluster decides which nodes are to survive. In the MySQL Cluster solution this is based on a heartbeat protocol. This heartbeat protocol contains all data nodes in the cluster. In MySQL Cluster the decision which nodes will survive is based on all node groups in the cluster, not just one.

A surviving set of nodes in MySQL Cluster must have at least one node in each node group. If it contains all nodes of at least one node group there is no risk of network partitioning and it will survive even if a majority of the nodes are down.

If there is a risk of network partitioning where no node group have all nodes surviving then if a majority of the previously alive nodes are still alive the cluster will survive. If there is a 50/50-situation an arbitrator is used to decide whether a cluster will survive or not.

In the trivial case of 2 data nodes in 1 node group and one of them fails, the surviving node will be able to continue if it can access the arbitrator and the arbitrator accepts its request to form a new cluster. The arbitrator is any of the NDB management servers or an API node, if the arbitrator fails, the cluster will select a new one immediately. Before the crash the nodes have agreed upon an arbitrator, at crash time all surviving node partitions will contact the same arbitrator to ask for permission to go on. Only one node partition will be allowed to proceed to avoid network partitioning.

In MySQL InnoDB Cluster the decision is part of the PAXOS protocol which means that it is a majority decision, thus in case of only 2 nodes being alive when a node fails a decision cannot be made and thus both nodes will enter read-only mode until the stopped node come back or until manual intervention adds a new node to the group. Thus MySQL Cluster needs 2 replicas for highly available operation and MySQL InnoDB Cluster requires 3 replicas for highly available operation.

The decision whether the surviving nodes will survive is based on the previously alive nodes in MySQL Cluster. Each node failure is a transaction in MySQL Cluster. Thus all nodes will see the failures in the same order. When a set of nodes fails we will decide if a majority of the previously alive nodes are still alive. This means that if we start with 4 replicas we will survive 2 nodes failing at the same time, after that we still have 2 nodes up and in this case we can still survive that one of those nodes fail. This means that MySQL Cluster can start with 4 replicas and reach 1 remaining replica and still continue to service updates. This comes from the benefit that nodes in MySQL Cluster fails as transactions.

By separating the decision as to which node will survive from the nodes that contain the actual data MySQL Cluster can run just fine with 2 replicas and will continue to service updates even in the presence of only 1 replica. MySQL InnoDB Cluster requires three replicas to handle one node failure. It cannot continue to service updates when 2 nodes have failed out of three since it cannot form a majority in that case.

The difference is that MySQL Cluster tries to maintain the cluster to be available for updates all the time whereas for MySQL InnoDB Cluster it is ok to enter into read-only mode for some time and involve manual intervention to decide which parts that should survive. Here it is pretty clear that MySQL Cluster is designed for write-intensive applications that continues to operate in most error conditions. MySQL InnoDB Cluster is designed for highly available applications that are read-intensive and where it is ok to temporarily not be able to update the data.

5.7   SHARDING DIFFERENCES

The next difference is about sharding. MySQL Cluster runs distributed transactions over all shards (== node groups) and it can run both updating transactions as well as read queries over multiple shards. This is not possible in MySQL InnoDB Cluster.

Partitioning among the shards differs, partitioning of data in MySQL Cluster is automatic using a hashing solution in MySQL Cluster. For MySQL Cluster sharding is transparent to the application although one can definitely get much better performance by using various hints as to where transactions are started and ensuring that the partition key is part of the index scans we perform (Partition Pruned Index Scan, will be described in more detail later).

For MySQL InnoDB Cluster sharding has to be solved by the application itself.

5.8   MULTI-MASTER DIFFERENCES

Next the MySQL InnoDB Cluster is mainly usable with a single updating master at a time. This means that the clients must divide between read transactions and updating transactions. Read-only transactions can run on any MySQL Server in the group whereas updating transactions can only go to the master MySQL Server. The group replication does support multiple masters, but this makes foreign key support no longer work fully (foreign key checks works, but foreign key actions are not propagated up to the replication layer currently). In practice a single master is the normal use case for MySQL InnoDB Cluster.

Group replication handles multi-master situations by using a sort of token ring solution. A node can update while holding the token. After releasing the token other nodes can update and we will have to wait with updates until we get the token again. In this manner conflicts are avoided by a sort of timesharing mode. The token can be held for several transactions, each time a server gets the token he gets a range of commits that he can do. Transactions can execute in parallel in all nodes but they must commit in order and if any conflicts occur the transaction that has had updates to its read set or write set must be updated. Group replication uses an optimistic concurrency control protocol whereas NDB uses a pessimistic concurrency control. Optimistic protocols often have advantages when concurrency is limited, but when conflict probability is high they will get frequent aborts whereas pessimistic protocols will handle conflicts well.

This is one more reason to stay away from multiple masters with MySQL InnoDB Cluster, the optimistic concurrency protocol makes applications harder to develop.

Design of load balancers for MySQL Cluster is easy. One can simply pick any MySQL Server for any transaction. All MySQL Servers (even if there are hundreds of them) can run equally well each transaction.

MySQL Cluster supports adding new node groups (== shards) online and reorganising the data to start using the new node groups as updating transactions continue to be serviced.

MySQL Cluster supports combining tables that are sharded and spread over many node groups with tables that are fully replicated and existing on all nodes in the cluster. This makes it possible to design applications that have both distributed parts and parts that are more centralised. Thus MySQL Cluster can handle a flexible application design.

5.9 DETAILED DIFFERENCES

If one node fails in MySQL InnoDB Cluster and in MySQL Cluster the cluster will continue to operate, a few transactions might be aborted in-flight and for MySQL InnoDB Cluster one need to use the new master MySQL Server for updates. MySQL Cluster will be immediately available for traffic again as soon as the node failure have been discovered.

At recovery after a complete cluster crash MySQL InnoDB Cluster will not lose any transactions if sync_binlog was set to 1. There is a chance for lost transactions when going from the group replication layer to the relay log, it is still not absolutely safe. MySQL Cluster will lose up to a few seconds of transactions in this case, but the recovered data will always be transaction consistent commit point. MySQL InnoDB Cluster will also lose a few transactions when sync_binlog is set to 0.

MySQL Cluster have been in production usage since 2004, we currently have many thousands of clusters in production usage in highly available applications and probably a lot more than that. MySQL InnoDB Cluster is a new product released as GA first in December 2016. Both are actively developed.

Interestingly the MySQL Cluster Manager (MCM) uses the PAXOS protocol implementation used in MySQL InnoDB Cluster to ensure that the steps used to manage MySQL Cluster is done in the same order on all participating machines.

5.10 What clustering solution to select

MySQL InnoDB Cluster is designed for users that use MySQL together with InnoDB. It is a natural extension of MySQL Replication to turn it into a high availability solution. It competes very well with other clustering solutions in the MySQL area, it does a very good job in providing a good high availability solution for the NoSQL area. It will serve as a natural extension for people currently using MySQL Replication with InnoDB to move to a new replication architecture.

5.10.1 Selection based on availability

The most important reason to choose MySQL Cluster is the higher availability it provides. Both solutions support a high availability, NDB have been battle-tested for 15 years.

MySQL Cluster requires only two replicas to stay available whereas MySQL InnoDB Cluster requires 3 replicas to stay highly available.

MySQL Cluster supports online reorganisation of data when new nodes are added. NDB supports adding and dropping indexes online and adding new columns can be done online. NDB is designed for constant uptime for both read and write. NDB supports online upgrade to a new version with no downtime while still handling reads and writes.

MySQL Cluster can be combined with MySQL Cluster Replication for disaster recovery and for any changes not possible to handle in an online cluster. These clusters can even run in multi-master mode with conflict detection and resolution.

MySQL InnoDB Cluster can be combined with asynchronous replication to other clusters. It is possible to replicate from MySQL Cluster to MySQL InnoDB Cluster and vice versa.

5.10.2 Selection based on real-time behaviour

NDB was designed for predictable response time and have gone through tough tests by demanding users to prove this. It can provide 100% of the responses within time limits of down to hundreds of microseconds for demanding telecom applications and financial applications.

Many of our users require 100% of the responses of complex transactions to complete within 10 milliseconds, this makes it impossible to use a solution based on disk-based storage.

MySQL InnoDB Cluster relies on one replication channel that handles one transaction at a time. If a large transaction is committed, this will affect the latency of all transactions queued up behind this long transaction.

5.10.3 Selection based on ease of application development

When using an application designed for InnoDB there are many advantages in using MySQL InnoDB Cluster. It is easier to design against MySQL Cluster in that all MySQL Servers are equal, no special master must be used for updates and all MySQL Servers see the most current data. This was the main reason why Oracle Open Stack decided to use MySQL Cluster for their HA offering.

The consistency model of NDB is that all applications see the updates immediately. The consistency model in MySQL InnoDB Cluster uses eventual consistency. This means that you cannot be certain to see your own updates. This makes application development considerably more difficult.

5.10.4 SELECTION BASED ON SCALABILITY

Both solutions scale very well for reads, for write scaling NDB will scale to many node groups (== shards) without changing the application code.

NDB can combine normal sharded tables that are synchronously updated with global tables that are fully replicated in the cluster for scalable application development.

MySQL Cluster scales to tens of millions of update transactions per second, MySQL InnoDB Cluster scales to tens of thousands of update transactions per second.

5.10.5 SELECTION BASED ON DATA SIZE

MySQL InnoDB Cluster is able to store more data per server, however since each server needs to contain the full data set it is limited to the size of one MySQL Server.

At the same time NDB can scale to many data nodes using hundreds of gigabytes per data node, the total size possible to store in MySQL Cluster and in MySQL InnoDB Cluster is on the same order of magnitude. If one uses disk data as well for much of the data in MySQL Cluster one can store terabytes per data node. MySQL Cluster has a more reliable recovery algorithm handling large data sets.

5.10.6 SELECTION BASED ON STORAGE ENGINE FEATURE SET

Both NDB and InnoDB supports all character sets supported by MySQL.

NDB has a limit on row sizes, the fixed size columns can be at most 8052 bytes. The total row size can be at most 14 kBytes.

InnoDB supports fulltext indexes, NDB doesn't. Both NDB and InnoDB supports GIS, only InnoDB supports a GIS index. Both NDB and InnoDB supports the JSON data type and indexes on virtual stored columns, InnoDB also supports storing it as a virtual column and having an index on it. InnoDB stores all data using a page cache and can thus scale to data sizes covered by the disks, NDB stores data in memory as default to ensure that NDB always delivers predictable response time. NDB can store non-indexed fields using a page cache backed by data on disks. Both NDB and InnoDB uses tablespaces to handle disk pages.

InnoDB runs all queries using a single thread that runs inside the MySQL Server. NDB runs queries in a number of threads that cooperate and queries are automatically parallelised when more than one partition is used in the query. NDB supports pushing down joins into the data node where they will execute with some level of parallelism.

InnoDB uses a clustered B-tree index for primary keys and separate B-tree index tables for secondary index. NDB always uses a main memory hash index for primary keys and unique keys. Ordered index is implemented using a main memory T-tree implementation. The unique indexes are global and stored in a separate table completely handled by NDB, the primary key hash index and the ordered indexes are part of each partition.

NDB and InnoDB uses slightly different consistency models as explained in the previous chapter on differences between NDB and InnoDB.

5.10.7 FINAL WORDS

MySQL Cluster was designed for telecom servers that require constant uptime, it was designed for scalability to a large number of nodes while still maintaining consistency of its data. Thus if you are aiming for a scalable application and plan to grow it to hundreds of nodes and want your application to see one common view of data then MySQL Cluster is a good hit.

Not surprisingly the original requirements in the design of MySQL Cluster are the key factors that will play in favor of MySQL Cluster in this selection.

There are many areas where MySQL InnoDB Cluster will be beneficial. It will be a more natural alternative for existing MySQL/InnoDB applications that require the feature set available in InnoDB.

Note that there are many areas where NDB is best used without mentioning its connection to MySQL. One such area is the implementation of file systems and block devices based on NDB. Another area is for designing scalable and highly available LDAP servers. In such situations an SQL database would not even be an option. Most of the telecom servers are areas where only NDB is a real option.

For file servers the reason NDB is such a useful solution is based on its division of the Query Server and the Data server. A file server solution will seldomly require any SQL queries, they would only be unnecessary overhead. These applications are best built using the APIs providing direct APIs to the data nodes of MySQL Cluster. The easiest to use of those APIs is ClusterJ for Java access. The fastest is the C++ NDB API. It is possible to access the data nodes directly from JavaScripts using the NodeJS API.

PART II

INTRODUCTION TO DATABASE CONCEPTS

CHAPTER 6

RELATION MODEL

Before introducing the model of how MySQL Cluster works we will introduce the terminology, this chapter introduces the relational model in a distributed system together with some concepts related to this that are used in NDB. The following chapter will introduce the model for distributed transactions and the terminology chapter will introduce the model we use for processors, computers and operating systems.

6.1 BASIC CONCEPTS

Table

Columns

Rows

Rows = records
Columns = attributes

A database is used to store information, this information is represented as values that can be of many different data types. More or less every conceivable database solution organises its data into *records*. A record can consist of one or more *attributes*. Synonyms for attributes are *columns* and *fields*. A synonym for record is *row*.

A column can only contain a single value according to the relational model.

In order to organise data it is common to employ some sort of schema to describe the data. It is possible to avoid the schema, in this case each row will have to contain the schema describing the row.

The relational model employs a strict schema which only allows storage of a single value per attribute and that each table has a fixed set of attributes. Representation of multi-valued attributes in the relational model is done by a separate table that can later be joined with the base table to retrieve the multi-valued attributes.

Person

SSN is Primary key
Name is Unique key
Department has index

Dep ID is Primary key

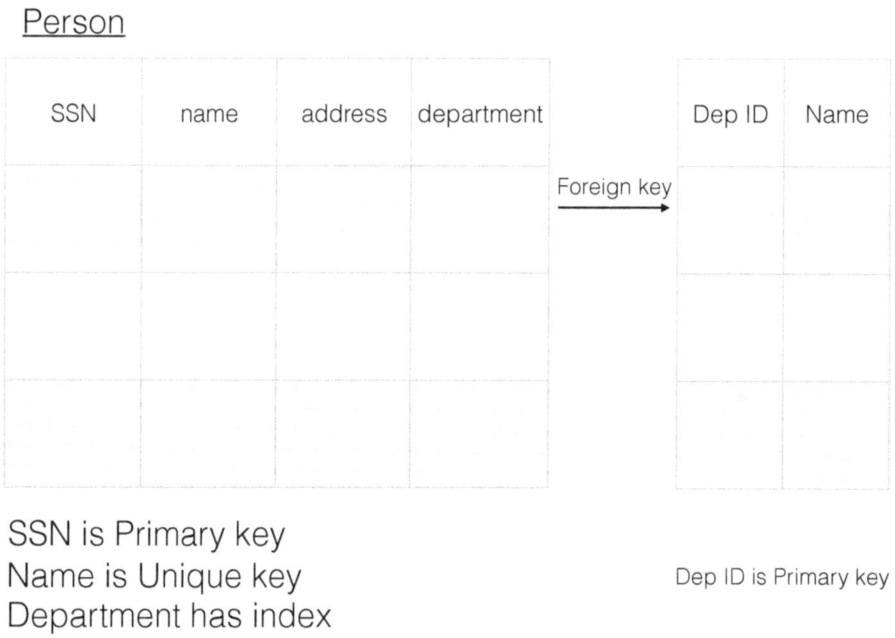

Another key concept in the relational model is primary key, this is a unique reference to a row in the table. If several unique identifiers exist in a table these are unique keys, only one primary key can exist in a table. Both primary key and unique keys are implemented using indexes that ensure uniqueness. In addition many non-unique indexes can be defined on a table.

Foreign keys defines relational constraints between tables in the schema. A foreign key above in the table person (child table) refers to a row in the department table (the parent table). The child table has a unique reference to the row in the parent table. Normally the columns defining the foreign key relation has an index defined on them (it is a requirement in NDB). The above figure shows an example of this.

There are other models where one describes the schema in each row. The popular format JSON follows this model.

The relational model was introduced in the 1970s by IBM. It is a simple model that provides nice mathematical properties that makes it easy to reason about the relational model and that makes it easy to develop complex queries against data and still be able to deduce how to compute the results of those queries.

One benefit of the relational model is that it is easy to reason about queries in this model. For example a select of a subset of the rows in a table and a projection only reading a number of columns delivers a query result which in itself is a table. A table can be joined with another table (or joined with a select-project of another table). The result of a join is again something that is a table. The result of a join can be joined with yet another table. In this manner a query can be arbitrarily complex. Sometimes this is called select-project-join. We have pushed some of this functionality down into the data server part and call the module that handles this DBSPJ where SPJ comes from Select-Project-Join. There are many types of joins, equality joins, semi-joins, cross product and so forth.

During the early phases of developing an application it is not crystal clear how the data model will look like. Thus the model constantly changes. As development progresses the model tends to be more and more fixed and changes are often expensive. This is true independent of how schemas are stored. This is just how development for any application happens.

If all records have their own schema we can end up with quite a messy data model at the end. In coding one talks about spaghetti code and similar here it is easy to end up with a spaghetti data model if there is no control of the development of the schema.

With MySQL Cluster we want to make it easy to change the schema dynamically in the early phases of development and in later phases of the development. At the same time we want to get the benefits of the relational model and its strength in handling complex queries.

We have implemented a data structure for records where it is easy to add and drop columns. The record representation is fixed per table, but it is easy to add and drop attributes on a table. The table can continue to be updated while these attributes are added (online drop column is not yet supported).

Thus in MySQL Cluster (as in MySQL) you define a *table* to consist of a set of *attributes* with a table name.

As most modern implementations of relational DBMSs MySQL and MySQL Cluster have added support for BLOBs (Binary Large OBjects) of various sizes and types such as GIS types and JSON objects (these are BLOBs that contain a self-described document, containing its own schema per document).

6.2 DISTRIBUTED RELATIONAL MODEL

MySQL Cluster is a distributed database as well. Thus the table has to be partitioned and replicated in some fashion as well. We selected horisontal partitioning in MySQL Cluster. Thus each row is mapped to one partition of the table. Each partition contains a subset of the rows, but it contains all attributes of the table for the rows it stores.

We use the term *partition* for the table partitions, but internally and in some documentation we have used the term *fragment*. We tend to nowadays use the term partition for the partitioning as seen by the user and to use the term fragment internally. One reason for this is that with fully replicated tables one partition is implemented as multiple fragments that are copies of each other.

6.3 REPLICATED RELATIONAL MODEL

MySQL Cluster employs replication to ensure that data remains available in the presence of failures. We need a model to map the replicas to nodes. In MySQL Cluster we have selected a mapping model that maximises the amount of node crashes we can survive. One could have employed a model where we spread the replicas in such a way that we optimise for fastest possible restart times. But the fastest restart time model can only handle one node crash which isn't good enough for high availability in a large cluster.

The model we have selected means that we group the nodes into node groups. One fragment is always fully replicated within one node group and there are no *fragment replicas* in any other node group. Thus if we have 2 replicas we can survive one node crash in each node group and with more replicas we can survive even more node crashes.

Node groups divides data in the same manner as done for sharding. Therefore one of the features of MySQL Cluster is that it handles auto-sharding.

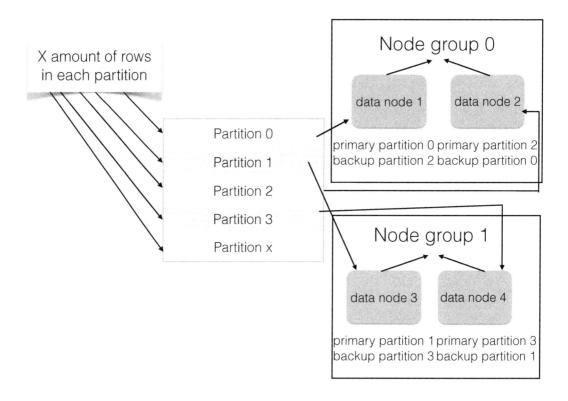

As the figure shows the row decides which partition the row goes into. The partition decides the node group the fragment replicas are stored in. Each partition has one *primary fragment replica* and one or more *backup fragment replicas* (only 1 replica is supported in which case there are no backup fragment replicas).

There can be a maximum of 48 data nodes and with 2 replicas this means a maximum of 24 node groups.

MySQL Cluster have its own heartbeat handling, when a node dies it will stop sending heartbeats, the neighbour nodes will discover the node failure and at failure discovery the surviving nodes that can communicate with each other will work together in definining a new cluster setup with the remaining nodes. We have to handle the case where network partitioning can occur. The simplest case is two data nodes and the network between those nodes is broken. In this case both nodes will attempt to form a new cluster setup. If both nodes are allowed to survive we will have two databases which is something we want to avoid.

To handle this situation we use another node in the cluster that doesn't own any data as *arbitrator*. This node will decide which set of nodes that should survive. The arbitrator is only contacted if a network partitioning is possible, the first one to contact it will win.

6.4 HASHMAPS

Tables in NDB use a concept called hashmaps. Hashmaps were introduced to make it easy to reorganize tables when new node groups are created. The algorithm we use to find the record based on a key is called distributed linear hashing and was named LH^3 in my Ph.D thesis. The linear hashing algorithm makes it possible to dynamically grow and shrink the hash table. There is one drawback for table reorganisation, the drawback is that when we have e.g. 6 partitions the first 4 partitions will contain 75% of the data (thus 18.75% per partition) and the last 2 partitions will contain 25% of the data and thus 12.5% per partition. Thus we won't have a balanced data fragmentation as is desirable.

The solution is hashmaps. We will hash into one of the 3840 buckets in the hashmap. Next we will map the bucket in the hashmap into the partition it should be stored in. When reorganising a table we simply change the mapping from hashmap bucket to partition. The fragmentation will thus be a lot more balanced than the traditional linear hash algorithm.

With MySQL Cluster we support online add of columns, online add/drop of tables, online reorganization of tables to handle new nodegroups introduced or to handle change of table distribution.

By default a table is divided into 3840 hashmap buckets. This means that if we have 8 partitions in a table each partition will house 480 hashmap buckets. If we add a new nodegroup such that we double the number of partitions, each partition will have 240 hashmap buckets instead. The original partitions will move away 240 out of the 480 hashmap buckets to the new partitions, the rest will stay. This is one more idea of hashmaps, to make sure that we can always reorganize data and that as much data as possible don't have to move at all.

The number 3840 is selected to make table distributions balanced in as many cases as possible without creating a hashmap which is too big. If we find the prime numbers in 3840 we see that

$$3840 = 2 * 2 * 2 * 2 * 2 * 2 * 2 * 2 * 3 * 5$$

Thus we can handle completely balanced distributions as long as the number of partitions can be made up a product of the prime numbers in 3840. E.g. if we have 14 nodes in the cluster we will not get perfect balance since 14 is 2 times 7 and 7 is not a prime number in 3840. The number of partitions for a default table is 2 times the number of node groups multiplied by the number of *ldm* threads (more on those later). But perfect balance will be achieved e.g. when we have 6 *ldm* threads and 16 data nodes (=> 192 = 2*2*2*2*2*2*3 partitions).

Balanced distribution on the partitions is desirable since this gives a good chance that CPU load distribution on the different *ldm* threads is balanced as well.

6.5 READ BACKUP REPLICA TABLES

In earlier versions of MySQL Cluster the focus was to provide a write scalable architecture. This is still the default behaviour. But we have added an option that makes it possible to have tables scale better for reading. This is an option when creating the table (or one can set the option in the MySQL Server if all tables should use this option). With this option READ_BACKUP=1 the reads can go to any fragment replica where the row is stored. There is a tradeoff with this in that write transactions will be slightly delayed to ensure that the reads can see the result of their own changes in previous transactions. We will explain more about the need for this special type of flags when we introduce the distributed transaction protocol that NDB uses.

6.6 FULLY REPLICATED TABLES

In MySQL Cluster 7.5 we introduced a new type of table which is called *fully replicated tables*, these tables can always read any replica for read committed queries. Normal tables in MySQL Cluster have different data in each node group. For a fully replicated table we have the same data in each node group. There might still be a number of partitions since each *ldm* thread can get its own partition, but each node group has the same set of fragments and they are replicas of each other. When a transaction changes a row in a fully replicated table it will change all replicas. It does this by using an internal trigger, the main fragment is first updated, a trigger ensures that all copy fragments are updated as well. All those changes are part of the same transaction, thus the update is atomic.

Fully replicated tables makes it possible to build simple read scalability into your applications. A natural architecture is to have one MySQL Server and one MySQL Cluster data node per machine that can communicate without using networking equipment. In this manner we can have up to 48 machines with the same data delivering many millions of SQL queries against the same data. Any changes are done to all replicas synchronously, no need to worry about replication lags and things like that.

Fully replicated tables can be reorganised, it is possible to start with a 2-node cluster and grow in increments of 2 until we reach 48 nodes. Similarly one can start with 3 replicas and grow in increments of 3 until we reach 48 nodes and similarly with 4 replicas. Reorganising a fully replicated table doesn't change the number of partitions, it only creates a number of new copy fragments of the partitions in the new node group(s).

CHAPTER 7

TRANSACTIONAL MODEL

Transactions is a concept that was developed many thousands of years ago to ensure that business transactions could be done in a safe way, such that buyer and seller could trust that they will receive what they expect from the business transaction.

In databases transactions have been an important concept since the first DBMS was developed. Using transactions makes it easy to reason about changes to your data.

7.1 BASIC TRANSACTION THEORY

An important part of the transaction theory is ensuring the *ACID* properties. A stands for *Atomic*, thus a transaction is either fully done or nothing is done. If the transaction is *committed* all operations of the transaction is performed, when the transaction is *aborted* no part of the transaction survives.

C stands for *Consistent*. Today many different models of consistency are discussed, but when we specify that a database is ACID we mean that transactions can be seen as happening one at a time although they happen in parallel, this is called *serialisable* in database theory. Most relational databases implement at least a subset of the requirements of serialisable transactions. Fully serialisable transactions can easily become a bottleneck, most database systems have a consistency level which is slightly lower.

Serialisability makes it easy to reason about correctness of changes and correctness of your data. Having a model that is close to this makes it easier to develop your application.

Each step in relaxing the serialisability requirement means that one will have to consider this in developing the application as it can no longer be treated as serial events happening to one set of data.

I stands for *Isolation*. It means that two different transactions is isolated from each other, a transaction make changes based on the state at the start of the transaction and will not see any changes of transactions that haven't yet committed. It can see the result of committed transactions, even if those have started after it since DBMSs do not support serial execution, but rather serialisable execution. In principle this means that a transaction happens instantly at commit time. Thus the transaction that committed before it is viewed as it happened before it. Isolation means that we're allowed to see results of transactions happening before us, but not after us.

D stands for *Durability*, most early database users were banks and the database used for monetary transfers. It is important that each individual transaction is safely stored even in the presence of crashes and similar events.

NDB is designed for ACID but does a few compromises. Serialisability is possible to achieve in NDB by the use of row locks. Many DBMSs ensure that ranges of rows can be protected. Given that the intended set of applications for NDB had no immediate need of this type of range locks, this is not supported. A range lock would make it very hard to meet response time requirements and applications could easily be made less scalable by misuse of range locks. Implementing range locks in a distributed architecture will limit the scalability of the DBMS even with a correct application usage.

In addition NDB supports a SQL mode called READ COMMITTED. This means that a transaction can read any row, even if it is currently being updated. If it is updated the read will return the latest committed value. This mode relaxes the serialisability requirement.

Durability requires the transaction to be committed on disk. This cannot be met while still meeting the response time requirements. An alternative model is used in NDB. The transaction is considered safe if at least two computers have received the transaction at commit time. If multiple nodes crash simultaneously a transaction could be lost. The restored system will always be a consistent database and if it is important to not report a successful transaction before it is durable on all disks in all nodes, there are API calls that make it possible to wait for this durability level.

This type of Durability is called Network Durable.

Most applications using NDB have many small transactions, each transaction have a value, they represent user changes and any disruption of the transaction model is a cost, but it is not the cost of a missed bank transfer of a billion dollar. NDB strives for the highest availability requirements and durability requirements while at the same meeting requirements of response times in the order of parts of a millisecond.

Transactions in NDB are fully atomic and transactions are isolated from each other.

Most DBMSs use transactions to update data. When updating data it is important to consider the state of the database at the time of the update. Those transactions require as much ACID capabilities as possible.

DBMSs are used for querying, analysing and many other things. Queries do not have the same requirements on consistency. A query could easily run for seconds, minutes or even hours. It isn't possible to use serialisable transactions for this.

There are two methods to support this. One method is that when scanning data you see the latest committed data, however the data isn't locked, so it might be concurrently updated. This model will always provide you with the most up-to-date version of the data. The returned data is not necessarily consistent with what the database contained at any specific point in time. This model is used by many DBMSs and will prioritise recentness of data for consistency. This mode is called *read committed* in MySQL. It is the model used in DB2 and normally in Microsoft SQL Server.

The other model is that the scan delivers the query results based on what the database content was at the start time of the transaction. This will deliver a consistent view of the database, but the view could be very old. Thus if a query runs for a minute, the query will not take into account anything of what changes have been made to the data in the last minute, it will only take into account those changes that were in the database one minute ago. This mode is called *repeatable read* in MySQL. It is used in MySQL/InnoDB and is used by the Oracle

DBMS.

NDB uses the *read committed* mode since NDB is designed for real-time data. Thus it is important to consider any changes happening while the query is running. Supporting *repeatable read* would mean extra memory overhead, extra processing overhead and even the risk of running out of memory due to long-running queries.

Both of the models have advantages and disadvantages. The *read committed* is better for analysing data in real-time and is a more efficient implementation. *repeatable read* has advantages in analysing the data when the data isn't moving so fast and it is ok to provide a result that is based on old data.

NDB is suitable for applications with fast-moving data.

7.2 LOCKING THEORY

Implementation of isolation can be done in numerous ways and the research literature is full of ideas on how to achieve isolation. The most common ways are pessimistic approaches that ensures that locks are held already in the prepare phase, the other set of popular approaches are optimistic approaches that hopes for the best and at commit time checks if the optimism was valid, if the optimisim was valid and no transaction has conflicted with ours the commit is done, otherwise if a conflict is found, at least one of the conflicting transactions have to be aborted.

The most popular approaches uses locks both for pessimistic and optimistic approaches, but also timestamps, and also timestamps combined with locks are other approaches and there are many more variants.

When implementing a distributed DBMS it is notable that the selection of the implementation method for isolation have a large impact on all the recovery algorithms. Selection of the concurrency control implementation to a large extent drives the implementation of the recovery algorithms.

Research have shown that optimistic approaches works well when there is low contention, but in high contention these approaches tend to fall apart since no work gets done since there is too often a conflict.

Pessimistic approach perform less optimal in low contention but continues to do fairly well in high contention scenarios.

In NDB the pessimistic locking approach was used. The main reason for this choice was simplicity. It is a lot easier to reason about things in recovery situations when one can hold a lock on a row, we make use of this both in node recovery situations and when reorganising a table.

The pessimistic approach is the most common approach in implementing distributed databases. But other approaches such as optimistic locking approaches are common as well. Another popular variant is the MVCC (Multi-version Concurrency Control) which combines timestamps and locks, it is an optimistic approach.

The most common approach when selecting the pessimistic approach is to use strict two-phase locking. What this means is that each transaction goes through two phases, one is the acquisition phase where locks are acquired. The second phase is the phase where locks are released. Using this approach one can prove that serialisability is achievable. The commit happens after the acquisition phase and before the release phase. In a distributed database the commit point is a distributed event as we will show later when describing the NDB transaction algorithm, thus it's a tad more complex.

7.2.1 DEADLOCK DETECTION

Using strict two-phase locking it is possible to reason about transactions using dependency graphs. A transaction T1 depends on a transaction T2 if T1 waits on T2 to release a lock. One important problem to consider when choosing this approach is deadlocks. A deadlock occurs when all of a sudden a set of transactions cannot proceed. In the dependency graph below we can see that there are 4 transactions and there are two deadlocks, first there is a cycle where T1 waits for T2, T2 waits for T3, T3 waits for T4 and T4 waits for T1. Additionally we see that T1 waits for T3 and thus we have a shorter cycle. Actually one can show that a deadlock occurs when a cycle is present in the dependency graph.

In order to get out of a deadlock the only method is to abort one or more transactions. In the case below we can abort T1, T3 or T4 to be able to proceed again. T2 isn't sufficient since it doesn't break the cycle between T1, T3 and T4.

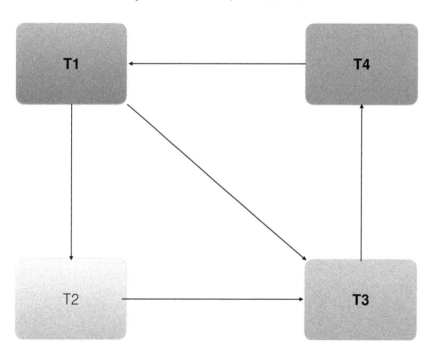

To avoid deadlocks one can use two approaches. The first is to avoid deadlocks, the second is to detect deadlocks and select an appropriate candidate for abort.

The most well-known method of avoiding deadlocks is to take locks in an order that all transactions uses. As an example we might have transactions that are required to take locks on one row in each table T1, T2 and T3. If all transactions take locks in the order T1 followed by T2 followed by T3, no deadlock is possible since no cycles can be present in the dependency graph. If one transaction decides to take a lock on a row in T3 and then one in T2, immediately a deadlock is possible.

The ordering of rows can happen in many different ways other than by table. Thus the application developer have the biggest influence on whether deadlocks will occur or not. One can have deadlocks that arise due to implementations of unique indexes, foreign keys, BLOBs, recovery and so forth.

Algorithms to detect deadlocks can be shown to be NP-complete. This means that it isn't possible to construct an algorithm with cost that is linear to the problem size. This means that the cost of detecting deadlocks increases exponentially as the number of potential deadlocks increases.

The practical consequence of this is that all DBMSs that can be involved in deadlocks have to implement a time-out based abort scheme. Thus deadlocks are not detected per se, rather the stop of progress of a transaction is detected and this leads to an abort of the transaction. This is safe and easy method of handling deadlocks. It means that some transactions will be aborted that were never involved in deadlocks. In a distributed database this can be used to detect transactions that have stopped progressing due to a node failure.

In practice it could be a good idea to discover the simplest deadlocks, the most common are the once having 2 participants, by avoiding these deadlocks to take time to discover we are removing one obstacle from the database. Trying to discover more complex wait graphs can easily consume too much CPU and network resources since the number of messages needed quickly grows. Even more so with more than 3 participants.

NDB implements a time-out based deadlock detection algorithm.

7.2.2 READ MODES

The next problem to consider in concurrency control based on strict two-phase locking is dirty reads. Dirty reads happens when a transaction T2 reads the non-committed values from a transaction T1 not yet completed. This means that T2 can read states that will never be committed, either T1 might update again the same row or the transaction T1 might be aborted in which case the value T2 read, never existed.

Using strict two-phase locking dirty reads will never happen as T1 holds an exclusive lock on the row and thus T2 cannot read it. As discussed before NDB supports the mode *read committed* in which case the transaction T2 will read the row which T1 is currently updating although it is exclusively locked. We ensure that those reads are not dirty in the sense that they read uncommitted values. They will always read the row as it existed before T2 started updating it. In this manner a dirty read as defined by the NDB API is a read of the latest committed value. This is what a normal SELECT query in MySQL will use when in the mode *read committed*. To use locking one uses SELECT .... LOCK IN SHARED MODE in which case all rows that are read will be read locked until the end of the transaction. It is possible to use SELECT ... LOCK IN EXCLUSIVE MODE to acquire exclusive locks on the rows read.

The next problem in concurrency control to consider is unrepeatable read. This happens when T1 reads the value of a row, then T2 updates the value and commits, next T1 reads it again and now it has changed. Using strict two-phase locking this isn't possible since the read lock from the first lock will prevent T2 from writing the row. Using *read committed* mode means that T1 might read the latest committed row and thus in this mode unrepeatable reads can happen. To prevent this one has to use SELECT ... LOCK IN SHARED MODE again from SQL.

MVCC (Multi-version Concurrency Control) does allow for reads to be repeatable, however if someone went in an updated the row in the middle of the transaction, it must be aborted to ensure a serialisable execution. If we ignore this problem we are running in a mode called *repeatable read*. This mode doesn't ensure a serialisable execution, it simply means that we can always repeat a read inside a transaction, in MySQL it means that we will perform all reads based on the value that the rows had at the start of the transaction.

NDB currently doesn't support this mode as discussed before.

As we have touched upon there are many different dependencies we can have. We can have a transaction that reads a row and another that writes the row. These can conflict, similarly for two writing transactions. two reading transactions cannot conflict since they do not change the value. Thus strict two-phase locking differs between shared locks and exclusive locks. Shared locks can be held by many transactions in parallel whereas exclusive locks can only be held one at a time.

7.2.3   OTHER LOCKING THOUGHTS

One could use a special lock for increments and decrements. This lock would conflict with shared and exclusive locks, but would not conflict with other increment locks. In a generic database used for SQL and many other use cases the difficulty in discovering those operations and the fact that it requires lock upgrade is an issue. We haven't implemented this approach in NDB.

The final thing we will discuss here is lock upgrades. Upgrading a lock from shared lock to an exclusive lock is an operation which is similar to getting a new lock, however it blocks others from touching the row, lock upgrades increases the risk of deadlocks more than simply taking an exclusive lock.

This is why MySQL supports SELECT ... LOCK IN EXCLUSIVE MODE to ensure that one can acquire the exclusive lock immediately and not perform any later lock upgrades.

7.3   DISTRIBUTED TRANSACTIONS

Since NDB is a distributed database any transactions must be implemented as distributed transactions. The most common method to implement distributed transactions is the two-phase commit protocol. This means that first all participants are prepared, then if all participants decided to accept the coordinator, they will decide to commit. This approach have a few problems, first of all if the coordinator fails while doing a commit the transaction is blocked until the coordinator comes back. The second problem is that this approach can easily cause deadlocks by sending lock requests to all replicas in parallel. Thus we can easily end up in a deadlock situation although the application is designed to avoid deadlocks.

To handle this we do two things, first to solve the blocking state when the coordinator dies, we implement a coordinator take over algorithm. Each time a transaction coordinator fails another node will collect the transaction state from the participants and will ensure that the transaction is completed. If this coordinator fails another coordinator will take over until we run out of nodes in which case the cluster have crashed and then we will perform cluster recovery.

The second problem we solve by combining the normal two-phase commit protocol with the linear two-phase commit problem. Linear two-phase commit means that we send the prepare phase in linear order, thus the transaction is started by the first node and it is committed by the last node. This approach decreases the number of messages needed to commit a transaction.

We keep one coordinator, but we use linear commit for each row update. Thus we always start the prepare phase by going to the primary replica first, then we go to the first backup replica and so forth until we reach the last backup replica from where we go back to the coordinator.

When committing we move through the nodes in reverse order. Thus we reach the primary replicas last in the chain as seen in the figure.

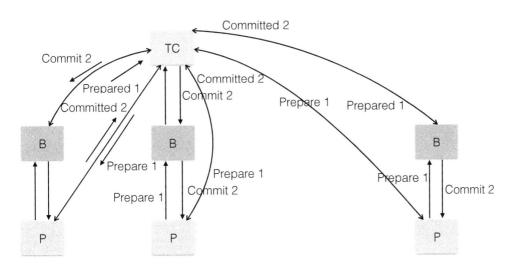

The interesting thing is when the actual commit point happens. As it turns out the actual commit point is when the commit message reaches the first primary replica. At this point the only thing that can make the transaction fail is a complete cluster failure. Since the cluster will survive as long as not all nodes in a node group fails, thus when all replicas have received the commit decision then at least one live node will know about the commit decision even in the presence of multiple node failures. If the cluster fails another algorithm will come into play, this algorithm is called the global checkpoint algorithm. It ensures that we will always recover a consistent database even in the case of a cluster crash.

In the coordinator take over protocol all nodes will be queried on any state of transactions from the crashed node. Thus we will not miss any knowledge about committed state information even in the presence of node failures.

Thus the commit point becomes theoretically well defined, but not easy to pinpoint practically.

The commit and complete messages are small messages, to avoid paying the price of the full overhead of a message we use a message called PACKED_SIGNAL, this message contains a few types of messages including COMMIT, COMMITTED, COMPLETE, COMPLETED and the response back to the coordinator in the prepare phase (called LQHKEYCONF) are all such piggybacked messages. This means that we save a lot of network bandwidth. In addition the NDB sending is performed for a set of signals and not just one signal. Thus we have double levels of piggybacking of messages in the NDB transporter module. Thus when the transaction throughput increases, the NDB efficiency increases.

This has the nice benefit that as NDB nears its saturation point it becomes more and more efficient. This is very important in building a highly available system. We will show more reasons for how NDB becomes more efficient as the load increases later in this book.

The commit protocol can deliver the acknowledge message to the API already after the commit phase and before starting the complete phase. At this point we know that the commit is safe and it can be communicated.

For tables where we want to support the ability to read from the backup replica we will wait until the complete phase is done before we send the acknowledge message to the application.

The reason is that there are still locks on the backup replica. Thus it is possible to start a read in the next transaction after the commit is done that will not see the updates we did ourselves. To avoid this anomaly we will wait a bit longer for tables that support read from backup replica. Read from any replica will be used for any reads that reads the latest committed results. It will not be used for locking reads, these will continue to use the primary replica for reading.

CHAPTER 8

COMPUTER MODEL

Modern computers are designed more or less as networks of processors that are interconnected in various ways. We will discuss configuration of MySQL Cluster a lot in this book and describing how to make optimal use of modern computers. To support this we will describe the computer model to ensure that the language is defined when describing CPUs, memories and networks. Given that this development is fairly new every processor manufacturer have invented their own language to describe their CPUs. Here we define a language that can be used to describe any type of CPU.

A modern CPU consists of multiple CPU cores. The largest Intel CPUs can have up to 28 CPU cores. The newest SPARC CPUs (M7) have 32 CPU cores. The newest AMD Epyc CPUs can have 32 cores in the high-end server models. Internally within one CPU core there can be one or more processors, we will call these processors CPUs. CPUs is what is seen by the operating system. The operating system knows about CPU cores, CPU sockets and so forth, but when a thread is scheduled to execute, it is scheduled to execute on a certain CPU within one CPU core.

Modern servers most often have more than one CPU chip, the most common is that each server have two sockets. These CPU chips used to be called CPUs simply, but we opt here to define these as a CPU socket, the CPU chip is placed into a CPU socket on the motherboard. Each such CPU socket houses a number of CPU cores which in turn houses one or more CPUs.

This defines the language where we use CPU, CPU core, CPU socket and computer to define ever larger parts of the computer. We will now describe how the current processors available on the market map into this language such that one can translate the language you are familiar with to the language used in this book.

In some sections we might use the term CPU thread instead of CPU to clarify that we are talking about one CPU inside a CPU core.

8.1   CPU CORE

The most commonly used processors to use to run MySQL Cluster are the x86 variants, and the SPARC variants. Other CPUs that are common today are ARM processors, these are mainly used in smartphones and in Raspberry PI and similar smaller designs. There have been attempts to develop servers based on ARM processors as well, but this market haven't taken on yet. NDB can work using *ndbd* on ARM processors, but NDB isn't supported on ARM processors.

It is possible to run MySQL Cluster on Power processors, there are likely still some compatability issues with those. Stewart Smith works on the Power architecture and have done a number of patches to MySQL to make it work better on Power machines. MySQL Cluster partially works on ARM and Power, but it is only officially supported on x86 and SPARC.

In this presentation we will focus on describing the processor architecture for modern x86 processors and modern SPARC processors.

We will start with the most common ones, the x86 processors. The vast majority of the server market is using Intel Xeon processors with various number of cores.

All modern x86 CPU cores use 2 CPUs per CPU core. Since 2017 this is also true for the AMD x86 processors using the new AMD architecture.

An important feature of those 2 CPUs is what they share and what they don't share. The figure below shows this for the x86 CPUs.

CPU core x86

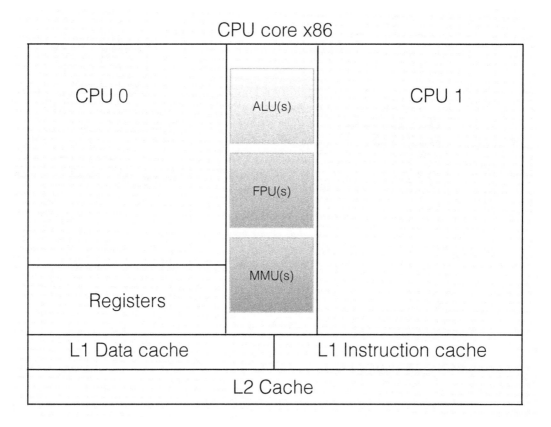

Each CPU has its own set of registers. Thus a CPU will always execute as if it was on its own. It will have more wait states compared to a CPU core with only one CPU since there are some shared resources as well.

Each CPU core has an L1 (Level 1) instruction cache, this is usually around 32 kBytes in size. Each CPU core has an L1 data cache as well, this is about the same size or smaller than the L1 instruction cache. Next there is an L2 cache which is used for both data and instructions in each CPU core. This is usually around 256 kBytes to 512 kBytes in size. All of those caches are shared between the two CPUs in the CPU core.

The CPUs share a set of computing resources such as ALUs (integer operations), FPUs (floating point operations) and MMUs (memory address calculations). Since each CPU can issue several instructions per cycle there is quite a few such resources inside a CPU core. This means that to a great extent a CPU will not be slowed down so much by another CPUs usage of computational resources.

The main reason that running two threads in parallel on the two CPUs doesn't provide twice the throughput is the sharing of the caches in the CPU core.

Modern CPUs have improved greatly in this area, in the first processors of this type that Intel came out with there was a slowdown due to parallel use of computational resources. This is much smaller now. The support for using both CPUs in the CPU core is now much improved.

Our experiments show that for the most part using both CPUs in the CPU core will deliver 50% more throughput compared to just using one CPU in the CPU core. It will pay off in almost all occasions to use all CPUs in the CPU core.

In x86 processors the advice is to use only one CPU per CPU core for *ldm* threads. This is based on only achieving a 10-20% speed up using the second CPU on the core. Given that adding *ldm* threads also increases overhead for scans, it is often a good idea to avoid using the second CPU in the core. The reason for the lack of speedup for *ldm* threads is that they are very efficient in using CPUs and thus the amount of computing resources is not sufficient to speed up with 2 CPUs per CPU core. There is more details on this in a later chapter.

The next level of CPU caches is the L3 cache. This is usually shared amongst a set of CPU cores and how many those are is different per processor variant. The AMD Epyc processor have 4 CPU cores that share an 8 MByte L3 cache. Intel CPUs have similar sets of sharing where a number of cores share an L3 cache, it is not the same for all Intel products. Thus it is hard to generalise there.

When we configure the NDB data nodes in how they map the various threads into CPUs, we need to take into account the consideration of which threads that should share CPU core. The NDB data node consists of a number of threads that all have an internal scheduler and each such thread can be heavily used. There are different thread types, one thread type to execute the data storage and recovery algorithm, another thread type to handle transaction coordination, one thread type to handle receive from the network, others to send to the network and others to handle other things such as IO, metadata and so forth.

One method that brings a bit of benefit (a few percent improvement of throughput) is to ensure that the two threads sharing a CPU core should be of the same type if possible. Thus we use the same instructions for both the CPUs and this has a positive effect on CPU caching.

Another variant to consider is to configure a thread which is using a lot of CPU with another thread that uses less CPU. This has the effect that CPU usage on the hot thread is going up when the other thread is more active than usual. There might not be sufficient amount of lightweight threads to share with the heavy threads.

Personally I usually start by distributing *ldm* threads and *tc* threads as well as *recv* threads and *send* threads on their own CPU cores, after that I fill in the threads to handle *main* thread, *rep* thread and *io* threads on a few CPUs that might share some CPU core with the heavy threads. More on this in a later chapter. In this chapter we will discuss what ids the OS gives to the various CPUs in the box to ensure that we can make a proper configuration of

NDB data nodes.

The next CPU we will discuss is the SPARC. The SPARC processors have for a while standardised on CPU cores with 8 CPUs. The reason for the difference is that SPARC processors is entirely devoted to the server market where throughput is king. Using 8 CPUs per CPU core gives a higher throughput, but it means a lower throughput per thread which would not work so well in the desktop and laptop CPUs where single-threaded performance is still vital. SPARC have nowadays a fairly good performance in single-threaded cases and there is some configuration variants where this can be put to use in NDB.

The standard of using 8 CPUs per CPU core is used by another server CPU manufacture in its Power processor.

The figure below shows how a SPARC CPU core looks like.

CPU core SPARC M7

ALU	FPU	MEM

CPU 0	CPU 1	CPU 2 . . . . . . CPU 7

L1 DataCache	L2 Instruction Cache
L2 Cache	

As can be seen it is the same model with the only difference that we now have 8 CPUs per core. We still have the same L1 caches, L2 cache and shared computational resources.

Doing experiments with the SPARC M7 processor I found that using 2 threads per CPU core gave about 50% improvement compared to using only 1 thread per CPU core. Increasing this to use 4 threads per CPU core (thus using 4 CPUs per CPU core) added another 50% throughput. Using 4 threads improved performance by around 125% compared to using only 1 thread per CPU core. Going beyond 4 CPUs per CPU core gave little extra advantage, less than 10% improvement. Thus for the most part it seems advantegous when used for MySQL

Cluster to simply treat SPARC CPUs as machines with 4 CPUs per CPU core and ignore the other 4 CPUs per CPU core. They could potentially be used for the MySQL Server process, but will not benefit the NDB data nodes to any great extent. The cost of the extra threads will cost more than the additional benefits of using 8 CPUs per CPU core for the NDB data nodes.

The SPARC CPU cores shares L3 caches for a set of CPU cores in a similar fashion to x86 processors.

8.2 CPU SOCKET

The next level for a processor is the CPU socket. This means one physical processor that contains a set of CPU cores. It could contain anything from 2 CPU cores in the most minimal configurations as e.g. in the Intel NUCs I have at home playing around with. It can go up all the way to 28 CPU cores in one CPU socket for Intel architectures.

For SPARC there are two variants. The SPARC M7 series that use 32 CPU cores per socket and the SPARC S7 series (Sonoma) that uses 8 CPU cores per socket.

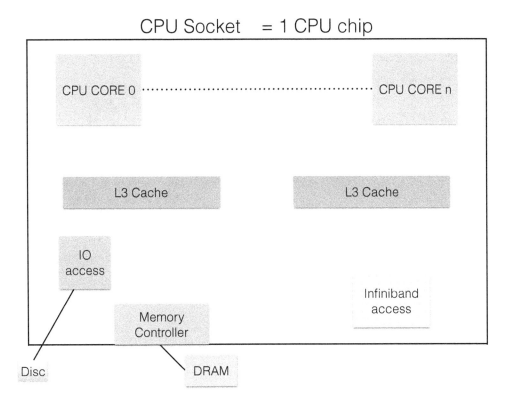

When defining a configuration it is important to consider CPU sockets. For NDB data nodes it is usually sufficient to house the CPU resources on one CPU socket. It is also important to consider bandwidth to processor memory. Each CPU socket have its own set of resources to access the memory in the machine. Each CPU socket can access all memory in the machine. But the bandwidth is bigger to the memory if all CPU sockets are used.

Thus having CPU sockets in mind for both memory and communication is important. It is important to consider this when dealing with MySQL Server configurations where it is fruitful to configure the MySQL Servers to use different CPU sockets for different threads.

8.3 COMPUTER

With one or more CPU sockets in the machine we are ready to look at other memory components. Naturally for a memory-based database the RAM memory is important. Memory is normally attached to a CPU socket and bandwidth to and from memory is usually high.

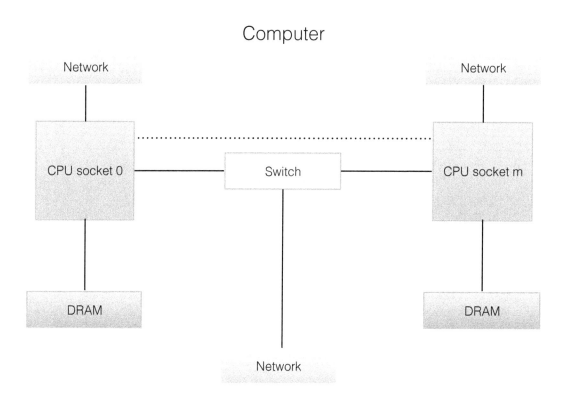

From an operating system point of view the memory is attached to processes. Each process can execute in a number of OS threads that all of them are able to access to the same memory.

The OS can provide shared memory between processes that could be used to communicate e.g. between a MySQL Server and an NDB data node when they are located on the same machine.

Files are stored independent of processes and are read and written through the file IO APIs of the OS. NDB use normal files to store recovery data and the data on disk parts.

8.4 COMPUTER NETWORK

The networking does mostly go through some sort of IO bus. NDB works best with high bandwidth networking. It is fully possible to run with Gigabit Ethernet, but it is possible to get the network to become a bottleneck in this case with as little as 2 CPU cores and most definitely with 4-6 CPU cores. For any server-like environment it is important to run MySQL Cluster on at least 10G Ethernet. Even Infiniband can be necessary in some cases which delivers currently up to 56 Gbit per second in bandwidth for normal installations.

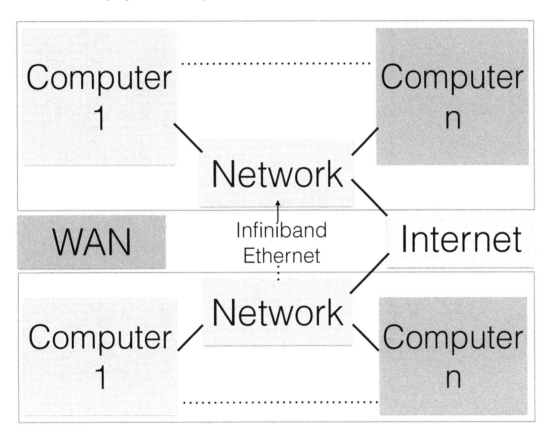

8.5 DISTRIBUTED DATA CENTERS

Many MySQL Cluster installations are done in large distributed data centers. In these centers one finds often a homogenous networking infrastructure where often it is efficient to communicate within one rack. Communication between racks has usually less bandwidth available and one should attempt to place an entire MySQL Cluster inside one rack. Modern cloud installations have worked hard to make it possible to communicate between all machines using the full bandwidth.

When using MySQL Cluster with replication between clusters one will often use installations in different parts in the country or world for higher availability. In this case the inter-cluster bandwidth is an important factor.

PART III

INTRODUCTION TO MySQL CLUSTER

## CHAPTER 9

MYSQL CLUSTER ARCHITECTURE

Now we move on to describing the architecture of MySQL Cluster. In the figure below we see a typical setup for a small cluster.

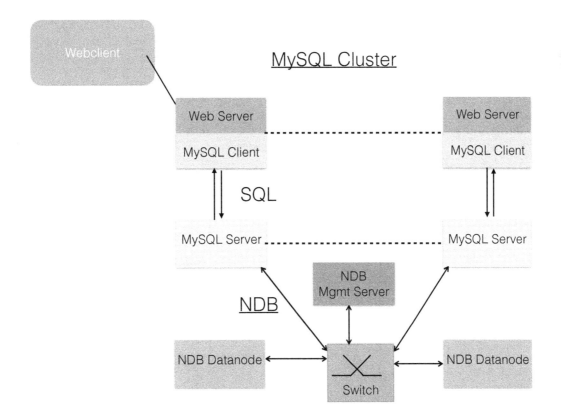

The web client contacts the Web Server, the web server contacts the MySQL Server to query data. The MySQL Server will parse the request and contact the data nodes to read or write the data. In addition we have a management server that contains the configuration of the cluster. Each node starting up contacts the management server (*ndb_mgmd*) to retrieve the configuration in the early phases of starting up the nodes.

The nodes that are part of the cluster can be divided into three types, the data nodes, the management servers and API nodes. All of these nodes have a node id in the cluster and communicate using the NDB protocol.

Data nodes comes in two flavors, the *ndbd* program and the *ndbmtd* program, the *ndbmtd* is the modern multithreaded version. We have kept the old *ndbd* program since it still has the best latency characteristics. It uses less resources, creating a minimal cluster setup is using *ndbd*. Thus *ndbd* will be useful in virtual machine setups with limited resources.

There is only one management server type *ndb_mgmd*, there can be one or two management servers, they are required to start up nodes, but as soon as nodes have started up they are only used for cluster logging. Thus if all management servers are down the data nodes and API nodes will continue to operate.

API nodes comes in many flavors. The most common one is of course a MySQL Server (*mysqld*). But we have also application specific API nodes that use some NDB API variant (will be described later).

A common environment is using MySQL Cluster with MySQL Servers. The figure below shows the setup in this case where a client calls the MySQL Server which in turn talks to the NDB data nodes.

MySQL Cluster

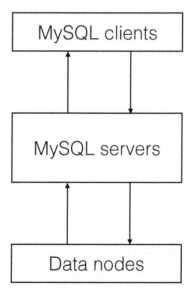

In this setup it is clear that MySQL Cluster is always a distributed solution. We have worked hard to optimise the communication between MySQL Server nodes and the NDB data nodes.

We'll discuss more later in how to setup optimal configurations of MySQL Cluster for various needs.

9.1 NODE GROUP CONCEPT (SHARDS)

A basic theme in MySQL Cluster is the use of node groups. The NDB data nodes are formed in node groups. When starting the cluster one defines the configuration variable *NoOfReplicas*. This specifies the number of nodes per node group. When defining the nodes in the cluster the data nodes are listed in the NDBD sections. The data nodes will be put automatically into node groups unless specifically configured to be in a node group.

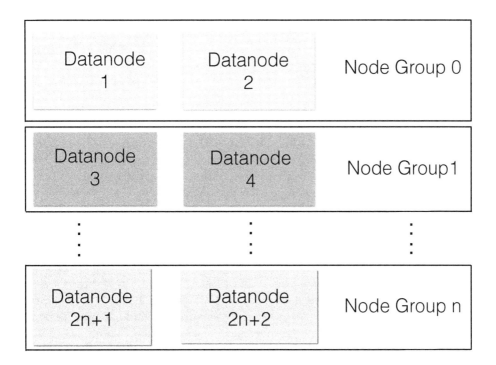

E.g. if we define 4 nodes with node ids 1,2,3 and 4 and we have *NoOfReplicas* set to 2, node 1 and 2 will form one node group and node 3 and 4 will form another node group.

Node groups works similar to shards. Thus all the nodes in a node group (shard) is fully replicated within the node group. Thus in the above example node 1 and node 2 will have exactly the same partitions and the same data. Thus all rows that exist in node 1 will also be present in node 2. The same holds true for node 3 and node 4. However none of the rows in node 3 and node 4 will be present in node 1 and node 2 (an exception is tables using the fully replicated feature).

The cluster continue to operate as long as we have at least one node in each node group up and running (there are some things to consider about network partitioning that we will discuss later). If all nodes in one node group have failed the cluster will also fail since we have lost a part of the data. This is one difference to sharding where each shard lives and dies independently of other shards.

MySQL Cluster supports foreign key relations between node groups and it supports
distributed queries over all node groups, the loss of an entire node group will make it difficult
to operate the cluster.

When NDB was designed there was a choice between spreading partitions over all nodes
and dividing into node groups. Spreading partitions means that we will always survive one
node failure, but it will be hard to survive multiple node failures. Spreading partitions would
mean faster restarts since all nodes can assist the starting node to come up again. Supporting
multi-node failures was deemed more important than to optimise node restarts, therefore NDB
use the node group concept.

9.2   PROGRAM TYPES

We will now discuss the various programs and what they contain. This includes the various
node types, but it also includes various management programs.

9.2.1   *ndbmtd*

The heart of MySQL Cluster is the data node. *ndbmtd* is the multithreaded variant of this.
The data nodes contains the code to handle transactions, it implements the various data
structures to store data, to index data. It implements all the recovery features. Thus most of
the innovations in MySQL Cluster is located in the data nodes. The remainder of the programs
is about interfacing the data node, managing the cluster and a few other things.

ndbmtd contains a fair amount of thread types. It has a number of threads to handle the
actual data and its indexes and the logging. These threads are called *ldm* threads. There are
a number of threads that handles transaction coordination and handles the interface towards
other nodes to a great extent. These threads are called *tc* threads. There is a set of *recv*
threads to handle receive from other nodes. Each thread handles receive from a set of nodes.
Communication to another node is through one TCP/IP socket. There is a set of *send* threads
that can handle send to any node. In 7.5 and later versions the send can also be done by other
thread types. It is still possible to configure with no *send* threads, this means that sending is
done by the threads that generated the messages.

There is a *main* thread, this is mainly used when doing metadata changes and it assists the
send threads. The next thread type is the *rep* thread, this thread is used for various things, but
it is mainly used for replication between clusters and when reorganising the data after adding
more data nodes to the cluster.

There is a set of *io* threads. These threads are used to communicate with the file system.
Since the file system access in most OSs was difficult to make completely asynchronous we
decided to break out file accesses into separate threads, in this manner the file system threads
can use the synchronous file IO calls and thus becomes much easier to handle from a portability
point of view.

There is a *watchdog* thread that keeps track of the other threads to ensure that they continue
making progress, there are two connection setup threads, one for connecting client and one
that acts as a server in the connection setup.

The *ndbmtd* threads (*ldm*, *tc*, *main*, *rep* and *recv*) contains a small operating systems,
they contain a scheduler and has memory buffers setup for communication with other threads

in an efficient manner. The programming of most threads is done using an asynchronous programming style where sending messages is a normal activity. There are coding rules for how long time a message execution is allowed to take (10 microseconds). To handle long running activities one have to use various sorts of continue messages to ensure that other activities gets access to CPU resources at predictable latency.

One nice feature of the data nodes is that the more load they get, the more efficient they become. When loading the cluster, the efficiency goes up and thus the nodes have an extra protection against overload problems.

The number of threads per type is configurable, most thread types can be changed with a configuration change followed by a node restart, but changing the number of *ldm* threads is a bit more involved and we'll look into that later.

Each thread handles its own data, thus in most cases there is no need to use mutexes and similar constructs to handle data. This simplifies programming and gives predictable performance. Even communication between threads is mostly done without mutexes since communication is mostly done using lock-free constructs with a single reader and single writer for each communication buffer. Mutexes and similar constructs are required to wake up sleeping threads, it is required for the send handling. There is special concurrency control to handle the data that represents the data distribution inside the cluster. This is using a mechanism called RCU (Read Copy Update) which means that any number of readers can concurrently read the data. If someone needs to be update the data it will be updated from the same thread always, there is a special memory write protocol used to communicate to readers that they need to retry their reads. This memory write protocol requires the use of memory barriers but requires no special locks.

One data node can scale up to more than 50 threads. A data node of that size will be capable to handle many millions of reads and writes of rows per second.

The cluster design is intended for homogenous clusters, the number of threads per type should be the same on all data nodes. It is possible to use a heterogenous cluster configuration but it is mainly intended for configuration changes where one node at a time changes its configuration.

It is possible to run several data nodes on the same machine.

9.2.2 *ndbd*

The *ndbd* program is performing exactly the same task as the *ndbmtd*. The difference is that in *ndbd* there is only one thread doing the task of the *ldm*, *tc*, *main*, *rep*, *recv* and *send* threads. Thus throughput is limited to what one thread can handle, throughput is severely limited in this case. Latency is improved since there is a lot less interaction between threads, only one thread is needed to wake up to do the task and it does everything.

For the same reason as it is not a good idea to have different configurations of ndbmtd's in the same cluster, it is not a good idea to mix ndbd's and ndbmtd's in the cluster other than as part of configuration changes.

9.2.3   ndb_mgmd

The NDB Management Server is a special program in MySQL Cluster which contains a small distributed database in its own that maintains the NDB configuration database with the configuration of all the nodes in the cluster. It stores the configuration data of the cluster. It supports changing the configuration data and the change will be done using a distributed transaction to ensure that all management servers gets the same updates.

The configuration changes will only be applied to other nodes when the nodes restart. To perform a configuration change requires two steps, first update the configuration in the management server(s), second restart the affected nodes.

The management server is also used for logging purposes. This logging is intended for management of the cluster and contains event reports of various sorts. There is also a set of commands that can be executed that generates output in the cluster log.

Since the management server is part of the cluster it can answer questions about current cluster state. There is a protocol called the NDB MGM protocol to communicate with the management server. It is a simple half-duplex protocol with carriage return to indicate a newline and two carriage returns to indicate the end of the message and that the sender is now expecting a reply. All the communication in this protocol is using the 7-bit ASCII character set.

This protocol has the ability to handle graceful shutdown of a node and startup of a stopped node.

It can only startup nodes if the program is still running, the data nodes can be started through an angle process that will survive when the data node crashes, this angle process will restart the data node process when told to do so by the management server.

A capability that both API nodes and management server nodes can handle is arbitration. Arbitration is used when nodes fail in the cluster to ensure that we can't get two clusters running after the failure. The simplest case is a two-node cluster (two data nodes that is), if one of them sees the other fail through missing heartbeats it will assume that the other node is dead. If the other node is alive, but the communication between the nodes is down, the other node might reason in the same way. In this case they will both contact the arbitrator, the first one to contact the arbitrator gets to continue and the second is told to die.

The cluster needs to decide on which node is arbitrator when nodes are up, a new arbitrator cannot be assigned at the time when a failure happens.

Thus the minimum configuration that can survive a failure of a data node is two working data nodes and one node that is currently arbitrator. If the arbitrator fails while the cluster is up, a new arbitrator is immediately assigned, normally there is some management server or API node available to handle this role.

9.2.4   ndb_mgm

The NDB Management client is a program that implements the NDB MGM protocol using the NDB MGM API. It provides a number of simple text commands to manage the cluster.

9.2.5 THE MySQL SERVER (*mysqld*)

The MySQL Server acts as an API node towards the data nodes and the management server. It can even act as several API nodes to ensure that it can serve the required traffic. One API node is limited by what one socket can deliver and what one receive thread in the NDB API can process. It is possible for larger cluster setups that the number of possible API nodes is the limiting factor in cluster throughput.

The MySQL Server interacts with the data nodes through the NDB API. The NDB API implements the NDB protocol to the data nodes. This protocol is a binary full-duplex protocol where the base message is a signal that has a small header and a payload. There is a fairly large number of predefined signals that can be carried.

One socket can be used by thousands of threads using multiplexing. Many threads can pack their own signals into the send buffers for each socket. Each signal has an address header that describes the receiver thread and the receiver block and a few other items.

9.2.6 *mcmd*

The MySQL Cluster Manager is a program which is used to assist users in more complex management of the cluster. It runs an agent program on each computer that have any MySQL Cluster program running. From this agent program it can start and stop individual programs, it can talk directly to the management client, the management server and so forth. It is not a node in the cluster, it performs all its activities through interfaces to the other programs. As soon as this program is started on all cluster machines it can be used to startup the cluster in a fully automatic fashion.

9.2.7 API NODES

API nodes comes in many flavors such as LDAP servers, DNS servers, DHCP servers, Hadoop File Server and the list can go on for a long time, it is limited to the imagination of application developers using MySQL Cluster.

9.2.8 MySQL CLIENTS

Programs that use MySQL APIs to communicate with the cluster is not part of the cluster as such. They are able to read and write the data in the cluster, but the cluster has no notion of when these nodes start and stop, they connect to a MySQL Server and perform a set of queries and when done they shut down the connection. Only the MySQL server knows of these programs as connections to the MySQL Server.

Any program that uses a MySQL APIs can potentially be used against MySQL Cluster as well. Whether it will work is of course dependent on a lot of things. Using a different database engine for an application is always a task that requires some work.

CHAPTER 10

MySQL Cluster APIs

To read, write and manage data and metadata inside MySQL Cluster one has to go through an API. Even when using SQL the query will have to be passed through an API before it reaches the NDB data nodes.

The most well known interfaces are all the interfaces that one can use to access any MySQL Server. All this interfaces works with MySQL Cluster by using tables that use NDB Cluster as the storage engine.

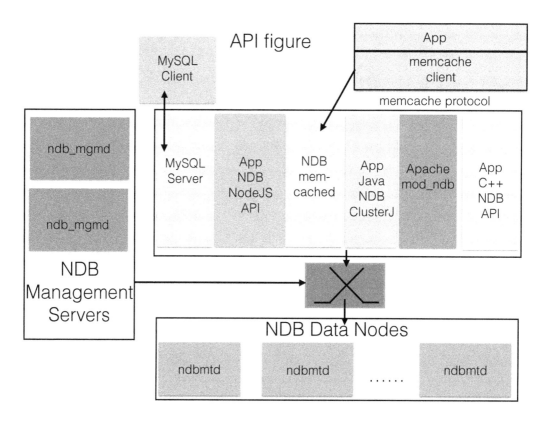

There are a number of direct interfaces that we maintain, these interfaces will go directly from the application to the data nodes. This means that we cut away the Query Server functionality and only use the Data Server capabilities. This is especially interesting when building a data service on top of MySQL Cluster. In this case it is probably more appropriate to say that one uses NDB Cluster. Examples we've seen when this is appropriate is in building an LDAP server, a file server for Hadoop File Service, a DNS server, a DHCP server and a lot of other functionalities. In this case we're building a service which is similar to the services a Query Server that can handle SQL does, but it is usually a bit more specialised in its use case. In the figure below we show a few examples of direct applications.

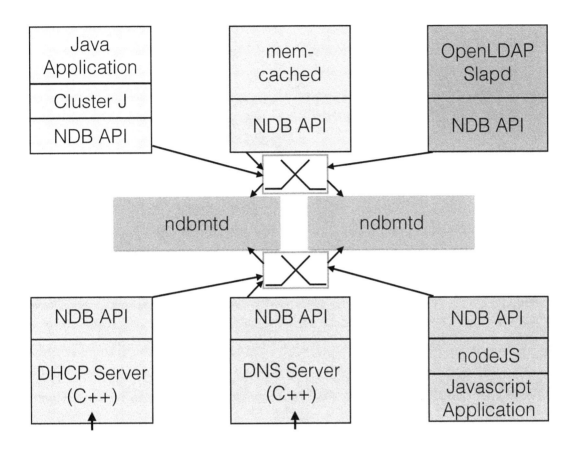

In this case one can use the C++ NDB API, this is the API that all other APIs are eventually going to use. This represents the shortest path to the data in NDB Cluster. The C++ NDB API is fairly complex to use directly, another interface which is quite direct but a lot simpler to program against is ClusterJ. ClusterJ is a Java API, it provides a simple object to relational mapping that makes it easy to work with NDB. There is also a direct mapping of the C++ NDB API available in Java.

Another interface that can be useful to develop high-performance web services is NodeJS. This interface makes it possible to contact the NDB data nodes from a JavaScript application.

In addition we have a memcached service built on top of MySQL Cluster which makes it possible to use NDB as a memcache server.

Programming against a direct NDB API can thus only be done in C++, Java and JavaScript. Most other languages have translation layers that would be possible to map the C++ NDB API to the respective languages. But programming in other languages than these currently requires going through the MySQL APIs.

10.1 MySQL APIs

MySQL Cluster is MySQL with NDB as a storage engine plus a lot more. Thus you can access NDB from any MySQL Server that is part of the cluster you are connecting to.

This has the effect that you can access MySQL Cluster from any API used to access a MySQL Server. We provide a list of some of those APIs and if there is any specifics about using MySQL Cluster from those.

10.1.1 Connector/J

Connector/J is a very well written Java API towards MySQL. It implements the JDBC interface. Programming in Java means that it is easy to mix using Connector/J for more complex queries and using ClusterJ for simple and more direct queries.

10.1.2 Connector/Net

Connector/Net provides an API towards the .Net environment. This environment provides access to the CLR (Common Language Runtime) from Microsoft and thus makes it possible to use many different languages available in Windows environments such as C#.

10.1.3 MySQL C API

The MySQL C API is the API you will use when using the MySQL client and it can be used directly from C and C++. There is also a MySQL C++ API. The C interface to MySQL is used to implement many of the APIs used from other languages.

10.1.4 MySQL API for languages

There is a MySQL API in PHP which is probably still the most popular API used for MySQL applications. There are APIs available for C++, Python, Go, Java, JavaScript and a few more.

10.2 Direct NDB APIs

Direct APIs will go directly to the NDB data nodes without passing the MySQL Server. Thus those interfaces are able to perform better. At the same time it means that one has to program against a lower-level interface. Direct APIs don't exist for all languages, the main direct API is the C++ NDB API which is the base that everyone uses to access the NDB data nodes. Most languages have escape routes such that one can call a function in C. Through these interfaces one can always access the C++ NDB API from all those languages.

As examples in Ruby it is possible to inline C and C++ code and to use something called Rice to access objects written in C++. Scala can access C and C++ code through JNI (Java Native Interface). Go also have a C interface.

10.2.1 ClusterJ: NDB API for Java

ClusterJ is a bit more than just a wrapper for the C++ NDB API. It does still go through the C++ NDB API on its way toward the NDB data nodes. But it provides an easy object-relational mapping interface to make it easy to work with.

Here one defines objects that are simply tables in NDB. These objects can be read from NDB and written down to NDB after setting the variables in the object.

A good example of an open-source product using ClusterJ is the HopsFS that implements the metadata server in the Hadoop filesystem (HDFS).

10.2.2 NODEJS: ASYNCHRONOUS NDB API FOR JAVA SCRIPTS

NodeJS makes it possible to quickly get up and running with MySQL Cluster to develop web applications using JavaScript programs.

10.3 MEMCACHED

We maintain a memcached server that implements the memcache API such that one can use MySQL Cluster to store any objects using the memcache API.

10.4 OPENLDAP

The OpenLDAP have a backend that provides access to NDB. A number of users have started from this backend and developed LDAP servers based on this.

PART IV

GETTING STARTED

In the following chapters we will get you started in installing and using MySQL Cluster. The first chapter will focus on developers. If you are completely new to MySQL Cluster and want to try it out, this is the chapter where you should start.

This chapter introduces a tool we have developed specifically for developers called MySQL Cluster Configurator (MCC).

To ensure that you can write integration tools with Chef, Puppet, Docket and many more orchestration tools we will cover the how-to on installing MySQL Cluster for various platforms in the second chapter. This chapter is useful if you want to get more hands-on experience in managing the MySQL Cluster software. It is a vital chapter to study if you have been tasked with setting up a DevOps environment for MySQL Cluster integrated with some application you are managing.

After installing software you need to understand the various programs in MySQL Cluster and how to start those. The third chapter in this part is about this. We will not attempt to be complete in our description here, for this we simply refer to the MySQL manual. This chapter will focus on the preferred ways of starting the programs.

To handle a DevOps environment it is important to understand handling of configuration files in MySQL Cluster, this is covered in the fifth chapter. Later in the book there will be a lot more description of how to set the various configuration parameters, these parameters will be important to understand in the late phases when setting up a production environment for MySQL Cluster.

Next we cover how to use Docker containers to run MySQL Cluster.

We cover how to build MySQL Cluster yourself. This is useful if you need to patch the MySQL Cluster software.

The final chapter in this part describes a few potential HW setups to operate NDB in.

Chapter 11

Getting Started for Developers

In this chapter we will focus on how to use MySQL Cluster Configurator (MCC) to get quickly up and running with MySQL Cluster. MCC is sometimes nicknamed the Auto Installer.

We will first show a detailed description of how to get a cluster up and running on a local Mac OS X box. This description can be immediately applied on Windows, Linux and even Solaris with minor tweaks.

A graphical download, install, configure and start of cluster is possible to complete in 4 minutes for an experienced user. For a new user it is likely that one wants to do things a bit more careful, but it will still be done within much less than 15 minutes.

MCC can assist you to quickly get a cluster up and running and it can handle tests of various simple management operations such as start and stop clusters. It has support to ensure that you get a good configuration for the hardware you are using.

We will show how to get going on a development machine where the entire cluster is in one machine.

11.1 Getting Started on Mac OS X

In this section we will demonstrate all the steps necessary to perform a download, installation, configuration and startup of the cluster on a Mac OS X computer.

Once your cluster is up and running you have access to two MySQL Servers on port 3316 and 3317 that both can be used to read and write the data in the cluster. You get access to 3 NDB API nodes that can be used to run various NDB tools towards the cluster. The actual data is stored in two NDB data nodes. All these programs run on the same machine in this simple case to test MySQL Cluster.

Mac OS X is a similar platform to Windows, it is mainly used for development. It is the platform I use myself to develop MySQL Cluster on. But more real-world testing I always bring to a Linux computer or a Solaris computer.

To install on Mac OS X is easy, one simply downloads the DMG archive of the version you are downloading, e.g. *mysql-cluster-gpl-7.5.8-osx10.12-x86_64.dmg* for the MySQL Cluster 7.5.8 version.

Once the installation is completed you should have a new directory called something like:

```
/usr/local/mysql-cluster-gpl-7.5.8-osx10.12-x86_64
```

This would be the installation directory for MySQL Cluster 7.5.8 and something similar would be the case if another version of MySQL Cluster was used. In this case the Mac OS 10.12 version was used to create the installation, but this installation can also be used on older and newer OS X versions.

We will show a detailed description of how to download MySQL Cluster on Mac OS X and how to get MCC up and running with a working cluster.

11.1.1 INSTALLING ON MAC OS X

To follow the process outlined below is simple. We still present it in all its detail to ensure that you don't get problems already in this early phase of getting to understand MySQL Cluster and what it can do for you.

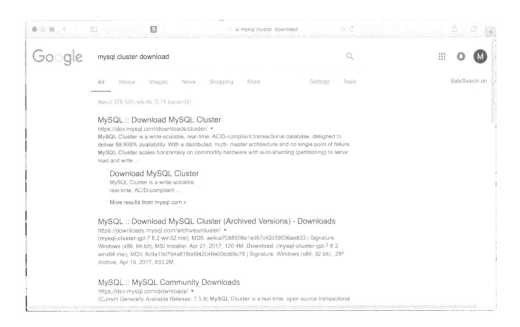

The first step is that we want to download MySQL Cluster. The easiest way to find out where this happens is to use Google. Enter "MySQL Cluster Download" as the search term. As the figure above shows the top result will be a reference to a download of the latest version of MySQL Cluster.

When you click on the top result you will come to a page, as shown below, where you are presented with a number of choices. The web page have already adapted to your operating system. Thus in this case it will show the possibilities for downloads of Mac OS X variants for MySQL Cluster.

There are two variants as you can see, the first variant is a tarball with all the necessary binaries. Personally I always use the DMG archive that comes with an installer. Clicking on a download of the DMG archive of MySQL Cluster brings you to the next page.

The next page presents you with a number of options. You can use an Oracle account to download the DMG archive and get some benefits from that as stated on the web page. You can also simply click on the link "No thanks, just start my download". If you do so the download of the 432 MByte DMG archive will start up.

The download will take a while, how long depends on the access speed you use. I have 100 Mbit per second download speed, for me the download takes about 1 minute. On a slow internet access it can easily take an hour or even more.

When you have clicked on the link you will see the progress bar in the Dock window.

When the download is complete this Download icon will indicate that the download is done. By clicking on the download icon and then clicking on the MySQL Cluster DMG archive the above popup window will appear. Here one should double-click on the .pkg file. This will start the MySQL Cluster installer. When the MySQL Cluster installer a new window appears as shown below.

The MySQL Cluster installer will go through a set of windows. The first one simply prepares you to the fact that you are installing MySQL Cluster and which version of MySQL Cluster you are installing. In this window you simply click Continue to proceed.

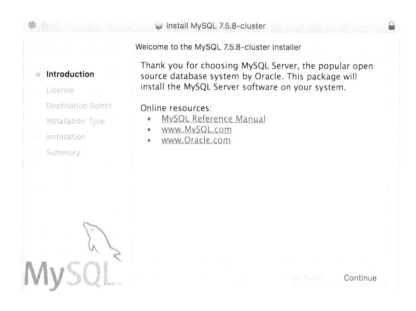

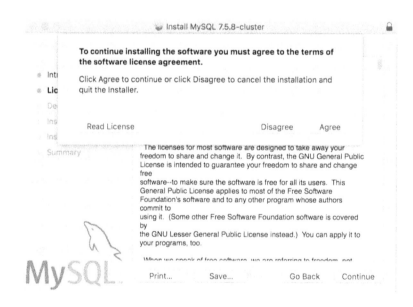

The next figure presents the GPL License for reading before clicking Continue again.

After clicking Continue you get a new question in the same window (as shown below) appears. Here you have to click Agree to the use of the GPL license.

Now before installing the MySQL Cluster installer will give you information about how large the installation is. Click Install. If you like to download the installation to a special installation directory you can provide that here. The default is the directory:

/usr/local/mysql-cluster-gpl-7.5.8-osx10.12-x86_64

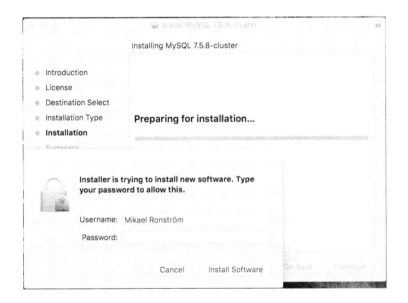

To install software on Mac OS X requires appropriate privileges and you have to provide your password before the actual installation starts up. Enter the password and then click "Install Software".

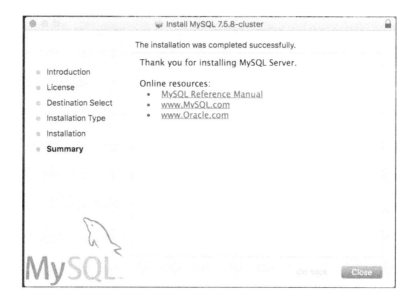

Now the installation starts. As part of this installation the installer will generate a random password to the MySQL Server. This ensures that the installation is secure. It will be presented in a popup window. It is very important to record this password before pressing OK. Otherwise it won't be possible to connect to the MySQL Server when starting it up. After recording the password you can press OK to continue the installation process.

When the installation is done the above window is presented. Click Close and the installation is complete.

11.1.2 STARTING A CLUSTER USING MCC

Now that the download and installation is complete we want to start up the MySQL Cluster Configurator. This will configure the cluster and start it up.

To start MCC requires running a Python script.

This Python script is called *ndb_setup.py*. It is located in the bin directory of the MySQL Cluster installation.

This program can be started in an easy manner from a terminal window. If you are not used to using the terminal application you can find it in the Launchpad under a symbol that describes multiple tools.

When clicking on this symbol in the Launchpad you will be presented with a set of system tools, click on the terminal symbol to start up a terminal window.

Now execute the *ndb_setup.py* script as shown in command window below.

In this version of MCC the pid file of MCC is created in the same directory as this script is started from. So to avoid having to start it as *sudo* we provide the full path to the python script and start it from our home directory.

As shown in the window below this will start up a web server on the localhost on port 8081.

MCC is currently undergoing heavy changes, these can be found in the latest MySQL Cluster 7.6 versions. It is ok to use the newer versions also to start up clusters using the MySQL Cluster 7.5 version of NDB.

The python script will immediately fire up a web page from where we can run MCC. At first MCC will inform that the Safari web browser isn't a web browser recognized by MCC and warn that not everything might work. In my testing I haven't found any problems in using the Safari Web browser with MCC, so you can simply click Close in the warning window to get to the welcome window of MCC.

Now you have arrived at the welcome window of the MCC. You can choose to either "Create a new MySQL Cluster" or you can continue working with an existing cluster. Given that we are starting from scratch here we will continue to create a new MySQL Cluster.

This brings us to a window where we can define a number of properties. We can define the name of the cluster which defaults to MyCluster. We can define a list of hosts to use in the MySQL Cluster. We will setup a cluster running on only our machine, the host 127.0.0.1 is appropriate which means that the cluster is local to this computer.

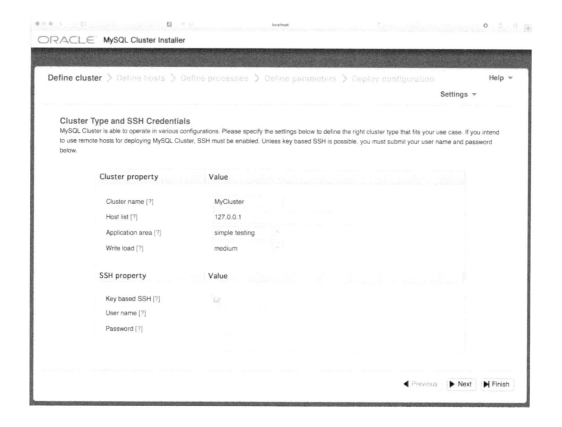

It is possible to define different levels for how to auto-configure the configuration through a scroll down window. We will choose the "simple testing" that will use about 25% of the memory resources on the machine. The "web application" and "realtime" options will both use all the memory in the machine with some different settings on real-time options.

Since I simply want to use it for development I will leave some memory for my development tools as well. In my case I have 32 GByte of memory, thus I can create a database of about 4 GBytes that is replicated locally on this machine and still have plenty of memory resources left.

I will set write speed to medium and I will keep the SSH property for setting up the cluster (on Windows it is a good idea to not use this property since an SSH server is normally not setup on Windows). The write speed can be set to low, medium and high.

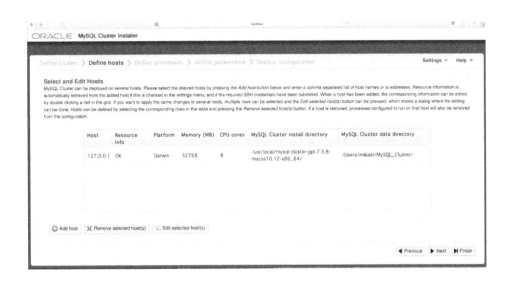

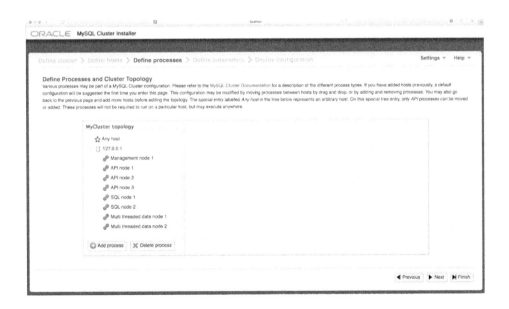

After clicking Next some magic happens and we discover the directory structure and we find the MySQL Cluster installation and we propose a data directory for the MySQL Cluster. We discover the amount of CPUs and the amount of memory in the machine. This is used as input to automatically setup the base configuration.

In this window we can enter more hosts if necessary, all hosts are auto-discovered. Click Next when done.

On the next window we are presented with a set of nodes that are suggested for the cluster. It will suggest 1 NDB management server, 2 NDB data nodes, 2 MySQL Servers and 3 slots for NDB API applications. We will go with this and thus we click Next.

On the next window we can edit the configuration. We can click on a node and edit the hostname, the node id and the data directory for all node types (except API nodes that only define node id and hostname). On management server nodes we can also edit the port number to connect to the management server. On MySQL Servers we can edit the port number to connect to it and the socket file to use for localhost connections.

By clicking on "Show advanced configuration options" and clicking on the Data Layer we can edit the configuration parameters of the NDB data nodes as seen in the figure above. These parameters are a lot more and there are many advanced configuration parameters that we will go through later in this book. Here we simply show the ability to change some of those settings from MCC.

If you already have a running MySQL Server on port 3306, it might be a good idea to change the port number of the MySQL Server. My Mac OS X installation has a MySQL Server running on port 3306, so I usually edit those and set them to 3316 and 3317 instead.

To change a parameter one should first click on the plus sign and then change either directly in text box or by clicking up and down arrows in text box.

Parameters to especially consider is *DataMemory*, *IndexMemory*, and *NoOfFragmentLogFiles*.

For an experiment defaults are likely to be fine, but these and others can be considered to be changed for more advanced development.

When we are done with our configuration we click Next in this web page.

Now we have arrived at the final window of MCC. This is the deploy and start window. In this case we will start to deploy the cluster. This means that we will install all the configuration files of the NDB management server(s) and all the configuration files of the MySQL Server(s). To perform this action click "Deploy Cluster".

After deploy is completed we will be informed that the deploy is completed and asked to close the popup window. After clicking this we are back to the above window again.

The below terminal window shows the high level view of the directories and files created for the various nodes that are created. If you want to edit the configuration file of the cluster (config.ini) or the MySQL Server config files (my.cnf), it is a good idea to do that now before starting up the cluster. There are many options available in both MySQL Server configs and in the cluster configuration that isn't settable through MCC. As you get more advanced you are likely to take this opportunity and add some more configuration options here.

When the configuration changes are done it is time to start the cluster.

To do this we click "Deploy and Start Cluster". This will kick off the startup of the cluster.

During the startup process we will get a popup window with a progress bar and information on what is currently starting up. First we will see the management server being started, next the first data node is started, next the second data node and as part of starting the second data node the data nodes will start an initial start together.

```
●  ●  ●                    ⚑ mikael — -bash — 80×24
Mikaels-iMac:~ mikael$ ls /Users/mikael/MySQL_Cluster/
1       2       49      53      54
Mikaels-iMac:~ mikael$ ls /Users/mikael/MySQL_Cluster/1
Mikaels-iMac:~ mikael$ ls /Users/mikael/MySQL_Cluster/2
Mikaels-iMac:~ mikael$ ls /Users/mikael/MySQL_Cluster/49
config.ini
Mikaels-iMac:~ mikael$ ls /Users/mikael/MySQL_Cluster/53
my.cnf  mysql   test    tmp
Mikaels-iMac:~ mikael$ ls /Users/mikael/MySQL_Cluster/54
my.cnf  mysql   test    tmp
Mikaels-iMac:~ mikael$
Mikaels-iMac:~ mikael$
Mikaels-iMac:~ mikael$
Mikaels-iMac:~ mikael$
Mikaels-iMac:~ mikael$
Mikaels-iMac:~ mikael$
Mikaels-iMac:~ mikael$
Mikaels-iMac:~ mikael$
Mikaels-iMac:~ mikael$
Mikaels-iMac:~ mikael$
Mikaels-iMac:~ mikael$
Mikaels-iMac:~ mikael$
Mikaels-iMac:~ mikael$
Mikaels-iMac:~ mikael$
```

When the management server and data nodes are started we will see the progress on starting the first MySQL server and finally we will see the second MySQL Server getting started.

Now MySQL Cluster is started, we get a report on this and we click Close.

In my case the startup took around 40 seconds. This would be fairly normal on a modern development machine.

After clicking Close we are back to the deploy and start window as shown below. As you can see the nodes now have different colors. The NDB management server, NDB data nodes and the MySQL Servers are all started and thus have green status. The NDB API nodes are currently not used, they are not started. Not started nodes have a red color. As you could see during the start of the data nodes the color of the nodes was yellow when they were started but still performing the node restart.

Now we show the high level file view when the cluster has completed its start. We can see that the NDB management server now has a cluster log, a node log, a pid file, the original config file and a new binary version of the config file. When a crash occurs the NDB data nodes will have a set of trace files.

The NDB data nodes have a pid file, a node log and a directory for the file system of the data node where we will have checkpoint files, meta data files, REDO log files, UNDO log files and tablespaces. More about that later.

In the MySQL Server directory we can see a traditional MySQL installation and there are 2 servers installed.

```
                          ⌂ mikael — -bash — 80×24
Last login: Sat Nov 19 12:37:50 on ttys001
Mikaels-iMac:~ mikael$ ls /Users/mikael/MySQL_Cluster/
1       2       49      53      54
Mikaels-iMac:~ mikael$ ls /Users/mikael/MySQL_Cluster/1
ndb_1.pid       ndb_1_fs        ndb_1_out.log
Mikaels-iMac:~ mikael$ ls /Users/mikael/MySQL_Cluster/2
ndb_2.pid       ndb_2_fs        ndb_2_out.log
Mikaels-iMac:~ mikael$ ls /Users/mikael/MySQL_Cluster/49
config.ini              ndb_49_cluster.log      ndb_49_out.log
ndb_49.pid              ndb_49_config.bin.1
Mikaels-iMac:~ mikael$ ls /Users/mikael/MySQL_Cluster/53
data                    mysql.socket            tmp
my.cnf                  mysql.socket.lock
mysql                   test
Mikaels-iMac:~ mikael$ ls /Users/mikael/MySQL_Cluster/54
data                    mysql.socket            tmp
my.cnf                  mysql.socket.lock
mysql                   test
Mikaels-iMac:~ mikael$ ▓
```

After downloading, installing and now starting up the cluster we are now ready to make use of MySQL Cluster for whatever purpose we had. We can access it from any normal MySQL application connecting to the 3316 or 3317 ports used in this setup.

We can access it from NDB tools or through some NDB application that access one of the internal NDB APIs. This could be e.g. a DNS server, an LDAP server, a DHCP server, a AAA server or any application you are developing.

To follow all these steps to download, install and startup MySQL Cluster on Mac OS X took me less than 4 minutes. Most of the clicks you need to do are fairly obvious and are quick. The most time consuming parts is the download of the DMG archive and the startup of the cluster. These consumed more than half of the time that expired.

If you want to use the MCC for development you can e.g. startup the cluster when you want to start up development (takes about 40 seconds). When you are done you can stop the cluster which takes around 20 seconds. If you want to start a completely new cluster you can simply erase the entire installation by issuing

```
rm -rf /Users/mikael/MySQL_Cluster
```

in my case. This will remove all configuration files, all data directories and will start everything from scratch.

11.2 Getting Started on Windows

Exactly the same process can easily be followed on Windows (and on Linux and Solaris as well for that matter). The installation windows will be very similar except that you will most likely choose the MSI installer package on Windows. We will not go through the details once more, we will only describe the main differences between Windows and Mac OS X.

Installing MySQL Cluster on Windows have two options from download sections. The first one is to run an installer program (.msi) that will install the binaries. One can also use the zip archives.

The most common use case for installing MySQL Cluster on Windows is to develop some application against it. The easiest model of development on Windows is to use the MySQL Cluster Configurator that was previously described.

The archive will create a directory with the installation files called:

mysql-cluster-gpl-noinstall-VER-winARCH

where VER is the version number of MySQL Cluster, e.g 7.5.6 and ARCH is i686 for 32-bit installations and x86_64 for 64-bit installations.

After completing the install one needs to start the Python program. In my Windows machine MySQL Cluster is installed on

C:\Program Files\MySQL\MySQL Cluster 7.5

for a 7.5-based installation. Python is installed as part of the MySQL Cluster installation to ensure that there are no issues with Python.

To start MCC one first opens a Windows Explorer window and goes to the directory provided above. In that directory there is a file shown as setup (setup.bat) that can be used to start MCC. To start MCC with debug options there is a setup-debug (setup-debug.bat) file.

To start MCC on Windows one right-clicks on the *setup* file in the Windows Explorer window and selects to run as administrator. Administrator privileges are needed since on Windows the NDB programs and MySQL Servers are started as services and to start a service requires administrator privileges.

One might have to add some stuff to ensure that the Windows firewall doesn't block the ports used by the NDB programs.

If Python is installed properly one can simply right-click on the ndb_setup.py file in the bin directory and select to run as administrator. It is preferrable on Windows to use the setup BAT files instead.

If you (as me) prefer to start programs from a terminal window (this gives possibilities to add options to the start of the program), on Windows you will likely use a PowerShell window for this. Start the PowerShell as Administrator.

Once the Python program is started the installation follows exactly the same procedure as on Mac OS X. When you get to the window where you describe the SSH property you should click away using SSH keys unless you are planning to setup SSH communication between your machines. It is possible to use SSH on Windows as well, but it is some extra work and I will not describe it in this book.

11.3 USING MYSQL CLUSTER CONFIGURATOR FOR DEVELOPMENT

If your objective is to develop and test an application running on MySQL Cluster it is quite likely that you are developing on Windows or Mac OS X. These are the most popular platforms for software development. Personally I develop everything I do on Mac OS X.

But developing and running is two different things, to deploy MySQL Cluster it is most likely that you are going to use Linux or Solaris or possibly an enthusiast might even choose to run on FreeBSD.

You can develop applications using the C++ NDB API, you can develop Java applications against the ClusterJ API and you can develop JavaScript applications using our direct NodeJS API (called Database Jones).

When you are done with the development for the day you simply click "Stop Cluster" to stop the cluster. If you want to start with the same cluster again the next day you simply click "Deploy and Start Cluster".

Now if you want to start from fresh again you can edit certain parameters, but not all parameters can be changed. Often in development you might want to remove all the data files created by the previous cluster installation as described above.

After this you can create a completely new cluster configuration completely unrelated to the previous one.

If you want to start and stop nodes individually it cannot be done from the auto installer. This can be done using the NDB management client and the *mysqladmin* program for MySQL Servers.

Chapter 12

Installing MySQL Cluster

Now that we described a simple graphical installation tool to get started for development of MySQL Cluster applications, it is now time to look more into how to install on platforms where you want to run production clusters. You can use these installation variants for development as well, but the description for Linux and Solaris is more focused on how it can be used in DevOps environments.

Naturally you could use the MySQL Cluster Configurator for development on Linux and Solaris as well, but this follows the procedure used on Mac OS X very closely and we assume you know how to use a terminal window if you are running Linux or Solaris. We won't mention anything more on this. The previous chapter showed a detailed look on how to install MySQL Cluster on Mac OS X and that description covers Windows in detail. We will focus this chapter on installing in Linux and Solaris.

There are many ways to install a cluster, but for now we will explain a manual installation to ensure that you get an idea of what happens when installing the cluster automatically.

The most important programs to install are the *ndbmtd* (the multithreaded NDB data node), *ndbd* (the single-threaded NDB data node), *mysqld* (the MySQL Server), *mysql* (the MySQL client), *ndb_mgm* (the NDB management client) and the *ndb_mgmd* (the NDB management server) programs. We also have a set of useful programs that might be of interest such as *ndb_import*, *mysqldump*, *ndb_top* and many different ndb_* programs that are various utilities for MySQL Cluster. There is also a set of important libraries, such as the NDB API library.

12.1 Installing using *yum*

Installing on *Oracle Linux*, *Red Hat*, *CentOS* and *Fedora* and a plethora of other distros depending on those are using the *yum* tool. MySQL has setup *yum* repos to install the latest MySQL and MySQL Cluster software.

12.1.1 Installing the RPM supporting *yum* tools

The first step in the installation process is to download an RPM package that is required to install using the MySQL *yum* repos.

The RPM package can be found at:

```
http://dev.mysql.com/downloads/repo/yum
```

There is a number of such RPM files. One for Red Hat 6/Oracle 6/CentOS 6 and one for Red Hat 7/Oracle 7/CentOS 7. There is a similar file for Fedora24, Fedora 25 and Fedora 26.

To install MySQL Cluster 7.5 one should use RPM packages that have a name starting with *mysql57-community-release*.

These packages are named as:

mysqlMYSQL_VERSION-community-release-OS_VERSION-RPM_VERSION.no-arch.rpm

Here MySQL_VERSION is 57, OS_VERSION is either el6 or el7 for

Red Hat/Oracle Linux/CentOS and fedora24/fedora25/fedora26 for various Fedora versions. RPM_VERSION is currently 11 and will be updated whenever a new version of the RPM package is released.

After downloading this RPM package we install the RPM package using the following command:

```
sudo rpm -ivh mysql57-community-release-el7-11.noarch.rpm
```

Use *rpm -Uvh* instead if it is an upgrade instead of a new install. After install a *yum update* (*dnf upgrade* for dnf systems such as Fedora) will update this RPM package.

All the commands normally require to be executed as root user and often this means that one puts a sudo before the command if executed from a non-root user.

After executing this command the default setting is to install MySQL 5.7 community version. We need one more step to ensure that MySQL Cluster 7.5 is installed.

To perform this we run the following set of commands:

```
sudo yum install -y yum-utils
sudo yum-config-manager --disable mysql57-community
sudo yum-config-manager --enable mysql-cluster-7.5-community
```

The first command installs the *yum-config-manager* that is part of the *yum-utils* package. The *yum-config-manager* can be used to disable and enable different MySQL versions.

An alternative is to edit the file as shown below (assuming one uses *vi* as editor):

```
sudo vi /etc/yum.repos.d/mysql-community-repo
```

In this file one sets *enabled* to 0 in the section for mysql57-community and set it to 1 in the mysql-cluster-7.5 section.

In order to make it possible to install minimalistic installations the *yum* packages have been divided into a large set of different packages. The packages are named as:

mysql-cluster community-PACKAGE_NAME

It is possible to use RPM packages directly to install MySQL Cluster, but using *yum* is much preferred since this have a lot more code to handle different problems during installation. There could be some reason to use it if one wants to install 32-bit versions. It is possible to use *yum* to install downloaded RPM packages.

As an example to install the data node package we would issue the command:

```
sudo yum install mysql-cluster-data-node
```

Installing on a VM to be used for NDB management server is equally easy. The command:

```
sudo yum install mysql-cluster-community-management-server
```

will install the *ndb_mgmd* binary.

Normally there will be three types of VMs in the cluster. The VMs used for data nodes, the VMs used for NDB management servers and the VMs used to run the MySQL Servers.

It is possible to have other VMs to run clients such as the NDB management client, the MySQL client, various VMs for NDB tools and VMs used for specialised NDB API applications.

Installing the MySQL Server package is a bit more involved. The command to do it is still as easy:

```
sudo yum install mysql-cluster-community-server
```

The problem is that the MySQL Server package depends on packages not normally accessible from a standard Red Hat installation. These are a set of Perl packages used by the MySQL client (the MySQL client is a dependency of the MySQL server package).

To handle this we need to install EPEL (Extra Packages for Enterprise Linux) packages in Red Hat before we execute the command to install the MySQL Server. This uses the following command on Red Hat 7 (similar commands on Red Hat 6):

```
sudo rpm -ivh \
http://dl.fedoraproject.org/pub/epel/7/x86_64/e/ \
epel-release-7-9.noarch.rpm
```

After this fuss we are finally done with installing the MySQL Server package on Red Hat Linux.

In most cases it is a bit more involved since very often there is an existing MySQL installation. In order to install the MySQL Cluster Server package on an Oracle 7 image in the Oracle Bare Metal Cloud the following commands will do the trick.

```
sudo rpm -ivh mysql57-community-release-el7-11.noarch.rpm
sudo yum install -y yum-utils
sudo yum-config-manager --disable mysql57-community
sudo yum-config-manager --enable mysql-cluster-7.5-community
sudo rpm -ivh \
http://dl.fedoraproject.org/pub/epel/7/x86_64/e/ \
epel-release-7-9.noarch.rpm
sudo yum remove mysql-community-{server,client,common,libs}
sudo yum install mysql-cluster-community-{server,client,common,libs}
```

If your servers lack accessibility to Internet you can download the RPM packages from MySQL websites and still use *yum install* to install the software in a similar fashion to when using the *yum* repos.

Note: On Fedora systems you should use *dnf* instead of *yum*.

12.2 INSTALLING USING *apt*

There is only one APT package currently. This package is currently named:

mysql-apt-config_0.8.9-1_all.deb

This package can be used to install on Debian 7.x/8.x/9.x and Ubuntu 14.04 LTS/16.04 LTS/17.04/17.10.

After downloading this package one should run the following two commands to prepare for installation of MySQL Cluster packages.

```
sudo dpkg -i mysql-apt-config_0.8.9-1_all.deb
sudo apt-get update
```

During installation of this package you will get a question of which MySQL component to use when installing. Here you should select *mysql-cluster-x.y* where x.y is the MySQL Cluster version, thus 7.5.

Before proceeding we need to install the following packages that is not automatically installed by the package:

```
sudo apt-get install python-paramiko libclass-methodmaker-perl
```

After this we can start installing the various cluster packages as described below. E.g. to install the data node package we execute the following command:

```
sudo apt-get install mysql-cluster-community-data-node
```

The generic name for packages described below are:

mysql-cluster-community-PACKAGE_NAME

More detailed instructions are available in the MySQL documentation at:

```
http://dev.mysql.com/downloads/repo/apt
```

12.3 Installing using *Zypper* on Suse

There is two different RPM packages used, one for Suse 11 and one for Suse 12. Only the Suse 12 variant supports MySQL Cluster.

The name of the RPM package is:

mysqlMYSQL_VER-community-release-slesSUSE_VER-RPM_VER.noarch.rpm

To prepare installation of MySQL Cluster packages on Suse 12 the following commands are executed:

```
sudo rpm -ivh mysql57-community-release-sles12-11.noarch.rpm
sudo rpm --import /etc/RPM-GPG-KEY-mysql
sudo zypper addrepo \
http://download.opensuse.org/repositories/\
devel:languages:python/SLE_12_SP2/\
devel:languages:python:repo
sudo zypper modifyrepo -d mysql57-community
sudo zypper modifyrepo -e mysql-cluster-community-7.5
sudo zypper refresh
```

First we add the MySQL SLES package to the *zypper* infrastructure. Next we need to add the key for the MySQL packages. MySQL Cluster relies on the *python2-crypto* and python-paramiko packages, we need a repository to ensure those things can be downloaded as part of the install process. Finally we switch to the MySQL Cluster packages and after that we refresh to get access to all packages within the MySQL Cluster package.

Now to install e.g. the data node package we run the command:

```
sudo zypper install mysql-cluster-community-data-node
```

12.4 MySQL Cluster packages

12.4.1 Installing NDB data node package

data-node is the component containing the *ndbd* and the *ndbmtd* program. For machines, VMs or containers that only run data nodes, this is the only package needed.

This package should only conflict with MySQL Cluster packages from other MySQL Cluster versions.

12.4.2 INSTALLING NDB MANAGEMENT SERVER PACKAGE

management-server is the component that contains the *ndb_mgmd* binary.

This package should only conflict with MySQL Cluster packages from other MySQL Cluster versions.

12.4.3 INSTALLING MySQL SERVER PACKAGES

server is the component containing the *mysqld*, the MySQL Server program, this package is required to use the *mysqld*, but on top of this *mysqld* also requires the *common* package.

Installing these packages can sometimes cause conflicts due to already existing packages installed (this could be either MySQL packages or MariaDB packages or Percona packages or some other MySQL packager). When installing the package there can be a conflict. To resolve this conflict it is necessary to remove the already existing package. Running MySQL, MySQL Cluster, Percona or MariaDB at the same time in the same machine isn't recommended since they use the same names of binaries and libraries but they aren't always compatible with each other. In order to use MySQL Cluster it is necessary to install a MySQL Server from the MySQL Cluster packages since no other MySQL Server is able to use the NDB storage engine.

As described below one might have to install the *libs*, *client* and *common* packages before removing some previous MySQL packages to handle dependencies that other programs have on MySQL packages.

12.4.4 INSTALLING CLIENT PACKAGES

client is the component installing the *ndb_mgm* binary and the *mysql* program (the MySQL client) and a set of other client tools.

Here one might run into conflicts with other packages having different *mysql* programs installed. These should be replaced by these packages.

12.4.5 INSTALLING LIBS PACKAGE

libs is the component installing the libraries. When installing these one can run into conflicts with previous installations. In order to resolve those conflicts it might be necessary to first install the *libs* package followed by removal of the conflicting package. An example could be that a program have been installed (e.g. *postfix*) already that depends on MySQL client libraries being available. The MySQL Cluster client libraries is ok to use with clients accessing other types of MySQL Servers.

There is a component called *libs-compat* that contains a backward compatible version of the libs package.

12.4.6 INSTALLING NDB CLIENT LIBRARY PACKAGES

ndbclient is the component installing the NDB client libraries, these are the libraries that contains the C++ NDB API. There is a *ndbclient-devel* component required for development against the NDB API with the necessary header files.

For development and running against the ClusterJ API one uses the *java* component.

Similarly there is a component *nodejs* for the NodeJS API for both development and running against. There is a component *memcached* to use the NDB memcached server.

These package should only conflict with MySQL Cluster packages from other MySQL Cluster versions.

12.4.7   OTHER PACKAGES

In order to use the MySQL Cluster Configurator one needs to install the component *auto-installer*.

When using MySQL Cluster for development one should install the *devel* component that contains various needed header files.

There are a number of packages to use MySQL embedded servers with MySQL Cluster. These are the *embedded* for MySQL Server, *embedded-devel* for development against embedded MySQL Server and *embedded-compat* for a backward compatible embedded MySQL Server. Support for the embedded server in MySQL Cluster will be removed in MySQL 8.0.

Finally there is a *test* component that can be used to run MTR tests against the MySQL Cluster.

12.5   INSTALL USING AN RPM PACKAGE

Installing from RPM packages can be done when a server has no internet access to directly use the *yum* repos.

To install a downloaded RPM package one uses the following command:

```
rpm -Uvh mysql-cluster-community-data-node-7.5.6-1.el7.x86_64.rpm
```

This command will install the *data-node* package for MySQL Cluster 7.5.6 on Oracle Linux 7 (or any Red Hat 7 compatible OS) using a 64-bit x86 package. It is still preferrable to use the *yum* tool in these cases when working with RPMs directly.

12.6   INSTALLING ON DEBIAN

Installing on Debian-based Linux distros can be done using *.deb* packages. This is useful if your server has no internet access and cannot use the MySQL APT resources. There is one package that contains everything, this has the name:

mysql-cluster-LICENSE-NDBVER-DEBIANVER-ARCH.deb

where LICENSE is either community or commercial, NDBVER is e.g. 7.5.6 for MySQL Cluster 7.5.6, DEBIANVER is e.g. debian8 for Debian version 8. ARCH is amd64 for 64-bit binaries and i386 for 32-bit binaries on x86.

To install this package one uses the *dpkg* command.

Here is the command to install MySQL Cluster 7.5.6 data node on a 64-bit x86 machine running Debian8.

```
sudo dpkg -i \
  mysql-cluster-community-data-node_7.5.6-1debian8_amd64.deb
```

12.7 INSTALLING TARBALLS ON LINUX

On all Linux versions you can install using tarballs with the MySQL Cluster binaries.

The name of the tarball to download is:

mysql-cluster-LICENSE-NDBVER-linux-glibc2.5-ARCH.tar.gz

where LICENSE is either gpl or commercial, NDBVER is e.g. 7.5.6 for MySQL Cluster 7.5.6, ARCH is either i686 for 32-bit binaries on x86 and x86_64 for 64-bit binaries on x86.

This tarball includes all libraries and binaries needed to run MySQL Cluster.

Now you need to unpack the tarball and copy the binaries and libraries to appropriate places and ensure that the PATH variables are updated if necessary. Normally one uses */usr/local/bin* to install binaries directly from a tarball, and */usr/local/lib* to install libraries directly from a tarball.

Remember to also ensure that binaries are made executable by using the *chmod* command. E.g. to make *ndbmtd* executable use

chmod +x ndbmtd

12.8 INSTALLING ON SOLARIS

The preferred manner to install on Solaris is by using a package in the Solaris PKG format. These packages are named:

mysql-cluster-gpl-VER-SOLARISVER-ARCH.pkg.gz

where VER is e.g. *7.5.6* for MySQL Cluster 7.5.6, SOLARISVER is e.g. *solaris11* for Solaris 11 and ARCH is either *x86_64* for 64-bit x86 and *sparc-64bit* for 64-bit SPARC machines.

To install these one first needs to unzip the file followed by installing the software using the *pkgadd* command.

```
gunzip mysql-cluster-gpl-7.5.6-solaris11-sparc-64bit.pkg.gz
pkgadd -d mysql-7.5.6-solaris11-sparc-64bit.pkg
```

By default this installs MySQL under the directory */opt/mysql*.

12.9 PREPARING TO RUN MYSQL CLUSTER ON LINUX

After installing the binaries and handling the dependencies to other packages we need a few more steps to prepare for running MySQL Cluster on Linux. Most of the information provided here can be applied directly on Solaris as well with some command names changed.

12.9.1 ADD LIBAIO LIBRARY

The MySQL Server depends on that a library supporting asynch I/O is installed on Linux. In many cases this is handled automatically, but in some cases it is necessary to do this during the installation process. On platforms supporting *apt-get* one would use the following command to install this library.

```
sudo apt-get install libaio1
```

12.9.2 ADD NEW MYSQL USER

The normal user to run MySQL Server and NDB management server and NDB data nodes on is the *mysql* user. It is quite ok to run on any user, but the standard method is to define a user *mysql* with proper rights to run MySQL Cluster.

To define this user one first needs to add new group *mysql*, this is done by the command groupadd or addgroup (command depends on Linux distros).

Next step is to add a user *mysql* to this group.

MySQL Cluster use a feature that some threads are given higher priority than others. On Linux this means that some threads are less nice than others, nice level can be decreased/increased on individual threads in NDB data nodes, in the MySQL Server, and in NDB API applications.

To be able to use this feature (MySQL Cluster will run just fine without it, but will be less performant in high-load situations) one needs the following lines in */etc/security/limits.conf* when using e.g. *Oracle Linux 7*, the same config file can sometimes be found in */etc/limits.conf*.

```
@mysql          soft    nice        -20
@mysql          hard    nice        -20
```

This means that the *mysql* user is allowed to use the *setpriority* call to decrease the nice level to -20. This is used by the receiver thread and send thread in the NDB API parts. It can be used by the data nodes to handle special configurations where certain threads are given a lower nice level than others.

12.9.3 PREPARE DATA DIRECTORIES FOR MYSQL SERVER AND DATA NODES

Before starting up the cluster each MySQL Server and each NDB data node and each NDB management server requires a directory prepared for running MySQL Cluster on.

DATA DIRECTORY FOR NDB MANAGEMENT SERVER

The standard directory used for the NDB management server is the directory */var/lib/mysql-cluster*. This directory will contain the cluster configuration file described later, it will contain the node log of the NDB management server. It will contain the cluster log that contains events generated on all nodes in the cluster that is reported as important to manage the cluster.

The binary version of the configuration database is stored in a place defined by installation directory by default. Therefore it is highly recommended to specify *--configdir* when starting the management server. It is easy to mistakenly look for these files in the data directory of the management server.

Naturally it is possible to use any directory for this. The directory should sustain the logging to the cluster log mainly and have disk quota to sustain this. Any normal disk subsystem should be able to handle this.

DATA DIRECTORY FOR THE MySQL SERVER

The standard directory for installing the MySQL Server is the directory */var/lib/mysql*. This directory will contain the InnoDB files, one directory for each database created in the MySQL Server, an error log file and a number of other files.

Running a MySQL Server mainly towards NDB storage engine means that there is very little use of the data directory for the MySQL Server. There are very few specific requirements on the disk storage used by this directory. Most of the data is logs, meta data about tables, indexes, foreign keys and so forth.

Naturally any directory can be used for the MySQL Server data directory. It is set in the MySQL configuration file or in a startup parameter of the MySQL Server.

DATA DIRECTORY FOR NDB DATA NODES

There is no standard directory for the data directory of NDB data nodes, the default directory is simply the directory from where the NDB data node is started. It is strongly recommended to always set the *DataDir* configuration variable in the cluster configuration.

This directory will contain the node log file, the various trace files described in a later chapter. It will contain the REDO logs, checkpoint files, metadata files and is the default directory to be used by NDB tablespaces.

Except for the NDB tablespaces used by NDB disk data, all files are mainly written to. Most of the writing is done with fairly large writes, the file system used to handle this data directory should be a file system that is good at handling massive writes. Most Linux file systems like *ext4* and *XFS* are ok to use, but *XFS* is preferred.

The data directory is given in the cluster configuration file. The size of this directory can grow significantly. A fair amount of log files, the size of the REDO log files, the size of the checkpoint files. The node log files are slowly growing, it is recommended to use a tool like *logrotate* to handle these logs.

The REDO log files are set in the configuration file and can thus be calculated and these are calculated from the start. The checkpoint files can grow up to about 2.5x times the size of *DataMemory* in the nodes. It is possible to use compression on the checkpoints to decrease the size about 2-3x.

Tablespaces and their data files and UNDO log files all have fixed sizes that are either set in the cluster configuration file or by command when creating those tablespaces and log file groups.

We need to store backups in the data directory of the data nodes. One backup contains the amount of data at time of backup, plus the logs generated while performing the backup which is dependent on the update speed of the cluster.

In summary this directory contains:

1. Node log (slowly growing)

2. REDO log

3. Local Checkpoint files

4. Meta data files

5. Tablespaces and UNDO log files

6. Backups

7. Trace files

Many of those things can be configured to use a different directory than the default ones where all directories reside under the data directory.

As an example we might want the tablespaces for disk data to be on a separate file system, similar for the UNDO logs of the disk columns. We might require the same thing for backup files and for local checkpoint files. The node log, trace files and REDO logs are always placed under the data directory.

The size of the REDO log is the multiplication of *NoOfFragmentLogParts* and *NoOfFragmentLogFiles* and *FragmentLogFileSize*. The default of those are 4, 20 and 256 MByte (thus 20 GByte).

The Local checkpoint files is around 2x the memory used for *DataMemory*, the backups are 1x *DataMemory* plus an amount that depend on update speed. Tablespaces are as big as you define its data files to be and the same holds for UNDO log files.

Trace files is usually around a few tens of megabytes at most, node logs are not generated at very high speeds, but in error situations they can generate log records faster and some sort of archiving of log files is necessary.

This file system needs to be fairly sizeable to fit all the necessary information. If multiple disks are available on the machine it is a good idea to use a RAID setup for this filesystem.

12.10   INSTALLING ON FREEBSD

FreeBSD is not a officially supported platform of MySQL Cluster. It is working pretty well. The only installation option on FreeBSD is to install using a software tarball. See the section on building MySQL Cluster later.

CHAPTER 13

STARTING PROGRAMS

This section will provide some details about how to startup the cluster and how to start individual programs. For a complete and updated list of the command parameters that can be used for each program the MySQL Reference manual should be consulted.

Most of the information in this chapter is likely to be put into whatever DevOps solution you will use for production. E.g. the MySQL Cluster Configurator takes care of all of these things. As an example the HopsFS development built a DevOps solution based on Chef and a tool they developed called Karamel. This uses a number of scripts and Ruby menues used by Chef to perform the installation automatically.

13.1 ORDER OF STARTING

To start a cluster we first start up the NDB configuration database. The configuration database consists of one or two NDB management servers (*ndb_mgmd*). It is sufficient to have one management server in the cluster. If the management server goes down the cluster will continue to operate. If one of the node fails and it tries to restart, it cannot come up again until a management server is up and running again. Therefore we also support using two management servers.

The management server writes the cluster log. This is a log with messages of interesting events happening in the cluster. If no management server is up and running there will be no cluster log messages written for the period when no *ndb_mgmd* is up and running.

When half of the nodes fail in the cluster an arbitrator is used to decide which part of the cluster will survive. This is normally handled by one of the NDB management servers, but it can also be done by any of the API nodes or MySQL Servers if no management server is up and running.

Normally for high availability installation there is at least two management servers defined in the cluster.

It is possible to start up NDB data nodes before the management server and also MySQL Servers. The NDB data nodes will simply wait until the specified management server is up and running before it starts. The NDB data node cannot complete the startup without access to a management server. The management server provides the cluster configuration to the starting nodes, this configuration is required to be able to start up the data node, the API nodes and any MySQL server using the NDB storage engine.

When starting a data node, a MySQL Server or an API node one can specify how long time to wait for a management server by using the parameters *--connect-retries* and *--connect-retry-delay*, *--connect-retry-delay* is given in seconds and defaults to 5. *--connect-retries* defaults to

12 and at least one attempt will be made even if set to 0. To wait forever one have set the number of retries to a very high number.

When all *ndb_mgmd*'s have been started the next step is to start up all the NDB data nodes (*ndbmtd* or *ndbd*). The first time they start up they will perform an initial start. When this initial start is completed the MySQL servers (*mysqld*) and API nodes can connect to the cluster. When all the MySQL servers and all API nodes have started up the cluster is ready for action.

Upgrade of a MySQL Cluster is performed in the same order. First restart the management server(s). Next restart the data nodes and finally restart the MySQL Servers and API nodes. A very safe path is to perform a rolling upgrade of the MySQL Cluster software one node at a time. One can restart one node per node group when restarting the NDB data nodes. The MySQL Servers and API nodes can be restarted as many or as few as the application can handle at a time.

13.1.1 NODE IDS

In MySQL Cluster each node need to have a node id. My personal preference is to control the node id selection myself when starting up the programs. This gives more control over node id allocation. If no node id is provided, the management server and data nodes will select a node id for you. This could possibly be used for MySQL servers and API nodes but certainly makes it harder to manage the cluster since all logs, all tables with log information (*ndbinfo* tables presented later in this book), all SHOW commands for the cluster, uses the node id to represent a node.

The possibility to dynamically choose a node id was mainly implemented to make it easy to get a cluster up and running. But to maintain a cluster, it is certainly easier if the node id is provided when you start up a program in the cluster.

When starting up a management server and a NDB data node you can provide this as a command line option with the parameter *--ndb-nodeid*.

The same is true in writing up the NDB configuration file that it isn't necessary to provide node ids in the configuration. In this case the management server will select the node ids. Again it is much easier to maintain the cluster if the config file already have node ids assigned to each node and where each node is using a node id when starting up.

A MySQL Server can startup using several node ids. In this case there is a MySQL Server parameter *--ndb-cluster-connection-pool-nodeids* that can be used to specify a comma separated list of node ids. To use more than one node id for one MySQL server use the parameter *--ndb-cluster-connection-pool* and set it to the number of node ids to use. The purpose of using more than one node id is that each node id uses one cluster connection and this connection has one socket, one receive thread and one send thread. By using multiple node ids the scalability of the MySQL Server is increased. At the same time one should not use too many. One cluster connection normally scales to around 8-12 x86 CPUs in a MySQL server.

MCM (MySQL Cluster Manager) always assigns each node a specific node id and uses the above features of the various nodes in the cluster.

For API nodes the node id is provided when creating an NDB cluster connection object. More about this when going through the NDB API.

NDB data nodes can only have node ids from 1 to 48. This means that it is a good idea to save those node ids for data nodes since we can add data nodes online in MySQL Cluster. The management servers are normally using node ids 49 and upwards. Thus a natural division of nodes is to use node ids 1 through 48 for data nodes, 49 through 50 for management servers and 51 through 255 is used by MySQL servers and API nodes.

13.2 STARTING *ndb_mgmd*

13.2.1 STARTING THE FIRST TIME

The first time that one starts the first NDB management server in a new cluster the NDB configuration file (*config.ini*) is used to create the NDB configuration database. One should first start the NDB management server where the config.ini file resides. To start this first NDB management server one uses the following command (assuming this management server is node id 49):

```
ndb_mgmd --config-file=/path/config/config.ini \
         --configdir=/path/to/config_database_directory \
         --ndb-nodeid=49
```

If a second management server is started, it will get its configuration from the first management server. Thus in order to start up it needs to know where it can find the first management server. This information is provided using the *--ndb-connectstring* parameter where a textstring is provided as *hostname:port*. If only a hostname is provided the default 1186 port is used. The second management server would be started using the command (assuming it is node id 50):

```
ndb_mgmd --ndb-nodeid=50 \
         --configdir=/path/to/config_database_directory \
         --ndb-connectstring=host_ndb_mgmd1
```

Notice that the initial NDB configuration database isn't created until all NDB management servers have started up.

When all management servers have started up in this way they will all have the same configuration stored in the NDB configuration database.

Notice that *--configdir* specifies the directory to place the NDB configuration database whereas cluster log is stored in the directory specified by the *DataDir* configuration parameter for the management server. It is normally a good idea to use the same directory for both of those things.

It is possible to start the second management server using the same command as for the first. This requires that both the first and the second management server uses exactly the same configuration file. More than two management servers won't work.

The default directory for writing the configuration binary files, is dependent on your build of MySQL Cluster. The builds provided by MySQL uses the directory */var/lib/mysql-cluster*. It is recommended to always set *--configdir* when starting the NDB management server.

The file name of this generated binary file is *ndb_NODE_ID_config.bin.SEQ_NUMBER* where sequence number is the version number of the NDB configuration database.

Each time the configuration changes a new file is created with one higher sequential number.

The *ndb_mgmd* program will ensure that all changes to the NDB configuration database is the same in all NDB management server.

In effect the *ndb_mgmd* maintains a very simple distributed database. It is created the first time one starts by using the *--config-file* option. This parameters points to the NDB configuration file.

If the directory already contains a binary configuration file the configuration file will be ignored. If it is desirable to start a new cluster from scratch one can scrap the old configuration and overwrite it with a new configuration using the *--initial* flag. This flag should not be used to update the configuration in a running cluster.

Starting with *--initial* will fail if another management server is still running with a different configuration file. So to actually change the NDB configuration database to a completely new value can only happen by restarting all management servers and preferrably also after stopping all data nodes and after that restarting the cluster from scratch.

13.2.2   Restarting the *ndb_mgmd*

If a management server fails one restarts it simply by executing the *ndb_mgmd* command again. Since it still has access to the configuration database it can find the other management servers and can thus ensure that any updates to the configuration database are applied before it starts to ship out configurations to starting nodes.

13.2.3   Changing the NDB configuration

In a previous section we showed how to start up with one or several NDB management servers. This installs the first version of the NDB configuration database. If a management server stops or crashes it can simply be restarted and it will come up with the same configuration or if another management server have been updated it will get the updated configuration from this management server.

This shows how to create the first configuration and how to keep the NDB configuration database up and running. It is desirable to be able to update the NDB configuration database as well.

Here is how an update of the configuration is performed. To update the configuration one starts with the *config.ini* file. We should save this configuration file properly. A good idea is to store it together with all management servers. If the file is lost it can be recreated by printing the configuration file. This will write a configuration file with all configuration variables displayed.

To update the configuration we edit the configuration file, this means that we can change configuration parameters for existing nodes. We can add new data nodes, new management servers and new MySQL Server and API nodes.

When we have updated the configuration we kill one of the NDB management servers. The pid of the management server is found in a pid-file in the directory specified by *DataDir*.

Next we restart it with a reference to the new configuration file and in addition we add the parameter *--reload*. The command would be

```
ndb_mgmd --config-file=/path/config/config.ini \
         --configdir=/path/to/config_database_directory \
         --reload \
         --ndb-nodeid=49
```

When this management server starts it will first start using the old NDB configuration database. Next it will compare the new configuration file to the old configuration file and will report in the cluster log what changes have been made. Other management server will be updated with the new configuration. If not all management server are up when this management server starts up it will wait until all management servers are up and running.

There is one special case where the *--initial* flag is needed instead of *--reload*. This is when you have started with one management server and want to add a second one. In this case one should first stop the running management server after changing the *config.ini* to include the new management server. Next one starts the management server with the *--initial* flag. Finally the new second management server is started pointing to the first one. The *--initial* flag should not be set when starting the second management server.

If for some reason one of the management servers is permanently down, it is possible to start up a management server that doesn't wait to synchronize with all other management servers. The permanently failed management server can be declared using the command line parameter *--nowait-nodes*. A list of node ids is provided in this parameter. Without this parameter a management server will not start up until all management servers have started up.

Management server that were dead at the time of change will get the new configuration when starting up (but to start it up it is required that the *--config-file* points to the new configuration file).

If the new configuration contains incompatible changes the configuration change will not be performed and the management server will stop with an error message. The same will happen when the new configuration file contains syntax errors or values out of range.

After this the configuration change is completed. Thus the NDB configuration database have changed. However nodes will not be informed of this change until they are restarted. To make all nodes aware of the new configuration all nodes in the cluster have to be restarted using a rolling upgrade procedure.

It is a good idea to keep the *config.ini* file used to change the config around until the next configuration change is needed. It is a good idea to keep it duplicated to avoid having to work with full configuration files that list all entries, also those that have the default value.

If problems occur when changing the config, try stopping both management servers before performing change. Another workaround that solves many issues is to always use *--config-file* also in second management server.

13.2.4 SPECIAL CONSIDERATIONS WHEN STARTING *ndb_mgmd*

One special case to handle is when the *ndb_mgmd* is started on a machine with several network interfaces. In this case it is important that the management server binds to the correct network interface. This can be specified using the parameter *--bind-address*. Here one specifies the *hostname* that the management server will bind to.

Normally the management server uses port 1186, if this is used no special configuration item is needed and no command line parameter. If a different port is to be used it is sufficient to change the configuration, the management server will pick up the port number from the configuration. If multiple management server are running on the same host they need to specify node id when they start up.

It is possible to use a *my.cnf* file to specify the configuration, to do this use the command line parameter *--mycnf*. No more information on this option is provided in this book. It's mainly used by internal test tools.

On all platforms except Windows the management server is started as a daemon by default. On Windows the management server should be started as a Windows service. However this requires administrative privileges, therefore this isn't default on Windows. To install *ndb_mgmd* as a Windows service one uses the command line parameter *--install*, by default the name is *ndb_mgmd* but one can provide a different name. This parameter should be the first name on the command line to ensure that other parameters are not missed when starting as a Windows service.

13.3 STARTING *ndbmtd*

The multithreaded data node uses the *ndbmtd* binary and the *ndbd* starts a binary that uses just one thread for all blocks (still separate threads for file handling and connection handling). All command parameters are the same for both those programs.

We will use ndbtmd in this presentation of how to start a data node in MySQL Cluster.

There are two things that normally is needed on the command line when starting up ndbmtd. The first is a reference to the NDB management server(s). This can either be provided through the environment variable *NDB_CONNECTSTRING* or by setting the parameter *--ndb-connectstring*. It is sufficient to use one of the management servers, but for higher reliability it is possible to list all hostnames of all management servers. The connect string is only used at start up to find the configuration. Once the configuration has been fetched all management servers will be connected to the data node. The hostname is normally sufficient in the connect string, but if a non-standard port is used (other than 1186) the port can be provided as *hostname:port* in a comma separated list.

Second we should specify the node id as described in a previous section. This ensures that we have control over the node id used by the processes running NDB.

```
ndbmtd --ndb-connect-string=host1,host2 --ndb-nodeid=1
```

Normally no more parameters are needed, the remaining parameters needed by the NDB data nodes is provided through the NDB configuration as delivered by the NDB management server.

13.3.1 DATA NODE FILES

The NDB data node will setup its work environment in the data directory as specified in the NDB configuration parameter *DataDir*. There will be one file there called:

ndb_NODEID.pid

where NODEID is the node id used by this node. This file contains the PID of the *ndbmtd* process. This file is used to ensure that we don't start two processes using the same data directory. There will also be a file called:

ndb_NODEID_out.log

This file is called the node log, this will contain the log message specific to this node. This log will contain a fairly detailed description of the progress of node restarts.

If a node failure occurs there will also be a file called:

ndb_NODEID_error.log

This file will contain a description of the errors that have occurred. If several failures occurs it will keep a configurable number of entries of node failures in the error log. This is by default 25.

In a crash there is a set of trace files created. These will be called:

ndb_NODEID_trace.log.ERRORID_tTHREAD_NUMBER

where ERRORID is the number of the error and THREAD_NUMBER is the number of the thread starting at 1. There is also a file called:

ndb_NODEID_trace.log.ERRORID

In *ndbmtd* this is the main thread, in *ndbd* it is the only trace file generated since there is only one thread.

The actual data is present in a directory called:

ndb_NODEID_fs

More about the files stored in this directory in a later chapter. We will go through the content of those files in a later chapter.

In debug builds of MySQL Cluster there is one more file called:

ndb_NODEID_signal.log

This file is used for special debug messages and will not be described any more in this book. To activate all these debug messages go into the file called SimulatedBlock.cpp and make the method *debugOut* always return true and then recompile the cluster code. It is nice tool when developing new features in MySQL Cluster.

13.3.2 SPECIAL CONSIDERATIONS WHEN STARTING *ndbmtd*

The above start method is ok for the first start and subsequent starts. There are cases when we want to start from a clean sheet with a clean file system. There are some rare upgrade cases that require a so called initial node restart. There might be rare error cases where this is necessary (e.g. some corruptness in the file system).

NDB can handle that one or several nodes in a node group starts from a clean file system. However at least one node in each node group need to retain the data in order for the cluster to be recoverable. One method of achieving this clean sheet is to place yourself in the data directory of the data node and issue the command *rm -rf * * (be careful to ensure that the data node isn't running when performing this command).

This command will wipe away all the files of that data node (except possibly some tablespaces that have been given a file name independent of the placement of the data directory). An alternative method is to use the command line parameter *--initial*. This will remove all data from the NDB data directory of the node, except the disk data files (tablespaces and UNDO log files). Removal of disk data files needs to be done manually before starting up an initial node restart.

It is possible to start up a mixed cluster with different number of nodes in each node group. The configuration must have an equal number of replicas in each node group and all these nodes need to be defined in the configuration. However when starting up the initial start of the cluster one can specify exactly which nodes to wait for in the startup. First use the parameter *--initial-start* and then add the node ids of the nodes you don't want to wait for using the *--nowait-nodes* parameter. This parameter gets a list of node ids that will not be waited for when starting up the cluster.

This option can be used if you have a cluster with uneven number of nodes available to start up. Say for example that you want to have a cluster with 15 data nodes with 3 replicas, thus 5 node groups of 3 nodes in each node group. But one machine had problems when delivered and you still want to get started in setting up your cluster. You define all 15 nodes in the cluster config, but when starting up with only 14 of them available one uses the above method to ensure that the cluster performs an initial start even without all cluster nodes being available for the initial startup. Each node that starts up have to use the same parameter for this to work.

When the data node starts up it will attempt to connect to the management server. If this fails it will make a number of retries with a certain delay between the retries. The number of retries to perform and the delay between each retry can be set using the parameters *--connect-retries* and *--connect-retry-delay*. Default is 12 retries with 5 seconds of delay between each attempt.

When starting up *ndbmtd* on a machine with multiple network interfaces it is a good idea to use the command line parameter *--bind-address* to specify the hostname (hostname or IP address) of the network interface to be used by this data node.

The *ndbmtd* is always started as a daemon on Unix OSs unless specifically told to not start as a daemon using the *--nodaemon* parameter or the *--foreground* parameter.

When running *ndbmtd* as a daemon you get two processes started for each *ndbmtd* (unless *StopOnError* is set to 0). The first process started is called the angel process. This angel process starts up the second *ndbmtd* process, the sole purpose of the angel process is to ensure that the data node can be automatically restarted if the config parameter *StopOnError* is set to 1. Thus the cluster will not need any manual interaction when a node fails. It will perform the node failure handling and after that it will immediately start the node again from the angel process.

On Windows the concept of daemon is replaced by Windows services. However to start a Windows service requires administrative privileges. This means that the default is to start *ndbmtd* not as a Windows service. To start *ndbmtd* as a Windows service one uses the command line parameter *--install* and the value of this parameter is the name given to the Windows service. Similarly the command line parameter *--remove* with name of service as the value of the parameter can be used to stop the Windows service. The *--install* and *--remove* parameters should be the first command parameter.

Notice that by default the *ndbmtd* will use a random port number to listen to. This makes the first configuration very easy to setup. However it makes it hard to setup MySQL Cluster in a secure environment with firewalls and so forth. To avoid this problem it is highly recommended to ensure that the NDB configuration option *ServerPort* is set to the desired port number to be used by the data node processes. As a suggestion use port number 11860 (easy to remember since 1186 is the default port number used by the NDB management server).

13.4 STARTING A MYSQL SERVER (*mysqld*)

Starting a MySQL Server in MySQL Cluster is not very different from starting a MySQL Server using InnoDB or any other storage engine. The only new things are that you need to add the parameter *ndbcluster* to the command line or to the MySQL configuration (usually named *my.cnf*. In addition you need to specify the NDB connect string to the management server such that you get the configuration of the cluster to your node(s). This works the same way as for *ndbmtd* and *ndb_mgmd* in that you specify the parameter *--ndb-connectstring* and set this equal to a list of hostnames where management server(s) resides.

Most parameters in the MySQL Server can either be set as command line parameter or as configuration parameters in a MySQL configuration file. Personally I prefer to use only command line parameter, most of the descriptions here assume using command line parameters, but it will work just as well to use the configuration files. My problem is simply that I run too many MySQL Servers on one box and thus using standard locations for configuration files won't work very well for me.

There are a great variety of parameters that can be configured when running the MySQL Server using NDB as the storage engine. In this section we will focus on just the most important ones and let the advanced ones be covered in a later chapter on configuration handling.

In most installations it is sufficient to have one cluster connection, for MySQL Servers running on larger servers it might be necessary to use more than one cluster connection. A good rule of thumb is to use about one cluster connection per 8-12 x86 CPUs. On a larger server with 20 cores one might need 4 cluster connections. To be able to know exactly which nodes that are tied to this MySQL Server one should specify the node ids to use when starting the MySQL Server. It is not necessary from an operational point of view, but it helps in managing the MySQL Server. For this one sets the parameter *--ndb-cluster-connection-pool*

to the number of cluster connections you will use and set the list of node ids to use for this
MySQL Server in the *--ndb-cluster-connection-pool-nodeids* parameter.

Starting up a large MySQL Server could look something like this:

```
mysqld --ndbcluster \
  --ndb-connectstring=ndb_mgmd_host1 \
  --log-error=/path/to/error_log_file \
  --datadir=/path/to/datadir \
  --socket=/path/to/socket_file \
  --ndb-cluster-connection-pool=4 \
  --ndb-cluster-connection-pool-nodeids=51,52,53,54 &
```

Note the ampersand sign at the end. The MySQL Server will run as a background thread if
you issue this ampersand. This is required to get back the terminal after starting the MySQL
Server. The above command assumes that you already initialised the data directory of the
MySQL server.

To initialise the data directory for a test run you can use the above command with an added
parameter *--initialize-insecure*. This command will perform a bootstrap of the data directory
and exit. After this command you can run the above command to start the MySQL server. To
initialize a secure MySQL server use the *--initialize* command parameter instead. In this case
a random password is generated that you will have to change when connecting to the MySQL
server the first time.

Setting the data directory, setting the error log file, setting the socket file are minimal things
required to get a proper MySQL server started in a test environment. There is a lot more to
starting MySQL servers that I will not go into any details about here. There are many books
and there is a MySQL reference manual that covers this in great depth. In a later chapter I
will go through the configuration settings that will be useful when starting a MySQL server to
be used with MySQL Cluster.

13.5 STARTING *ndb_mgm*

ndb_mgm is a tool that can be used to send commands to the NDB management server.
To run this tool we only need to know how to connect to the management server. This
uses the normal *--ndb-connectstring* parameter. In Unix one can set the environment variable
NDB_CONNECTSTRING to specify the whereabouts of the management server.

The most commonly used command in the management client is SHOW. This command
shows the status of the cluster nodes. As an example MCC when it reports the status of the
nodes in the cluster, it uses this SHOW command at regular intervals.

The management client is the tool that is used to start up a backup and report on the
progress of the backup.

It is possible to gracefully shut down NDB data nodes and NDB management servers. It is
not possible to shut down API nodes and MySQL Servers.

Another common command used here is to check memory usage status.

There is a command call DUMP, first one specifies the node to send the command to, ALL means all nodes. Next one specifies the DUMP code and after that one can send a set of parameters to the DUMP command code. This DUMP command is sent to the proper data node and each DUMP code represents a different command. Most of these commands will print various debug information to the cluster log. These commands are mostly used in situations when trying to figure out why cluster is not working correctly. At times working with the MySQL support team the customer can be asked to execute some of those commands.

More details on these commands in a later chapter.

13.6 STARTING *mcmd*

mcmd is the program that MySQL Cluster Manager (MCM) uses. One instance of this program need to execute on each machine in the cluster. The *mcmd* program must be started before the cluster starts up in order to make full use of the program. It is possible to take control of an existing cluster as well. But the normal operation is to use MCM already from the start.

Chapter 14

MySQL Cluster configuration files

There is only one configuration file that is absolutely needed for MySQL Cluster. This is the cluster configuration file that specifies the nodes that are part of the cluster and a number of configuration parameters for those nodes.

In MySQL it is normal to also use a special configuration file, *my.cnf* instead of using startup parameters. This file isn't absolutely necessary. Personally I tend to avoid using this since I often get problems in that the MySQL Server finds configuration files that I didn't know about and that causes the setup to be different than I intended. Therefore in the benchmark scripts that I will present later in this book I avoid using the MySQL configuration file.

The configuration file handling for MySQL servers also presents an issue when starting up several MySQL servers on the same machine.

Using the MySQL configuration files makes the starting of the MySQL Server, NDB management server, NDB data nodes and NDB management client easier since most of the parameters can be specified in this file. So for most users this is still the preferred method of providing startup parameters to the MySQL server.

We will start by shortly describing the format of the files and after that describing each file in more detail. The actual configuration parameters will be covered in later chapters since there is a lot of them and some of them requires a fair bit of explanation of how they work and why they exist.

14.1 General rules for MySQL configuration files

A configuration file consists of a number of sections. A section starts like this:

[ndbd]

The cluster configuration file have the following sections that can be used.

[ndbd] or *[db]*

[api] or *[mysqld]*

[ndb_mgmd] or *[mgm]*

[tcp]

api and *mysqld* are synonyms as are *ndb_mgmd* and *mgm* and *[ndbd]* and *[db]*.

The *ndbd, ndb_mgmd, mysqld* sections each represent nodes in the cluster, one section per node. One can specify default sections like this:

[ndbd default]

The default sections are normally at the beginning of the file to avoid having to write every changed parameter for each node.

The *tcp* section represents the communication between two nodes. There is no need to use the *[tcp]* sections other when communication between two nodes use different configuration than other communication.

Currently only TCP/IP communication between nodes is possible. Historically there has been a *[sci]* and *[shm]* communication variant. These are no longer used, but *[shm]* might be reintroduced in the future.

Section names and configuration parameters are case insensitive in the cluster configuration file.

After #, the text following this on the rest of the line is treated as a comment.

The *my.cnf* file uses the same parsing rules for the configuration, also here there are sections provided in the same fashion and comments can be provided. One major difference is that section names and configuration parameters are case sensitive in the *my.cnf* file.

14.2 CLUSTER CONFIGURATION FILE

Here is a simple example of a cluster configuration file.

The reasoning behind this minimal configuration file is the following.

The NDB management server must be possible to find for all other nodes. This node must have a static IP address attached to it. The same goes for all other NDB management servers if there is more than one defined in the cluster. This IP address is specified in the *Hostname* configuration parameter.

The NDB data nodes must have a static IP addresses to ensure that they can be found by other data nodes and the NDB management servers and all the other API nodes. It is required to assign a *Hostname* to all data nodes in the configuration file.

It isn't strictly required to set a *Hostname* on the NDB management server but it is strongly recommended.

It is recommended to use IP addresses in the configuration. This avoids any availability issues with DNS servers while running MySQL Cluster.

The MySQL Servers and API nodes can connect from anywhere. The main reason to set *Hostname* parameter here is to limit the accessibility from any other computer.

Given that MySQL Servers have predefined places and need to have a static IP address for MySQL clients to find them, it makes sense to define *Hostname* for MySQL Servers as well.

For API nodes that are used to run various NDB tools it is only necessary to set the *Hostname* if you want to limit cluster access for security reasons.

It is strongly recommended to set *DataDir* for both data nodes and management servers although it isn't strictly required.

Similarly it is strongly recommended to set *NodeId* for both data nodes and management servers since otherwise it will be very hard to manage the cluster. The same applies to MySQL

Servers. There is no specific need to set *NodeId* on API nodes other than to control the number space used by *NodeIds*.

```
config.ini

# Data node defaults
[ndbd default]
DataDir=/path/to/datanode/dir
DataMemory=4G
DiskPageBufferMemory=1G
ServerPort=11860

#NDB management server defaults
[ndb_mgmd default]
DataDir=/path/to/mgm/dir

#The management server node
[ndb_mgmd]
NodeId=49
Hostname=192.168.1.100

#The first data node
[ndbd]
NodeId=1
Hostname=192.168.1.101

#The second data node
[ndbd]
NodeId=2
Hostname=192.168.1.102

#The first MySQL Server
[mysqld]
NodeId=51
Hostname=192.168.1.103

#The second MySQL Server
[mysqld]
NodeId=52
Hostname=192.168.1.104

# 3 API nodes for use by NDB tools
[api]
[api]
[api]
```

There are 2 parameters that define the memory usage that is strongly recommended to setup. These are the *DataMemory* and *DiskPageBufferMemory*. *DataMemory* is the memory used for in-memory tables and hash indexes. This sets the maximum size of the in-memory data of the cluster installation. It is not possible to insert into more than 95% of this memory space to ensure that we can always recover properly.

DiskPageBufferMemory is the memory used for caching disk pages.

If you are using disk data it is quite likely that you want to setup the configuration parameters *InitialTablespace* and *InitialLogfileGroup*.

With those parameters we have a pretty good basic configuration setup that is tuned to your computer. There is still some more advanced configuration details that you want to add before going into production, these details are covered in later chapters after going through more about the internals of MySQL Cluster.

14.3 MYSQL CONFIGURATION FILE

```
my.cnf

[mysqld]
ndbcluster
ndb-connectstring=192.168.1.100

[ndbd]
connect-string=192.168.1.100
nodeid=1

[ndb_mgmd]
connect-string=192.168.1.100
config-file=/path/to/config/file
nodeid=49

[ndb_mgm]
connect-string=192.168.100
```

The MySQL configuration file (*my.cnf*) contains parameters to the various programs executed in MySQL Cluster. The *[mysqld]* section contains parameters to be used by *mysqld* when starting. The *ndbcluster* and *ndb-connectstring* are mandatory here so they are good candidates to place into *my.cnf*.

The *[ndbd]* is used by *ndbd* and *ndbmtd*. The *connect-string* parameter is good to place here. If only one data node is used per host it makes sense to place the data node id here as well.

The same reasoning applies to the *[ndb_mgmd]* section, here the placement of the configuration files *config-file* seems like a useful parameter to place in *my.cnf*.

There is a section for the *ndb_mgm* program and here it makes sense to specify the *connect-string*.

One of the complexities of the *my.cnf* is that it can execute several *my.cnf* files before using the command run-time parameters.

This is the order that the search for *my.cnf* is done.

1. /etc/my.cnf

2. /etc/mysql/my.cnf

3. $MYSQL_HOME/my.cnf

4. defaults-extra-file

5. ./my.cnf

6. ./mylogin.cnf (only MySQL clients)

The *defaults-extra-file* is specified as a command parameter. This means that potentially up to 6 different configurations files are processed and only after that the run-time parameters are processed. As is clear it is easy to forget about one of those instances of the MySQL configuration file. The complexity here comes from that a distribution might have preinstalled some of those configuration files with values that you don't want to have there.

As long as you are careful about how to handle those configuration files they can be of great help. Personally I have often felt it easier to only use command parameters since all the starting and stopping of programs is executed by scripts anyways. This means that your environment have to use its own configuration file. This is how the DBT2 benchmark scripts works as I will show later in this book.

The *defaults-file* command option can be used to specify the one and only *my.cnf* file to read. To start without any configuration file at all one uses the option *--no-defaults-file*.

CHAPTER 15

MySQL Cluster and Docker

There is numerous reasons why one may want to use Docker to run MySQL Cluster. Our MEM team used Docker since it was such an easy way to setup and tear down clusters for testing purposes. Another reason to use Docker is that removes the need to worry about any other MySQL installations.

The Docker image is completely independent of the other binary installations on the machine since it carries a minimal Linux implementation. In this sandbox you can create a minimal and sufficient environment to run your applications.

Yet another use case is to use Docker to create a VPN network where the cluster access is completely controlled within Docker.

The official MySQL Cluster docker containers are found at:

```
https://hub.docker.com/r/mysql/mysql-cluster/
```

In order to use this you should first use the *docker pull* command to fetch the proper version of MySQL Cluster docker scripts. The below fetches the latest version of MySQL Cluster.

```
docker pull mysql/mysql-cluster
```

To fetch a specific version e.g. MySQL Cluster 7.5 use instead the command:

```
docker pull mysql/mysql-cluster:7.5
```

These docker instances uses a slim installation of Oracle 7. It uses special minimal RPM packages designed for Docker usage. These packages are available at

```
http://repo.mysql.com/yum/mysql-cluster-7.5-community/docker/x86_64
```

In this directory there is an RPM package that contains a full MySQL Cluster installation with all relevant binaries and libraries. The MySQL Cluster docker scripts will use these RPM packages transparently.

The docker container expects a volume to be provided that will be using */var/lib/mysql* internally in the Docker container. There is a simple *my.cnf* provided at */etc/my.cnf* and a simple cluster configuration file at */etc/mysql-cluster.cnf*.

The docker container has an entrypoint script that can start an NDB management server, an NDB data node, a MySQL Server, an NDB management client and any other program in the MySQL Cluster installation.

In order to use your own *my.cnf* you should insert the following part in your Docker startup command:

```
-v /path/to/your/own/my.cnf:/etc/my.cnf
```

and similarly to replace the cluster configuration file add the following:

```
-v /path/to/your/own/mysql-cluster.cnf:/etc/mysql-cluster.cnf
```

It is recommended that you replace both of these, but it is only necessary to replace the cluster configuration file when starting up the NDB management servers.

To use your own data directory you should map your own data directory to the internally used */var/lib/mysql*. This is done again using the *-v* switch as shown here:

```
-v /path/to/your/own/datadir:/var/lib/mysql
```

The configuration database is placed in the directory */usr/mysql-cluster*. It is necessary to place also those in a volume that is handled outside of the docker container. A good idea is to use the data directory for this as well, so add the following to the startup command as well.

```
-v /path/to/your/own/datadir:/usr/mysql-cluster
```

An alternative to this is to add *--configdir=/var/lib/mysql* at the end of the startup command of the docker container for the management server.

For users on systems with SELinux enabled it might be necessary to allow the Docker container to mount the external files and volumes. This can be done using the command:

```
chcon -Rt svirt_sandbox_file_t /path/to/file
and
chcon -Rt svirt_sandbox_file_t /path/to/dir
```

15.1 USING DOCKER TO AVOID INSTALLATION PROBLEMS

In the case where you simply want to use the Docker container as a solution to the problem of installing MySQL Cluster. In this case no installation of MySQL Cluster is necessary, it all happens inside Docker. In this case you want to use your own set of configuration files, your own data directory and your own networking.

You start a NDB management server by using the following command:

```
docker run -d \
   --net=host \
   -v /path/my.cnf:/etc/my.cnf \
   -v /path/config.ini:/etc/mysql-cluster.cnf \
   -v /path/datadir:/var/lib/mysql \
   -v /path/to/your/own/datadir:/usr/mysql-cluster \
   --name=mgmt1 \
   mysql/mysql-cluster ndb_mgmd --ndb-nodeid=49
```

If you want additional parameters to the startup call you can add those at the end. E.g. if you want to add *–initial* or *–reload* to the startup of the management server or as in example above *–ndb-nodeid=49*.

There is a similar command for starting up NDB data nodes where *ndb_mgmd* is replaced by *ndbd* or *ndbmtd* and the mapping of the cluster configuration file is removed and changing the name of the container. When starting the data node containers it is necessary to specify the node id as well.

When starting with *ndbmtd* it is necessary to specify *--nodaemon*. For *ndbd* this is handled automatically. Running as daemon in a docker container is currently not handled.

```
docker run -d \
   --net=host \
   -v /path/my.cnf:/etc/my.cnf \
   -v /path/datadir:/var/lib/mysql \
   --name=ndbd1 \
   mysql/mysql-cluster ndbmtd --ndb-nodeid=1 --nodaemon
```

One special thing here is that the node log, both from the management server and the data nodes is piped to *stdout* in the docker container. To read the node logs you can use the following command (this one reads the node log the first data node).

```
docker logs ndbd1
```

To run a MySQL Server replace *ndbmtd* by *mysqld* and change the name of the container. We set the node id of the MySQL server using *--ndb-cluster-connection-pool-nodeids*.

```
docker run -d \
   --net=host \
   -v /path/my.cnf:/etc/my.cnf \
   -v /path/datadir:/var/lib/mysql \
   --name=mysqld1 \
   mysql/mysql-cluster mysqld --ndb-cluster-connection-pool-nodeids=51
```

15.2   USING DOCKER ON A SINGLE HOST

In the single host case you can use the default Docker bridge network or define a separate Docker network for your tests. The command to create such a new Docker network is very simple:

```
docker network create mynet --subnet=192.168.0.0/16
```

After this you can use the IP addresses in the range 192.168.0.0 to 192.168.255.255 for your Docker network.

```
docker run -d --net=mynet \
  -v /path/my.cnf:/etc/my.cnf \
  -v /path/datadir:/var/lib/mysql \
  --name=datanode1 \
  --ip=192.168.0.1 \
  mysql/mysql-cluster ndbd
```

Above is the command to start an NDB data node and connect it to the Docker mynet network.

Using this network it is easy to run one command per node you want to start in the cluster. Obviously it is as easy to tear down this network and there will be no sign of any MySQL Cluster installation afterwards. This is good for testing MySQL Cluster in a sandboxed environment.

15.3   USING DOCKER OVERLAY NETWORK

In order to run Docker containers using a Docker overlay network requires the use of key-value store. Docker supports a number of different key-value stores such as *Consul, etcd* and *ZooKeeper*.

One thing to remember when using a key-value store to handle the Docker network is that you have created a dependency on this key-value store to be up and running for your cluster to operate. If you are aiming for the highest availability this might not be desirable.

To start a MySQL Server in an overlay network called my_overlay_net is done using the command:

```
docker run -d --net=my_overlay_net \
  -v /path/my.cnf:/etc/my.cnf \
  -v /path/datadir:/var/lib/mysql \
  --name=mysqld1 \
  --ip=192.168.0.51 \
  mysql/mysql-cluster mysqld  --ndb-cluster-connection-pool-nodeids=51
```

Setting up a Docker network is documented in the Docker documentation. Once the network have been setup and the key-value store have been started, it is possible to start Docker containers using this network in exactly the same fashion as you did for a local docker bridge network.

15.4 USING DOCKER SWARM

Docker Swarm is another method to build Docker networks. Currently this doesn't support MySQL Cluster since it cannot use static IP addresses on containers. There is some discussion on the NDB forum on how to overcome this problem.

15.5 SETTING THE PASSWORD ON MySQL SERVER CONTAINER

The MySQL Server is started in secure mode. You need to discover the password and change it. To do this (assuming that the MySQL Server container is called mysqld1) uses the command:

```
docker logs mysqld1 2>&1 | grep password
```

Next you use this password to connect a MySQL client to the MySQL Server using the command:

```
docker exec -it mysqld1 mysql -uroot -p
```

After the command has executed you will be asked for the password and after that you are connected to the MySQL Server. Now it is time to change the password. Use this MySQL command to do this:

```
mysql> ALTER USER 'root@localhost' IDENTIFIED BY 'NewPassword';
```

15.6 RUNNING THE NDB MANAGEMENT CLIENT

To run a client requires using an interactive Docker terminal. This is done using the *docker exec -it* command where *-i* makes it interactive and the *-t* allocates a pseudo-TTY for the Docker container.

To start a NDB management client one issues the command assuming we use the *mynet* network.

```
docker exec -it --net=mynet mysql/mysql-cluster ndb_mgm
```

After this you can verify that the cluster is up and running by running the *show* command.

15.7 USING DOCKER TO LIMIT MEMORY RESOURCES

If we want to run several cluster programs on the same machine or VM it is useful to set limits on the memory usage of each program. The NDB data node consumes quite large memory resources whereas other programs usually use a lot less.

As an example we might want to colocate an NDB data node and a MySQL Server on the same machine. The MySQL Server have no limit on how much memory it could use. By limiting the memory usage of the MySQL Server we can protect the NDB data node from a run away MySQL Server while still running in the same computer or VM.

Docker has this capability, when starting a Docker container it is possible to limit its memory usage.

If we want to run a NDB data node combined with a MySQL Server and we have a machine with 32 GByte of memory, we can start them up in the following manner:

```
docker run -d --net=host \
  -v /path/my.cnf:/etc/my.cnf \
  -v /path/datadir:/var/lib/mysql \
  --name=mysql1 \
  --ip=192.168.0.51 \
  --memory=4G \
  --memory-swap=4G \
  --memory-reserve=4G \
  mysql/mysql-cluster mysqld
```

```
docker run -d --net=host \
  -v /path/my.cnf:/etc/my.cnf \
  -v /path/datadir:/var/lib/mysql \
  --name=datanode1 \
  --ip=192.168.0.1\
  --memory=24G \
  --memory-swap=24G \
  --memory-reserve=24G \
  mysql/mysql-cluster ndbmtd --ndb-nodeid=1 --nodaemon
```

These two programs are now limited to using at most 28 GByte of memory and they cannot steal memory from each other (leaving 4G of memory for OS and other programs). This can be a good way of testing how MySQL Cluster behaves in an environment with a certain memorys size.

15.8   Using Docker to limit CPU resources

In MySQL Cluster we have the ability to control on a detailed level which CPUs that a certain thread is using. This is especially true for the NDB data node. If we want to ensure that two programs run on different CPUs we can again use Docker to do exactly that.

We expand on the previous examples and assuming that we run on a machine with 8 CPU cores with 16 CPUs we could start the machines as below.

```
docker run -d --net=host \
  -v /path/my.cnf:/etc/my.cnf \
  -v /path/datadir:/var/lib/mysql \
  --name=mysql1 \
  --ip=192.168.0.51 \
  --memory=4G \
  --memory-swap=4G \
  --memory-reserve=4G \
  --cpuset-cpus=0-3,8-11 \
  mysql/mysql-cluster mysqld
```

```
docker run -d --net=host \
  -v /path/my.cnf:/etc/my.cnf \
  -v /path/datadir:/var/lib/mysql \
  --name=datanode1 \
  --ip=192.168.0.2\
  --memory=24G \
  --memory-swap=24G \
  --memory-reserve=24G \
  --cpuset-cpus=4-6,12-14 \
  mysql/mysql-cluster ndbmtd
```

Here we have dedicated 24 GByte of memory and 3 CPU cores to the NDB data node. We have dedicated 4 GByte of memory and 4 CPU cores to the MySQL Server. This means we left 4 GBytes of memory and 1 CPU core dedicated to the OS and other programs.

In this manner we can use Docker to get a controlled run-time environment. Thus Docker can be used both to get a controlled environment for installation as well as for as execution. In both of those examples we are running the NDB programs directly on top of the host file system and on the host networking. We're using Docker to not having to worry about installation of MySQL Cluster programs and we also use Docker to ensure that the MySQL Server and the NDB data node can run concurrently without interfering with each other on the same host other than using the same disks and network.

15.9 USING DOCKER AND CGROUPS TO CONTROL CPU AND MEMORY

Instead of using Docker parameters it is possible to connect a Docker container to a cgroup. This means that all the resource constraint that are possible using cgroups are available for configuration.

Probably the most important thing here is that it makes it possible to allocate CPU resources exclusively to a Docker container, cgroups is the only method of exclusively locking CPU resources in Linux.

The Docker parameter for this is *--cgroup-parent=cgroup_name*.

CHAPTER 16

BUILDING MySQL CLUSTER

Developing MySQL Cluster is something that could interest some people. Obviously I am one of those :)

There are a few things that need to be installed in your development machine in order to be able to build MySQL Cluster, this includes the need for header files for readline and ncurses libraries.

1. CMake

2. make

3. C++ compiler

4. Bison

5. ncurses (in ncurses library or separate) library

6. Boost library

7. readline library

8. Java JDK

9. NodeJS JDK

MySQL Cluster is built using CMake, you need a sufficiently fresh version of CMake installed. Normally the one you get from your operating system package manager should be sufficient.

The actual compilation is driven by make, gmake of a normal stable version should suffice here.

You need a C++ compiler, which one differs a bit dependent of the OS you are using. On Mac OS X, you need to install the XCode packages which will install an LLVM compiler that is compatible with gcc. On Linux, you will install a stable gcc version (including g++), using the very latest compiler versions might be problematic since MySQL Cluster is mainly tested with stable compiler versions. On Windows, Visual Studio 2013 or higher is used.

The build of MySQL Cluster requires a bison program to convert the SQL yacc file to C code.

The MySQL client program uses the readline library which in turn is built on top of the ncurses library and normally included in this library.

Some new NDB tools in MySQL Cluster 7.6 use the ncursesw library to implement some ASCII graphs for top-like NDB tools, this library is sometimes included in the ncurses library and sometimes it is a separate library.

MySQL Cluster 7.5 is based on MySQL 5.7 which is using BOOST 1.59.0. This is used to implement the Geo support in the MySQL Server.

To compile MySQL Cluster you need to download a source tarball from the MySQL Cluster download section. Alternatively you can clone a branch of the GitHub tree for the MySQL Server. The branch for 7.5 is called mysql-5.7-cluster-7.5.

16.1 LINUX

We have a prepared Perl script to execute the build of MySQL Cluster. This script is the script *compile-cluster* placed in the *storage/ndb* directory. To compile, place yourself in the top directory of the MySQL Cluster source. Then issue the following command:

```
cd mysql-5.7-cluster-7.5
storage/ndb/compile-cluster
```

This script will start by running CMake. If any of the programs or libraries are not installed it will stop with a report on what is missing. The boost library needs a path, you can use the parameter –with-boost=BOOST_PATH. I normally setup the BOOST_ROOT environment variable to point to the BOOST library using the command:

```
export BOOST_ROOT=/path/to/boost
```

I normally place this command in the shell startup script (e.g. *.bashrc*).

Personally when I develop I will normally not need the ClusterJ installation, this can be removed from the compilation by setting the environment variable WITH_NDB_JAVA_DEFAULT. Similarly one can remove the need to compile the NodeJS API through the environment variable WITH_NDB_NODEJS_DEFAULT.

The following commands will remove the need for compiling Java and NodeJS.

```
export WITH_NDB_JAVA_DEFAULT="0"
export WITH_NDB_NODEJS_DEFAULT="0"
```

If you want to run an autotest environment it is necessary to compile with error insertion activated (obviously not active in production compiles). This is done through the parameter *--autotest*.

To compile a debug compilation add the parameter *--debug*.

After compiling using this command it is sufficient to use make from the proper directory after making code changes. If you need to install into a specific directory one can use the *--prefix* parameter to set the installation path.

16.2 Solaris

Compiling on Solaris works the same way as on Linux except that one uses gmake, gtar and so forth instead of make and tar. It is important to use the GNU tools and not the Solaris built int tools.

16.3 FreeBSD

Building MySQL Cluster on FreeBSD works as on Linux. NDB isn't supported on FreeBSD, so building your own binaries is the only method of using NDB on FreeBSD and other BSD variants.

16.4 Mac OS X

This is the development platform I use, it is a fair amount of work to setup the environment for development since one needs to install XCode and a number of other tools. Describing this is outside the scope of this book, it is straightforward to install the above tools, but it is a fair amount of work and takes some time.

Once installed all the necessary tools the procedure to compile is exactly the same as on Linux.

16.5 Windows

If you are brave enough to try to get MySQL or MySQL Cluster to compile on Windows you should probably teach me how to do it. I have worked with a Windows developer and we have a tool that runs Sysbench on Windows from a source tarball. This takes care of the building of MySQL Cluster on Windows and the execution of the Sysbench program. The script that does this is a PowerShell script which is available in the *dbt2-0.37.50.15* benchmark tarball that will be described later in this book.

CHAPTER 17

HW SETUPS FOR MYSQL CLUSTER

In this chapter we will discuss the mapping of the MySQL Cluster programs to computers. This mapping is a bit dependent on what the cluster is used for. In some cases the best configuration is to use one computer per program instance, there are other cases where it is optimal to colocate the instances.

We will go through the most common variants, their advantages and disadvantages. In all cases when it says Computer it can be replaced with VM/cloud instance.

17.1 SINGLE HOST SETUP

This configuration is mainly intended for development purposes. It is easy to setup (see chapter on Getting Started how to use the MySQL Cluster Configurator to achieve this in a few minutes). It will not deliver the desired availability for a production cluster.

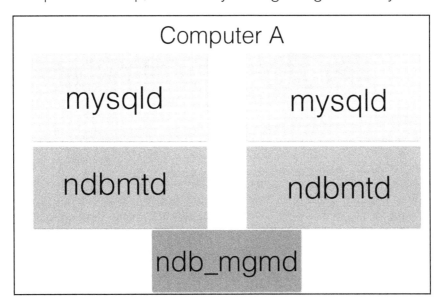

Simple test setup/In-memory storage engine for MySQL

The setup is very simple, one simply runs all nodes, the management server(s), the data node(s) and the MySQL Server(s) on one box, for development purposes one might use different

VM instances or Docker instances for this.

17.2   NDB as an In-memory storage engine for MySQL

This setup is a fairly unusual setup, it is a production setup for a MySQL Server using the
NDB storage engine. The advantages that NDB provides in this example is that it can handle
large sizes of main memory providing low latency access to all of this memory.

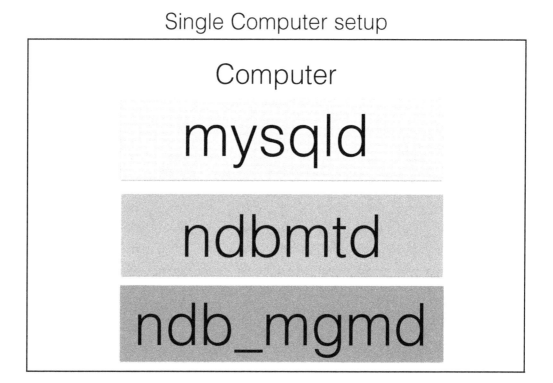

One advantage that makes this configuration worthwhile to consider is the ability of MySQL
Cluster to support parallel queries for many types of queries. It is a model that can handle
hundreds of thousands of transactions per second of simple transactions while still processing a
set of complex queries in the background.

In this we only need a very simple configuration with 1 data node, 1 management server and
a number of cluster connections for the MySQL Server, all located on a single host most likely
containing lots of memory.

17.3   Minimum configuration for AlwaysOn

What is the minimum setup for an SQL application to use MySQL Cluster in a high availability
setup?

The minimum configuration for high availability requires three computers. The reason is that we need a third computer to vote in case one of the computers dies suddenly, this avoids the problem with a partitioned network.

Given that it is a setup for an SQL application we want to make sure that the MySQL Servers are colocated with the NDB data nodes. Given that a minimum requirement for high availability is to use two replicas of the data we use two computers that have both a MySQL Server and a data node colocated. One of these computers also handle one management server. Finally we need a third computer where we only run a management server. This node should have the ArbitrationRank set highest to ensure that the cluster chooses this node to be the arbitrator at all times. When we change the configuration we should use another management server to reload the new configuration in this case.

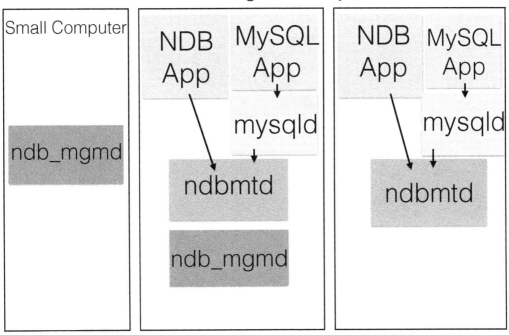

The MySQL Server should set the *--ndb-read-backup* flag to 1 to ensure that all tables use the read backup feature that ensures that we can read the local replica in almost all cases.

In this setup we achieve that NDB becomes a local storage engine to the MySQL Server, but at the same time this configuration provides synchronous replication such that both MySQL Servers instantly see all changes made by the other MySQL Servers.

Thus any of these three computers can fail and the cluster will continue operating, it will even survive some cases where two out of the three computers fails.

It is ok to use only one management server in the third computer as well. The only drawback of this is that nodes cannot start while this managment server is down.

17.4 SETTING UP MYSQL CLUSTER FOR SECURE OPERATION

Security in MySQL Cluster is often achieved by ensuring that computers executing NDB data nodes and computers accessing those computers are located in a phyiscally separate network. Another approach is to use virtual private networks (VPNs).

We can control in the NDB configuration from where the computers can access the data nodes of MySQL Cluster. It is possible to allow any computer to access MySQL Cluster nodes.

One manner to build a MySQL Cluster is to place the NDB data nodes and NDB management servers in one VPN that can be accessed from NDB API nodes (MySQL Servers typically).

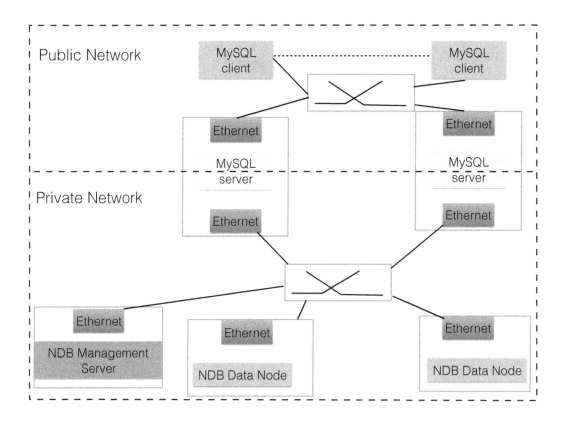

As the figure shows the MySQL Servers are connected both to the public network and to the private network used by MySQL Cluster. To access a MySQL Server one typically uses port 3306 and ensures that the MySQL Server binds to the hostname of the public network interface. This can be done using the MySQL configuration variable *--bind-address*.

When the MySQL Server access the NDB data nodes it uses the hostname of the private network interface instead. This is setup in the NDB configuration. When connecting to the

NDB management server from the MySQL Server it is necessary to ensure that one uses the private network interface. This is accomplished setting the MySQL configuration variable *--ndb-connectstring* to use specifically the private network interface when it connects to the NDB management server.

To do this one writes the NDB connect string as

--ndb-connectstring="bind-address=private_ip_addr_mysql_server,

private_ip_addr_mgm_server:1186"

By setting up the network like this the NDB nodes are protected from all outside access except accesses going through the MySQL Server. The security in this case relies on setting up the MySQL Server in a secure way using proper passwords, users and so forth. There is a number of commercial plugins available to increase security of MySQL Servers. These are also available when using MySQL Cluster.

In this configuration it is important that any API nodes are only able to connect from IP addresses in the private network.

17.5 SCALING OUT FROM THE SIMPLE HA SETUP

The minimum AlwaysOn configuration can quite easily be scaled out to a larger number of computers. It can scale to at least 48 computers that is the current limit of the number of data nodes.

It is not possible to have more than two management servers. These two management servers can either be all on separate computers or colocated with the data nodes and MySQL Servers.

As the previous figure showed we start with a set of computers that each contains a MySQL Server and a data node. These computers are grouped into groups with as many computers as we have replicas (NDB supports 1 to 4 replicas). Each group will have all data nodes of one node group in NDB.

Assume that we use 2 replicas and that we started with 6 computers. In this case we grow the cluster in steps of 2 new computers. We go from 6 computers, to 8 computers, to 10 computers and so forth. When adding computers we follow the procedure defined in the chapter on online configuration changes.

We will now continue to show various variants of how to scale up MySQL Cluster for various needs.

17.5.1 STANDARD HA SETUP FOR SQL APPLICATIONS

First of all a standard HA setup for SQL applications for write scaling will separate the MySQL Server from the NDB data nodes. Thus the minimum AlwaysOn configuration for this setup uses 4 computers.

17.5.2 SETUP FOR WRITE SCALABILITY OF SQL APPLICATIONS

One simple manner to get a write scalable cluster for SQL applications is to avoid using the *--ndb-fully-replicated* configuration flag and possibly even the *--ndb-read-backup* flag and still use colocated data nodes and MySQL Servers. It might still be some tables that should be fully replicated, but for the most part in this case the tables should use the default partitioning and replication setup for NDB tables.

In this we scale the standard HA setup for SQL applications by adding either more MySQL Servers or more NDB data nodes or both. The NDB data nodes have to be added in steps of the number of replicas used in the cluster.

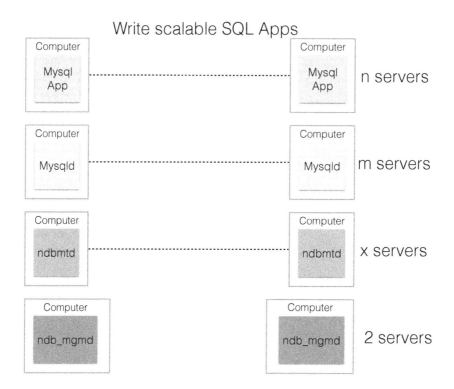

In this case some of the arguments to colocate MySQL Servers and NDB data nodes are no longer valid since local access will be a lot more uncommon. Each transaction could write data in any node group and thus local access will be fairly uncommon.

Even with mostly local accesses it is often the case that the load is unbalanced such that we need more MySQL servers compared to the number of data nodes. So it might still be useful to avoid colocation of the data nodes and the MySQL servers.

In this case it could make sense to setup a cluster with a set of computers running NDB data nodes, another set of computers running MySQL Servers and finally a smaller set of computers running NDB management servers.

This has advantages in that the computers can be optimised for their specific use case. It means that the memory usage of MySQL Servers cannot affect the data nodes. In many cases the number of MySQL Servers will be greater than the number of data nodes or at least the number of CPU cores required in the MySQL Server layer is usually higher.

In this case we have four layers of computers, the first layer is the application layer, the second layer is the set of MySQL Servers receiving the SQL queries and the third layer the NDB data nodes containing the data of the cluster. The management servers are a separate small cluster to handle the configuration database of the cluster.

As we can see in the figure this setup has a lot more nodes and can scale to a larger number of computers.

17.5.3 SETUP FOR WRITE SCALABILITY OF NDB API APPLICATIONS

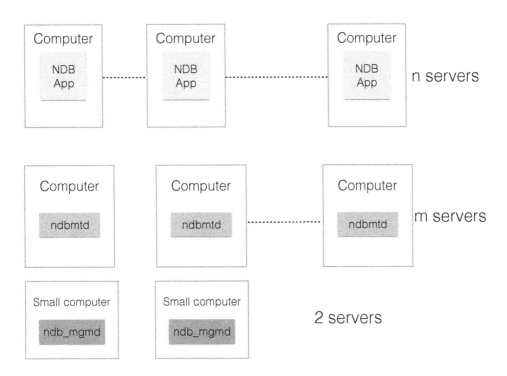

When setting up MySQL Cluster for a write scalable NDB API application it is not so important to colocate nodes. The locality of accesses from one NDB API application node is not high at all. One example of this application type is the implementation of Hadoop HDFS in HopsFS. Each transaction in this case is mostly local to one node group, the different transactions started are using many different node groups.

Each node in the cluster is a separate computer. Each NDB API application node thus requires a fair bit of computational effort to handle the actual application. Usually it doesn't require so much memory though since it mostly gets the data from the NDB data nodes.

In the HopsFS case this is a Name Node handling client requests for file system metadata in HDFS. This layer can scale to a large number of nodes, up to hundreds of computers. These computers need a large computational capacity but doesn't require so much memory. It requires an absolute minimum of a file system.

The NDB data nodes is located in a separate set of computers that require a fair amount of computational capacity and in addition they require a large memory and a very capable file system. The number of such computers are counted in tens of computers. As an example in HopsFS 8 data nodes can scale to handle the load from almost 50 Name Nodes. Each node group of data nodes can handle a set of 12 Name Nodes.

17.5.4 SET UP OF MySQL CLUSTER FOR READ SCALABILITY

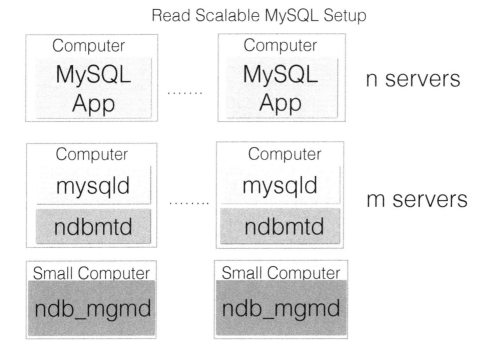

Setting up MySQL Cluster for read scaling means that we want to ensure that each MySQL Server can talk directly to a data node residing on the same computer. This means that most of the communication can happen inside a computer.

Communication with other computers is still needed for all recovery operations, for all updates, but the system is much less reliant on the network to always deliver high performance compared to a write intensive application.

The same configuration applied in a virtual machine environment or cloud simply replaces the computers by virtual machines.

Given that this configuration is designed for read scalability it is quite likely that one wants to use fully replicated tables. In this case one should set the configuration parameter *--ndb-fully-replicated* on all MySQL Servers to ensure that all tables are created as fully replicated tables.

17.6 SET UP OF MySQL CLUSTER FOR MULTI-CLUSTER APPS

This configuration is a bit less common, but is perfectly suitable in some cases. In this case the NDB management servers together with the NDB data nodes forms independent clusters. However the NDB API nodes can connect to several clusters. Developing a large application using the native NDB APIs (C++ NDB API or ClusterJ using Java) can sometimes benefit from this approach where different clusters can be used to scale, one can use a functional separation of the clusters, where a cluster contains data coupled to a specific functionality in the application.

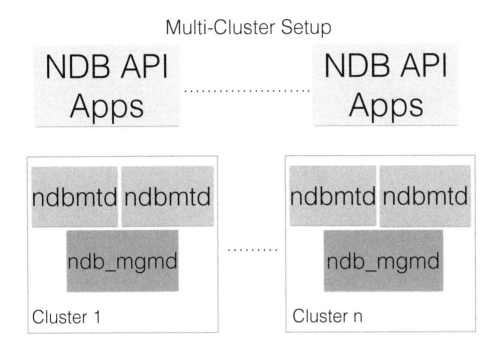

Horizontal separation simply means using shards that is a cluster rather than a single server and the other approach is to use functional separation. Both of those approaches are used by users of MySQL Cluster and even the combination of the two.

Part V

MySQL Cluster as a SQL engine

In order to understand the features of MySQL Cluster and its storage engine NDB we will look at the SQL commands available to define tables and their support structures such as tablespaces, UNDO log files and the parts of a table like columns, indexes, primary keys and so forth.

This is important to understand since even applications using the NDB API will query tables that have been mostly defined in SQL.

We will cover basic SQL statements, row format, foreign keys, disk data columns, BLOB handling. We will deal in some detail about the various table options that are available when creating a table in NDB.

We will cover how various MySQL concepts such as stored procedures, views and so forth are handled in NDB and we will cover ALTER TABLE statements.

Chapter 18

Basic SQL statements

18.1 Create a table

18.1.1 Simplest form of table

Creating a table happens in a normal CREATE TABLE statement in MySQL. What makes the table become a table in NDB is that we add that ENGINE=NDB (NDBCLUSTER is a synonym of this and both are case insensitive). Here is a very simple table created in SQL.

```
mysql> CREATE TABLE t1 (a INT) ENGINE=NDB;
```

This table is about as simple as a table can be in MySQL Cluster. It contains one column which is a 32-bit integer attribute. Here is the first distinction of tables in NDB, all tables in NDB must have a primary key. So when this table is created it is created with two attributes, the first is the column *a* and the second column is the hidden primary key which is an 8-byte unique key.

18.1.2 Simple table with primary key

Moving on to a bit more sophistication we create a table with a primary key.

```
mysql> CREATE TABLE t1 (a INT PRIMARY KEY) ENGINE=NDB;
```

This table contains only one column *a* and this has a distributed hash index which is the primary access method that all tables use. Here is now the second distinction of tables in NDB, a table that defines a primary key index defines two indexes on the table, the first is the distributed hash index and the second is an ordered index (a T-tree index data structure) which is local to each fragment replica.

By definition a primary key cannot have any columns that can have NULL values.

18.1.3 Simple table with only primary key hash index

Moving to the next level of sophistication we define a table with only a primary key index, one column *a* and nothing more.

```
mysql> CREATE TABLE t1 (a INT PRIMARY KEY USING HASH)
mysql> ENGINE=NDB;
```

By adding USING HASH to the index definition we clearly specify that the index will only be a hash index. The reason that normal primary key indexes are also containing an ordered index is that almost everyone using a database expects an index to be an ordered index always. Since the base primary key index in NDB is a distributed hash index it means that we add another index to ensure that newcomers to NDB get what they expect from an index.

18.1.4 SIMPLE TABLE WITH PRIMARY KEY HASH INDEX AND AN INDEX

Now we move on to a table with also an additional index and an additional column.

```
mysql> CREATE TABLE t1 (a INT PRIMARY KEY USING HASH, b INT KEY)
mysql> ENGINE=NDB;
```

This adds a new column *b* and an ordered index on this column. This is a pure ordered index and there is no hash index involved in normal indexes.

18.1.5 SIMPLE TABLE WITH PRIMARY KEY HASH INDEX AND A UNIQUE INDEX

Now we move to a unqiue index and a primary key index.

```
mysql> CREATE TABLE t1
mysql>    (a INT PRIMARY KEY USING HASH, b INT UNIQUE KEY)
mysql>    ENGINE=NDB;
```

Unique indexes is the third sophistication of NDB tables. Unique indexes are implemented as a special unique index table that have the unique index as primary key and the primary key is the field in this table. In addition the unique key definition adds an extra ordered index on the table in the same fashion as the primary key. The reason is that the unique key index is the normal distributed hash index used for all tables. Thus it isn't an ordered index and we add this to make life easier for newbies to MySQL Cluster.

The above definition adds the following: a table t1 with a column *a* and a column *b*, also the distributed hash index on the column *a* and an ordered index on the column *b*.

In addition another table t1_unique (it is not its real name, we simply use it here as a possible name) that have the column *b* as primary key using a distributed hash index and another column *a*.

We add an internal trigger from table t1 to table t1_unique, this trigger fires every time we perform an insert to insert into the unique table and every time there is a delete a trigger is fired to perform a delete in the t1_unique table. At updates two triggers are fired that performs an insert of the new value in the unique index table and a delete of the old value in the unique index table.

Behind this fairly simple definition of a simple table using a primary key and a unique key we have a fairly complex index structure and trigger handling to ensure that all indexes are kept in synch with each other. The unique index is updated transactionally within the same transaction as the update of the base table.

18.1.6 A simple table with a generated primary key

In MySQL a concept called *auto_increment* is used to generate unique keys in increasing value. For InnoDB tables the step is 1 between inserted rows always. In NDB we can have multiple APIs and multiple MySQL Servers hitting the table at the same time. We have implemented *auto_increment* as one row in a special system table. When we get the next key from this table we get a range of keys. By default this range is set to 1 key. This is a configurable item in the MySQL Server configuration option *ndb-autoincrement-prefetch-sz*.

The default here is set to ensure that people used to MySQL isn't surprised by behaviour of NDB. However for any real MySQL Cluster application it is quite likely that this value should be set to at least 32 to ensure that the updates of the rows to get a new unique key isn't becoming a bottleneck. If insert rates on the table is beyond a thousand inserts per second and even smaller than that if latency is high between nodes in the cluster this value must be increased to avoid running into a bottleneck when creating unique keys. Setting the value to 1024 means that millions of inserts per second can be sustained on the table. It can be set to at most 65535.

Here is the syntax used to create a table with autoincrement on the primary key.

```
mysql> CREATE TABLE t1 (a INT PRIMARY KEY USING HASH AUTO_INCREMENT)
mysql> ENGINE=NDB;
```

18.1.7 More complex tables

Using the simple examples we can move on to very complex tables. The limit is that we can have at most 511 columns in a table and the sum of the column sizes must be less than 8052 bytes for the fixed size columns, 14 kBytes for the maximum row size of all columns. BLOB tables are treated a bit special, we'll cover those later in this chapter. We can have up to 64 indexes per table as well.

NDB can store any field type available in MySQL and using any character set available in MySQL. A word of caution here is to remember that complex character sets use more than one byte per character.

The syntax used is the same syntax used for any tables in MySQL. We will describe later some specialisation available to NDB tables.

Tables in MySQL Cluster can have GIS columns, but cannot have GIS indexes, they cannot have fulltext indexes. NDB tables can have JSON attributes, it is possible to have stored generated columns that are indexed in NDB, it is not possible to have an index on a virtual generated column in NDB tables.

18.2 Altering a table

Once a table have been created we can use ALTER TABLE to modify the table. Some of the changes to the table can be done using a copying alter table statement and some can be done as online alter table statements.

18.2.1 ONLINE ALTER TABLE STATEMENTS

Our aim for MySQL Cluster is that NDB tables should always be available for read and write after its creation.

There is one caveat to this. Due to the internal software structure in the MySQL Server it isn't possible to write to a table in the same MySQL Server as the change is happening within. What this means is that in order to create a highly available cluster it is a good idea to have a special MySQL Server used to execute online ALTER TABLE statements.

The fact is that the NDB data nodes allows for writes to be performed on a table where indexes are added, columns are added or the table partitioning is changed. However the actual MySQL Server where this change is performed only allows reads of this table. This is due to internal locking in the MySQL Server that is hard to get around. The MySQL Server assumes that even online operations are not truly online. To execute truly online ALTER TABLE statements these should be executed from a MySQL Server purely used for metadata statements. NDB is actually more online than what one MySQL Server can be. Other MySQL Servers can thus continue to operate on the table using reads and writes since these MySQL Servers are not aware of the locks inside the MySQL Server that performs the change.

The following things can be changed as online alter table statements.

1. Add an ordered index

2. Add a unique index

3. Drop an ordered index

4. Drop a unique index

5. Add a new column

6. Add a foreign key

7. Drop a foreign key

8. Reorganise table to use new node groups

9. Add partitions to a table and reorganise

10. Set the Read Backup feature on the table

11. Rename table

Things that specifically isn't supported as online alter table statements are:

1. Remove a primary key

2. Change primary key columns

3. Change columns

4. Drop column

Primary keys are the vehicle we use to control all online changes to a table. Changing the primary key of an existing table is not possible. Drop column could be implemented, but it would require tables to use a very dynamic data structure that have a high CPU overhead.

It is likely that even more ALTER TABLE statements will be possible to perform as online alter table statements as development of MySQL Cluster moves on.

The syntax used to ensure that we only allow an online alter table statement performed is the following:

```
mysql> ALTER TABLE t1 algorithm=inplace, add c int
```

In this case we want to add a new column c to a table t1. By adding the *algorithm=inplace* syntax we ensure that the operation will only be successful if we can perform it as an online alter table statement.

Another method is to set the configuration option

ndb-allow-copying-alter-table to 0, this has the effect of not allowing copying alter table and failing any ALTER TABLE that attempts to use a copying alter table. By default this option is set to 1.

18.2.2 COPYING ALTER TABLE STATEMENTS

In some cases we want the table recreated as a new table and the old table data to be moved to the new table. In this case the syntax used is the following:

```
mysql> ALTER TABLE t1 algorithm=copy, add c int
```

In this case the change will be performed as a copying alter table statement even if an online alter table statement is possible.

It is possible to set the configuration option *ndb-use-copying-alter-table* to 1 to get the same effect as providing the syntax *algorithm=copy*. By default this option is set to 0.

18.3 QUERYING A TABLE

Querying an NDB table is using normal SELECT statements. Here we focus on the syntactical parts of SELECT queries and there is nothing special about SELECT queries for NDB. They are using the same syntax as any other table in MySQL.

18.3.1 SELECT COUNT(*) QUERIES

One specific variant of queries have a special treatment in NDB. This is the *SELECT COUNT(*) from table* query. In this case we want to know the number of records in the table. Actually there is no method to get the exact count of this since we cannot lock the entire table in the entire cluster. It is possible to lock a table in one MySQL Server but this doesn't prevent other MySQL Servers or API nodes to update the table.

There are two methods to get the approximate row count in the table. The first one is the optimised one that uses a local counter in each fragment to keep track of the number of rows in a partition of the table. This method is quick and provides a good estimate. The other method is to scan the entire table and count the rows in the table. This method is comparably very slow.

The optimised method is default, to use the slow method one can set the MySQL Server configuration option *ndb-use-exact-count* to 1.

18.3.2 CONFIGURATION OPTIONS THAT AFFECT SELECT QUERIES

The configuration option *ndb-join-pushdown* set to 1 means that we will attempt to push joins down to the NDB data nodes for execution and setting it to 0 means that we will not even attempt to push down joins to the NDB data nodes. It defaults to 1. More on pushdown join in a later chapter.

The option *ndb-force-send* can be set to 1 to ensure that we attempt to send immediately to the NDB data nodes when we have something ready for sending in our connection thread. If not we will give the responsibility to the sender thread or send based on how much data is waiting to be sent and how many have attempted to send before us. This adaptive send method can sometimes provide better throughput but can increase latency of some queries. It is set to 1 by default.

The option *ndb-batch-size* gives a boundary on how many bytes that is allowed to be sent to the MySQL Server node as part of a scan query before we return to the MySQL Server to handle the returned rows. By default it is set to 32 kByte.

ndb-index-stat-enable enables use of index statistics. It is on by default.

The configuration option *ndb-cluster-connection* sets the number of API node connections that the MySQL Server will use, by default it is set to 1. But for larger MySQL Server that goes beyond 8-12 CPUs it is a good idea to use multiple API node connections per MySQL Server to make the MySQL Server scale to use more CPUs. The connection threads will use different cluster connections in a round robin scheme.

18.3.3 QUERY CACHE AND NDB

Query Cache will be deprecated in MySQL 8.0.

In principle NDB supports the MySQL Query Cache. However it is strongly recommended to no longer use the Query Cache in MySQL. The code is still working but it hasn't been updated for modern servers, it will create a bottleneck in the MySQL Server already after using 2-4 CPUs in the MySQL Server.

To ensure that the Query cache isn't part of any query handling make sure to set the MySQL configuration option *query-cache-size* to 0 and *query-cache-type* to off. This will ensure that the query cache is completely disabled.

We will not discuss the Query Cache any further in this book, we will assume that these two configuration options are always set. If you decide to still venture on using the Query Cache the MySQL manual can provide some more details on how to do that.

18.4   Writing to a table

There are many different ways of writing to a table in MySQL such as INSERT, DELETE, UPDATE. MySQL also supports REPLACE, INSERT INTO DELAYED and a few other variants.

These statements use the same syntax for NDB tables as they do for normal MySQL tables. There are a few configuration options that can be used to change the behaviour of those writing SQL statements.

The configuration option *ndb-use-transactions* is specifically designed for large insert statements. Given that large transactions might be too big to handle for NDB, those statements can be split into multiple transactions. NDB can handle a number of thousand row updates (configurable how many) per transaction, but for extremely large insert statements (such as LOAD DATA .. INFILE) that loads an entire file in one statement it is a good idea to split those extremely large transactions into more moderately sized transaction sizes. When this is set to 1 (default setting) the large insert statements will be split into multiple transactions. LOAD DATA INFILE will always be split into multiple transactions.

18.5   Transactions

Everything in MySQL Cluster is performed using transactions of varying sizes. In MySQL one can run in two modes, the first is the autocommit mode which means that each SQL statement is treated as a transaction.

The second variant is to enclose all statements belonging to a transaction by BEGIN and COMMIT (ROLLBACK if necessary to roll back transaction).

NDB supports using autocommit and the BEGIN, COMMIT and ROLLBACK handling in MySQL. NDB doesn't support using XA transactions. NDB doesn't support savepoints.

18.6   Drop/Truncate Table

A table can be dropped as in any normal MySQL table. We will drop tables in a graceful manner where the table is completing the running queries before the table is dropped.

No special syntax is used for dropping tables in NDB.

MySQL supports dropping all tables in a database by dropping the database where the tables reside. This is supported by NDB.

18.7   Indexes

NDB support three different types of indexes. Normal primary key indexes consists of both a distributed hash index and an ordered index on each fragment replica. Unique key indexes implemented as a separate table with the unique key as primary key and the primary key as columns in the unique index table (these also have an ordered index on the unique key). All normal indexes are ordered indexes.

Indexed columns in NDB must be stored in main memory, columns that are stored on disk using a page cache cannot be indexed. All tables must have a main memory part and at least one primary key hash index.

It is possible to define a pure hash index for primary keys and unique keys by using the keyword USING HASH in SQL.

NDB supports adding and dropping indexes on a table as an online alter table statement. This statement can either be an ALTER TABLE statement or a CREATE INDEX statement.

18.7.1 INDEX SIZES

In many DBMSs the size of an index is dependent on the number of fields in the index. This is NOT true for NDB. In NDB the size of a distributed hash index and an ordered index is a constant overhead. The reason is that we only store a row id reference in the index and not any values at all.

In the hash index we store one word per row that is used for some bits and also used to find the lock owner when we have ongoing transactions on the row. There is also one additional words with a row page id. Each row entry is 8 bytes. In addition the hash index has some overhead in how those 8 bytes are found that adds a few more bytes to the overhead. There is a container header of two words for each container and there is around 5-10 entries per container. There will also be some free space between containers since those are stored in a number of fixed places and the placement into the pages is more or less random based on the hash of the key. Around 15 bytes of overhead one should account for in the hash index per row. One important part of the hash index is that we store a part of the hash in the index. This makes it possible to skip rows that are not equal faster compared to a lookup of the primary key.

```
hash(PartitionKey) % Number of Hash maps = distribution_id
distribution_info(distribution_id) -> Set of nodes storing replicas
hash(PrimaryKey) >> 6 = Hash index page id
hash(PrimaryKey) & 63 = Hash index page index
tree_lookup(Hash index page id) -> Physical page reference
get_mem_address(physical_page, page index) -> Memory adddress to container
```

In the box above we show how the partition key is hashed to find the hash map to use for the row. The hash map is used to translate into the partition id and this will give a set of current alive nodes storing the replicas for this row.

When we get to the node we use the hash on the primary key (often the same as the partition key unless the table was created with a specific partition key). We use part of the hash to find the page id where the bucket of the key element is stored in. A second part is used to find the page index in the page. The page and page index will point to the first container in the hash bucket.

Each bucket consists of a linked list of containers, normally there is only one container, but there is no specific limit to how many containers there can be.

The container header contains references to the next container in the bucket if one exists and a few other bits. Each container contains anywhere between zero and eleven key elements. Each key element contains a reference to the row and a part of the hash of the key and a few more bits. A key element is 8 bytes in size. Most of this stores the row id, but there are also scan bits and hash bits and some other bits.

The hash pages are 8 kBytes in size, if we cannot store any more container in the same page as the linked list we can use overflow pages that only store overflow containers.

Given that the containers can be wildly different in sizes we have implemented a variant where we can have containers both starting from the left and from the right. Thus we can have 2 containers in each container entry in the page. Each container entry is 112 bytes. The sum of the sizes of the containers in the container entry is always 112 bytes or less.

At the bottom of each page we have eight overflow containers, these can also be filled from both ends.

The overhead of the hash index is around 15 bytes per row. A significant part of this comes from the element and container overhead. The rest is empty unused slots and memory areas that comes through the random nature of the hash index.

The hash index is used in all primary key lookups and unique index lookups. It is used for full table scans and a number of scans that are part of metadata changes.

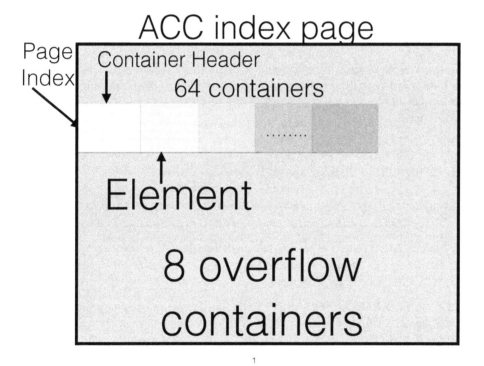

The ordered index is implemented as a T-Tree. A T-tree is similar to a balanced binary tree. A balanced binary tree stores the pointers to rows only in the leaf nodes. The T-tree stores pointers to rows in all index pages. The T-tree index uses mini-pages that are 256 bytes in size (these mini-pages are stored in the *DataMemory*).

Each such mini-page contains a header, it contains a reference to a new mini-page for those keys that are smaller than the left pointer. It contains a reference to a new mini-page for those keys that are larger than the right pointer. The pointers are row ids that contain the boundary values.

For those keys that are between the left and right the reference to the row is found among the up to 22 references in the mini-page. The search within those 22 references uses a binary search algorithm.

In addition the mini-page also stores a subset of the left and right key values. These are used to avoid having to go and read the rows for the most part. This subset of the keys is an important optimisation of the index operation.

These mini-pages are stored in a binary tree structure that is kept balanced. When we are searching the index and we come to a container we have three choices. Go left, stay or go right. The most common is to go left or right since it is only at the end of the search that we stay in the same index mini-page.

The benefit of the T-tree structure compared to a binary tree is that it saves memory in that only 2 pointers are needed per 22 entries. It also brings benefits that we can avoid going to the actual rows in many cases where it is sufficient to use the subset of the key to discover whether to move left or right or stay.

The overhead of an ordered index stays at around 10 bytes per row. Most of this memory is used for the row reference.

The main use case for the ordered index is to perform range scans.

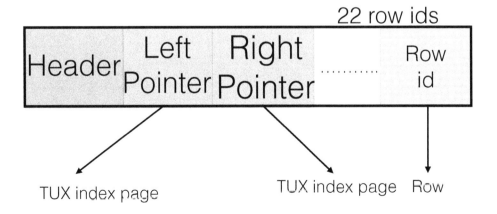

18.8 FOREIGN KEYS

NDB support foreign keys between tables. More on this in a separate chapter on NDB foreign keys.

18.9 OPTIMIZE/ANALYZE TABLE

OPTIMIZE table command can be used on NDB tables to remove any fragmentation on variable sized rows and dynamically formatted row. It cannot defragment the fixed size part in memory since this would change the row id of a row and this is a very important part of the recovery algorithms in NDB.

The ANALYZE table command is used to build up the index statistics on an NDB table. It can generate large speedups on some SELECT queries.

18.10 BLOBs

NDB supports BLOBs of any size. We will describe this in more detail in a specific chapter on BLOBs for NDB.

18.11 ROW FORMAT OF NDB TABLES

NDB supports a few row formats for its tables. We will describe those and the effect of them in the next chapter.

18.12 DISK DATA COLUMNS

NDB supports storing non-indexed columns on disk. We will describe this in more detail in a separate chapter.

18.13 MySQL REPLICATION OF NDB TABLES

NDB supports using MySQL Replication in a fairly advanced manner. We'll cover this in a specific part of this book.

CHAPTER 19

NDB ROW DATA STRUCTURE

A database is about storing data for easy accessibility. Most DBMS have some special tricks to store data and indexes in a format suitable for the application categories that the DBMS focus on. NDB is no different, we have heavily optimised index data structures for primary key access. We have also added a standard index for ordered access to data.

Much of the source code in NDB is focused on the distribution aspect and reliability aspect, so we probably focus less on data structures than many other DBMSs do. In this chapter we will go through the data structures we use for rows, hash indexes and ordered indexes.

19.1 ROW FORMAT

NDB stores rows in two different formats. FIXED format and DYNAMIC format. The term FIXED format is somewhat a misnomer. It means that fixed size columns is stored in the fixed size part of the row and variable sized columns are stored in the variable sized part of the row.

To understand the concepts here we will introduce the data structure of the rows in NDB. Every row in NDB has a fixed size part. Most tables also have a variable sized part. All tables with disk columns in addition have a fixed size disk data part.

The fixed size part of the row contains a row header and all the fixed size columns that are using the FIXED format.

The variable sized part contains all columns that have a variable size. The variable sized part have two parts. It has one part for columns that always have at least a length. It has a second part where all columns using the DYNAMIC format are stored.

Columns stored in the dynamic format will not be stored at all if they are NULL or have the default value. This means that new columns with dynamic format can be added to a table without any need to change the row storage at all. This is why we can support add column as an online operation. Columns using the dynamic format will have a bit more overhead when they are stored and the execution overhead will be a bit higher as well for them (around 40% more CPU used in retrieving data from row storage, this is only a small part of the execution time for a row operation except when performing scans that touch very many rows).

There is one more reason to use the dynamic format, the row storage for those columns can be compacted using OPTIMIZE TABLE. Columns that are stored in the fixed row part is not possible to move around and thus cannot be compacted.

The disk columns are always stored in a fixed format, this row part is always of the same size for all rows of a table. Disk columns can thus not be added and dropped as online operations.

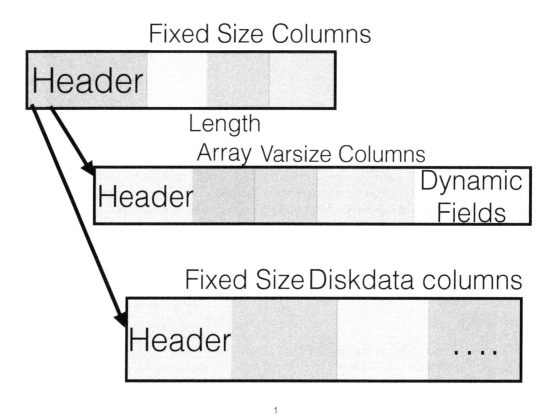

The row header contains the following information:

The first word is used to refer to the operation currently owning the record. This operation might be part of a linked list of operations that have operated on the row in the same transaction. If the row isn't currently involved in a transaction the first word contains the special value RNIL which is a variant of NULL that is equal to 0xFFFFFF00. Internally in NDB we use relative pointers, thus 0 is a valid pointer. Thus we had to use a special NULL value and this value is RNIL. It is heavily used in the NDB code.

The second word contains the tuple header bits. 16 bits are used as a version number which is used by the ordered index to keep track of which row version it is. The other 16 bits are various indicators for the row such as if it has a variable sized part, if it has a disk part, if it has grown in the transaction, some bits referring to local checkpoints and so forth.

The third word contains a checksum of the fixed size part of the row.

The fourth word contains the global checkpoint identifier of the last update of the row. This is an important part used in node recovery to know which rows that need to be synchronised in the starting node.

The fifth word contains NULL bits. If no NULLable columns exists in the table this word doesn't exist. Each column that is NULLable have one bit in the NULL bits, if more than 32 NULLable columns exist in the table there will be more than one NULL bit word.

Finally we have the reference to the variable sized part of the row and the disk part of the row. Each of those are 8 bytes in size to accomodate large main memory sizes and large disk data sizes.

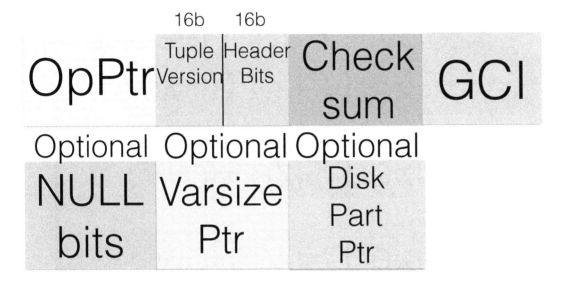

The base header that will be there for all tables is 16 bytes in size. With NULLable rows in the table there will be at least one NULL bit word extending the size to 16 bytes. Most every table uses a variable sized part extending the header size to 28 bytes. If the table uses a disk part the row header extends to 36 bytes.

The most common tables will have a 28 byte row header size (NULL columns exist, have VARCHAR fields and have no disk columns).

The fixed size part of the row is fixed in size at table creation. It doesn't need to contain any columns at all, but it will always contain the row header. A table always has a fixed size part since this is the entry point to the row. The fixed size part is addressable using a row id. This row id stays constant, a tuple is not allowed to move, the row id of all replicas of the row must use the same row id. At insert the primary replica will assign the row id and this will be sent to the backup replica to ensure that it uses the same row id. This is an important requirement for the synchronisation phase of a node restart.

The fixed size part is stored in fixed size pages.

32kByte Page

128Byte PageHeader
Fixed Size Row
⋮
Fixed Size Row
⋮
Fixed Size Row

Row Address = Page Address +128+RowSize*PageIndex

The variable sized part of the row is stored in a variable sized page. Given that it is variable in size we address it through a page directory starting at the end of the page. This page directory contains one word per row, 2 bytes is the index where the row starts in the page, the second 2 bytes is the length of the variable sized part of the row.

Now the variable sized part contains two parts. The first is the variable sized columns. Each such column have 2 bytes that contains the index of the column inside the variable size. The length of the item can be calculated using the next 2 bytes. The start of the column can be quickly found.

This means that all variable sized columns will use at least 2 bytes all the time, but no more than this is needed. NULL bits for variable sized columns is stored in the fixed size part of the row.

We also have a dynamic part, in this part of the row the absence of a column means that its value is NULL. Thus NULL columns consume no space. It means that it is very easy to add a new column in the dynamic part of the row. It needs to be added with NULL or a default value as its starting value. The dynamic part is stored at the end of the variable sized part of the row.

The variable sized part also contains a reference back to the fixed part to ensure that anyone can move the variable sized part when necessary.

The variable sized part is stored in variable sized pages. These pages are addressed using an

Varsize Array
n+1 Lengths n columns

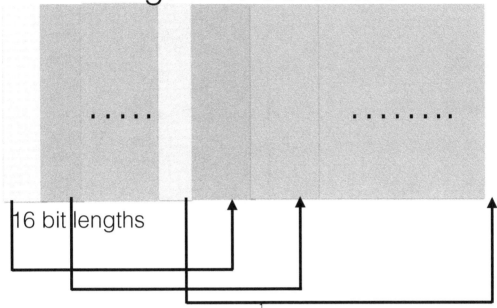

16 bit lengths

index to the page. This index resides at the end of the page. Each index entry is 32 bits in size, 16 bits is the size of the entry and 16 bits is a pointer inside the page to the row part. As mentioned the first 8 bytes in the variable sized part is an 8 byte reference to the fixed row part. The overhead of using a variable sized part is 12 bytes in the variable sized row part in addition to the 8 bytes in the fixed size part, thus in total 20 bytes of overhead per row.

As described above there is also a 2 byte overhead for each variable sized column to store the length of the column.

The disk format is fixed in size. All columns are stored using their maximum size.

19.2 FIXED ROW FORMAT

Using the fixed row format means that the column (or all columns if it is applied on the table) is stored in either the fixed size part of the row or in the variable sized part of the row.

Thus the storage for the column is always present, even if set to NULL.

There are many ways to achieve that a column is stored in FIXED format. First there is a configuration variable that sets the default of the column format. This is the MySQL Server configuration option *ndb-default-column-format*. It can be set to *FIXED* or *DYNAMIC*.

By default it will be set to FIXED, normal tables will use the fixed size row format. One can also set the property *column_format* on the column when creating the table or when altering

Variable Sized Page

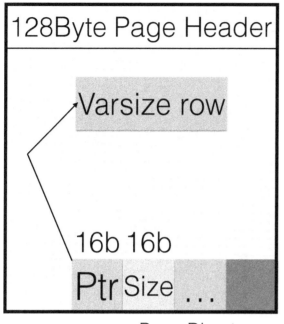

Row Address =
Page Address+
RowPtr

RowPtrAddress =
Page Address + 32768
- Page Index*4

Page Directory

the table. Here is an example of this.

```
mysql> CREATE TABLE t1 (a int column_format FIXED, b int)
mysql> engine=ndbcluster;
```

19.3 DYNAMIC ROW FORMAT

The Dynamic row format means that the column is stored in the dynamic part of the row. This means that it is easy to add new columns in this part. The column format have a much higher overhead in both storage and in computing necessary to read and write it. The actual read and write of it increases by 40% for the actual read/write part of the transaction. However for a primary key lookup this part is such a small part of the cost that the overhead decrease to much less than 5% whereas for a full table scan that more or is entirely about reading rows will see this 40% drop in performance.

Chapter 20

Foreign Key handling

Foreign keys is a concept in SQL that enables the application to create constraints on the data in the tables.

A foreign key is defined on the table that is referred to as the child table. The parent table is the referenced table. The parent table must be created before the child table can create a foreign key referencing it.

The idea with a foreign key is that the child table have a reference in its table that gives a unique reference to a row in the parent table. The reference consists of one or more columns, normally these columns are simply the same columns as the primary key of the parent table.

We will call the columns in the child table the reference columns and the columns in the parent table the referenced columns.

Here is a simple example of a foreign key constraint.

```
mysql> CREATE TABLE tab_parent (a int primary key) engine NDB;
mysql> CREATE TABLE tab_child (a int primary key, b int)
mysql> INDEX (b)
mysql> FOREIGN KEY (b) REFERENCES tab_parent(a)
mysql> ON UPDATE SET NULL
mysql> ON DELETE SET NULL
mysql> ENGINE NDB;
```

The first table in this example, the parent table, has only one column, the primary key column a, this is the referenced column. The second table, the child table has a reference to the parent table in column b, this is the referencing column, and it has its own primary key column a.

It is required that the foreign key columns in the child table have an index defined on the referencing columns. This is required to ensure that the foreign key actions can be executed efficiently. Note that there can be multiple rows in the child table referring to the same row in the parent table. Thus the naming parent-child. There is only one parent row, but there can be multiple child rows referring to the parent.

The parent table must have a primary key or a unique key defined on the referenced columns.

In InnoDB it is sufficient to have an index defined on the parent table. But again the reference to the rows in the parent table should be referring to one and only one row, for all practical use cases the parent table should have a primary key index or a unique key index defined on the parent table for the referenced columns (also true for InnoDB).

The foreign key constraint is either checked immediately when the change is done or checked in a special pre-commit phase before the actual commit starts, but after all modifications have been prepared in the transaction. This is done through a read on the parent table, if the read fails the transaction is aborted.

If the reference columns are set to NULL no trigger will be fired, the trigger fires already in the prepare phase, the transaction coordinator either executes it immediately or stores the trigger until the pre-commit phase and when the pre-commit phase starts it will send off all stored pre-commit triggers.

Thus the child table have a trigger defined on changes of the reference columns. The trigger fires on all INSERTs and on all UPDATEs that change the reference columns. A DELETE cannot cause any inconsistency in this case, so no need to trigger at DELETEs.

The updates on the referencing columns and inserts into the child table are checked immediately except when we are using *ON UPDATE NO ACTION*. In the *NO ACTION* case the check is deferred until the pre-commit phase. In the checks in the pre-commit phase we check the final value committed and ignore any intermediate states we have passed through during the execution of the transaction.

The handling of *NO ACTION* differs from InnoDB. The handling in InnoDB for *NO ACTION* is the same as for *RESTRICT*. In NDB we decided to follow many other DBMSs that use *NO ACTION* to indicate that checks are deferred to commit time.

Now if the row in the parent is deleted or if the referenced columns are updated it will affect the child row as well. Here we have a number of different options of what to do. We can *CASCADE* the changes to the child table such that they continue to refer to the correct row. We can *SET NULL* on the referencing columns (only if setting those to NULL is allowed). We can *RESTRICT* the change (the transaction will be aborted).

We define this when we define the table. The default is *RESTRICT*. We define *ON DELETE* to specify what to do when a row in the parent table is deleted. We specify *ON UPDATE* to specify what happens when we change the referenced columns and when we update the referencing columns in the child table and when we insert into the child table. For the child table the only option that differs is *NO ACTION* that defers the check to the pre-commit phase. All other options means that changes in the child table are immediately verified.

When *CASCADE* is used we rely on foreign key handling to remove the rows in the child table when a delete occurs in the parent table.

CASCADE is potentially a very dangerous mode. One delete could delete an entire database since the cascading delete could lead to a new delete which in turn leads to a new cascading delete and so forth. If this option is used it is important that the application developer have very good control over his changes.

ON UPDATE CASCADE is only supported if the referenced columns form a unique key. It will be rejected if the referenced columns form a primary key. The reason is that it isn't possible to update the primary key in NDB, an update of the primary key is performed by first dropping the row and then reinserting the row.

SET NULL can trigger a fair amount of updates, in this case the change can at least not cascade into even more tables. Setting it to NULL in the foreign key trigger ensures that at least the tables have no incorrect references.

The *RESTRICT* is used when the application expects to take care of any changes to ensure that they start with a consistent database and ends with a consistent database. However the application developer wants the MySQL Server to ensure that the changes are consistent. This is in my view the proper usage of foreign keys in an application with requirements on predictable latency.

NO ACTION is the same as *RESTRICT* except that for *RESTRICT* the check of the foreign key relation is immediate whereas for *NO ACTION* it is deferred to commit time. This means that using *RESTRICT* you should always drop or change the child rows before the parent rows. Using *NO ACTION* it is sufficient to ensure that the entire transaction is consistent, the order of changes do not matter.

In NDB, foreign keys are checked and verified in the NDB data nodes. Thus if you define a foreign key on a table, this foreign key relation will be checked and maintained by transactions performed from applications using direct NDB API applications as well as SQL applications.

This means that updating the primary key in a parent table that have a primary key on the referenced columns is only possible using the *SET NULL* option. For *RESTRICT* and *NO ACTION* the DELETE trigger and INSERT trigger will ensure that the update of the primary key is disallowed and *ON UPDATE CASCADE* on a primary key is not even allowed.

Foreign keys have a fairly high overhead in that all changes requires checks and those checks will extend the time for the transactions. It is seldomly used for very time-critical applications. It is a great aid in quickly developing new applications that need to maintain consistency of the database.

Most applications using foreign keys in InnoDB should transfer easily into NDB since for foreign keys the differences between InnoDB and NDB are very small.

Foreign keys can be created when creating the table. Foreign keys can be created using the *ALTER TABLE* command. They can also be dropped as part of the *ALTER TABLE* command. Both creation and dropping of a foreign key is an online operation that can happen while the table is updated.

Dropping a table while it is involved in a foreign key relation is not allowed since that would be a breach of the foreign key constraint.

InnoDB supports a special parameter called *foreign_key_checks* that disables all foreign key checks if set to 0. This will not have any effect on NDB. Once a foreign key have been defined in NDB it will perform the foreign key checks. Foreign keys can be created and dropped as online operations in NDB, this removes the need to use this parameter.

Foreign keys is well integrated with MySQL Cluster Replication. Even if the slave side doesn't have the foreign keys defined on the tables, the triggered actions will still be performed on the slave side since all row operations that are part of a transaction will be sent to the binlog. The binlog stores all row changes for a transaction and this means that the slave side do not need to understand how those row changes came about.

Foreign key relations can only exist between tables using the same storage engine, thus the foreign key relations from an NDB table must refer to another NDB table.

20.1 FOREIGN KEY CONSIDERATIONS

Given that one focus of NDB is real-time applications it is important to consider how to use foreign keys. Foreign keys is a strong concept to support application constraints. Foreign keys uses triggers to secure that any inserts, updates and deletes leaves the database with its constraints still maintained.

Foreign keys can create problems in three ways. The first is that a delete can trigger a delete of a record that in turn triggers another delete and so forth (called cascading deletes). Thus transaction sizes even for a single row change can grow to become any size. Often implementing application functionality directly using foreign keys is easy, but it requires that one analyses the data usage to ensure that not too big transactions are created that create problems with real-time aspects of NDB.

The preferred options to avoid these large transactions are *RESTRICT* and *NO ACTION*.

The second problem is when creating the foreign key on a live table. If we create the foreign key in a system that are constantly changing data, it means that we cannot be absolutely sure that foreign key constraints are valid when we created the foreign key. We worked hard on ensuring that building a foreign key is done correctly such that if data is consistent, the foreign key constraints should be ok when the foreign key is created.

The third potential problem is when dropping a foreign key. In this case we drop the triggers at some point in time, after this drop we no longer maintain the foreign key relation. Such a drop is not possible to serialise towards all other parallel changes in a distributed database without a global cluster lock which isn't desirable in a real-time database that is supposed to be AlwaysOn.

The recommended manner to use foreign keys is to create them when creating the tables and dropping them when dropping the tables and ensuring that the cascading actions don't cause extremely large transaction sizes.

We do work hard to ensure that both create and drop of foreign keys can be done in a safe way also while done in parallel with application changes of the data.

CHAPTER 21

BLOB HANDLING

BLOBs are treated in a special manner in MySQL Cluster. The reason is that NDB is a real-time engine. This means that working with large BLOB's isn't desirable for the NDB data nodes. Working with large objects would create challenges around buffer management. A single read of a row would have to be scheduled in several steps.

To avoid these problems we split the BLOB into a number of parts and work with one part at a time.

Currently NDB data nodes doesn't support storing the entire BLOBs as part of the original row. A large BLOB must be split into multiple parts and these parts are stored in different rows.

A BLOB (or TEXT) field creates a VARCHAR column that can be up to 256 bytes in the table itself. If the BLOB is smaller, no more parts are needed. If the BLOB is larger, the BLOB is split such that the first 256 bytes is stored in the table itself, the rest is stored in a separate table for the BLOB column. Each row in this table contains a VARCHAR that can store up to 2 kBytes of the BLOB. E.g. a BLOB of 12.8 kBytes will be stored partly in the table itself (256 bytes), there will be 6 rows that use the entire 2 kBytes and a final row that stores the remainder which is about 0.55 kBytes in size. The last 7 rows are stored in a special table that is only used for this BLOB column. Each BLOB column adds one more table in NDB. It is important to remember this when considering the amount of metadata NDB has to store.

One reason for storing the extra rows in a separate table is to make it easier to add and drop BLOB columns. Adding a BLOB column can be made as an online operation by adding the VARCHAR column to the base table using the dynamic row format and creating a new table for the BLOB parts.

The part rows use the same partitioning key as the base table and partly the same primary key as the base table with an added columns for part id. Thus the BLOB rows will be stored in the same places since the BLOB tables use the same partitioning scheme.

Some of the problems of BLOBs comes from load regulation. If we store a BLOB that is 100 MByte in size it is obvious that if someone tries to write the entire BLOB as one operation or reading the BLOB as one operation as this would put an enormous load on the network for a short time, most likely stopping many other operations from progressing. To avoid this we will definitely want to send parts of a large BLOB at a time over the network even if at some time the whole BLOB is stored inside the table row.

Using BLOBs for fields that normally isn't very large is not the optimal solution in MySQL Cluster. For example if the majority of the BLOBs are about 1 kBytes in size it makes sense to create a VARCHAR(2048) or something like that instead.

However for storing objects that can be fairly large the BLOB implementation is quite ok. We ensure that reading and writing of BLOBs is split into many operations to ensure that the network isn't overloaded by single BLOB operations.

Concurrency control of BLOB columns is a bit special due to this split of the column, this will be covered in the coming chapter on Concurrency Control.

When executing a transaction that changes a BLOB it is important that one operation record per BLOB part is needed, in the example above with a BLOB of 12.8 kByte in size there are 7 additional operation records when writing a BLOB. In MySQL 5.7 all BLOB operations from SQL either write or read the entire object.

A natural thing for many BLOB columns are to store those as disk data columns. The main consideration here is that each extra BLOB part has to store the primary key part in main memory, thus the main memory used for each BLOB part is about 50-60 bytes dependent on the size of the primary key. If we need to store about 1 TBytes of BLOBs we still need to have about 30 GBytes of main memory storage.

CHAPTER 22

DISK COLUMNS

Disk columns are columns that are stored on disk and is only cached in main memory when reading and writing them. Columns stored in main memory are pinned to a main memory location at startup and stays there as long as the node is up and running. Both the main memory columns and the disk column are still checkpointed and written to disk to be recoverable.

The main reason we decided to implement disk columns was to extend the size of databases that we can support. We have so far decided not to spend time on implementing disk-based indexes. The reason is that our focus have been on supporting applications that require predictable latency to queries and updates while maintaining a very high availability. While disk-based indexes would extend our reach to new users, it would not add to our unique selling points which are very high availability and predictable response times in a strongly consistent distributed environment with high throughput.

With the development of persistent memory, fast NVMe drives and SSD drives the picture is quickly changing. The use of persistent memory modules that come out in 2018 with Intel Cascade Lake will make it normal for a server to have 1 TByte of memory that can be used by NDB.

The development of SSD's and NVMe's plays very well into our unique selling points. Given that they can respond in tens of microseconds and can sustain hundreds of thousands of IO operations per second (IOPS) we can use these as main storage for many more columns.

Cloud machines like the one provided through the Oracle Cloud are perfect fits for running large MySQL Cluster installations with very low and predictable latency as well as very high availability using our new features for making use of the availability domains in the cloud. These machines come equipped with 768 GByte of memory and tens of TBytes of NVMe drives.

It is strongly recommended that all tablespaces are created on SSD devices or NVMe devices. The reason is simply that this will bring a thousand times better throughput and a hundred times better latency compared to using hard drives. Access to disk for disk data is always one page at a time (currently 32 kBytes in size), thus access to the disk is always random access. Random access to hard drives is limited to around 200 accesses per second and this is very unlikely to be sufficient for normal NDB applications. For an SSD it is possible to achieve tens of thousands of random accesses per second and for NVMe devices it is even possible to achieve hundreds of thousands of random accesses per second. Clearly one should avoid using use hard drives for disk columns for production usage.

Hard drives are still an ok fit for REDO logs, UNDO logs, backups and local checkpoint files. The reason is that those are strictly written and read using sequential access. Thus the hard drives can sustain their full disk bandwidth. Hard drives are also less likely to wear out due to constant writing.

For larger systems where write speeds beyond 100 MBytes per second are needed, SSDs are needed to be able to sustain the high write speeds for logs, backups and checkpoints.

Many applications store fairly large chunks of data in BLOB's and in variable sized character strings. There could be large amounts of statistical data in integers stored as information in the database. Often these columns are not indexed, these columns represent natural use cases for disk columns in NDB.

One remaining limitation of disk columns is that it isn't possible to extend with new disk columns as an online alter table statement. It is also not possible to move a column from a disk column to a main memory column in an online alter table statement.

22.1 ROW FORMAT FOR DISK COLUMNS

The main memory row has a reference to the disk data part of the row. This reference is kept consistent by the recovery algorithms such that the row is connected also after recovery. The disk part also has a back reference to the main memory row. The reason for this is to ensure that we can perform scans in disk order. Thus we read the pages on disk and find the main memory part rather than the opposite (improves sequential reading of the disk).

The disk data part of the row is currently always a fixed size row. All fields, also the variable sized fields are stored as fixed size columns with the column size as the maximum possible size of the column.

22.2 TABLESPACES

The actual data in a disk column is stored in a tablespace. Each table that have disk columns is using one tablespace. There can be several tablespaces in a cluster. Each tablespace will exist with the same size on all data nodes in the cluster. The relative file name of the tablespace file(s) will be the same on all machines.

Tables allocate extents from the tablespace. The size of an extent is decided when the tablespace is created. By default the extent size is 1 MByte. Once an extent have been allocated to a table it stays in this table until the table is dropped and a local checkpoint after the drop table have been completed.

All disk data rows are stored in pages of 32kByte in size. The pages move back and forth between disk and main memory as pages. The pages are maintained by the Page Manager and uses a page cache to store the pages while in memory. The size of this page cache is given in the NDB configuration option *DiskPageBufferMemory*.

Each tablespace contains a few pages describing each extent, to support fast decisions on where to place new rows, these pages are always in the page cache. The extent pages have a 4-word header for each extent and in addition they have 4 bits per page in the extent providing some state information of how full the page currently is.

This means that with a 4 TByte tablespace with 1 MByte per extent we will have 4M extents in the tablespace and each extent will use 20 bytes in main memory. Thus the extent pages will use about 80 MByte of the page cache.

It is recommended to have at least a few gigabytes of page cache when using disk columns in a larger scale. When pages are involved in updating transactions they will be temporarily locked into main memory when the commit operation starts and will remain locked until the UNDO log have been written to disk. This is to ensure that we follow the WAL principle of writing to the log before we write the actual disk data pages.

For writes to the data pages we use the *NO STEAL* approach. This means that we only write committed changes to the data pages. During the transaction the data resides in memory buffers and only at commit time is the changes written into the page cache and even later the data is flushed to disk.

Tablespaces consists of one or more data files. Size of existing data files cannot be changed, but new data files at any size can be added as online operations to a tablespace.

22.3 UNDO LOG

The disk data uses the WAL principle (Write Ahead Logging). Thus before we write any disk data page we must write an UNDO log record to ensure that we can roll back the pages to the state at the start of a local checkpoint.

The UNDO log files are stored in a special tablespace called Logfile Group. At the moment the implementation only supports one Logfile Group. There can be multiple log files in this Logfile group and new log files can be added as online operations.

22.4 SYNTAX FOR DISK DATA

When using disk data we first need to create an UNDO logfile group. Second we need to create at least one tablespace that uses this UNDO logfile group. After that we can create the tables that makes use of this tablespace.

22.4.1 UNDO LOG SYNTAX

When creating an UNDO log file group we need to add at least one file to it. We provide the size of it using the INITIAL_SIZE keyword. Each logfile group will also use an UNDO log buffer, the size of this we specify when creating the UNDO log.

```
CREATE LOGFILE GROUP lg1 ADD UNDOFILE 'lg1.dat'
        INITIAL_SIZE 4G UNDO_BUFFER_SIZE 32M engine=ndb;
```

This creates a logfile group *lg1* that is stored in the file *lg1.dat* (this file is stored in the DataDir of the data node (more control can be applied using *FileSystemPath* or *FileSystemPathDD*. The size is 4 GBytes and the UNDO buffer is 32 MBytes in size.

Given that only one UNDO log file group is allowed one might as well create this already at initial start of the cluster. This happens using the NDB configuration variable *InitialLogfileGroup*.

Here is an example of how to set this variable:

```
InitialLogfileGroup=undo_buffer_size=32M;lg1.dat:4G;lg2.dat:4G
```

This creates an initial logfile group called *DEFAULT-LG* with two files *lg1.dat* and *lg2.dat* both 4GByte in size. The UNDO buffer is set to be 32 MBytes in size. When creating an initial tablespace it is possible to specify the logfile group name. But since *InitialTablespace* cannot refer to any other than *DEFAULT-LG* this is not a good idea.

At any time we can add more log files to an existing logfile group. This is done by using an ALTER LOGFILE GROUP command.

Here is an example:

```
mysql> ALTER LOGFILE GROUP lg1
mysql> ADD UNDOFILE 'lg2.dat'
mysql> INITIAL_SIZE 4G
mysql> engine=ndb;
```

The setting of InitialLogfileGroup is equivalent to these two example queries CREATE LOGFILE GROUP and ALTER LOGFILE GROUP. The last example creates a new log file that is 4GBytes in size. It uses the same UNDO buffer, there is only one UNDO buffer per logfile group, it isn't possible to change that here.

Another good reason to use *InitialLogfileGroup* is that it means that the memory for the UNDO log buffer is not taken from the memory specified in the NDB configuration option *SharedGlobalMemoryPool*.

22.4.2 TABLESPACE SYNTAX

Creating a tablespace adds the first datafile to the tablespace. When creating the tablespace one needs to refer to the logfile group to be used with the tablespace. It is necessary to set the extent size (defaults to 1MByte). Extents are allocated to a table from the tablespace, an extent is the allocation unit when allocating disk space to a table.

```
mysql> CREATE TABLESPACE ts1 ADD DATAFILE 'ts1.dat'
mysql> INITIAL_SIZE 16G
mysql> EXTENT_SIZE 16M
mysql> USE LOGFILE GROUP lg1
mysql> engine=ndb;
```

The above statement creates a tablespace named *ts1* with a first data file *ts1.dat*, the data file is 16 GByte in size and uses an extent size of 16 MByte and uses logfile group *lg1*.

```
mysql> ALTER TABLESPACE ts1
mysql> ADD DATAFILE 'ts2.dat'
mysql> INITIAL_SIZE 16G
mysql> engine=ndb;
```

The above statement adds another datafile to the tablespace *ts1* with the file called *ts2.dat*, the file will have an initial size of 16 GByte.

In the same fashion as with logfile groups it is possible to create an initial tablespace for the cluster using the NDB configuration file. In this case the configuration variable is called *InitialTablespace*.

Here is an example of its use:

```
InitialTablespace=name=ts1;extent_size=16M;ts1.dat:16G;ts2.dat:16G
```

This creates the same tablespace as the CREATE TABLESPACE command and ALTER TABLESPACE command did together. The name is optional, if not provided the name will be *DEFAULT-TS*. It will always use the default log file group *DEFAULT-LG*. Thus when specifying *InitialLogfileGroup* one should not specify any other name on the logfile group.

22.4.3 CONTROLLING WHICH COLUMNS ARE STORED ON DISK

By default all columns are stored as in memory columns. One can set the storage type of a column by specifying either STORAGE MEMORY or STORAGE DISK. This can be set on the table, if it is set on the table it is applied on each non-indexed column.

Here is an example:

```
mysql> CREATE TABLE t1 (a int, b int storage memory)
mysql> engine=ndb
mysql> storage disk
mysql> tablespace ts1;
```

This creates a table with a hidden primary key stored in memory with 2 attributes, the first *a* stored on disk and the second *b* stored in memory.

22.5 PAGE MANAGER

The Page Manager maintains the page cache. It uses a modern page cache algorithm. We will attempt to provide a basic understanding of this algorithm.

Each page in the page cache has a page cache record in the Page Manager. Each such page cache record goes through a number of states before it has a page connected to it.

At first a main memory page must be bound to the page cache record. Once this have been done the page must be mapped to a disk page. For new pages this is trivial since the page content on disk can be overwritten for new pages. For existing pages the page is mapped to the disk page by reading the page from disk (page in).

In order to find a clean page to use for binding to a page cache record it might be necessary to first "clean" the page. Cleaning the page means that it might need to be written to disk before the page can be used for another disk page (page out).

A basic part of the algorithm is that we have 10x as many page cache records as we have pages in the page cache. We maintain those pages in a linked list ensuring that we know the "hotness" of a lot of pages that are not present in the page cache.

As a page is used by the application we increment the usage counter of the page. This counter is maintained for pages that have been paged out as long as the page cache record haven't been removed as well.

Thus we can see patterns of reuse that are longer than our page cache size can handle.

22.6   CONSIDERATIONS FOR DISK DATA TABLES

22.6.1   INITIALISATION OF FILES

Files can be added to both logfile groups and tablespaces as online operations. The addition of a new file will take some time. The file is created as part of the command to add the file. It will be created with its initial size. To ensure that the file system have allocated space for the entire size of the file, we will write the entire log file or tablespace file as part of adding it. Even though the operation to add a new file is an online operation, care is needed to ensure that the disk bandwidth used to initialise the file doesn't harm the ongoing transactions.

22.6.2   PLACEMENT OF DISK DATA FILES

It is possible to specify the full path of a file when adding a file to a logfile group or tablespace. It is not necessary advisable though since all machines might not look exactly the same.

If only a file name is provided, and the path is derived from the configuration parameter in the following order.

DataDir is normally a variable that should be set in the NDB configuration. If not, it will use the working directory of the NDB data node process. The default is to place all the files used by the data node process under this directory.

By specifying the NDB configuration option *FileSystemPath* all the disk data files will be moved to this directory. However if *FileSystemPathDD* is set this directory will be used instead.

The algorithm to choose directory for a data file in a tablespace is as follows. If configuration option *FileSystemPathDataFiles* is set use this directory, else if configuration option *FileSystemPathDD* is set use this directory, else if configuration option *FileSystemPath* is set use this directory, else if configuration option *DataDir* is set use this directory, else use the working data directory of the data node process.

The algorithm for choosing directory for UNDO log files is the same except for the first step where *FileSystemPathDataFiles* is replaced by *FileSystemPathUndoFiles*.

22.6.3   DISKIOTHREADPOOL

One more important thing to consider for disk data is the number of OS threads to use to read and write pages in the UNDO log files and tablespace files. This number is set through the NDB configuration variable *DiskIOThreadPool*. By default it is set to 2. It is quite likely that this parameter should be increased, in particular when using SSD's and NVMe's to store the tablespaces and logfile groups.

22.6.4 DISKPAGEBUFFERMEMORY AND DISKPAGEBUFFERENTRIES

Two important parameters are *DiskPageBufferMemory* which is simply the amount of memory dedicated to the page cache. *DiskPageBufferEntries* is the multiplication factor for how much memory we will have of old page cache entries that have been evicted from the cache. This is set to 10 by default. Thus we have 10 page cache entries for each actual page in the page cache. Since each such record consumes roughly 84 bytes (around that) it means that we use about 2.5% of the page cache memory to keep a record of old page cache entries. We could potentially increase this slightly or decrease it slightly but most likely this value is a good trade off. The more page cache we have, the better its hit rate will be.

Note that the MySQL manual could be a bit confusing when describing the *DiskPageBuffer-Entries* option.

22.6.5 LOCAL CHECKPOINTS FOR DISK DATA

Local checkpoints ensure that all dirty disk data pages are written to disk. This is important to ensure that we can cut the REDO log and the UNDO log for disk data pages. The algorithms used to handle disk data is described in a fairly detailed manner in a large comment in *pgman.cpp* and some comment in *pgman.hpp*. In *Backup.cpp* a very detailed description of the local checkpoint algorithm as such is provided. When a fragment replica is checkpointed, its main memory data and its disk data is checkpointed together, to ensure that the references between them stays correct after a restart. The most detailed comments are always in the latest version of NDB.

To ensure that we don't oversubscribe too many writes due to local checkpoints we will never have more than 1 MByte of outstanding page writes due to local checkpoints (LCPs) per *ldm* thread.

22.6.6 FOREIGN KEYS IN NDB DISK DATA TABLES

It is fully possible to use foreign keys on tables with disk data attributes. It is important to consider the implications of cascading actions for these tables. If a cascading action tries to change too many rows we could easily hit the limit for transaction sizes for those tables. It is important to take this into consideration when designing your schema. Foreign key cascading actions can easily lead a simple transaction to update all rows in a table and this can cause havoc for transaction latency and it can easily lead to overload problems.

This problem is present for main-memory tables, for disk data tables it will be even worse since all deleted rows will cause disk pages to become dirty and in the need of disk writes in the next local checkpoint.

Chapter 23

Table options

A default table using the NDB storage engine will be created such that we get balanced reads when we always read the primary replica. We create one partition per *ldm* thread per each node in the cluster, all columns are stored in main memory and we use REDO logging on the table.

There are options available when creating the table that makes it possible to change these defaults.

23.1 Read Backup feature

The transaction protocol in NDB is designed such that we first commit the update and as part of this we release the lock on the primary replicas but we still retain the locks on the backup replicas, next we send the commit acknowledge to the application. In parallel with that we complete the transaction by removing the memory allocated for the transaction and release the locks on the backup replica.

If we read the backup replica immediately after performing a read it is theoretically possible to not see our own updates to a row if we read using Read Committed (this reads the latest committed row, a locked row is still not committed). Thus default tables always use the primary replica to read in Read Committed mode to avoid this anomaly.

When deciding how to make it possible to read the backup replicas we opted for making this a table option. For tables that use this option we will delay sending the commit acknowledge to the application until we've completed the transaction and released the locks on the backup replicas. Thus tables using this table option will always be able to read the backup replicas when reading in Read Committed mode.

An alternative would have been to always be able to read from the nearest replica and allow for random reads that will not see your own updates. This will have the best throughput for both read and write. But we decided to value the feature to see your own updates higher than the absolutely shortest response time.

An example application is an application using SQL that have two data nodes, two MySQL Servers and each MySQL Server is colocated with one data node. In this case all SELECT queries can be completely localised to one computer and we have no network bandwidth worries for the application, only updates traverse the network to the other node.

In this example application it is very clear that if the application is doing heavy read activity it is a good idea to use this Read Backup feature. For tables that do a lot of writes the choice is not as obvious since the Read Backup feature delays response to the writes. It doesn't affect the throughput, but it does affect the latency of write transactions.

23.1.1 READ BACKUP SYNTAX

When creating the table the following should be placed in the comment section of the CREATE TABLE statement.

COMMENT="NDB_TABLE=READ_BACKUP=1"

It is also possible to set this as a MySQL configuration option. By settting the configuration option *ndb-read-backup* to 1 all tables created in the MySQL Server will be using this property (it will not affect tables that are changed using ALTER TABLE).

It is also possible to set this property in an ALTER TABLE statement. If only this feature is changed in the ALTER TABLE statement the change will be an online alter table statement.

When used in an ALTER TABLE statement only properties actually changed in the COMMENT section will be changed. E.g. if the READ_BACKUP feature was previously set and we now change some other property in the comment section, it will not affect the value of the READ_BACKUP property after the ALTER TABLE statement.

23.2 FULLY REPLICATED TABLES

A similar feature to Read Backup is fully replicated tables. A fully replicated table means that the table will have one replica in each node of the cluster instead of one replica per node in a node group. If we have an 8-node cluster with 4 node groups with 2 nodes in each, we would normally have splitted the table into at least 4 parts (possibly more parts). However for a fully replicated table each node group will contain the full table and all data will be fully replicated in all 8 nodes of the cluster.

The table is implemented as a normal table where updates use an internal triggering that always first updates the first node group and then an internal trigger ensures that all the other node groups also receive the update. The changes are always transactional, thus we always guarantee that we write all available replicas.

This is very nice for clusters that want to scale reads. We can have up to 48 data nodes that are colocated with MySQL Servers using a shared memory transporter thus scaling reads to many millions of SQL queries towards the shared data. We can still handle hundreds of thousands of updates on this data per second.

Another type of usage for fully replicated tables is so called dimensional tables, small fact tables that are often used in SELECT statements but rarely updated and used together with large tables containing references to these smaller tables.

Fully replicated tables gives a lot more options for how to design scalable applications using MySQL Cluster. In particular we expect it to enhance performance when executing complex join operations that makes use of the pushdown join feature presented in a later chapter.

23.2.1 FULLY REPLICATED TABLE SYNTAX

When creating the table one uses the comment section to set the fully replicated table property as shown here in the CREATE TABLE or ALTER TABLE statement.

COMMENT="NDB_TABLE=FULLY_REPLICATED=1"

It is possible to set it as a configuration option in the MySQL Server with the *ndb-fully-replicated* variable. This will ensure that all tables in the MySQL Server use the fully replicated table property when creating new tables while this configuration option is set. This option will have no effect on ALTER TABLE statements.

Setting a table to be fully replicated also means that it will have the read backup property set. Reads on a fully replicated table can use any node in the cluster for reading.

When setting this feature in a table using ALTER TABLE it will use a copying alter table statement.

It is possible to reorganise the fully replicated table to handle new added node groups as an online alter table using the command *ALTER TABLE algorithm=inplace, REORGANIZE*. No downtime is needed to scale the cluster to use new node groups for fully replicated tables (similar with normal tables).

23.3 PARTITIONING OF TABLES

MySQL Cluster is a distributed DBMS, thus all tables are always partitioned even if not specifically declared to be so. The default partitioning key is the primary key. If no primary key exists a unique key is used as primary key. If neither a primary key nor a unique key is defined on the table a primary key is constructed with an extra hidden column added, this column has a unique value that is a sequence number.

The MySQL Server supports specifying partitioning. With MySQL Cluster we only support one variant of partitioning and this is *PARTITION BY KEY*. It is possible to specify *PARTITION BY KEY()* in which case the primary key is used. Otherwise a list of columns is defined as the partitioning key. These columns must be a subset of the columns used for the primary key.

It is often a good idea to be careful in selecting the partitioning key. Often it is good to have the same partitioning key in a set of tables. A good example of this is the TPC-C benchmark. All of the tables in TPC-C (except for the item table that describes the products) has a warehouse id as part of the table. The customers are linked to a warehouse, a warehouse is connected to a district, orders and order lines comes from warehouses and stock is also per warehouse.

In the TPC-C benchmark it is natural to use the warehouse id as the partitioning key. In todays world of big data it is very common to use a sharding key to split up the application. To find the proper partitioning key for a set of tables is the same problem as when selecting a sharding key for a set of databases that works together in a shard.

In HopsFS that implements a meta data server for a distributed file system on top of NDB Cluster the partitioning key for the inodes table is id of the parent inode. Thus all inodes of a certain directory are all in the same partition.

MySQL Cluster has a number of similarities with a sharded set of databases. The main difference is that NDB is much more tightly integrated and supports queries and transactions that spans many shards.

By default the number of partitions is set to ensure that the primary replicas of each fragment is balanced on all *ldm* threads in all nodes of the cluster. In a cluster with 2 replicas,

2 node groups and 4 *ldm* threads this means that the default table will have 16 partitions in those 16 *ldm* threads. Thus since each partition has two replicas it means that each *ldm* thread will handle one primary fragment replica and one backup fragment replica.

If we add another node group this means that we will add another 8 partitions. To perform this change one uses the command below on each table.

```
mysql> ALTER TABLE tab_name algorithm=inplace, REORGANIZE PARTITION;
```

It is possible to create a table with a specific number of partitions. In this case there is no guarantee of any balance at all among the *ldm* threads. In this case it is possible to add a specific number of partitions as an online operation.

The variant that is recommended is to use the keyword *PARTITION_BALANCE* to set a balanced number of partitions. We will describe these in a section below after some introductory remarks on how we partition.

23.3.1 HASHMAP PARTITIONING

One important feature of MySQL Cluster is the ability to add new nodes to the cluster with the cluster up and running. In order to take advantage of these new nodes we must be able to perform an online reorganisation of the tables in the cluster. What this means is that we need to add more partitions to the cluster while the cluster is fully operational and can handle both reads and writes.

In order to ensure that such an online reorganisation can execute without requiring extra memory in the already existing nodes a scheme was invented called hashmap partitioning.

The partitioning happens by calculating a hash value based on the partitioning key values. Normally this value would be using linear hashing to decide which partition a row is stored in. However the linear hashing algorithm is not sufficiently balanced for our requirements. It will grow nicely, but it will not grow in steps that are adequate for our needs.

Another layer was invented called a hashmap. Each row is mapped into a hashmap, by default there are e.g. 3840 hashmaps in a table. If we have 4 partitions each partition will have 960 hashmaps. If we decide to add 4 more partitions there will be 8 partitions and in that case we will instead have 480 hashmaps per partition. Each partition will need to move 480 hashmaps to another partition (thus half of the data).

The hashmaps are balanced as long as the number of partitions is evenly divisible with the number of hashmaps. The number 3840 is equal to 2*2*2*2*2*2*2*2*3*5. For a large number of selections of number of node groups and number of *ldm* threads in MySQL Cluster it will be divisible with 3840 although not all. If they are not divisible it means a small imbalance (and thus loss of memory in some nodes that are less occupied than others). The impact is small even when there is an imbalance.

23.3.2 USER DEFINED PARTITIONING

The MySQL Server makes it possible to define Hash partitioning, List partitioning, Range partitioning and Range column partitioning. These are not supported by MySQL Cluster but they can still be made to work in a partial manner.

To use those types of partitioning one need to start the MySQL Server with the *--new* parameter.

When using these types of partitioning the data is only accessible from the MySQL Server. The reason is that the partitioning function is currently not possible to push down to the data nodes in NDB. This means that the normal backup isn't sufficient to backup the tables. It is necessary to backup the *frm*-files in addition, where the partitioning ranges and functions are saved.

It isn't possible to change the partitioning, this means that add partition, drop partition and reorganize partition doesn't work with those tables other than as offline operations.

Since MySQL Cluster is very much focused on online operation we have decided to not support this type of partitioning although it still works.

23.4 CONSIDERATIONS FOR SELECTING NUMBER OF PARTITIONS

Normal tables are distributed with equal burden on all *ldm* threads in the cluster. To achieve this each *ldm* thread has one primary replica of the table and also a backup replica. Thus with a 4-node cluster with 4 *ldm* threads per node there will be 16 partitions in the table and thus one primary replica and one backup replica per *ldm* thread.

For large tables and for tables that are heavily updated this makes sense. If we have many small tables that are rarely used it would make sense to have fewer number of partitions for these tables. In this case mostly to minimise the amount of files to open and close at checkpoints and the amount of schema memory to use.

It also makes a lot of sense to decrease the number of partitions in a table where range scans are often performed on all partitions. Assume we run on a large cluster with 8 data nodes where each data node contains 16 LDM threads. In this case a default table distribution maps the table into 128 partitions. For primary key reads and writes this have no negative impact, for partition pruned index scans neither. If you have written a highly scalable application this have very little consequence.

So in other words if you have written an application that makes use of the sharding key (== partition key) in all queries, the application is scalable even with very many partitions.

For an application that uses a lot of queries that don't define the sharding key on index scans and the scan is looking for small amount of data the overhead will be high since there is a startup cost of each ordered index scan. In this example one needs to execute 256 index scans, one on each partition.

In this case if the table is small and the table isn't a major portion of the CPU load, it could make sense to decrease the amount of partitions in the table.

By setting the partition balance we can adjust the number of partitions in a table.

Selecting a high number of partitions means that we spread the load of accessing the table evenly among the *ldm* thread. Thus we minimise the risk of any CPU bottlenecks.

Selecting a high number of partitions increases the overhead of each index scan that is not pruned to one partition and similarly for full table scans. The choice of partitioning scheme is a balance act between balanced CPU usage and minimum overhead per scan.

Selecting the default mechanism also provides a possibility to use extra CPU threads to rebuild ordered index as part of a restart. The default mechanism is the natural selection for a highly scalable application. But for less scalable applications and special tables it might make sense to change the partitioning scheme to a scheme that have a smaller overhead for less optimised queries.

23.5 PARTITION BALANCE

Using partition balance we can decrease the previous example to use 4 partitions instead of 256 partitions. Each partition is located in one LDM thread which can be executed by one CPU. Thus it is important to ensure that for tables with a lot of usage one should be careful to not decrease the number of partitions too far.

Even before version 7.5 it was possible to set explicit number of partitions on a table. In 7.5 we added a number of special table options to change the number of partitions in the table. These options are designed to ensure that we still get balanced load among the *ldm* threads. Setting specific number of partitions is still possible but this gives less balance between the nodes and the *ldm* threads.

We have two dimensions of balance. We can balance for usage with Read Primary replica, thus we want primary replicas to be balanced among the nodes and *ldm* threads. We can balance for usage with Read Any replica and in this case we balance the replicas among the node groups and *ldm* threads.

The second dimension is whether to balance one all *ldm* threads or whether to only balance between the nodes/node groups.

23.5.1 ONE PRIMARY PARTITION PER EACH LDM IN CLUSTER, *FOR_RP_BY_LDM*

This is the default mechanism, it stores one primary fragment replica in each *ldm* thread in each node. Thus the total number of partitions is the number of nodes multiplied by number of *ldm* threads.

Balancing for read primary replica on each *ldm* thread is the default behaviour. Thus we will get one partition for each *ldm* thread in the cluster. Thus if we have 4 nodes and 4 *ldm* threads per node we will have *4 * 4 = 16* partitions in the table.

This will always bring perfect balance among the *ldm* threads and this is why this is the default option.

This option have the most partitions among the standard partitioning options. This is desirable for a default option since it makes it easier to parallelise restarts execution.

This option is called *FOR_RP_BY_LDM*.

23.5.2 ONE PRIMARY PARTITION PER LDM PER NODE GROUP, *FOR_RA_BY_LDM*

This is the natural mechanism to use for read backup tables and fully replicated tables, it stores one primary fragment replica in each *ldm* thread in each node group. Thus the total number of partitions is the number of node groups multiplied by number of *ldm* threads.

If we mainly use the read backup feature and mainly use Read Committed and not *SELECT*

... *LOCK IN SHARED MODE* so much, it is sufficient to balance the load by ensuring that each *ldm* thread have one fragment replica per table. Since all fragment replicas are almost used as much there is no special need to have multiple fragment replicas per *ldm* thread.

Thus in the case of 4 nodes with 4 *ldm* threads we will have 16 fragment replicas and with 2 replicas this means we will have 8 partitions per table.

This partitioning balance is interesting for tables that have a fair amount of scans on all partitions that still need it to be balanced on all *ldm* threads.

This option is called *FOR_RA_BY_LDM*.

23.5.3 ONE PRIMARY PARTITION PER NODE, *FOR_RP_BY_NODE*

This mechanism stores one primary fragment replica in one *ldm* thread in each node. Thus the total number of partitions is the number of nodes.

In case we decide to not balance a table among *ldm* threads we still want it balanced among all the nodes. Not balancing among nodes would mean that we would use different amount of CPU resources in different nodes and this would create imbalances that would be hard to predict for a user.

Under the hood we will try to balance those tables among the *ldm* threads although this will not be perfect in any sense.

We can still decide whether to balance for read primary replicas or for read of any replica. This one balances for read of primary replica. For a normal cluster with 2 replicas this means that each node have 2 fragment replicas in two different *ldm* threads. This sometimes strike a nice balance between CPU resources available for the table and minimising the number of partitions in the table.

Thus in the case of 4 nodes with 4 *ldm* threads we will have 4 partitions per table.

This option is called *FOR_RP_BY_NODE*.

23.5.4 ONE PRIMARY PARTITION PER NODE GROUP, *FOR_RA_BY_NODE*

This is the minimal mechanism, it stores one primary fragment replica in one *ldm* thread per node group. Thus the total number of partitions is the number of node groups.

This partitioning option is the one that gives the least amount of partitions. Thus it is very useful for tables that have mostly index scans on all partitions and for small tables rarely used but still desiring balance among the nodes in the cluster.

It is useful to decrease overhead of many small tables in the cluster while still maintaining a balance of memory usage on all nodes in the cluster.

Thus in the case of 4 nodes with 4 *ldm* threads and 2 replicas we will have 2 partitions per table.

This option is called *FOR_RA_BY_NODE*.

23.5.5 SYNTAX FOR PARTITION BALANCE

This table option is only settable in the COMMENT section when you create a table and when you alter a table.

COMMENT="NDB_TABLE=PARTITION_BALANCE=FOR_RA_BY_NODE"

It is possible to set several properties in the comment section at the same time like this:

COMMENT="NDB_TABLE=READ_BACKUP=1,

PARTITION_BALANCE=FOR_RA_BY_NODE"

Going from a partition balance to another can be done as an online alter table operation if the number of partitions increase. It will be a copying alter table statement if the number of partitions decrease.

The partitioning balance can be used for fully replicated tables. It is not possible to change the PARTITION_BALANCE as an online alter table option for fully replicated tables. It is possible to add new node groups to the fully replicated table as an online alter table statement.

23.6 SETTING EXPLICIT NUMBER OF PARTITIONS

As mentioned previously it is still ok to explicitly set the number of partitions. This provides no guarantees on balance, but we will still attempt to balance the load among nodes and *ldm* threads as much as possible.

Once a table have set a specific number of partitions it cannot be changed to any other partitioning option as an online alter table statement. It cannot be reorganized using the REORGANIZE keyword. It can increase the number of explicit partitions as an online alter table statement.

Thus the setting of explicit number of partitions gives the user complete control over the number of partitions per table if this control is desirable. It does not provide control of the placement of these partitions.

The PARTITION_BALANCE options makes it possible to control the number of partitions even when adding new node groups and still maintaining a good balance between the nodes and the *ldm* threads.

Setting explicit number of partitions is done using the normal partitioning syntax. Adding e.g PARTITIONS 4 after specifying the PARTITION BY KEY and the list of fields for key partitioning gives explicit number of partitions.

23.7 NO REDO LOGGING

Normally all tables are fully recoverable. There are applications where data changes so rapidly that it doesn't make sense to recover the data. An example is a stock exchange application where data is changed hundreds of thousands of times per second and the amount of data is very small. Thus in the case of a cluster crash and returning a few minutes later the data is no longer current.

In this case we can optimise the table by removing writes to the REDO log and removing writes to the local checkpoints for the table. This removes around 30% of the overhead in performing updates on the table.

23.7.1   NOLOGGING SYNTAX

To enable this feature can be done as a table option. This table option can not be changed as an online alter table statement. It uses the COMMENT section in the same fashion as the read backup, partition balance and fully replicated features.

COMMENT="NDB_TABLE=NOLOGGING=1"

By setting the MySQL configuration option *ndb-table-no-logging* to one we ensure that all tables created in this connection will use the NOLOGGING feature.

23.8   SCHEMA CONSIDERATIONS

We've already mentioned that all primary keys and unique keys by default define an extra ordered index on top of the distributed hash index that is always part of a primary key and unique key. Adding *USING HASH* to an index definition is a method to avoid the ordered index if it isn't needed.

We've discussed to use disk columns for columns that you don't expect to add any indexes to. This is useful if you have a fast disk, such as SSDs or NVMe's to store your tablespaces in. Using hard drives is technically ok, but the difference between the access time to a hard drive and the access time to memory is so great that it is very unlikely that the user experience will be any good.

Nowadays there are disks that can handle many, many thousands of IO operations per seconds (IOPS), while at the same time the access time is measured in tens of microseconds. These are useful even when compared to using memory.

We've discussed the possibility to use fully replicated tables in some cases to get faster access for read and various partitioning variants.

One more consideration that we haven't mentioned is to consider the recovery algorithms.

In MySQL Cluster all deletes, updates and inserts are written to a REDO log. This REDO log is a logical change log, thus the amount of log information is proportional to the actual change made. Only the changed columns are logged in the REDO log.

In addition we execute local checkpoints, these will write all the rows at checkpoint time. Rows that are updated very often will only be written once per checkpoint. The checkpoint always writes the full row.

Similarly for disk columns we write an UNDO log where the size of what we write is dependent on the total column size. The consequence of this is that the amount of data we write to the checkpoints is dependent on the size of the rows.

This means that if we have information that is very often updated there can be reasons to put this data in a separate table to avoid having to checkpoint columns that are mostly read-only. Naturally there can be many reasons for those columns to be in the same table as well and for most applications this particular issue is not a concern at all. As with any optimisation one should measure and ensure that it is worthwhile using it before applying it.

CHAPTER 24

MySQL Concepts in NDB storage engine

There are quite a number of different concepts that exists in MySQL. These concepts are developed such that they work for any storage engine. There is one thing that differs with NDB compared to a traditional MySQL storage engine. This is the fact that the NDB storage engine is connected to a cluster. In this cluster there can be many more MySQL Servers, creating something in one MySQL Server doesn't automatically create it in all MySQL Servers connected to the cluster. In this chapter we will discuss many of those concepts and how they work in NDB.

24.1 MySQL Queries

Queries are the normal *SELECT, INSERT, UPDATE, DELETE* queries and a few more special query variants. These queries are used to read and write the data. This is an area where the syntax used to query tables in e.g. InnoDB and in NDB is the same. The performance characteristics will differ and as mentioned the consistency model differs, but a query executed will be executable towards NDB and other storage engines. A query is executed in one MySQL Server and as soon as it has executed it is gone, there is no relation to other MySQL Servers for the query.

24.2 MySQL Databases

MySQL Databases are created from the MySQL Server. A database is automatically created in the cluster when it is created in one MySQL Server. Under the hood there is no special handling of different databases in NDB. The database is present in the internal table name of tables in NDB. This is the only handling of databases in NDB.

24.3 MySQL Triggers

Triggers comes into play with writes to the database. A trigger is fired and completely handled within one MySQL Server. This is the case for NDB.

NDB does currently not propagate the trigger definition to all other MySQL Servers. If one wants a trigger to be executed on the table in the cluster it is necessary to add the trigger on all MySQL Servers in the cluster.

MySQL triggers is something to be a bit careful with. The reason is that it is only executed in MySQL Servers. Given that tables in MySQL Cluster can also be accessed using the NDB API, ClusterJ and other direct APIs, it is important to consider this when using triggers.

If triggers are used to maintain some sort of constraint, this constraint must be maintained also by direct NDB applications that are not using the MySQL Servers.

24.4   MySQL Views

Views are a method to make it appear as if a table exists that is only a view of the real data. Views could be used for security reasons or to make it simpler to access data.

Views works perfectly fine with NDB but it is important to remember that if a view is used in all MySQL Servers in the cluster, it has to be defined in all MySQL Servers in the cluster.

If a round robin router is used in front of the MySQL servers and the queries use a view it places special requirements that one has ensured that all those views are created in all MySQL Servers before they are used.

There are no problems related to views for the cluster, the views will not be seen from the NDB API, the NDB API will only see the real tables. A view is used when executing a query to translate the query into a more complex query. Thus the view is only related to the execution of a specific query. Thus views works fine with NDB as for any other storage engine. The only thing to remember is that a view is local to one MySQL Server and is not automatically replicated to other MySQL Servers in the same cluster.

24.5   MySQL Events

Events are a method to have special actions happen at predefined times. This again works perfectly fine with MySQL Cluster.

In this case it is not necessarily a good idea to install the event on all MySQL Servers. Events are often some actions that need to be taken at certain intervals. The action is quite likely an action for the cluster and not for one specific MySQL Server.

Since events often need to execute once per time period for a cluster it seems more likely that it is necessary to install the event in a few MySQL Servers. At the start of the event processing one could check some special event table that ensures that the event is only executed once per time period. In this manner the MySQL Servers will discover that someone else already has executed the event.

It is fairly straightforward to handle MySQL events in MySQL Cluster and it is fairly easy to even make events such that they are highly available.

24.6   MySQL Stored Procedures

Stored procedures is defined per MySQL Server. If it is needed in all MySQL Servers, it has to be created in all MySQL Servers.

Defining a stored procedure is local to the MySQL Server it is executed on. There is nothing special with stored procedures for NDB, they are executed as any other stored procedure in MySQL. A stored procedure is a language to execute several SQL queries with one query call. The interpreter for this SQL language executes within one MySQL Server.

The impact on NDB by stored procedures is the same as if there was an application program executing multiple SQL queries towards one MySQL Server.

24.7 MySQL Functions

MySQL functions is very similar to stored procedures. There is nothing special about using MySQL functions for NDB compared to a MySQL Server using InnoDB.

24.8 MySQL User Management

User management in MySQL Cluster can be handled as a cluster-wide property. It is also possible to handle it separately for each MySQL Server in the cluster.

To prepare the cluster for distributed user management, the user table have to be converted to an NDB table. We won't go through the details of how to do this in this book, check the MySQL manual if you want to use distributed user management.

24.9 MySQL Transactions

Executing transactions in MySQL translates into transactions in NDB. Any transaction executed in MySQL Cluster involving only NDB tables will be executing a distributed transaction in the NDB data nodes. There is no support for transactions with multiple storage engines in one transaction.

24.10 Savepoints

In MySQL we can declare savepoints in a transaction that we can roll back to. This is not supported for transactions involving NDB tables, a rollback will always roll back the transaction entirely.

24.11 MySQL Prepared Statements

Prepared statements are a way to avoid parsing and optimizing a query each time it is executed. This means that the MySQL Server will store a part of the query plan for the execution of the query and use this the next time the user wants to execute this query. This works fine for NDB tables, there is nothing special about MySQL Cluster here. Each MySQL Server prepares queries independent of all other MySQL Servers in the cluster.

24.12 MySQL Explain statements

MySQL has a special statement called EXPLAIN. This statement is used by the database developer to understand how a specific query is executed. There are some variants that are specific to MySQL Cluster using NDB tables. One thing is that we can pushdown a join to the cluster. This means that a large part of the join execution is handled in the NDB data nodes.

Explains list one line per table in a join operation and lists how this table is accessed and how it is joined to the other tables. A set of tables can be pushed down as a whole to the NDB storage engine such that they are executed together. If this pushes down evaluation of some conditions the speedup can be quite significant.

There are other things such as condition pushdown, execution of batched key access and many other techniques that will have a major impact on query execution time and that can be viewed in the EXPLAIN statement. There are many more details on this in the MySQL manual that explains in more detail how the EXPLAIN command works in MySQL Cluster.

24.13 TABLE LOCKS

At the moment the lock tables and unlock tables are only handled locally in one MySQL Server. We currently do not support lock tables that lock tables over the entire cluster. It only locks it within one MySQL Server. The only safe way of excluding access to a table is to use the single user mode described in the chapter on NDB management client.

24.14 XA SUPPORT

MySQL Cluster doesn't support running transactions in XA level.

CHAPTER 25

ALTERING A TABLE

In this chapter we will cover how we can change the meta data in MySQL Cluster. In most cases it can be done as an online operation.

Any time spent altering meta data and not allowing writes to the tables in parallel means downtime. Therefore much resources have been spent to ensure that most normal meta data changes can be done online.

One problem is that the storage engine API doesn't allow for a true online operation in the MySQL Server that performs the meta data change. Thus as will be discussed in a later chapter it is necessary to perform meta data changes in a specialised MySQL Server that is only used for meta data changes (at least at the time the meta data changes are performed).

25.1 ONLINE META DATA OPERATIONS

25.1.1 ONLINE CREATE TABLE

Creating a new table and dropping a table is obvious online operations. All meta data operations are performed as distributed schema transactions. For example when creating a table we create a base table, zero or more ordered indexes, zero or more unique index tables, zero or more BLOB tables, zero or more foreign keys and internal triggers to keep indexes up to date. All of those are created atomically.

This requires a stepwise approach where each step in the creation process is recorded on disk to ensure that we can roll forward or roll it back in recovery situations. Due to this stepwise approach the create table statements takes a bit of time. A few tables per second can be created in MySQL Cluster. Speed of meta data operations isn't the focus in NDB, the availability for reads and writes during those operations is rather the focus.

If MySQL Cluster Replication is activated it will be an integral part of the create table statement to ensure that the create table is replicated to the slave clusters. This increases the time to execute the create table statement. The create table statement have to be synchronised with all MySQL Servers that are used for binary logging and we have to synchronise writes of data and meta data changes.

From this we deduce that meta data operations are online, but they are not necessarily fast. The focus of meta data operations is that they are properly synchronised with all cluster nodes and synchronised with slave clusters. NDB is focused on applications where meta data changes are done in relation to software upgrades that happen, but are rare compared to the number of user data transactions and queries.

25.1.2 ONLINE DROP TABLE

Drop table is an online operation. One complication for drop table is when scans on the table is still ongoing at the time when the drop table is issued, we can also have a number of internal recovery operations that could be ongoing for the table. In this case we might have to wait for a short time until the drop table is completed. As part of drop table we remove all files that are specific to the table and extents of any tablespaces are free'd up as part of drop table. Similarly the memory connected to the table is released.

25.1.3 ONLINE CREATE ORDERED INDEX

Adding a new ordered index starts by creating a new index table. This involves adding internal triggers on update, delete and insert operations that ensure that the ordered index is kept up-to-date.

This operation is online such that no writes will be blocked by the creation of this new index. The operation will take some time, the table have to be scanned and for each row the row will be inserted into the index and internal triggers will ensure that the index is kept up-to-date.

During an update we know if the ordered index scan build has reached the row we are updating since each row has a row id and the build scan is scanning in row id order. The index contains a sorted list of row ids. The sort order is based on the index columns and whether the index is ascending or descending.

The creation of a new ordered index can take substantial time for large tables, but it will run without interfering with user transactions other than that it will use new memory resources and will use CPU resources for the index build.

Ordered indexes are always in memory, all ordered indexes are rebuilt as part of all node restarts and cluster restarts. This rebuild is an offline build that happens when the node isn't involved in any transaction.

The *ndb_restore* program have the ability to create new ordered indexes that are built as an offline operation. Thus the creation of the index is much faster, but it isn't an online operation. A restore of a backup isn't expected to happen in parallel with user transactions.

25.1.4 ONLINE DROP ORDERED INDEX

Dropping an index only releases the memory and removes the meta data about the index. As when you drop a table we will wait for up to 5 seconds for any scans that are still using the ordered index.

25.1.5 ONLINE CREATE UNIQUE INDEX

Creating a unique index means creating a real table. The table is special in that it cannot be accessed as a table, it can only be used to access the main table.

Internally it is a normal table. This table have a hash index as all other tables in NDB. It doesn't have any other indexes. It is possible to handle cases where a column amongst the unique index columns value can be NULL.

The table is recoverable if the main table is. There is a trigger from the main table to the unique index table ensuring that any updates on the unique index columns in the main table will be reflected in the unique index table. An update leads to both a delete and an insert. An insert leads to an insert in the unique index table and a delete leads to a delete in the unique index table.

25.1.6 ONLINE DROP UNIQUE INDEX

Dropping a unique index is similar to dropping a table, it removes the memory, the files and the internal triggers for the unique index table.

25.1.7 ONLINE CREATE/DROP FOREIGN KEY

A foreign key have two components. The first component is an index on the reference columns in the child table. The second component are triggers that verify that the foreign key constraint isn't broken by any updates.

As part of creating a foreign key one needs to scan the data to verify that existing data meets the foreign key constraints.

25.2 ONLINE ADD COLUMN

Adding one or more new columns to a table can be an online operation that is merely changing the meta data. For the operation to be online the column must be an in-memory column and it has to use the DYNAMIC format. In addition the new columns must be NULLable columns or they need to have a default value. NULL or the default value is the value of all rows for the new column after adding the column.

The internal row structure have three variants of implementing a column. One variant is fixed size, in this case the column have a fixed size which is the maximum size of the column. The second variant is variable sized columns. In this case there is at least two bytes for the column that provides the pointer to the column within the row and if NULLable there is also a bit in the NULL bit array. Both of these variants can only be added when the table is created or when the table is altered using the offline algorithm (the offline algorithm creates a new table and copies data over to the new table).

The third variant is to place the column in the DYNAMIC part. In this part columns are only present if they have a value different from the NULL or default value. So adding a column in this part can happen by simply changing the meta data and there is immediately a new column in the row. Accessing a column in the DYNAMIC part is more costly, but a lot more flexible.

When defining a column it is possible to specify whether it should be using the FIXED format, the DYNAMIC format or if it should use the DEFAULT format. The default format is the FIXED format.

When adding a new column one can specify whether the column is an in-memory column or if it is a disk column. The default is in-memory columns, the default can be changed on the table level by setting the STORAGE to DISK on table level.

25.3 ONLINE CREATE TABLESPACE

Tablespaces are used to store the disk columns. Each table with disk columns need to use a specific tablespace. Tablespaces can be added as part of the configuration using the *InitialTablespace* configuration variable. In this case the tablespace is added as part of the initial start of the cluster.

New tablespaces can be added as online operations. A tablespace cannot be used until it has been created, a tablespace can only be used in a table if the table is created after the tablespace is created.

In a tablespace we can have one or more data files. The first data file is always added as part of creating the tablespace.

When a tablespace is created one needs to define the extent size. The extent size is the unit of allocation from the tablespace to a table. When an insert to a table needs a free page and there are no more free pages in the extents connected to the table, a new extent have to be allocated from the tablespace. When creating a tablespace one sets the size of the tablespace by setting the initial size of the tablespace. This is the size of the first file added to the tablespace.

Creating a tablespace can be a lengthy process since the data file will have to be initialised. The reason for this is that otherwise the OS will not ensure that the actual disk space needed for the file is allocated and this could cause the tablespace to become full even without using the full size specified.

25.3.1 ONLINE ADD DATAFILE TO TABLESPACE

It is possible to add new data files to an existing tablespace. The only things to set here are the file name of the new data file and the initial size of the data file (the size cannot be extended after it is added, only new files can be added).

25.3.2 DROP TABLESPACE AND DATA FILES

Data files and tablespaces can be dropped as online operations as well. But they can only be dropped if they are completely empty. Extents allocated to a table can only be released by dropping the table. The allocation from a table is not directed to any specific data file. It is only practical to drop an entire tablespace, individual data files can only be dropped immediately after they were added before they had been used the first time.

25.4 ONLINE CREATE LOGFILE GROUP

Disk columns need an UNDO log in addition to the tablespace. The UNDO logs are managed by the logfile group that each tablespace need. When creating a tablespace one need to define a logfile group this tablespace is using. Currently we can only have one logfile group.

A logfile group can be created from the configuration by using the configuration parameter *InitialLogfileGroup*. It can also be created using an SQL command. Either way we need a first log file, we need to set the size of the UNDO log buffer size connected to this logfile group and we need to set the initial size of the log file.

Log files are initialised when created, the command is online, but will take some time.

25.4.1 ONLINE ADD LOGFILE TO LOGFILEGROUP

New log files can be added at any time to the UNDO log. We need to set the name of the file and the initial size of the file. Also here the file needs to be initialised when added and the command is an online command.

25.5 ONLINE ADD NODE

Most users of MySQL Cluster will start out with a small 2-node cluster with 2 replicas. If the usage of the cluster increases it is important to be able to add new nodes to the cluster.

To add a new node there are two steps needed. First of all one can only add entire node groups currently. If the cluster uses 2 replicas we have to add 2 nodes at a time. After adding a new node group the existing tables need to be reorganised to use the new node group(s).

25.5.1 ADD A NEW NODE GROUP

The first step in adding a new node group is to add the new nodes to the configuration. These new nodes should be configured with *NodeGroup* configuration parameter set to 65536. Thus the node is not part of any node group. Thus other nodes will setup the communication paths to these nodes, but the nodes will not yet be used to store data. New tables created will not attempt to place table partitions into those nodes yet.

In principal it is possible to add these new nodes early on, the only problem with this is that the nodes will have to allocate memory for all send buffers to these nodes.

The change of configuration is covered in the chapter on programs and more specifically in the section on the NDB management server.

Adding a new node group is an online operation and it is a schema transaction that is atomically done. It is executed using the *ndb_mgm* client. The command to add two new nodes 3 and 4 to an existing cluster with node 1 and 2 in the first existing node group is done like this:

CREATE NODEGROUP 3,4

After this command is completed the new node group is created and used when new tables are created. The creation of a new node group is a fairly quick operation.

The creation of tablespaces and logfile groups are performed during the first start of the new nodes. This is not part of the creation of new node groups. Starting up a new node for the first time can take some time to complete even though no data needs to be transferred to the node during restart.

It is possible to drop a node group, but it can only be done if the node group is empty.

25.5.2 NEW TABLES

Immediately after creating a new node group any new table will use the new node group.

25.5.3 REORGANISE EXISTING TABLES

After adding one or more new node groups it is recommended to reorganise existing tables as well. This is done one table at a time by issuing the command:

```
mysql> ALTER TABLE tab_name algorithm=inplace, REORGANIZE PARTITION;
```

This command will be done online. It will take some time since the entire table have to be changed.

The algorithm used follows this procedure.

1. A number of new partitions are created in the new node groups

2. A table scan is started in each previously existing node

3. For each row we decide if the row should be copied to the new partitions

4. Wait for scan to complete

5. Start a new table scan on the previously existing node

6. Each row that was copied over will now be deleted

7. Wait for scan to complete

In parallel with this we ensure that each transaction will write to both the old node group and the new node group. In effect some of the rows will be in two partitions at the same time during the change.

Fully replicated tables are reorganised in a different manner. In this case there is no need to delete any rows since a new node group will increase the number of replicas.

25.6 OPTIMIZE TABLE

Optimize table is a command that removes fragmentation from the in-memory columns for the variable sized parts. A row in MySQL Cluster consists of up to 3 parts. The first part is the fixed part. The fixed part cannot be compacted since the row id is the reference to the row. Changing the row id would be very complex since it would create complex interactions with scan operations that happens in parallel with optimize table. The second part is the variable sized part of the rows. This stores all variable sized components and all dynamic columns. This part can be fragmented and this part is compacted by an *optimize table* operation. The third part is the disk columns part which are fixed size. Currently we don't support returning an extent to the tablespace. This part is not compacted as part of an *optimize table* operation.

Fixed size columns are much faster, but *DYNAMIC* columns are more flexible. If compacting memory is most important, one should use the *DYNAMIC* keyword on columns (or on the entire table). It is possible to set a configuration parameter such that all tables are created with *DYNAMIC* columns as the default.

25.7 REORGANISE TABLE

It is possible to reorganise a table also when the number of *ldm* threads have changed. Similarly if we change the *PARTITION_BALANCE* strategy from e.g. *FOR_RA_BY_NODE* to *FOR_RP_BY_NODE* a reorganise action can be performed. It is only possible to increase the number of partitions in a table, thus no decrease of number of partitions is currently possible as online operations.

An important thing to consider is that performing a reorganise table isn't a safe operation unless we're doing it in conjunction with add nodes. The reason is that we increase the memory size during the reorganise operation. For add node this is ok since the memory allocated is in new nodes that had no data previously. If we run out of memory during the reorganise operation we will roll back the change. This is not the most well tested part of MySQL Cluster. So one should ensure that there is sufficient amount of memory to perform the reorganise operation. Again reorganise operations in conjunction with add node are safe in this respect.

25.8 OFFLINE META DATA OPERATIONS

There are a few things that can only be done as offline operations. For the most part these things should be avoided. It is necessary to set a configuration variable in the MySQL Server to even allow those operations. The reason is that it is necessary to be aware of that an offline operation is invoked.

An offline operation requires some careful considerations. In MySQL Cluster we don't support locking a table in the entire cluster. The only safe method to use offline operations is to ensure that we have entered a special single user mode. If you are able to control all access to the cluster you can ensure that the table isn't updated. If you only access from MySQL Servers you can use

LOCK TABLES table_name READ;

This needs to be entered in all MySQL Servers in the cluster in that case.

25.8.1 SINGLE USER MODE

From the NDB management client there is a command to enter single user mode. This is primarily intended for safe use of *ALTER TABLE* statements that use the copy algorithm.

The command is *ENTER SINGLE USER MODE 55*.

Thus the API node with id 55 is now the only API node allowed to send requests to the cluster.

For offline operations you first enter single user mode for the MySQL Server. When starting this special MySQL Server you should ensure that it is started with the node id set in the startup parameters. Thus any changes this MySQL Server does while in single user mode is safe.

After completing the necessary changes you exit single user mode through the command:

EXIT SINGLE USER MODE

25.8.2 Operations that require offline operations

1. Drop column

2. Change to/from disk column

3. Change character set

4. Change column size

5. Change column data type

6. Change column memory placement

7. Truncate table

Drop column requires an offline operation.

To move a column from in-memory to disk or to move it from being a disk column to being an in-memory column requires an offline operation. This could include creating an index on the column as well when moving to in-memory.

Changing the character set of a column or of a table requires an offline operation.

Modifying a column to a new data type or change the size of a column requires an offline operation. Also moving from fixed size part to the *DYNAMIC* part.

All of these operations requires using the copy algorithm, thus a new table is created and row by row is copied over to the new table. When the copy is done the new table becomes the table and the old table is dropped.

Truncate table is an offline operation that will first drop the table and next the table is created again.

25.8.3 Online solutions to offline operations

Many users that need everything to be online often uses MySQL Cluster Replication. They have more than one cluster that is operational. These changes are often correlated to software changes. Often such a change starts by taking a backup in the cluster to change. Next the cluster is taken offline. Next the cluster software is upgraded. Next the meta data is restored again. In this restore it is possible to perform changes of column sizes, column data types, column storage, and how the columns are stored, columns can be dropped and columns and indexes can be added.

Next the data is restored again. The cluster is brought up again using binary log from the cluster that is still operational.

Next the second cluster need to be changed to the new software and new meta data. More details about how this can be achieved in detail will be provided in the chapter on *Multi-Site MySQL Cluster*.

Part VI

Concepts in MySQL Cluster

In the next set of chapters we will cover a number of very important concepts in MySQL Cluster. They are not absolutely necessary to understand NDB from an SQL view, but it certainly helps to understand those matters when designing scalable applications using MySQL Cluster.

The first chapter is the replication protocol used in MySQL Cluster. It is based on the traditional two-phase commit protocol where we have made it a non-blocking protocol. It is also designed to handle predictable latency while at the same time providing a consistent recovery from cluster crashes.

Many new implementations of DBMSs have opted to use various replication protocols based on quorum and various forms of eventual consistency. In MySQL Cluster we provide strong consistency at scale to ensure that application developers do not have to worry about where to send their requests.

The next chapter shows how MySQL Cluster routes read and write requests. This is performed in a transparent manner to the application. But to design applications that scales to millions of transactions per second it is essential to understand this chapter.

The development of the cloud in various forms have made data center implementations streamlined such that clouds have several data centers per cloud region. We have designed features in MySQL Cluster that takes into account the placement of nodes within a region in a cloud. This ensures that we can improve scalability of cloud installations and also provide the optimal latency of queries executed in a cloud.

Any scalable DBMS will have to consider how the consistency of the data is handled. In MySQL Cluster we have designed for easy application development where applications can see their own writes and that the data is immediately visible. All consistency models have different advantages and disadvantages and in the chapter on Concurrency Control we describe how we handle this in MySQL Cluster.

The final chapter in this part goes through a feature that is currently unique in the MySQL world, the ability to parallelise query execution. This is a feature with many names, but it is about pushing down joins from the MySQL Server to the data nodes. In this chapter we describe how this is done and the advantages this provides and also the current set of limitations of this feature.

## CHAPTER 26

NON-BLOCKING 2PC

A popular protocol to replicate changes between nodes in a distributed database is the two-phase commit protocol. Recently many systems have implemented other protocols that are more complex and most of them require three phases. The idea with the third phase is to avoid that the protocol is blocking.

In the two-phase commit protocol a node is blocked in the *prepare* phase until the transaction coordinator have spread its decision on whether the transaction was committed or not.

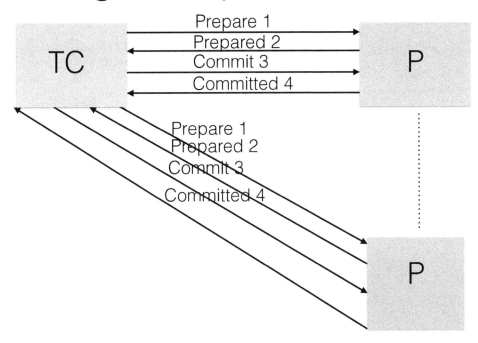

Original 2-phase Commit

The block here could mean that nodes have to keep locks for a long time waiting for a node to recover. This is not a desirable feature of a replication protocol.

We have also added a third phase, the complete phase. It is possible to reply to the application already after the second phase. We discussed this in an earlier chapter where we described the Read Backup feature.

26.1 Idea behind new two-phase commit protocol

In NDB we kept some of the ideas of the two-phase commit protocol, but we also changed a lot of important details in it.

Distributed commit combined with linear commit

One variant of the two-phase commit protocol is called linear commit protocol. This protocol sends the *prepare* message from first participant to last participant in serial order. Instead of returning to the transaction coordinator to commit the transaction, the transaction is committed in the last participant. Next the commit message is sent in serial order back to the first participant.

Linear 2-phase commit

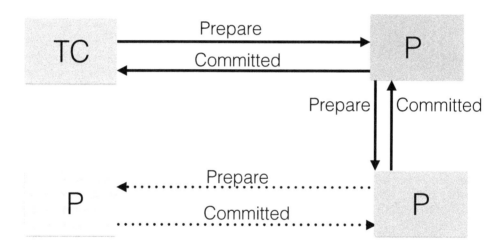

The original two-phase commit protocol uses $4 * n$ messages to complete a transaction (where n is the number of participant nodes in the transaction. The linear two-phase commit protocol uses $2 * (n - 1)$ instead. Thus the linear commit protocol saves more than half of the messages. This is very important for throughput.

At the same time latency of the original two-phase commit protocol is shorter. The latency of the original two-phase commit protocol is the latency of two rounds of parallel messages whereas the linear commit protocol gets longer as the number of nodes increases.

Given that we want to achieve scalability AND predictable latency it would be beneficial to use a combination the original protocol and the linear commit protocol.

Before presenting our new protocol, we mention that we use primary copy locking. Thus we need to lock the primary replica row before we lock the backup replica row. Failure to use this order can easily lead to deadlocks that could have been avoided.

Our idea is to use linear commit for one row, but to use the original commit protocol on each row. Thus the number of messages we will send will be $2 * m * (r + 1)$ (where m is number of rows in transaction set, and r is the number replicas). If we were to use the original commit protocol only we would send $m * 4 * r$.

An example with m, number of rows set to 10 and number of replicas (r) set to 2 will give 80 messages for original protocol and 60 messages for our new protocol. The latency of our protocol is much better compared to the linear commit protocol. The latency of our protocol is slightly worse to the original commit protocol. Given that we decreased the cost of communication we expect to get this latency loss back at high loads. We use a lot of piggybacking to ensure that the real number of messages is a lot lower.

DESCRIPTION OF NEW PROTOCOL

The figure below shows the new transaction protocol.

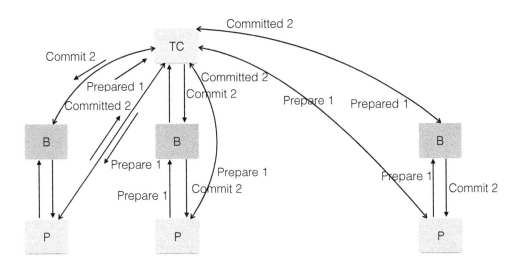

The idea is to start the *prepare* phase by going to the primary replica, this ensures that we minimise the risk of deadlocks. The risk of deadlocks is high in the original two-phase commit protocol since we can lock the replicas in different order for different transactions. This can lead to a deadlock even when the application has ensured a transaction ordering that is free from deadlocks.

The use of linear commit is important not only to minimise number of messages, but also to ensure that we avoid distributed deadlocks that make it very difficult to scale the application even if properly designed.

Next we move to the backup replicas and from there back to the transaction coordinator.

Now when it is time to commit the transaction we use the reverse linear order. The idea with this order is that it makes it possible to release the locks on the primary replica already in the commit phase. This has the advantage that if we route reads to the primary replica we can report transaction commit to the application already after the commit phase and still see our own updates. If we want to read any replica we still have to wait for the complete phase to complete before reporting the commit to the application.

The complete phase releases the locks in the backup replica. It also releases the memory attached to the transaction in the form of copy rows and operation records used to contain transaction state. A certain level of parallelism is used in the transaction commit where several rows can be committed in parallel and likewise for the complete phase.

26.2 ACHIEVING A NON-BLOCKING COMMIT PROTOCOL

Before we move on to prove that the new protocol is a non-blocking we need to make a few observations.

First, the transaction coordinator is no longer the commit point in the transaction. Instead the commit point is when the first primary replica decides to commit the transaction. Before the commit message arrives at the primary replica it has passed through all backup replicas. Thus at the commit point all replicas have decided on the commit.

All replicas reside within one node group in NDB, if all nodes within a node group fails, the cluster will also fail. Thus at a node failure that doesn't bring down the cluster we are certain that there is information in the surviving nodes to find out whether the transaction should commit or abort.

Thus we are never blocked by any node failure that doesn't cause a crash of the cluster.

If the cluster crashes completely we will always need recovery before transactions can start again. We can never become blocked in this case. Thus our commit protocol is a non-blocking protocol if we can make use of the information in the transaction participants to complete transactions after node failures.

We implement a *take-over protocol* to rebuild the transaction state of transactions that lost their transaction coordinator to ensure that we can always decide on commit or abort of any ongoing transactions in the cluster. More on this protocol below.

We have shown that our new two-phase commit protocol is a non-blocking protocol. There is no node failures that can cause transactions to hang waiting for nodes to recover before the transaction can complete.

If nodes are missing to complete the transaction it also means that there is insufficient amount of nodes to keep the cluster up and running. If the cluster crashes it will perform recovery and recover those transactions that are durable also on disk.

26.2.1 TAKE OVER PROTOCOL

The *take-over protocol* asks all nodes in the cluster to send information about any ongoing transaction where the failed node is transaction coordinator. The node asking is the master node that will take over the completion of these transactions.

After receiving all information about a set of transactions the new transaction coordinator will decide whether the transaction should be committed or aborted based on how far it got in the process. If any node heard a commit decision it will be committed. The new transaction coordinator will also inform the API of the transaction outcome.

This protocol will ensure that the transactions ongoing in the failed node, at the time of the crash, are completed before we report the node failure handling as completed. When node failure handling is completed we thus have none of the transactions still lingering in the surviving data nodes, they are all committed or aborted.

Similarly the API nodes have been informed of the transaction outcome with one exception. The exception is when using the read backup feature, in this case the transaction outcome is reported at complete. This means that the only remaining part of the transaction is the transaction coordinator when going to send the commit message. This transaction is handled by the message about the node failure handling being complete. If the transaction coordinator have failed and the node fail handling is completed and we haven't heard anything about transaction outcome, we know that the transaction is committed since this is the only reason for the transaction outcome message to not arrive.

We keep special commit ack information in the data nodes to ensure that the API can always be informed of the transaction outcome if the API itself survives.

26.3 GLOBAL CHECKPOINT PROTOCOL

NDB is designed for applications that require latencies that cannot be achieved when writing to a hard drive as part of the commit protocol. SSDs wasn't around at the time NDB was designed.

NDB uses Network Durability to implement the *D* in the term *ACID* (Atomic, Consistent, Isolated, Durable). Thus at commit time the transaction is committed in memory of multiple computers, thus it can survive any single point of failure of an entire computer and in many cases even multiple node failures.

26.3.1 FIRST PHASE OF GLOBAL CHECKPOINT PROTOCOL

Some mechanism is also required to ensure that the cluster recovers to a consistent state also after a complete cluster crash. It is not sufficient to simply write out the transaction logs to disk as soon as possible. To recover a consistent state of the database we need something more as well.

What we implemented here is a sort of group commit transaction. We call this group commit a *global checkpoint* (GCP). Each GCP is a consistent recoverable point at a cluster crash. We also use *micro GCPs*. These are not recoverable after a crash, they form *epochs* used to send batches of transaction over to a slave cluster.

We use *global checkpoints* for many things in our recovery mechanisms. Each time a transaction is about to commit it asks for a *global checkpoint id* (GCI). Normally it gets one of those immediately. If we are in the process of starting a new *GCP* there could be a small wait.

The process to start a new *global checkpoint* is the following. The master data node decides to create a new *global checkpoint*. It sends a message called *GCP_PREPARE* to all nodes in the cluster (including itself). It responds with a *GCP_PREPARECONF* message, next the master data node sends *GCP_COMMIT* to all nodes.

At reception of the *GCP_PREPARE* message the nodes starts blocking committers from proceeding. All the *prepare* phase activities are allowed to continue which means that the impact on throughput and latency is minimal. Impact on throughput is low since there will be more room for *prepare* messages, thus we can still keep the CPUs busy. Impact on latency is low since it only introduces an extra delay of a two-phase message and given that committers are blocked a little bit more CPU is available to handle this message faster. After 15 years of operation of the cluster we still have had no issues with this initial phase of the *global checkpoint protocol*. One more reason is that queueing the commits for a short time introduces a sort of batching of commits that improves throughput.

At reception of *GCP_COMMIT* the nodes will immediately resume the commit of the stalled transactions.

Now that we have created a new *global checkpoint* we have also at the same time completed the previous one. Given the two-phased approach we are certain that we get a proper serialisation point between the *global checkpoints*. We know that a *global checkpoint* contains a set of transactions and all these will either be recovered completely or not at all.

This means that when we recover a node we use the GCI to recover to know which transactions to restore.

Each COMMIT record in the transaction log (in our case only a REDO log) is tagged with the GCI of its transaction. We also use the GCI to make synchronisation of a starting node and a living node easy. We recover the starting node to a certain GCI, after that only the rows in the living node with a higher GCI need to be sent to the starting node to synchronize the rows in the nodes.

26.3.2   SECOND PHASE OF GLOBAL CHECKPOINT PROTOCOL

The second phase makes the completed GCI durable on disk. This phase starts already when receiving *GCP_COMMIT*.

The first step is that each node needs to wait until the transaction coordinators have completed the processing of all transactions belonging to the completed GCI. Normally this is fast since it mostly involves networking messages and memory operations. Large transactions have the possibility to increase the time for this phase. Commits of transactions changing many rows with disk columns can represent a challenge.

When all transactions in the *GCP* in the node are completed we will send the message *GCP_NODEFINISH* back to the master data node.

When all nodes have finished the commit phase of the *global checkpoint protocol* the next phase is to flush the REDO logs in all nodes. The message *GCP_SAVEREQ* is sent to all nodes to ask them to flush the REDO log up to the GCI. The REDO log implementation need to keep track of where the last commit message for this GCI is stored to know how much REDO log needs to be flushed.

When the flush of the REDO logs is complete the nodes respond with *GCP_SAVECONF*.

At this point there is enough information to recover this GCI. To simplify the recovery we use one more phase where we write a small system file that contains the recoverable GCI. This is accomplished by sending *COPY_GCIREQ* to all nodes that will respond with *COPY_GCICONF* when done.

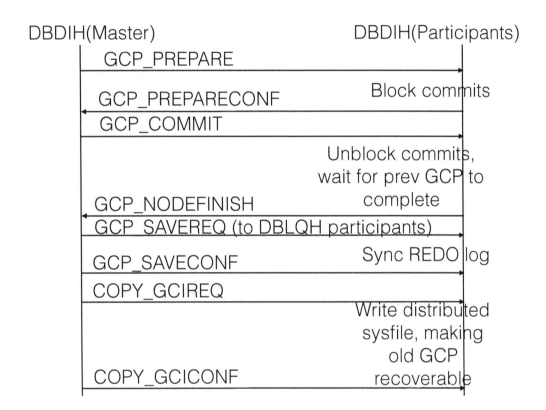

26.4 HANDLING CLUSTER CRASH

At a cluster crash we will use the information from the system file to discover which GCI to restore. To restore the data we will first install a local checkpoint. This local checkpoint will know how far back in the REDO log we need to start to ensure that we recover the data. More on the details of this in a later chapter.

Next we execute the REDO log executing all log records belonging to restored tables and with GCI smaller or equal to the restored GCI.

After that we have restored a consistent database, before the recovery is completed we execute a local checkpoint to avoid strange issues with multiple node crashes close to each other.

26.5   Impact of Read Backup feature

As mentioned the Read Backup feature changes the protocol slightly in that the response to
the API is done after the complete phase instead of after the commit phase. Thus making the
protocol into a true three-phase commit protocol. Only when reading primary replicas can we
use the optimisation to respond already after the second phase of the commit protocol.

26.6   Conclusions

The NDB transaction protocol is a bit involved since we have many different requirements on
it. The requirements are:

1. Avoid deadlocks using primary copy locking

2. The protocol must be non-blocking

3. It must be able to handle multiple node failures in all protocols

4. It must be able to handle multiple node failures in node failure handling

5. Minimise overhead of transaction protocol by decreasing amount of messages

6. Avoid writing to disk as part of commit phase to achieve predictable latency

7. Restore a consistent database after a cluster crash

8. Handle node restarts

Important to understand here is how the transaction protocol and the *global checkpoint
protocol* is actually both parts of the implementation of transactions.

What we have done is that we first use a special two-phase commit protocol to ensure that
we achieve Network Durability (committed in memory of several computers before sending
commit message to the application).

Next we perform a group commit of a set of transactions and make those transactions
durable.

Interestingly although I invented the ideas, it is really useful to describe those protocols to
fully understand how the protocols are interconnected. The ideas evolved over a period of 25
years, so even for me it is good to go back and revisit the basic requirements to understand
why we have the set of protocols we have.

Most DBMSs integrate everything into one commit protocol and possibly do some group
commit optimisations. For NDB this wasn't an option since the telecom database requirements
meant that we could not wait for disk during the commit processing. To provide the durability
without using disk we made use of the Network Durability concept instead that commits in
memory of several computers.

At the same we still needed to recover something also after a complete cluster crash. We
needed a protocol to make the transactions durable also on disk. Also this disk durable state
needed to be consistent and thus the *global checkpoint protocol* was invented.

CHAPTER 27

ROUTING OF READS AND WRITES

An important part of a distributed DBMS is how to route reads and writes within the various nodes in the distributed DBMS.

In MySQL Cluster we distribute data using a hash algorithm using a hash map. Each partition of each table is fully replicated within one node group of the cluster. Each partition is also located within one *ldm* thread within the nodes in this node group. The location of data is decided once we have created a table.

However reads can be routed differently if we are using the Read Backup feature or if we are using the fully replicated feature.

The transaction coordinator can be placed in any node in the cluster. Any MySQL Server can be choosen to execute a query in MySQL Cluster.

27.1 CHOOSING THE MySQL SERVER

With MySQL Cluster every MySQL Server is capable of handling each transaction. There is no specific need to choose a special MySQL Server for read and write transactions. We have special MySQL Servers for replicating between clusters and it is possible to have special MySQL Servers for handling meta data changes (although not required). But there is no need to use a special MySQL Server for normal read and write transactions.

The natural choice here is some sort of normal round robin scheme. There are many methods to implement the handling of this round robin scheme. One method is to use methods in the MySQL APIs. For example the JDBC API towards MySQL supports listing many different MySQL Server and performing a round robin on them.

The second option is to use the MySQL Router.

One more option is to use a standard load balancer in front of the MySQL Server. Thus the set of MySQL Servers used have a single IP address and a single port to access. In e.g. the Oracle Infrastructure Cloud this is a normal service that you can connect to your infrastructure. It is possible to set this load balancer up such that it is highly available.

If you are developing an application that use the NDB API, it is necessary to have a similar mechanism on top of your application nodes.

From a MySQL client we have no way of guessing the best MySQL Server to use. This requires knowledge only available through the NDB API.

The principle to use to get best scaling is to spread the load among the MySQL Servers in the cluster.

27.2 Choosing the node of the transaction coordinator

It is possible to choose any node as transaction coordinator. But there is great value in choosing a transaction coordinator that is close to the data of the transaction. The principle of choosing transaction coordinator based on locality means that we are minimising the latency of the transaction and avoiding as much as possible oversubscribed network links that can cause bottlenecks.

27.2.1 Choosing at NDB API level

Using the NDB API it is possible to provide a hint about where to place the transaction coordinator. The hint we provide is the table object and the primary key to use for access. Provided the primary key and the table object we can calculate the partition identity and through this and the table object we can deduce the nodes where the replicas are stored. This is not exact knowledge since e.g. an ALTER TABLE REORGANIZE can change this on the fly without immediately informing the NDB API. It is only a hint, the impact of an erroneus hint is that the transaction will take slightly longer time to execute.

A key hint provided to start the transaction

We will select a node from one of the data nodes that have a replica. The selection depends on a few things, it depends on if we are using the read backup feature, it depends on if we are using the fully replicated feature.

If the table have the read backup feature we can select any of the data nodes with a replica. We will select the one that is considered most close. This is using a configuration parameter called *Group* on each transporter (this parameter should normally not be set by user). By default on a TCP transporter this is set to 55. When we start an API and the transporter is an TCP transporter we will check if the TCP transporter can use a localhost connection. If it can it drops the *Group* down to 54. We can change the *Group* all the way down to 5 if we have set the node to be our neighbour. This is done by setting the configuration parameter for the MySQL Server *--ndb-data-node-neighbour* to the node id of our closest neighbour.

All of this assumes that we have set *--ndb-optimized-node-selection* to 3 which is the default value. This parameter is there to be able to get backwards compatible behaviour with older versions. This parameter should normally not be changed.

In short we will select the node among the replicas and we will prioritize first our data node neighbour, next any node that can connect using localhost, and finally any other node.

If the table is fully replicated we will perform the same algorithm, but this time using all nodes that have a replica (normally all data nodes in the cluster).

No key was provided

When no key is provided we have no hints, we will select a node based on the closeness of the node as described above. This time the nodes to choose among is the full set of data nodes in the cluster.

27.2.2 Choosing at the MySQL Server level

From a MySQL Server we have integrated the hint mechanism of the NDB API in the following manner. When starting a transaction the first query will decide the key to provide in the hint. If the primary key of a table is given in the first query we will use this as the key in the hint mechanism. For range scans, full table scans and pushdown joins we will not have any key provided.

27.3 Choosing the *tc* thread

The *tc* thread is always choosen after the node have been choosen using a round robin scheme.

27.4 Choosing the data node for reading

For tables without the read backup feature we always use the primary replica to read with the exception for some BLOB reads as explained in the BLOB chapter.

For tables with the read backup feature we first attempt to read from a replica residing in the same data node as the transaction coordinator is placed in. Otherwise we always read the primary replica.

27.5 Choosing the *ldm* thread

The *ldm* thread is decided by the row used. We will use the same *ldm* in all nodes in the node group for a certain partition. Thus there is nothing to choose here.

27.6 Choosing the data nodes for writing

This is completely determined by the row to write. We will always write all available replicas and these replicas have a strict order where one replica is primary replica and the other are backup replicas that are organised in a certain order. Thus there is nothing to choose here.

CHAPTER 28

CONCURRENCY CONTROL

For an application developer it is important to understand the concurrency control model used by a DBMS. There are two approaches to concurrency control, there is an optimistic approach and there is a pessimistic approach. The optimistic approach is used when low number of conflicts between changes are expected. The optimistic approach goes ahead and does the updates without checking for other updates. At commit time the transactions are checked for conflicts, if any two transactions are in conflict one of them has to be aborted.

The pessimistic approach tries to ensure, already before commit, that we don't cause any concurrent actions on the same object to occur. Most commonly this employs a method called strict two-phase locking. This means that there is first a lock phase where the applications grab their locks and after getting all locks the transaction is committed (or aborted) whereafter all locks are released whereafter no one is allowed to lock any more rows in this particular transaction.

The rule of strict two-phase locking is that no locks are taken after the first row has been unlocked.

The pessimistic approach have much higher chance of handling a highly concurrent system better.

There is a great variety of different methods for both optimistic and pessimistic algorithms. Most of them is based on either locking or some timestamp method. It is one of the most well researched topics in the area of DBMSs.

So what to use? We opted for the pessimistic approach. The main reason for this was a number of factors. I read many, many research articles on the topic of concurrency control and there are tons of research papers in this area. The concurrency control mechanism used in most DBMSs is the strict two-phase locking.

The optimistic approach have a serious impact on application development. Any DBMS using the optimistic approach have to handle many more aborted transactions. In the pessimistic approach the only aborted transactions that comes about from concurrency control is due to deadlocks. These are much less frequent than conflicts. A conflict using the pessimistic approach causes a delay, but not an aborted transaction. Applications using the optimistic approach have to be written with the understanding that aborts are common, this makes it even more difficult to port an application to a new DBMS than otherwise would be the case (it is difficult enough as it is).

In addition the optimistic approach has the disadvantage that the CPU cost per transaction increases as load increases and the chance of conflicts increase.

Using the optimistic approach would have had an impact on all recovery algorithms. It is a lot easier to reason about recovery algorithms when using locks compared to when using the optimistic approach. Given that our focus is online algorithms for all metadata changes, it made a lot of sense to try to use simpler algorithms. As an example the ability to lock a row for a short time is used in the node restart algorithm when synchronising the live node with the starting node. This short lock makes it very easy to reason about the node restart algorithm.

For these reasons we opted to use the standard strict two-phase locking approach that acquires locks in the prepare phase and releases the locks in the commit phase and continues to release the locks in the complete phase.

28.1   ROW LOCKING

The approach in NDB is to use row locking. We always access records using a hash index when any type of lock is needed. We can scan using the hash index, but we can also scan in row order and in disk data order. In the two latter cases we have to ask the hash index for a lock on the row for each row we scan when a lock is needed.

In the hash index we implemented our row locks. If a scan comes from an ordered index and needs to lock the row it will use the hash index to get the lock. Most DBMS use a hash index to implement the lock data structure, in our case this hash index is also used as an access data structure, not just to handle locks.

NDB has no support for range locks. This is required to fully support serialisability. Thus we support serialisability on everything except range queries. Our analysis of the applications that NDB focused on suggested that serialisable mode for range queries was of limited use in the analysed applications.

Supporting range locks in a distributed database imposes serious scalability problems. Locking a range using hash partitioning requires locking the range in all nodes and the alternative to use range partitioning only supports range locks on the columns in the partition key. Range partitioning is much harder to make scalable in a distributed system. This is a major reason why most classic SQL DBMSs use a shared disk implementation to scale the DBMS. Shared nothing have a number of algorithms that are harder to implement such as range locking, deadlock handling and so forth.

The choice between shared nothing and shared disk is a trade off where you have to select what matters most to you. When implementing MySQL Cluster what mattered most was the time to handle a node failure. With shared nothing we were able to get this down to a small number of seconds and even below a second in a real-time environment. For shared disk it is hard to get this number down this far given that all nodes do not have access to the latest updates, the latest updates can only be retrieved from the logs. Thus shared disk can never be as fast to recover as shared nothing.

Another benefit of shared nothing is that it doesn't require a shared nothing file system. Interestingly all shared disk implementations are implemented on top of a file system that is more or less a shared nothing database. This is why it makes sense to build a file system on top of NDB.

When developing NDB we decided to go for shared nothing and thus decided that we will not support range locks in all situations.

If the application has special needs to lock certain parts of the database, it is possible to implement this by ensuring that the access to those parts always go through a specific record. Thus special records can be used in the same fashion as a read-write mutex is used in lower-level designs.

In essence it is possible to handle all locking needs using NDB, but it might require a bit more work on the application level to get the most fancy lock variants.

A good example of this is HopsFS that had a special problem where they needed to support the *mv* command. This moves a whole hierarchy of directories. This was implemented by performing the move step by step and using application level locks while doing so. Every DBMS is implemented for a sweet spot and the engineers have to decide on which requirement is the most important for them. The aim of MySQL Cluster is to meet the highest availability requirements and at the same time extreme performance requirements for key lookups. We are aiming long-term to provide a very good parallelisation of complex queries since this is such a good fit in the NDB architecture.

For the same reasons no sharded NoSQL system supports range locks. Since NDB is a distributed system that automatically supports up to 24 shards using 2 replicas, it is a natural choice to not support range locks in NDB.

In conclusion all rows in NDB can be locked either exclusively (when updating or when using exclusive lock mode for reads) or locked for reads. It is possible to read the latest committed value without using locks.

28.2   Consistency Models

DBMSs mainly uses two different consistency models. The first model is the one implemented in NDB that performs read using *read committed* mode. The second popular consistency model in DBMS is to use *repeatable read* mode. We will explain those two variants, they both provide a consistency level that uses transactions to update the data.

Most of the *NoSQL* systems employs something called eventual consistency. Eventual consistency means that updates are not transactional, eventual consistency is more about replicating changes. In NoSQL systems all updates are first employed on a master node, after that various methods are used to replicate those changes to other nodes in the system.

Eventual consistency can not be combined with distributed transactions. One can keep the locks in the master node for such a long time that the changes are also employed in the nodes replicated to. But the term eventual consistency only promise that each node replicated to will eventually be consistent with the master node. Thus the only node where you can see the latest changes are in the master node.

InnoDB Cluster, Galera Cluster, MongoDB are examples of systems that uses eventual consistency. In InnoDB Cluster the other nodes have received the logs of the changes when the transaction is committed, but the other nodes have not yet updated the actual data at commit time. Reads that are sent to other nodes than the master node will not see the latest writes.

Thus a major difference between systems employing eventual consistency is that the application have to know in detail what the concurrency implications are due to the eventual consistency. This makes it a lot harder to implement a scalable application using NoSQL systems compared to using MySQL Cluster.

We will now try to explain how *read committed* differs from *repeatable read* and why the choice for NDB to use the *read committed* mode was a natural choice.

Repeatable read means that the query results will be the result that would result if the database was frozen at the start time of the query. This means that the query can be repeated again and again and the result remains the same. During the query execution there is no locks on the database, what happens is rather that the DBMS have to save the old row until the query is completed.

This have two consequences. The first consequence is that the database size will grow, rows have to be kept until all queries have completed that was started at the time when the row change happened. The combination of long-running queries and high update rates will cause a high increase of storage needs. With MySQL Cluster we have a focus on in-memory data, thus we would get too much RAM used for old rows.

Additionally to use *repeatable read* requires adding a timestamp to each row, thus even more use of memory resources. It adds CPU overhead to handle all those extra old rows although this is not a major issue.

The second part is that *repeatable read* will not deliver results that is based on the latest changes. Thus *repeatable read* is completely focused on delivering consistency at the cost of recentness. The *read committed* mode focuses on delivering the most recent changes at the cost of complete consistency of the result.

Delivering a completely consistent result and up-to-date result can only be achieved with massive locks in the database, thus this is not an alternative for any scalable application.

So which mode is most appropriate is dependent on the application. But for the type of applications that NDB was developed for, the *read committed* mode is the preferred one.

28.3 READ COMMITTED MODE

The model used in NDB is called *read committed* mode. Thus we will read the latest committed row. There could be one or two row versions at any point in time (except for transactions that update the same row many times). There is one row when the row isn't currently updated and there is two rows when a transaction is currently changing the row.

A *read committed* read will read the old committed rows in cases where the user is currently updating the row. These reads are lock-free.

When performing a read of the database in *read committed* mode we will always read the latest committed row, so even when running a long-running query the result of the query will be impacted by changes in the database.

28.4 LOCKING AND UNIQUE INDEXES

Unique indexes are simply a special table that have the unique key columns as primary key and the primary key of the main table is the remaining columns. Thus we can with one key lookup translate the unique key to the primary key.

When we read the unique key we use a shared lock to ensure that no one is allowed to delete or insert the row we are looking for while we are performing this translation. As soon as we have found or completed the read of the main table we can release the lock on the unique index row. The NDB storage engine has special code to ensure that we release those unique key locks immediately after returning from the read/write of the main table.

We need to use this shared lock also when the read of the main table is using the *read committed* mode.

Reading through the unique index and updating the main table can happen in parallel. Given that those comes from different directions it is possible for them to cause a deadlock. These are normally rare, but frequent inserts and deletes of rows in a table using a unique key and at the same time reading this table using the unique key can cause deadlocks to occur. Deadlocks cause no harm other than timing out, but constitutes a problem to consider to achieve predictable latency of an application.

The best use of unique keys is to use them primarily for constraint checks. In this case they are only used during inserts and updates to ensure that only row with a given unique key exists. In this case we cannot have deadlocks due to reads using unique key since we never use such reads.

28.5 Locking and BLOB tables

Locking for BLOB tables is a bit special since the BLOB consists of multiple rows in MySQL Cluster. The first row accessed is always the main row, any changes of any BLOB requires holding an exclusive lock on both the main row (even if no part of it is updated) and on the BLOB parts that are updated.

Reading of a BLOB is a bit special, especially when using the *READ COMMITTED* mode. Normally this mode requires no locks for reading since we always ensure that the read is reading the latest committed values. For BLOBs this method doesn't work since reading rows with BLOBs requires reading multiple rows.

The manner used here is that we take a shared lock on the main row of the BLOB table. Next we read the BLOB parts one by one. By holding the shared lock on the main row we ensure that no one is allowed to change any BLOB parts while we are reading the BLOB parts.

In addition the reads on the BLOB parts use a special lock mode when reading the BLOB parts. This mode takes a lock while reading the row, but releases the lock before sending the result back to the NDB API. This has the effect that we ensure that the read is consistent, if we would have read the BLOB parts using the latest committed we could read an old version of the BLOB through a race condition.

The short-lived lock is almost certain to be successfully acquired immediately, but in rare situations it might have to wait for some commit messages from an old transaction to arrive before it can start the read.

The effect of this is that BLOB tables have less concurrency than ordinary tables, but they will still be consistently read and updated.

Another positive effect of the above is that reads of BLOB tables are always done using any replica independent of the table mode for READ_BACKUP.

Chapter 29

Parallel Query

Many SQL queries are performed with some amount of parallelism in NDB. It happens when the SQL queries uses scans that are not limited to scanning a single partition.

It can happen as part of table scans, it can also happen as part of more complex scans that are linked together. These linked scans is a variant of a parallel join algorithm. The scanning of data in the data nodes can be parallelised to the same level as the number of *ldm* threads in the cluster. The result rows are sent to the single MySQL Server that has a single user thread that is executing the query, but much of the filtering of the rows can be parallelised.

This parallel join algorithm is a bit more advanced compared to a parallel nested loop join. The best descriptive name for it is to call it a parallel linked scan algorithm.

29.1 Full table scan in NDB

Scans comes in a number of flavors, the first one is the full table scan. It will read each and every row in the table and apply a search filter on each row to see if it should be returned to the application. These scans are automatically parallelised such that they execute on a set of partitions in parallel. For example if the table contains 1 million rows and is divided into 8 partitions, eight concurrent scans will be started that each will scan around 125k rows. Conditions from the SQL query can be pushed to this scan such that only a subset of the rows is returned to the MySQL Server. When the row returns to the MySQL Server it has to be evaluated by the single thread that the SQL query is executed within, but during the table scan we can have up to eight CPUs running in parallel on filtering out the rows to be returned. This happens automatically, no special action is needed to make this happen, it is the default behaviour.

We will go through in more details later what conditions that can be pushed down as part of a scan (the same condition pushdown can be applied on a primary key or unique key request to flag if the read row is to be returned to the application).

29.2 Range scan in NDB

Next the same thing applies to range scans. Ordered indexes in NDB are implemented per partition. Thus in order to perform a range scan the same scan algorithm is used as for full table scan except that we scan in index order between two boundaries. NDB can also start multi-range scans using one scan operation. These scans can also have conditions pushed down and the scan can be parallelised.

29.3   Partition pruned range scans

We have a special case which is very important, this is the partition pruned range scans. In this case the range scan is not performed on all partitions, it is rather performed only on one partition. There is an easy condition for when this pruned partition scan happens. As part of the condition the partition key must be fully set. For example in TPC-C there are lots of tables that contain a warehouse id. One manner to set up the tables in TPC-C is that all tables use the warehouse id as the partition key. Now any query that has a condition that contains *warehouse_id = variable/constant* will now be able to perform a partition pruned range scan. By retrieving the warehouse_id from the query we can figure out which partition to scan. We know that the data cannot be in any other partition and we can thus prune away all the other partitions.

This technique is what almost all Big Data applications is using when they are sharding. With NDB it is possible to set up the cluster tables to be easily sharded. If all or at least most of the tables in a database or application uses a common partition key this becomes a sharding key of the application inside NDB.

As an example in HopsFS where a file system meta data layer was implemented a clever partition key was selected that made it possible to ensure that almost all scan queries, e.g. the scan used to perform *ls* (list the files in a directory in Unix) was always directed to only one partition and thus no extra overhead was created in starting up many parallel scans since each parallel scan only accessed one partition each.

29.4   Pushdown joins

In a number of situations we want to perform queries that span the entire data set. In this case we are most likely analysing the data and we are scanning major portions of the data to find some specific property of the data. In this case the fact that scans are automatically parallelised is good and decreases the latency significantly in processing complex queries.

In the descriptions below we use the term scan, but often a scan is a key lookup. In the presentation below this would simply be a special scan that can return 0 or 1 rows.

Now in MySQL Cluster we have made another step forward. We implement a technique where these scans can be linked. Say that we start with a scan of table t1, this scan provides 10.000 rows. Now we want to join the table t1 with the table t2, from each of those 10.000 rows we get a key that is used in the condition for table t2 and we perform a new index scan for each of those 10.000 rows. This index scan can also be a key lookup, it can also be a full table scan and the scan can also be partition pruned such that it only scans one partition. Let's say that each of those 10.000 scans now gives us 3 more rows back, thus we now have 30.000 rows from t2. Now we can continue and use data from table t2 to join it with a table t3 in exactly the same manner.

Using this technique we can execute arbitrarily complex queries. In our testing of this we've used heavily a query that we got from an early user of MySQL Cluster. In the early days of MySQL Cluster this query took something like 6 seconds to execute (in those days MySQL had almost no batching techniques, the query was more or less executed one row at a time). Now in MySQL Cluster 7.5 using the normal technique of single table scans performed in sequence and always returning to the MySQL Server the query takes 1.2 seconds to execute in a very small cluster with one data node and one LDM instance. Using condition pushdown we are able to avoid much of the interaction with the MySQL Server and most of the filtering is done before sending it to the MySQL Server. Using these techniques the query can be executed in 0.2 seconds instead. With a few more *ldm* threads, e.g. 4 of them the query is executed in 50 milliseconds. This query scans and analyses many tens of thousands of rows as part of the query execution, mostly in the data node.

One can perform more odd variants of joins using this technique, so for example if one starts by reading table t1 and based on the data retrieved in table t1 we can immediately start fetching the data in table t2, table t3 and so forth.

29.4.1 LIMITATIONS OF PUSHDOWN JOINS

The conditions used in joining tables that are part of the pushed down query must use equality conditions. The columns used in those equality conditions must be of exactly the same data type. It is currently not possible to use pushdown joins if any of the columns retrieved by the query is a BLOB column. Subqueries can sometimes inhibit the pushdown of the join from happening. One can use *show warnings* after executing the query to discover any problems in handling the pushdown of the join. Likewise the *EXPLAIN* command can be used to discover exactly how the pushdown join is handled.

Pushdown of joins can only occur in read only queries that are not using any locking constructs such as *LOCK IN SHARED MODE* or other similar construct. The join execution must be lock-free, so it cannot lock rows as part of the join execution which would be required if it is part of an updating transaction where the result can be used to update rows in a scan takeover.

29.4.2 DETAILS OF PUSHDOWN JOINS

A complex join can be divided into multiple parts that are pushed down to NDB. As an example assume that the MySQL Server comes up with a plan that does a 5-way join, for each row in the inner join of this 5-way join we have a subquery that is in itself a 4-way join. Now the 5-way join can be handled with a scan on the first table and for each row in the first table we execute a pushed down 4-way join to the NDB API.

Thus even if there are specific parts that makes it impossible to handle the entire query in the NDB data nodes, we can still send parts of the query at a time down to the NDB data nodes.

The MySQL Server does the query optimisation before the joins are pushed down to the NDB data nodes. The query optimisation doesn't take the distribution aspects into account. However once NDB decides to push a join down to NDB data nodes it can decide using some heuristics to reorder the join order of the tables.

Aggregation, group by and order by processing is currently not handled by pushdown joins. Thus all the rows to be put into the group by processing must be returned to the MySQL Server as part of the join processing. This makes the MySQL Server user thread a bottleneck for complex queries using group by, at least if many rows are used to calculate the aggregates. The parallel filtering can still make those queries go significantly faster using pushdown join.

29.4.3 PUSHDOWN OF JOINS AND FULLY REPLICATED TABLES

Fully replicated tables are a bit special, these tables are replicated in all data nodes. Thus a join where all tables are fully replicated can be handled in a completely local execution where the entire query execution is processed within one data node.

The same is true for a table using the read backup feature and executing in a cluster with only one node group (e.g. 2 nodes with 2 replicas).

This means that we can execute the entire query without performing any communication with other computers if the MySQL Server and data node are colocated.

A normal join execution starts up a number of parallel join execution parts that each take care of a subset of the query. This is handled by limiting each subquery to only scan a subset of the partitions on the first table. The result of the query in this is case is a union of the subqueries and can thus easily be merged back again. E.g. the first query part could take the first partition of the first joined table and join this table with the full tables of the remainder of the joined tables.

The join execution for each query part will be controlled from the node where the primary replica of the partitions used in the first table resides. This is independent of if this first table is fully replicated or not. The remainder of the reads will always go to the same node if a replica is stored on the node, otherwise it will go to the nearest replica available.

Execution of pushdown joins will often spread over all nodes to make use of all nodes and *ldm* threads in the cluster.

MySQL Cluster can be limited by Gigabit Ethernet very easily and even with 10G Ethernet it is fairly easy to overload the network in a dual socket server. Thus it makes a lot of sense to try to ensure that queries are executed as much as possible in the same node as the query was issued from.

29.5 CONDITION PUSHDOWN

Pushdown of conditions to the NDB data node can happen in cases where we compare with constants either for equality, greater than and so forth and ranges of the same. We can perform checks if the column is NULL or not, we can perform like conditions and we can compare string values if they are of the same collation.

This can be used both for full table scan, index scans and key lookups and it can be part of a pushdown join execution. It is a very powerful concept when it gets used.

CHAPTER 30

SPECIALISED MySQL SERVERS

When configuring a cluster it is useful to have a set of specialised MySQL Servers. The first is a specialised MySQL Server for metadata operations. Most of the operations in NDB are possible to perform as online operations such adding a column, adding nodes to the cluster, reorganising data partitions for a table, adding and dropping indexes and tables.

The MySQL Server code is not designed for truly online operations. This means that when performing an ALTER TABLE on a table, the table is read only in the MySQL Server performing the ALTER TABLE operation while the table can be both read and written in all other MySQL Servers and API nodes.

Thus it makes sense to use a specialised MySQL Server for metadata operations. For high availability it makes sense to have two of those in different machines.

The next is MySQL Cluster Replication. Normally the binlog records are generated in the MySQL Server from where the update operation was issued. This is not the case for NDB. In NDB the operations are executed in the data nodes and after that a change log is shipped to the MySQL Server that has defined replication to be set up.

In almost all cases it is desirable to have at least two MySQL Servers used for replication to make sure we can handle failover to another MySQL Replication server in cases of node failures.

When metadata operations are performed in a MySQL Server the binlog of those events are shipped in a special manner between the MySQL Servers. We support sharing the binlogging MySQL Server and the MySQL Server performing the metadata operation.

The recommended minimum configuration for MySQL Cluster is to have two data nodes on separate machines, four MySQL Servers on two different machines (could be the same as the data node machines) and two NDB management servers, all on different machines. In addition a few API node slots should be configured to enable the various NDB tools to also access the cluster concurrently with the MySQL Servers.

The MySQL Servers used for metadata operations and replication will use very little memory and CPU resources, it will not be any issue in having those colocated on the same machine with a MySQL Server used for normal query processing.

This type of configuration avoids many hickups that could otherwise happen in combination with meta data changes.

For bigger clusters it is not necessary to add any more specialised MySQL Servers nor any more NDB management servers, it is enough to add new servers with data nodes and MySQL Servers used for query services.

PART VII

TOOLS TO IMPORT AND EXPORT DATA

Importing and exporting data is important when starting up new database services. We will focus our description here on how one can import data into MySQL Cluster, but also some words on how to export data out of NDB. We will also cover backup and restore from one NDB cluster to another, or to use a backup to restore data after some problem.

There are many possible variants for import and export, we will focus on describing the ones that are the recommended methods. These chapters will provide an overview of methods to import and to export data from or into MySQL Cluster, also how to backup and restore in NDB. It will not even attempt to make a detailed description of the tools themselves. This is nicely covered by the MySQL manual, no need to replicate that effort here.

We will focus our description on the preferred methods.

CHAPTER 31

IMPORT DATA

There are at least four methods to import data into NDB. A very efficient method exists by using CSV files as input. CSV files can be produced by most DBMS and in particular MySQL can produce it either using *mysqldump* or using *SELECT .... INTO OUTFILE 'file.name'*.

Backup files produced by NDB is a second method to import data into NDB, this is often used in conjunction with replication between clusters. Of course also when restoring a backup that will be covered in more detail in a later chapter.

A third method is to use a dump produced by *mysqldump* or *mysqlpump*. *mysqldump* and *mysqlpump* produces a file full of SQL statements (*mysqldump* can dump data both in SQL format and in CSV format).

Next one can alter a table to become an NDB table if the data is moved from e.g. InnoDB in a MySQL Server already connected to the cluster.

31.0.1 IMPORTING METADATA

If the data is imported from another DBMS then the tables and databases must be manually created in MySQL Cluster before starting the import.

If we import the data from another MySQL database using InnoDB or other storage engine we can use the following commands to create the NDB table for the import.

```
mysql> CREATE DATABASE ndb_db;
mysql> USE ndb_db;
mysql> CREATE TABLE ndb_table LIKE mysql_db.mysql_table;
mysql> ALTER TABLE ndb_table engine=NDB;
```

First ensure that the database to be used by the new NDB tables are created. Next create an empty table with the same table definition as the table we are importing in this database. Finally convert this table into an NDB table. We should make any necessary changes to the table definition in the ALTER TABLE command to suite your NDB installation.

If data is to be transported from one MySQL installation to another the most natural program to use for importing the MySQL tables and databases is the *mysqldump* command.

```
mysqldump --no-data --databases db_name > db_name.sql
```

The above command will write all table definitions and the database definition into a dump file. The *--no-data* option means that no rows from the table will be dumped, only the

CREATE TABLE and CREATE DATABASE commands.

To install these tables into the MySQL Cluster installation simply use the MySQL client like this:

```
mysql < db_name.sql
```

After executing this command it is still necessary to perform an ALTER TABLE command on each table to convert them into NDB tables.

31.1 *ndb_restore* USING BACKUPS

ndb_restore is a tool that have existed since version 2.1 of NDB Cluster. It is the complement of the feature in NDB to backup its data. It takes the backup files as input and uses the data files and log files to restore the database content using an API program. Several *ndb_restore* instances can operate in parallel to restore the data. There is one backup file per node per LDM. With 4 nodes and 4 LDMs per node there will be 16 backup files. More information on how to use this tool in the chapter on restore.

31.2 IMPORTING FROM MYSQLDUMP FILES

The dump produced by *mysqldump* contains files full of SQL statements. To import the data from a dump one simply pipes the dump file to the *mysql* client program that will then execute one SQL statement at a time.

This will become a single-threaded approach to importing and is thus likely to take a very long time. One approach to this is to split the data file into multiple files. This can be accomplished with a fairly simple shell script. After that one restores using those files in parallel.

31.3 ALTER TABLE

If the export is from the same MySQL Server as the import is done into we can use ALTER TABLE to convert from one storage engine to another. It is one command per table.

31.4 *mysqlimport*

mysqlimport is another tool that can be used for importing data into NDB.

Chapter 32

Export data

The main method for exporting data out of NDB is the backup feature. Backup is the only method to export data from NDB in a consistent manner. A backup consists of two sets of files. The first set of files is containing the rows scanned from NDB. The second set of files contains REDO or UNDO logs that makes the backup consistent to the starting point of the backup (UNDO logs used) or the point in time when the backup is completed (REDO logs used).

Backup was mainly designed to provide a method for restoring the data in NDB, in either the same cluster or in another cluster. It is an important tool in setting up replication between clusters, it is a very important tool to restore a cluster after failures due to corrupted data.

The data in the backup files can be used to restore a database exactly as it looked at the time of the completion or start of the backup.

It is straightforward to restore it to another MySQL Cluster instance or the same MySQL Cluster instance. To restore to another database such as InnoDB, Oracle and so forth is a bit less straightforward.

ndb_restore can be used to output the data in CSV format, it can also be used to output the row changes as SQL statements. There are a few obstacles. The backup takes a backup with data in the same representation as in NDB. This is not a problem in most cases, but it does represent an issue when dealing with BLOBs. BLOBs store the first 256 bytes of the data in the main table. This data is represented correctly. The remainder of the BLOB data is stored in a separate BLOB table with up to 2048 bytes per row in this table. There is one BLOB table per BLOB column.

It is a challenge when exporting data from NDB to another DBMS to piece together the BLOBs again. In addition the change logs cannot be represented in CSV format since they represent inserts, deletes and updates. They can be represented in the SQL format that *ndb_restore* can also produce.

The conclusion is that transporting data consistently to another DBMS requires that the data isn't updated during the export process. In this case we can use the *mysqldump* and we can use *SELECT ... INTO OUTFILE*.

When transporting data to another NDB cluster, backup is the preferred method.

32.1 *mysqldump*

One method of exporting data from NDB (and from any other MySQL storage engine) is to use the mysqldump tool. The problem in using this tool for NDB is that it doesn't generate a consistent data point. To be able to export data properly using *mysqldump* it is important that NDB isn't allowed to be updated while performing the *mysqldump* if a consistent data point is required in the export.

mysqldump can generate its export format as SQL statements, text files (CSV files) or as XML files. *mysqldump* can be used to transport data from any MySQL installation into any other DBMS including other MySQL instances.

mysqldump can be used to export data from MySQL/InnoDB and import it into MySQL Cluster. In this case it is important to NOT use the option *--single-transaction*. This will create very large transactions which can cause the import to fail due to lack of resources for extremely large transactions.

To dump data into a dump file is straightforward, to dump one database one uses the following commands. The first command generates an SQL file with the CREATE TABLE statements required to create the tables in the database, it also generates the CREATE DATABASE command for the database exported.

```
mysqldump --no-data --databases \
   database_name > database_name_tables.sql
mysqldump --no-create-info --no-create-database \
   --databases database_name > database_name_data.sql
```

The default output from *mysqldump* is SQL INSERT statements. CSV files can be produced using the *--tab=DIRNAME* parameter. It is also possible to provide the output in XML format using the *--xml* parameter.

32.2 SELECT INTO OUTFILE

Another method of exporting data from NDB and from any other MySQL storage engine is to use the SQL command *SELECT ... INTO OUTFILE*. This command can select the full or parts of a table and export it into a CSV file. The command can be used with any SELECT query. For exporting data the normal use case would be the command.

```
mysql> SELECT * from table_name INTO OUTFILE 'table_name.csv';
```

This command will not produce a consistent data point for NDB, for InnoDB it will, also for InnoDB one have to ensure that no updates are performed when using this method to export data since there will be no consistency between different tables. Each table will require its own file.

Using this method one file per table will be produced. It is fairly straightforward to parallelise the production of these files by executing several such commands for different tables in parallel.

The command SHOW DATABASES can be used to discover all databases in MySQL. For each database one can then use SHOW TABLES to get all the tables in MySQL. For NDB all tables in the cluster will be listed in this manner.

CHAPTER 33

BACKUP

Any highly available DBMS requires a backup service. In NDB this was implemented already in version 2.1 of NDB Cluster. So it has been around for more than 15 years in NDB.

Starting a backup is easy. It is started from an NDB management client.

```
ndb_mgm --ndb-connectstring=mgm_host
ndb_mgm> START BACKUP
```

This command kicks off the execution of a backup in the entire cluster. When the backup is completed it will report back to the NDB management client a completion report. The completion report contains some statistics about the backup execution such as how many records were backed up, how many log records were written to the backup as part of the backup, which is the starting global checkpoint identifier and what is the last global checkpoint identifier and how many bytes were written.

The backup can take considerable time to execute if there is a large amount of data in the cluster. The speed of writing backups is controlled by the same set of configuration parameters that control the local checkpoint speed, thus *MinDiskWriteSpeed* and *MaxDiskWriteSpeed*.

The result of the backup is written into a set of files per node. The first file is called *BACKUP-nodeid.backupid.Data*.

This file contain the data backed up. Next there is a file called *BACKUP-nodeid.backupid.ctl*. This file contains the metadata of the tables backed up. Finally there is a file called *BACKUP-nodeid.backupid.log*. This file contains all changes since the backup was started.

33.1 BACKUP ALGORITHM

A backup is executed starting from a specific global checkpoint. All changes from this global checkpoint until the last global checkpoint triggers a write to the log file mentioned above.

The backup scans each table partition to find all records in the database. Before the data is scanned we record all table definitions in the control file of the backup.

To restore a database from a backup means first restoring the tables from the control file, next the data file is processed to insert all rows in the database again. Finally the log is executed to install all changes during the backup execution. The log is needed to ensure that the backup is a transaction consistent checkpoint at the last global checkpoint. It is possible to define the backup point to the be first global checkpoint if desirable. This means that the log will record how to UNDO the actions happened during the backup rather than how to REDO the actions.

33.2 THE START BACKUP COMMAND

It is possible to specify for how long to wait until control is returned such that new commands can be issued in the NDB management client. It is possible to use:

1. START BACKUP NOWAIT

2. START BACKUP WAIT COMPLETED

3. START BACKUP WAIT STARTED

WAIT COMPLETED is the default setting. NOWAIT means that we don't wait at all. The completion report will still be reported back to the management client even if new commands have been issued.

WAIT STARTED means that we wait for backup to start, but not wait for it to complete.

Next it is possible to change whether backup is taken at start of backup or at finish of the backup.

1. START BACKUP SNAPSHOTSTART

2. START BACKUP SNAPSHOTEND

SNAPSHOTEND is the default.

33.3 ABORTING A BACKUP

If for some reason we discover that the backup cannot proceed it is possible to abort it. This is performed from the NDB management client as well by using the ABORT BACKUP command.

```
ndb_mgm --ndb-connectstring=mgm_host
ndb_mgm> ABORT BACKUP backupid
```

This command causes all backup files so far created by the backup to be deleted.

33.4 BACKUP FILE PLACEMENT

The backup files are by default placed in the directory *BACKUP* under the NDB data nodes data directory. There will be one such directory in each data node in the cluster. For each backup a new directory is created under this directory called *BACKUP-backupid*.

Often it is a good idea to place the backup files in a directory you decide on yourself. In this case set this directory in the cluster configuration parameter *BackupDataDir*.

33.5 Backup configuration

Most of the configuration parameters are shared with the local checkpoint process. These are the following parameters:

1. *BackupWriteSize*

2. *BackupMaxWriteSize*

3. *BackupDataBufferSize*

BackupWriteSize is the default size of the blocks written to disk. By default this is set to 256 kBytes.

BackupMaxWriteSize is the maximum size of the blocks written to disk. By default this is set to 1 MByte.

BackupDataBufferSize is the size of the memory buffer where rows are placed when scanning the tables before being sent to the disk. This is set to 16 MBytes by default.

There is usually very little reasons to touch those variables. Increasing those variables increases the variability of the CPU load during backups and local checkpoints. Decreasing them increases the overhead for writing to disk during checkpoints and backups.

The final configuration parameter that is strictly used by the backup and not by the local checkpoint process is the *BackupLogBufferSize*. This is where all changes are recorded during the backup process. This is set to 16 MBytes by default. If the bandwidth to the disk have occasional dips it is useful to increase this buffer size. If a change occurs and there is no room in the log buffer the backup will be aborted.

There is one such log buffer of the configured size in each *ldm* thread. Similarly for the data buffer. The data buffers only share the configuration parameters with checkpoints, they do not share the actual data buffers.

33.6 Backup file management

Once a backup is completed, the files created are in the hands of the DBA. There is no automatic maintenance of those files. Thus it is important to not execute a backup when there is no file space on the device.

For stability reasons it is a good idea to place the *BackupDataDir* on a separate device from the NDB data directory. This ensures that creating backups cannot jeopardize the operation of NDB. Filling the disk device means that there will be no space for checkpoints anymore and this can lead to a crash of the node and even of the entire cluster. By placing backups on a separate device this is no longer possible.

33.7 Backing up metadata in MySQL Cluster

It is possible to use the backups to recreate tables in MySQL. In many cases it is advisable to use backups only for the data part of the backup and instead use *mysqldump* for the metadata part.

```
mysqldump --no-data --databases \
    list_of_database_names > backup_metadata.sql
```

The above command dumps the table definitions together with the CREATE DATABASE commands to restore the databases used by MySQL Cluster. By placing NDB tables in their own database this makes it possible to only perform a backup of the NDB tables used by the MySQL Server and avoid all local tables that might exist at the same time in the MySQL Server.

mysqldump can also be used to dump other things such as stored procedures, stored functions, triggers, views and so forth. These MySQL objects are not part of the NDB backups. The NDB backups only backup the tables and their data.

CHAPTER 34

RESTORE

In this chapter we will discuss how to restore a backup. Restore uses a program called *ndb_restore*. This program always have as input, files generated by a backup from MySQL Cluster.

In its normal usage *ndb_restore* is applied to a system that currently is empty. Thus before restoring it is assumed that the user have performed an initial start of the cluster.

It is possible to use restore also as an import. It is however essential to understand that the tables restored in this process is not usable until the entire restore process have completed. Trying to use them before this gives unpredictable behaviour. Other tables not affected by the restore can still be used in a predictable manner.

To start this program we need to know at the very least the following things:

1. Placement of NDB management server(s)

2. The node id of the data node being restored

3. The backup id

4. The path to the backup files

To restore we go through a number of steps.

1. Restore meta data

2. Disable indexes

3. Restore data for each data node

4. Rebuild indexes

We need to restore the metadata before we insert the data. Next we recommend that one disables indexes before restoring data. If there are unique indexes in the backup this is a must. The reason is that otherwise the unique constraint cannot be guaranteed.

Remember that a backup first scans the tables and records rows in the backup files. Since the scan can go on for a long time there is no consistency among the records in this scan. The consistency comes after also applying the backup log file where all changes since the start of the backup are recorded. When this is performed we have restored a consistent database. Restoring the data happens in two stages where first the scanned rows are inserted and in the second step the log is applied. Thus during insertion of scanned rows the unique index constraint is not guaranteed to be valid. Thus it is a must to disable unique indexes before restoring data and to rebuild the unique indexes after the data have been fully restored.

For ordered indexes it is not a must to use disable of indexes before the restoring of the data. At the same time the parameter *--disable-indexes* applies to both unique indexes as well as ordered indexes. Second it is faster to use disable indexes followed by rebuild indexes also for ordered indexes. My recommendation is to always use this procedure.

The second reason to disable indexes while restoring data is that it is faster to perform those three steps compared to restoring data with indexes active. Rebuild indexes can be parallelised even beyond the number of *ldm* threads and also rebuilding indexes requires no communication while doing it and there is a higher chance of CPU cache hits while rebuilding indexes compared to when you insert one row at a time.

All phases except the restore data phase requires only one invocation of *ndb_restore*.

Here is the set of commands used to restore a 2-node cluster where the data nodes are 1 and 2 and the backup id is 10. The two invocations of *ndb_restore* with *--restore_data* can run in parallel.

```
ndb_restore --connectstring=mgm_host --nodeid=1 \
  --backupid=10 --backup-path=/backup/path/dir \
  --restore_meta
ndb_restore --connectstring=mgm_host --nodeid=1 \
  --backupid=10 --backup-path=/backup/path/dir \
  --disable-indexes
ndb_restore --connectstring=mgm_host --nodeid=1 \
  --backupid=10 --backup-path=/backup/path/dir \
  --restore-data
ndb_restore --connectstring=mgm_host --nodeid=2 \
  --backupid=10 --backup-path=/backup/path/dir \
  --restore-data
ndb_restore --connectstring=mgm_host --nodeid=1 \
  --backupid=10 --backup-path=/backup/path/dir \
  --rebuild-indexes
```

To restore data for a complete cluster we have to invoke *ndb_restore* one time for each node in the cluster producing the backup. If there were 4 data nodes in the cluster where the backup was taken, we need to invoke *ndb_restore* 4 times to restore the data.

All of these *ndb_restore* instances can run in parallel, it does however require one API node per instance in the NDB configuration. The other steps in the restore process must be sequential, thus we need to complete restoring meta data before we disable indexes. We need to disable indexes before we start the parallelised restore of data and we need to complete all the restore data parts before we rebuild the indexes.

During the restore process used above the indexes are not updated, this is however not known by the MySQL Server. Using the MySQL Server during the restore process can provide inaccurate data since only the primary key index is correct, thus only primary key lookups and full table scans are providing correct data.

During restore the data in the tables isn't consistent.

34.1   RESTORING METADATA

Here we have two options. We can restore the metadata from the backup taken in NDB. In this case we need to execute the following command before restoring the various parts.

```
ndb_restore --connectstring=mgm_host --nodeid=N \
  --backupid=B --backup-path=/backup/path/dir \
  --restore_meta
```

This command is only executed once for any of the nodes that produced the backup. It must be executed before the invocations of *ndb_restore* using *--restore_data*.

After executing this *ndb_restore* commands it is important to issue a SHOW TABLES command to ensure that meta data is synchronized with the various MySQL servers in the cluster and that the new tables are properly replicated to the slave side.

The other option is to restore the metadata from an SQL file that was produced by *mysqldump*. This command is very simple, it uses the MySQL client and the SQL file to send SQL commands to a MySQL Server that recreates those metadata objects as below:

This is the recommended approach since it is synchronized with MySQL Cluster Replication and automatically synchronizes the MySQL servers in the cluster such that they have the same meta data.

```
mysql < restore_meta.sql
```

The above command can also be used if it is desirable to restore other MySQL objects.

34.2   PARTIAL RESTORE

If only a subset of the tables or databases are to be restored it is possible to specify those with the parameters:

1. *--exclude-databases*

2. *--include-databases*

3. *--exclude-tables*

4. *--include-tables*

Exclude databases and tables are used to specifically specify all the databases and tables that must not be restored, all other tables and databases are restored. Include databases specify those tables and databases that are to be restored, no other tables and databases are restored.

When specifying a table in include and exclude tables one must specify both database name and table name with a dot between them as *dbname.tablename*. One can specify these parameters multiple times or use a comma separated list of database and table names.

34.3 RESTORE FOR UPGRADE

Restoring a backup can be a method to perform various software upgrades and also changes to the schema. Thus the data must not be entirely consistent with the new schema.

Restoring for an upgrade means that we create tables that have differences to the original tables, but they are populated using the same data.

--exclude-missing-tables means that any tables that are missing when performing a restore is ignored. Normally the restore will fail if it tries to insert or change data in a table that haven't been created before the restore of data starts. In a similar fashion we have *--exclude-missing-columns* that ensures that fields that have been removed are ignored when importing the data from the backup.

The parameter *--lossy-conversions* is set to indicate that it is ok to lose information in a field when inserting data from the backup. Examples could be converting from integer to unsigned integer, changing to strings of shorter length.

A few changes are allowed without any special startup parameters to *ndb_restore*. These are:

1. Changing row format (FIXED to DYNAMIC and vice versa)

2. Changing storage type from DISK to MEMORY and vice versa

3. Changing the default value of a column

4. Changing the partition key

To "promote" a column means to store it in a data type that is similar but larger. E.g. a string type that is longer. If we promote a fixed size CHAR column to a variable size column, we can specify the parameter *--preserve-trailing-space*. Thus the trailing spaces in the CHAR column that are required in a CHAR column are also transported into the VARCHAR column. To enable promotion of variables it is necessary to set the *--promote-attributes* parameter.

There is a limit to how many types of conversions can happen at the same time. We can convert columns from VARCHAR to TEXT columns, but it isn't possible to convert from MEDIUMINT to BIGINT at the same time. Conversions from one VARCHAR to another VARCHAR and conversions from BINARY to VARBINARY can be performed without this restriction.

In older versions of MySQL Cluster only fixed size strings was supported, when performing a restore of a backup from such an old NDB version *ndb_restore* will automatically convert VARCHAR fields to variable sized columns. If the old fixed size variant needs to be retained one should use the parameter *--no-upgrade*. It is most likely never needed.

The options *--skip-broken-objects* and *--skip-unknown-objects* can be used to ignore unknown objects and also some broken objects. This can happen in downgrade situations.

It is possible to change the name of a database during restore, the parameter *--rewrite-database* will provide the old database name as the first parameter and separated by a comma, the name of the new database name. E.g. *--rewrite-database=dbold,dbnew*. This option can be repeated for each database that should change name.

Setting the parameter *--skip-table-check* is equivalent to setting the parameters *--lossy-conversions* and *--exclude-missing-columns* and *--promote-attributes* and *--skip-unknown-objects*.

34.4   Restore as part of MySQL Cluster Replication

Setting up a new slave cluster from an operational master cluster always starts with restoring a backup. There are some parameters specifically related to replication when performing a restore.

First of all it is necessary to set the parameter *--no-binlog* to ensure that the restored data isn't replicated back to the master cluster. This is only required if we replicate from the cluster from where the backup was taken.

To ensure that the *ndb_apply_status* table on the slave have the correct information we need to execute the final *ndb_restore* step with the flag *--restore-epoch*. This inserts only one entry into *ndb_apply_status* table with the proper *epoch* number restored by the backup. Thus it doesn't matter in which command to execute this since the *epoch* number is available in all backup files.

The example in a previous section of restoring to a cluster with two data nodes will now be changed into the following parameters to support starting up MySQL Cluster Replication.

```
ndb_restore --connectstring=mgm_host --nodeid=1 \
  --backupid=10 --backup-path=/backup/path/dir \
  --restore_meta --no-binlog
ndb_restore --connectstring=mgm_host --nodeid=1 \
  --backupid=10 --backup-path=/backup/path/dir \
  --disable-indexes --no-binlog
ndb_restore --connectstring=mgm_host --nodeid=1 \
  --backupid=10 --backup-path=/backup/path/dir \
  --restore-data --no-binlog
ndb_restore --connectstring=mgm_host --nodeid=2 \
  --backupid=10 --backup-path=/backup/path/dir \
  --restore-data --no-binlog
ndb_restore --connectstring=mgm_host --nodeid=1 \
  --backupid=10 --backup-path=/backup/path/dir \
  --rebuild-indexes --no-binlog --restore-epoch
```

More details on starting up replication channels in the part on Global Replication.

34.5 RESTORING DISTRIBUTED PRIVILEGES

Restoring distributed privileges can be done using the *ndb_restore* program. It is not done by default.

To invoke the restoring of also those tables it is necessary to add the parameter *--restore-distributed-privileges*. It is important that this parameter is specified in all invocations of *ndb_restore*. Also the distributed privilege table needs to be created as a table and the data from various nodes must be restored.

34.6 VARIOUS OTHER USE CASES FOR *ndb_restore*

The normal (and default) use case is to restore the data into the cluster using the NDB API. This is handled by the above shown *--restore_data* parameter. You can also use the parameter *--restore_meta* parameter, in this case only the metadata of the backup is restored.

If you want to view the data before you restore it, you can use *--print_data* and *--print_meta* to view data or metadata respectively. *-print_data* only prints the scanned tables, not the logged changes, these are printed when using the parameter *--print_log*. The parameter *--print* is equivalent to setting all three of those print parameters.

ndb_restore can output SQL statements for all operations it performs. *ndb_restore* can also output the information in a CSV file. To do this first use the parameter *--print_data* followed by the option *--tab*. This creates a file called *table_name.txt* for each table in the backup.

It only prints the data files, not the backup log files. This approach have some limitations since it doesn't make sense to write the log files to CSV files. These logs represents changes in the database since the start of the backup. Thus to restore something consistent using these CSV files requires that the database wasn't updated during the execution of the backup that is restored (thus log is empty).

The output of the CSV files can be changed using:

--append means that we are appending to a file rather than writing a new file from scratch.

--fields-enclosed-by sets the character that can be used to separate fields.

--fields-terminated-by sets the character used to terminate a field.

--lines-terminated-by sets the character used to terminate a line.

--hex ensures that binary fields are printed in hexadecimal format.

34.7 SPECIAL PARAMETERS FOR *ndb_restore*

The transactions used by *ndb_restore* are always a single row per transaction. These transactions are sent in batches with a parallelism of 128. To increase or decrease the parallellism set the *--parallellism* parameter.

To set frequency of progress reports the *--progress-frequency* parameter can be used. The default is 0 which means no progress reporting. It is set in seconds. The verbosity of the output can be changed using the *--verbose* parameter. It can be set between 0 and 255 and the default is 1.

Part VIII

MySQL Cluster APIs

The most important API in MySQL Cluster is the C++ NDB API. Currently all access to the NDB data nodes goes through this interface.

The MySQL Server accesses NDB data nodes through the MySQL Storage engine API. This API is implemented using the NDB API. Through the MySQL Server it is possible to access the NDB data nodes through any MySQL API. There are so many MySQL APIs that I don't even know all of them myself. There is an API for most programming languages.

There are three direct NDB APIs. This means APIs that do not need to pass through a MySQL Server to get to the data. Quite a few applications have been written on top of the C++ NDB API. Some of those have implemented an LDAP server that can be accessed through an LDAP API.

There is also numerous applications developed on top of ClusterJ. ClusterJ is a very nice Java API that implements access to NDB rows as Java Objects. This API was used among others by the HopsFS that implements the meta data service for a Hadoop file system (HDFS).

There is also direct NDB API available from the NodeJS programming language.

We will go through the three direct APIs to the NDB data nodes, one in each chapter with most focus on the C++ NDB API.

CHAPTER 35

C++ NDB API

Now we have completed the view of MySQL Cluster from the SQL point of view. The SQL view always depends on lower level constructs in its implementation. All accesses to data in tables, metadata about tables and retrieval of configuration data goes through the NDB API.

In MySQL there is a storage engine concept to allow many different implementations of the database engine. We have mapped the storage engine interface to our NDB API interface in the NDB storage engine.

The NDB API is implemented in C++, it is possible to write applications directly towards this C++ API. We have implemented special interfaces on top of the NDB API for Java (ClusterJ) and for JavaScript (Database Jones, a Node.js API towards NDB) that we will describe in subsequent chapters.

The aim of this chapter is to describe the NDB API from a high level to make it easier to understand how to write NDB API programs. There is a large set of example programs available in the directory *storage/ndb/ndbapi-examples* in the MySQL Cluster source tree. In this chapter we focus all attention on using the *NdbRecord* variant of the NDB API, some of the examples are old and uses the column format where one column at a time is provided. The new record format is faster, but the old column format is still supported and can thus still be used.

There is documentation of the NDB API available that is for the most part retrieved from the header files using Doxygen. Some parts are skipped in the documentation since they are treated as internal parts of the NDB API. These are safe to use, but have a higher risk of being changed in future versions since they are deemed as internal parts of the API.

Most of the early research work on NDB was centered around the NDB data nodes and how to implement those. In early 1998 the implementation of the data node parts was nearing completion and we started considering how the application code would interface the data nodes.

The NDB data node was written to handle requests asynchronously. We did not expect that application developers wanted to work with an asynchronous API towards NDB. Thus we decided to make a synchronous API. For the most part this decision has been a correct decision, implementing the NDB storage engine requires a synchronous API and using a synchronous API is a lot simpler compared to an asynchronous API.

At the same time the asynchronous API can be used to implement fairly elegant implementations and the code will be a lot easier to optimise. We ended up handling key operations using an asynchronous API that is used by a few users and by a number of our internal tools. It has also been used in a number of benchmarks we have developed to showcase the throughput possibilities of NDB.

At this point scan operations can only be accessed from the synchronous NDB API part.

35.1 META DATA OPERATIONS

The NDB API contains code to handle all interactions with the NDB data nodes including normal user transactions as well as event handling and meta data operations.

It is not recommended to use the meta data part of the NDB API directly in a user application. It is recommended to create all tables using the MySQL Server. Creating a table through the NDB API means that it isn't possible to use it from the MySQL Server. It is a lot simpler to use the SQL syntax to create tables, drop tables, create indexes, foreign keys and so forth.

The MySQL server will also take care of synchronising table changes with slave clusters.

Thus a normal NDB API application will contain code to both connect to a MySQL Server to create the necessary tables and other meta data for the application and the NDB API part to work with those tables.

We will not go through the meta data part of the NDB API in this book and will instead go through the specific syntax required for handling table creation and so forth of NDB tables in the MySQL Server.

Thus it is recommended to always have at least one MySQL Server in an NDB Cluster even if the MySQL Server isn't used at all for normal transactions or queries.

35.2 INITIALISING THE NDB API AND MySQL CLIENT API

Before any interactions with the NDB API it is necessary to initialise the NDB API first. This happens through a call to the method *ndb_init()*.

Similarly it is necessary to initialise the MySQL client API before using it by calling *mysql_init()*.

35.3 CONCURRENCY IN THE NDB API

In 1998 most computers were using a single CPU or possibly two CPUs. Concurrency was limited, however it was necessary to handle many concurrent threads accessing the NDB API.

We decided to create a C++ class called Ndb that is used by one thread. There can be many Ndb objects that can be operated on from many different threads at the same time. But one Ndb object can only be operated on by one thread at a time. Thus this object must be handled with care. It is possible to use it in different threads, but only in one thread at a time. If using it in many threads, it is necessary to protect the move of the Ndb object to another thread.

The Ndb object uses a set of classes that we call the Transporter classes. These classes are responsible for taking the information from one Ndb object and converting it to the NDB protocol and later send this information to the NDB data nodes. It is responsible to receive data back from the NDB data nodes and read the NDB protocol and place the results back into the objects handled by the Ndb object.

In the first implementation of the NDB API and all the way up to MySQL Cluster version 7.2

the Transporter layer used a very simple concurrency control by implementing a Transporter mutex that ensured that only one thread at a time was able to interact with the transporter parts.

After a few years this became a bottleneck and to avoid this bottleneck we made it possible to have several API nodes within one API program. In the MySQL Server this is a configuration variable called *--ndb-cluster-connections*. In 7.2 and earlier versions each API node scaled to about 1.5 CPUs when running a simple benchmark using the NDB API directly (using the MySQL Server means it scales to more CPUs since the MySQL server code will use quite a few CPUs to handle query processing). So e.g. to run a benchmark in a 8-CPU environment was made possible by using 6 API nodes (or cluster connections as they are called in the NDB API). Each cluster connection uses their own node id and can be seen as independent nodes in most management views from NDB.

Now with the multi-core revolution that started around 2006-2007 the number of CPUs per machine escalated very quickly. Thus it was necessary to implement a more scalable concurrency control of the Transporter part. This was implemented in MySQL Cluster 7.3 and makes each API node or cluster connection scale a lot more. So e.g. for the Sysbench benchmark each cluster connection scales to more than three times as many CPUs as before. For DBT2 it was even more where it scaled to more than seven times more CPUs.

Now it is possible to to use only four cluster connections even when running a MySQL Server using 64 CPUs when executing the Sysbench benchmark.

The major limiting factor now in the Transporter part is that there is only one thread at a time that can execute the receive part of the Transporter part.

35.4   NDB CLUSTER CONNECTION

The *Ndb_cluster_connection* object is the starting point for all NDB API programs. When creating this object it is necessary to specify the NDB connect string. The NDB connect string is used to fetch the cluster configuration from the NDB management server. It is possible to specify multiple NDB management servers in the connect string to increase the chance for a successful configuration retrieval. It is possible to specify a specific node id to use by this cluster connection. If not specified the management server will pick a node id that is available currently in the configuration.

To use specific node ids is not absolutely required. In my view it is recommended to use it as much as possible. For management servers and data nodes I recommend to always use it since the node id is connected to a state saved on disk. It will simplify management of the cluster if all processes start up using a specific node id. This requires setting the node id in the configuration for these node types.

For MySQL Servers and long running API programs it is a good idea to use specific node ids. Using MySQL Cluster Manager it is required to use node ids for all data nodes, management servers and for all MySQL Servers.

The normal procedure for the *Ndb_cluster_connection* object is to first create the object specifying the NDB connect string and possibly node id as well. Next a connect call will fetch the NDB configuration from a management server. Next a call to *wait_until_ready* will wait until we are connected to at least one NDB data node.

After these calls our API program is now a part of the cluster and will show up when we list the nodes in the current cluster.

35.4.1 Auto reconnect

Once the NDB API has established communication to the data nodes it will automatically balance the load on the connected data nodes. If a data node is no longer connected we will automatically try to reconnect to this node without any need for the user of the API to interact. It is possible to disable this behaviour if desirable.

35.4.2 Selection of data node to communicate with

Each transaction is handled by one specific data node. There is a number of things impacting the decision which data node to choose. The first consideration is whether the user have provided a hint when starting the transaction, if he has, we will use this hint to connect to the data node if possible.

The hint doesn't say which data node to connect to, it rather specifies a primary key in a specific table, this primary key is mapped to a node using a hashing function and some data distribution hints provided to us from the data nodes when we started using the table. These are hints that are very stable, but they can change e.g. during an add node operation. There is no guarantee that they will be 100% accurate. If they are incorrect, it is not a problem since the data node will get the correct nodes to read and write data from, independent of which data node the transaction is started from. The data nodes always have a correct view of the data node distribution of each table.

If no hint is provided we use a round-robin scheme to ensure that we spread the load on all data nodes.

When using SQL we always use the first SQL statement of a new transaction as the way to provide the hint. If the first SQL statement specifies a primary key to use for a table we will choose this as the hint for the transaction we start.

Setting data node neighbour

In case we haven't specified a hint about where to place the transaction coordinator we can set the node id of the closest data node in the configuration. This will be used in those cases.

If a MySQL Server has the same IP address as a data node it will automatically become the neighbour of this data node and will prefer transactions to use this data node unless a hint has been provided.

However in some situations we know that two nodes are close to each other but they use different IP addresses. This could happen e.g. when we use a Docker network setup where each node have its own IP address but some IP addresses are actually located on the same physical server or even the same virtual machine.

In this case one can provide the data node neighbour through the *set_data_node _neighbour* call on the *Ndb_cluster_connection* object.

In the MySQL Server one can set this node id through the *ndb-data-node-neighbour* configuration variable.

The main use of the data node neighbour concept is for query processing where we are issuing complex SQL queries. In this case most likely no primary key is provided, round robin would be used unless a data node neighbour is selected.

Using a data node neighbour is important if the network between the computers have limited bandwidth. Using a node local to the computer means that we don't have to use limited bandwidth available in connecting between computers in the cluster.

Combining this feature with the possibility to read from backup replicas and possibly even using fully replicated tables makes the API node very strongly connected to the neighbour data nodes in their interaction for all query processing and makes it possible to build query processing that scales in an excellent manner when adding more and more MySQL Servers and NDB data nodes.

35.4.3   LOCKING RECEIVE THREAD TO SPECIFIC CPU

It is possible on Linux, Solaris and Windows to lock threads to specific CPUs. In the NDB API we have the possibility to use this feature in the NDB API by calling the function *set_recv_thread_cpu* on the *Ndb_cluster_connection* object. The API call is prepared for multiple receive threads per NDB cluster connection. Currently we only support one, the array always should be 1 in length in this call.

It is possible to specify the CPUs to use for NDB cluster connections in the MySQL Server configuration. For this one uses the *ndb-recv-thread-cpu-mask* configuration variable. In this variable one can list e.g. 0,2-4 to specify that CPU 0 is used for the first cluster connection, 2 for the second, 3 for the third and 4 for the fourth. The number of CPUs here must be at least the number of cluster connections specified in the configuration variable *ndb-cluster-connection-pool*.

There is a call *set_recv_thread_activation_threshold* that specifies how many API threads that should be concurrently used for the receiver thread to take over receive processing. Setting CPU locking means that it can be a good idea to set this to 1 to ensure that the receive thread is used for all receive handling when multiple threads are active. There is a corresponding MySQL configuration parameter called *ndb-recv-thread-activation-threshold* for this as well.

By default there is no CPU locking for receive thread and the activation threshold is set to 8.

Locking the receive thread to a specific CPU improves performance if it is combined with locking the MySQL server process or the NDB API program to use other CPUs and not the CPUs used by receive threads. It is also necessary to control other programs in the computer that uses large CPU resources, one should also control interrupt handling to avoid those CPUs. If this cannot be done one should not use CPU locking of receive threads.

35.5   NDB OBJECT

The Ndb object is the starting point for all NDB interactions. As mentioned this object should not be used from more than one thread at a time. When waiting for a response back from the NDB data nodes it is important to not use this object while waiting.

Concurrency in the NDB API comes from three places. First it is possible to use multiple cluster connections, second it is possible use multiple threads per cluster connection using separate Ndb objects. Third it is possible to handle multiple operations and even multiple transactions per interaction using the Ndb object.

The Ndb object is a placeholder for transaction objects, operation objects and many other objects used by the Ndb object. Objects are created through the Ndb object and destroyed by the Ndb object.

Before starting to use the Ndb object it has to be created and it is necessary to call the method *init()*.

When creating the Ndb object one specifies two things, first the

Ndb_cluster_connection object used and second a string containing the database name used by the Ndb object. It is possible to change the database name used later on.

The *init()* method has one parameter that is set to 4 by default, the parameter specifies the maximum number of transactions that can be active in parallel on the Ndb object. Using the asynchronous API or using batching with one Ndb object it is possible to handle up to 1024 transactions in parallel from one Ndb object.

Here is a simple code example skipping all error checks for creating the cluster connection and the first Ndb object.

```
Ndb_cluster_connection *cc =
  new Ndb_cluster_connection(connectstring, node_id);
cc->connect();
cc->wait_until_ready(timeout, wait_after_first_node_connected);
Ndb* ndb_obj = new Ndb(cc, "database_name" );
ndb_obj->init();
```

35.6 SETTING UP A ROW

Before a user transaction can be called we need to setup a row data structure. The NDB API also contains a variant where one takes care of one column at a time. I will only describe the NDB API to handle things using the *NdbRecord* columns since this is nowadays the recommended use of the NDB API.

To setup a row we need a reference to the table and the columns we want to operate on.

The first step is to get an object from Ndb of the type *NdbDictionary::Dictionary* that is retrieved using the call getDictionary() on the Ndb object.

Next this dictionary object is used to get a table object of type *NdbDictionary::Table*. This is retrieved by using the call *getTable(tableName)* where tableName is a string with the table name.

Next we use the table object to retrieve one or more column objects. This is retrieved by using a set of calls of the type *getColumn(colName)* where colName is a string containing the column name.

Next we create a record specification object that maps each column into a buffer from where data to set will be read or data read will be inserted when read from NDB.

This is an object of the type *NdbDictionary::RecordSpecification*. We create an array of such objects with as many members in the array as the number of columns we want to access.

We create an Ndb record by calling *createRecord* on the dictionary object. This method have as input the table object, the record specification array, the number of entries in the record specification array and the size of the *NdbDictionary::RecordSpecification* object (needed for backwards compatibility since there used to be an older variant of the record specification object).

This call returns an object of the type *NdbRecord* that can now be used in user transactions. It is also possible to set up a row for access through an ordered index or a unique index. In this case we need both the index object and the table object in the call to *createRecord*.

Here is a very brief example of the above.

```
struct row_buffer
{
  int col1;
  int col2;
};

....

NdbDictionary::Dictionary* dict_obj= ndb_obj->getDictionary();
NdbDictionary::Table *tab_obj = dict_obj->getTable("table_name");
NdbDictionary::Column *col = tab_obj->getColumn("column_name");
NdbDictionary::RecordSpecification spec[2];
spec[0].column = col;
spec[0].offset = offsetof(row_buffer, col1);
spec[0].nullbit_byte_offset= 0;
spec[0].nullbit_bit_in_byte= 0;
spec[1].column = col;
spec[1].offset = offsetof(row_buffer, col2);
spec[1].nullbit_byte_offset= 0;
spec[1].nullbit_bit_in_byte= 0;
NdbRecord *pk_record =
  dict_obj->createRecord(tab_obj, spec, 2, sizeof(spec));
```

For each element in the column array it is necessary to set the column object retrieved previously in the variable *column* and an offset to the column in the buffer provided in a variable called *offset*. There are variables called *nullbit_byte_offset* and *nullbit_bit_in_byte*. These two numbers point out which bit in the null bits of the record that is used to represent the NULL state of the column. These are ignored for columns that are declared as NOT NULL. Thus *nullbit_byte_offset* is the number of bytes from the start of the row.

Thus the row buffer must have space allocated for both the column values as well as for NULL bits. It is recommended use at least 32 bits for the NULL bits to avoid misaligned column values. Similarly for all column values it is recommended that they are aligned on 32-bit boundaries for efficient access without misaligned traps. On a SPARC it is necessary to use this alignment.

35.7 TRANSACTIONS

Every interaction involving reading or writing user tables in NDB uses transactions. A transaction goes through a number of steps, first it is created, next it is executed and the final execution specifies either commit or abort, it can be executed multiple times before abort/commit and finally it is closed.

35.7.1 START A TRANSACTION

Starting a transaction means that we allocate one connection record in one of the DBTC threads in the cluster. Once such a record have been allocated by an API node the API node keeps the connection record. This means that only the first time the start transaction involves a distributed interaction with the NDB data nodes. Most startTransaction calls are local calls that grabs a connection record from a linked list of free connection records and there is one such linked list per data node in the cluster.

The start transaction can be without any parameter *startTransaction()*. In this case a round robin mechanism is used to decide which data node to start the transaction in, if we have a neighbour data node (either with same IP address as API node or by setting *data_node_neighbour* in the cluster connection object), we use the neighbour node.

START TRANSACTION WITH HINT

To start a transaction with a hint on where to start the transaction is a very important feature of MySQL Cluster. This is important to write scalable applications using MySQL Cluster. As an example HopsFS mapped a hierarchical file system on top of a 12-node MySQL Cluster. In order to get this to scale it was important to ensure that operations such as *ls* (list files in a directory) could execute using a scan on just one partition of the table. HopsFS solved this by using the parent directory as the partition key for the table.

Similarly TPC-C have a warehouse id that is part of all tables that can be used to make TPC-C scale perfectly if the warehouse id is used as a partition key. Selecting the proper partition key is important to design scalable applications in NDB.

There are two reasons for this. The first is that if one makes a transaction that updates many rows that have some connection (this is what happens in TPC-C and in HopsFS and in almost all applications), it is very valuable to place the transaction coordinator on the same node as the primary replica location of the rows to be updated. This will significantly decrease the overhead of communication within the cluster during the transaction.

The second is that we can perform ordered index scans that has an equality bound on the partition key, or a full table scan with such an equality bound. These scans only need to scan one partition of the table since all rows sought for will be housed in the same node. By placing the transaction coordinator on this node, we can avoid communication to get to this partition since the partition is placed on the same node.

Decreasing the number of partitions that is required to scan gives us a lower startup cost for the scan. Each additional partition to scan brings an additional small cost to the query execution.

Decreasing communication needs is always important to create scalable distributed applications whether it is a *NoSQL* database, a shared disk relational DBMS, or a shared-nothing DBMS such as MySQL Cluster. Modern hardware makes communication cheaper and makes it easier to write distributed applications, but it will always be beneficial to write your application to minimise the communication needs.

To start a transaction with a hint we use a variant of the *startTransaction* call that use a few parameters. It uses a table object of the type *NdbDictionary::Table* as input that is created by calling the method *getTable(tableName)* on a *NdbDictionary::Dictionary* object. The second parameter is NULL-terminated array of objects of the type *Key_part_ptr*. The *Key_part_ptr* object is a simple struct containing a void pointer and a length of the pointer. This data represents the distribution key or partition key of the table defined by the table object. These are checked against each other that they are consistent.

There is also a method that uses a *NdbRecord*, this is not part of the public NDB API, but is used by the NDB storage engine. The *NdbRecord* here is a record of the primary key of the table used. Here is a simple example to start a transaction with a hint given this interface.

```
NdbRecord *ndb_rec = ....
Ndb *ndb_obj = ....

NdbTransaction *trans_obj = ndb_obj->startTransaction(ndb_rec,
                                                      row_buffer,
                                                      NULL,
                                                      0);
```

The two last parameters specify a buffer to be used for hashing. By specifying NULL as pointer to the buffer we ensure that the *malloc* call is used, otherwise one has to ensure that the buffer is large enough for the hash function call. In the public function described above these two parameters defaults to NULL and 0. But they can be specified explicitly also in this call.

If a buffer is provided it must be large enough to contain all columns in their maximum size and the buffer must be aligned to a 64-bit boundary to be used in these calls. So the buffer should be fairly large if provided. The hash function must work on an expanded row to ensure that different representations of the same word uses the same hash value (there are many character sets that have multiple ways to write the same word).

If no such pointer is passed the NDB API will have to use *malloc* and *free* to allocate and release the memory needed for executing the hash function.

It is also possible to start a transaction on a specific node id and instance id, but normally the application will have no knowledge of the table distribution such that this will be of any use whereas using the partition key will be very useful.

35.7.2 DEFINE OPERATIONS

After starting a transaction we define a set of operations for the first interaction with the NDB data nodes. We will go through in detail how this is done below, these could be operations on a specific record using either a primary key or unique key, it could be scan operations that scan a part of a table using either a full table scan or an ordered index scan. Scans can be used to write rows where we find the rows to write through a scan.

35.7.3 EXECUTING A TRANSACTION

After defining one or more operations it is now time to execute the operations. When executing key operations one can decide whether it is time to commit the transaction while executing it. It is possible to commit with a set of operations, it is also possible to commit with an empty set of operations. Committing an empty set of operations will commit all operations executed since the start transaction call was made.

When a transaction has completed executing a commit of a transaction it is no longer possible to continue using the operation in any other manner than to close the transaction.

The call to execute is made on the *NdbTransaction* object received in the *startTransaction* call. The method is called *execute* and the only required parameter is whether to commit, not commit or abort. The value sent in to commit is *NdbTransaction::Commit*, to execute but not commit yet one uses *NdbTransaction::NoCommit* and to abort a transaction one uses *NdbTransaction::Rollback*. We can provide a second parameter that specifies how to handle errors during transaction execution.

Setting this second parameter to *AbortOnError* means that no errors at all are allowed. *AO_IgnoreError* means that we will commit as much as is possible to commit, thus for most errors we will continue the transaction even if one part of the transaction fails. The default setting for the abort option is that it can be set on a per operation basis. However explicitly setting it in the *execute* call overrides the operation setting.

It is possible to set a third parameter with a force send flag. By default this is turned off. In the MySQL Server this is controlled by a configuration parameter in the MySQL Server.

Scan operations use *execute* as part of starting up a scan. The continuation is however different after the startup of the scan. A scan can handle any number of rows so there is an API to control the fetching of rows to the API that we will describe below.

35.7.4 CLOSE A TRANSACTION

After committing a transaction one needs to close the transaction to make all allocated resources available again. If the transaction had not been committed yet and the NDB data node is waiting for more input the NDB API will abort the transaction as part of the *closeTransaction()* call.

A call to start a transaction with a hint immediately followed by a call to get the node id of the transaction coordinator (using *getConnectedNodeId()*) followed by a call to close the transaction is a quick way of discovering which node the primary replica record belongs to. This method is used by the *flexAsynch* benchmark program and the *ndb_import* program (introduced in 7.6) to distribute queries to different threads where each thread is handling one data node.

35.8   Key operations

To define a key operation is straightforward after setting up the row. One calls a method on the *NdbTransaction* object and it returns an *NdbOperation* object.

35.8.1   Insert tuple

To insert a row we call the method *insertTuple* that requires four parameters. The first is the *NdbRecord* object for the primary key and the second is a pointer to the memory buffer for the primary key columns. The third parameter is the *NdbRecord* for the rest of the columns and the fourth is the memory buffer for these columns. The memory buffers must contain the data to be inserted in all columns before the call.

In a sense one can see the *NdbRecord* objects as the meta data descriptions of a row object. The memory buffers contains the actual data that is interpreted according to the *NdbRecord* object.

There is a variant where only two parameters are needed where the primary key columns are combined with the rest of the columns. This only exists for the *insertTuple* call and not for other types of calls.

The buffer can be reused for other purposes immediately after the call since the data have been saved in the NDB API and no data is to be returned in this case.

35.8.2   Update tuple

Exactly the same as inserting of a row except that instead we use the call *updateTuple* with the same parameters and we still need to set all columns before the call. Also here the buffers can be immediately reused.

35.8.3   Write tuple

The *writeTuple* call will perform an insert if the row didn't exist before or update if the row previously did exist. All required columns need to be part of the record specification since it can become an insert. Also here the buffer can be immediately reused.

35.8.4   Delete tuple

The call *deleteTuple* uses the same parameters, but the fourth parameter can be skipped if no read is performed while deleting the row. The record specification for the entire row is still required in this call.

35.8.5   Read tuple

The call *readTuple* will perform a read of one tuple. The parameters are still the same as when calling insert, update and write of a tuple. It is not ok to reuse the second memory buffer provided in the fourth parameter until the read has been completed. The memory buffer is here used to return the data read from NDB. It is important to still set the primary key fields before calling *readTuple*. The first memory buffer can be immediately reused after the call.

It is possible to set lock mode in this call, more on this below in the section on scans.

35.8.6 OPERATION OPTIONS

In addition the above calls can all set a result mask which is a bit mask indicating which parts of the record specification to use. It is an array of bytes where bits are set in column id order. If a bit is set in this array of bytes it indicates that the column is used for either update or read dependent on the operation type.

There is a possibility to set special options for the reads and writes, more on such options below. There are two parameters for this, one that is a pointer to the options object and a second that contains the length of this options object.

35.9 SCAN OPERATIONS

There are two types of scan operations, full table scans and ordered index scans.

35.9.1 ORDERED INDEX SCANS

Ordered index scans normally use a range scan that specifies a start position and an end position for the range scan. These ranges are defined on the columns defined in the ordered index. Multiple ranges are possible to specify in a scan operation.

To specify an ordered index scan we use a call to *readIndex* on the transaction object that returns an *NdbIndexScanOperation* object. The parameters passed in this call defines the ordered index record specification and another record specification for the data returned in the scan. Optionally one defines the lock mode, a bitmask of the columns in the record specification that are to be read, a bound object of the type *NdbIndexScanOperation::IndexBound* and finally an option object with its length.

The bound object can be defined after this call in a separate call on the scan object returned from *scanIndex* using the method *setBound* where the record specification of the ordered index and the bound object is the parameters.

Multiple index ranges can be defined, various sort orders can be defined. These are specified in the options parameter specified below.

35.9.2 FULL TABLE SCAN

A full table scan will scan all rows in a table and there are three ways to do this, scan through hash index, scan through main memory rows and scan through disk data records.

After starting the transaction one can start a full table scan by calling *scanTable* on the transaction object. This call will return an object of the type *NdbScanOperation*.

This requires at least one parameter, this is the record specification of the row to be retrieved from the table, not all columns need to be part of this specification only the columns of interest.

The second parameter is the lock mode of the scan. Default lock mode is *LM_Read* that means that a row lock will be held on the row from it is scanned until we move onto the next row. *LM_Exclusive* means that we have a row lock, but here an exclusive lock instead.

LM_CommittedRead means that no lock is held at all while scanning, the last committed value of the row is read instead.

LM_CommittedRead is the default setting for SELECT queries in MySQL for the NDB storage engine. The NDB storage engine only supports the setting *READ_COMMITTED*.

To use *LM_Read* from SQL one uses *SELECT ... LOCK IN SHARED MODE* and to use *LM_Exclusive* from SQL one uses the syntax *SELECT FOR UPDATE ....* The final setting that one can use is *LM_SimpleRead*, thus the row is locked while reading it, but before sending it to the API the lock is released. This behaviour is default for reading BLOB tables from the MySQL Server. BLOB tables are a bit special in how they handle these lock modes, see the chapter on concurrency control in MySQL Cluster.

Lock mode can be set on the *readTuple* calls above when defining a read operation using primary key or unique key. It cannot be set on write operations since these operations are always using an exclusive lock.

The third parameter is the result mask. This parameter can be used to define the set of columns (in column id order) to be used in the scan. This is useful if we are using a standard record specification that contains all columns and we want to specifically set a different set of columns for this scan operation.

The fourth parameter is the scan options, there are many different ways to perform the scan, we will go through those options below.

35.9.3   THE ACTUAL SCAN PHASE

The scanning is started by calling *execute* on the transaction object with *NdbTransaction::NoCommit* as parameter.

Next the actual scanning happens in a loop where we constantly call the method *nextResult* on the *NdbScanOperation* object. This method requires a pointer to a memory buffer from where the data can be read. Thus the NDB API uses its own memory and returns a pointer to this memory.

The second parameter is important, if true it states that a fetch is allowed. Thus if it is false we will only return rows that have already been fetched from the NDB data node. By looping with this set to false we know that we won't release locks on rows that we have scanned with *nextResult*, we know that the memory buffers that was returned from previous *nextResult* calls are still valid. This gives us an opportunity to perform write operations on these rows before releasing the lock on the rows. It makes it possible to get this done in a batching mode where up to almost one thousand rows can be scanned locally before the next interaction with the NDB data nodes need to happen.

The third parameter is whether to use force send flag when starting a new fetch. If we are ok to pass on to the next row immediately we will set fetch allowed to be true and this is set after completing the actions required on rows that we have scanned without starting a new fetch.

For read queries we can simply call *nextResult* in a simple loop until we get the result that no more rows exists.

There is a variant of *nextResult* called *nextResultCopyOut* that instead of getting a pointer to a memory buffer sends in a buffer where it asks the NDB API to store the row fetched. Other than that it works exactly the same way as *nextResult*.

35.9.4 SCAN WITH TAKEOVER

Scan with takeover means that we use the row fetched in a scan to either update or delete the row. This should only be used if the scan uses the lock mode *LM_Exclusive*. If used with only *LM_Read* it can cause a deadlock to occur since the lock must be upgraded.

When using scan with takeover it is necessary to use a double loop, an outer loop that uses *nextResult* with fetch allowed set to true and an inner loop that uses *nextResult* with fetch allowed set to false. When the inner loop exits or as part of the inner loop we need to handle all the updates and deletes performed as part of the scan.

To delete the row that was reported in the scan operation it is done through the call *deleteCurrentTuple*, updates are using the call *updateCurrentTuple*. The take over can be made by any transaction, it need not be the same transaction as the scan is executed in.

35.10 OPTIONS

There is a whole range of options that can be set for both scan and key operations that affects the operation of the key lookups and scans. We will cover these here, we will explain them in the context of key lookups, but they can also be used for scan operations. The difference is only that the options class is called *NdbOperation::OperationOption* for key lookups and it is called *NdbScanOperation::OperationOption* for scan operations.

The option identifiers are called *OO_** for key lookups and they are called *SO_** for scan operations.

35.10.1 SCAN FLAGS

Scan flags are an integral part of a scan. It is set by the option *SO_SCANFLAGS* and by setting the option variable *scan_flags* to a proper value. This option is only available for scan operations.

Several flags can be set by OR:ing them together. The following flags are supported:

SF_TupScan

This option is only applicable to a full table scan. It scans the tuples in row id order instead of the default order imposed by the hash index.

SF_DiskScan

This option is only applicable to a full table scan on a table with disk columns. In this case the scan can be done in the row order on disk pages. This can be beneficial since it can decrease the amount of fetching disk pages for a table scan.

SF_OrderBy

Given that an ordered index scan is parallelised on a number of partitions the rows can be returned in non sorted order. Each partition will return rows in the order sorted by the index.

The NDB API has the capability to sort the rows before returning them to the application. This requires running with full parallelism, thus this flag cannot be combined with *SO_Parallel*.

It requires all partitions to return data such that the sort can be performed before returning data to the application. This will have an impact on scan throughput.

SF_OrderByFull

Same flag as *SF_OrderBy* except that the flag implies that all index columns are added to the read set of the scan.

SF_Descending

This is only applicable to an ordered index scan. By default ordered index scans are done in ascending order, with this flag the order is instead descending.

SF_MultiRange

This applies to ordered index scans where multiple index ranges are scanned. In this case this flag must be set.

SF_ReadRangeNo

If multiple ranges are scanned this flag enables reading the range number for a row that has been delivered through the API.

SF_KeyInfo

If a scan is performed using the lock mode *LM_Read* one can specify this flag. It will send back key information to the API that enables a take over operation to be defined using the call *lockCurrentTuple*. This is necessary if we want to retain a read lock on a row already scanned.

This flag is enabled by default when using the lock mode *LM_Exclusive*.

35.10.2 SCAN BATCHING

Normally the size of batches sent back to the API is limited by configuration parameters on the API node. It is possible to override these defaults by setting the option *SO_BATCH* and set the option variable *batch* to the number of rows per batch that is desired.

This option is only available for scan operations.

35.10.3 SCAN PARALLELLISM

By default a scan will use the maximum parallelism available. This means to scan all partitions in parallel up to a limit of how many partitions that can be scanned in parallel.

By setting the option *SO_PARALLEL* we can set an explicit limit on the parallelism for a scan. We set the limit in the variable *parallel* on the options object.

This option is only available for scan operations.

35.11 SCAN PARTITIONING INFO

There is an option *SO_PART_INFO* available that is never used. Its use is related to multiple ranges defined in a query where all ranges use the same partition. This is a feature used by the user defined partitioning scheme not supported but still implemented. The MySQL Server implements this without using any option.

Only available in scan operations.

35.11.1 REDO LOG QUEUEING

All write operations are written into a REDO log. As part of the prepare phase we write them into a REDO log buffer. This buffer could be full. If this happens we have different choices. One choice is to abort the transaction. The other option is to queue the operation before executing it and wait for REDO log buffer to be available.

The default behaviour for this is set as part of the cluster configuration of the API node. Through setting an option OO_QUEUABLE and OO_NOTQUEUABLE (note spelling error here). we can change to either queue or not queue for a specific transaction. The same option should be used for all operations in a transaction.

This option is only available for writing key lookups.

35.11.2 EARLY UNLOCK

The normal behaviour for a transaction is to release locks at commit. BLOBs in NDB are implemented as separate tables.

For a normal table using READ COMMITTED mode requires no locks. For a BLOB table we need to first get a lock on the base table followed by a read on the BLOB table where we read with a simple lock.

For BLOB tables this lock on the base table is unlocked immediately after completing the read of the BLOB table.

The mechanism to unlock rows before commit is available to an application. Such behaviour has an impact on the transactional correctness of the application, so if used, it should be used with care.

When the operation is defined one uses the flag *OO_LOCKHANDLE*. Later when we want to unlock the row we call getLockHandle on the operation object followed by a call to unlock on the transaction object using this handle. The unlock row operation will be sent the next time we call *execute*.

```
NdbTransaction *ndb_trans = .....
NdbOperation *ndb_op = ....
NdbOperation::OperationOptions options;
options.optionsPresent =
  NdbOperation::OperationOptions::OO_LOCKHANDLE
...
Execute ndb_op operation towards NDB data node
...
NdbLockHandle *lock_handle = ndb_op->getLockHandle();
ndb_trans->unlock(lock_handle);
```

This operation is only available to key lookups.

35.11.3   DISABLE FOREIGN KEY CONSTRAINTS

The MySQL Server provides the capability to temporarily disable foreign key constraints. This is implemented as an option in the NDB API. By setting the option *OO_DISABLE_FK* this is achieved, if it is set on an operation it is set on the transaction in the NDB data node, it is always a transaction property.

Use of this feature means that it is possible to create an inconsistent database, it is important that you understand what you are doing when using this feature.

This feature is only available to key lookups.

35.11.4   DEFERRED CONSTRAINTS

In the SQL standard constraints are checked at commit time, deferred constraints are the default behaviour. In MySQL the constraints are checked immediately by default and InnoDB only supports immediate check of foreign key constraints.

NDB supports deferring constraint checks (unique key constraints and foreign key constraints) to commit time. This is controlled in the MySQL Server by setting the MySQL configuration parameter *--ndb-deferred-constraints* to 1. It is always used in the slave applier for MySQL Cluster Replication since this packs a number of transactions together, only the result at commit time is certain to pass the constraint checks.

It is possible to use deferred constraints in the NDB API as well by setting the option flag *OO_DEFERRED_CONSTAINTS* (note spelling error here).

This feature is only available to key lookups.

35.11.5   SAVE DATA IN OPERATION OBJECT

It is possible to save a reference to any data structure in the operation object. This is done by setting the option *OO_CUSTOMDATA* and setting the variable *optionData* on the options object.

This is used by NDB for handling conflict detection in the slave applier. But it could be used for anything really.

Later on you can retrieve this pointer through the call *getCustomData()* on the same operation object.

This option is available to both scan operations and key lookups.

35.11.6   PASS A VALUE TO THE EVENT API

It is possible to pass a 32-bit value from the NDB API to the NDB Event API. This is passed in any update, insert or delete operation. When this operation triggers an event that is sent to the node receiving the events, this value is passed and can be read through the call *getAnyValue* on the event operation object.

To set this value use the flag *OO_ANYVALUE* and the variable *anyValue* on the options object.

This is used as part of the MySQL Cluster Replication implementation to pass information from the NDB API that issued the change to the slave applier. For more information on the content in the any value data see the code files *sql/ndb_anyvalue.h* and *sql/ndb_anyvalue.cc*.

If the cluster isn't using replication to another cluster and the application needs to transport some value to the event API it is possible to use this value.

This feature is only available to key lookups.

35.11.7 OPERATION BOUND TO SPECIFIC PARTITION

It is possible to bind an operation to only be executed by one partition. For example if one needs an estimate on the number of rows one can scan one partition and assume that the the other partitions have roughly the same data distribution.

In this case one sets the flag *OO_PARTITION_ID* and sets the partition id that is scanned or used in the variable *partitionId* on the options object.

This option is available to both scan operations and key lookups.

35.11.8 GET SPECIAL VALUES

Normally an operation retrieves column values from the row. It is also possible to retrieve metadata values about the row and its partition. These columns are called pseudo columns internally in NDB. These pseudo columns all relate to the current row read or written in a key lookup or in a scan operation. By performing a scan operation on all partitions of a table it is possible to get table values for many of those items.

A few of those pseudo columns are only intended for internal use cases.

This option is available to both scan operations and key lookups.

```
Uint32 row_gci;
Uint32 row_size;
....
NdbOperation::OperationOptions options;
NdbOperation::GetValueSpec extra_gets[2];
extraGets[0].column = NdbDictionary::Column::ROW_GCI;
extraGets[0].appStorage = &row_gci;
extraGets[1].column = NdbDictionary::Column::ROW_SIZE;
extraGets[1].appStorage = &row_size;
options.optionsPresent =
  NdbOperation::OperationOptions::OO_GETVALUE;
options.extraGetValues = &extra_gets[0];
options.numExtraGetValues =
  sizeof(extra_gets)/sizeof(extra_gets[0]);
...
Pass reference to option in call to readTuple/insertTuple/...
```

In the example above we perform a normal key lookup operation where we are reading a number of normal row columns (not shown in example above) and in addition we want to know the last GCI the row was updated and we want to know the size of the row.

These extra columns are added to the columns read by this operation as shown above and the same pattern applies to a whole range of metadata columns.

These columns are also accessible from SQL, their name in this case is as below with *NDB$* prepended, e.g. *NDB$ROW_GCI*.

FRAGMENT

This will return the id of the partition of the row returned. It is a 32-bit column.

FRAGMENT_FIXED_MEMORY

This provides the total amount of memory used for the fixed part of the rows in this partition (we use the term fragment internally in NDB as synonym for partition in most cases). In reality we are reading the information on the specific fragment replica where the operation was executed. It is a 64-bit column.

FRAGMENT_VARSIZED_MEMORY

This provides the amount of variable sized memory for the partition. A row has a fixed memory part, an optional variable sized part and an optional disk part. The partition also have a primary key hash index and possibly also a set of ordered indexes. It is a 64-bit column.

ROW_COUNT

This returns the current number of rows in the partition. A row is seen in this view when the row insert have committed. It is a 64-bit column.

COMMIT_COUNT

The number of commits in this partition since the node was started (or partition was created) is reported in this variable. It is a 64-bit column.

ROW_SIZE

Returns the size of the row read. It is a 32-bit column.

RANGE_NO

This is only applicable to ordered index scans. Ordered index scans can use multiple ranges, in this case this column returns the number of the range that the row is returned from. It is a 32-bit column.

DISK_REF

This is the reference to the disk part. It contains a file id, a page id and a page index. It is a 64-bit column.

RECORDS_IN_RANGE

When executing an ordered index scan this column will calculate an estimate of how many rows that exist in the range specified in the scan. The intended use for this is to calculate index statistics used to optimise queries in the MySQL Server. The column type is an array of 4 32-bit values.

The first value is the number of entries in the index (all rows in the partition except rows that have a NULL value in an index column). The second is the number of rows in the range, the third value is the number of rows before the range and the last value is the number of rows after the range. All these values are estimates.

ROWID

The column type is an array of 2 32-bit values. The first 32-bit value is the fragment page id and the second is the page index. This number must be the same in the primary replica and the backup replicas.

ROW_GCI

This value is the GCI identifier of the transaction that last updated this row. It is a 64-bit column, although the value will always fit in a 32-bit variable.

ROW_GCI64

It is a 64-bit column. The higher 32 bits is the same as returned in ROW_GCI. The lower is the extra GCI bits used in the conflict handling of the MySQL Cluster Replication. More on this later.

ROW_AUTHOR

When a table is involved in conflict detection handling we add this extra flag that indicates if the row was written last by the slave applier or not. It is a 32-bit column.

ANY_VALUE

This reads the any value set by the *OO_ANYVALUE* above. It is a 32-bit column.

COPY_ROWID

The column type is an array of 2 32-bit values. It is the same as ROWID except that this is the row id for the copy row, this row id might differ in the replicas.

LOCK_REF

This provides a reference to the lock object. The highest 16 bits of the first 32-bit value is the node id where the lock resides. The lowest 16 bits of the first is the fragment id, the second word is the operation record reference in the LQH block and the third word is a part of the unique id in the LQH block of the operation.

This is used under the hood for unlocking a row before commit. It is intended only for internal use of the NDB API.

OP_ID

This returns the unique id inside the LQH block of the operation currently executed. It is currently not used for anything. It is a 64-bit column.

FRAGMENT_EXTENT_SPACE

The column type is an array of 2 32-bit values. These two numbers together form a 64-bit value. This value represents the number of extents the partition have that are free.

FRAGMENT_FREE_EXTENT_SPACE

The column type is an array of 2 32-bit values. These two numbers together form a 64-bit value. This value represents the amount of free rows available in the free extents already allocated to this partition.

35.11.9 SET SPECIAL VALUES

This is very similar to getting special values. The difference is that the option flag is *OO_SETVALUE*, the object used to set the values are NdbOperation::SetValueSpec instead of NdbOperation::GetValueSpec. The number of set values is set in *numExtraSetValues* and the set value object is stored in *extraSetValues* as shown below.

```
NdbOperation::OperationOptions options;
NdbOperation::SetValueSpec extra_sets[2];
....
options.optionsPresent =
  NdbOperation::OperationOptions::OO_SETVALUE;
options.extraSetValues = &extra_sets[0];
options.numExtraSetValues =
  sizeof(extra_sets)/sizeof(extra_sets[0]);
```

This feature is only available to key lookups. As an example it can be used to set the *ROW_AUTHOR* field above, see the NDB storage engine code for an example.

HIDDEN KEY COLUMN

When a table is created without a primary key, the NDB storage engine will add a column that is an 8-byte column where we generate a unique id of the row when inserting it. This column is always placed last in the set of columns.

PARTITION ID FOR USER DEFINED PARTITIONS

For tables with user defined partitioning the MySQL Server calculates the partition id and sets it in the first column id after the last column (or after the hidden key column).

ROW_AUTHOR

ROW_AUTHOR can be set by slave applier thread for tables involved in conflict detection.

OPTIMIZE

This column is used as part of implementation of OPTIMIZE TABLE. By setting this column to a proper value the NDB storage engine instructs the NDB data node to move the variable sized part to a prepared place to remove fragmentation of the variable sized memory. It is not intended for normal use cases. It is a 32-bit column.

35.12   INTERPRETER COMMANDS AS PART OF NDB API OPERATIONS

The final option that one can use is so advanced that it merits its own section. This is the execution of interpreted programs. All read and write operations can run an interpreted program as part of their operation.

The most common use of this feature is to push down scan filters to NDB data nodes. Thus the MySQL Server has a condition it wants to push down to the data node. This is handled such that the conditions is translated into an interpreted program.

This interpreted program is sent as part of the read/write operation down to the data node owning the data. When reading or writing the row this interpreted program is executed and for scan filters it decides whether to read the row or to skip the row and move on.

For write operations it could be used e.g. to increment an integer field rather than performing a read followed by a write. There is no way currently to get this optimisation from the MySQL Server, but it is possible to write an NDB API program that builds an interpreted program that does this.

The interpreter is a very simple register machine with 8 registers. It is possible to read a column value into a register, it is possible to load constants into registers, it is possible to add, subtract registers. It is possible to define labels and it is possible to branch dependent on a register value to a label. It is also possible to define a subroutine and call it.

To enable pushdown of LIKE constructs, this is also available as a interpreter instruction.

To use this one creates an NdbInterpretedCode object. For use of things like increment column one should use the functions of the NdbInterpretedCode object directly. For definition of condition filters one should use the NdbScanFilter class.

```
NdbInterpretedCode code(...);
... Define interpreted program
options.optionsPresent =
  NdbOperation::OperationOptions::OO_INTERPRETED;
options.interpretedCode = &code;
```

35.12.1   NDBSCANFILTER

The *ha_ndbcluster_cond.cc* contains lots of uses the NdbScanFilter functions. Also read *NdbScanFilter.hpp* to see more how one can use this object.

The general idea of using the NdbScanFilter is that you define groups of conditions. The start of this filter group is started by calling the function *begin*. The parameter to this specifies whether the conditions inside the group should use AND, OR, NOR, or NAND. One condition inside this group could then be a new group of conditions. One could view *begin* and *end* calls as left parenthesis (*begin*) and right parenthesis (*end*) in a textual condition.

The actual conditions are defined by a call to the function *cmp*. This starts by defining the comparator type (e.g. larger than, equal and so forth). Next the column to compare with. Next the value to compare with. This value is represented by a *void** pointer with a length. No length bytes are expected in the value representation.

The comparator could also be LIKE and NOT LIKE. In this case the value could contain % and ? wildcards.

There is also methods to check for NULL and for NOT NULL.

35.13   Scan example

Here is an example where we delete all rows using an ordered index on the primary key and in addition a scan filter. All the rows that pass are part of the index scan and matches the scan filter are returned and deleted.

At first we start a transaction, we create a scan object that contains the record specification of the index and one record specification of the columns to read. We use exclusive lock since we are going to delete the rows as part of the scan.

We define the lower bound to be 1 and we include 1 in the range. We define the upper bound to be 100 and we don't include the 100 in the range.

Next we also define a scan filter using an equal condition on one of the columns in the table. This scan filter will generate an interpreted program that will skip the row unless the scan filter is passed.

Using the above mentioned option *SO_SCANFLAGS* it is possible to specify that rows are returned in various sorted orders, it is possible to define multiple ranges and to get the range number of returned rows.

We have a double loop where the outer loop is making calls to the NDB data node and the inner loops handles the rows returned from this call to the NDB data node.

We execute the deletes once per outer loop, but we wait with committing the transaction until the scan is completed.

```
NdbRecord *primary_key_record = ...
NdbRecord *columns_record = ...
...
trans_obj = ndb_obj->startTransaction();
scan_obj = trans_obj->scanIndex(primary_key_record,
                                columns_record,
                                NdbOperation::LM_Exclusive);
unsigned lower_bound = 1;
unsigned upper_bound = 100;

NdbIndexScanOperation::IndexBound key_range;
key_range.low_key = (char*)&lower_bound;
key_range.low_key_count = 1;
key_range.low_inclusive = true;

key_range.high_key=(char*)&high;
key_range.high_key_count=100;
key_range.high_inclusive=false;

key_range.range_no=0;
scan_obj->setBound(primary_key_record, key_range);

NdbScanFilter scan_filter(scan_obj);
scan_filter.begin(NdbScanFilter::AND);
scan_filter.cmp(NdbScanFilter::COND_EQ,
                column_id,
                (void*)column_value,
                column_length);
scan_filter.end();

trans_obj->execute(NdbTransaction::NoCommit);
while (scan_obj->nextResult(true)) == 0)
{
  do
  {
    scan_obj->deleteCurrentTuple();
  } while (scan_obj->nextResult(false)) == 0);
  trans_obj->execute(NdbTransaction::NoCommit);
}
trans_obj->execute(NdbTransaction::Commit);
trans_obj = ndb_obj->closeTransaction();
```

35.14 NDB Event API

The NDB API contains an Event API that makes it possible to subscribe to all changes of a specific table. Each time a transaction is committed an event can be generated for each row that have been changed. These events are collected together for a specific global checkpoint and sent to the API node(s) that are listening to the events. There can be many listeners to the same event. This is used by NDB to inject events into a MySQL binlog to get the changes into the MySQL Replication infrastructure. It can be used by applications to wait for certain events and create actions based on those events. There are countless applications of how to use events.

The events are asynchronous events, they will arrive as soon as possible, but there is no specific guarantee on when they will arrive. Normally a cluster uses *micro GCPs* that are created with 100 millisecond delay. Therefore it is expected that events are delayed for at least around hundreds of milliseconds and in overloaded systems it can take longer.

The data node will buffer events in a buffer, if the API node is not fast enough to consume the events, the event will eventually fail. In this case the API node will be informed that the event reporting failed.

35.14.1   CREATE EVENT

The first step is to create an event of type *NdbDictionary::Event*. To create such an event it needs a name and it needs a table object of type *NdbDictionary::Table*, the table object is retrieved by name from the *NdbDictionary::Dictionary* object.

Next one adds one or more table events, one can set the event to wait for inserts, deletes, updates or all of those. This uses the method *addTableEvent* on the event object.

The event specifies which columns that will be sent to the event listener as part of each event. This uses the method *addEventColumns* on the event object.

For insert events the after value is sent, for delete events the before value is sent and for update events both the before value and the after value of those columns are sent.

If the table contains BLOBs that one want to hear when they are updated it is necessary to call the method *mergeEvents* on the event object before creating it in the NDB data nodes. This method can be called with the flag set to not merge events from the BLOB tables.

Setting merge events to true have the impact that several writes on the same row within one global checkpoint will be merged into one event.

BLOB events are reported as mentioned above when merge events have been set, but it is necessary to read the BLOB fields using the *NdbBlob* object to see their value.

The next step is to create the event in the NDB data nodes. This happens through a call to the method *createEvent* on the *NdbDictionary::Dictionary* object using the event object as parameter.

Now the event is created in the NDB data node and can be used to listen to events.

35.14.2   DROP EVENT

Events are dropped from the NDB data nodes by calling the method *dropEvent* on the *NdbDictionary::Dictionary* object using the event name as the parameter.

35.14.3 CREATE EVENT OPERATION

Now that the event exists in the NDB data nodes we can create an event operation to listen to the events. This is done through a call to the method *createEventOperation* on the Ndb object using the event name as parameter.

It is necessary to call the method *mergeEvents* on the event operation object to specify whether it is desirable to get events merged or not. This merge setting activates the merging, but the merge flag need to be set also on the event object when the event is created in the data nodes. If not set also there there will be events missing from the data node making it impossible to merge events properly.

As part of setting up the event operation object we need to define objects of type *NdbRecAttr* to provide the before value (using *getPreValue*) and after value (using *getValue*) for each column we are interested in.

Finally we need to call *execute* on the event operation object.

35.14.4 WAIT FOR EVENTS

To listen to events one now calls the method *pollEvents* on the Ndb object using the number of milliseconds to wait for wakeup if no events occur. This method returns a positive number if events occur.

If events occur one calls the method *nextEvent* on the Ndb object to retrieve one event. This method returns the event operation previously defined. This object is now filled with information from the event and the user can use methods in this object to retrieve the information about the event type (insert, delete or update) and what columns that changed with their before value and after value.

The *NdbRecAttr* objects can be used to discover if attributes have changed, if they are set to NULL and the column value.

When the program is no longer interested in listening to events it drops the event operation by calling *dropEventOperation* on the Ndb object using the event operation object as parameter.

35.14.5 NODE FAILURE HANDLING OF EVENTS

Events are generated in all data nodes. It is only the node that have been selected as primary event sender that will send his event to the API node. If a data node fails that was primary event sender the other nodes will ensure that the API node gets the information from one of the remaining live nodes instead. Thus all nodes keep the buffers for the events of a global checkpoint until the API node have confirmed that it has received those events. All this happens automatically without any user interaction.

35.14.6 NDB API EVENT EXAMPLE

Here is an example of how to write an event handler loop for a specific table and a number of specific columns.

```
const char *col_names[2] = { "col1", "col2" };
NdbDictionary::Dictionary *dict_obj ndb_obj->getDictionary();
NdbDictionary::Table *tab_obj = dict_obj->getTable("table_name");
NdbDictionary::Event event_obj("event_name", *tab_obj);
event_obj.addTableEvent(NdbDictionary::Event::TE_ALL);
event_obj.addEventColumns(2, col_names);
event_obj.mergeEvents(false);
dict_obj->createEvent(event_obj);
NdbEventOperation *op = ndb_obj->createEventOperation("event_name");
op->mergeEvents(false);
NdbRecAttr *col_after[0] = op->getValue(col_names[0]);
NdbRecAttr *col_before[0] = op->getPreValue(col_names[0]);
NdbRecAttr *col_after[1] = op->getValue(col_names[1]);
NdbRecAttr *col_before[1] = op->getPreValue(col_names[1]);
op->execute();
while (true) {
   int r = ndb_obj->pollEvents(1000);
   while (r > 0 && (op = ndb_obj->nextEvents())) {
     ... Handle event
   }
}
ndb_obj->dropEventOperation(op);
dict_obj->dropEvent("event_name");
```

35.15 Pushdown Join

A part of the NDB API is the handling of the complex query operations. It is possible to push parts of a join query down to the NDB data nodes. This makes use of a form of linked table scans.

The first table is either using a primary key operation, unique key operation or a scan operation. Each row that is found in this first table is sent to the second table in the join order. Normally the first table is a scan operation in a pushdown join operation.

For each row found in the first table the results is sent to the NDB API, at the same time the columns needed for evaluation further down the join evaluation is sent along in a new join that involves all tables except the first table.

In this manner the query is recursively executed. If the join evaluation contains filtering parts this can lead to a very high parallelisation. If very little filtering is performed the NDB API will still be a major bottleneck since there is a limit to how fast the NDB API can process queries.

This pushdown join interface to the NDB API is used by the NDB storage engine, it is not intended for use by normal NDB API applications. I won't go through any more details how this part of the NDB API works.

35.16   ASYNCHRONOUS API

The asynchronous NDB API is currently only applicable to the key operations. It is not possible to use it for scan operations.

It only differs in how transactions are executed. Instead of a single *execute* there are three calls. These calls must be preceded by a call *executeAsynchPrepare* that prepares the defined operations for execute.

A normal *execute(...)* call will normally perform three actions:

1. Prepare defined operations for execute

2. Send prepared operations

3. Poll for completion of sent operations

With the normal synchronous API it is possible to execute multiple transactions in parallel, but the normal use case is to use one transaction at a time. The above poll will always wait for all sent operations to complete.

Using the asynchronous API it is expected to have many concurrent transactions outstanding at any point in time and the poll doesn't have to wait for all actions to complete, it is sufficient to wait for a few actions (by default one) to complete.

35.16.1   *sendPollNdb*

sendPollNdb is more or less the same as calling execute with one major difference. The sendPollNdb can be asked to wake up before all transactions have completed. Thus the asynchronous interface can be used to work with hundreds of interactions in parallel per thread. Thus fewer threads are needed to operate the interactions, the fewer threads can thus use more batching and thus higher throughput can be achieved.

35.16.2   *sendPreparedTransactions*

If the thread will take care of any other business while NDB is working it can use the *sendPreparedTransactions* call to send the prepared transactions but not waiting for their completion.

35.16.3   *pollNdb*

This can be used in conjunction with *sendPreparedTransactions*. When returning from other activities it is possible to poll for those transactions already sent to be completed.

35.17   *flexAsynch* ARCHITECTURE

The *flexAsynch* program is a benchmark program we've used to showcase hundreds of millions of reads and tens of millions of write operations per second. It uses a special model for how to achieve extremely high throughput. It can be used in other programs only requiring access to key operations.

Chapter 36

ClusterJ, API for Java and Scala

ClusterJ is the name of our direct access to the NDB data nodes for Java programs. ClusterJ is implemented on top of the C++ NDB API. The first layer on top of the NDB API is a JNI (Java Native Interface) layer that maps the C++ NDB API onto a Java NDB API.

Thus it is possible to program directly against most of the NDB API even from Java if desirable (this layer is called ndbjtie internally). ClusterJ adds another layer that makes it considerably much easier to program against NDB.

I am personally quite fond of the ClusterJ interface even though I rarely program in Java myself. Interestingly ClusterJ can also be used from the Scala programming language. All Java libraries can be called from Scala.

The ClusterJ layer provides an object-relational mapping that is similar to Hibernate.

To explain how to use ClusterJ we will start with the initialisation methods followed by the classes created to map tables or parts of tables into Java objects. The next step is to go through the use of the *Session* object that controls accesses to NDB. We will go through some details on how to control searches in NDB from the *Session* object. We will also provide a number of examples of how to use the ClusterJ API.

There are plenty examples provided in the MySQL source tarball. The test suite for ClusterJ contains a large set of examples of how to use the ClusterJ API.

A fairly sizable application that uses ClusterJ is HopsFS that we covered a bit earlier. This implements a Hadoop file system on top of NDB. It replaces the name nodes of the HDFS (file system in Hadoop) with a set of name nodes that use ClusterJ and store its data in NDB data nodes. This code can also be used as an example of how to write a ClusterJ application.

This code is available on *github.com* and can be downloaded from there using the following command:

```
git clone https://github.com/hopshadoop/hops-metadata-dal-impl-ndb
```

36.1 Installing ClusterJ

The simplest method of installing ClusterJ is by using the Linux repos as described in an earlier chapter. The name of the repo to install is *java*. Installing a full MySQL Cluster application will contain ClusterJ as well.

Currently there is no prepared Docker file ready for ClusterJ.

36.2 COMPILING CLUSTERJ APPLICATIONS

When compiling ClusterJ applications we need to have the *jar* file clusterj-api.jar in the class path. We provide the class path using the option *-classpath*. There are three main places where the Java jar files for MySQL Cluster are installed. This is either in the *share/mysql/java* directory under the install directory of MySQL. This is where older versions of MySQL Cluster placed it.

Newer versions of MySQL Cluster place it in the *share/java* under the MySQL Cluster installation directory.

The MySQL Linux repos install the JAVA jar files for MySQL Cluster under the directory */usr/share/mysql/java*.

In addition in newer versions the file names are tagged with a version number. Thus the jar file is called clusterj-api-7.5.4.jar in MySQL Cluster 7.5.4. Searching for *clusterj-api-CLUSTER_VER.jar* is the most appropriate on recent MySQL Cluster versions.

The program to compile Java code is *javac* that requires installation of the proper Java JDK for this. ClusterJ requires use of Java version 7 or version 8.

Here is the command used to compile my small test program.

```
javac \
  -classpath $CLUSTERJ_INSTALL_DIR/clusterj-api-$CLUSTER_VER.jar:. \
  myClusterJApp.java
```

The extra . in the classpath ensures that the compiler looks for a Customer.java or Customer.class in the same directory as my main program.

36.3 EXECUTING A CLUSTERJ APPLICATION

Executing a Java application using ClusterJ requires access to at least two things. One is the *clusterj.jar* that is located in the same directory as the *clusterj-api.jar* described in the previous section.

The second thing we need access to is the NDB API library. We provide the path to this library in *java.library.path*. This library is normally found in the *lib* directory in the MySQL installation directory in newer versions. In older versions it can be under *lib/mysql* instead.

The following command will run your new ClusterJ application. The extra . directory ensures that classes already compiled in your local directory will be included in the compile or execution of your ClusterJ application. The command to start your ClusterJ application becomes more complex for bigger projects. Java code is executed by the *java* binary.

```
java \
  -classpath $CLUSTERJ_INSTALL_DIR/clusterj-$CLUSTER_VER.jar:. \
  -Djava.library.path=$MYSQL_INSTALL_DIR/lib \
    myClusterJApp
```

36.3.1   PROPERTIES FILE

All the properties that can be changed in the *Properties* object are documented in the MySQL Cluster documentation at

   https://dev.mysql.com/doc/ndbapi/en/mccj-clusterj-constants.html.

We will go through the most interesting ones in this section. When creating a session factory (one such per cluster connection) we need a *Properties* object as input. The recommended manner to fill in this object is by using a properties file. Normally this file would be called *clusterj.properties* and be placed under the same directory where your application resides. But given that this is under control of the application developer it could be named differently and be placed elsewhere as well.

After reading the file and filling in the properties it is also possible to change those settings programmatically in the *Properties* object.

com.mysql.clusterj.connectstring

The connect string to the NDB management server(s) is a necessary setting that most installations is required to set. It can be used to set hostname(s) of management server(s) (defaults to localhost), port number (defaults to 1186).

com.mysql.clusterj.database

This parameter defines the default database to use when working against NDB. Defaults to *test.*

com.mysql.clusterj.connection.pool.size

If more than one cluster connection it can be set here. One cluster connection scales to some level, but if the program is required to use a full server one might need a few more cluster connections to scale. Defaults to 1.

com.mysql.clusterj.connection.pool.nodeids

To improve management of the cluster it is a good idea to have stable node ids on NDB API programs that execute for long times. For short lived programs it can be ok to get any node id.

This parameter can list a number of node ids to use for the cluster connections. The number of node ids should be the same as the size of the pool of cluster connections. It is also possible to only set one node id, in this case the node ids used are starting at this node id, e.g. if set to 55 and the pool size is 4 we will use the node ids 55, 56, 57 and 58.

Is not set by default.

com.mysql.clusterj.connect.autoincrement.increment

When using tables with autoincrement columns this parameter specifies how much we will step the autoincrement between each insert. Defaults to 1.

com.mysql.clusterj.connect.autoincrement.offset

This represents the starting value for the autoincrements. Defaults to 1. The intended use case for non-default settings of autoincrement increment offset is for MySQL Cluster Replication where both clusters can be used to insert new rows at the same time. By ensuring that the clusters use the same increment, but different start values (= offsets) we can ensure that they won't generate the same autoincrement value.

com.mysql.clusterj.connect.autoincrement.batchsize

An API node allocates a batch of autoincrement values at a time. This parameter specifies how many values we retrieve per batch. Set by default to 10.

com.mysql.clusterj.connect.retries

Specifies the number of retries before we give up on connecting to a management server. A negative value means that we will never give up. We will continue until we succeed with the connection setup. Set by default to 4.

com.mysql.clusterj.connect.delay

Specifies the delay after an unsuccessful attempt until we make another attempt to connect to the management server(s). Defaults to 5 seconds.

com.mysql.clusterj.connect.verbose

This will write a bit more verbose printouts during connect process if set. Defaults to not set (= 0).

com.mysql.clusterj.connection.reconnect.timeout

The NDB API is designed for automatic reconnect at failures. This parameter specifies how many seconds to wait until we reconnect after a network failure. The default value is 0, thus we won't attempt to reconnect. It is worth considering changing this value. The timeout is used to wait for all Session objects to be closed before a reconnect is performed.

There is a method *reconnect* on the SessionFactory object that can be used to change this value programmatically.

com.mysql.clusterj.max.transactions

The maximum number of transactions that can be handled by one Session object. This is an important parameter to increase if using the asynchronous NDB API. This API is not accessible from ClusterJ. Thus in this case the only manner to use many transaction objects is through multiple open scans. Thus by default we can have at most 3 open scans in parallel. If more are needed this parameter must be incremented. There is no reason to decrease it. It is set to 4 by default.

com.mysql.clusterj.connect.timeout.mgm

The time we will block waiting for a connection from a data node. When we timeout here we will check the timeouts before and after if they have expired, if not we will retry the blocking connect attempt. Defaults to 30000 milliseconds, only multiples of 1000 are allowed.

com.mysql.clusterj.connect.timeout.before

This represents the time to wait for the first data node to connect before giving up. Defaults to 30 seconds.

com.mysql.clusterj.connect.timeout.after

After the first data node have connected, this is how long we will wait for all data nodes to connect. Defaults to 20 seconds.

com.mysql.clusterj.byte.buffer.pool.sizes

By default memory blocks used to store BLOB parts are pooled within ClusterJ. To save memory at the expense of more processing one can set this value to 1. This means that buffers for BLOB objects will be using normal malloc and free calls during their usage.

com.mysql.clusterj.connection.recv.thread.cpuids

Each cluster connection (SessionFactory) have one receive thread. This receive thread executes all signals arriving from the NDB data nodes. Thus the receive thread is a potential bottleneck for scalability of the NDB APIs. It is thus a bottleneck due to that only one CPU can be used to execute these signals. The way to scale this is to use multiple API nodes, this gives access to multiple receive threads.

Given that this receive thread executes so much it can be beneficial to execute it in the same CPU all the time. This parameter specifies a list of CPU ids, the number of CPUs listed here must equal the pool size.

The default setting is that no CPUs are provided, thus no CPU locking is used.

It is possible to set/unset this programmatically on the SessionFactory object using the call *setRecvThreadCPUids*. The input to this call is an array of CPU ids of *short* type. The size of the array must be the same as the number of cluster connections used (pool size above). The CPU locking is unset by using the CPU id -1. It is set by setting a CPU id recognized by the OS in the array.

com.mysql.clusterj.connection.recv.thread.activation.threshold

This parameter specifies the threshold for how many Session objects (NDB objects) that are active in a cluster connection before the receive thread is activated to take over execution of signals. Before this threshold the user thread will take care of the receive thread work (still only one thread at a time can handle the receive thread work). By default this is set to 8. If we lock CPUs it might be useful to set this to 1 instead.

It is possible to set this programmatically on the SessionFactory object using the call *setRecvThreadActivationThreshold*.

36.4 CLUSTERJ ANNOTATIONS

One of the first step in defining your ClusterJ application would be to map the table objects in your database towards a set of Java classes. These classes are mapped to the table definition using annotations. Normally such classes maps all columns of the table, but it is also possible to only map a subset of the columns and indexes to the class.

It is possible to define several classes that maps to the same table. One can see these classes as different views on the tables.

Each column of the table has a get-method that returns the value of the field of the Java type that maps to the SQL type stored in NDB. Similarly there is a set-method for setting the value of this column.

36.4.1 @PERSISTENCECAPABLE

Before the class is defined we define that the class is a persistent class. The only attribute of interest to this annotation is the name of the table in NDB.

36.4.2 @PRIMARYKEY

One can either define the entire primary key with all its columns before the class, but it is easier to simply add a *@PrimaryKey* annotation before defining the get and set method of the column. No attributes are needed on the annotation if provided inside the class.

36.4.3 @COLUMN

In many cases it is not necessary to provide any *@Column* annotation. The default name of the column is the name found in the get and set call.

Now we have enough to give a very simple example. As shown in this example it is necessary to import all annotation types used in the java file.

The example table can be created using the following MySQL command:

```
CREATE TABLE customer (
  customer_id INT PRIMARY KEY NOT NULL,
  name varchar(255) UTF8,
  KEY name_index(name)
  ENGINE=ndb
);
```

In the example below we have a table *customer* with two columns. The first one *customer_id* is an integer that is also the primary key. The second field *name* contains the name of the customer. There is an index on this column.

Since we want to use the method names getId and setId for getting/setting the customer id, we describe the column using the *@Column* annotation. This is required when the name of the column in NDB is different from the names of the methods.

```
import com.mysql.clusterj.annotation.PersistenceCapable;
import com.mysql.clusterj.annotation.PrimaryKey;
import com.mysql.clusterj.annotation.Column;

@PersistenceCapable(table="customer")
public interface Customer {
  @PrimaryKey
  @Column(name="customer_id")
  int getId();
  void setId(int id);

  String getName();
  void setName(String name);
}
```

We add the *@PrimaryKey* annotation before the *customer_id* column to indicate that this is the primary key of the table.

The column *name* requires no mapping since it uses the same name on the methods as the name of the column in the database. There is an index on the column, this is discovered automatically by ClusterJ.

ClusterJ will automatically discover the partition key of a table to ensure that scans can avoid scanning all partitions when the partition key is provided.

36.4.4   @LOB

BLOB columns is mapped using the *@Lob* annotation type. This is used both for text BLOB's that can use the *String* type in Java and binary BLOB's that can use the *byte []* type. The *@Lob* annotation is provided as part of class definition right before the BLOB column.

36.4.5   @PROJECTION

One table can be mapped to more than one class. If a class will not contain all columns one should provide the *@Projection* annotation before the persistence definition. At a minimum a class must contain the primary key or possibly a unique key. Without this information in the object it isn't possible to persist the object in the database.

36.4.6   @NOTPERSISTENT

It is possible to add variables in the Java class that is not persistent and thus not mapped to any database column. In this case one adds the annotation *@NotPersistent* before the attribute is declared with its access methods.

36.4.7   NULL VALUES

Columns that can contain NULL values can handle NULL values differently. One method is to signal with an exception if the column isn't set before the object is flushed to the database. Another method is to set the value to the default value if no value have been provided. Here are two examples of this.

```
@Persistent(nullValue=NullValue.DEFAULT)
public Integer getX();
public void setX(Integer int_val);

@Persistent(nullValue=NullValue.EXCEPTION)
public Integer getY();
public void setY(Integer int_val);
```

36.5 STARTUP EXAMPLE CODE

```
import com.mysql.clusterj.ClusterJHelper;
import com.mysql.clusterj.SessionFactory;
import com.mysql.clusterj.Session;
import com.mysql.clusterj.Query;
import com.mysql.clusterj.LockMode;
import com.mysql.clusterj.query.QueryBuilder;
import com.mysql.clusterj.query.QueryDomainType;
import com.mysql.clusterj.query.Predicate;
import com.mysql.clusterj.query.PredicateOperand;
import java.io.File;
import java.io.InputStream;
import java.io.FileInputStream;
import java.util.List;
import java.util.ArrayList;

public class TestClusterJ {
    ... Implementation of test methods
    public static void main(String[] args) throws Exception {
        File propertiesFile new File("clusterj.properties");
        InputStream inputStream = new FileInputStream(propertiesFile);
        Properties properties = new Properties();
        properties.load(inputStream);
        SessionFactory sessionFactory =
        ClusterJHelper.getSessionFactory(properties);
        Session session = sessionFactory.getSession();
        .... Call test methods
    }
}
```

To start up a ClusterJ application it is necessary create one SessionFactory object. From this object we create Session objects that are used to interact with NDB. The Session object is mapped directly to the Ndb object in the C++ NDB API as explained in the previous chapter. Ndb objects are mapped to cluster connections in a round robin fashion by the SessionFactory object.

To create a SessionFactory requires that we prepare a *Properties* object. We assume this object comes from reading the file *clusterj.properties*.

Equipped with a Session object we are ready to work with data in NDB.

36.6 SESSION OBJECT

We get a session object from the session factory object. The session object is mapped to the Ndb object in the NDB API. It can handle one transaction at a time and multiple rows can be fetched and updated in parallel when interacting with NDB data nodes.

36.6.1 INSERTING A ROW

We use a simple example based on the Customer class that we defined in the previous section. To insert a new object we create a new object of type Customer, next we assign values to all columns. Finally we call the *persist* function, the function *makePersistent* is equivalent to the *persist* function.

```
Customer newCust = session.newInstance(Customer.class);
newCust.setId(100);
newCust.setName("Mikael");
session.persist(newCust);
```

If the session has no transaction started yet, the *persist* call will perform the actual transaction in an NDB data node that inserts the new customer row into the database.

Thus if no transaction is started in the Session object we execute in autocommit mode where each operation is executed as a separate transaction.

36.6.2 UPDATING A ROW

There are two variants of how to update a row. The first method is a so called blind update. This means that we don't read the row before we update it. We simply overwrite all values in the updating class.

This example shows that the only difference to an insert is that we call *updatePersistent* instead of *makePersistent*.

```
Customer newCust = session.newInstance(Customer.class);
newCust.setId(100);
newCust.setName("Mikael");
session.updatePersistent(newCust);
```

The other variant is a read before the update. In this case we perform the read by using the *find* call. In this case we only need to update the columns that will change. All the other ones will be persisted with the same column values as was read. Given that we are planning to update the row after reading it, we use exclusive lock mode already at the read to avoid deadlocks, in addition we have to explicitly use a transaction to ensure that the lock is held also after returning from *find*. Default mode is autocommit, thus *find* will by default commit before returning (thus no locks are held when returning).

```
session.setLockMode(LockMode.EXCLUSIVE);
session.currentTransaction().begin();
Customer newCust = session.find(Customer.class, 100);
newCust.setName("Mikael");
session.updatePersistent(newCust);
session.currentTransaction().commit();
```

The *find* call will always go immediately to the NDB data node and fetch the row.

One more variant is to issue multiple reads before we go towards the data node to fetch the rows. In the below example we use the load method (only prepares for a read) several times followed by a *flush* call that performs the prepared operation. The load method can only be used when an active transaction is ongoing.

Since we have a transaction started, the calls to *updatePersistent* will not take effect until we call commit, at commit both updates will be sent in one batch to the data nodes.

When a transaction is started only *find, flush* and *commit* will start communication with the data nodes.

```
session.setLockMode(LockMode.EXCLUSIVE);
session.currentTransaction().begin();
Customer newCust1 = session.newInstance(Customer.class);
Customer newCust2 = session.newInstance(Customer.class);
newCust1.setId(100);
newCust2.setId(101);
session.load(newCust1);
session.load(newCust2);
session.flush();
newCust1.setName("Mikael");
newCust2.setName("Mikael");
session.updatePersistent(newCust1);
session.updatePersistent(newCust2);
session.currentTransaction().commit();
```

Hopefully these examples provides some insights into how one can batch interactions with NDB data nodes when designing ClusterJ applications.

We will show an alternative to using the transaction interface to batch updates. This uses the *updatePersistentAll* interface that takes a set of rows to persist through updating.

```
List<Customer> updatedInstances = new ArrayList<Customer>();
Customer newCust1 = session.newInstance(Customer.class);
Customer newCust2 = session.newInstance(Customer.class);
newCust1.setId(100);
newCust1.setName("Mikael");
newCust2.setId(101);
newCust2.setName("Michael");
updatedInstances.add(newCust1);
updatedInstances.add(newCust2);
session.updatePersistentAll(updatedInstances);
```

The *updatePersistentAll* takes a list of objects to update instead of a single object. In this case we don't use explicit transactions, instead we use the autocommit mode. Thus the *updatePersistentAll* will perform the updates and commit in one interaction.

36.6.3 DELETING A ROW

Deleting a single row using autocommit is very similar to an update except that it is only necessary to update the primary key of the object and use the call *deletePersistent*.

```
Customer newCust1 = session.newInstance(Customer.class);
newCust1.setId(100);
session.deletePersistent(newCust1);
```

We can use the read before delete in the same fashion as for updates and similarly we can use the batch interface to perform multiple deletes in a batched operation as shown in example below.

```
List<Customer> deletedInstances = new ArrayList<Customer>();
Customer newCust1 = session.newInstance(Customer.class);
Customer newCust2 = session.newInstance(Customer.class);
newCust1.setId(100);
newCust2.setId(101);
deletedInstances.add(newCust1);
deletedInstances.add(newCust2);
session.deletePersistentAll(deletedInstances);
```

36.6.4 READING A ROW

To read a row we can either use the *find* call or the *load* call. Both read an object based on the primary key and load it into a Java object.

find will execute immediately in the NDB data node whereas *load* will execute asynchronously at the next interaction with an NDB data node (*find*, *flush*, *query* or *commit* calls). As mentioned above *load* can only be used when an active transaction is ongoing, it cannot be used in autocommit mode.

Thus the *load* call is easy to use for batching a set of reads whereas *find* might be a bit easier to program against given that the interaction is immediate.

load use an object where at least primary key have been filled in by a *newInstance* call or the object have been returned by previous *find* call or from a query.

36.7 TRANSACTIONS

Each Session object can have one current transaction at most. This transaction can be found by calling *currentTransaction()* on the Session object. This transaction object can be used to start a transaction using the *begin()* call, to commit a transaction using the *commit()* call, to abort a transaction using the *rollback()* call.

It is also possible to set the transaction into a mode where it can only be rolled back by calling the method *setRollbackOnly()* on the transaction object. The status of this flag can be checked with a call to *getRollbackOnly()*. If this rollback only flag is set when *commit()* is called, the transaction will be rolled back.

One can check if a transaction is currently active by calling *isActive()* on the transaction object.

36.7.1 HINTS WHERE TO PLACE THE TRANSACTION

Normally the hint to place the transaction coordinator is automatically derived from the first operation in the transaction. If for some reason we want something different we can set the hint through a call to the method *setPartitionKey* on the Session object.

This call needs two parameters, the first is a class that is a mapping towards an NDB table. The second is an object that maps to the primary key of this table. In our examples the primary key is an integer, a number works fine as object.

For multi-column primary keys we need to create an *Object[]* type with one entry for each primary key column and the type for each column should correspond to the primary key column used. The order of the columns is the order defined when annotating the mapped object.

```
session.setPartitionKey(Customer.class, 100);
session.persist(newCust);
```

36.8 CREATING A QUERY

Queries are scanning a table, either using an ordered index or through a full table scan. The interface in ClusterJ doesn't explicitly specify using a table scan or an index scan. It will use an index scan if possible and otherwise it will use a table scan. ClusterJ doesn't support queries against multiple tables in the same query.

Thus ClusterJ contain a simple query optimiser that will decide the index to use through analysing the conditions.

If it is necessary to execute complex queries against NDB from a Java application one should simply use SQL through the MySQL JDBC connector. It is perfectly possible to mix using ClusterJ and using JDBC. Some of the ClusterJ test programs does exactly that. Using the MySQL JDBC connector for NDB tables works perfectly fine.

The execution of a query in ClusterJ goes through a number of steps.

1. Create a QueryBuilder object

2. Create a QueryDomainType object for the persistent class

3. Create parameters needed by query (optional)

4. Specify query condition (optional)

5. Create Query object

6. Set parameter values (optional)

7. Set skip and limit (optional)

8. Set scan ordering (optional)

9. Execute the query

10. Handle query result

We start with a simple example based on our usual Customer table.

```
QueryBuilder qb = session.getQueryBuilder();
QueryDomainType<Customer> qdc =
  qb.createQueryDefinition(Customer.class);
PredicateOperand id_low = qdc.param("id_low");
PredicateOperand id_high = qdc.param("id_high");
PredicateOperand searched_name = qdc.param("searched_name");
Predicate left = qdc.get("id").between(id_low, id_high);
Predicate right = qdc.get("name").equal(searched_name);
qdc.where(left.and(right));
Query<Customer> qc = session.createQuery(qdc);
qc.setParameter("id_low", 100);
qc.setParameter("id_high", 102);
qc.setParameter("searched_name", "Mikael");
List<Customer> results = qc.getResultList();
```

In this example we created a QueryBuilder object and based on this we created a
QueryDomainType for our Customer class that is a persistence class for the customer table.

We created one condition to return all Customers with *id* between 100 and 102. We use this
as the left predicate. We add another predicate that we only want to return Customers with
the name Mikael. We use AND between those predicates and create the query object.

100, 102 and Mikael was all parameters that could have been instantiated using input
variables to a function, so this could be extended to a function very easily.

After setting the parameters we are ready to execute the query. *getResultList* will execute
the entire query at once. Thus when using this interface it is important to ensure that sufficient
amount of memory is available to handle the full result of the query.

The name used for columns is the name of the attribute in the class, thus not necessarily the
column name used in the table. Here we use *id* and not *customer_id* as the column name is in
the table.

36.8.1   *QueryDomainType* CLASS

get

get use the name of the column in the class to represent this in a query. The actual value is in
the database, thus different for each row. It returns a PredicateOperand object.

param

We can introduce parameters in our query. Before executing the query these parameters must
get a value set through the Query object. It returns a PredicateOperand object.

where

A Predicate is constituting the search condition. This predicate is boolean expression of
predicates where each predicate represents a search condition. It returns the QueryDomainType
object itself.

36.8.2 *PredicateOperand* CLASS

Many different search conditions can be applied here. Normally the

PredicateOperand returned from the *get* call on the QueryDomainType object is used as base object and a number of methods are available to compare it with one or more other PredicateOperands. Mostly these will be PredicateOperands returned from the *param* call, but could also be another PredicateOperand returned from the *get* call.

The conditions that can be applied are *equal, greaterThan, greaterEqual, lessThan, lessEqual, between* (have low and high PredicateOperand), *in* and *like*.

in is used to represent a list of values, this is the same as a number of equality conditions that ORed together. In this context *in* is the same as calling *equal*, but calling *in* provides more context and makes it easier to choose the right execution plan for the query.

like has a parameter that is a string that can contain % and ? to form a LIKE expression.

We also have methods to check for NULL values, *isNull* and *isNotNull*.

36.8.3 *Predicate* CLASS

A predicate can be combined with other predicates to form a new predicate and also a predicate can be negated. We support *and, or* and *not*. Given these we can form any boolean expression since all other boolean expressions can be converted to a set of those.

36.8.4 *Query* CLASS

Before moving on to executing the query we need to set the parameter values defined in the query.

setParameter

The parameter is provided as a string value and the value is of any type, but it must be conformant to something that can be compared to its other operands.

setLimits

The *setLimits* call sets the *skip* parameter to specify how many rows to skip before considering the result rows and the *limit* parameter specifies the maximum number of rows that will be returned to the application.

Must be called before executing the query.

setOrdering

This call corresponds to an ORDER BY call in SQL. The first parameter defines whether we should use ASCENDING order or DESCENDING order (Ordering.DESCENDING). ASCENDING is default.

After that the columns are listed in the order that we sort them on, we first sort on the first column and so forth.

The columns listed must be the columns in an ordered index. It is not necessary to specify all of the columns, but the order of the columns must be the same as the order specified in the index. Thus we don't support general sorting of rows, but we support ordering of results from many index partitions that are scanned in parallel. In our example we could have used this method.

In our example above both the ordered index on the primary key and the index on the *name* column could have been used. With the below call we enforce that the index on the *name* column is used.

```
qc.setOrdering(Ordering.DESCENDING, "name");
```

getResultList

This call is a quick way of executing the entire query in one call without having to iterate the results. The returned result is a list of the Customer objects.

deletePersistentAll

This is another method of executing the entire query in one call. In this case all the rows that we find in the query will be deleted. In this case we should ensure that we call *setLockMode* to set it to use the EXCLUSIVE mode before executing this query, otherwise deadlocks can easily occur.

Remember to switch back the lock mode after completing the transaction when switching to EXCLUSIVE lock mode.

execute

In case the result is too big to handle in one call we can call *execute* instead. In this case we set the parameters in the call to *execute* in the order they were defined in the query definition.

This call returns a *Results* object. By calling *iterator()* on this object you will get an *Iterator* on Customers (in our example) that can be used to iterate through the results of the query.

explain

Given that ClusterJ have a simple query optimiser it is also necessary to provide input to the user of how the query is going to be executed. Thus just before executing the query we can call *explain* to discover how this query is to be executed. The result is of the type *Map<String, Object>*, it is possible to call *toString* on this object to get a textual representation of how the query is executed, which index is used, what type of index is used and what scan type is used.

36.9 COLUMN TYPE MAPPINGS

Mappings between MySQL data types and Java data types are described in the following web page. For the most data types there is a natural mapping to a Java data type. However in Java there are no unsigned data types. Thus mapping MySQL unsigned data types to Java isn't straightforward.

https://dev.mysql.com/doc/ndbapi/en/mccj-using-clusterj-mappings.html

36.10 CLUSTERJ RECONNECT

When a cluster connection loses the connection to the cluster we have to close all open sessions before we can reconnect. The reason is that when we reconnect to the cluster, it could have restarted, thus there is no guarantee that we connect to a cluster in the same state as before. We discover this condition by calling *getState()* on the SessionFactory object. If the state is RECONNECTING or CLOSED we have lost connection to the cluster, if we discover this we should start closing Sessions.

Losing connection to the cluster means losing connection to all data nodes. As long as we are connected to at least one data node the cluster connection is still ok.

If we discover that we lost connection to the cluster we can call *reconnect* on the SessionFactory object. This initiates a reconnect independent of the settings used in the ClusterJ properties.

It is important to close Sessions before reconnecting since a cluster restart could potentially return the cluster with changes in meta data and data. Thus we need to start from a clean slate by closing all Session objects first. Otherwise we might use incorrect cached data in the Session object.

It is even possible that an initial cluster start was performed while we lost connection, no cached data in ClusterJ can be trusted if we lose all connections to the cluster.

The error code 4009 means that we lost cluster connection. 4010 indicates a node failure, thus most likely the cluster connection is still ok.

36.11 DYNAMIC MAPPING OF ROWS

The description of the ClusterJ so far has only described the case where the programmer knows the tables in the database. In this case one can use static mappings. It is also possible to use dynamic mappings in ClusterJ to access also tables that wasn't known at the time when the program was developed.

Chapter 37

Node.js API

The NDB API for use in Node.js applications is called Database Jones. It is a direct NDB API that can be used to develop real-time Node.js applications on top of NDB.

Node.js is a server-side implementation of the JavaScript language. JavaScript was developed to handle interactive web pages. Since so many people learned this language, it is now also used in web server development.

Database Jones is aimed at supporting web server applications that want to provide a scalable MySQL Cluster solution.

With Database Jones it is possible to have hundreds of web servers connected to the same cluster, using MySQL Cluster Replication it is possible to scale this even further by having many read clusters.

Given that NDB has very good write scalability it would be particularly interesting for applications that puts a heavy write load on the database.

With this in mind a sample application was developed that mimic a simple *tweet* application. The sample application is a very simple web server that accepts simple HTTP requests and shows how to program such an application towards NDB using Database Jones, the NDB adapter for Node.js.

Database Jones is developed in a separate *git* tree, this tree is named *mysql/mysql-js*.

This tree contains the NDB adapter called *ndb*. It also contains an extension of the *mysql* adapter. The description of the API can be used both towards the *mysql* adapter and towards the *ndb* adapter. The main interest in this book is the *ndb* adapter that connects directly to NDB using the C++ NDB API. Node.js can map C++ calls to Node.js calls in a layer similar to the JNI layer for Java.

In this chapter we will go through how to install Database Jones, how to get the sample application up and running and go through some very basic use cases for the API.

Programming in Node.js is asynchronous, this works very well with NDB since NDB is designed as asynchronous engine beneath the hood. At the same time it is a bit more complex to reason about asynchronous programs, it can take some time to get used to for someone that is used to sequential programming.

37.1 Installing Database Jones

As mentioned in the chapter on how to install MySQL Cluster there is a component in the Linux repos called *nodejs* that installs Database Jones. You can follow the same procedure as shown there to install the *nodejs* component. After preparing the repos for MySQL on Linux in a Red Hat-based Linux it is sufficient to run the command:

```
sudo yum install mysql-cluster-nodejs
```

We will also describe here how to install the Node.js NDB adapter from *github.com* where the development tree resides.

To install from *github.com* we need to install git at first. We also need an installation of MySQL Cluster. What we need here is the NDB API library that is used by *ndb* adapter.

Next step is to install Node.js. On my Mac OS X I simply wrote *brew install node* to do this. It should be easy enough to find out how to do this on your machine and operating system. Database Jones is working on Linux and Mac OS X primarily.

Now we have the *npm* program that we can use to install the *mysql* adapter if we want that one installed. It is not necessary since all API operations can be performed using the *ndb* adapter. The *ndb* adapter cannot be used to create, drop and alter tables.

To install the *mysql* adapter use the following command:

```
npm install mysql
```

37.1.1   PREPARING TO INSTALL THE *ndb* ADAPTER

To install the *ndb* adapter we need to compile the C++ code that maps Node.js calls to C++ NDB API calls. This is done using a Node.js module called *node-gyp*. To install this use the command:

```
npm install -g node-gyp
```

node-gyp requires Python 2.7. On Linux we need a *make* tool and a compiler such as *gcc*.

On Mac OS X we need to install the XCode environment, this contains both a compiler and make tools.

37.2   INSTALLING *ndb* ADAPTER

We start by preparing *git* to use symlinks and next we download *mysql/mysql-js* from *github.com* and prepare to install the *ndb* apapter using the following command.

```
git config --global --add core.symlinks true
git clone http://github.com/mysql/mysql-js
cd mysql-js/jones-ndb
```

At first we need to configure the *ndb* adapter using the command:

```
node configure
```

During execution of this command we need to point to the MySQL Cluster installation such that we find the NDB API library.

Now we are ready to build the *ndb* adapter using the command:

```
node-gyp configure build -d
```

It is normal to get a warning that *$MYSQL_INSTALL_DIR/lib/mysql* don't exist. In newer versions of MySQL this no longer exists.

37.3   THE TWEET SAMPLE APPLICATION

With Database Jones installed we can now make some experiments in how to use it. Node.js is a language developed for web pages that have been developed to also be used in web servers. A natural example application is a tweet application.

The sample application is available in the directory *samples/tweet* directory.

For simplicity we will start up a cluster using the MySQL test tool MTR. Go to your installed MySQL Cluster installation and the mysql-test directory and run the command.

```
cd $MYSQL_INSTALL_DIR/mysql-test
./mtr --start ndb.ndb_basic
```

This starts up a MySQL Server on port 13001 and a NDB management server on port 13000 together with two data nodes.

At first we need to create the tables. We run the following command in the *samples/tweet* directory.

```
mysql --protocol=tcp --port=13001 -uroot < create_tweet_tables.sql
```

Now the *tweet.js* program contains a web server that we will start on port 7800. Node.js is a programming language that is interpreted, there is no need to compile it before running it. The compilation is done by the Node.js execution environment.

Before we do this we need to set the environment deployed to use the MTR setup. To do this we perform the following commands:

```
export JONES_ADAPTER="ndb"
export JONES_DEPLOYMENT="mtr"
export LD_LIBRARY_PATH="$MYSQL_INSTALL_LIB/lib"
node tweet start server 7800
```

Now we have a web server running on port 7800. If we run on Mac OS X we need to change the *LD_LIBRARY_PATH* to *DYLD_LIBRARY_PATH*.

In the last line *node* is the Node.js execution environment. *tweet* means that the file *tweet.js* is executed. *start server 7800* are the three startup parameters to this *tweet* program.

export needs to be replaced by *setenv* on some shell implementations.

This is the general method of executing a Node.js program.

```
node my_program_name program_parameters
```

This will execute the program in *my_program_name.js*. Since Node.js is an interpreted language, there is no need to compile the program before executing it. The compilation happens on the fly.

The next step is to populate the database with the initial data. This is performed using the script *demo_populate.sh*. This script is hardcoded for some reason to use the *mysql* adapter. If you haven't installed the *mysql* adapter you need to manually change to use *ndb* adapter on one of the first lines in this script (the export command).

Now we run the *demo_http_get.sh* that runs some http requests such as this one:

```
curl http://localhost:7800/tweets-about/carthage
```

The variable JONES_DEPLOYMENT affects what deployment is choosen from the file *jones_deployment.js* in the top directory for this test run.

37.4   CONNECTIONPROPERTIES

The first part of the program always calls require with *database-jones* as parameter. The next step is to create an object of type *ConnectionProperties*. This object decides how to connect to MySQL Cluster.

mysql_host, *mysql_user*, *mysql_port* and *mysql_password* contains the parameters needed to connect to the MySQL Server using the *mysql* adapter.

None of these are needed for the *ndb* adapter. But they could be used to create tables from the *ndb* adapter using a MySQL Server.

It is also possible to set *mysql_charset*, *mysql_socket*, *mysql_sql_mode*, *mysql_pool_size* and a few debug parameters on the *mysql* adapter. These are not possible to set on the *ndb* adapter.

37.4.1   COMMON CONNECTIONPROPERTIES

There is only one common ConnectionProperties for the *mysql* and the *ndb* adapter. This is the *database* property. This is by default equal to *test* for both adapters.

37.4.2 *ndb* CONNECTIONPROPERTIES

ndb_connect_retries

Defaults to 4. This is the number of retries we will perform to connect to the NDB management server before giving up. A negative value here means that there is no limit on the number of retries, it will be retried indefinitely.

ndb_connect_delay

This represents the delay between attempts to connect to the cluster. By default it is set to 1 second.

ndb_connect_verbose

If set this variable ensures that printouts to the console is made of progress on cluster connect setup. By default it is set.

   ndb_connect_retries, *ndb_connect_delay* and *ndb_connect_verbose* are all passed to the call where the cluster connection is made.

linger_on_close_msec

This parameter sets a timeout on how long we will wait before we start closing the cluster connection when the connection was closed. By default this is set to 500 milliseconds.

use_ndb_async_api

Setting this to true means that we are going to use the asynchronous NDB API functionality to increase the parallelism in using the NDB API. By default this is set to false.

use_mapped_ndb_record

Setting this to true means that we keep results fetched from NDB in NDB API buffers, otherwise they are copied out to JavaScript objects. Defaults to true.

ndb_session_pool_min

Each cluster connection uses a pool of NDB objects (Each Session object in the *ndb* adapter maps to one NDB object. This parameter sets the minimum number of objects in this pool. It defaults to 4.

ndb_session_pool_max

This parameter sets the maximum number of objects in the NDB object pool. By default it is set to 100.

ndb_session_concurrency

The maximum number of transactions in an NDB session, only one is visible to the user, but multiple may be started before the current have finished. Defaults to 4. If the asynchronous API is used it is recommended to increase this parameter to 1024 since the asynchronous API can run many transactions in parallel.

37.4.3 CREATING A CONNECTIONPROPERTIES OBJECT

This object is created by calling ConnectionProperties with the first parameter set to a string with either *ndb* or *mysql* dependent on which adapter is used.

The second parameter is not needed, if it is not set a default object is returned. Next the application can change this object programmatically as desired before proceeding.

The second parameter can also be a function in which case this function is used to fill in the variables in this object.

The second argument can be a string pointing to which deployment to use (several can be defined).

The deployment is found in a file called *jones_deployment.js*. An example file of this is found in the top directory of the *mysql-js* installation.

The search starts for this file starts in the directory containing the currently executing main source file. Next it tries in the directory above and continues until it reaches the root of the file system. It attempts to find it in the directory that is the current working directory.

```
Alternative 1:
  var con_prop = new db_con.ConnectionProperties("ndb");
  con_prop.database = "new_db";

Alternative 2:
  function set_prop(props) {
    props.database = "new_db";
  }
  var con_prop = new db_con.ConnectionProperties("ndb", set_prop);

Alternative 3:
  var con_prop = new db_con.ConnectionProperties("ndb", "test");
```

37.5 CLUSTER CONNECTION OBJECT

After calling require on Database Jones and creating a ConnectionProperties object, we are ready to create a cluster connection object.

For the *mysql* adapter this object is simply a pool of connections the MySQL Server. Each session will be represented by a connection to the MySQL Server.

For the *ndb* adapter this object creates a cluster connection. Thus we can use multiple such objects for one Node.js server since NDB supports having multiple cluster connections from one program.

Each cluster connection will have its own SessionFactory returned and when a Session object is created it will use an NDB object to map the Session calls to NDB API calls.

The call to create the SessionFactory object is created using two parameters, the

ConnectionProperties object and a mappings object. The mappings object can be an array of table mappings that can be used by the cluster connection.

37.5.1 TABLE MAPPINGS

Table mappings in Database Jones is very similar to the annotations used in ClusterJ. In our example we will use the Customer table. At first we need to create a function to fill in the Customer object. In this example the JavaScript object have two fields *id* and *name*. The table uses the column names *customer_id* and *name*.

This object can be created when reading the row from the database when it is called without parameters, it can also be called from application logic with proper parameters. By checking the first parameter for *undefined* we can derive whether to set the variables.

```
function Customer(customerId, customerName) {
  if (customerId != undefined)
  {
    this.id = customerId;
    this.name = customerName;
  }
}
```

The simplest method to map this table would be the following code.

```
var db_con = require("database-jones");
var cust_map = new db_con.TableMapping('customer').
  applyToClass(Customer);
```

Now this won't work since the *id* is stored in a column called *customer_id*. We need to define also the field mappings like this:

```
var db_con = require("database-jones");
var cust_map = new db_con.TableMapping('customer');
cust_map.mapField("id", "customer_id");
cust_map.mapField("name");
cust_map.applyToClass(Customer);
```

Here we provide a mapping between the *id* used in the JavaScript object and the *customer_id* used in the table.

It is also possible to specify a *Converter* object that converts between database types and JavaScript types. It is also possible to set a field to not be persistent. For more details on this see the documentation in the *database-jones/API-documentation* directory.

It is not necessary to specify indexes in the table mapping. For all key lookup operations (both read and write) all primary key columns must be specified in the object. Alternatively all columns of a unique key column must be specified. Otherwise an exception is generated on the call on the Session object.

The table mappings will use all columns of the table. If the table changes such that a new column is added while the cluster connection is up and running the new column will not be part of the mapping. Thus schema modifications and software upgrade must be closely aligned.

37.6 Startup example

```
var db_con = require("database-jones");
var con_prop = new db_con.ConnectionProperties("ndb", "test");
function Customer(customerId, customerName) {
  if (customerId != undefined)
  {
    this.id = customerId;
    this.name = customerName;
  }
}
table_maps = [];
var cust_map = new db_con.TableMapping('customer');
cust_map.mapField("id", "customer_id");
cust_map.mapField("name");
table_maps.push(cust_map.applyToClass(Customer));
function successFunction() {
  ...
}
function failFunction() {
  ...
}
function exampleOperation(session) {
  ...
}
db_con.connect(con_prop, table_maps).
  then(function() { return sessionFactory.openSession()}).
  then(exampleOperation, failFunction);
```

The Node.js API has a lot of similarities to the ClusterJ API. This isn't surprising since the ClusterJ architect was involved also in designing the Node.js API.

There is a main difference though in that Node.js is a language designed for asynchronous operation. Each time we call a function that accesses the NDB data node we can use callbacks to continue the execution. This makes it possible to perform rather complex interactions with several steps with a few lines of simple code.

We use the standard promises design pattern in some of those examples. The reason is that most of the asynchronous calls in Database Jones return a promise that is Promises/A+ compatible.

The idea with promises is that they return either with success plus a return value or it returns with a failure and a return value. The return value can be multiple objects.

Putting these things together our example codes will always use the following startup code. Here exampleOperation will be replaced by the operation we want to show an example of in coming sections. We use the SessionFactory returned by the connect call to create a Session object to use in our examples. We ignore the error handling function and the function to use at success here.

37.7 SESSION OPERATIONS

37.7.1 INSERTING A ROW

The below example shows a very simple example of an insert row. We create a new Customer object and call the method *persist* on the Session object. This performs an insert of the provided object.

```
function insertOperation(session) {
  newCust = new Customer(100, "Mikael");
  session.persist(newCust).
    then(successFunction, failFunction);
}
```

37.7.2 UPDATING A ROW

To update the row instead of inserting we simply replace the *persist* function with the *update* function.

```
function updateOperation(session) {
  newCust = new Customer(100, "Mikael");
  session.update(newCust).
    then(successFunction, failFunction);
}
```

37.7.3 DELETE A ROW

To delete a row we only need to specify the primary key and we use the *remove* function to perform the delete operation.

```
function deleteOperation(session) {
  newCust = new Customer(100);
  session.remove(newCust).
    then(successFunction, failFunction);
}
```

37.7.4 WRITE A ROW

To write a row (insert if row with same primary key doesn't exist and update if it previously existed), one uses the *save* method.

```
function writeOperation(session) {
  newCust = new Customer(100, "Mikael");
  session.save(newCust).
    then(successFunction, failFunction);
}
```

37.7.5 READ AND UPDATE A ROW

Now we move on to a slightly more advanced example. In the previous examples we executed in autocommit mode. Only one operation was executed in the transaction, there was no need to introduce any transactions. Now we move onto a transaction where we first want to read the row, followed by an update of the row where want to change the name of the customer.

In this case we create a new function changeCustomer to handle the change of the customer name.

We introduce a transaction that we begin before reading the row and complete after updating it. The method *currentTransaction* returns the transaction where we can apply the functions *begin()*, *commit()*, *rollback()*. We can also set the transaction to be only abortable by a call to *setRollbackOnly()* and we can check if it is only abortable by calling *isRollbackOnly()*.

We set the Session to now work with exclusive locks on reads to ensure that the transaction doesn't deadlock after attempting to perform a lock upgrade from shared lock to exclusive lock. The lock modes that can be set are EXCLUSIVE, SHARED and NONE. NONE corresponds to READ COMMITTED.

When a transaction is started on the Session object the call to *update* will return immediately, it will be executed by the next operation that requires an interaction with the NDB data nodes (calls to *flush*, *find*, *commit* or *rollback*).

```
function readOperation(session) {
  this.session = session;
  function changeCustomer(customer, name) {
    customer.name = name;
    session.update(customer);
  }
  var customerName = "Mikael";
  var customerId = 100;
  var customer = new Customer(customerId);
  session.currentTransaction().begin();
  session.lockMode(EXCLUSIVE);
  session.find("customer", customer).
    then(changeCustomerName(customer,customerName)).
    then(session.currentTransaction().commit()).
    then(successFunction, failFunction);
}
```

37.7.6 BATCHING MULTIPLE OPERATIONS

In this example we show how to batch two insert operations into one execution towards the NDB data nodes.

To do this we introduce a batch object by calling the method *createBatch* on the Session object. This object have more or less the same interface as the Session object except that the calls are batched for later execution instead of executed immediately.

To execute the batched operations we need to call *execute* on the batch object.

```
function insertMultipleRows(session) {
  batch = session.createBatch();
  newCust1 = new Customer(101, "Mikael jr");
  newCust2 = new Customer(102, "Mikaela");
  batch.persist(newCust1);
  batch.persist(newCust2);
  batch.execute().
    then(successFunction, failFunction);
}
```

We can also batch multiple keyed reads using the same batch interface as shown here. After reading the rows we want to update them again after changing the customer names.

```
function insertMultipleOps(session, cust1, cust2) {
  cust1.name = "Michael jr";
  cust2.name = "Michaela";
  batch.update(cust1);
  batch.update(cust2);
  batch.execute().
    then(session.currentTransaction().commit()).
    then(successFunction, failFunction);
}
function readAndInsertMultipleRows(session) {
  session.currentTransaction().begin();
  session.lockMode(EXCLUSIVE);
  batch = session.createBatch();
  var newCust1 = Customer(101);
  var newCust2 = Customer(102);
  batch.find("customer", newCust1);
  batch.find("customer", newCust2);
  batch.execute().
    then(insertMultipleOps(session, newCust1, newCust2)),
        failFunction);
}
```

37.7.7   SCANNING ROWS

There is also an interface to scan tables through an ordered index. To perform this we need to first create a query object. When creating the query object we can supply the table name or a table mapping object.

This method returns a Query object. Through this query object we can define the query search condition. We define one predicate per call. All functions that define predicates return a query predicate that can be passed into a new predicate function.

The conditions supported are *eq* (equality condition), *ne* (not equal), *gt* (greater than), *ge* (greater than or equal), *lt* (less than), *le* (less than or equal), *isNull, isNotNull*.

There are numerous functions to join two predicates.

and(predicate) (if both predicates are true), *or, andNot* (this query predicate with the negation of the parameter predicate), *orNot, not.*

```
function handle_results(err, results) {
  if (err) { ... } // Error code
  else     { ... } // Successful code
}
function query_definition(query) {
  query.where(query.name.eq("Mikael"));
  return query.execute("order" : "desc");
}
function scanCustomers(session) {
  session.createQuery("customer").
    then(query_definition(query)).
    then(handle_results(err, results),failFunction);
```

In the example we use the short form where *query.name* refers to the *name* column. This means the same as *name = "Mikael"*. In the execute we define the query to be executed in descending order. It is also possible to set a limit in the same manner that limits the number of rows to return. Also *skip* that skips the first number of rows before starting to report rows.

Default *order* is no order, default *limit* is several billions of rows and *skip* defaults to 0.

The result of the *execute* method is returned with an error condition and an array of result objects. The result objects are in this case a set of Customer objects.

37.7.8 JOIN OPERATIONS

There is an interface to define join operations using Database Jones. This uses the Projection interface. This code is a bit less stable than the rest of the code, I will skip describing it here. It is documented in the same place as the rest of the code.

We recommend using SQL to execute complex queries such as joins between tables, as this is the most well tested method of executing complex queries. If the query is complex it makes sense to pay the little extra cost in shipping it over to the MySQL Server for execution.

37.8 FINAL COMMENTS

The above examples were developed to show one way of using Database Jones to develop a web application. More complete examples are found in the *samples/tweet* directory.

The API that Database Jones supports makes it possible to access NDB in many more variants than I have shown here. These examples are there to get you started to develop more interesting applications using Database Jones.

The complete API documentation is found in the *database-jones/API-documentation* directory.

Part IX

Global replication

CHAPTER 38

INTERNALS OF MYSQL CLUSTER REPLICATION

Before we move into a description of how MySQL Cluster Replication works, it is important to understand the internals of asynchronous replication in NDB.

MySQL Cluster Replication is built on top of MySQL Replication. There are some major differences to how NDB uses MySQL Replication compared to how other storage engines use it. In other storage engines the events that are written into the binlog (the MySQL replication log) in the same MySQL Server where the write occurs.

This is not possible using NDB since we can have API nodes that write into NDB without using a MySQL Server. In addition we could have tens or even hundreds of MySQL Server in one cluster. It isn't possible to write a log in only one of the MySQL Server where the changes occurs.

Instead we use specialised MySQL Servers that I will call MySQL replication servers. To ensure high availability we strongly recommend to always have at least two such MySQL replication servers in each cluster.

These servers receive events from data nodes and write them into the binlog.

There might even be more pairs to accomodate replication to different clusters or replicating different parts of the database in different directions.

MySQL Replication uses a binlog server that gathers all logs of writes in the database. In the other cluster a slave server retrieves log records from the binlog server and writes them into the slave cluster.

In this chapter we will focus on how MySQL replication servers communicate with the NDB data nodes. The communication between MySQL replication servers and setup of those will be covered in the next set of chapters.

38.1 DATA NODE TRIGGERS

In the NDB data node we have a trigger mechanism that is used for a diverse set of purposes. It can be used to maintain local T-tree indexes, it can be used to maintain global unique indexes, it can be used to maintain foreign keys, it is used during online reorganisation of table partitions.

For MySQL Cluster Replication we have asynchronous triggers that gather and send information about committed changes in NDB data nodes.

Each time a write of a row (update, insert, delete) is committed it can trigger an asynchronous write of the change to a local module called SUMA (SUbscriber MAnagement).

There are multiple *ldm* threads that can commit row writes. In the NDB architecture these log messages of a committed row write are called events and the user can get access to those events from an NDB Event API.

The SUMA block is executing in one thread, the *rep* thread.

38.2   Epochs

As discussed in an earlier chapter we commit operations in groups that are committed to a durable media (files on top of hard drives, SSDs or other persistent media).

These groups are called global checkpoints and occur at configurable intervals, by default 2 seconds. For MySQL Cluster Replication we have one more grouping of transactions into something internally called *micro GCPs*. The name we use in documentation is *epochs*. *Epochs* is a term that was described in the research literature on replication between databases already more than 25 years ago.

By default we have 20 *epochs* for every global checkpoint. Thus they arrive with 100 milliseconds intervals.

38.3   Epoch Buffers

The SUMA block in each node organises the *events* in a number of Epoch Buffers. We can have multiple epoch buffers. Epoch buffers are maintained only in memory.

As soon as an epoch is completed we can send the epoch over to the requester of the events. In this case the requester is a MySQL replication server. It could be any other application that uses the NDB Event API. As an example HopsFS uses the NDB Event API to maintain a searchable index in ElasticSearch to files stored in HopsFS.

We work together with the other data nodes in the same node group to send an *epoch* over to the MySQL replication servers.

When all the MySQL replication servers have acknowledged receiving the *epoch*, and the other data nodes in the node group have acknowledged that it has completed its transfer to the MySQL replication servers.

The data nodes in a node group share the responsibility to send the *epochs* to the MySQL replication servers. If a data node fails the other data node(s) in the same node group must complete the sending of the buffer.

In the figure below we see the protocol to transfer *epochs* from the data nodes to the MySQL replication servers. In this figure we have 2 MySQL replication servers and two data nodes in the node group. There could be up to 4 data nodes in one node group (max 4 replicas in NDB). There can be any number of MySQL replication servers although normally it would be 2.

In this figure we only show how one node group transfers its epoch data to the MySQL replication server. All node groups must do this, this is performed independently of each other. Thus as soon as one node group has completed the transfer of *epoch n* we can release the epoch buffers for this *epoch* in the nodes in the node group.

As we see in this picture both the data nodes in the node group gather all data for the *epoch* in its epoch buffers. When the buffer is complete and the transfer of the previous *epoch* is

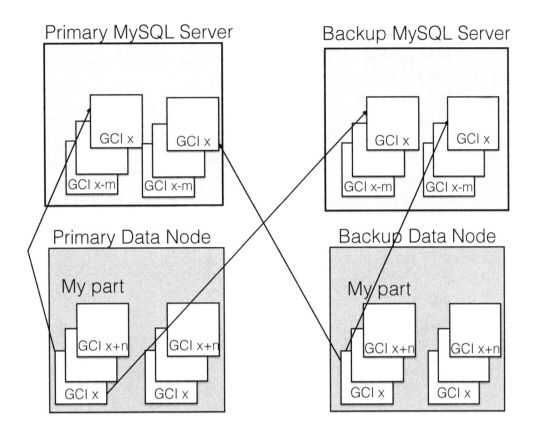

completed we start sending our part of the epoch buffers to the MySQL replication servers. We send our part to all the MySQL replication servers. The other data node sends all its parts also to all the MySQL replication servers.

When a MySQL replication server have received an epoch buffer from one node group it acknowledges this to the data nodes. The MySQL replication server will send this acknowledgement when it has received the *epoch* from the entire cluster.

As soon as a data node receives the confirmation from all MySQL replication servers about receiving all *epoch* data it can release the epoch buffers connected to this epoch.

We need to have sufficiently large epoch buffers to gather epochs even in situations when node crashes slows things down, short bursts of high update rates and a few larger transaction.

These values are configurable through *MaxBufferedEpochs* that limits the number of *epochs* we will buffer, by default set to 100, thus a bit more than 10 seconds of buffering. *MaxBufferedEpochBytes* sets the limit on the buffer sizes for epoch buffers. By default this is set to 25 MBytes. These are important parameters to configure, in a cluster that handle a hundred thousand transactions per second we could write 50 MBytes per second or more and thus it would be a good idea to extend buffer size in this case to 500 MBytes instead.

Running out of epoch buffers means that the replication channel is at risk. Running out of epoch buffers in all data nodes in a node group means that the MySQL replication servers cannot continue replicating and thus the entire replication channel will be lost. In this case the replication channel must be restarted.

Thus it is very important to ensure that the epoch buffers are large enough. Failure of a replication channel will not stop transactions in a cluster from proceeding. Thus operation of the local cluster have higher priority than the event handling.

38.4 SEND BUFFERS

There is a lot of data sent from the data nodes to the MySQL replication servers that act as binlog servers. Similarly there is a lot of data sent from MySQL replication servers to the NDB data nodes when they act as slave appliers.

The send buffers to communicate between MySQL replication servers and NDB data nodes are more likely than others to run out of send buffers.

Send buffer memory can be configured per link between nodes if desirable to change the send buffer for those links to a higher value compared to other nodes.

38.5 MYSQL REPLICATION SERVER INTERNALS

We will skip most of the details on how MySQL replication works. There is a lot of detail about this that can be gathered from the MySQL manual and from many books on MySQL.

NDB uses a special thread called the injector thread that acts as the thread that writes into the binlog. This runs an eternal loop reading NDB events and inserting those into the binlog files.

When writing into the binlog files a memory buffer is used. To ensure that this writing doesn't become a bottleneck it is possible to set the binlog cache size through the MySQL option *binlog-cache-size*. By default this is set to 32 kBytes. It is more or less mandatory to set it higher. Another important parameter to consider setting is the size of the binlog files. If file size is too small there will be too many hickups when files are changing. At the same time it is not good with very large files since then it becomes difficult to purge the binlog files. It is set through the MySQL option *max-binlog-size* that defaults to 1 GByte which should be ok for most use cases. The MySQL binlog files must be purged manually.

The slave applier uses two main threads. The slave IO thread that reads over the network from the MySQL replication server in the other cluster. It stores the information in relay log files. The slave SQL thread reads from the relay log and creates NDB transactions to insert one *epoch* at a time.

Epochs are written into the slave clusters as one transaction. The reason is that this is the only consistency points. In the middle of applying an *epoch* the database isn't consistent, to avoid inconsistency problem the entire *epoch* is written as one transaction.

The relay log files are automatically purged as soon as they have been used.

38.6 LIMITATIONS OF MYSQL CLUSTER REPLICATION

There are many parts of the replication between clusters that are single threaded. This means that there are limits to how many transactions per second can be handled. The most demanding write applications can get problems in using MySQL Cluster Replication.

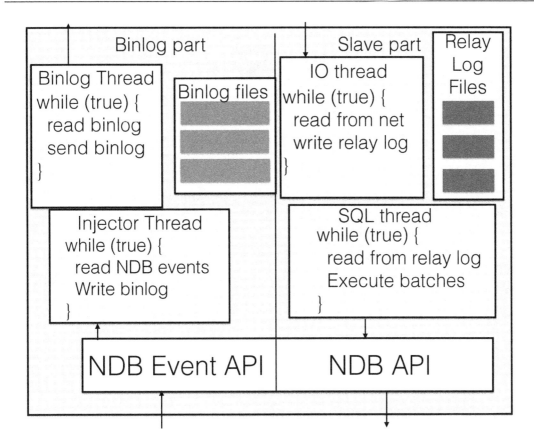

With a proper setup of MySQL Cluster Replication it should be possible to reach at least well beyond 100.000 row writes per second.

At the same time many of our users, and even the most demanding users have been able to use the MySQL Cluster Replication. Many found good ways to shard their applications such that they have one cluster per shard.

The first potential bottleneck is the *rep* thread. This thread receives change information from the *ldm* threads and buffers this information to send it on to the API nodes that have subscribed to those changes. I've never seen this become a bottleneck, but to ensure it doesn't become a bottleneck one can lock this thread to a CPU no one else uses.

The next step in the chain is the MySQL replication server acting as a binlog server. There are two main threads that perform a lot of work in this part. The receive thread for the NDB API and the injector thread. To achieve the best possible throughput here one should use a dedicated MySQL server that uses one cluster connection and the MySQL Server should be locked to 4 CPUs such that both the receive thread and the injector thread can use their own CPU. The other two CPUs are used to send data to the slave MySQL server(s).

To ensure that the injector thread doesn't perform any of the receive thread activity one should set *ndb-recv-thread-activation-threshold=0*. This ensures that all receive activity is handled by the NDB API receive thread and not by any other thread at all.

On the slave side it is important to set *slave-allow-batching* since without this setting the throughput of the slave applier is decreased by a magnitude. Similarly on the slave side it is important to use a dedicated MySQL Server to achieve optimal performance. This server should be locked to 4 CPUs to ensure that the slave IO thread, the slave SQL thread, the NDB API receive thread and send activitity can work in parallel. Also here one should set *ndb-recv-thread-activation-threshold=0* to ensure that the slave SQL thread doesn't have to handle any NDB API receive thread activity.

If one uses one VM per MySQL Server in a cloud setup one should use a VM with 2 CPU cores for the MySQL replication servers to achieve optimal throughput. If they act as both master and slave replication servers we should use 4 CPU cores for optimal throughput.

This is a method to ensure that they are locked to their own CPUs without having to use specific locking to CPU when starting the MySQL Server. Otherwise one can use *taskset* or *numactl* on Linux.

In the NDB data node it is important that there is sufficient amount of *tc* threads such that the *tc* thread used to execute the *epoch* transactions are not sharing the *tc* thread with too many other activities. This is the least likely performance bottleneck.

CHAPTER 39

MULTI-SITE MYSQL CLUSTER

MySQL Cluster is designed for Local Area Network (LAN) environments. It is possible to have nodes a few kilometers away from each other and still get a good user experience as is the case within a cloud region.

There are a number of reasons to make use of multiple clusters that contain the same data. Each cluster uses synchronous replication between nodes in the cluster. MySQL Cluster Replication uses asynchronous replication between the clusters.

A few reasons to use MySQL Cluster Replication are:

1) The application must survive even earthquakes and other such drastic problems. An earthquake will impact a fairly large area and other types of problems such as local conflicts, local unrest is affecting larger areas than a LAN or cloud region will cover.

For the absolutely highest availability it is of utmost importance to have availability beyond what a single cluster can provide.

This is the reason many of our high-profile users use MySQL Cluster Replication. A telecom operator cannot accept that the phone service or mobile internet service is disrupted completely by one catastrophic event. The application has to be built to handle such catastrophic events.

2) The application needs 100% uptime in all types of software upgrades. Many applications upgrade not only the DBMS when upgrading, they might decide to upgrade their application and they might even decide to move one data center from one place to another. A fail-over cluster can be very useful in all of those cases.

MySQL Cluster is designed to handle most software changes without downtime. But there is still some things we don't support that might be needed such an online drop column. In this case another cluster can be used to perform an online upgrade. Next the clusters are swapped and the first cluster is brought online and after that the second cluster can be brought down to upgrade that as well.

3) MySQL Cluster Replication can be used to build a true globally distributed database where updates can be performed in any cluster anywhere in the world. Given the latency between systems on a global scale it is not possible to wait for commit until all clusters have accepted the transaction. Instead we use a conflict detection scheme. MySQL Cluster supports a number of different conflict detection schemes.

The globally distributed database setup can be used in companies that operate over multiple continents and need a cluster on each continent that can act as master cluster.

Even with a single master cluster one can use conflict detection to ensure that failover to a new master cluster can be done without downtime. In this case the conflicts only occur in the short time that two clusters are both master clusters.

4) Replication to a different storage engine of MySQL. We will not cover this in any detail in this book. It should be straightforward to do with the descriptions in this chapter.

39.1 MySQL Replication

The asynchronous replication between clusters is built on top of MySQL Replication. It reuses most of the basic things about MySQL Replication such as a binlog, a relay log, master MySQL Servers and slave MySQL Servers. There is a set of differences as well.

First of all NDB only supports row-based replication. The meta data changes are replicated using statements, but all data changes are replicated using row changes.

The row changes are not generated in the MySQL Server (remember that NDB can be accessed also from NDB API applications), rather they are generated inside the data nodes. The data node generates events for row changes and transports them to a specific MySQL Server that handles replication between clusters.

MySQL Cluster uses a concept called epochs to transport changes over to the slave cluster. Epochs are a sort of group commit, it groups all changes to the cluster committed in the last time period (100 milliseconds by default) into one epoch. This epoch is transported to the slave cluster and applied there as one transaction.

MySQL using InnoDB relies on GTIDs to handle replication consistency. NDB gets its replication consistency from its use of epochs.

In research papers about database replication, there are two main themes on how to replicate. One is the epoch style, this requires only sending over the epochs and apply them to the slave cluster. The actual replication is simpler in this case. The problem with this approach is that one need to create epochs, this puts a burden on the master cluster. In NDB this isn't a problem since we already have an architecture to generate epochs efficiently through our global checkpoint protocol. Thus using epochs is a natural choice for NDB.

The other approach has smaller impact on the master, it instead requires that one keep track of the read and write sets and ensures that the slave applier has access to this information. This is a natural architecture for a DBMS where it is harder to change the transaction architecture to create epochs.

Both architectures have merits and disadvantages, for NDB epochs was a very natural choice. For MySQL using InnoDB the approach using GTIDs to serially order transactions (still lacks the read sets) was the more natural approach.

MySQL Cluster Replication actually supports more features compared to MySQL Replication. The features we support in this area are very advanced. The lead developer in this area took his Ph.D in this area about 20 years ago and presented a distributed replication architecture at the VLDB conference in Rome more than 15 years ago.

This is an area that we have developed in close cooperation with our telecom users that all require this feature and have built a lot of support functionality around it.

39.2 ARCHITECTURE OF MySQL CLUSTER REPLICATION

As a first step we will describe the nodes required to setup replication between clusters. Given that almost all applications of NDB is high availability applications, we will only consider replication channels that have a primary and a backup channel.

A replication channel always depends on a master MySQL Server and a slave MySQL Server. Thus to have a primary replication channel and a backup replication channel means that we need at least two master MySQL Servers and two slave MySQL Servers to replicate from one NDB Cluster to another NDB Cluster.

In active-active architectures replication goes in both directions. This can be accomplished with the same set of MySQL Servers or it can be accomplished with indepedent MySQL Servers. There is no difference in this choice, in this description we will assume that the four MySQL Servers are responsible for only replicating in one direction.

Thus active-active replication will require four or eight MySQL Servers for two NDB Clusters. Circular replication require four MySQL Servers per NDB Cluster.

39.2.1 SPECIALISED MySQL SERVERS FOR REPLICATION

The optimal design for the MySQL Servers used for replicating to a slave cluster and also for the MySQL Servers that applies the binlogs in the slave cluster, is that those MySQL Servers are specialised servers only used for replication. These specialised MySQL servers can also be used for performing schema changes.

39.2.2 BASE ARCHITECTURE

The base architecture is replicating from one NDB Cluster to another NDB Cluster. Here we have a set of local MySQL Servers and a set of data nodes in each cluster that are local to that cluster. There are two MySQL Servers in the master cluster that receives the events from the master cluster and both stores the events in their binlog.

There is a slave cluster, also with a set of local MySQL Servers and data nodes. In addition it has two slave MySQL Servers. These two MySQL Servers are receiving replication events from one of the MySQL Replication Servers in the main cluster. Only one of those is active at any time. Failover between those slave MySQL Servers happens on epoch boundaries. Thus if one replication channel fails, the other can deduce which epoch that have been applied and start from the next epoch after that.

If the master cluster fails or if both replication channels fail, we will fail over to the slave cluster. Again using epochs this is straightforward, we discover which is the last epoch we received in its entirety and we will continue from there.

The application must also be redirected towards the new master cluster before the failover is completed.

39.2.3 ACTIVE-STANDBY CLUSTERS

Active Standby clusters is the most basic configuration used primarily for high availability, complex software upgrades, hardware upgrades and so forth. No conflict detection is required since there is only one active cluster at a time.

MySQL Cluster Replication Architecture

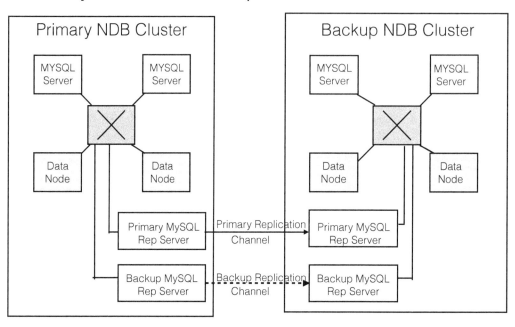

39.2.4 READ-SLAVE CLUSTERS

In this case there is no failover handling. The replication is done to increase read throughput. We could have more than slave cluster.

39.2.5 MULTI-LEVEL READ-SLAVE CLUSTERS

With high throughput of writes it can be hard for one master cluster to replicate to all other slave clusters. In this case one might have multiple levels of replication.

Thus the master cluster replicates to a set of clusters, each of those clusters in its turn can replicate onto another set of NDB Clusters.

39.2.6 ACTIVE-ACTIVE CLUSTERS

Active-Active clusters replicate in both directions. This means that we can get conflicts. Thus it is important to decide how to handle those conflicts, we will go through the options available in the chapter on globally distributed databases using MySQL Cluster and in the chapter on extremely available solutions with MySQL Cluster.

A special case of this architecture is when we normally run in Active-Standby mode, but during the failover we run in Active-Active mode. To support this, is one of the reasons we support conflict detection in the Active-Active setup.

Multi-level Slave Clusters

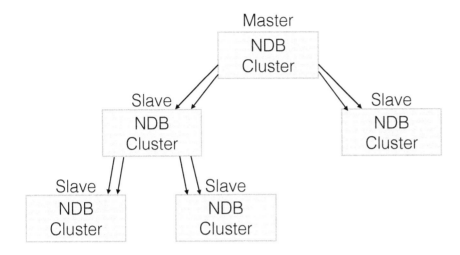

39.2.7 CIRCULAR ACTIVE-ACTIVE CLUSTERS

With more than two active clusters we build the replication in circular fashion. This still requires conflict detection handling. We will cover this in the chapter on globally distributed databases.

39.3 TABLES USED BY MySQL CLUSTER REPLICATION

MySQL Cluster Replication uses a set of internal tables to provide information about replication status. These tables are created when installing a MySQL Server.

The *ndb_binlog_index* table is an InnoDB table that is local on each MySQL Server used to replicate cluster tables to another cluster or another storage engine.

The *ndb_apply_status*, *ndb_schema* and *ndb_replication* tables are NDB tables.

All those tables belong to the *mysql* database.

39.3.1 *ndb_binlog_index table*

The *ndb_binlog_index* table contains an index to what have been written in the local binlog in a MySQL Server handling MySQL Cluster Replication. This table is created by the MySQL installation program.

One row is created per *epoch* executed, even empty epochs leads to a row written in this table. In this case *next_position* and *next_file* is pointing to the same position as the start position (*Position*) and start file (*File*).

```
CREATE TABLE ndb_binlog_index
(
  Position bigint unsigned NOT NULL,
  File varchar(255) NOT NULL,
  epoch bigint unsigned NOT NULL,
  inserts int unsigned NOT NULL,
  updates int unsigned NOT NULL,
  deletes int unsigned NOT NULL,
  schemaops int unsigned NOT NULL,
  orig_server_id int unsigned NOT NULL,
  orig_epoch bigint unsigned NOT NULL,
  gci int unsigned NOT NULL,
  next_position bigint unsigned NOT NULL,
  next_file varchar(255) NOT NULL,
  PRIMARY KEY ('epoch','orig_server_id','orig_epoch')
) ENGINE=InnoDB DEFAULT CHARSET=latin1;
```

The *Position* field specifies the start position of the epoch in the binlog and *File* is the filename of the file where the start position is placed.

The *epoch* lists the 64-bit id of the epoch number consisting of a 32 bit GCI number and a 32-bit *micro-GCI*. The GCI is also reported in its own column.

inserts, *updates*, *deletes* and *schemaops* counts how many of those operations that the epoch consist of.

next_file and *next_position* point to the position and file of the next epoch after this one.

orig_server_id is a variable updated when the *ndb-log-orig* MySQL server variable is set to 1 (defaults to 0). In this case it is set to the originating server id of this epoch and *orig_epoch* contains the epoch number in the originating cluster. Each MySQL replication server must have its own unique server id. The responsibility to make it unique and setup the replication configuration lies on the DBA. The server id is set when you start up the MySQL replication server using the *--server-id* parameter.

When circular replication is used, each epoch will generate as many entries in this table as there are clusters in the circle. Assume that *epoch* 13 is originated in cluster A, now this *epoch* is applied to cluster B in *epoch* 209. Thus *epoch* 209 will generate two rows in this table. One that is the *epoch* 13 originated from cluster A, this will have *epoch* set to 209, *orig_epoch* set to 13 and *server_id* set to the server id of the originating MySQL replication server in cluster A. The second is the *epoch* generated from transactions in cluster B. This will generate a row with *epoch* set to 209, also *orig_epoch* is set to 209 and *server_id* is set to the server id in cluster B where this transaction is written to the binlog.

These multiple entries in the *ndb_binlog_index* table are used by the conflict detection code as we will later discuss.

39.3.2 *ndb_apply_status*

The *ndb_apply_status* table contains rows that describe *epochs* that are written into the cluster by a slave applier. Updates to this table is not generated by events in the cluster, it is generated by a MySQL replication server acting as a binlog server. Thus in the master cluster this table will be empty, the table will be filled in the slave cluster when applying the *epoch* in the slave. This table has a primary key that is the server id, thus each *epoch* will overwrite the values in this tables. Only the latest applied *epoch* is represented in this table for each server id.

Each epoch contains one write into this table, even empty epochs if the MySQL server option *ndb-log-empty-epochs* is set.

```
CREATE TABLE ndb_apply_status
(
    server_id int unsigned NOT NULL,
    epoch bigint unsigned NOT NULL,
    log_name varchar(255) binary NOT NULL,
    start_pos bigint unsigned NOT NULL,
    end_pos bigint unsigned NOT NUL
    PRIMARY KEY (server_id) USING HASH
) ENGINE=NDB DEFAULT CHARSET=latin1;
```

server_id contains the server id from the MySQL Server generating the binlog entry for the epoch. Thus it is the server id of the MySQL replication server in the master cluster. The information stored in this record is the following.

epoch is the epoch number in the master cluster. The *log_name* is the file name of the start position of the epoch. *start_pos* and *end_pos* are the start and end position in the binlog of the epoch.

Given that transactions are applied atomically and this write is part of the epoch transaction, it is possible to deduce if an epoch have been applied in the slave cluster by looking at this table.

Normally the writes to this table isn't replicated from the slave cluster. But for globally distributed database implementations using multi-master it is necessary to also replicate these changes on towards the next cluster to ensure that conflict detection can work correctly.

This is controlled by the *ndb-log-apply-status* variable. If the server id is the same as written it will be ignored to avoid replication loops.

39.3.3 *ndb_schema*

Schema changes (CREATE TABLE, RENAME TABLE, DROP TABLE, ALTER TABLE, ...) are replicated as well. They are replicated through the aid of the *ndb_schema* table. When a schema change is executed a row is inserted into the *ndb_schema* table. This table is never replicated to the slaves.

Each MySQL Server listens to events on this table. Thus each MySQL Server will hear about any schema modifications as part of the schema change process. In addition each MySQL Server listens to events that provide detailed information about the resulting table(s) from the event.

The schema change is not necessarily executed in the same MySQL Server as where the binlog is written. By writing a row in the *ndb_schema* table we transport information to the MySQL replication server(s) about the schema change. We also ensure that the schema change is executed in a specific epoch.

The table provides a column called *slock*, this column is a bitmap that is updated by each MySQL Server when they hear about the schema change. Thus through this table we ensure that all MySQL servers are informed of all metadata changes. If a MySQL Server is down when the schema modifications occurs, it can find about this schema change in the recovery phase by looking into this table.

```
CREATE TABLE ndb_schema (
    db varbinary(63) NOT NULL,
    name varbinary(63) NOT NULL,
    slock binary(32) NOT NULL,
    query blob NOT NULL,
    node_id int unsigned NOT NULL,
    epoch bigint unsigned NOT NULL,
    id int unsigned NOT NULL,
    version int unsigned NOT NULL,
    type int unsigned NOT NULL,
    PRIMARY KEY USING HASH (db,name)
) ENGINE=NDB DEFAULT CHARSET=latin1;
```

In this table we record the database name in *db*, the table name in *name*, the actual query executed is inserted into the *query* column. The query might be a bit rewritten for multi-table schema changes since *ndb_schema* will only contain single-table schema changes.

node_id contains the node id of the MySQL Server that executed the schema change. *id* contains the table id, *version* contains the table version and *type* contains table type. *epoch* contains the epoch number of the schema change.

39.3.4 *ndb_replication*

The *ndb_replication* table has two major use cases. The first is that it can be used in normal replication setups to control which tables that are to be replicated and what data to replicate. The table doesn't exist by default, thus the user must create the table and fill it with data for it to be used. If the table doesn't exist the MySQL server settings through the options control what to replicate and by default no conflict detection is used.

The table should be placed in the *mysql* database and below is the CREATE TABLE command used to create it.

```
CREATE TABLE ndb_replication (
  db varbinary(63),
  table_name varbinary(63),
  server_id int unsigned,
  binlog_type int unsigned,
  conflict_fn varbinary(128),
  PRIMARY KEY USING HASH (db, table_name, server_id)
) ENGINE=NDB PARTITION BY KEY(db,table_name);
```

db

Database name, could contain % and ? such that the database name is regular expression. In this case the columns will apply to all tables that have a database that fit the regular expression.

table_name

Table name, can also contain regular expressions.

server_id

If this is set to 0 it applies to all MySQL replication servers in the cluster. If set to a non-zero value it only applies to the server id listed in the table.

binlog_type

The values used here are defined in *sql/ndb_share.h*. The values are used to set the way we binlog. There are three configuration options that control this for the default setting. These are *ndb-log-update-as-write*, *ndb-log-updated-only*, and *ndb-log-update-as-minimal*.

ndb-log-update-as-minimal are OFF for all options except 8 and 9 below for which they are set. The 8 and 9 settings can only be used in conjunction with the conflict detection functions *NDB$EPOCH2* and *NDB$EPOCH2_TRANS*.

Setting this to 0 (NBT_DEFAULT) means that the server defaults rules. This is default if no row for a table exists or if the entire *ndb_replication* table is missing.

Setting it to 1 (NBT_NO_LOGGING) means that the table or set of tables will not be logged in the binary log.

Setting the value to 2 (*NBT_UPDATED_ONLY*) means the same thing as when *ndb-log-updated-only* and *ndb-log-update-as-write* are set. Thus only changed values are sent in events to MySQL replication servers and thus only changed columns are written into binlog. This is the recommended value for tables that are replicated using MySQL Cluster without conflict detection. Using default settings of the configuration options will use this binlog type.

Setting this to 3 (*NBT_FULL*) lead to that the full row is sent in an event from the data node and written into binlog. We will still only write the after image. Same behaviour as when *ndb-log-updated-only* is set to OFF and no other changes to default settings.

Settting this to 4 (*NBT_USE_UPDATE*) or to 6 (*NBT_UPDATED_ONLY_USE_UPDATE*) lead to that updates are logged as updates and inserts as writes. This is the setting one gets by setting *ndb-log-update-as-write* to OFF and *ndb-log-updated-only* to ON.

These settings are the one to use for replication to another storage engine.

Setting this to 7 (*NBT_FULL_USE_UPDATE*) lead to the same as setting 6 but the *ndb-log-updated-only* is set to OFF.

This is the setting when using conflict detection with either of the functions *NDB$OLD(column_name)* and *NDB$MAX_DELETE_WIN(column_name)*.

8 (*NBT_UPDATED_ONLY_MINIMAL*) is the setting used for replication with conflict detection using either of the conflict detection functions *ndb$EPOCH2* or *NDB$EPOCH2_TRANS*. It writes updates as updates and writes only the changed columns in the after image and only the primary key columns of the before image.

9 (*NBT_UPDATED_FULL_MINIMAL*) is the same as 8 except that all non-primary key columns are written in the after image. This can be used to replicate to older versions of MySQL Cluster. The option *ndb-log-update-as-minimal* was introduced in MySQL Cluster 7.5.7.

conflict_fn

This specifies the conflict function, this will be covered in the chapter on globally distributed database.

39.4 EPOCHS

MySQL Cluster uses a concept called *epochs* to replicate transactions. An *epoch* is a group of transactions that are serialised to execute before the next epoch and after the previous epoch as described in earlier chapters.

We achieve these transaction groups by blocking transactions from starting to commit when we receive a prepare message from the master node, after the master node have received a response from all nodes it will send a message that transactions are allowed to start committing again.

Transactions can be in three states. They can be running operations such as read, insert, update and delete, but haven't yet reached the commit point. The second state is that they have reached the commit point and the third state is that they are executing the commit. Transactions can continue committing if they have passed the commit point and they can continue executing in the prepare phases. The performance isn't affected a lot by creating these transaction groups that are the *epochs* used for replicating to a slave cluster.

Epochs are created at a configurable interval. By default this interval is 100 milliseconds. By settting the cluster configuration parameter *TimeBetweenEpochs* we can decrease or increase the interval for the creation of *epochs*.

Some of the *epochs* are also used to create a global checkpoint that the cluster can restore from in the case of a complete cluster crash. This is configurable by the cluster configuration parameter *TimeBetweenGlobalCheckpoints*. This is set to 2000 milliseconds by default.

As mentioned before the *epoch* is executed as one transaction in the slave cluster.

39.5   SETTING UP A REPLICATION CHANNEL BETWEEN TWO CLUSTERS

In order to handle the more complex replication scenarios we will first show the basic building block of setting up a single replication channel. To make it even easier this channel is brought up before starting any operations on the master cluster.

At first it is highly recommended to start by setting the MySQL server parameter *slave-allow-batching* to 1 in the MySQL Server in the slave cluster where the binlog is applied. This allows the slave thread to execute many operations in parallel and is very important to keep up with the update rates in the master cluster.

39.5.1   STARTING UP THE MySQL REPLICATION SERVERS

At first the MySQL Server in the master cluster must be started with a number of MySQL server options set properly. The master must set a unique server id using the parameter *server-id*, it must activate the binlog through setting the *log-bin* option to the base filename of the binlog files. The NDB storage engine must also be activated through setting the option *ndbcluster*. NDB only supports row based replication, it is necessary to set the option *binlog-format* to MIXED. This will automatically use row based replication for normal operations.

The *ndb-log-updated-only* option is important to have ON (which it is by default), this will ensure that the NDB data nodes will only send changed columns to the MySQL replication servers after a write transaction is completed.

ndb-log-update-as-write converts updates to writes to ensure that execution of the binlog is idempotent. This is on by default and should be kept on.

So the default behaviour is to record all updates as writes with only the changed columns recorded. This setting is good unless you are using any of the conflict detection setups, this will be covered in a later chapter. If you replicate to another storage engine it is important to set *ndb-log-update-as-write* to 0.

Setting *ndb-extra-logging* to 99 might be useful if you want more understanding of what goes on in the MySQL replication server.

In the master MySQL server we should ensure that file writes are synchronised to disk to ensure that the *epochs* are written to disk as soon as they are completed. This means we need to set *sync-binlog* to 1.

In this chapter we assume that you are setting up the infrastructure for a highly available MySQL Cluster solution. As shown in the following chapter we should set the option *ndb-log-empty-epochs* to ensure that we can write an easy script to discover when we need to fail-over the replication channel.

Thus starting up the MySQL replication server in the master cluster should at least contain the following options.

```
mysqld --server-id=$id
       --log-bin=mysql-bin
       --sync-binlog=1
       --ndbcluster
       --binlog-format=MIXED
       --ndb-log-empty-epochs=ON
       --binlog-cache-size=1M
```

The MySQL replication server in the slave cluster must also set a unique *server-id*, it must set the *ndbcluster* option. If it only operates as a slave it doesn't need to configure the binlog. To avoid that the slave replication starts before we are ready it is important to add the option *skip-slave-start*. The slave applier should use batching to increase speed of the applier, setting the *slave-allow-batching* to 1 means that we can use batching of operations at the slave.

Thus starting up the MySQL replication server in the slave cluster should at least contain the following options.

```
mysqld --server-id=$id
       --ndbcluster
       --skip-slave-start
       --slave-allow-batching
```

39.5.2   CREATING A USER ON THE MASTER MySQL SERVER

Given that the slave server needs to connect to the master MySQL server, it is necessary to setup a special replication user on the master MySQL Server. This is recommended for security reasons.

```
mysql> GRANT REPLICATION SLAVE ON *.*
mysql> 'user'@'hostname'
mysql> IDENTIFIED BY 'password';
```

39.5.3   SET THE REPLICATION CHANNEL STARTING POINT ON THE SLAVE SIDE

Before the slave applier can start it needs to know the following things:

1. Hostname of master MySQL Server

2. Port number of the master MySQL Server

3. Username that the slave will use on the master MySQL Server

4. Password of this user on the master MySQL Server

5. The starting binlog file on the master MySQL Server

6. The starting position on the master MySQL Server.

When starting replication from a new cluster an empty file name means the starting binlog file and this file starts at position 4. The command executed in the slave MySQL Server now is the following.

```
mysql> CHANGE MASTER TO
mysql> MASTER_HOST='master_host',
mysql> MASTER_PORT=master_port,
mysql> MASTER_USER='slave_user',
mysql> MASTER_PASSWORD='slave_password',
mysql> MASTER_LOG_FILE='',
mysql> MASTER_LOG_POS=4;
```

There is also a set of options in the CHANGE MASTER TO command to setup a secure communication between the slave and the master using SSL options.

39.5.4   START SLAVE APPLIER

Now we are prepared to start our replication channel. We execute the command

```
mysql> START SLAVE;
```

in the slave MySQL Server. Now the replication channel have started and any transactions executed in the master cluster will be applied in the slave cluster through the slave MySQL Server.

39.5.5   IMPORTING A BACKUP FROM THE MASTER CLUSTER

Bringing up a replication channel in a live cluster is not that much more complex. All the preparations are exactly the same except for one thing. We must first import the entire data set from the master cluster followed by catching up with the binlog in the master cluster.

Eight steps are required here:

1. Ensure that the binlog has been started on the master MySQL Server

2. Execute a backup in the master cluster

3. Create any databases needed in the slave cluster not yet present there

4. Reset the slave in the slave MySQL Server

5. Restore the backup in the slave cluster

6. Discover the last *epoch* that was in the backup

7. Discover the start position in the binlog for the first *epoch* not in backup

8. Set this position in the *CHANGE MASTER TO command*

9. Start the slave applier

The binlog is started immediately when the MySQL Server is started with *log-bin* set.

To execute a backup in NDB is very simple, we provide more details on this in the chapter on backups in NDB. It is enough to connect to the NDB management server using a management client and issue the command *START BACKUP*. After some time the command is completed.

Now before restoring the backup ensure that any *CREATE DATABASE* commands are issued on a MySQL Server connected to the slave cluster. Databases are not stored in NDB backups. If metadata was restored using data from *mysqldump* that also restored databases this is not necessary.

To restore the backup in the slave cluster is covered in detail in the chapter on *Restore in MySQL Cluster*. Essentially we install a backup from the master cluster, we ensure that the *ndb_apply_status* table is up to date and we ensure that the restore is not logged to any binlogs.

Now ensure that the slave is reset before we setup the replication channel to ensure that the old slave settings aren't interfering. This is performed through the following command in the slave MySQL Server.

```
mysql> RESET SLAVE;
```

Now to discover the last *epoch* in the backup we use the command in slave MySQL Server (or any other MySQL Server connected to the slave cluster).

```
mysql> SELECT @latest:= MAX(epoch) FROM mysql.ndb_apply_status;
```

We have now read the last *epoch* number that have been restored in the slave cluster.

Equipped with this information we can now use the *ndb_binlog_index* table in the master MySQL Server to discover the binlog position where to start the slave applier.

We execute the following query in the master MySQL Server where *@latest* comes from the previous command and *@file* and *@pos* is what we are looking for.

```
mysql> SELECT @file:=SUBSTRING_INDEX(next_file, '/', -1),
mysql>        @pos:=next_position
mysql> FROM mysql.ndb_binlog_index
mysql> WHERE epoch = @latest;
```

Now we take those two parameters back to the slave MySQL Server and use those to set the binlog file and binlog position from where the slave MySQL Server should start applying the binlog.

```
mysql> CHANGE MASTER TO
mysql> MASTER_HOST='master_host',
mysql> MASTER_PORT=master_port,
mysql> MASTER_USER='slave_user',
mysql> MASTER_PASSWORD='slave_password',
mysql> MASTER_LOG_FILE=@file,
mysql> MASTER_LOG_POS=@pos;
```

Now we are now ready to start the slave applier.

```
mysql> START SLAVE;
```

After starting the slave applier it will take some time before the slave cluster has caught up with the master cluster. The slave cluster will never entirely catch up since replication is asynchronous. But the replication lag will start with as long time as it takes to restore the backup and this could potentially take a fairly long time, definitely minutes and potentially even hours in larger clusters. The replication lag should be possible to get down to seconds.

The MySQL manual contains an example script written in Perl called

reset-slave.pl that automates parts of this process.

39.6 POINT-IN-TIME BACKUPS

Normally the second cluster is used for fail over cases. If the master cluster is able to sustain a high load and the slave cluster can only survive the update load, in this case it could be interesting to use the slave cluster to provide a point-in-time backup solution for MySQL Cluster.

To install such a point-in-time backup at the master cluster one starts with a backup, next one uses the slave cluster to catch up unto the point in time that should be restored.

The MySQL manual have a detailed description how to handle this.

39.7 READ SLAVE CLUSTERS

The above setup could be directly used for Read Slave Cluster setups. In this case it might even be ok to avoid a fail-over replication channel between the master cluster and the slave cluster. Loss of the replication channel means that the slave cluster cannot be used until it has been restarted and come back again.

For a slave cluster used only for extra read capacity this can be agreeable. The master cluster can thus sustain more clusters instead of sustaining fail-over replication channels.

39.8   CHARACTERISTICS OF SLAVE APPLIER FOR NDB

The slave applier is the slave applier used by MySQL Replication. This applier is single-threaded. At the same time this single thread works on very large batches where transactions spanning the last 100 milliseconds is applied in one large transaction.

Given that the NDB API can sustain very high levels of batching, the performance of this single thread is extremely good. More than a hundred thousand operations per second can be handled through this single thread.

MySQL Cluster Replication can be used for most application using NDB. The exception is applications requiring many hundreds of thousands of write operations per second or even going into millions of write operations per second.

39.9   PURGING MySQL REPLICATION FILES

MySQL Replication uses binlog files that have a specific size, after completing the write of one binlog file, the file is closed and a new one is written to instead. It goes on like this as long as the replication continues. A binlog file can also be closed and a new one created through restarting the MySQL Server.

MySQL will never delete any binlog files automatically, it can delete them on command, but the command must be executed by the DBA. Thus the DBA must always have a strategy for how to delete the binlog files.

In case the slave clusters are not used for fail-over scenarios it would be sufficient to keep the binlog files until all slave clusters have applied the binlog file.

Thus to calculate which files to delete at any point in time one would issue the following query towards the *ndb_apply_status* table in each slave cluster to deduce what *epoch* have been applied in the slave cluster.

```
mysql> SELECT @latest:= MAX(epoch) FROM mysql.ndb_apply_status;
```

Now take the minimum of all the *@latest* from all slave clusters. Next use the following query on the *ndb_binlog_index* table in the master cluster.

```
mysql> SELECT @file:=SUBSTRING_INDEX(next_file, '/', -1),
mysql>          @pos:=next_position
mysql> FROM mysql.ndb_binlog_index
mysql> WHERE epoch = @minimum_latest;
```

Now the *@file* variable contains the last file that need to be retained. All files before this one can be deleted.

Now if we have a fail-over scenario it is essential to be able to fail-over after a complete crash of the master cluster. It is important to be able to handle simultaneous crash of the master cluster and the slave cluster used for fail-over. In this case we can restart one of the clusters using a backup from the master cluster followed by applying the binlog up to the end of the binlog.

To ensure that the binlog can be used together with a backup one checks the *StopGCP* number output from the backup at completion. In the example below the *StopGCP* is 3845.

```
ndb_mgm> START BACKUP
Waiting for completed, this may take several minutes
Node 2: Backup 1 started from node 1
Node 2: Backup 1 started from node 1 completed
 StartGCP: 3839 StopGCP: 3845
 #Records: 193234 #LogRecords: 12349
 Data: 20519789 bytes Log: 1334560 bytes
```

An *epoch* number is formed by using the *StopGCP* as the 32 most significant bits of a 64-bit number and 0 as the 32 least significant numbers. Use this *epoch* number in the same manner as above to calculate the binlog file that can be deleted using the above query on the *ndb_binlog_index* table.

In the fail-over case we have to ensure that all slave clusters can survive a master cluster failure and we need to be able to handle a restore from backup, thus we need to retain files needed for both the above cases.

When we are deleting a binlog file it is important to also delete all entries in the *ndb_binlog_index* table for this file as well. Running the *PURGE BINARY LOGS* will ensure that this is done in a correct manner.

```
mysql> PURGE BINARY LOGS TO 'mysql-bin-009';
```

Thus an important script in the DBA toolbox for MySQL Cluster Replication is a script that automates the above to ensure that we purge binlog files in the MySQL replication servers in the master cluster.

Chapter 40

Global Fail-over Architecture

This is probably the most common reason to replicate between different clusters. In this scenario it is necessary to setup more than one replication channel between the clusters. We use this scenario for increased availability, thus it is important that the replication itself doesn't hurt availability and thus we need at least two replication channels. In this chapter we will always discuss how to use two replication channels, one is the primary replication channel and one is the standby replication channel. To setup with 3 or even 4 replication channels is not any major concern and the required changes to the decription in this chapter should be small.

We assume here that both clusters are designed such that they can be used as the master cluster after a fail-over.

40.1 Setup for fail-over scenario

The setup for a fail-over scenario is exactly the same as the setup for a single replication channel. The only difference is that we set it up for two pairs of MySQL Servers instead of only one. We will call the operational pair the primary replication channel and the fail-over replication channel we will call standby replication channel.

It is important to start up both MySQL replication servers in the master cluster. These two MySQL replication servers will have very similar content in their binlog files. We can however never trust they use exactly the same positions. Thus when setting up the slave MySQL Server on the standby replication channel we always have to use data from queries executed in the master MySQL Server on the standby replication channel and vice versa for the primary replication channel.

The last two commands, the *CHANGE MASTER TO* and the *START SLAVE* command must only be performed on the primary replication channel.

These commands cannot be executed on the standby replication channel. Doing so would lead to two slave appliers trying to insert the same data in parallel and could cause all sorts of troubles.

The standby replication channel is not used until it is time to perform a fail-over from the primary replication channel to the standby replication channel.

40.2 Discovering failure of a replication channel

What could cause a replication channel cutover to start using the standby replication channel?

If either the master MySQL Server or the slave MySQL Server on the primary replication channel fails, we need to cut over to the standby replication channel.

A cutover can also be caused by a network failure that stops the master MySQL server and the slave MySQL server on the primary replication channel from communicating with each other.

Indeed it can also be caused by a lost connection from the master MySQL Server towards the data nodes in the master cluster. If this happens it will insert a special gap event called *LOST_EVENT*. When the slave applier finds this record in the binlog it will immediately stop applying the binlog and thus stop the slave.

Given that these failures can be complex and require a view from several independent systems it can even be worthwhile to make the decision to cutover as a manual decision.

40.2.1 IMPORTANT THINGS TO WATCH

In both the VM of the master MySQL Server and the VM of the slave MySQL Server it is important to see if the process is still up and running. In Linux this can be achieved with a fairly simple script using the *ps* program. In my iClaustron hobby project I am using the following command to watch if a process is up and running.

```
ps -p $SEARCHED_PID -o command | \
  grep $SEARCHED_PROCESS | \
  wc -l |
  sed -e 's/ //g'`
```

SEARCHED_PID is the *pid* of the MySQL server process in this case,

SEARCHED_PROCESS is mysqld in this case. If this returns 1 the process is still running, if it returns 0 it means that the process has for some reason stopped.

Returning 0 here means that the cut-over should be initiated. If 1 is returned it simply means that we need to gather more information, the process is still running, but is it making progress is another question we need to ask.

An alternative method is to issue a simple command to the MySQL Server, if it returns a result it is up and running and if it doesn't we can attempt to reconnect and if we cannot connect to the MySQL Server it is likely that it has stopped.

```
mysql> SELECT @latest:= MAX(epoch) FROM mysql.ndb_apply_status;
```

If the value of this have changed in the slave cluster since the last call we know that we are making progress. If the value is the same we have made no progress, but that is still not necessarily an indication that the replication channel have failed.

Now if we discover that no *epochs* are applied in the slave cluster we can check the status of the slave applier by issuing the command *SHOW SLAVE STATUS* in the slave MySQL Server. This will most likely provide details on why the replication channel is not working properly.

One reason the slave has not advanced the *epoch* number could be a large transaction running. In this case the *SHOW SLAVE STATUS* command will show that the slave applier is busy executing. In this case we will simply wait one more time slot.

Another thing the command could show is that the slave has stopped. In almost all cases this should lead to a cut-over to start.

ndb-log-empty-epochs

To use the approach where we check the *ndb_apply_status* table, it is necessary to set MySQL server option *ndb-log-empty-epochs* to ON. This ensures that we will write to both the *ndb_binlog_index* table on the master and to the *ndb_apply_status* table on the slave even when an epoch is empty.

This will increase the idle load slightly, but this should normally not be any major issue. Any type of constant health check increases the idle load a bit.

40.2.2   Thoughts on an automatic discover fail-over script

A simple script to handle fail-over is to have a connection to the slave MySQL Server.

Next step is to decide on the time to wait between checks of the replication channel. Let's say we use 10 seconds here.

Every 10 seconds perform the following.

1. Issue a read of latest *epoch* from *ndb_apply_status* in slave MySQL Server

2. If *epoch* has changed since last 10 second check we stop with OK

3. We issue a SHOW SLAVE STATUS to check the state of the slave applier

4. If the state is stopped we start a cut-over of the replication channel

5. If the state is that we are executing we will stop with OK

The check if any *epochs* have been applied will discover all types of failures of the primary replication channel. In a sense this command is sufficient to perform a health check of the state of the primary replication channel. Given that a new *epoch* is created once per 100 milliseconds we simply need to decide how long time we think that it is ok to wait for an *epoch* to complete. This is affected by the size of the largest transactions executed, it is also dependent on what type of ALTER TABLE statements that are replicated across the channel.

40.2.3   Thoughts on a replication channel cut-over script

The first step is to ensure that the slave applier in the slave MySQL server is stopped. Normally this is simple enough using the *STOP SLAVE* command. It is a bit more complicated if the slave MySQL Server doesn't respond. If so we can ensure that the slave is stopped by killing the slave MySQL Server.

After ensuring that the slave applier in the currently active replication channel has stopped we perform the usual logic to discover from where to start the standby replication channel.

This means issuing the following command in the slave MySQL server in the standby replication channel.

```
mysql> SELECT @latest:= MAX(epoch) FROM mysql.ndb_apply_status;
```

Next we use the *@latest* in the command towards the master MySQL Server in the standby replication channel.

```
mysql> SELECT @file:=SUBSTRING_INDEX(next_file, '/', -1),
mysql>         @pos:=next_position
mysql> FROM mysql.ndb_binlog_index
mysql> WHERE epoch = @latest;
```

If this command returns the empty string it could be because this MySQL replication server is a bit behind, if this is suspected we could check more states or simply wait a bit more. A more common reason is that returning an empty string simply means that the replication channel didn't record this *epoch*. In this case the replication channel is broken since both the primary and the standby replication channel is broken.

A broken replication channel means that one have to start from a backup again, the backup must be taken after the stop since we lack binlog information for some period around the stop time.

Now in the successful case where we did find the *epoch* we use the *@file* and *@pos* from this query in the following command towards the slave MySQL server in the standby replication channel.

```
mysql> CHANGE MASTER TO
mysql> MASTER_HOST='master_host',
mysql> MASTER_PORT=master_port,
mysql> MASTER_USER='slave_user',
mysql> MASTER_PASSWORD='slave_password',
mysql> MASTER_LOG_FILE=@file,
mysql> MASTER_LOG_POS=@pos;
```

We are now ready to resume slave applier operations in the slave cluster by issuing the *START SLAVE* command in the slave MySQL Server in the standby replication channel.

```
mysql> START SLAVE;
```

Now the standby replication channel have been promoted to primary replication channel.

40.2.4 Handling GAP events

GAP events or *LOST_EVENT* is something inserted in the binlog when the MySQL replication server have lost the ability to write the binlog. The most common reason for this, using NDB, is that the binlog server have lost connection to the master cluster or that the binlog server could not keep up with the replication and ran out of event buffer memory.

When the slave encounters a GAP event in the binlog it will stop. When this happens we will soon discover that the replication channel have stopped. After discovering that this happened due to a GAP event we will perform a normal cutover to the other replication channel.

If the standby replication channel had a GAP event even before the primary replication channel we will not find any record for the current *epoch* in the *ndb_binlog_index* table in the binlog server in the standby replication channel. Thus the replication channel is broken and we will need to start it up from scratch again.

If the standby replication channel had a GAP event at exactly the same place as the primary replication channel we will be able to start the standby replication channel. But it will stop immediately on the GAP event. In this case we will compare the binlog position we have stopped at, if this is the same as when we started it, we will not attempt to cutover the replication channel since we know that it will not work.

If the standby replication channel had a GAP event further on in the binlog we will treat it as the first GAP event and will execute the above procedure for that GAP event as well. There is no way of knowing if this GAP event is enough to enable us to cutover the original primary replication channel, thus we will try and see if it works.

40.3 Discover failure of a cluster

To fail over to the slave cluster entirely after a failure of the master cluster requires discovery logic of when the master cluster have failed.

To discover that a cluster have failed is a fairly complex process given that there are many potential variants where we can have partial failures.

We need to have a perfectly working slave cluster for a fail over to be of any use. Thus we need to check the operations of both the master cluster as well as the slave cluster.

There are two simple methods of checking that a cluster is up and running. The first uses a MySQL client to perform a simple operation and the other uses an NDB management client to check the cluster status.

40.3.1 Checking status through MySQL client

We can use the MySQL replication servers to also check the status of the cluster. A simple *SELECT* query towards the cluster will show if the cluster is up. If the query succeeds the cluster must be up.

```
mysql> SELECT a_column from an_ndb_table where pk=a_key;
```

If the cluster fails we can attempt the same query also towards the other MySQL replication servers.

40.3.2 CHECKING STATUS THROUGH NDB MANAGEMENT CLIENT

Another possibility to check cluster status is using the SHOW command in the NDB management client. This command reports the status as it is seen from the management server we contact to issue the *SHOW* command.

```
ndb_mgm> SHOW
Cluster Configuration
---------------------
[ndbd(NDB)] 2 node(s)
id=1    @192.168.1.9  (5.7.19-ndb-7.5.8, Nodegroup: 0, *)
id=2 (not connected, accepting connect from 192.168.1.10)
[ndb_mgmd(MGM)] 1 node(s)
id=49   @192.168.1.8  (5.7.19-ndb-7.5.8)
id=50   @192.168.1.9  (5.7.19-ndb-7.5.8)
[mysqld(API)]   2 node(s)
id=51   @192.168.1.9  (5.7.19-ndb-7.5.8)
id=52   @192.168.1.10  (5.7.19-ndb-7.5.8)
id=53 (not connected, accepting connect from 192.168.1.9)
id=54 (not connected, accepting connect from 192.168.1.10)
```

If the cluster is up and running at least one of the data nodes (ndbd(NDB) above) will be presented with its hostname, its MySQL Cluster version and its node group id. Nodes that are considered down are listed as not connected, data nodes can also be listed as being in a start phase.

If none of them are up and running this management node considers the cluster as down.

40.3.3 BUILDING BLOCKS FOR DISCOVER CLUSTER FAILURE SCRIPT

A natural building block is to use a MySQL client at first to check the cluster status. As long as this is successful we need not do anything more. If it is unsuccessful we can try the same thing from another MySQL replication server in the same cluster. If this is not successful either we move on to attempt with the first management server in the cluster. If it considers the cluster as down as well we proceed and check with the remaining management servers connected to the cluster.

If all MySQL replication servers and all NDB management servers connected to the cluster all report the cluster as not up, we will deduce that the cluster is down.

This will be a signal to fail over to the slave cluster.

40.3.4 APPLICATION ASSISTANCE IN FAIL-OVER DISCOVERY

Applications can consider the cluster useless even if the cluster is still up and running. One such case happens when we run out REDO log (the application receives error code 410), this turns NDB into a read-only database that is normally not an acceptable state and can lead to a fail-over to the slave cluster.

We can discover this state by turning the heartbeat query into an update query (possibly even updating disk columns).

We can also run out UNDO log for disk columns, there are various memory buffers that one can run out of that causes intermittent failures.

The application logic can also participate in the discovery process to discover when a cluster is no longer in an acceptable state and thus requiring a fail-over to the slave cluster.

40.4   CLUSTER FAIL OVER

If we discover that the master cluster have failed we need to fail over to the slave cluster. This requires the slave applier to complete the application of the log records that was produced in the master cluster before it failed.

Once this is completed we will stop the slave using the *STOP SLAVE* command.

Now the slave cluster is up and running, the master cluster is down, at this moment the live data is in the slave cluster. There is one major problem still though. All applications are still connected to the main cluster where no action is happening.

The next step is application specific, all application logic must be transferred from the main cluster to the slave cluster. For web server applications this usually involves redirecting the load balancers to the MySQL Servers of the slave cluster.

Chapter 41

Globally Distributed MySQL Cluster

In this chapter we will describe a scenario where MySQL Cluster is used to implement a globally distributed database with a set of clusters that can even be on different continents.

This scenario supports updates made in any cluster, thus it is a multi-master solution on a global scale. The problem with this scenario is that the latency to detect conflicting updates is on the order of a second for a truly global case due to the speed of light.

In a truly globally distributed database it is not a good idea to use strong consistency as we do internally in one cluster in NDB. We need to use a model for eventual consistency. So we could have conflicting updates in this setup.

It is still a good idea to limit the possibility of conflicts by routing queries and transactions to clusters dependent on the data to be read or written. The responsibility of this is on the application.

The ideas for a globally distributed database does not cover cases where we support transactional consistency on a global scale. The latency in a globally distributed database makes that not tractable.

Instead we solve the problem on a row-by-row basis.

NDB does support a transactionally consistent method, this is only intended for short duration where we have network partitioning or are performing a switchover from one cluster to another or extremely rare conflicts. We will cover this in the next chapter.

The question is how to handle conflicts that will occur in such a setup.

MySQL Cluster supports a number of ways to handle conflicts.

1. Most recently updated wins (Automated conflict resolution)

2. Conflicts require manual resolution

3. Primary cluster wins (Automated conflict resolution)

41.1 NDB$MAX_DELETE_WIN(column_name)

This option is to have a simple decision based on a value of a specific column that acts as a timestamp. The update with the highest timestamp or value of this column will win. This requires adding such a timestamp column to each table that requires conflict detection. Decision is done on a row level.

The timestamp column is updated by the user and maintained by the application developers.

The conflict logic is very simple, when a replication event for an update comes and there is an existing row already, the update will be applied if the value of this column is higher than the value in the existing row. If it is not higher, a conflict occurred and the update or write is not applied. The conflict is logged in an exceptions table (explained later in this chapter) if one exists.

This is by far the simplest conflict handling function. The user need to ensure that the timestamp column is properly set and deletes must be handled with care. The conflicts are automatically resolved, the conflicts can in parallel be logged to an exceptions table.

There is no special significance in this scheme for where the update comes from. All clusters are equal in priority. Thus we can have any number of clusters in this setup and they can be organised in a lot of different configurations.

41.1.1 INSERT-INSERT CONFLICTS

If an insert is replicated into a cluster where the row already exists we have a conflict. This is a bit special, Insert-Insert conflicts should always be worked around. One manner this can be done in MySQL is using autoincrement functionality where different clusters will never generate the same key.

41.1.2 DELETE-DELETE CONFLICTS

A delete in this case is treated as if the timestamp column is always higher than the existing row. Thus deletes will always succeed.

There is also an old variant called *NDB$MAX(column_name)* that treats deletes as if they always have a lower timestamp column compared to the existing one. Thus deletes never succeeds. We don't recommend using this variant.

41.2 *NDB$OLD(column_name)*

When checking if an update is in conflict using *NDB$OLD(column_name)* we get the before value of the row from the updating cluster, we get the current value of the row from our cluster. If those two values differ we have a conflict.

This conflict handling function doesn't automatically perform conflict resolution. It is expected that the application have defined an exceptions table and that the application uses this table to resolve the conflicts.

As an example if the row version is 2 and now both Cluster A and Cluster B wants to update the row to version 3. Thus both clusters will have a success in executing this change in their own cluster. When the replication event arrives in the other cluster both those events will see a conflict. Both clusters will have a logged entry in the exceptions table. The end result of these two transactions is that the clusters have different data. The application logic using the information in the exceptions table is required to bring the database back into a consistent state.

To use *NDB$OLD(column_name)* without defining any exceptions table doesn't make sense.

NDB$OLD(column_name) can be used in many different replication configurations. It can be used in circular replication setups with more than two clusters involved.

41.2.1 Insert-Insert conflicts

If an insert is replicated into a cluster where the row already exists we have a conflict. The before value in this case is NULL, it is clearly different from whatever value we are inserting in the timestamp column.

41.2.2 Update-Update conflicts

In this case we have a before value from the originating cluster and the row to be updated have a value in the current cluster updated. If these values are the same no updates have interfered and caused any conflict. If the values differs it means that some other update successfully changed the row in this cluster and thus we have a conflict.

41.2.3 Delete-Delete conflicts

If we are trying to delete and find that the row is already deleted, we can deduce that the value of the column have changed and thus we have a conflict.

41.3 *NDB$EPOCH2*

The previous conflict detection function only uses a special column set by the application to deduce whether conflict occurs or not. *NDB$EPOCH2* discovers conflicts based on a timestamp generated by NDB internally through our *epoch* based timestamps. If *epochs* are generated at intervals of 100 milliseconds we get a conflict window that is 200 millisecond for a circle of two clusters.

Now *NDB$EPOCH2* uses a Active-Standby approach. There is always one primary cluster and the rest of the clusters are secondary clusters. Updates applied in the Active cluster, the primary cluster, cannot conflict. Only updates that originates in a secondary cluster can be in conflict. Thus the rule is that the primary wins all conflicts.

NDB$EPOCH2 can only be used with two clusters, one acting in the role as primary cluster and one acting in the role as secondary cluster.

NDB$EPOCH2 is still a row-based conflict detection mechanism. Thus only the rows that conflict are affected by the conflict detection.

There is an older variant called *NDB$EPOCH*, this doesn't handle delete conflicts properly. This is solved in *NDB$EPOCH2* by keeping track of deleted rows for some time before removing them completely. There should be no need to use the *NDB$EPOCH* method any more.

41.4 Conflict detection tables

Before conflict detection can be activated we must create a number of tables to handle conflict detection. It is mandatory for *NDB$EPOCH2* since the existence of an exception causes a number of extra hidden columns to be added to the table when created. The exceptions table must always be created before the table itself is created.

For *NDB$OLD(column_name)* there is no practical use without it. For

NDB$MAX_DELETE_WIN(column_name) it is optional to create an exceptions table.

These tables should all be defined as using the NDB storage engine.

41.4.1 EXCEPTIONS TABLES

If the name of the user table is *my_example_table*, the table name of the table that stores the conflicts must be named *my_example_table$EX*. A $EX is added at the end of the table name. The table and the exceptions table should be in the same database.

This table have four mandatory columns that are defined first. It is strongly recommended to call those *NDB$server_id*, *NDB$master_server_id*, *NDB$master_epoch* and *NDB$count*. The server id is the id of the MySQL replication server where the conflict was detected. The master server id is the server id where the conflicting operation was inserted into the binlog and master epoch is the epoch number that was used when this was inserted into the binlog. The *count* is a simple counter to ensure that each conflict is a unique entry in the exceptions table. These four columns are the primary key of the exceptions table.

Next we have three optional columns, the first one is called *NDB$OP_TYPE*. This is an ENUM that lists the operation type of the conflict. It can be either of WRITE_ROW, UPDATE_ROW, DELETE_ROW, REFRESH_ROW and READ_ROW.

The second is another ENUM that lists the cause of the conflict. It can be any of ROW_DOES_NOT_EXIST, ROW_ALREADY_EXISTS, DATA_IN_CONFLICT, TRANS_IN_CONFLICT. It is called *NDB$CFT_CAUSE*. TRANS_IN_CONFLICT can only occur in the *NDB$EPOCH2_TRANS* method we will discuss in the next chapter.

The third is a BIGINT that is unsigned. This column is called *NDB$ORIG_TRANSID*. It is a 64-bit value and represents the transaction id in the originating cluster. This is only interesting for conflict handling using transactions that we will discuss in the next chapter.

Now after those optional columns we need to list the primary key columns in the order they are created in the original table. They should use the same data type in the exceptions table as in the original table.

Now for each column in the table that isn't a primary key one can define an additional 2 columns. The first is the original column value ($OLD). The second is the after value of this column ($NEW).

Now let us show an example. We have a table defined as below:

```
CREATE TABLE test.my_example_table (
  pk int unsigned not null,
  data varchar(255) not null,
) ENGINE=NDB;
```

In this example we only want to use a simple conflict detection based on the row value. Thus no need for the transaction id in the conflict table.

We define the exceptions table as:

```
CREATE TABLE test.my_example_table$EX (
  NDB$server_id int unsigned,
  NDB$master_server_id int unsigned,
  NDB$master_epoch bigint unsigned,
  NDB$count int unsigned,
  NDB$OP_TYPE ENUM ('WRITE_ROW', 'UPDATE_ROW', 'DELETE_ROW',
                    'REFRESH_ROW', 'READ_ROW'),
  NDB$CFT_CAUSE ENUM ('ROW_DOES_NOT_EXIST', 'ROW_ALREADY_EXIST',
                      'DATA_IN_CONFLICT', 'TRANS_IN_CONFLICT'),
  pk int unsigned not null,
  data$OLD varchar(255) not null,
  data$NEW varchar(255) not null,
  PRIMARY KEY (NDB$server_id,NDB$master_server_id,
               NDB$master_epoch,NDB$count)
) ENGINE=NDB;
```

Now equipped with this information about a row conflict the application developer can write code that uses data from the exceptions table to resolve the conflict.

The primary key of the exceptions table are mandatory columns. At least a part of the primary key of the table is mandatory. The remainder of the columns are optional. What columns that are stored in the exceptions table depends on what is needed to resolve the conflicts. This is defined by the users requirements and thus these columns are optional all of them.

41.4.2   NDB_REPLICATION TABLE

To setup conflict detection handling we need a row in the *ndb_replication* table. The columns in this table was presented earlier. To use conflict detection we need to have an entry in this table for each table involved in conflict detection (one row can handle multiple tables).

The *binlog_type* column should contain a 7. Thus updates are logged as updates and thus the entire before and after image is logged. This setting is used with *NDB$OLD(column_name)*, *NDB$MAX_DELETE_WIN(column_name)*.

The column *conflict_fn* contains the selected conflict function. The ones that we should select are either of:

NDB$OLD(column_name), *NDB$MAX_DELETE_WIN(column_name)*,

NDB$EPOCH2, *NDB$EPOCH2_TRANS* (handled in the next chapter).

The server id in this table should be set to 0 to ensure that all MySQL replication servers in the cluster handle conflict detections.

41.5   SETUP FOR CIRCULAR REPLICATION

The setup for circular replication is very similar to setting up a primary and standby replication channel.

41.5.1 *IGNORE_SERVER_IDS*

The first major difference is that circular replication means that the changes in one cluster
will eventually return to the cluster. In MySQL replication this is handled by checking the
originating server id of a transaction to be applied, if the server id is our own id we will ignore
the transaction since it originated in the MySQL Server we're in and thus is already in the
database.

Now with MySQL Cluster we need to check that the originating server id isn't in the list of
server ids used by MySQL replication servers in the cluster.

We show an example here. In the figure below we have a cluster A with four MySQL
replication servers with server ids 1 through 4. We have a cluster B with four MySQL
replication servers with server ids 5 through 8. Cluster C also have four MySQL replication
servers with server id 9 through 12.

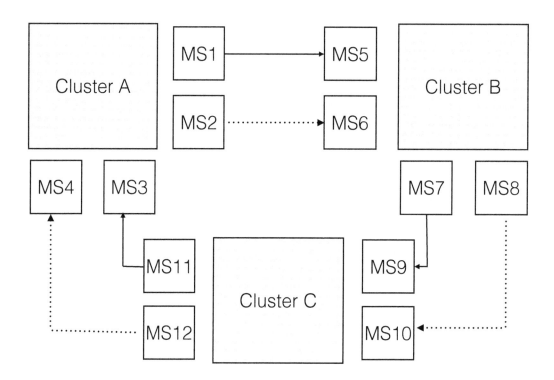

As shown in the figure we have setup a primary replication channel between cluster A and
cluster B using MySQL replication servers with server id 1 and 5, the standby replication
channel uses server ids 2 and 6.

The cluster B and cluster C has a primary replication channel setup between MySQL
replication servers with server id 7 and 9, the standby replication channel use server ids 8 and
10.

Similarly cluster C is connected to cluster A through a primary replication channel between

MySQL replication servers with server id 11 and 3, the standby replication channel use server ids 12 and 4.

Thus in cluster A we have two slave appliers, one of which is active at a time. These are using server ids 3 and 4. However the originating server ids is either 1 or 2. Thus we have to add a list of server ids to ignore.

The easiest manner is to simply ignore all MySQL replication servers that is connected to this cluster. When setting up the slave in cluster A for server id 3 and 4 we will use the following *CHANGE MASTER TO* command.

In reality one could have settled for server id 1 and 2. But setting it to 3 and 4 means that we are prepared if we start using those servers as binlog servers as well.

```
mysql> CHANGE MASTER TO
mysql> MASTER_HOST='C_host',
mysql> MASTER_PORT=C_port,
mysql> MASTER_USER='slave_user',
mysql> MASTER_PASSWORD='slave_password',
mysql> MASTER_LOG_FILE=@file,
mysql> MASTER_LOG_POS=@pos,
mysql> IGNORE_SERVER_IDS(1,2,3,4);
```

This command will ensure that the slave applier will break all cycles by avoiding to accept any replication events that originated from server ids 1 through 4.

The other slaves in this example requires a similar *CHANGE MASTER TO* command, listing the server ids present in their cluster.

41.5.2 *ndb-log-orig*

By default the *ndb-log-orig* option in the MySQL Server isn't set. If a MySQL Server is used to write the binlog in a circular replication setup for MySQL Cluster it is essential that this variable is set. It ensures that the *ndb_binlog_index* is updated with one entry for each *epoch* that is propagated from other clusters to this cluster in addition to the entry for the part of the *epoch* originating in this cluster.

Thus if for example we have 3 clusters in a circular replication we will have 3 entries per *epoch* in each MySQL replication server that writes the binlog.

41.5.3 *log-slave-updates*

In a circular replication setup we must set the option *log-slave-updates* on all MySQL Servers acting as binlog servers. Thus on server id 1,2,5,6,9 and 10 in the above example.

41.5.4 *ndb-log-apply-status*

In a circular replication using conflict detection we need to see the full view of all cluster's apply status. To handle this we will replicate any changes to the *ndb_apply_status* table, they will be logged with the same data except that the originating server id will be changed into the server id that writes the binlog in the replicating cluster.

Thus it is very important to ensure that this option is set in all binlog servers in the circular replication setup.

41.5.5 *ndb-log-update-as-write*

When not using conflict detection it is recommended to use writes for updates to make the updates idempotent. With circular replication channel we should not use writes for updates. Thus we need to set *ndb-log-update-as-write* to OFF for circular replication setups in all binlog servers.

41.6 *ndb-log-update-as-minimal*

When using the *NDB$EPOCH2* or *NDB$EPOCH2_TRANS* function it is not necessary to record the entire before image. It is sufficient to record the primary key of the before image and it is enough to record updated columns in the after image. To achieve this behaviour we set the *ndb-log-update-as-minimal* to ON. This MySQL option should only be used for those two conflict detection setups.

NDB$OLD(column_name) and *NDB$MAX_DELETE_WIN(column_name)* requires the full before image and it requires updates to be recorded as updates. Therefore this option cannot be set for those conflict detection functions. Normal replication between clusters requires only the changed columns of the updated row and record those as a write row. So one should not use this option for this setup either.

41.7 INSERT-INSERT CONFLICTS

Two inserts trying to insert the same primary key value will always be treated as if they are in conflict. The conflict will be logged in the conflict detection tables.

41.7.1 USING AUTOINCREMENT

Autoincrement have a feature that is intended for insertion into multiple clusters active at the same time. We allocate autoincrements with a certain step between id allocation. The step should be equal to the number of clusters we are using. Next we specify the autoincrement offset, this describes the number of the cluster. Thus if we have 3 clusters they should all have autoincrement step set to 3, the offset they should have is 0, 1 and 2. All MySQL Servers in each cluster should use the same numbers.

CHAPTER 42

EXTREMELY AVAILABLE SOLUTIONS

Using MySQL Cluster in a single cluster solution it is possible to get 99.999% availability. There are some complex software upgrades and configuration changes and cluster crashes that could cause downtime.

Now using the failover mechanism from one cluster to another as presented in an earlier chapter here brings the availability up to 99.9999%. Thus only 30 seconds downtime per year.

One remaining reason for downtime is switching over from one cluster to another. This can happen in complex software and hardware upgrade situations. In this situation the application might be in read-only mode for a short time while switching over write activity from one cluster to another.

For most users this 99.9999% availability is sufficient. But for a few users even the downtime for a switchover from one cluster to another is desirable to remove. One such case could be a network operator that provides services that might have to restart ongoing connections if the database is not available for updates for a while.

Such an operator might operate one cluster on the west coast of the US, another cluster is operated on the east coast.

Now in normal operation the west coast cluster handle the customers that are currently in the west and the east coast cluster handles customers in the east.

Now assume that the west coast cluster has to be brought down for some kind of management activity such as hardware upgrade, software upgrade, complex configuration changes.

In the case of a normal setup with an operating cluster and a standby cluster ready to fail over to, there would be a short read-only mode affecting customers in the west in this case.

To handle this type of switchovers NDB supports a conflict detection mechanism that enables this type of management operation to complete without any downtime at all.

The problem in this case is that it is hard to switch over all application nodes at the same time to start using the east coast cluster. The routing of application requests is a distributed decision made in many different nodes at the same time, it is hard to change these decisions all at exactly the same time.

In order to solve this we must accomodate for updates to arrive from both the west coast cluster and from the east coast cluster at the same time, operating on the same data.

Thus conflicts can occur. In this case we want to have a much stricter consistency. We operate normally in strong consistency mode. We want to continue operating in this mode even when updates can go to any of the two US clusters.

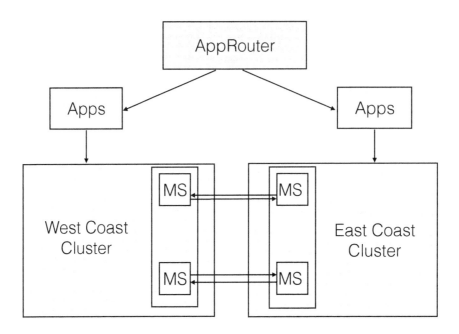

This means that any conflicts must roll back entire transactions that are in conflict. We need to use reflecting replication events to implement the conflict resolution. In addition we want to also protect important reads by ensuring that we log in the binlog also events about reading a row with an exclusive lock. In effect this is implemented such that those reads perform an update of a hidden column.

Now the number of conflicts generated in a setup like this during switch over to a new cluster can be substantial. Thus we don't expect this conflict detection mechanism to be used to support a generic update anywhere solution.

The idea is that the conflicts are generated in a short period where the switch over is executed. As soon as the switch over have completed, the resolution of the conflicts can quickly complete and the remaining east coast cluster is fully operational and accepting updates from all US users without any risk of conflicts.

42.1   SETTING UP TRANSACTION-BASED CONFLICT DETECTION

It is set up exactly the same way as *NDB$EPOCH2* except that this conflict detection function is called *NDB$EPOCH2_TRANS*. We need to set two more MySQL server options *ndb-log-transaction-id* and *ndb-log-exclusive-reads*. We need to define exception tables as explained in the previous chapter and insert rows in the *ndb_replication* table to define the replication setup.

It is also necessary to set the *ndb_slave_conflict_role* systems variable as shown below.

42.1.1 *ndb-log-transaction-id*

In order to use the conflict detection function *NDB\$EPOCH2_TRANS* it is necessary to set the option *ndb-log-transaction-id* in all MySQL replication servers used as binlog servers. With this option set the binlog server will insert a transaction id for each entry in the binlog. This enables tracking which updates that were updated in the same transaction.

42.1.2 *ndb-log-exclusive-reads*

To ensure that we can also discover reads of conflicting data we have introduced the ability to log exclusive reads of records in the binlog. This is a useful feature for conflict detection that relies on transactions for conflict discovery.

To achieve a fully consistent handling of transactions it is required to cover not only write-write dependencies between transactions, it is also required to cover read-write dependencies. To ensure that a dependency is inserted into the binlog a read must be performed using an exclusive lock.

42.1.3 *ndb-slave-conflict-role*

The role of a primary cluster is very important for both *NDB\$EPOCH2* and *NDB\$EPOCH2_TRANS*. This role is under control of the user through the MySQL system variable *ndb_slave_conflict_role*. Setting this to *PRIMARY* in all MySQL replication servers in a cluster makes this the primary cluster. All other clusters should set this variable to *SECONDARY* instead in all MySQL replication servers.

Now an important scenario we can operate here is that before any switch over is required the setting of this variable is set to PASS. PASS means that we don't look for conflicts, we apply the log records in the slave applier as they arrive.

Thus this setting is very similar to a normal fail over setting with two clusters that are operational.

Now if we want to shut down the west coast cluser, we start by stopping the slave appliers in both the west and the east coast cluster. Next we set the *ndb-slave-conflict-role* to NONE, immediately followed by setting it to SECONDARY. Next we do the same thing in east although here we set it to PRIMARY role instead.

Finally we startup the slaves again.

42.1.4 EXAMPLE STARTUP OF MySQL REPLICATION SERVER

Here is an example of the startup of a MySQL Server that is both handling the binlog server part and the slave part for one of the cluster using the *NDB\$EPOCH2_TRANS* function.

```
mysqld --log-bin=mysql-bin
       --skip-slave-start
       --server-id=1
       --binlog-cache-size=1M
       --ndb-log-update-as-write=OFF
       --ndb-log-orig=ON
       --log-slave-updates=ON
       --ndb-log-apply-status=ON
       --ndb-log-transaction-id=ON
       --ndb-log-exclusive-reads=ON
       --ndb-log-empty-update=ON
       --ndb-log-update-as-minimal=ON
```

42.2 CHARACTERISTICS OF THIS SOLUTION

The only supported configuration of this is when there are two clusters, one is PRIMARY and the other is the SECONDARY cluster. All updates in the PRIMARY cluster will succeed, all updates in the SECONDARY cluster will be checked by the slave applier in the PRIMARY cluster. If a conflict occurs it will be logged in the exceptions table.

In addition the conflict resolution is automatically started by ensuring that all rows involved in the transaction is restored to the value in the primary cluster. This is implemented by a special replication event performing a reflecting operation.

As long as write operations continue to come into both clusters we can still get new conflicts. We will start to heal the database immediately through reading the exceptions table and implementing the user decided conflict resolution.

42.3 CONFLICT HANDLING

Now we are prepared to handle conflicts. Now the application logic can ensure that the traffic is moved from the west coast cluster to the east coast cluster. For a period the updates can go to any cluster and conflict detection will discover any problems with consistency.

When the switch over have completed and no more traffic goes toward the west coast cluster we need to wait for all conflict resolution tasks to complete. Once they complete we are ready to bring down the west coast cluster.

Bringing back the west coast cluster again after completing the management changes is done in the same fashion as bringing online any cluster, see the chapter on Global Failover architecture for this.

This variant maintains transactional consistency of our data. Thus any conflicting updates that are not accepted are rolled back in its entirety, not just the row that had a conflict, but the transaction as well.

The rollback is implemented through a reflecting replication event.

Thus we need a mechanism here to rewrite transactions. Every conflicting transactions that is rejected have to be handled using special code reading the conflict detection tables and deciding on how to handle the conflicts.

Any kind of such logic is beyond this book, it requires a detailed understanding of your application requirements and what the actual meaning of those conflicts means.

The function *NDB$EPOCH2_TRANS* is the conflict detection method used in this case. There is an older variant called *NDB$EPOCH_TRANS* that have the same flaw as the *NDB$EPOCH* around delete operations, so it should be sufficient to focus on *NDB$EPOCH2_TRANS*.

The conflict detection is the same as for *NDB$EPOCH2* using *epochs* as timestamp.

Conflict handling is a lot more complex compared to the other conflict detection function.

42.4   MORE COMMENTS

It is possible to use this mechanism also for cases where we have very small conflicts between the clusters, potentially could be used to handle network partitioning cases with smaller timespans.

PART X

MANAGEMENT OF MySQL CLUSTER

We provide many ways to look at what is going on within MySQL Cluster. The most important manner to see what is going on inside the data nodes is by using the ndbinfo tables. We will go through all of those tables, what they contain and how their information can be used.

We have also made a few special tools that provide an easy view of some graphical information through a normal terminal interface using so called ASCII graphs. The first tool implemented in this fashion is *ndb_top* that displays the CPU usage of various threads in an NDB data node. This is available only in the 7.6 distributions of MySQL Cluster but can be used against a 7.5 cluster as well.

The management client provides a number of commands to the management server to view cluster state, manage backups and perform graceful shutdowns of nodes as well as starting them again.

We also have two types of system logs that contain a lot of information about specific events in MySQL Cluster. Most of these log messages are of informational nature, but there is also some warnings and error messages sent this way. It is also possible to print various messages to the cluster log through DUMP commands in the management client.

The node logs are mostly quiet, they do however report a fair amount of information during node restarts and various warning messages. We will go through some of those messages.

CHAPTER 43

NDBINFO TABLES

Managability of MySQL Cluster 7.5 is something we have worked hard on. One of the most important features here are the *ndbinfo* tables that export lots of internal information about data node behaviour to the DBAs.

These tables are all accessed as normal tables in the *ndbinfo* database. They are read-only tables that can be used in any place in a query where one selects from a table. They are accessed from a MySQL server.

There are currently 39 different tables exporting many different types of data useful in understanding NDB operations. In addition there is a set of views on these tables.

We will describe them all here, some in more detail and some we will gloss over. The manual have descriptions of every table and every column in these tables. In this chapter we will focus on explaining reasons why you could be interested in a specific table and drill a bit deeper into some specific tables and columns.

New *ndbinfo* tables are constantly added as we see the need to make information about the cluster accessible. It is a fairly simple process to add a new *ndbinfo* table.

43.1 REASONS TO USE *ndbinfo*

There are many reasons to use *ndbinfo* such as understanding how the cluster is getting used, understanding the dynamic behaviour of it, solving various problems with your application, understanding NDB itself, the hardware, the OS and so forth. It is important to get an understanding if the current configuration is appropriate and thus knowing when it is time to make various configuration changes. These configuration changes can include adding more nodes to the cluster.

43.1.1 UNDERSTANDING HOW THE CLUSTER IS USED

The most common use case is for the DBA to understand how much the cluster is used. Is it running close to its limits or is there plenty of resources?

There are many types of resources to manage, CPU resources, memory resources, disk resources, internal buffer resources and so forth.

43.1.2 SOLVING APPLICATION PROBLEMS

One typical problem that can happen in a database application is that we get problems with locks. Hot locks can easily lead to deadlocks, lower throughput and many other issues. Other problems could be related to that we use more memory in the application than expected.

In addition we might need to watch the exact behaviour of the cluster in a live situation. This helps us understand what our application code does to the database.

Query analysis can be performed on the MySQL level. Some query analysis can also be performed by watching statistics from *ndbinfo*.

43.1.3 FINDING SCALABILITY ISSUES

If an application is designed properly it can scale to the full cluster size of 48 data nodes. Very few applications reach that level of scalability. Understanding how to improve scalability requires understanding what impacts scalability.

ndbinfo can assist in this work by providing statistics about the number of local operations (operations where the transaction coordinator is in the same node as the data) versus the number of remote operations (not a local operation).

CPU statistics gives hints on which threads that are most active, there is also thread information about the number of signals executed per loop and other things that gives a better understanding of the behaviour of NDB.

43.1.4 SOLVING PROBLEMS WITH MySQL CLUSTER

Some of the tables in *ndbinfo* provide very detailed information about important internal data structures in NDB. When users report issues, the *ndbinfo* tables is one tool that can be used to analyse these issues.

NDB developers can use the tables to understand the dynamic behaviour of the programs in various situations. This can lead to new ideas on development for MySQL Cluster.

43.1.5 UNDERSTANDING CONFIGURATION ISSUES

Configuring a DBMS can be challenging. It is important to get a tradeoff between the usage of memory, CPU and disk resources and find an appropriate configuration that fits the application.

43.2 HOW NDBINFO WORKS

The *ndbinfo* tables are implemented using a special scan operation in the NDB API. It sends the scan operation to all nodes in the cluster using the table id as key to this scan. Each node will send the scan to every thread and every block in each thread. For the most part these query parts will return no rows.

If the block recognizes the table id as something that it has data for it will send the data in one or more rows per signal until all data have been provided.

There is no indexing of *ndbinfo* tables for the moment. The MySQL Server can apply any search conditions as on any SQL query, the actual data returned to the user will only be the requested subset of the table.

The *ndbinfo* scans are performed in NDB data nodes, the information retrieved is only coming from the data nodes. Thus any information in *ndbinfo* tables about MySQL Servers and API nodes are sent from those nodes to the data nodes.

The lowest level in *ndbinfo* is the base tables. All these base tables can be accessed directly using the table name *ndb$base_table_name*. The list of base tables and their columns is listed in the file *NdbinfoTables.cpp* in the directory *storage/ndb/src/kernel/vm*. These tables can be accessed using SQL, but they are not listed when you use the *SHOW TABLES* command in the MySQL client.

Most of the ndbinfo tables are fairly straightforward mappings of these tables into the available ndbinfo tables. The mappings are defined in the file *ndbinfo.sql* in the directory *storage/ndb/tools*. This file contains definitions also of the base tables.

Some of the ndbinfo tables are a bit more complex mappings where we use a bit of mapping integers to names, perform some join operations and so forth. Some of the tables in ndbinfo are also views.

As in any monitoring software there is an overhead when asking for monitoring information. For the most part the *ndbinfo* queries are cheap and will only return a limited amount of rows. There are some examples that could potentially return a substantial amount of rows.

In particular all tables that lists data about fragments and the fragment replicas can potentially contain millions of rows in a large cluster with many tables. These should be used with some level of care.

At the same time the *ndbinfo* implementation is done in such a way as to ensure that the queries against *ndbinfo* cannot overload the cluster. Thus there is a fair amount of serialisation. Thus if the *ndbinfo* query returns a large result, the query will take longer time.

Each query will scan one node at a time, each round trip to this node will retrieve at most 256 rows and at most 65535 bytes (both those sizes are configurable as MySQL options). It is also possible to make the *ndb$...* tables visible through SHOW TABLES by setting a MySQL option.

For the most part it is ok to query often. The *ndb_top* program that will be discussed in a later chapter uses a query against the *cpustat* table in *ndbinfo*. It issues such a query once per second and the load from this is barely noticable.

The performance schema in MySQL has a considerably higher overhead even when not queried. The *ndbinfo* tables only give an overhead when actually queried. All the statistics reported is gathered all the time and are most of the time simple variables that are incremented while performing other operations on the same data structures. The performance overhead from statistics in NDB is very small.

The manual contains information about all stable tables in *ndbinfo*. The base tables can change from version to version and can even disappear and new one can be added. So any tools developed towards *ndbinfo* should only use the official *ndbinfo* tables.

But for debugging and other purposes it can at times be useful to know about the base tables as well. Here we list also the base tables and their purposes.

Most of the detailed information on columns I will skip here. It can be found in the MySQL manual and in the files I mentioned above found in a source tarball of MySQL Cluster.

43.3 METADATA TABLES

43.3.1 *ndb$tables* AND *ndb$columns*

These tables lists the tables and columns in the *ndbinfo* database.

43.3.2 *dict_obj_info*

This table contains a list of meta data objects stored in the cluster. This includes objects for tables, ordered indexes, unique indexes, system tables, various trigger types, tablespaces, log file groups, data files for tablespaces, undo log files for log file groups, foreign keys.

For most tables about meta data it can be useful to join the table id with the id in this table to find out about the name of the table and by also joining with *dict_obj_types* we can get the type name of the table.

Some objects such as BLOB tables have a parent object. These are listed in this table. We can get the table version from this table.

43.3.3 *dict_obj_types*

The *dict_obj_info* has a column called *type*. This is the type of object (e.g. table, ordered index, unique index, event object and so forth). The *dict_obj_types* table have a mapping from type id to type name. Joining with this table can be very useful when there is an interest in what type of object we are looking at.

43.3.4 *table_info*

This contains information about table distribution, flags about reading from backup, fully replicated table, and at which GCI the table was created and so forth.

43.3.5 *ndb$stored_tables*

This is the base table listing information retrieved from the DBDIH block. It contains a fair amount of flags on table distribution, special hidden columns. There is a fair amount of detailed flags available in the base table that is not available in *table_info*.

43.3.6 *table_distribution_status*

This table contains information also from DBDIH. This information has a lot more status variables on local checkpoints, online table reorganisations, status of the table and number of partitions and fragments (can be changed through online reorganize of the table). Contains the same information as the base table except that in the base table you get the type of the table. This can be found also in the *dict_obj_info* table.

43.3.7 *table_fragments*

This contains one row for each table fragment stored in NDB. This is the information that NDB uses to decide from where to read the data. The information is the same as in the base table *ndb$table_fragments*.

This table can be used to discover table distribution, it can be useful to understand what goes on if the load is unbalanced in the cluster.

We have both partition id and fragment id in this table. For most tables this is the same. But for fully replicated tables there is a difference between fragment and partition.

Partition is the division of data seen from the users point of view. Fragments contain the data of partitions internally in NDB. Fully replicated tables store a partition in multiple fragments, one fragment for each node group. All other tables store partitions in one fragment and thus for those tables partition and fragment are synonyms.

43.3.8 *ndb$table_fragments_all*

This contains the same information as the *table_fragments* table. The difference is that the *table_fragments* only retrieves information from the current master data node in the cluster.

The table distribution is stored in the DBDIH block in each node. This information should always be the same in all nodes. This base table can be used to verify that the table distribution information is correctly set in all nodes. This table can be useful in researching potential issues with table distribution.

43.3.9 *table_replicas*

This contains one row for each fragment replica in NDB. Each fragment is stored in a set of fragment replicas, one fragment replica per node in the node group where the fragment is stored. Most of the information in this table is low level information used by NDB in recovery situations and is thus not so important for a user. This table is mostly intended for support cases where one can check this table to get a detailed glimpse into what is going on inside the DBDIH block.

43.3.10 *ndb$table_replicas_all*

Same information as in *table_replicas* but here the information is fetched from all nodes, not only from current master data node.

43.4 CONNECTION INFORMATION

A table was added in 7.5.6 to ensure that MySQL Enterprise Manager had a way to discover the cluster when connecting to one of the MySQL Servers.

43.4.1 *processes*

This is an important table in some cases. This is a table for cluster discovery. By pointing a tool to one of the MySQL servers in the cluster you can automatically find out where all the cluster processes are placed. Each node that is currently up and running is listed in this table.

A node can be a data node. In this case we get pid of the data node process and the pid of the angel process as well. In the *service_URI* column we can see the hostname of this node.

The same information is available also for NDB management servers. In addition the *service_URI* column here also contains the port number to connect to this management server.

For MySQL servers we get information about hostname to connect to the MySQL server and the port it listens. We also get information of its *server-id*.

Here we can have multiple node ids using the same MySQL Server, they are separated by specifying which cluster connection they use in the *service_URI* column, in addition they have different node ids.

For MySQL servers the port number is the port that MySQL clients use to access MySQL.

One example usage of this table is to write your application such that it connects to one of the MySQL Servers first, from this server we get the rest of the MySQL Servers connected to this cluster, we also get the NDB management servers. From this we can ensure that we can automatically set up round robin lists of MySQL Servers to connect to for those MySQL connectors that support load balancing (e.g. JDBC connector).

43.5 CONFIGURATION INFORMATION

It can be useful to discover the configuration from a MySQL client as well.

43.5.1 *config_params*

This table contains a list of all configuration parameters and information about their name, description, default values, min value, max value, type information and whether the parameter is default or not.

This table can be useful to join with when checking the configuration in the cluster at the moment.

43.5.2 *config_nodes*

This table contains a list of all configured nodes in the cluster with their node type, node id and the hostname where they are allowed to execute from.

43.5.3 *config_values*

Each node receives a full configuration from the NDB management server. This information is only updated when a node restarts. Thus during a configuration change the configuration can differ in the nodes. This table can be used to view the current configuration stored in each node. We can only get this information for data nodes.

43.6 TRANSACTION INFORMATION

Transactions and the operations that they consist of are very important to analyse. We want to have statistics on how they behave to see long-term trends.

We need to understand latency issues. An important characteristic of NDB is predictable latency. We want to enable you to track latency in the NDB data nodes to understand if latency issues are coming from the NDB data nodes or if they are added somewhere else in the software stack.

For application development it is important to see views on what is going in more detail currently in the cluster. We have tables that show the current locks, the currently executing operations and the currently executing transactions.

43.6.1 Transaction statistics

counters TABLE

The counters table contain statistical counters from DBLQH, DBTC and DBSPJ. DBTC is the transaction coordinator so every transaction starts and ends here. Most every operation starts and stops here as well. The exception is committed reads using key lookups. In this case the query is routed to the owner of the data and the query never returns to DBTC. DBSPJ works together with DBTC to handle complex join queries. DBLQH handles the actual reads and writes and scans of data. Thus they are incremented only in the nodes that contain the data used in the queries. DBTC is incremented in whatever node the transaction is executed from.

In DBTC we collect information about transactions, commits, reads, writes, simple reads, aborts, full table scans, ordered index scans (range scans), local reads and local writes.

The meaning of a local read is that it reads data where DBTC is located in the same node as the data. Remote reads is the opposite where we don't have the data locally accessible. A local write is where the transaction coordinator is on the same node as the primary replica of the row to be write.

Each operation contains an interpreted program for execution. For reads this is normally one word (32 bits) per column read and for writes it is normally one word per column plus the new column value. A delete normally have no interpreted program sent at all. In some cases an interpreted program is sent as well that could be for example the filters in a scan. For joins that are pushed down it contains the join execution plan. These words are summed together in the counter named ATTRINFO.

Partition pruned scans will only scan one fragment since the partition key is bound in the index scan. There is currently no specific statistics about partition pruned scans in DBTC, there is more information in DBSPJ about those things for pushdown joins.

DBLQH counts the number of operations (one per row access and one per scan). In addition it collects detailed information about when an overload occurs. Overload occurs when a row operation is initiated in DBLQH and the communication to the nodes receiving (TC node, API node, event API nodes for updates) the query result is overloaded.

The following simple query collects the total amount of each counter for the entire cluster grouped on the counter name.

```
mysql> select counter_name, sum(val) from counters
mysql>    group by counter_name;
```

And the following query counts the total amount of transactions started in the cluster (includes both aborted and committed transactions and ones not yet completed) since the cluster was started.

```
mysql> select counter_name, sum(val) from counters
mysql>    where counter_name = 'TRANSACTIONS'
mysql>    group by counter_name;
```

The counters table provides an easy way to get transaction and operation statistics with easy queries. By executing a certain query with some time in between, for example the above query on transactions, will provide the current execution rate. E.g. if the above returns 10200 and 5 seconds later it returns 24200 we have executed 2400 transactions per second during these 5 seconds. By summing READS, WRITES and SIMPLE_READS we get the total number of key lookups and TABLE_SCANS provides the number of scans. These are interesting measurements to understand the throughput in the cluster for the moment.

If the application throughput is low and the cluster is performing many operations it can be interesting to drill down on what low level queries the application generates.

tc_time_track_stats

Every time a transaction or an operation is completed we measure the time it took to execute it. We put the result in a histogram that starts at 50 microseconds and goes upto 14.3 seconds in 32 logarithmic steps.

We measure response time for queries, transactions, scans, fragment scans and so forth. Each entry in this histogram is one row in this table, the row lists the upper bound for the row, the lower bound is two thirds of the upper bound.

The below query collects the amount of transactions that have completed within 500 microseconds and the total amount of transactions executed, both since the nodes were started.

```
mysql> select sum(transactions) from tc_time_track_stats
mysql>    where upper_bound < 500
mysql> union
mysql>    select sum(transactions) from tc_time_track_stats;
```

By collecting this information regularly we can discover if the the percentage of transactions with higher latency goes up or down.

Transaction latency includes time the transaction is waiting for the application.

By focusing on a specific type of operation, e.g. *write_key_ops* we can see the latency is for individual operations that have no interaction with the API nodes as part of the latency.

43.7 LIVE TRANSACTION INFORMATION

43.7.1 *cluster_locks*

Every locked row in the cluster is reported in this table, with information about the table it waits for and other things. Useful to discover application problems with concurrency.

43.7.2   cluster_operations

This lists every operation currently ongoing in NDB. There can be millions of those, thus this table is mostly intended for exploratory usage. Probably most interesting as education tool for NDB.

43.7.3   cluster_transactions

Same as *cluster_operations* except that it logs all ongoing transactions. Probably most interesting as education tool for NDB.

43.7.4   server_*

The *server_locks*, *server_operations*, and *server_transactions* are equivalent to the *cluster_** tables except that they log only those locks, operations and transactions that was initiated on the MySQL Server from where the query originated.

These tables are views on the *cluster_** tables.

43.8   MEMORY INFORMATION

We have a few *ndbinfo* tables that can be used to gather information about memory usage. In particular those gives insights into how we should configure the variable *SharedGlobalMemory*, *DataMemory* and *LongMessageBuffer* and many other configuration parameters that affect memory usage.

43.8.1   resources

For the most part this table shows how much memory is allocated statically to a number of memory pools. A fair amount of the memory in NDB is allocated in various pools. We are constantly adding more and more resources to these pools. There are still parts of the memory that is allocated without assignment to a special pool.

The generic reasoning is that a pool can reserve memory, this memory can not be shared with other pools. Each pool have a maximum allowed memory, if 0 there is no upper bound. The reserved memory for a pool is allocated when the data node starts.

The extra memory that a pool can allocate is coming from the memory allocated according to the configuration parameter *SharedGlobalMemory*. This memory is allocated when the data node starts. Almost no memory at all can be allocated after the data node starts. The data nodes manage the memory while up and running.

Allocation of memory at startup takes considerable time. In addition to allocating the memory we touch the memory before we move on with the start. The reason is that we need to ensure that the memory is allocated for real and not just in some swap area. This is necessary to achieve the predictable latency. It is possible to lock the memory in the data node such that it cannot be swapped out. This is achieved by setting the *LockPagesInMemory* configuration parameter to 1.

This *ndbinfo* table shows how much memory is reserved to a pool, how much memory the pool can allocate at most (0 means no limit) and how much memory is currently allocated to it. All the memory used above the reserved space is coming from *SharedGlobalMemory*. The table lists the number of pages (32 kByte pages) for this resources.

When a log file group for disk data is created the memory space for the UNDO log buffer is taken from the *SharedGlobalMemory*. If a log file group is created as part of the configuration, the memory for the UNDO log buffer is automatically added to the memory allocated for *SharedGlobalMemory*.

JOB_BUFFERS are used for communication between blocks inside the NDB data node, it is also used when sending to other nodes. This can be a fairly sizable memory chunk since it is important to not run out of memory for internal communication. The size of this memory is dependent on the number of threads in the data node. It is not configurable in any other way, all its memory is reserved and nothing extra can be allocated.

TRANSPORTER_BUFFERS is the memory used to buffer data before it is sent over the network (using TCP/IP sockets or shared memory). This is configurable and depends on *SendBufferMemory* and the number of threads in the data node. It can also be set directly through the configuration parameter *TotalSendBufferMemory*.

This memory is shared for communication with all nodes. The buffer used towards one node can use extra memory segments if available. It can allocate up to 25% more memory from *SharedGlobalMemory* compared to its configuration if necessary and if available.

DISK_RECORDS have no memory permanently attached to it, it allocates memory from the extra memory available through *SharedGlobalMemory*. This is used for all page and file operations associated with disk columns and stores request information.

QUERY_MEMORY have no reserved memory, it has no upper bound on its allocation. It is memory used for executing complex join queries in the NDB data nodes. It allocates its memory from *SharedGlobalMemory*.

DISK_PAGE_BUFFER is the disk page cache. All its memory is reserved and no more can be allocated. The size is set through the configuration parameter *DiskPageBufferMemory*.

DATA_MEMORY is the memory used for in-memory data. This is the pool that the user want to pay special attention to since running out of memory in this pool means that no more data can be stored in NDB. There is a limit such that during normal operation one cannot allocate more than 95% of this memory. The rest is only available during restarts. During a restart it is possible that we have a small increase in memory during the various restart phases. To ensure that we don't run out of memory during recovery, we ensure that not all *DataMemory* is used during normal operation.

FILE_BUFFERS are used for REDO log buffers. This is configured with the configuration parameter *RedoBuffer*.

43.8.2 *memoryusage*

The memory usage gives information about *DataMemory* again, it also provides information about *LongMessageBuffer*. The *LongMessageBuffer* is an important resource that is used for longer signals sent internally. When a message arrives that is a long message it allocates a memory segment from this resource, it is held until the signal have been executed, similarly resources are allocated when long signals are sent and released when put into the send buffers of the transporters. It is important to have a sizeable amount of memory available for this purpose, especially in a data node with much traffic and large amount of data being transported in and out of the database.

Tracking the amount of memory used for the long messages, to compare it with the total available memory, is a vital management operation to discover issues before they happen.

43.8.3   *ndb$pools*

This table contains information not represented in any *ndbinfo* table. The reason is that most of this information is in the process of being moved towards the above *resources* table. From the beginning NDB had all its data in large memory arrays with fixed size of all of them. We have been moving data piece by piece from these fixed size arrays to pools instead. There is still a significant number of those fixed arrays remaining. Many of those can be seen in the *ndb$pools* table.

Moving those arrays into pools makes NDB less susceptible to various configuration mistakes and makes NDB much more capable in adapting to different user needs. The aim is to move the most memory consuming resources first, this ensures that the ones with fixed arrays can be allocated to ensure that they won't run out of memory.

Therefore this table represents mostly things that is not stable over many versions of MySQL Cluster. Thus the table is not a good idea to become part of the *ndbinfo* table.

It does still contain lots of information about how much memory resources that are allocated in NDB for various purposes. The table specifies the configuration parameters that these array pools are dependent on when allocated. There can be up to four configuration parameters affecting them. Some of them are static and not changeable as well.

43.9   THREAD STATISTICS

The internal architecture of the NDB data nodes uses several different thread types. Each thread type handles a functional part. Almost all databases today use multiple threads per program (some use many programs working together on one computer).

NDB use a model internally where execution is divided functionally into a number of different thread types. We have one set of threads handling receiving from the network, another set of threads handling sending to the network, a set of threads handling transaction coordination and routing of query processing, a set of threads handling the local database parts, a set of threads handling interaction with the OS file system.

There are thread types that always have only one thread. It is the *main* thread, handling management of meta data and some restart functions. The *rep* thread, handling events and proxy functions for the other thread types and a set of restart functions and functions related to online reorganisation of data parts. The name *rep* is short for replication since the events are used to implement replication between clusters.

We keep track of the use of these threads in several dimensions.

In the *cpustat* one can track the exact amount of CPU usage that each thread has used for all thread types except the *io* threads that interact with the file system. The OS has exact knowledge about when a thread is active and when it isn't, this information NDB retrieves through the API to the OS information.

In addition for those threads, NDB also tracks the wall clock time that these threads are active. If the wall clock time is close to, or equal to the time reported by the OS there is very little contention for CPU resources. If the wall clock is much higher than the time reported by the OS, there is much contention on CPU resources. Contention on CPU resources means that the throughput can vary quite a lot over time. To avoid this NDB provides the capability to lock each thread type to individual CPUs or groups of CPUs (including the *io* threads).

In addition we have the *threadstat* table that provides statistics on how block threads (all thread types except *io* and *send*) execute. Block threads executes signals in a loop, below is a simple pseudo code to show how this loop looks like.

```
while (true) {
  c_loop++
  gather signals to execute
  for each signal { execute_signal, c_exec++ }
  if (no more signals to execute) {
    c_wait++
    sleep to wait for signals to arrive
  }
}
```

In the pseudo code we have shown where the columns *c_loop*, *c_exec* and *c_wait* are updated. If the number of signals executed for each signal gathering is high we make very efficient use of the CPU. Similarly we want to execute as many signals as possible before we go to sleep. This is one reason why NDB data nodes becomes more and more efficient as load increases.

A thread that goes to sleep is woken up by another thread that wants to communicate with it. The *recv* threads are woken up when data arrives on a socket. Waking up a thread is quite fast, it takes at most a microsecond or two. But if it happens a lot it could hamper performance. NDB provides the possibility to spin for a few microseconds before going to sleep. This removes the need to wait for a wakeup at the expense of not returning the CPU to the OS. In a system with CPUs exclusive to the NDB data nodes it can be useful. In a shared environment where NDB shares CPUs with other programs it is not a good idea to use it.

Tracking the *threadstat* table is an important tool to see if it is useful to employ spinning.

43.9.1 *blocks*

This table contains a mapping from block number to block name that can be useful to join with.

43.9.2 *threads*

This contains a mapping from thread number to thread name and thread description that i useful to join with.

43.9.3 *threadblocks*

This table shows exactly which blocks that execute in which threads. Most blocks execute in more than one thread.

43.9.4 *threadstat*

In addition to the statistics on the execution loop it provides information about signals sent of different priorities, how much OS time is reported on each thread.

43.9.5 *cpustat*

This lists the CPU usage, both real from the OS and wall clock time per thread in percentage of the last second. This table is used as input to the *ndb_top* tool.

43.9.6 *cpustat_50ms*

This table provides 20 measurements, one per 50 milliseconds. Each measurement lists the amount of time spent in user mode, system time and idle time as reported by OS, it reports amount of time executing and sleeping according to wall clock. It provides the amount of time spent sending, spinning, waiting for buffers when no buffers available and the time since the last measurement.

The measurements are in microseconds.

43.9.7 *cpustat_1sec*

This is an aggregation of *cpustat_50ms* and reports one row per second for each thread the last 20 seconds. The columns are exactly the same.

43.9.8 *cpustat_20sec*

This is an aggregation of *cpustat_1sec* and reports one row per 20 seconds for each thread the last 400 seconds.

43.10   Node information

We have a few tables that show information about nodes.

43.10.1   *nodes*

This table has one row per data node. It shows node id, uptime in seconds, the node status (e.g. STARTED), start phase currently executing (0 when alreadys started) and the version number of the cluster configuration it uses.

This table can be used instead of the SHOW command in the NDB management client to see the status of data nodes.

43.10.2   *membership*

This is another table that shows information about the node group of a data node and various information related to selection of master node in the cluster and arbitrator.

When nodes enter the cluster, they do so one at a time. Each node gets a unique id based on when they started. The node with the lowest such id is always the master node in the cluster.

This table shows the master role, the succession order for who becomes the next master. The master role is called president in the heartbeat protocol. In higher level protocols the president is called master. One node handles both the presidency and the master role in a number of protocols. It is normally not a role that requires a lot of work, but it is required to know who is in charge of a protocol. Otherwise it is very hard to figure out what to do in error situations.

This table also presents the arbitration data. The president selects the arbitrator. The table shows which node is president, the state of arbitration and which nodes are the potential successor if the current one fails.

This table provides a view on the heartbeat order. Each node sends a heartbeat to its right neighbour and expects a heartbeat from its left neighbour. This table shows who is left and right neighbour. The selection of neighbours is also based on the order of joining the cluster.

43.10.3   *arbitraror_validity_detail*

This table is a view on the *membership* that focus on only the arbitration data.

43.10.4   *arbitraror_validity_summary*

Yet another view on the *membership* table that presents the arbitrator, its ticket, its status and the number of nodes that agree about it.

43.11   RESTART INFORMATION

Analyzing restarts is important. We have a table called *restart_info* that provides information about 19 different restart phases and how many seconds they took to execute.

This is an important tool to understand recovery performance in your NDB setup. Most of the crucial phases benefit from parallelising to many *ldm* threads.

43.11.1   *restart_info*

The information about the latest restarts is available in this table. It can only report data about node restarts. Inital cluster start is not logged and neither is complete cluster restarts.

Most of the times measured in these phases is very short. But we provide the details about each phase to ensure that we can understand what is going on in the cluster also in the not so normal states.

Only one row per node can exist. If the table is used during a node restart it will report 0 in those parts of the restart that haven't started yet. If the node haven't made any node restarts since the master node started there will be no records in this table about that node.

The first column *secs_to_complete_node_failure* keeps track of the current time used to complete the node restart.

A node restart consists of the following stages:

First the cluster must complete the node failure handling. This ensures that all nodes know about the failed node. A node with the same node id cannot join again until this is completed. It includes cleaning up all transactions where the failed node was transaction coordinator. It usually takes a few seconds. When this stage is completed the node is allowed to allocate its node id again.

After allocating the node id, the node must perform its initial startup code. The major time consumers here are allocation of memory (can take about 1 second per GByte of memory) and for initial node restarts there is also initialisation of REDO logs and disk data files.

Entry into the heartbeat protocol also takes a bit of time since only one node is allowed to enter at a time. A few seconds it will take per node that is restarting in parallel.

secs_until_wait_for_ndbcntr_master is the time it took to get permission to start from the master. Normally this is immediate, but only node at a time is allowed to copy the meta data from the master node. There could be some wait here for other nodes to complete their meta data copying.

secs_wait_for_ndbcntr_master is the time it took to wait for master to allow to continue the restart. Normally immediate.

secs_to_get_start_permitted is the time it took to receive the permit also from all other nodes. Normally immediate.

secs_to_wait_for_lcp_for_copy_meta_data is the time it took to wait until we can copy the meta data from the master node. The meta data is locked for a short time during startup of a local checkpoint.

secs_to_copy_meta_data is the time it took to copy the meta data. Normally not a very long time unless there is a large amount of tables and other meta data in the cluster.

secs_to_include_node is the time it took to include node in various cluster protocols such as local checkpoint and global checkpoint. Normally immediate.

secs_starting_node_to_request_local_recovery is the time it took for the starting node to start requesting to restore its data. Normally immediate.

secs_for_local_recovery is the total time it took to restore fragments, execute UNDO log, execute REDO log and rebuild indexes.

secs_for_restore_fragments is the time it took to restore the local checkpoint files from disk. Each *ldm* thread can restore about one million rows of about a hundred bytes per second. Roughly 100-200 MBytes per second is restored here per *ldm* thread. This phase can take several minutes to complete if the database is hundreds of GBytes.

secs_undo_disk_data is the time it took to execute the UNDO log. The UNDO log is used to ensure that the disk data rows are synchronized with the in-memory rows before we start executing the REDO log to generate a consistent checkpoint of the local data. The time it takes to perform this part is dependent on the length of the checkpoint before crash and the amount of writes to disk data before the crash.

secs_exec_redo_log is the time it took to execute the REDO log.

secs_index_rebuild is the time it took to rebuild all ordered indexes. This is heavily parallelised since it can easily become a major time consumer with many ordered indexes.

secs_to_synchronize_starting_node is the timing of an important phase where we synchronize our data with a live node in our node group. The time it takes to perform this phase is very much dependent on how much changes occurs after the crash until our restart comes to this point.

secs_wait_lcp_for_restart contains the time it took to wait for a local checkpoint to complete that we are part of. It is necessary to participate in a local checkpoint before we complete the node restart. Without a completed local checkpoint our node would not be recoverable and we could create an unrecoverable cluster if we were to continue running the cluster without the aid of a recoverable node.

A local checkpoint is started as soon as possible when a node is in this wait state. But we allow some extra time before we start a local checkpoint if other nodes are close to coming to this state.

secs_wait_subscription_handover is the final step in a restart. This synchronizes the new node with all MySQL replication servers and other API nodes that uses the NDB Event API. If such an API node or MySQL server is currently down this phase will time out after two minutes.

total_restart_secs is the total time the restart took.

43.12 LOCAL CHECKPOINT INFORMATION

We have a few tables that provide information about the local checkpoint characteristics and REDO logging. The *disk_write_speed_aggregate_node* table is a natural place to start looking. This table contains a summary per node of disk write speed of local checkpoint and REDO logs. It has columns for last second, last 10 seconds and last 60 seconds.

The *disk_write_speed_aggregate* table have more detailed information. First it provides the information per *ldm* thread. It provides standard deviation of the aggregate numbers.

The disk write speed of a local checkpoint is set by an adaptive algorithm. It is slowed down when the CPU usage is too high, it is slowed down when we see a too high IO lag on the REDO log. Each second we make adjustments to the disk write speed of local checkpoints. If no slowdown is performed we will use the maximum disk write speed as configured by *MaxDiskWriteSpeed*. Slowdowns can slow it down to *MinDiskWriteSpeed*. The current disk write speed is reported in this table in the column *current_target_disk_write_speed*. At restarts we can use *MaxDiskWriteOtherNodeRestart* or *MaxDiskWriteSpeedOwnRestart* as the maximum local checkpoint speed.

The *disk_write_speed_base* table contains the base data for the disk write speed of local checkpoints and REDO log for the last 60 seconds.

All the speeds are reported in bytes per second.

Watching those tables together with the table *logspaces* is useful to track if the size of our REDO log is sufficient. If it isn't we can either make it bigger (increased time for recovery), or we can increase the disk write speed (increased CPU overhead for checkpoints).

Increasing the disk write speed is handled by the *DiskWriteSpeed* parameters.

Increasing the REDO log size must be performed using an initial node restart since NDB currently doesn't support changing the size of the REDO log as an online operation. It does support this for the UNDO log.

43.13   DISK PAGE CACHE INFORMATION

NDB have a normal disk page cache used to access data for disk columns. The *diskpagebuffer* have statistics for the accesses to this page cache.

43.13.1   *diskpagebuffer* TABLE

There is one row for each *ldm* thread, in addition there is one row for the *rep* thread. This is the last thread, the so called extra PGMAN worker thread. It is the proxy block of PGMAN that is used to read and write the extent pages. The extent pages are read in at creation of the data file of a tablespace. Once it has been read, it will not be swapped out again from the page cache. Thus the extra thread (the one with highest *thr_no*) will eventually only perform page writes.

The column *pages_written* contain the number of pages written due to congestion in the page cache, the write is needed to remove a dirty page from the page cache to be able to read in new pages from disk.

The column *pages_written_lcp* is the number of pages written as part of a local checkpoint. This is a normal write where the page was written to and the next local checkpoint will write the page to ensure that we can cut the UNDO log and the REDO log.

The counter *pages_read* is incremented every time a page completes a read from disk.

The counter *log_waits* shows the operation of the WAL protocol for disk data pages. Thus if a page is made dirty by an updating transaction an UNDO log is written. The page cannot be written until the UNDO log entry have been flushed to disk. If we attempt to write before the UNDO log have been flushed, this counter is incremented.

page_requests_direct_return counts the number of times that the page cache contains the row and it is returned immediately.

page_requests_wait_queue is the number of times we request a page and the page have been requested already, but not yet arrived into the page cache. We wait in the queue for this page to be delivered.

page_requests_wait_io is the number of times we request a page and we have to start an IO request to fetch it from the disk.

page_requests_direct_return divided by the sum of

page_requests_direct_return, *page_requests_wait_io* and

page_requests_wait_queue is the page cache hit rate.

By making regular SELECTs against this table we can gather the page cache hit rate as it changes over time.

43.14 COMMUNICATION INFORMATION

To keep track of communication speed and potential overload problems in the communication paths we have the *transporters* table to our disposal.

43.14.1 *transporters*

There is one row for each communication link. Each data node is linked to all other nodes. There are no links between API nodes and there are no links from the NDB management servers to other nodes (other than when fetching the configuration from the NDB management server).

The row is identified by the node id and the remote node id of the communication link. Communication links between the data nodes is reported from both data nodes. This communication link can be a bottleneck in heavy update scenarios.

status is the status of the link, CONNECTED when connected and CONNECTING when not connected. It can also be in some intermediate states while disconnecting.

When the status is CONNECTED we also have a hostname of the remote node.

We provide *bytes_sent* and *bytes_received* as counters that are constantly decreasing. To measure the current transfer rate we need to make constant queries against this table.

Every time a connection uses more than 60% of the configured *SendBufferMemory* it enters the slowdown state. The *slowdown* column is 1 if it is in this state and 0 otherwise. The *slowdown_count* is incremented every time we enter this state.

In the slowdown state any scan operations using this connection will automatically have its batch size set to a minimum to avoid overloading it even more.

Every time a connection uses more than 80% of the configured *SendBufferMemory* it enters the overload state. The *overload* column is 1 if it is in this state and 0 otherwise. The *overload_count* is incremented every time we enter this state.

Any attempt to start a new transaction or a new scan in this state will lead to an error indicating that the send buffer is overloaded.

We also track the number of times we connected between those nodes.

43.15 STATUS OF REDO AND UNDO LOGS

The REDO log and the UNDO log are important to track. If we run out of buffer space for any of those logs we will have to abort transactions.

The *ndb$logspaces* and *ndb$logbuffers* tables have one additional column *high* that records the highest use so far of the log space/log buffer.

43.15.1 *logspaces* TABLE

This is a simple table that have one row for each log. The REDO log thus have one row per log part (by default 4 of those) whereas the UNDO log only have one row since there is always just one part.

In *total* we have the total size of the log part and in *used* we have the current usage.

Using this table it is very easy to see the percentage of the various log parts that are currently in use.

The columns in this table are *node_id*, *log_type* which is either REDO or DD-UNDO, *log_id* that is 0 for REDO logs and 10 for UNDO logs, *log_parts* is always 0 for UNDO logs and it is the log part id for REDO logs (starting at 0).

43.15.2 *logbuffers* TABLE

This table has similar columns where the most important ones are *total* and *used*. It represents the memory buffer for the UNDO log buffer and the REDO log buffer for each *ldm* thread. The log part id for REDO logs starts at 1 and is equal to the number of *ldm* threads.

43.16 FRAGMENT STATISTICS

We have a number of tables that list information about all the fragment replicas in the cluster. There can be quite many of those fragments in a large cluster with many nodes, it is recommended to use these tables with care.

The base tables have the same information, the *ndbinfo* tables are views that have joined to retrieve a bit useful information about table names and object types. The base tables for those tables are *ndb$frag_locks*, *ndb$frag_operations* and *ndb$frag_mem_use*.

43.16.1 *locks_per_fragment*

This table have lots of statistics about how many accesses of various types that a specific fragment have received. We have columns tracking the number of requests with exclusive lock and other columns showing how many of those requests are immediately ok, how many put us in a lock queue with successful ending and how many locks that result in an aborted transaction. Similar columns for shared locks.

There is also a column on how many milliseconds that we spent waiting for row locks in each fragment and how many milliseconds we spent waiting that resulted in aborts.

This table can be useful to get an overview of how many lock issues we have in our application. If we discover that we have issues we can drill down on those using the *cluster_locks* and *server_locks* table that shows the current locks and the waiters for those.

43.16.2 *operations_per_fragment*

This table gives very detailed statistics for each fragment. We can see number of key reads, updates, writes, deletes and number of key lookups that failed.

We can see total number of bytes of interpreted programs we send, total number of key information we send, total number of instructions executed in the interpreter by key lookups and total number of bytes returned to the application from key lookups.

For scan operations we record number of scans, number of rows examined while scanning and number of rows returned from scans, also number of bytes returned from scans, number of bytes interpreted program received, number of index bound bytes received for scans, total number of interpreted instructions executed as part of scans, total number of queued scans and current number of active scans and current number of queued scans.

Finally the number of commits on this fragment. There is a lot of statistics we can derive for each fragment.

This table can be used to get a very detailed view on what tables and fragments that are being used and in what way they are used. One should not query this table with a small delay between each query since the overhead for querying this table is fairly high, especially if the number of tables and nodes are high.

43.16.3   *memory_per_fragment*

This table gives a very precise view on how much memory is allocated to each table fragment.

fixed_elem_alloc_bytes is the number of bytes allocated to the fragment for fixed size rows in total. This is always a multiple of 32 kBytes since 32 kByte pages are allocated to fragments.

var_elem_alloc_bytes is the number of bytes allocated to the fragment for variable sized rows in total. This is also a multiple of 32 kBytes.

hash_index_alloc_bytes is the number of bytes allocated to the fragment for the hash index. This is always a multiple of 8 kBytes since a quarter of a 32 kByte page is the allocation unit for hash pages.

fixed_elem_size_bytes is the size of the fixed size part of the table and *fixed_elem_count* is the number of rows in the fragment (each row has a fixed size element, thus this is a count of the rows as well as a count of the fixed size parts in the fragment).

fixed_elem_free_bytes is the number of free bytes available in the already allocated space for the fixed size part of the rows. This free size is equal to *fixed_elem_free_count* multiplied by *fixed_elem_size_bytes*.

var_elem_free_bytes is the number of free bytes on already allocated variable sized pages.

var_elem_count is the number of variable sized parts allocated to the table.

43.17   ERROR MESSAGES

The *error_messages* table is a static table that reports all errors in NDB. It lists the *error_code*, the description of the error (*error_description*), the error status (*error_status*), the classification of the error (*error_classification*)

This table can be used to quickly translate an error message to something hopefully understandable.

43.18   SUMMARY OF *ndbinfo* INFORMATION

ndbinfo is a useful tool to gather information about CPU usage, memory usage, network usage, disk usage, buffer spaces, log spaces, about meta data and detailed information about table fragments and transaction statistics and live information about transactions.

Chapter 44

NDB management client *ndb_mgm*

The NDB management client has a few useful commands. The management client is used to start and stop nodes, show cluster status, and shutdown the cluster.

The commands to handle backups using the NDB management client is covered in the chapter on Backup.

The management client is used to add new node groups to the cluster and can also drop node groups that are still empty. This is covered in the chapter on online configuration changes.

It is possible to set the cluster in single user mode, this means that only one API node is allowed to be active.

The management client can be used to change the filters for what gets printed in the cluster log. The DUMP command provides a possibility to print lots of debug messages to the cluster log, most of those are undocumented since they require fairly deep understanding of the cluster code to be useful.

The HELP command lists all the commands supported and e.g. HELP RESTART will provide specific help on the RESTART command.

For someone that wants to understand more about NDB internals there is a set of commands listed in HELP DEBUG that shows various ways of logging signals in the data nodes. In a special compile mode it is possible to inject errors in the data nodes for efficient testing of cluster.

There is a command to get rid of node ids that haven't been freed through the command PURGE STALE SESSIONS.

All the management client commands are also available through the NDB Management API, this API is a C API.

The command client remembers the history of commands and these can be retrieved by using up arrow and down arrow.

44.1 SHOW command

The simplest command is *SHOW* that displays the configured nodes and their current status.

When a node isn't started it lists the hosts that are allowed to connect.

When a node has started it lists the MySQL version it started upon. In addition it also lists node id and hostname connected from for connected nodes.

For NDB data nodes it also lists the node group each data node belongs to.

Below is an example output from a small cluster started from MTR where there is one NDB management server, 2 data nodes and 14 API nodes. In this case there are 2 MySQL servers started with 3 cluster connection each, thus 6 API nodes are connected from 2 MySQL servers. The remaining 8 API nodes are available for connections from localhost.

```
ndb_mgm> show
Cluster Configuration
---------------------
[ndbd(NDB)] 2 node(s)
id=1 @127.0.0.1  (mysql-5.7.19 ndb-7.5.7, Nodegroup: 0, *)
id=2 @127.0.0.1  (mysql-5.7.19 ndb-7.5.7, Nodegroup: 0)

[ndb_mgmd(MGM)] 1 node(s)
id=49 @127.0.0.1  (mysql-5.7.19 ndb-7.5.7)

[mysqld(API)] 14 node(s)
id=51 @127.0.0.1  (mysql-5.7.19 ndb-7.5.7)
id=52 @127.0.0.1  (mysql-5.7.19 ndb-7.5.7)
id=53 @127.0.0.1  (mysql-5.7.19 ndb-7.5.7)
id=54 @127.0.0.1  (mysql-5.7.19 ndb-7.5.7)
id=55 @127.0.0.1  (mysql-5.7.19 ndb-7.5.7)
id=56  @127.0.0.1  (mysql-5.7.19 ndb-7.5.7)
id=57 (not connected, accepting connect from localhost)
id=58 (not connected, accepting connect from localhost)
id=59 (not connected, accepting connect from localhost)
id=231 (not connected, accepting connect from localhost)
id=232 (not connected, accepting connect from localhost)
id=233 (not connected, accepting connect from localhost)
```

44.2   START/STOP COMMANDS

NDB management client cannot stop and start processes. For this an agent is required such as used by the MySQL Cluster Manager. It can however stop processes. It can also restart a data node and a management server. Data nodes have an option to run with a special angel process. In this case the data node is started from the angel process. When the data node stops, the angel process can restart the data node again.

Thus the management client can be used to start and stop data nodes and management servers after the programs are started. This is heavily used in the NDB test programs where we can control start and stop of programs completely from the test program once all the cluster programs have started.

The management client have no capability to start and stop application programs and MySQL servers.

All START/STOP/RESTART commands start with a node id, if ALL is used instead of a node id the command applies to all nodes (data nodes and management servers, only data nodes for START command).

For example to restart node 2, use the following command:

```
ndb_mgm> 2 RESTART
```

44.2.1 STOP COMMAND

The STOP command is used when it is desired to stop the program completely in a node, thus stopping both the data node and the angel process.

This command will by default perform a graceful shutdown. This means that an attempt will be made to ensure that no interference with user transactions happen. Transactions have a few seconds to complete before the transactions are aborted to continue the node shutdown.

The command *STOP -a* means a more abrupt stop where we will not ensure that committed transactions are safe on durable media. The use of this is mostly for testing purposes and not for production purposes.

Normally a STOP command will be aborted if the stop of the node means that the entire cluster is shut down. In order to shut it down in even in this case use the command *STOP -f*.

44.2.2 RESTART COMMAND

The restart command is very useful in situations where it is necessary to change the configuration or for some other reason one needs to restart a data node or a management server.

The command first does a STOP, this stop can be affected by the parameters *-a* and *-f* similar to the STOP command. The START is normally immediate after the STOP. But using the flag *-n* it is possible to return without restarting until a START command is executed.

There is an option to restart using the *-i* flag. This flag means that an initial node restart will be performed. This flag should be used with great care since it will remove the entire file system of the data node. The node will get all its data from other live nodes in the cluster.

44.2.3 START COMMAND

The START command can be applied on a data node that have been started with the option *--nostart*. This option means that the data node program will start, but the data node startup will not start until instructed to do so by the management client.

It is possible to reach this state through the RESTART *-n* command as well. This makes it possible to stop a node and at some later time restart it again.

44.2.4 SHUTDOWN COMMAND

The SHUTDOWN command shuts down all data nodes and management servers using a graceful shutdown.

44.3 REPORT COMMAND

The REPORT command can report backup status, memory usage and print the current event log.

Here is an example of the output from the three different reports that can be printed. The event log is cut since it can be quite long.

The memory report reports IndexMemory and DataMemory usage.

```
ndb_mgm> 2 REPORT backupstatus
Node 2: Backup not started

ndb_mgm> 2 report MemoryUsage
Node 2: Data usage is 1%(10 32K pages of total 950)
Node 2: Index usage is 1%(10 32K pages of total 950)

ndb_mgm> 2 REPORT EventLog
2017-09-20 14:11:48 Node 2: CM_REGREF from Node 1 to our Node 2. ..
2017-09-20 14:11:51 Node 2: CM_REGREF from Node 2 to our Node 2. ..
......
2017-09-20 15:06:22 Node 2: Node Sent Heartbeat to node = 1

ndb_mgm>
```

44.4 STATUS COMMAND

The easiest way to explain the STATUS command is by showing an example. This example also gives examples of some of the other commands.

The example starts with the same cluster as the SHOW command displayed. Node 2 is one of the data nodes and it is up and running when the example starts. In this case the status is *started* and the version of the data node software is also provided.

Next we perform the RESTART command, as can be seen this command doesn't return until the command is completed. We used *RESTART -n* to see how it looks when the node is not started. The status in this case is *not started*.

The next step is to start node 2 again. The command returns when the start have been initiated and we can check the status of the restart. In this case the status is *starting* with some additional information about the start phase it has reached.

When the start completes we will get a printout of this even though the management client has already returned.

```
ndb_mgm> 2 status
Node 2: started (mysql-5.7.19 ndb-7.5.7)

ndb_mgm> 2 restart -n
Node 2: Node shutdown initiated

Node 2: Node shutdown completed, restarting, no start.

Node 2 is being restarted

ndb_mgm> 2 status
Node 2: not started (mysql-5.7.19 ndb-7.5.7)

ndb_mgm> 2 start
Database node 2 is being started.

ndb_mgm> Node 2: Start initiated (version 7.5.7)

ndb_mgm> 2 status
Node 2: starting (Last completed phase 100) (mysql-5.7.19 ndb-7.5.7)

ndb_mgm> Node 2: Started (version 7.5.7)

ndb_mgm>
```

44.5   PROMPT COMMAND

In some cases it might be useful to have several windows with management clients and it might be necessary to change the command prompt. The PROMPT command changes the prompt.

44.6   ENTER SINGLE USER MODE COMMAND

ENTER SINGLE USER MODE node_id is a command that can be useful if it is required to perform an offline ALTER TABLE change.

When single user mode is entered, only the API node that was given in the command is allowed access to the cluster. Normally changes in the cluster are performed using online operations. This command provides a safe way of performing bigger changes using ALTER TABLE that cannot be performed while updating the cluster. It leaves one MySQL Server with access to the cluster, this can be used for read while the ALTER TABLE is performed.

After completing the offline operation one goes back to normal mode by using the command EXIT SINGLE USER MODE.

44.7 CLUSTERLOG COMMAND

The CLUSTERLOG command controls what log messages that will end up in the cluster log.

The commands CLUSTERLOG ON, CLUSTERLOG OFF and CLUSTERLOG TOGGLE are used to change the on and off status of the various severity reports of the cluster log.

The severities are DEBUG, INFO, WARNING, ERROR, CRITICAL, ALERT.

ON sets it to ON, OFF sets it to OFF and TOGGLE changes the state from ON to OFF or from OFF to ON dependent on the state at the time of the command.

This command changes what is reported by the management server. By default all severities except DEBUG are reported.

In addition we have a number of log categories. These are STARTUP, SHUTDOWN, STATISTICS, CHECKPOINT, NODERESTART, CONNECTION, ERROR, INFO, CONGESTION, DEBUG, and BACKUP.

Each of those categories can have their own log level that can be set with a CLUSTERLOG command.

We provide an example where we set the log level of NODERESTART and BACKUP to log level 8.

```
ndb_mgm> 2 clusterlog noderestart=8 backup=8
Executing CLUSTERLOG NODERESTART=8 on node 2 OK!
Executing CLUSTERLOG BACKUP=8 on node 2 OK!

ndb_mgm>
```

44.8 DUMP COMMAND

The DUMP command is mentioned when using the HELP DEBUG command. It can create printouts to the cluster log, to the NDB data node log and it can even perform some intrusive changes of variables in the code to perform workarounds of difficult problems.

This command is not normally used by developers or DBAs, it is mostly intended for MySQL support that can use this to gather information about a special issue. The DUMP commands forms a signal sent to various blocks in the data nodes. The code in those blocks to handle those signals is the documentation of what can be done using the DUMP command.

44.9 EXIT/QUIT COMMAND

The EXIT command exits from the NDB management client as well as the QUIT command.

44.10 CONNECT COMMAND

The CONNECT command can be used to reconnect to the management server or to connect to a different management server. The parameter to the CONNECT command is a connect string, thus *host[:port]*.

This command can be useful to see if all management servers agree on the cluster status.

44.11   PURGE STALE SESSIONS

In the history of MySQL Cluster there was at times issues that a node id was kept allocated for longer than it was supposed to. As a workaround for those situations the PURGE STALE SESSIONS command was developed. This purges any sessions from node ids that are no longer used.

It should hopefully not be needed, but the command still exists.

CHAPTER 45

CLUSTER LOG AND NODE LOGS

Printing information is something most programs do a lot to ensure that it is possible to troubleshoot problems when they occur. NDB is no different in this respect. It is very easy to add new log messages, these log messages are not documented as such, they should be viewed as free text explanation of events in the software.

The NDB management server(s) prints the cluster log. There are simple functions in the NDB software to print a message in the cluster log. Look for *infoEvent* calls in the block code.

The NDB data nodes prints node logs. These are a bit more detailed in some aspects.

The MySQL Server has an error log that is used to write log messages, these can also come from the NDB storage engine.

45.1   THE CLUSTER LOG

The cluster log is found in a file normally called *node_49_cluster.log* if the node id of the management server is 49.

It contains all sorts of messages about what is going on. To provide a flavour of what it contains we first show the printouts in the cluster log at the very first initial start.

The first segment of the log shows what node id the management server uses and what port it is using. It reports the version number and informs that we start from an initial configuration. After this the first configuration generation is created with version number 1. If the management server is restarted it will reuse the configuration in the binary configuration file created. To change the configuration we will go through in a later chapter in some detail.

```
2017-09-23 15:48:38 [MgmtSrvr] INFO     -- Id: 49, Command port: *:1186
2017-09-23 15:48:38 [MgmtSrvr] INFO     -- Node 49: Node 49 Connected
2017-09-23 15:48:38 [MgmtSrvr] INFO     -- MySQL Cluster Management
   Server mysql-5.7.19 ndb-7.5.7 started
2017-09-23 15:48:39 [MgmtSrvr] INFO     -- Node 49 connected
2017-09-23 15:48:39 [MgmtSrvr] INFO     -- Starting initial
   configuration change
2017-09-23 15:48:39 [MgmtSrvr] INFO     -- Configuration 1 commited
2017-09-23 15:48:39 [MgmtSrvr] INFO     -- Config change completed!
   New generation: 1
```

We have broken the long lines to make the examples readable, some of the messages in the logs can use very long lines.

A few seconds later here the NDB data nodes 1 and 2 start up. They allocate a node id before they can start up. After receiving their node id they convert the connection to the management server to an NDB connection that can be used to send signals between the management server and the data nodes.

Each start phase completion is reported into the cluster log. A message that starts with *Node 1:* means that it is a message generated by node 1 and sent to the cluster log for logging. When it isn't preceded by this, it is a message coming from the management server itself.

We will skip showing the time and MgmtSrvr for the rest of the messages, they are there in each line. I will also skip INFO and – for all lines that are INFO messages.

```
Nodeid 1 allocated for NDB at 127.0.0.1
Nodeid 2 allocated for NDB at 127.0.0.1
Node 49: Node 1 Connected
Node 49: Node 2 Connected
Node 2: Start phase 0 completed
Node 1: Start phase 0 completed
Node 1: Initial start, waiting for 2 to connect,
   nodes [ all: 1 and 2 connected: 1 no-wait:  ]
Node 2: Initial start, waiting for 1 to connect,
   nodes [ all: 1 and 2 connected: 2 no-wait:  ]
Node 1: Communication to Node 2 opened
Node 2: Communication to Node 1 opened
Alloc node id 51 failed, no new president yet
Node 2: Node 1 Connected
Node 1: Node 2 Connected
Node 1: Initial start with
   nodes 1 and 2 [ missing:  no-wait:  ]
Node 1: CM_REGCONF
   president = 1, own Node = 1, our dynamic id = 0/1
WARNING  -- Failed to allocate nodeid for API at
   127.0.0.1. Returned error: 'Id 51 already allocated by
   another node.'
```

The cluster log reports what type of start each node is performing, it reports what nodes have already connected and which nodes are required for the restart to proceed. Thus first both node 1 and node 2 reports that they want to perform an initial start, but they are waiting for both nodes to connect. Once they connect to each other, node 1 (lowest node wins when no president has started yet) is selected as president.

Node 51 is a MySQL Server attempting to connect to the cluster. For an API node to be able to allocate a node id, the cluster must be up and running. Therefore the allocation will fail. The MySQL Server will continue to regularly try, the log will receive a fair amount of messages of failed allocations of node id from MySQL Servers that start before the cluster have started. This is not a problem, it is simply something we log.

```
Node 2: CM_REGCONF
  president = 1, own Node = 2, our dynamic id = 0/2
Node 1: Node 2: API mysql-5.7.19 ndb-7.5.7
Node 2: Node 1: API mysql-5.7.19 ndb-7.5.7
Node 2: Start phase 1 completed
Node 1: Start phase 1 completed
Node 1: System Restart:
  master node: 1, num starting: 2, gci: 0
Node 1: CNTR_START_CONF:
  started: 0000000000000000
Node 1: CNTR_START_CONF:
  starting: 0000000000000006
```

CM_REGCONF is received when we completed entering the heartbeat sending. When we reach this state we have completed memory allocations and memory initialisations in the nodes.

Next a new start phase is completed and we report a System Restart (all cluster nodes starts, no cluster is up and running). Since gci is 0 here, it is a System Restart from an initial start that we call inital start.

Next the nodes connect on the next layer where we deduce that node 1 considers no previous nodes started and that node 1 and 2 are starting. The 0000000000000006 is a hexadecimal number representing a bit map of all nodes starting. Bit 1 is 2 and Bit 2 is 4 and 2+4 is 6.

```
Node 1: Local redo log file initialization status:
#Total files: 16, Completed: 0
#Total MBytes: 192, Completed: 0
```

Next we receive a report on each log part that is initialised in each node. This initialisation can take some time.

```
Node 2: Start phase 4 completed (initial start)
Start phase 4 completed (initial start)
```

We continue receiving reports on completed start phases from all starting nodes.

The cluster log will switch to a new file when the file is full (1 MByte in size). It is configurable how many cluster log files that you want to save before they are overwritten. If you want to save the cluster log files for longer time it is necessary to copy them to another place.

The old cluster log file is automatically renamed when starting a new cluster log file. This has the same name with e.g. *.3* added. It will increment this number for each new cluster log file created. When reaching the maximum number of cluster log files it will start at one again.

```
Node 1: Make On-line Database recoverable
  by waiting for LCP Starting, LCP id = 2
Node 1: Local checkpoint 2 started.
  Keep GCI = 1 oldest restorable GCI = 1
Node 1: LDM(1): Completed LCP, #frags = 4
  #records = 1037, #bytes = 33264
...
Node 1: Local checkpoint 2 completed
Node 1: Make On-line Database recoverable
  by waiting for LCP Completed, LCP id = 2
...
Node 1: President restarts arbitration thread [state=1]
...
Node 1: Start phase 101 completed (initial start)
Node 1: Started (mysql-5.7.19 ndb-7.5.7)
Node 2: Started (mysql-5.7.19 ndb-7.5.7)
Node 2: Prepare arbitrator node 3 [ticket=1cc90001aec87e2a]
Node 1: Started arbitrator node 3 [ticket=1cc90001aec87e2a]
Node 2: Communication to Node 51 opened
```

After completing the recovery, we need to make the database recoverable by performing a local checkpoint. Execution of location checkpoints is reported in the cluster log regularly. The log will be filled with these in normal operation.

For each local checkpoint we return number fragments checkpointed, number of records written as part of this checkpoint and number of bytes written in this checkpoint.

Phase 101 is the last restart phase and at the end of the restart we start up the arbitrator node to ensure that we can survive at least one node crash.

When the node has started a lot of messages about communication between nodes being opened, node id allocated and connected are logged.

```
Alloc node id 51 succeeded
Nodeid 51 allocated for API at 127.0.0.1
Node 51: mysqld --server-id=1
Node 2: Node 51 Connected
Node 1: Node 51: API mysql-5.7.19 ndb-7.5.7
```

For MySQL Servers that starts up we can see the server id of the MySQL Server.

When a table is created we receive reports about phases it passes through in creating the table.

When the cluster have entered a started state and tables have been created, the logging quiets down. Now it is mostly regular checkpoints that gets logged.

This stays until we decide to restart a node or some other event happens.

The majority of the events logged in the cluster log are related to start of the cluster, failed nodes or nodes that disconnect, restart of a node, local checkpoints.

Most of the reporting is intended to be readable messages that can be understood with some background in NDB.

It is possible to get logs about even more events by changing the cluster log levels as discussed in the previous chapter.

Naturally the cluster log also have information about various error situations.

Personally I find the node logs more interesting to look at to analyse problems since it often contains a lot more details about what happened. But the cluster log is a good place to start your investigation of what is going in the cluster since it has a helicopter view of what goes on.

45.2 MANAGEMENT SERVER NODE LOG

The management server also reports a bit of information in its node log. Most of this information is also recorded in the cluster log, there is rarely much of interest in this log except when there is a problem in starting up the management server.

45.3 DATA NODE LOGS

If for some reason there is an issue with starting a node, stopping a node, a node crash or some error situation, it is usually in the data node logs that most information can be retrieved about the problem.

The data node logs are mostly focused on restarts, node failures, and error situations. In particular one can often see problems in the node log with regard to watchdog issues. These occur often when the OS misbehaves and doesn't schedule the process or one of the threads in the process. It is not uncommon for this to happen for seconds at a time in certain situations. Since NDB is a real-time system, it will quickly detect those problems since each node have to send heartbeats regularly to other nodes. NDB will not work very well if the OS runs like syrup and constantly fails to make to progress.

The node logs are constantly written to, it is important to regularly copy them away and to empty the file. Otherwise there is a risk that the file system runs out of space for logging. A popular Linux tool to handle this is *logrotate*. This can be used together with *cron* to ensure that the log file is constantly rotated and that the log is backed up if required.

We will now show examples of output in the node log, there is some information in their that is useful for various purposes. In all those examples we will skip any timestamps and INFO strings. Some of the messages have this header of time and type of message, some messages have no such header info.

A data node starts up first with the angel process, this process connects to the management server and allocates a node id. Next the angel forks a data node process that runs the actual data node. The angel stays around waiting to start up failed data node.

As seen below the node log contains the host and port of the management server, the node id allocated and the PID of both the angel process and the data node process.

```
Angel connected to 'localhost:1186'
Angel allocated nodeid: 1
Angel pid: 71526 started child: 71530
Normal start of data node using checkpoint and log info if existing
Configuration fetched from 'localhost:1186', generation: 1
Changing directory to '/path/datadir/ndbd.1'
ThreadConfig: input: main={count=1},tc={count=3},ldm={count=4},
   io={count=1},rep={count=1},recv={count=2},send={count=2}
   LockExecuteThreadToCPU:  => parsed: main,ldm,ldm,ldm,ldm,
   recv,recv,rep,tc,tc,tc,send,send
```

Next the data node process changes current directory to the data directory of the data node. We always get a report of the threads that the data node will start up. In this case there is four *ldm* threads, three *tc* threads, 2 *send* threads, 2 *recv* threads, one *main* thread, and one *rep* thread.

```
....
mysql-5.7.19 ndb-7.5.7 --
A monotonic timer was not available on this platform.
Memory Allocation for global memory pools Starting
Adjusting system time manually, or otherwise (e.g. NTP), may
   cause false watchdog alarms, temporary freeze, or node shutdown.
numa_set_interleave_mask(numa_all_nodes) : no numa support
Ndbd_mem_manager::init(1) min: 248Mb initial: 268Mb
Touch Memory Starting, 6220 pages, page size = 32768
Touch Memory Completed
Adding 195Mb to ZONE_19 (1, 6219)
Memory Allocation for global memory pools Completed
```

Next we receive some redundant information skipped here, we report the version number. In this case I start on Mac OS X where no monotonic timer is available so I get an apprioate information what to consider to avoid problems in this case.

The global memory manager allocates most of the memory used in NDB. After allocation of the memory, it is touched to ensure that the memory pages are allocated. This ensures that we don't run out memory space in normal operations. Touching the memory can take about 1 second per GByte, thus it can be a fairly lengthy process.

```
Started thread, index = 0, id = -1, type = NdbfsThread
Loading blocks for data node run-time environment
Starting Sending and Receiving services
Started thread, index = 1, id = -1, type = SocketClientThread
Started thread, index = 2, id = -1, type = WatchDogThread
Started thread, index = 3, id = -1, type = SocketServerThread
```

Every thread started in the startup has some sort of printout attached to it. Above we
see the first instance of the NDB file system threads, these handle the interaction with the
file system and there can be quite a few such threads although they are not using the CPU
so much. These threads are there to ensure that also the file system can be accessed using
asynchronous signals.

We start a watch dog thread, a thread that connects as a client to other nodes through a
socket and thread handling our socket server that waits for other nodes to connect to us. The
socket client thread is regularly trying to connect other nodes where we take the client role in
the socket setup.

```
Starting the data node run-time environment
thr: 0 (main) DBTC(0) DBDIH(0) DBDICT(0) NDBCNTR(0) QMGR(0)
  NDBFS(0) CMVMI(0) TRIX(0) DBUTIL(0) DBSPJ(0) THRMAN(0)
  TRPMAN(0) THRMAN(1) realtime=0, spintime=0,
  max_signals_before_send=300, max_signals_before_send_flush=110
First START_ORD executed to connect MGM servers
Received second START_ORD as part of normal start
Disconnect all non-MGM servers
Start excuting the start phases
Sending READ_CONFIG_REQ to index = 0, name = CMVMI
Start initiated (mysql-5.7.19 ndb-7.5.7)
```

For the block threads we receive information about which block objects it handles, the
thread parameters on realtime setting, the signal scheduler settings. These are configured
through the *SchedulerResponsiveness* parameter, higher setting will increase responsiveness and
thus decrease the maximum number of signals executed before flush and before send. Above
printout comes from Mac OS X where thread ids are not available. On Linux a thread id is
also reported for the thread that can be used e.g. in *perf* scripts that we will discuss later in
this book.

```
Ndb kernel thread 2 is stuck in: Unknown place 0 elapsed=11
Watchdog: User time: 3  System time: 16
thr: 12 (send)
NDBFS/AsyncFile: Allocating 310392 for In/Deflate buffer
Started thread, index = 18, id = -1, type = NdbfsThread
```

Above we have a typical warning message that can happen easily in an environment that
cannot handle the real-time requirements. The watchdog here reports that one of the thread
with id 2 is stuck in an unknown place and the time that passed by since last it was seen. The
watchdog will report threads that don't show up within 100 milliseconds. It will not crash the
node until a much longer time have passed by, log messages of this kind can show up every now
and then.

A message about kernel threads being stuck is an indication of CPU overload and should be
avoided if real-time responsiveness is desirable.

Very early in our development we had such a case where the user had a crash due to the watchdog firing at 2am every night. After some investigation it turned out that at time the machine backup was started and it consumed almost all the memory resources in the machine and made the data node go into swapping mode. This is one reason why we have the configuration parameter *LockPagesInMainMemory* that ensures that all our memory will stay in memory and never be swapped out even in such cases where heavy programs are started at the same time. In the same fashion modern VM technology can be used to protect the data node programs from other programs getting access to its dedicated CPU resources. Docker have some protection against this as well, Docker can also protect that we get a certain share of the CPUs.

```
READ_CONFIG_REQ phase completed, this phase is used to read
configuration and to calculate various sizes and allocate
almost all memory needed by the data node in its lifetime
Not initial start
Start phase 0 completed
Phase 0 has made some file system initialisations
Starting QMGR phase 1
DIH reported initial start, now starting the Node Inclusion Protocol
```

Phase 0 of the restart sends a signal *READ_CONFIG_REQ* to all blocks. This signals gives the chance for early initialisation of objects, it allocates any objects not allocated from the global memory space and it calculates sizes of various pools based on configuration and thus various other calculations based on the configuration.

In phase 1 QMGR will insert us into the heartbeat protocol.

```
Include node protocol completed, phase 1 in QMGR completed
Start phase 1 completed
Phase 1 initialised some variables and included node in cluster,
locked memory if configured to do so
Asking master node to accept our start (we are master, GCI = 0)
We are performing an initial start of the cluster
System Restart: master node: 1, num starting: 2, gci: 0
CNTR_START_CONF: started: 0000000000000000
CNTR_START_CONF: starting: 0000000000000006
NDBCNTR master accepted us into cluster, start NDB start phase 1
```

QMGR handles the lowest layer of the cluster node management. The next layer is handled by the NDBCNTR block. We are informed of which node became the master node, how many nodes are starting and their node ids in the form of a bitmap.

After being accepted by the master node to start we proceed on with the restart.

```
LDM(1): Starting REDO log initialisation
LDM(1): Completed REDO log initialisation of logPart = 0
LDM(1): Completed REDO initialisation
Schema file initialisation Starting
Schema file initialisation Completed
NDB start phase 1 completed
Start phase 2 completed
Phase 2 did more initialisations, master accepted
   our start, we initialised the REDO log
```

This is an initial start, so now it is time to initialise the REDO log files to ensure that we have access to the full space of the REDO log files. This can take considerable time in the first initial start, it is only done in an initial start and initial node restart.

```
Grant nodes to start phase: 3, nodes: 0000000000000006
Start NDB start phase 2
NDB start phase 2 completed
Start phase 3 completed
Phase 3 performed local connection setups
Grant nodes to start phase: 4, nodes: 0000000000000006
Start NDB start phase 3
LDM(1): Completed old Redo head invalidation on log part 0
LDM(1): All redo actions complete (apply, invalidate)
Start invalidating: Part 0, Head: file: 0, page: 1,
   Invalidation start:
   file: 0, page: 1, actual start invalidate: file: 0 page: 1
```

As part of the restart we have to apply the REDO log and before that we might have to invalidate a part of the REDO log that was written, but didn't survive the crash. We get reports about where this happens.

```
LDM(1): Completed old Redo head invalidation on log part 0
LDM(1): All redo actions complete (apply, invalidate)
NDB start phase 3 completed
Starting with m_restart_seq set to 1
Start phase 4 completed
Phase 4 continued preparations of the REDO log
Grant nodes to start phase: 5, nodes: 0000000000000006
NDB start phase 4 completed
Creating System Tables Starting as part of initial start
Node 2 have reached completion of NDB start phase 4
Creation of System Tables Completed
Start NDB start phase 5 (only to DBDIH)
```

m_restart_seq is the number of the restart and ensures that we can separate this instance of the node from any earlier instance of this node that already failed. Other nodes might have signals received from the old instance. So we need some protection to ensure that we don't get confused by old signals still progressing through the cluster even after a node failure.

In an initial restart we create some system table and fill it with data.

```
NDB start phase 5 completed
Start NDB start phase 6
NDB start phase 6 completed
Start phase 5 completed
Phase 5 Created the System Table
Phase 5 waited for local checkpoint to complete
Grant nodes to start phase: 6, nodes: 0000000000000006
Start phase 6 completed
Phase 6 updated blocks about that we've now reached
  the started state.
Grant nodes to start phase: 7, nodes: 0000000000000006
President restarts arbitration thread [state=1]
Activating bucket 0 in SUMA
Start phase 7 completed
Phase 7 mainly activated the asynchronous change events
  process, and some other background processes
```

Here we might get confused since start phase 5 completes after NDB start phase 6 have completed. The reason is that start phase is managed by the subblock Missra in NDBCNTR that sends phased signals to each block in the data node. This is controlled by the signals STTOR and STTORRY.

When NDBCNTR receives such a start phase from Missra it starts off zero, one or more NDB start phases.

The reason for separation of lower layer cluster management and database cluster management both in heartbeat setup and early phases and also later phases of the restart is historical.

In the early days before the NDB architecture had settled down the idea was that NDB would be just one susbsystem running in the virtual machine. Thus the STTOR/STTORRY handles the start of the virtual machine whereas NDB_STTOR and NDB_STTORRY handles the start of the database machine.

This idea has been completely abandoned for almost 20 years, the distinction today between the layers is not as clear anymore. But the design works fine, thus there has been no specific need to change this part, also it would be quite hard to change it given the implications it would have on upgrade of the cluster software due to the impact on the NDB protocols it would have.

In the late restart phases we startup the event API handling and the arbitration thread ensuring that we can survive split brain scenarios.

```
Grant nodes to start phase: 8, nodes: 0000000000000006
Start NDB start phase 7
Foreign Key enabling Starting
Foreign key enabling Completed
NDB start phase 7 completed
Start phase 8 completed
Phase 8 enabled foreign keys and waited forall
  nodes to complete start up to this point
Grant nodes to start phase: 9, nodes: 0000000000000006
Start phase 9 completed
Phase 9 enabled APIs to start connecting
Grant nodes to start phase: 10, nodes: 0000000000000006
Start phase 49 completed
Grant nodes to start phase: 50, nodes: 0000000000000006
Restart complete, updated local sysfile
Start phase 50 completed
Grant nodes to start phase: 51, nodes: 0000000000000006
Start phase 101 completed
Phase 101 was used by SUMA to take over responsibility
  for sending some of the asynchronous change events
Grant nodes to start phase: 102, nodes: 0000000000000006
Node started
Started arbitrator node 49 [ticket=176a00019a4cb559]
Allocate event buffering page chunk in SUMA, 16 pages,..
```

Here is the final phase of the initial start where foreign key handling is started up and a couple of more phases to synchronise special parts of the data nodes. After starting the arbitrator on node 49 (the NDB management server) the restart is done.

45.3.1 FINDING NODE LOG MESSAGES IN CODE

If you are interested in understanding a bit more about the NDB code you can do this by adding more messages to the node log. Most normal information messages are added through a call such as shown below:

```
g_eventLogger->info("Insert normal printf logic here");
```

By doing a grep as below you can quickly find all the examples of node log messages in our code base.

```
cd $MYSQL_SOURCE_DIR
cd storage/ndb/src
grep -r 'g_eventLogger->info' *
```

Replacing info by debug shows all debug messages, warning shows all warning messages and critical for critical messages.

45.3.2 WRITING TO NODE LOGS

Every write to the node log presents a potential problem. It can fail due to various problems with the disk. To avoid crashing the data nodes in those situations, we implement the actual log writing in a special log writing thread. If the log writes fails after a number of retries, the log message is thrown away and the data node can continue to operate. Similarly if the log writing buffer is full, the message is thrown away in this thread.

45.4 SUMMARY OF LOGS

The data node logs and cluster log contain lots of information. The above was presented mostly as an example. It presents information about restarts, node failures. It is heavily used by developers printing debug information during analysis of bugs and new feature development.

In MySQL Cluster 7.4 a major effort was spent on ensuring that supportability of the product was increased by improving the understandability of the restart messages. Many more new messages was printed to ensure that it is possible to follow the restart phases in some detail. A new *ndbinfo* table was developed that keep track of node restarts in a live system and one can see progress of restarts.

There are many different DUMP commands that can be used to print detailed information on various topics to analyse error situations. These are mostly intended to aid MySQL support to assist users with various sorts of problems.

The good news is that NDB is open source, the code is available and so anyone can learn those detailed logging messages as well and become an expert in supporting a MySQL Cluster installation.

The cluster log messages are documented and all of them are described in the MySQL manual. This is not the case for messages in the node logs. These are not documented, rather the aim of those is to be as self-describing as possible and the amount of messages in the node logs can at times be a bit higher.

CHAPTER 46

TROUBLESHOOTING NDB

You have managed to get a cluster up and running, maybe you have even managed to get the cluster into production usage. All of a sudden a crash occurs unexpectedly. What to do about it?

MySQL Cluster is designed for continous operation even in the presence of bugs and failures. In most cases the crashed node comes up again and you are back to a replicated setup after a short time. After that you can analyse your log files to see what went wrong.

There has been cases where a node has failed and the node failed to start up again. After working with the error logs and the remaining nodes it is possible at times to work around the problem to avoid system downtime. Oftentimes the cluster can stay up and running for weeks and months even with a node down. With two replicas it will stay up for years and years.

MySQL Cluster inherited extensive crash logs from its AXE inheritance. In AXE the CPUs generated writes into a jump address memory that showed the last few thousands jumps in the assembler code before any crash. We took this concept to the C++ world by writing a set of scripts called *jam()* with a few variants. Each such macro will write an entry into a memory area that shows which source code file and which line in this file that we visited the last microseconds before the crash. We record a few thousand such macro calls before the crash. This has a CPU overhead, but it is an overhead that is well worth the effort in quickly finding bugs.

In addition since NDB is a message oriented architecture and we use memory for send buffers, it is possible to generate signal logs for the last few thousand signals. This can take us back milliseconds before the crash and in some cases even seconds back.

NDB data nodes using *ndbmtd* has a multithreaded architecture. Here each thread is generating its own crash output. It is even possible to follow messages that pass between threads in many cases, in cluster crashes it is possible to follow messages going between nodes in the cluster if the configuration of the transporters uses Signal Ids.

In addition a very important tool for analysing the behaviour of data nodes is the node logs and cluster logs. These are printouts that goes to special log files, the cluster logs gather all logs for the cluster and the node logs gather logs from all threads within one node (there is a node log also for the management server, and the MySQL Server have its error log).

The MySQL server and the NDB API doesn't have the same facilities of crash logs. At the same time a crash in the MySQL Server using NDB is a crash of client software, thus it represents very little risk for you of losing your data. It is much more important to care for the risk of losing data in data nodes.

When debugging and developing NDB we use a set of tools to printout debug messages in data nodes and in the MySQL Server we use the same tools that are used by the rest of the MySQL Server.

With this combination we have the upper hand on any bug caused by temporary glitches. It is usually detected and found rather easy with those tools.

The crash principle in NDB is a bit different to the crash principle of the MySQL server. The MySQL server goes a long ways to avoid crashing the MySQL server. The reason is that a normal MySQL server that fails means downtime for the user application.

An NDB data node that goes down doesn't represent any downtime in a standard NDB configuration. A standard configuration of NDB always have 2 replicas of all the data in the data nodes. Thus a crash can be handled without any downtime seen by the user other than that a few transactions will have to be executed again.

In NDB we employ the fail fast methodology. Thus our production code is filled with asserts that ensure that the data structures in NDB are always consistent. As soon as something is wrong we immediately crash. We see it as better to crash and come back to a stable state rather than to continue operating with data in a state that the code isn't prepared to handle. Continuing in this state could jeopardize the database since we might corrupt data when integrity of our data structures has been breached.

46.1 Data node crash output

When a crash occurs we gather a number of logs before the program is completed.

Each thread writes a trace file that contains a combined jump trace file and a signal log file. The node log is maintained continously and so is the cluster log.

Crashes can occur for a myriad of reasons. The crash could come through internal problems in our code. These cases are normally found through some assert in the code.

Other cases can be that we attempted to perform a configuration change that simply didn't work. Often there is a clear error message in those cases explaining the problem.

We can crash in cases where we overextend the memory buffers in the node. This is rather uncommon that we crash for this reason, in this case we normally drop the connection to a node instead in this case. We employ various techniques to avoid crashing in this case. In an overload situation it rarely helps to crash, this usually leads us into an even bigger issue.

A crash is recorded in an error log with a reference to the crashing thread and its trace file.

In order to display the use of those files I inserted a very easy crash case in a version I am currently developing. The below is just to show how the various log files looks, that you know where to look (we have cut some lines to make the output readable in the book format).

46.1.1 Error log

The error log contains a short description of the error that occurred. This describes the time of the failure, the status of the failure (how large impact did it have), an explanation of the problem. In this case it was caused by an assert in the DblqhMain.cpp.

In the error log we can see the exact condition that was checked in the error check and at what line in the code the assert happened. Obviously we need to use source code from the same version to be able to analyse any reports about code lines.

```
Time: Thursday 19 October 2017 - 20:17:09
Status: Temporary error, restart node
Message: Internal program error (failed ndbrequire)
   (Internal error, programming error or
    missing error message, please report a bug)
Error: 2341
Error data: DblqhMain.cpp
Error object: DBLQH (Line: 8084) 0x00000002 Check lqhRef == 0 failed
Program: ndbmtd
Pid: 2526 thr: 3
Version: mysql-5.7.19 ndb-7.5.7
Trace file name: ndb_1_trace.log.1_t5
Trace file path: /path/datadir/ndbd.1/ndb_1_trace.log.1 [t1..t11]
***EOM***
```

In this case the output was generated by the *ndbmtd* program. The *ndbd* program only have one thread and thus only uses one trace file. *ndbmtd* uses multiple trace files.

In the above case we have crashed in node 1, thread id 5 and there was threads t1 through t11. The first thread is the *main* thread and its trace file is called *ndb_1_trace.log.1*. The second thread is the *rep* thread, this thread has its trace files written into *ndb_1_trace.log.1_t1*. Next comes the *ldm* threads (4 in my case), these end with t2 -> t5. After that comes the *tc* threads. In our case we had three of those, thus t6 through t8. There is in our case two *recv* threads, these gets their input into t9 and t10.

In the above test we got a crash log in the last of the *ldm* thread. We get the pid, the thread count and the version number generating the crash output.

46.1.2 JAM

The output of the *jam()* macros is listed in the above trace files. To make it easier to read the lines around the crash the last line touched before the crash is the last line listed before the signal logging starts. Thus signals are listed in the *jam()* output going backwards in the file. A good idea to read the trace file is to search for Signal and start from there.

```
---> signal
DbtupMeta.cpp          00661 00718 00906 00908 00812
DblqhMain.cpp          04077
```

Each new signal is listed in the *jam()* output and each time we jump into a new file we change into a new line with the name of the source file listed. Next we display the line numbers we have touched. In some cases we can list a 16-bit number instead in the *jam()*. An example could be that we want to list which node we are processing, in this case the number doesn't refer to a code line.

46.1.3 SIGNAL LOG

The signal log have a lot more information in it. Each signal carries a header with receiving block number and name, receiving node id, receiving signal id and the global signal number and the name of the signal and its priority. Here *r.bn* is short for receiving block number. 247/4 means block number 247 (DBLQH) and *ldm* thread instance 4 (starting at 1). *r.proc* means receiving processor id, that is our node id. Each signal carries a signal id, each new signal executed in a thread increments this number. Similarly *s.bn*, *s.proc* and *s.sigId* is the senders identity. Thus we can find the exact signal that sent this signal if we suspect that it did something wrong in sending signal.

The rest of the signal output depends on the signal. Many signals have special signal printers attached to them (LQHKEYREQ below has that). These print the various fields and flags in text and a bit better readability compared to a hexadecimal dump of the signal data that is the default if no special printer is available.

LQHKEYREQ is the signal sent from DBTC to read, update, delete, write or insert rows using a primary key. In this case we are performing an insert. We can see the transaction id, the table id, the back reference to DBTC and a number of other fields.

```
--------------- Signal ----------------
r.bn: 247/4 "DBLQH", r.proc: 1, r.sigId: 11937
    gsn: 316 "LQHKEYREQ" prio: 1
s.bn: 245/1 "DBTC", s.proc: 1, s.sigId: 81
   length: 13 trace: 0 #sec: 2 fragInf: 0
 ClientPtr = H'00002b20 hashValue = H'27680d04 tcBlockRef = H'02f50001
 transId1 = H'00000000 transId2 = H'00000001 savePointId = H'00000000
 Operation: Insert
 Op: 2 Lock: 0 Flags: CommitAckMarker
   ScanInfo/noFiredTriggers: H'3fffb
 AttrLen: 0 (0 in this) KeyLen: 0 TableId: 2 SchemaVer: 1
 FragId: 7 ReplicaNo: 0 LastReplica: 1 NextNodeId: 2
 ApiRef: H'00fb0001 ApiOpRef: H'00000000
 AttrInfo:
```

We have developed many prototypes of even more advanced signal loggers that can be used also when not crashing. These can be very helpful in learning about how signal flows for various functions are implemented. This is true even for me with 20 years of experience of developing NDB. There are commands in the NDB management client accessible using HELP DEBUG to provide such signal logs.

What we have found again and again is that the crash logs does more than 90% of the functions needed to understand what goes on. It is often simpler to insert a simple assert somewhere in the code and have it crash at some point where you want to see the workings exactly before the crash. Therefore none of those prototypes have been productified. We even had an advanced signal database tool implemented in Java already in the 1990s for this purpose and we have done some efforts in a similar fashion a few years ago as well.

46.1.4 NODE AND CLUSTER LOG

We covered the node and cluster log in the previous chapter.

46.1.5 WATCHDOG

An important part of the execution environment is that we always ensure that threads do not stop from proceeding. We check this from a special watchdog thread. Every thread must register into shared data structures that this thread will see. If a block stays away for more than a minute or two the node will crash because of this.

Warnings are printed by the watchdog already after 100 milliseconds. These warnings should be taken seriously, they are usually an indication of the OS environment you are running in. Thus if the OS have a lot of CPU contention these messages can quickly start appearing.

46.1.6 LOG WRITING

A number of cases occurred at user sites where logging itself could cause the watchdog to fire off. This happened in cases with overloaded disks and other similar OS issues.

To prevent this from happening all log writes have been moved to a special log writing thread. The execution threads will never do any form of IO operations other than those that assist in sending to the network and the *recv* thread that will take care of the network reading.

46.1.7 NDBREQUIRE

A very commonly used macro in the NDB data node code is called *ndbrequire*. This is an assert function, it is executed even in a production environment. Its cousin *ndbassert* is only executed in a debug environment. For the most part we prefer *ndbrequire* since we want to fail fast if there is an error in any data structure. Thus *ndbassert* is more for testing stupid tests that sometimes can be good to have in a development phase to find some silly errors.

ndbrequire can only be used in block code, in other code we have another macro called *require*.

46.2 DEBUGGING MySQL CLUSTER

Debugging NDB code is about using the above tools. I have used the above tools to solve many thousands of complex bugs over the years. In all other software I have written I have almost always been forced to write lots of special debug statements scattered all over the code, and as soon as the code is in production these printouts are gone.

The above mechanisms makes it possible for us to work efficiently with users that experiences problems in the field. Many times these logs can be sufficient to solve the issues.

There is still a need for printing debug macros however as a debugging tool and in the NDB API and in the NDB storage engine we use the MySQL server debugging tools that provides a good insight into how the server works.

For the NDB data nodes there is many ways to write log messages. Most of them end up in the node log. There is also another mechanism that end up in a special log called signal log, this log can be used to combine signal logging and normal debug printouts.

Below is a preferred method I have used heavily the last few years.

46.2.1 DEBUGGING USING DEBUG MACROS

During a project to implement Partial local checkpoints, that are part of 7.6.4, I used special debug macros a lot in my development.

The reason is that in this project, it was often the case that the bug was in the production of checkpoints. The bug wasn't discovered until the restart though. Thus we have no chance of discovering the error through signal logs.

In this case I used a wide range of debug macros that can be selectively activated during development.

Here is an example of the definition of such a debug macro. It is important to include the header file *EventLogger.hpp* and *extern* declare the event logger object *g_eventLogger*.

```
#define DEBUG_EXTRA_LCP 1
#ifdef DEBUG_EXTRA_LCP
#define DEB_EXTRA_LCP(arglist) \
  do { g_eventLogger->info arglist ; } while (0)
#else
#define DEB_EXTRA_LCP(arglist) do { } while (0)
#endif
```

Now we can use this macro in the code to print a line to the node log that contains a timestamp and also these logs are serialised to ensure that each line is printed in full without interruption from other log writes.

When the code is ready we can simply remove this code by commenting out the line above defining DEBUG_EXTRA_LCP and the code is no longer executed, neither in debug nor in production builds.

To use it in the code one uses a normal printf format. Important to note is that it requires double parenthesis around the statement.

```
DEB_EXTRA_LCP(("(%u)op_type: %u, newestGci: %u, "
              "tableId: %u, fragId: %u",
              instance(),
              tcPtrP->operation,
              regFragptr->newestGci,
              regFragptr->tabRef,
              regFragptr->fragId));
```

CHAPTER 47

ONLINE CHANGES OF CONFIGURATION

NDB was originally designed for telecom applications. A telco application is extremely well tested before it is put into production. In those situations it was expected that the configuration had already been tried out before starting it up in a production environment. In a test environment one can stop the cluster and change the configuration and run a new test.

In a telco production environment configuration changes will normally happen in conjunction with software changes and other changes. So a rolling restart of the cluster to change the configuration is ok.

The need of changing configuration while up and running haven't been a focus earlier. Rather we have used the fact that any node can be restarted without impact on the cluster operation. Thus we can reconfigure through various node restarts.

There is ongoing work to make it easier to configure and reconfigure NDB that will arrive in future versions of NDB.

47.1 CLUSTER CONFIGURATION

The cluster configuration contains the full configuration of all data nodes in the cluster. It describes the configuration of how to communicate between nodes in the cluster. It defines the set of nodes of various types that we have in the cluster. A few parameters is defined for the NDB API part in the API nodes. The API nodes often have their own set of configuration parameters that is application specific. We will describe the MySQL Server configurations that are specific to NDB.

Each node that starts in the cluster retrieves the current cluster configuration from one of the management servers. The startup of the node is using this configuration. To change anything in the configuration normally a node restart of the node is required. Given that the cluster can operate even in the presence of node restarts, this isn't critical for the availability of the cluster. It means that it will take more time to reconfigure the cluster though.

The cluster configuration is stored in a configuration database that is maintained by the management server. The method to update this configuration database is by using the procedure described here and in a previous chapter on handling of the *ndb_mgmd* process.

47.2 ADDING NODES TO THE CLUSTER

Every node sets up communication to the other nodes as part of their startup. It is currently not possible to add nodes to communicate with, for an already started node. One reason we are a bit careful about this is that adding a new communication link requires new memory buffers and we try to avoid memory allocations in a live node since it can easily disturb the operations in the running node.

To add a node (or several ones), it must first be added to the configuration through a distributed configuration change. Next all nodes must be restarted such that they can communicate with the new node.

47.3 MANAGING THE CONFIGURATION DATABASE

The configuration database is stored in the set of management servers. The easiest manner to explain how this database is managed is to describe the workings of the management server at startup.

The workings of the management servers is not so well described in the MySQL documentation, so I provide a fairly detailed description of both how it works and how it is intended to be used. Problems in changing the configuration is probably the most common question on the various forums for MySQL Cluster.

When a management server starts up it will start by retrieving the command line parameters. The next step is to read the configuration.

47.3.1 *--skip-config-cache*

If the startup option *--skip-config-cache* have been provided we will always read the user provided *config.ini* (or whatever name of the configuration file that was specified in the startup parameters). This mode disables the configuration database, the management servers will no longer work together to check the configuration, the configuration will not be checked against any previous configuration.

Personally I would never use this mode for any production cluster, I would only use it for setups with a single management server. I use it when running my benchmark scripts. The reason is that I always start my benchmarks from a completely new cluster, so I skip all the complexity of managing configuration versions. For the rest of the description here we will assume this setting has not been used.

47.3.2 *--configdir*

Next step is to check that the configuration directory is created. This was specified in the startup parameter *--configdir*. The default setting is dependent on the build of MySQL Cluster. For your own builds you can define it with -DMYSQLCLUSTERDIR in the CMake definition of the build. It is recommended to always set this parameter when starting the NDB management server.

47.3.3 GET NODE ID

Next we will get our node id. First we will check the startup parameters, this is the preferred method of setting the node id.

Next we will check the configuration binary files. These files have a node id in their name, as long as there is only one node id in all the files stored in this directory we can proceed after verifying that another management server isn't already started using this particular hostname.

If no binary files exist we will check in the user provided configuration file. It will look for a management server executing on the host we are starting from.

If we have multiple management servers running on the same host it is mandatory to set the node id when starting the management servers.

47.3.4 INITIAL CONFIGURATION CHANGE

Next we will check if the *--initial* option was provided. In this case we will verify the new configuration and if ok we will delete all saved configuration binary files, if not ok the management server won't start.

The intention of the *--initial* flag is to use it when installing a new cluster in the same place as a previous one. Thus the old configuration is removed and a new one installed without checking that the change from one configuration to another is ok. This flag only matters if *--config-file* was set. This option is not intended for any form of upgrade procedure. It is intended for use when creating a new cluster where we already had a previous one.

As an example the old cluster could be based on a configuration with *NoOfReplicas* set to 1. Now we have completed the testing with just one replica and now we want to extend the cluster to using two replicas. In this case we need to take a backup of the cluster and restart the cluster from initial state. In this case one can use the *--initial* flag to overwrite the old configuration without any checks of upgradability at all.

Next we attempt to read the latest binary configuration file. If no one exists we will read the user provided *config.ini* and create the first version of the binary configuration file. In this case we must perform a distributed initial configuration change transaction. This will not be performed until all management servers have started up. It is possible to specifically exclude one or more management servers using the *--no-wait-nodes* parameter.

If neither a binary configuration file exists and we didn't specify a configuration file we assume that another management server has started up with a configuration. We fetch it from there, if this is not the initial version we will simply write it down to our *configdir* and the management server is started.

If it was fetched from a remote management server and it was the initial version we will wait to complete the startup until initial distributed configuration change transaction have completed.

For an initial configuration change to be executed all management servers must be up and running. There can be a maximum of two management servers.

If one node attempts to perform an initial configuration change and another node is not attempting to perform an initial configuration change the node attempting to start an initial configuration change will stop.

To start a new configuration when an existing was around it is necessary to start up with *--initial* in all management servers AND all management servers must provide the same new initial configuration. Otherwise the change to a new initial configuration will fail.

When starting up the first time all management servers must be in an initial state, but only one of them is required to specify a configuration file.

When all nodes have started and it is verified that they can start an initial configuration we proceed with a change configuration request.

47.3.5 NORMAL MANAGEMENT SERVER STARTUP

If we find a binary configuration file and we didn't specify *--reload* the startup is done. No
configuration change was requested. The management server is immediately ready to accept
new requests for the configuration from starting nodes.

Now if *--reload* was specified we must also specify

--config-file=/path/to/config, if not provided the *--reload* parameter will be ignored.

47.3.6 CHANGE CONFIGURATION REQUEST

When a management server have been started with *--reload* and a new configuration file was
provided through the *--config-file* option we will attempt to change the configuration. We
will verify that the configuration actually has changed. We will write the diff of the new
configuration and the old configuration to the node log of the management server. Next we will
start a change configuration request.

There is two other methods available to start a change configuration request. Both are
available through NDB MGM API. The first one is called *set config* and sends an entire new
configuration to change into. The second is called *reload config* and sends the file name of the
new configuration. The file must be present in the host of the management server this request
is sent to.

A few test programs use this feature to test things related to configuration changes.

For a DBA to change the configuration the below procedure can be used to change any
configuration parameter. Ensure that the old *config.ini* is backed up before starting the change.

```
ndb_config --ndb-connectstring host[:port]
           --print_config_ini > config.ini
```

After that one edits this file to change the parameters as desired and starts the procedure by
restarting a management server with *--reload* and providing the *--config-file* parameter pointing
to the new *config.ini* file.

A transaction is used to change the configuration. First a diff is built from the old to the
new configuration. It is not allowed to change the type of a node. E.g. we cannot have node id
2 as a data node and change it to become an API node. This is an illegal change.

The new generation of the configuration change must be one more than the previous. This
protects against multiple changers of the configuration trying to change it at the same time.
This can happen if someone performed a change of the configuration while the management
server was down.

In addition the cluster name cannot change and neither are we allowed to change the primary
management server. The primary management server is the last management server that
performed a change of the configuration by using *--reload*, it is cleared if a change is performed

through the NDB MGM API. Thus when using this procedure one should always use the same management server to change the config.

When changing the configuration it is important to consider a few configuration parameters that have special rules for their change. We will go through those parameters in the next section.

After these checks the management servers together execute a configuration change and if all goes well they decide jointly on a new configuration database version and each management server writes this new version into a binary configuration file using the new version number as part of the file name.

47.3.7 SPECIAL CONFIGURATION PARAMETERS

The types of special rules for changes are the following. Some configuration parameters require a restart of the node to take effect. This is currently the case for every configuration parameter.

A set of configuration parameters requires a initial node restart to be changed.

There is a set of configuration parameters that require a full cluster restart to be changed correctly and there is a few configuration parameters that cannot be changed other than through a completely new cluster installation.

NoOfReplicas

NoOfReplicas is a parameter that cannot change once the cluster have been started up. The placement of the data nodes into node groups depends on this parameter and it is required that all node groups have the same number of nodes the number of replicas.

NoOfFragmentLogParts

NoOfFragmentLogParts is possible to change, but it requires an initial node restart to change it. The number of partitions in a table is defined by the number of log parts in the master node when the table is created. Normally all nodes in the cluster share the number of log parts.

The change of number of log parts can be done and will affect the number of log parts. However it won't change the number of partitions in already created tables. NDB supports increasing the number of partitions in a table, but it doesn't support decreasing the number of partitions in a table. In addition the fragments are mapped to a log part, this log part will not change even if the number of log parts change. Thus we cannot decrease the number of log parts since that would mean that some fragments have no place to go.

In practice changing the number of log parts can be done if it is changed to a higher number of log parts. But the change will only effect the new tables created after changing the number of log parts in all nodes through a rolling initial node restart.

NoOfFragmentLogFiles

Number of fragment log files can be changed, but it requires an initial node restart to be successful since we would forget about the old REDO log files and in addition we might fail the recovery if we change this without an initial node restart. The data node will stop the restart if it discovers that a change has been performed of the number of fragment log files without performing an initial node restart.

FragmentLogFileSize

Same as for *NoOfFragmentLogFiles* it can be done, but requires an initial node restart.

InitFragmentLogFiles

This parameter only affects if files are to be written entirely as part of an initial node restart or not. Thus it can be changed at any time, but will only change the behaviour of initial node restarts and initial cluster starts.

The following parameters also only affect behaviour of initial node restarts and can thus be changed at any time, but the effect will only be seen on the next initial node restart/start.

```
InitialLogfileGroup
InitialTablespace
```

Diskless

This is mostly a test parameter and for use cases where we will never bother with restoring from disk. It is only possible to change through installation of a new cluster. In principle it will work also with an initial node restart.

DataDir

Moving any directories around means that we will no longer find any of our files for recovery. Thus this can only be done through an initial node restart. This holds true also for the following similar parameters.

```
FileSystemPath
BackupDataDir
CompressedLCP
FileSystemPathDD
FileSystemPathDataFiles
FileSystemPathUndoFiles
```

A problem with those parameters is that changing those means that we have no way of checking that the change is correct when the node starts up. Any information about what we started with in previous starts is only accessible in the recovery files and if we moved those to a new location we will not have the capability to verify that they have changed.

Here we will notice that it won't work since the node recovery will fail in one way or the other.

Hostname

Changing the hostname of a node is possible, but given that the entire data node is moving it has to be done through an initial node restart.

It is possible to change the host of a data node without an initial node restart. It requires that the new host have access to the file system of the old host. This is often true in most cloud environments using block devices. In addition the new host must reuse the same hostname/IP address as the previous node.

This is outside the scope of any things MySQL Cluster software deals with, it is done without the NDB software noticing that things have changed.

ServerPort

The port used to connect to a data node cannot be changed. This would require this to be changable dynamically since the *ServerPort* can only change when it is starting up. Since that requires the node to be down, the other nodes cannot also be required to be restarted to update their config.

PortNumber

PortNumber of a management server can be changed, but it requires the use of multiple management servers. The management can move entirely to a new location while the other management servers are up and running. While the management server is down the remaining management servers can change the configuration for the moving management server.

NodeId

The node id of a data node cannot change. Similarly *Nodegroup* cannot change of a data node.

MaxNoOf*

Most of the parameters that specifies the maximum number of objects of various kinds can be changed at any time. It is always safe to change them to a higher value. Changing them to a lower value might fail if not enough memory is available to restart the node. This mainly applies to configuration parameters relating to meta data objects.

ThreadConfig

Most of the things about ThreadConfig can be changed in a node restart. One has to pay special attention to the number of *ldm* threads however. The number of *ldm* threads cannot be set higher than the number of log parts. Normally the number of *ldm* threads should be equal to the number of log parts.

HeartbeatIntervalDbDb

This applies also to *HeartbeatIntervalDbApi*.

This can be changed dynamically. All the nodes must have very similar numbers. The heartbeats are sent with the interval that defaults to 1500 milliseconds. After four missed heartbeats, after around 6 seconds we will fail due to missed heartbeats.

This means that doubling or cutting in half or smaller changes of the heartbeat interval should be safe. One should still change in all nodes through a rolling restart such that they have the same value.

Through multiple steps it is possible to change the heartbeat interval to any value.

47.4 PROCEDURE TO PERFORM ONLINE CONFIG CHANGES

To change the configuration in the cluster requires more than one step. The first step is to change the configuration database as described above. This step doesn't change the running configuration. To change the configuration in the running cluster the nodes must be restarted to read in the new configuration.

To ensure that this change can be performed without downtime we use a rolling restart procedure. This means restarting the data nodes in a sequence. It is important to NOT restart all data nodes at the same time. This would give downtime. The idea is rather to restart one node per node group at a time. In a two-node cluster one first restarts the first data node, when this restart is completed we restart the next data node. In larger clusters one can stop one node per node group at a time to perform the rolling restart.

MySQL Cluster Manager have very good support for performing rolling restarts without much user interaction. Using the management client one can perform the rolling restart through a set of RESTART commands that will perform a graceful shutdown of the nodes (ensures that impact on running transactions is minimised).

Dependent on the change we might also need to restart the API nodes and the management servers.

It is not recommended to change the configuration in the cluster by restarting all nodes at the same time.

The reason for this is that the restart of a node with the new configuration might fail. It is not possible to check the correctness of a change without actually performing a node restart. This is especially true in the case when we want to decrease some resource. In this case it is very important to ensure that the cluster can survive such a configuration change by performing a node restart with the new configuration.

For example if we want to remove some *DataMemory* from each data node and allocate more memory resources for some other resource such as the *DiskPageBufferMemory* it is important to verify that the new *DataMemory* setting is ok by performing a node restart with the new setting. A cluster restart would in this case fail the entire cluster and in worst case the cluster might become unrecoverable, this would not normally happen, but restarting using node restarts is a lot safer in those cases. If any form of corruption would occur due to the configuration change one can always restore the data in the data node by using an initial node restart after changing back to the old configuration.

Normally the configuration changes are safe and should not have any dire consequences, at the same time it is hard to analyse and test every conceivable configuration change that is possible. It is a good idea to follow a safe procedure that never puts the data in NDB at risk.

One possibility might simply be that the memory is overcommitted with a new configuration and this is not possible to test before the change is made. It is usually a good idea to use the configuration parameter *LockPagesInMainMemory* to ensure that we don't get problems with swapping when changing the configuration.

If the node restart fails, one should analyse the node logs and error logs to see why it failed. In many cases there is a proper error message written in those cases. If it fails and it is not possible to deduce why the change failed, then change back to the original configuration.

It is a good idea to consider filing a bug report or write a forum question in the case where the error messages are not easy to understand in those cases. This will help us improving the product to make it easier to manage.

47.5 ONLINE CHANGES OF MySQL SERVER CONFIGURATION

Changing the configuration of a MySQL Server can often be done as an online operation. The MySQL Server can change its configuration using various SET commands. The MySQL manual contains a detailed description of each configuration variable and how they can be changed and the scope of those variables. Some variables exist per connection and some are global in the MySQL Server. This is true also for the NDB specific configuration options in the MySQL Server.

47.6 ONLINE ADD MySQL SERVER

Adding a MySQL Server requires adding a new node to the configuration. The first step here is to add this new node in the configuration using the above procedure to change the configuration database. Next a rolling restart of all the data nodes is performed as described above. After this procedure the cluster is ready to use the new MySQL Servers.

Exactly the same procedure can also be used to add new API nodes.

As usual one should put special care in deciding if these new nodes should have their node id and hostname set in the configuration. Setting those provides for a safer cluster setup and a more managable cluster.

Often it is a good idea to configure with more API nodes than necessary. This commits a bit more memory to the send buffers and receive buffers in the nodes, but if that is ok, it eases the burden of adding new MySQL Servers or API nodes as desired.

To add new API nodes doesn't require restart of MySQL Servers and other API nodes. There are no communication links between those nodes.

47.7 ONLINE CHANGE OF DATA NODE CONFIGURATION

Changing most of the configuration parameters in the data nodes requires a change of the configuration database followed by a rolling restart of all data nodes.

An exception here is if we only want to change the configuration of one data node or a subset of the data nodes. This is rarely something that should be done since most of the time it is best to let the data nodes have the same configuration.

47.8 ONLINE ADD DATA NODE

The most advanced configuration change is adding data nodes. This requires several steps to be performed.

First the new data nodes must be added to the cluster configuration. It is required that they are added using a node group id of 65536. This says that the nodes are not belonging to a node group, so thus they will not yet store any data.

Next a rolling restart is required to ensure that the new nodes are added to the configuration. This rolling restart must also restart all API nodes, all MySQL Servers and all management servers in the cluster. These nodes also need to setup connections with their buffers to the new data nodes. It is important to restart those to prepare them to use the new data nodes.

After this configuration change the new nodes exist in the cluster. It is possible to perform this configuration change as a preparatory step and only make use of those new data nodes long after. They will consume a bit of memory in the nodes to handle send and receive buffers, but other than that there is no special cost of having them in the configuration.

When starting a cluster initially the configuration parameter

StartNoNodeGroupTimeout will specify how long time we will wait for those nodes to startup before we start the cluster. They are not absolutely necessary to startup the cluster. This parameter is by default set to 15000 milliseconds (15 seconds).

The next step is to startup the new nodes. They should be started with the *--initial* flag to ensure that they initialise all the files before coming online.

Next we create new node groups using those new data nodes.

Here is an important thing to consider when adding data nodes. Data nodes are always added in groups at the size of *NoOfReplicas*. With 2 replicas we add the nodes in groups of two nodes. We can add several node groups in one go, but we cannot add single data nodes with missing nodes in the node group.

A new node group is formed of the new nodes by using a command in the management client. Assume we had 4 nodes to start with in 2 node groups. Now we want to add two more nodes with node id 5 and 6 to form a new node group. The command to do this is:

```
CREATE NODEGROUP 5,6
```

Now we have created new node groups. Existing tables don't use those new node groups at the moment. Any new tables created after this command will start using those new node groups.

Now it is possible to reorganise the tables to use those new data nodes.

The algorithm to reorganise a table is specifically developed to ensure that it doesn't increase memory usage on the existing nodes while the reorganisation is ongoing. This makes it quite a lot safer to make this change.

One table at a time is changed by using the command in the MySQL Server used for meta data operations.

```
ALTER TABLE table_name REORGANIZE PARTITIONS;
```

After completing this command for a table it is recommended to also issue the command:

```
OPTIMIZE table_name;
```

This ensures that the space for the rows that was moved to the new node groups is reclaimed such that it can used also by other tables in the cluster. Otherwise the memory will remain allocated to the partitions in the existing tables.

It is recommended to perform a backup before starting this add data node operation.

The above algorithm to reorganise data in the cluster can also be used to make use of new REDO log parts after changing the configuration parameter *NoOfFragmentLogParts*. This change is however not entirely safe since there is no preallocation of the memory required to performed the change. In this case the data is moved from one partition in a data node to another partition in the same data node. Since data is replicated in both partitions during the change this requires additional memory during the change.

It is not recommended to use this command at this point in time. If used it is important to ensure that sufficient memory is available to perform this change otherwise the cluster will be stuck in a situation that is very hard to roll back from. The software will attempt to roll back the change, but there is not a lot of testing of this scenario in our development, thus we do not recommend using it. It should only be used when adding new data node groups.

PART XI

RECOVERY IN MySQL CLUSTER

The next set of chapters deals with something that we put a lot of effort into, how to handle failures in MySQL Cluster. Failures of nodes in MySQL Cluster are expected, but we work hard to ensure that these failures only cause temporary failures, and that the cluster is operational again within milliseconds for software failures and within seconds for a hardware or operating system failure.

The first chapter in this part goes through how we handle node failures in the cluster, which failures lead to cluster crashes and how we handle network partitioning problems.

Next we go through our recovery architecture. It contains a large amount of protocols required to handle node failures, starting up nodes and recovering data in a crash situation.

Next we go through what the user can do to improve the restart times. To understand we go through the major time-consuming parts of the restarts and how to get information about how much time is consumed in each phase of the restart.

The next chapter goes through the start types we use and in which situations they are used.

The restart of an NDB data node goes through a set of phases, we go through the details of these phases and also point to some places in the code where we cover those things in even more deep detail.

CHAPTER 48

CRASH HANDLING

So what type of crashes can we handle in MySQL Cluster? At the beginning of NDB development we had to choose between optimising on fast restart times or surviving a maximum amount of crashes. We decided to focus on surviving as many crashes as possible.

This led to the introduction of node groups. Thus each node group contains one part of the entire database, there is no data shared between node groups (except of course fully replicated tables that are replicated in all node groups). Each node in a node group contains the full data set handled by that node group. The node group concept is more or less the same as the sharding concept used in Big Data applications. The main difference is that sharding is done from the application level and each shard is a stand-alone DBMS that have no synchronisation with other shards.

In NDB the shards (node groups) are all part of the same DBMS and we support both transactions between shards and queries over all the shards in the NDB Cluster. Thereby NDB supports cross-shard transactions, cross-shard queries, cross-shard foreign keys, cross-shard unique indexes while still being able to operate very efficiently using partition pruned index scans that ensure that applications can scale.

NDB supports Online Add Node as described earlier, this means that we can dynamically add new node groups (shards) and we can even reorganize the data in all tables as an online operation while still allowing data to be updated in any manner. Thus NDB support on-line resharding.

An alternative could have been to split out partitions over all nodes in the cluster. In this case all nodes would assist the node starting up, at the same time this architecture would never survive more than one crash at a time. As soon as a second node failed the cluster could not continue to operate.

The node group concept makes it possible to survive the cluster as long as at least one node per node group is still up.

48.1 REPLICATION INSIDE A CLUSTER

The most basic configuration variable in a MySQL Cluster installation is the *NoOfReplicas* variable. This can be set to 1, 2, 3 and 4.

1 means no replication at all and is only interesting when used in a one node cluster when NDB is used as a storage engine for MySQL or as a very simple fast hash table. It can be interesting for application development to minimize resources used during development.

2 replicas is the standard use case for MySQL Cluster and currently the only supported replication configuration. The software can handle also 3 and 4 replicas as well.

48.2 FAILURES SUPPORTED FROM A FULLY FUNCTIONAL CLUSTER

Assume that we have a fully functional cluster, all nodes in all node groups are working. Question is how many failures we can support.

The following rules apply in order: 1) If all nodes in one node group have failed we cannot survive (obviously happens with any failure with 1 replica).

Observation: If 1) is false this means that we have at least one node per node group that is still alive.

2) If at least one node group is fully alive we will survive the set of crashes.

Proof: From observation we can conclude that no node group is completely failed, also we have at least one node group fully alive. Thus the failed nodes cannot survive on their own since they will be missing at least one node group completely. Thus rule 1) means that they will not survive.

3) If no node group is fully dead, but also no node group is fully alive, an arbitrator will decide whether the cluster is able to survive.

Proof: Rule 1) through 2) shows that we have no completely missing or available node group. We have two sets of nodes that both could potentially survive. In this case we would have to crash both if no arbitrator was available or risk network partitioning.

To resolve this situation NDB have an arbitrator role that is used in only this situation.

48.2.1 EXAMPLES OF FAILURES

The most simple example is a cluster with 2 data nodes in one node group. A failure here of only one node requires an arbitrator. Thus the arbitrator is required for the most common and simple example of them all. This means in reality that we need to ensure that the arbitrator is placed on its own node and not colocated with any of the two data nodes.

This is why MySQL Cluster requires at least 3 computers to provide a highly available service. With only 2 nodes we can only survive software failures and 50% of the hardware failures (this covers a lot of cases and isn't that bad). The third computer only needs to run a *ndb_mgmd* program or a simple NDB API application. Thus it can be a much less resourceful computer compared to the data nodes.

In a cluster of 2 replicas with multiple node groups we can survive a crash of one node per node group, but no crashes of two nodes in the same node group. This example shows an obvious reason why it isn't a good idea to place two nodes from the same node group on the same computer. By default node groups are formed from the order in the configuration file or by the order of node ids. By default the two data nodes with the lowest node ids are placed in the first node group (with 2 replicas) and similarly moving forward.

It is possible to specify the node group id for a data node to arrange them in node groups under user control. It is necessary that the config contains as many nodes in each node group as there are replicas in the cluster (set by *NoOfReplicas*).

48.3   ARBITRATOR

The arbitrator is only used in one and only case. This is the case when two clusters can be formed with nodes from all node groups. The arbitrator must have been set up before the crash happens. All live nodes must agree on which node is arbitrator before the crash happens.

When a node discovers a need to ask the arbitrator for permission to continue the node asks the arbitrator for his vote. The arbitrator will say yes to the first node and after that he will say no to the other nodes coming after that. In this manner only one cluster can survive.

Once the arbitrator have voted it cannot be used any more as an arbitrator. Immediately after using the arbitrator the nodes surviving must select a new arbitrator (or the same arbitrator again).

Arbitrator is selected from the set of management servers, API nodes and MySQL Servers in the cluster. The configuration variable *ArbitrationRank* is set on those to provide guidance on which nodes will be selected as arbitrator. Setting it to 0 means the node will never be selected as arbitrator and nodes with rank 2 will always be selected before nodes with rank 1.

48.4   EXTERNAL ARBITRATOR

It is also possible to write your own arbitrator and integrate it with MySQL Cluster. This could be useful e.g. if you absolutely cannot get hold of a third machine for the cluster and you feel safe that you can decide which machine is the one that should survive. It could also be useful when integrating NDB with some Clusterware.

At the time that the data node discover that it has to ask an arbitrator to pick the data node to survive, it will log a message to the cluster log instead of sending a message to our arbitrator.

Continuing after wait for external arbitration, node: 1,2

where 1,2 is a list of the nodes to arbitrate between. It is a list of the node ids for the data nodes to decide which are to survive.

The action that the external clusterware should now perform is to check for this message in the cluster log. When it discovers this message it should ensure that one of the data nodes in the list is properly killed. The surviving node will then assume that it won the arbitration and the other node will be crashed. It is important to consider having a management server in both machines in this case.

For this to work the *ArbitrationTimeout* needs to be set to at least twice the interval required by the clusterware to check the cluster log. The configuration variable *Arbitration* is set to *WaitExternal* for this to happen.

48.5   HANDLING STARTUP AND NETWORK PARTITIONING

When starting after a crash we can provide information about how to proceed. There are a number of configuration variables and startup parameters to data nodes that specifies how to handle startup.

StartPartialTimeout specifies how many seconds we will wait before starting up a partial cluster. The cluster must not be partitioned, thus at least one node group must be fully started. But not necessarily all nodes in the cluster are needed to perform a partial start. This configuration parameter defaults to 30 seconds.

StartPartitionedTimeout specifies how many seconds to wait before we decide to start a partitioned cluster. In this case we can come into a situation of two network partitioned clusters. By default this parameter is set to 60 seconds. It is highly recommended to set it to 0 which means that it will never start up in a partitioned manner.

--nowait-nodes=list specifies a set of nodes that isn't necessary to wait for. This is a manual intervention where the DBA (DataBase Administrator) knows that these nodes are not up and running and thus there is no risk of network partitioning coming from avoiding those nodes. It is ok to start a partial cluster as soon as at least one node group have all nodes, or all nodes except nodes specified in this list. At least one node per node group must be specified to be able to start at all. This parameter is only a startup parameter for the NDB data nodes.

Another special case is handling of nodes belonging to node group 65536. Data nodes belonging to this node group are not part of any node group. They are put into the configuration such that at a later time we can run the command in the management client to add node a new node group. These nodes are not vital to start a cluster. We can set the time to wait for those nodes to start with the configuration parameter *StartNoNodeGroupTimeout*. The default value of this configuration parameter is 15 seconds.

48.5.1 HANDLING NETWORK PARTITIONING

NDB tries to avoid network partitioning for a cluster. The only possible manner to get a partitioned cluster is to have the configuration parameter *StartPartitionedTimeout* set to a non-zero value. This makes it possible to start two parts of the same cluster that have no knowledge of each other. We don't recommend using this option.

To even more ensure that we cannot get into strange situations in this situation we will record the nodes that form in this case. We will not allow the nodes that got excluded to enter back into the cluster other than through an initial node restart.

A similar approach is performed when using the *--nowait-nodes* parameter.

NDB definitely tries to avoid partitioned clusters and focuses on the Consistency and Availability in the CAP theorem. However NDB supports global replication, in this case we can survive in a network partitioned state where two clusters that replicate to each other are both continuing to operate after the network has been partitioned. Later when the network heals the normal replication will ensure that changes are replicated in both directions and that conflicts are properly handled. Thus local NDB cluster focuses on the C and A in the CAP theorem whereas replication between local NDB clusters handles the P part in the CAP theorem.

Our most demanding users always combine a local NDB cluster with replication to one or more other local NDB clusters to provide the very highest availability.

CHAPTER 49

NDB RECOVERY ARCHITECTURE

NDB recovery architecture is an important part of the NDB internal architecture. This is what makes it possible for NDB to deliver availability of 99.9999% (Class 6 availability).

There are a number of parts of the architecture that work collectively to achieve this. To start with there is a transaction protocol, this is based on a combination of a standard two-phase commit protocol and a linear commit protocol to minimize the number of messages sent during the commit phase. We perform a lot of piggybacking of these messages to ensure that packets sent are as big as possible.

The standard two-phase commit protocol is blocking at node failures, this is clearly not a desirable feature of a highly available DBMS. To avoid this we have added a transaction discovery protocol at node failures. When a transaction coordinator fails, the information about the transaction is lost. To rebuild this information a new take-over transaction coordinator is selected. It is always the master data node (the oldest data node living gets this responsibility and more specifically the first *tc* thread instance in this data node). This new transaction coordinator will retrieve information from all Local Data Managers (LDMs) about any transaction they had ongoing with the failed coordinator. A part of this information is the state of the transaction. Using this information the new transaction coordinator is able to complete all transactions that were ongoing in the failed transaction coordinator. In addition it will inform the API about the outcome of the transactions.

NDB have a special signal called *TC_COMMIT_ACK*. This signal is used to ensure that we keep information about the outcome of the transaction until we're safe that the API have heard about it. Thus the API should always hear about the transaction outcome if it was positive. An absence of any message about its outcome means that the failure happened before the transaction had completed and is thus an indication of an abort.

If the API node fails during the transaction there will be no one to report the outcome of the transaction to. It is possible to solve this as well. But this requires an application level solution where each transaction need to write e.g. the transaction id into a special transaction table. Every transaction would have to insert a row with the transaction id as key. After completing the transaction and after ensuring that all parties have been informed of its success the row must be deleted in a separate transaction.

The handling of failed transaction coordinators can be divided up into multiple phases if very many transactions were ongoing at the time of the node crash.

Given the requirements on response times on the order of hundreds of microseconds it was clear that committing write transactions to disk in the commit phase isn't desirable. Rather we ensure that a transaction is safe by committing it in several computers (nodes). This is called Network Durability. Rather than committing to persistent media we commit to multiple network locations.

At the same time it is necessary to restore a consistent database after a complete cluster crash. To ensure this, we added a global checkpoint protocol. This can be seen as a type of group commit protocol. The global checkpoint protocol ensures that transactions are committed to a durable media. This is a phase that happens in the background after the user have received the commit acknowledge. The application can wait for a certain global checkpoint to complete if desirable.

We create a new global checkpoint by using a two-phase commit protocol. First we prepare all nodes for a new global checkpoint, at this point no transaction is allowed to pass the commit point, in the second phase the new global checkpoint is installed and transaction can start committing again. Thus each transaction belongs to a global checkpoint and each transaction that is serialised after another transaction is belonging to a later global checkpoint or the same global checkpoint. This ensures that any recoverable global checkpoint is always a transaction consistent point.

As part of the global checkpoint we ensure that it is recoverable, this happens by forcing the REDO logs written as part of this global checkpoint to disk in all data nodes and later updating a system file that contains a recoverable global checkpoint identity such that we know which global checkpoint that is recoverable.

The recovery of NDB is very much tied to the transaction protocol, the handling of failed transaction coordinators and the global checkpoint protocol. Now if we had access to eternal REDO logs this would be sufficient, but we don't, we need to perform checkpoints (we call those local checkpoints or LCPs). These checkpoints ensure that a version of each row is written to disk such that we can cut the REDO log tail and ensure that we don't run out of REDO log.

The local checkpoint protocol have to take special precautions to handle the fact that a row could consist of both main memory parts and parts that reside on disk. Now these four protocols (transaction protocol, failed coordinator protocol, the GCP protocol and the LCP protocol) take us a long way towards a recoverable NDB. However more is still needed. First of all we need to know which tables, indexes, partitions, foreign keys and other meta data objects that are to be restored.

For this purpose NDB have a schema transaction protocol. This allows for almost arbitrarily complex schema changes to be performed as online operations by performing a technique based on internal triggers.

In addition we need a heartbeat protocol and a node failure protocol. One important part of the distributed transaction theory is that node failures have to be handled as transactions. This means that any transaction have to be serialised in relation to the node failure. To achieve this we use the heartbeat protocol to quickly discover nodes that have failed and we use the node failure protocol to collectively decide on which set of nodes that failed together using a two-phase protocol. We detect node failures in many other ways such that most node failures that are detected by the heartbeat mechanism is either due to real hardware failures or are due to some sort of overload mechanism or an operating system that have stalled our process (was fairly common in early versions of virtual machine implementations).

These seven protocols takes us even further but even more is needed. All recovery protocols contain a master role. This master role must be quickly resumed by some other node when a failure happens. All nodes must select the same master node. Thus in order for this to always happen we have a node registration protocol where nodes always enter the cluster in a specific order that everyone knows about. This node registration protocol is used to select the new master always as the oldest member in the cluster. This registration protocol is part of the heartbeat protocol. An important part of all protocols except the registration protocol is that they all need to handle the following cases.

1. Single node failure of participant

2. Multiple node failures of participants

3. Single node failure of master node

4. Multiple node failures, including a failure of the master node

5. Failure of new master in master take-over handling

When nodes fails and the master is still alive we need to maintain information in the master about ongoing state changes. If a node fails we will normally fake a response signal from the failed node to ensure that the protocol doesn't stop.

For all protocols where the master fails, we start by asking for information about protocol state for this protocol in a discovery protocol. Thus the new master can build up the protocol state such that it can proceed with handling the failed nodes as part of the master takeover protocols.

These eight protocols are the ones that ensure that the protocol to start up nodes can work. We will in addition describe two additional parts of the recovery architecture, the first is the graceful node shutdown protocol and the second is the watchdog mechanism.

The startup as such is in a sense a protocol as well and we will describe it. The startup protocol is a complex set of operations that are linked together, we will describe this in a separate chapter.

Now we will move into describing the ten protocols that form the foundation of the NDB recovery architecture. Each of them has some set of complexity involved in it.

The code itself has fairly extensive documentation of the restart process. This documentation is describing the actual implementation whereas this description describes the workings on a functional level fairly independent of its implementation. The restart process is described in the source file *storage/ndb/src/kernel/blocks/ndbcntr/NdbcntrMain.cpp*.

49.1   TRANSACTION PROTOCOL

As mentioned we use a variant of the two-phase commit protocol with a special protocol to handle failure of transaction coordinators.

The protocol relies on that we always go first to the primary replica before we enter any backup replicas with a write operation. This has the advantage that the transactions are serialised on the primary replica rows. Going to all nodes in parallel means that the risk of deadlock is much higher since we could have two transactions performing a write operation on the same row and coming to the rows in different order they might both be successful in locking the rows in the first replica and thus both will face a deadlock when arriving at the second replica. This is avoided by all operations first going to the primary replica. This is a well known technique in distributed transaction theory and is called primary copy locking. Using this technique it is possible to prove that it is possible to create serialisable transactions. To create fully serialisable transactions one need to implement range locks which NDB doesn't. NDB will perform serialisable transactions as long as no updates of ranges are involved in the transaction.

The figure below shows the normal transaction protocol.

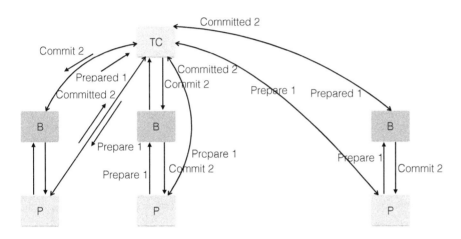

As one can see from this figure the order at commit time is the opposite. Here we commit first on the backup replicas whereafter we commit on the primary replica.

The idea with this order is that the commit point is reached when we arrive at the last replica for commit. Thus not until then are we free to release any locks on the rows in the transaction.

49.1.1 REDO LOGGING IN TRANSACTIONS

We get durability of transactions from the REDO log. At the time a transaction has committed all replicas have been updated, thus all reads after this commit will see the new data. Thus we are Network Durable after commit by relying on multiple computers to have the transaction stored in memory. The REDO log will be synchronized as part of the global checkpoint protocol. In order to make a transaction Durable both on network and on multiple persistent medias we rely on writing the REDO logs to disk as part of the global checkpoint protocol.

49.2 Transaction coordinator failure protocol

When developing the transaction protocol it was obvious that the two-phase commit protocol as such is blocking. One variant used in another distributed telecom database developed in the 1990s was to use a backup transaction coordinator.

I wasn't satisfied with this solution. This solution would still fail if we had two simultaneous node failures.

Instead I opted for designing a special failure protocol to rebuild the transaction state at failures. This is possible since the NDB data nodes are part of an integrated system. This is not possible in most modern database solutions where each data server is an independent database as well. E.g. there is no manner for how to rebuild a transaction state in MySQL InnoDB Cluster, in Galera Cluster, in MongoDB or in any other database technology that builds a distributed database from a number of independent database servers. This technique was called federated databases in the past.

However in NDB we can ask each transaction participant about its transaction state. The signal *LQH_TRANSREQ* is sent from the take over *tc* thread to all *ldm* threads in the cluster. Each *ldm* thread (or more accurately each *LQH* block instance) will go through all transactions that was ongoing. For each operation it finds that used the failed node as transaction coordinator it will send the information about this transaction to the take over *tc* thread.

When all operations have been found it will inform the take over *tc* that it has completed its scan of transaction operations.

Using this information it is possible to rebuild the transaction state and ensure that the transaction is either committed or aborted. It is not possible to continue the transaction after building up this state. The transaction must complete as part of the node failure handling, either aborting it or committing it.

The protocol is designed such that it can handle a subset of the transactions at a time if the *take over tc* doesn't have sufficient memory to handle all at the same time.

49.3 Global Checkpoint protocol

When a transaction have committed it is necessary to ensure that it is still durable when all nodes of the cluster fails. The solution to this comes from using logs that are flushed to durable disk media. In NDB it is sufficient to flush the REDO logs to disk to make the transactions durable.

However in flushing the REDO log records to disk it is important that we ensure that the restored data is transaction consistent. To recover a transaction consistent point it is not sufficient to randomly flush REDO log records. It is necessary to ensure that all transactions up to a certain point is restored and no transaction after this point.

NDB creates such a point using the global checkpoint protocol. In NDB we create a global checkpoint (identified by a GCI, global checkpoint identifier) regularly. By default a new global checkpoint is created once per 1-2 seconds. It is possible to create those more often and less often, if we create them more often less transactions are lost in a cluster crash at the same time we have to perform more disk flushes and execute the global checkpoint protocol more often.

The global checkpoint protocol is controlled by the master node in the cluster (the oldest node in the cluster). It starts by sending a *GCP_PREPARE* message to all nodes in the cluster. At reception of this message the node stops committing transactions. It is still ok to continue preparing transactions and it is still ok to continue committing transactions that have already passed the commit point. Each node replies to the master indicating that they have completed the GCP prepare phase.

The master node waits for all live nodes to respond back, when they have, the master node immediately sends a *GCP_COMMIT* message to all live nodes. At reception of this message the queued transactions can start up again, they will get the new GCI as will any transactions committed after receiving this message.

Using this protocol we know that any transaction in GCI *n+1* is serialised after all transactions belonging to GCI *n* and earlier GCIs. The reason is that at the point when a transaction reached the commit point (at this point it has acquired all necessary locks) for a transaction in GCI *n+1* it knew that all transactions belonging to GCI *n* will either be before it in serialisation or independent of it. If it is independent of it, it is serialisable to it since it can be placed before both and after the transaction and thus it can surely be placed after. If there is a dependency it is certain that transactions belonging to GCI *n* to be before since they acquired the lock definitely before any transaction belonging to GCI *n+1* due to the global checkpoint protocol where we ensure that all nodes freeze commits for a short time to ensure that we get a serial order of global checkpoints.

The prepare and commit phase have done the job of ensuring that we have a transaction consistent point available for recovery.

Before a global checkpoint can be used in recovery it has to be flushed to disk first.

The flushing happens in a second phase of the global checkpoint protocol. At first we send a message to all nodes instructing each node to send a response back when all transactions belonging to the given GCI has completed. When all nodes have responded to this message we are sure that all transactions belonging to the GCI have either reached the REDO log or its buffers in all nodes. This phase is combined with the *GCP_COMMIT* phase. There is no need to immediately respond to *GCP_COMMIT* so we respond when all transactions belonging to the GCI have completed.

If a large transaction is committed as part of this GCI, this wait can take some time since a lot of commit and complete messages have to be sent as part of this phase. Normally it will be very quick. The only impact of this delay is that it will take a bit longer to make the GCP durable on disk.

The next step is to send *GCP_SAVEREQ* to all nodes instructing them to flush all log parts up to the GCI. When all nodes have responded to this message we know that the GCI is recoverable.

It is perfectly possible that some log records belonging to GCI *n+1* is flushed to disk as part of this. There is no serial order of GCPs in one specific REDO log. This is not a problem, at recovery we know which GCI we are recovering and we will skip any log records with a higher GCI than the one we are recovering.

The final problem is to ensure that we can easily discover which GCI is recoverable. This phase sends a *COPY_GCIREQ* message to all nodes, this message will write a special file called *P0.sysfile*. It is written in a safe manner in two places to ensure that it is always available at recovery. This last phase isn't absolutely necessary, but to avoid it would require scanning all REDO logs before we start recovery, we opted for this simpler variant instead.

These four messages back and forth from the master node will ensure that a global checkpoint is recoverable.

The global checkpoint protocol is a corner stone of the recovery architecture in NDB. The first two phases are used for creating *micro GCIs*. These *micro GCIs* are used for creating epochs in MySQL Replication for NDB. Thus we replicate one *micro GCI* at a time over to the slave cluster.

49.4   Local checkpoint protocol

The approach in MySQL Cluster 7.5 and earlier versions is that the entire database is written to disk during each LCP. There is a lot of modifications to this in the 7.6 DMRs.

Starting point of LCP

The starting point of the LCP is an important point. The data in the database at start of the LCP must be retained in a fuzzy manner in the LCP on disk. What this means is in this case is that exactly the rows that are present at the start of the LCP of a fragment must exist in the fragment LCP on disk. If a row doesn't exist at the time of the start of the LCP it cannot exist in the LCP on disk either. The actual row data might be different. After restoring the LCP we will execute the REDO log to bring the data content to the global checkpoint that the data node had written before it crashed.

In a system restart this is the data recovered, in a node restart we also need to synchronize the data with a node that is alive with the most up to date version of the data.

Local checkpoints also write the disk data parts. The references from the main memory row at start of the LCP and the reference from the disk row back to the main memory part of the row must be retained in the LCP on disk. The disk data reference from main memory row doesn't change unless the row is deleted. If a row is deleted before it was sent to the LCP, the row will be copied and queued up for immediate sending to the LCP on disk.

The disk data parts use an UNDO log to ensure that the data pages of the table partition has exactly the rows at start of the LCP. This is accomplished by writing an UNDO log record representing the start of the LCP. Next each change of the row is UNDO logged. Each time we make an update to a disk data page we will update the page LSN (Log Sequence Number). This ensures that when the page is written to disk we know which UNDO log records need to be applied and which can be ignored.

Write phase

The actual writes to disk of the LCP happens in a fuzzy checkpoint. We start by writing the main memory row parts. We perform a full table partition scan such that all rows will be retrieved. We retrieve up to 6 rows at a time, we have some special mechanisms to ensure that LCP writing has higher priority at very high loads to ensure that LCP writing is done at the rate we need it to be. If we have filled our quota for LCP writing we will back off from writing until we get more quota to write again. We get a new quota once per 100 milliseconds.

The LCP simply takes the row format as it is and copies it to disk. The operation to write the row is very simple. It must copy the fixed size part of the row first and next the variable sized part of the row.

When the writing of the main memory parts are done we record the maximum global checkpoint identifier that was written during this write phase. The LCP is not usable for restore until this global checkpoint is restorable. We cannot remove the LCP files from the previous LCP of this table partition until we are sure that this global checkpoint is restorable.

Actually the LCP of a table fragment isn't considered complete until the entire LCP is completed. The reason is that disk columns are checkpointed at the end of the LCP and before those are checkpointed the LCPs aren't completed. Thus we will have to store 2 local checkpoints per fragment on disk at the end of an LCP.

Next step is to write the disk data pages that are dirty to disk. The UNDO log will ensure that those pages are transported back to the start of the LCP at recovery, we need not care about what is written on those pages while we are checkpointing, the UNDO logger will handle that.

LONG-RUNNING TRANSACTIONS

Each operation in the REDO log consists of two parts. The prepare part and the commit part. We will execute the REDO log operation when we find a commit entry. The commit entry will refer to the prepare entry. The prepare entry is written at prepare of the write operation, if a long time goes by after preparing before committing the transaction we will have to keep the change records in memory as well as we cannot cut the REDO log tail beyond the prepare records we have written for prepared transactions. Long-running transactions can lead to that we miss finding prepare entries in the REDO log buffer when executing REDO logs. They can slow down restart execution.

NDB isn't intended for long-running transaction applications. A certain amount of long-running transactions can be handled by proper configuration, but it isn't intended to perform transactions that takes several minutes to complete or that changes more than 10% of the database in one set of transactions running in parallel. Again it is possible to configure it for that, but it will use more memory and disk resources. A better approach is to divide your changes into appropriately sized transactions (can still be fairly large) that executes without awaiting user input.

GENERAL THOUGHTS ON LCPs

The execution of LCPs is controlled by the master node. The nodes will send a report about completed checkpoints to all data nodes. We retain this information in the *DIH* block, and use it at recovery to decide which LCP to use in restore.

An LCP only writes down the row content, no information about indexes is written to checkpoints, instead the indexes are rebuilt during restart.

The whole purpose of the LCP protocol is to cut the REDO and UNDO log, this happens after completing a full LCP on all table partitions. The actual point in time when this cut is performed is at the start of the next LCP. At this point we move both the REDO log tail forward as well as the UNDO log tail.

49.5 SCHEMA TRANSACTION PROTOCOL

It is recommended that all tables are created from a MySQL Server. If they are created from the NDB API they cannot be used from the MySQL server since the MySQL Server creates an FRM file that needs to exist for a table to be accessible. This will change in MySQL Cluster 8.0 since MySQL 8.0 implements a Data Dictionary.

In NDB, schema operations are smaller than SQL statements. For example when adding a new table it might consist of a new table, a new hash map, a new set of indexes (hashed and ordered). It might also add foreign keys to the table.

In NDB we have implemented the possibility to declare a set of those schema operations as a schema transaction. The schema transaction is executed in a number of phases, each phase have an abort operation as well that makes it possible to roll back a schema transaction.

The implementation is fairly general and we can probably some time in the future even move towards schema transactions involving multiple tables. However for the moment it is limited to supporting the subset of DDL operations that MySQL Cluster supports for NDB tables.

This schema transaction implementation is something we have worked hard on in many versions of MySQL Cluster. The current implementation of schema transactions is the fourth generation of the meta data implementation in NDB.

The first phase was very simple and had most of the data hard coded, this implementation had severe issues already early. We substituted it with a new implementation that used a serialised format for sending over schema information. The third generation of the meta data implementation standardised on handling of schema operations where each operation had a set of methods and each of those methods had a callback used to execute it.

The fourth phase implemented a protocol that executes each step of the schema transaction in lock-step mode. This means that a schema transaction is defined in a specific order and we keep track of exactly what in this order that have completed and what haven't. This makes it possible at recovery to see exactly which steps that have already executed. Many of those steps also have to be synchronised to disk in the cluster.

Schema transactions are not super fast, but they are reliable and can handle arbitrarily complex schema transactions.

A schema transaction has a commit point, if it passed this point the transaction will be rolled forward even in the case of node restarts and system restarts.

The most complex schema transaction we support is most likely the operation to reorganize a table to make use of new node groups added since the table was created.

This involves creating a set of new fragments on the new node groups. It also means that we have to copy over the data from the old table partitions to the new table partitions.

49.6 NODE REGISTRATION PROTOCOL

The node registration protocol is an important part of the node recovery handling. We can only add one node at a time to the cluster. This protocol is described in some more detail in the source file *storage/ndb/src/kernel/blocks/qmgr/QmgrMain.cpp*.

The nodes currently in the cluster must agree on the node to add next. The reason is that nodes have a dynamic order id. Thus we know which nodes is the currently oldest node in the cluster. We will always select the oldest node in the cluster as the master node in the cluster.

49.7   HEARTBEAT PROTOCOL

The heartbeat protocol uses the order of nodes acquired by the node registration protocol and always sends heartbeats to the next node in the dynamic order. Similarly it expects to receive heartbeats from the node before it in dynamic order. The newest node will send heartbeats to the oldest node and vice versa the oldest node will expect heartbeats from the newest node.

Heartbeats have a special signal. Normally this signal isn't used. Every signal received from a node is treated as a heartbeat, so the transport layer assists in the heartbeat protocol. The reason was that in high load cases the heartbeat signal sometimes got so far into the send buffer that the heartbeat timeout happened before it got to the other node.

49.8   NODE FAILURE PROTOCOL

Node failures are discovered in numerous ways. If a data node closes the TCP/IP socket to another data node, the other node will treat this as a node failure. Missing heartbeats for more than the heartbeat period (four times the heartbeat timeout) will trigger a node failure handling protocol.

Sometimes a node behaves in a weird manner, in this case the node might be shut down by another node sending a shutdown signal to it.

When the node failure protocol starts, it sends a prepare message to all nodes with the list of failed nodes. A node receiving this message will be able to add to the list of failed nodes. It will not be able to remove nodes from the list.

When all nodes have replied to this we might have a new set of failed nodes. If so we send another round of prepare messages. Eventually the set of nodes will agree on the failed nodes. After that we will commit the node failures. Thus each node failure set is agreed upon by all surviving nodes in the cluster. Thus we can trust that all nodes see the same view on the list of nodes alive after the node failure transaction is completed.

Now that we have decided on the set of failed nodes we will start handling the node failures. This includes handling each and every distributed protocol.

In particular it involves handling the failure of the transaction coordinator in many transactions as described in the section above.

49.9   GRACEFUL SHUTDOWN PROTOCOL

A crash shutdown works just fine for many cases. However we have implemented a graceful shutdown to ensure that no transactions are aborted during a planned shutdown of a node.

A graceful shutdown is initiated from the NDB MGM client (*ndb_mgm* binary).

A graceful shutdown will ensure that no more transactions are started in the node. It will allow for already started transactions to complete before it shuts down the node. If transactions are still running after a few seconds they will be aborted.

49.10 Watchdog handling

Every thread in the NDB data nodes are protected by a watchdog thread. For most of the time
the watchdog is not showing up at all. As soon as a thread is non-responsive for more than 100
milliseconds we will get printouts of this in NDB. Watchdog printouts can come due to bugs in
NDB code, but it can also come if the OS have problems in delivering a real-time experience.
During early phases of restart it is fairly normal to get some printouts of some watchdog issues
during memory allocation.

If the watchdog doesn't hear any progress in a thread for the watchdog timeout (about one
minute) it will crash the data node. If this happens it is usually due to an NDB bug where we
end up in some loop that we don't get out of. The watchdog thread is there to ensure that we
will come out with a crash even if there is no crashing code.

49.11 Node restart activities

During restart we use the LCP to restore the rows. We bring the disk data parts back to their
starting point by applying the UNDO log. Next we run the REDO log to recover the node to a
specific GCP. After this we rebuild the ordered indexes.

After this we come to a very important part of the recovery, we have a node that is recovered
to an old but consistent GCP. At the same time we have a live node that has continued to
update the rows.

The next step is to synchronize the live node with the starting node. We didn't want to
rely on any logs for this part. This would require us to keep the logs for a very long time, it
would complicate the REDO logs since we would need to read and write them at the same
time. In addition any synchronization using logs requires a point in time where we have to stop
transactions to allow the node to participate in transactions again.

To avoid all of this we instead rely on synchronising the starting node using the data in the
live node. In MySQL Cluster 5.1 we implemented a mechanism that synchronizes row ids. We
ensure that rows in all replicas share the same row id. Each row has a GCI that specifies the
last GCI it was written. This makes it easy to scan all rows in the live node in row id order.

For each row in the live node that is stamped with a GCI that is higher than the restored
GCI in the starting node we start a synchronization of the rows. We must handle deleted rows
as well, thus even deleted rows must be synchronized with the starting node. If an entire page
of row ids have been deleted the row ids of this page will be synchronized with the live node.

When we are about to synchronize the rows we start by taking a shared lock on the row in
the live node. After this we send a write operation to the starting node with the row content
(or a delete operation). We rely on signal ordering such that we can release the row lock
immediately after reading the row and not wait for the write operation to complete.

During the synchronization phase the starting node participates in each transaction. If a
transaction handles a row that have not yet been synchronized we will act as if we successfully
performed the change. If the transaction happens after the synchronization of the row, we will
change the row as for a normal write operation.

In my Ph.D this mechanism was proven to be correct by reasoning about the various
operations that can occur in a transaction.

During this synchronization phase the REDO log is not active for any fragment. When all fragments have been synchronized we activate the REDO log for all fragments.

The final step in ensuring that data is recoverable in the starting node we wait until the starting node have participated in an LCP. After this have happened the node is recoverable again and the node can survive even if the live node would die.

49.12 Initial node restart activities

The default behaviour of an initial node restart is very similar to a node restart. The only difference is that it restores GCI 0, thus all fragments are empty.

This means that the synchronization phase have to synchronize all rows.

By setting the configuration parameter *TwoPassInitialNodeRestartCopy* to 1 we change the recovery for initial node restarts. This is the recommended setting and is default in 7.6.

With this setting the synchronization happens in two phases. The first phase synchronizes all rows from the live node. There is no ordered index created in this first phase. Thus this synchronization phase is faster.

Next we execute a parallel ordered index build. It is much faster to build indexes in parallel compared to building them while inserting rows.

The last phase is a normal synchronization that uses the GCI that happened immediately before the first synchronization phase started.

Chapter 50

Optimising restart times

As a DBA for a highly available MySQL Cluster installation you are likely to have requirements on restart times for MySQL Cluster. In this chapter we will discuss the options available to impact restart times.

The restart has around 20 different phases, most of those phases are fairly quick. There is an *ndbinfo* table that gives information on restarts and the exact time we spent in these different phases.

Here we will focus on the most important phases that consumes most of the time.

50.1 Early phases

Most of the early phases are normally executed quickly. There are occasions when they can take some time.

The first phase is to allocate a node id. This phase can wait for the node failure handling to complete. When a node fails the transactions need to be completed for all ongoing transactions this node was responsible for. A number of protocols need to be completed before the node failure handling is complete. As long as the node failure handling is still ongoing in the cluster it won't be possible to allocate the node id.

Next phase is to be included into the heartbeat protocol. The registration of a new nodes takes 1-3 seconds. If many nodes start in parallel this phase might take some time.

Next we have to wait until all nodes required for the restart are up and running. For a node restart this is normally very short. In a cluster start or a system restart of the cluster enough nodes have to be available for the start to be able to proceed. This phase might have to wait for nodes to start up.

Next there is a short phase waiting for permission to be included into the cluster followed by waiting for an appropriate time to copy the meta data over to the starting node. Starting up an LCP might block the start of a node for a short time, in 7.3 and older versions this time was considerable, but in 7.4 and newer versions it is at most a few seconds normally.

The next phase copies over the meta data, the length of this phase is dependent on the amount of tables and other meta data in the cluster. It is normally a very short phase.

Next we have a phase to include node in a number of important protocols. Next a phase to start up the local recovery of a node.

After these phases we move into the phases where the actual database recovery happens. This is where most restarts spend a majority of their time.

50.2 LOAD DATA PHASE

The first phase that can take considerable time is the load data phase. This phase reads in the data from the local checkpoint files. This phase executes in parallel on all LDM threads. The time it takes for this phase is directly dependent on the amount of data to restore. With records of a few hundred bytes in size it is likely that each LDM thread will be capable of sustaining a few hundred thousands records per second and even up to a million records per second. Thus we can sustain several million records per second during this recovery phase. Thus even a database of of 200 GByte should be loaded within 3 minutes. This requires the file system to be able to sustain reading more than 1 GByte per second from disk into memory.

The user considerations for this phase are:

1. Ensure disks can sustain the speed used by the LDM threads

2. Ensure that the number of LDM threads is sufficient in the data node

3. Ensure that the larger tables are spread among all LDM threads

Most of the considerations are fairly automatic, the only considerations that are important is to select the proper hardware, both regarding CPU resources and disk resources and ensure that the amount of LDM threads is sufficiently high to meet the requirements on restart times.

50.3 UNDO LOG EXECUTION

The UNDO log execution is only used for disk data tables. The amount of UNDO logs is directly dependent on the amount of changes to the disk data content in NDB.

The execution of the UNDO log starts by reading the UNDO log in the *rep* thread. Next one looks up the table and fragmentation identity in the page. This read of a page in the extra PGMAN block is necessary to be able to route the log message to the correct LDM thread.

The LDM threads executes the UNDO logs in serial mode.

A normal rule is to try to configure the data nodes such that a local checkpoint takes about 5 minutes to execute. If this is the case the UNDO log should be possible to execute in no more than a few minutes. The UNDO log execution needs to read the pages from disk to change them. Thus the disks used for the UNDO log and more particularly for the data files of the tablespace should be high performance disks.

The user considerations for this phase are:

1. Ensure disks used for tablespaces can read data pages quickly

2. Ensure disks used for UNDO log can read and write sequentially at sufficient speed

3. Ensure that the number of LDM threads is sufficient in the data node

4. Ensure that the data nodes are configured to complete LCPs at predictable time

50.4   REDO LOG EXECUTION

After finishing loading data and executing the UNDO log we are ready to execute the REDO log.

The amount of REDO logs to execute is completely dependent on the amount of writes performed before the crash time combined with how long time have passed since the last local checkpoint of the table partitions to restore.

Executing a REDO log record takes similar time to executing the operation except that no distributed commit is necessary. The code used to execute the REDO log operations is the same code used to execute normal user transactions.

To keep the time for executing the REDO log records low it is important to keep the time of executing a full local checkpoint short. This can be accomplished by using higher disk write speeds. It is possible to increase CPU usage during normal operation to decrease restart time and so it is possible to increase throughput during normal operation at the expense of longer restart times.

50.5   REBUILD ORDERED INDEXES

Rebuilding ordered indexes is a completely CPU bound activity. We will use all CPUs available in the configuration or a high number of parallel threads that will make use of most of the available CPU resources. It is not possible to parallelise to more than two times the number of LDM threads. Again to decrease the restart time it is a good idea to set the number of LDM threads appropriately.

This is configurable through configuration variable *BuildIndexThreads*. This is by default set to 0. This can be set to 128 to fully parallelise ordered index builds.

50.6   REBUILD UNIQUE INDEXES

The unique indexes are implemented as normal tables that are maintained using internal triggers using the transaction protocol. There is no specific need to rebuild unique indexes during recovery, it is rebuilt as any normal table. A unique index table doesn't have any ordered indexes on it, thus there is no specific ordered index build processing.

The hash index is built and maintained by the process that installs checkpoints and by the REDO log execution and by the copy fragment execution. All of these processes use exactly the same code path that any normal transaction is using.

50.7   COPY FRAGMENT PHASE

After completing the rebuild of the ordered indexes we have restored an old version of the database. However to get from here to an up-to-date version we need to synchronize each row with a live node. This is the aim of the copy fragment phase where one table partition at a time is brought on-line.

The copy fragment phase knows the last global checkpoint that the restored data contains. Thus no rows with older GCI (global checkpoint identifier) are required to copy from the live nodes to the starting node. Each row has a GCI field where we stamp the GCI that updated this row. Thus the live node will scan all rows in the table partition and check for each row if the GCI field contains a GCI higher than the GCI restored on the starting node. We know the GCI where we have all rows restored for each of the table partitions.

This phase will scan all rows in the live node and copy over all changes to the starting node. This will happen in parallel in each LDM thread in the live node and the starting node.

Before the copying of a fragment starts up, the distribution handler will ensure that the starting node will participate in all transactions. This ensures that after copying a row it will be kept up-to-date.

During the copy fragment phase we will have to write UNDO logs for all changes to disk data parts. After completing the copy fragment execution we will enable the REDO logs for each fragment.

The time for the copy fragment is again dependent on the number of LDM threads. It is highly dependent on the load in the live node while performing this phase. If the live node is busy serving user transactions this will give less CPU time for the restart of the starting node. There will always be progress, this phase will eventually complete also in highly loaded clusters.

50.8 LOCAL CHECKPOINT PHASE

After completing the copy fragment phase we have restored an up-to-date version of the data. We cannot yet recover the node without assistance from the live node(s). To make it recoverable on its own we need to perform a local checkpoint. This is a normal LCP that all nodes alive is participating in.

After completing this phase we have a data node that can recover on its own without aid of other nodes.

50.9 INITIAL NODE RESTART

Initial node restart is a bit special and need to be considered. In this case there is no data to start with. All the data comes from the live nodes through the copy fragment execution.

In this case we can use two phases by setting the configuration parameter

TwoPassInitialNodeRecovery. The first phase copies over all rows of the table partition. This phase doesn't enable the starting node to participate in transactions. After copying all data over we will start the rebuild index phase.

When the rebuild ordered index phase is completed we are in the same state as after rebuilding the ordered indexes for a normal node restart. Thus we continue with a second phase of copy fragment, this is performed in the same fashion as the traditional one. We have kept track of the oldest GCI we have data for, we need not copy rows over with GCI older than this GCI.

There is a configuration variable enabling this two-phase approach for initial node restarts.

50.10 Handling MySQL Replication Servers

The final phase in the restart is to setup the MySQL replication server. The new node needs to be known by the MySQL servers that act as replication servers to ensure that they know that they can go to this node to fetch event records. This phase requires the MySQL Replication servers to be up and running, otherwise we will wait for a configurable time which is two minutes by default before we proceed and announce the node as restarted.

50.11 Final words

There is an *ndbinfo* table called *restart_info* that records the times of each the 20 phases of a restart and how long time it takes. This can be used to understand which phase of the restart is your problem and considering how to improve the speed of recovery in this part.

After going through all restart phases we see that enabling as many CPUs to work on the restart in parallel as possible is important to shorten restart times. This can be accomplished by using machines with more CPUs and configuring to use more LDM threads. At the same time more LDM threads means more partitions of the tables and thus a higher startup cost for table scans that are not able to use pruned partition scans.

We can spend resources on executing faster LCPs during normal operation to decrease restart times and similarly we can increase throughput of normal operations at the expense of longer restart times.

For example by having a very large REDO log we can decrease the disk write speed and spend more resources on normal transactions. Thus the time to execute the UNDO log and REDO log will take longer and this in turn will increase the time for synchronizing the live nodes since they had more time to drift apart.

Contrary by setting a very high disk write speed we will ensure that LCPs execute rapidly and thus we can decrease the time spent in executing UNDO logs, REDO logs and synchronization of starting nodes. This will come at the expense of using more CPU time during normal operation to write LCPs.

CHAPTER 51

NDB STARTUP

There are four types of NDB startup. Initial start of the cluster, node restart after a node failed where the rest of the cluster is operational, system restart that restarts the cluster after the entire cluster failed or was shut down. The final variant is an initial node restart that is a node restart where the node starts from scratch.

This chapter will also discuss the start phases used when starting a data node.

51.1 INITIAL START

Initial start is the very first start of a new cluster. Before starting we have prepared a configuration file and we have prepared machines, OS and file systems to house the database files for NDB.

An initial start takes some time primarily to initialise the REDO logs, the system tablespace and the UNDO log files. The reason for those to take time is that we ensure that the entire file is written. Since those files can be very big it can take some time. If we don't write them at initial start the file system doesn't guarantee that the necessary file space is allocated. It is possible to use some configuration variables that avoids writing all of the files, but this doesn't guarantee that we have the file space. Thus if using those configuration variables we can run out of REDO log file space in the middle of writing to the REDO log.

Other than that the initial start is fairly quick and completed in less than a minute. A very large node could consume some time allocating memory, normally it takes about one second per gigabyte of memory allocated.

51.2 NODE RESTART

If a node shut down, or failed, while the rest of the cluster is operational, the restart is normally using a node restart.

A node restart starts by a local recovery up to the point where the node failed. The data has continued changing after the node failed. After the local recovery has been completed we synchronize the data with a live node in the same node group.

This synchronization is done row id by row id. Each row in NDB has at least a small fixed size memory header part. It can also have a variable sized memory part and a fixed size disk part. The row id of a row is the logical address of the fixed memory part of the row. Pages in a fragment starts at page 0 and continues upwards. Each page contains a set of rows, the number of rows per page is dependent on the amount of columns that use the fixed size part of the row. The fixed size part has faster access, but it is less flexible in memory operations.

When a node is restarting it synchronizes row id by row id. For this synchronisation to work it is essential that a row has the same row id in all replicas. There are extremely rare cases when an insert fails to allocate the row id on the other replicas, this is a temporary error 899 that we've worked very hard to remove as much as possible. It is now so rare that one should report it as a bug if it occurs.

There are a number of cases to handle at synchronisation, the row in the starting node and the live node could be the same and there is nothing to do. We discover this by checking the GCI on the row. The starting node has all the updates up to a certain GCI, so any row in the live node that has the same GCI or a lower GCI have no need of synchronisation.

If the row has changed it is possible that a row id exists in the live node that doesn't exist in the starting node, in this case we have to insert the new row in the starting node. The opposite can happen where we need to delete the row in the starting node. The next is that the row can have been updated, in this case we have two different cases. If both rows have the same primary key one simply updates the row with the new information in the row. It is possible that the primary key differs (this can happen when the original row is deleted followed by a new insert that uses the same row id as the old row). If the primary key differs we have to first delete the old row in the starting node followed by an insert of the new row.

The local recovery first reads in a checkpoint, applies the UNDO log on the disk data parts, synchronises these pages to disk after completing the UNDO log execution. Next the REDO log is executed from the local REDO log. Next any ordered indexes are rebuilt.

The synchronisation is performed with a live node. During the synchronisation phase (copy fragment phase) no REDO logs are generated. After the synchronisation phase is completed the started node has exactly the same data as the live node(s) in the node group. The data is not recoverable yet though. The final step is to write a checkpoint that makes the data recoverable.

51.3 SYSTEM RESTART

A system restart is a restart that involves all nodes of the cluster. During a system restart the cluster is not available. The nodes perform the same actions as during a node restart except that there is no need to run the synchronisation phase. After executing the REDO log and rebuilding the ordered indexes and performing a local checkpoint the cluster is operational again.

51.4 INITIAL NODE RESTART

The final restart variant is initial node restart, this is a node restart that starts from a node that has an empty file system.

This can be used in a number of cases. The first case is if the file system of the node was corrupted. In this case one can start the node from scratch again after repairing the file system and removing all old files of the node.

In some cases it is necessary to use this restart type for complex upgrades.

Downgrade support is an important feature in a system that is required to always be available). If there is something that is not working correctly during an upgrade or after the upgrade, this could be problem in MySQL Cluster, it could be application issues since one often upgrades the application software at the same time. Supporting downgrade is important for applications that really care about uptime of their applications.

One can use initial node restart to upgrade computers. One takes down the old node, replaces it with a new node and gives it the same IP address and restarts the node from scratch. In this manner it is possible to upgrade the node to use a more recent hardware.

51.5 NDB START PHASES

NDB restart is controlled at a number of different levels. At first we need to start up the virtual machine that controls the execution of the actual database code.

51.5.1 STARTING NDB VIRTUAL MACHINE

The NDB virtual machine consists of a set of threads, there is a set of threads called *ldm* threads. *ldm* stands for Local Data Manager. These threads take care of handling the actual data, the REDO log, the hash indexes, the ordered indexes. This is the heart of the data node process. There can be between 1 and 32 such threads.

The next thread type is the *tc* threads that deals with transaction control. There can be up to 16 such threads.

There is one *main* thread that handles meta data, takes care of a number of restart activities. There is always one of this thread type.

Next there is one *rep* thread, this thread takes care of asynchronous replication and event reporting of data changes. It is possible to subscribe to changes and get asynchronous event signals for every data change in the database. It also takes care of the UNDO log handler, some proxy functions of the various blocks (proxy functions are used to handle control functions involving multiple threads).

The above threads are called block threads. These threads almost entirely spend their time executing signals sent to blocks residing in their thread. A block is a set of data and code, only one thread is executing at a time in a block except for some actions by the *tc* threads that need to access some shared data structures that are updated by the *main* thread. We will go through the most common signal flows in NDB in a later chapter.

There is a number of *recv* threads. These can also execute signals, but they also handle all the actions to receive data on the sockets connecting the data node to other nodes in the cluster. The *recv* threads communicate with other threads using the same mechanism used to communicate between any block threads. This mechanism is a memory buffer unique for communication between two distinct block threads. The only synchronisation mechanism needed for this communication is carefully placed memory barriers.

There is a set of *send* threads. These can't execute signals, they are only used to send signals to other nodes that the block threads didn't take care of by themselves. They communicate with other threads using mutexes and signals.

There is a large set of file threads, these threads makes it possible to access the file system using synchronous file operations by code written as asynchronous signals sent between blocks. They communicate with the NDBFS block residing in the *rep* thread using mutexes and signals.

There is a watchdog thread checking that threads continue to make progress.

Before the actual database start phases can start we need to start all those threads, this includes setting up CPU locking and thread priorities for these threads. We need to initialise the communication subsystem. We need to setup the communication subsystem to communicate between threads, we allocate most of the memory (some of it is allocated during the first phase of the database start as well) before the actual database start phases start.

At a high level one can say that we start the virtual machine first before we start the actual database engine.

A very important thing that happens even before this is to read the configuration from the NDB management server. The configuration contains information about how many threads of various types to use, how much memory of various types to allocate and all sorts of other things.

Reading the configuration is done over the network by connecting to the NDB management server. This is why the address information where to find the NDB management server is normally supplied as a command parameter when starting the *ndbmtd* program.

One special variant of the NDB data node is to use the *ndbd* program. This program has one and only one block thread and this thread take care of the activity of the send threads and receive threads.

51.5.2 PHASES USED TO START THE NDB DATA NODE

When the virtual machine has completed starting up it is time to start up the actual database engine. This is controlled by a block called *Missra* that is a sub-block of NDBCNTR. This block starts by sending a signal called STTOR with phase 1 to all blocks, one block at a time. The block takes care of the action to be performed in phase 1 and in addition it sends a signal STTORRY where it reports which phases the block is interested in. When a block exists in multiple threads it will execute the phase in each thread in a serial manner. Thus the execution order of a startup is completely deterministic internally in a node.

In addition a starting node communicates with other live nodes and with other starting nodes. This communication is necessary to synchronise the startup to ensure that recovery is done in the correct way.

In the block NDBCNTR, a large comment explains the various start phases and what they do. At a high level the first phase does some memory allocation and a lot of data initialisation. The second and third phase builds up a number of data structures, most of the work in those two phases have been removed in newer versions of MySQL Cluster.

Phase four through six performs the actual database recovery. There is some additional synchronisation in phases between seven and one hundred followed by a phase that ensures that the new data nodes takes it share of the work for event handling. This phase requires the API nodes to be available to complete. If they are not available a wait of 2 minutes will happen before the event part of the restart is completed.

## PART XII

INTERNALS OF NDB CLUSTER

In the next few chapters we will go through the internal architecture of NDB, both of the data nodes and of the NDB API.

NDB uses a message passing architecture, it is implemented in C++ using classes. But most of those classes are fairly big classes that we call blocks. Messages are addressed with a 32-bit address label. The messages are called signals. The most essential part of NDB is about blocks and signals. We start by describing how these blocks and signals are mapped in the data nodes. Next we describe them in the API nodes.

To understand the presentation of the most important signal flows, we next introduce the blocks in the data nodes.

We present the most important signal flows to provide an understanding of what happens in NDB when a query is executed towards NDB.

NDB is a database, thus presenting the most important data structures we use is important. This includes the data structure of our rows, our hash index our ordered index and our data structures for row locks.

To implement this architecture we have implemented two different virtual machines, one is optimised for machines with 2 CPUs and one is scalable to more than 50 CPUs. We will go through the workings of these two virtual machine implications.

We will discuss some other important internal architecture components used in many parts of NDB such as internal triggers, the transporter architecture used for communication and our principles for memory allocation.

CHAPTER 52

DATA NODE ARCHITECTURE

The data nodes in NDB is heavily inspired by the AXE architecure at Ericsson. The architecture is a message passing architecture where messages (called signals) are transported from one module (called block) to another module.

Messages have a destination address, this is a 32-bit number that similar to an IP address is used for routing the message to its destination. The message also carries a source address and the messages carries data.

52.1 BLOCK AND SIGNAL ARCHITECTURE

52.1.1 BLOCKS

The idea with a block is that it has its own data and its own code. In AXE the blocks were implemented in PLEX, this programming language did not allow for any type of code sharing and data sharing. Our blocks are implemented as C++ classes and they can share some common base classes to handle various common data structures such as hash tables, memory pools and so forth.

For the most part though the blocks contain their own code and their own data. This has the advantage that errors are quite isolated from each other. Given that the interface to a block is intended to use messages all the time, a bug can only affect other blocks by sending erroneus data. This makes it easier to find bugs in NDB.

Reading the code requires an understanding of how messages are routed. In the code a signal is passed using a block reference. There is very little in the code that indicates where this signal goes. It is important to document signal flows to make it easier to understand the code. At the same time there are many ways to create signal flows to assist new developers to understand the signal flows.

52.1.2 BLOCK REFERENCES

When a signal is sent we use a number of methods called something like *sendSignal* mostly. A signal is using a 32-bit block reference as its destination address. This address is divided into a number of parts. The lowest 16 bits is the node id. At the moment we can only use 8 of those bits, but the architecture is designed such that it can grow to clusters with 65535 nodes.

The 16 upper bits is a block address inside a node. They are interpreted a bit differently in data nodes and in API nodes.

In an API node the block address is used to get the Ndb object from an array, the array address is the index to this array. This array starts with index 32768. There can be at most 4711 Ndb objects in one cluster connection. Since Ndb objects are designed to be used in one thread this is the limit on the number of parallel threads to be used per cluster connection. At the same time the practical limit is much smaller. There is very little reason to use thousands of threads per cluster connection.

There are three special API blocks, block number 2047 is used for sending packed signals. Block number 4002 is used for sending signals to the cluster manager and 4003 is used for configuration change signals between management servers.

In a data node the lowest 9 bits of the block address is the block number, for example DBLQH have the block number 245. We can have up to 512 blocks, currently we have 24 blocks, there is lots of space in this part of the address space.

The upper 7 bits constitutes a thread id of the block. Each thread can contain its own DBLQH instance for example. This means that we can have up to 128 threads of each thread type.

When a signal is sent the software looks at the destination node, if it isn't our own node we pass the signal to the sending of distributed signals. If the destination node is our own node we check the thread id combined with the block number to get the destination thread number. Next the signal is passed into a signal queue of the destination thread.

52.1.3 ASYNCHRONOUS SIGNALS

Most signals sent are asynchronous signals. These signals are not executed immediately, they are put into a signal queue of the thread. This signal queue is called job buffer.

Asynchronous signals can be sent on two priority levels, A is high priority and B is normal priority. The priority of a signal affects the scheduling of a signal execution in a data node, it doesn't affect how it is put into buffers for sending to other nodes and it doesn't affect scheduling on an API node.

52.1.4 SYNCHRONOUS SIGNALS

We can also send synchronous signals, in practice those are function calls that use the same protocols as signals. They are always executed in the same thread, but might in a few situations execute on blocks that belong to another thread (mostly true when looking up the distribution information from a transaction coordinator).

In some cases we can also use direct function calls on other blocks in the same thread. This is mainly used for the most optimised code paths and mostly in the *ldm* thread.

52.1.5 SCHEDULING RULES

A thread executing signals on blocks use a scheduler to handle execution and communication with other threads. When a signal is executed in a block it is always calling a method that looks like this:

```
void
BlockName::executeSIGNAL_NAME(Signal *signal)
{
    .....
}
```

The scheduler is not using a time sharing model here. It is the responsibility of the block to not execute for too long. There are coding rules that a signal should not execute for more than at most 10 microseconds and almost all signals should be executed within 1-2 microseconds.

Thus even if hundreds of signals are waiting in the job buffer, they will be executed within a few hundred microseconds.

This scheduling model have advantages when combining primary key queries with long running scan operations. Scan operations handle a few rows at a time when being scheduled, after that they will be put last in queue again. This means that they will not block the execution of key lookups for very long time. This architecture is an important part of our solution for predictable latency in NDB.

To handle background activities that requires a certain percentage of the CPU resources we have implemented methods to check job buffer levels and make use of high priority signals in cases where it is necessary to run for more extended times. This is currently used by our local checkpoint algorithms to guarantee a certain progress there even when the load from traffic queries is very high.

52.1.6 PARALLELISING SIGNAL EXECUTION

Given that each signal starts a new thread of execution, it is extremely easy to parallelise activities in NDB. If one signal is sending one signal it is one thread of execution, but if one thread sends two signals, it has in principle created a new thread of execution.

Thus creating a new thread of execution has a cost measured in nanoseconds. We use this when executing a scan operation. If we have 16 partitions in a table, a scan will send off parallel scan operations towards all partitions from the transaction coordinator.

It is important to not start threads in an unbounded manner. This would overload the job buffers. We have design principles that state that a signal cannot start more than 4 new signals in the same thread. And even signals to other threads one have to be careful with. For the above scans we limit the amount of scans that can execute in parallel by the *MaxNoOfScans* configuration parameter, this parameter can not be set higher than 500.

52.1.7 SIGNAL DATA STRUCTURE

Signals come in a number of flavors. The easiest signals carry from 1 to 25 32-bit unsigned integer values, the signal has a specific length. These are sometimes called short signals.

Many years ago we added long signals, they can come with up to 3 extra parts. The total size of a long signal can be up to around 28 kBytes in size.

In some cases it is necessary to send even longer signals. In this case we use a concept called fragmented signals. This is a signal that is sent through many long signals. Each such long signal is received and handled and the memory is stored in a buffer waiting for all parts to arrive before the signal is executed.

These fragmented signals are fairly rare and mainly used in various meta data operations. Normal traffic signals are carried in long signals in almost all cases.

52.2   Receive handling in Data Node

In a multithreaded data node we have one or more special thread(s) that handles the sockets communicating with other nodes (more on single-threaded data nodes later). Signals are received on a socket, we use a special connection setup protocol to get started. After that each signal carries a fixed 12 byte header that ensures that we can easily find where the signal ends and where the next signal starts.

Any signal can be destined for any thread and any block in the data node.

Each thread have one job buffer for each thread that can communicate with it. The receiver thread have one job buffer to write its signals into for each thread handling signals in the data node. We call these threads block threads.

These job buffers can be written into without using any mutexes, they are mapped such that each job buffer has one thread writing into it and one thread reading from it. In this case it is possible to design algorithms for buffer read and write that only uses memory barriers to secure a safe communication between the threads. Only high priority signals are sent to a shared job buffer protected by a mutex.

The *recv* threads sleep on an *epoll_wait* call on Linux and similar constructs on other OSs. Thus as soon as a message arrives from a node the *recv* thread will wake up and handle it.

It is possible to specify that the *recv* thread should spin for a while before going to sleep again, this has the possibility of decreasing latency in low load scenarios. It is also possible to set the thread priority of the *recv* thread a bit higher to ensure it isn't forced to go to sleep when it still has a job to do in high load scenarios.

52.3   Send handling in Data Node

Sending signals to another node is handled through send buffers. These buffers are configurable in size. A block thread executing messages that is sending a signal will simply copy the signal into one of those send buffers and continue execution.

After executing a number of signals the scheduler will ensure that the send buffers local to its thread is made available for sending. This includes signals sent to other threads in the same node. The number of signals before this happens is controlled by the configuration parameter *SchedulerResponsiveness*. Setting this value higher means that we will execute for longer time before we make them available.

After executing even more signals we will return to the scheduler loop. The number of signals before this happens is controlled by the *SchedulerResponsiveness* parameter. If the job buffer is empty we will always return to the scheduler loop (this is the most common reason of course).

The scheduler loop handles checking for delayed signals (signals that are sent with a delay of a specific number of milliseconds)). In addition it handles packing of send buffers when necessary. It handles sending of packed signals, these are signals where several small signals are packed into one signal, these signals avoid the cost of signal scheduling for a number of very common signals and avoids the cost of the 12 byte overhead for each signal sent to another node over the network.

The scheduler of a block thread calls a method *do_send* to activate sending of the messages. The actual sending of a message is normally configured to be done by one or more send threads. If no send thread is configured, the sending will be handled by the block threads.

In MySQL Cluster 7.5 we added the possibility for sending to be done by block threads even when a send thread is configured. This is handled by an adaptive algorithm. If a thread is very lightly loaded it will wake up once per millisecond to see if it can assist in sending messages. If a thread is an overloaded state (roughly above 75% load) it will offload all sending to the send threads. If the thread is not overloaded, it will send to as many nodes as the thread itself was attempting to send to.

In practice this algorithm usually leads to that the *tc* does a lot of assistance to send threads since they go through this scheduler loop quite frequently. The *main* and *rep* threads are usually lightly loaded and wake up every now and then to ensure that we keep up with the load on the send threads. This ensures that the node can keep up with the send load even when configured with a single send thread and lots of block threads. The *ldm* threads usually assist the send threads a bit while not overloaded, if any threads is overloaded, it is usually the *ldm* threads. The *recv* threads do not assist the send threads.

When a node wants assistance from send threads to execute, it will wake a send thread up. The first send thread will be woken up if available, next the second and so forth. Thus the load on the send threads is higher on the first send thread and lowest on the last send thread.

The send threads have as their sole purpose to send signals. They grab a global mutex to see if any nodes are scheduled for signal sending. If so they grab the node from the list, release the mutex and start sending to the node. If no nodes are available to send to, the send thread will go to sleep. The global mutex keeping track of nodes that need signal sending is one of the two hot mutexes in the NDB data node. The other hot mutex is the mutex protecting allocation and release of send buffers by the various threads.

These mutexes can have a small impact on performance, up to 5% when running with very large data nodes (at least 16 *ldm* threads).

When the data nodes are overloaded, the block thread will be a bit more eager to assist the send threads.

52.4 NDB CONNECTION SETUP PROTOCOL

Whenever a socket is setup between a data node and an API node or other data node, the following connection setup protocol is used to ensure that the other side is an NDB node as well.

First the client side (the API node or the data node with the highest node id) sends a *ndbd<CR>* message, next it immediately sends a *ndbd passwd<CR>* message and waits for a response from the server side. The server responds to these messages with *ok<CR>*. After this the client side sends *2 1<CR>* assuming 2 is the node id of the client side and 1 means TCP/IP socket used for communication. The server side responds with the same message with its node id and a 1.

If any side finds a problem with this setup protocol it will close the connection. If both sides are ok with the setup protocol they will now enter into a full duplex mode where both can send signals at full speed. In most cases the receive side of the socket is handled by some receive thread and the send side of the socket is handled by some send thread.

52.5 NDB SIGNAL HEADER DEFINITION

When the connection between two nodes are setup the only thing carried on the sockets are signals. These signals are sent using the following format.

The signal always starts with 3 words (a word is 32 bits) that form a header. If the configuration specified that the connection would use signal ids, the header will be four words instead where the fourth word is an id of the signal sent, each signal sent to the other node increments the id. This signal id can be used to improve signal logging capabilities. It is not on by default in a cluster.

After the header the normal signal data comes. This can be up to 25 words. The number of words is specified in the header part.

After the normal signal data we have the lengths of the optional 3 segments that the signal can carry, each length is a word. The number of segments is specified in the header part. There can be zero segments.

Next the segment data comes, this is always a number of words.

After the segment data there is an optional checksum word. By default this is not on, but it can be activated through a configuration parameter on the communication section.

Header word 1:

1. Bit 0, 7, 24, 31 Endian bits

2. Bit 1,25 Fragmented messages indicator

3. Bit 2 Signal id used flag

4. Bit 3 Not used

5. Bit 4 Checksum used flag

6. Bit 5-6 Signal priority

7. Bit 8-23 Total signal size

8. Bit 26-30 Main signal size (max 25)

Bit 0,7,24 and 31 in the first header word are all set if the communication link is using big endian, otherwise they are 0. Currently it is not possible to mix little endian machines with big endian machines in the cluster.

Fragmented messages are multiple messages that should be delivered as one message to the receiver of the message. In this case bit 1 and 25 represent a number between 0 and 3.

0 means there is no fragmentation, or in terms of fragments, this fragment is the first and the last fragment.

1 means it is the first fragment in a train of fragments.

2 means it is not the first fragment, but also isn't the last fragment.

3 means it isn't the first, but it is the last fragment.

Header word 2:

1. Bit 0-19 Signal number (e.g. API_HBREQ)

2. Bit 20-25 Trace number

3. Bit 26-27 Number of segments used

4. Bit 28-31

The signal number is the id of the signal sent. This will be used to ensure that the correct function is called in the data node and in the API node.

Trace number is a feature that can be used to trace signals for a specific train of signals. Each signal sent carries the trace number of the signal executed currently. It can be used to follow a special event like a scan operation through the data nodes. It has been used in special implementations, but there is no support for this type of tracing in the current source trees.

The number of segments is used to discover long signals and also segments in fragmented signals. It gives the number of segment sizes after the short signal data and how many segments of data to read in at the end of the signal.

Header word 3:

1. Bit 0-15 Sender block id

2. Bit 16-31 Receiver block id

The receiver block id is used to direct the signal to the proper Ndb object in the API nodes and the proper thread and block in the data nodes. the sender block id is occasionally used by blocks when executing a signal.

CHAPTER 53

API NODE ARCHITECTURE

In a previous chapter we went through the NDB API. This is the C++ API used to access NDB. In this chapter we will look at the implementation aspects of this API. In particular what we have done to map the block and signal architecture to a synchronous API. We have an asynchronous API part as well that fits very well with the block and signal model.

The C++ NDB API is a fairly normal object-oriented library. It is using blocks and signals as a way to route messages to the appropriate thread and software unit in the data nodes.

The original NDB API used a structure where we had one mutex that protected the entire send and receive part of the NDB API. When we fixed this in MySQL Cluster 7.3 we had a number of choices.

We needed to separate the send and receive logic and ensure that they could execute without interfering with each other. We had to make a number of choices on where to execute the actual signals. The signals have as destination the Ndb objects or some other object linked to this object. It is possible to let user threads execute the signals.

We decided to let the signals be executed by the receive logic. The reason is that we could improve our latency in this case. We could see that the alternative approach would increase latency of the NDB API. At the same time the scalability of the approach where user threads execute the signals is better, so it is a trade off. In iClaustron, my hobby project, I went for the scalability option instead.

Thus there are two main scalability limitations of the current NDB API limitation. The first is that all signals arriving have to be received and executed by a single thread that handles both receiving on the socket as well as executing the signal itself.

The second limitation is that one API node is using one TCP/IP socket. One socket have a fair amount of states where only one or two CPUs at a time can work on the socket. Thus one socket have limitations on number of packets received per second and the bandwidth that such a socket can maintain.

The solution to both these problems is to use multiple API nodes for one program. E.g. the MySQL Server can define any number of cluster connections that will work independent of each other.

53.1 CLUSTER CONNECTION

The cluster connection is maintaining one API node and as mentioned already, there can be multiple API nodes in one program.

One cluster connection contains all the structures required to communicate with each data node in the cluster and each management server.

Thus the cluster connections have one receive thread handling signals arriving to the API node. It has one send thread that can take over send handling when the socket is overloaded at the time when the user thread tries to send. Finally it has a thread to handle cluster management activities, such as heartbeats.

53.2 USER THREADS

User threads are not under our control in most cases. The MySQL Server is an exception where one thread is created per connection to the MySQL Server (except when the thread pool is used). These threads execute all the normal NDB API calls and we wake those threads up when we have completed executing all signals that we were requested to execute to handle the NDB API calls. User threads handles most of the send and receive handling in cases of low loads. The higher the load becomes, the more the receive thread will jump in to assist in executing the signals received.

53.3 NDB API SEND THREADS

Send threads in the NDB API only send when the socket cannot keep up with the amount of signals we attempt to execute. Normally the send threads are sleeping. But in high load cases they can be quite busy sending signals that it was assigned to handle.

53.4 NDB API RECEIVE THREADS

The receive threads is the heart of the NDB API implementation. Receive handling is a property that is controlled by a mutex. Any user thread can take this responsibility if no other thread already has grabbed this responsibility. This improves latency in single-threaded use cases.

When many user threads are active at the same time, the receive thread is becoming active. The threshold to this is set by the MySQL Server variable

--ndb_recv_thread_activation_threshold. By default this is set to 8. One problem that we can get with the receive thread is that it is a thread that uses much more CPU compared to the other MySQL Server threads.

This means that the normal Linux scheduler will give it a lower priority compared to the rest of the threads. This is not beneficial to the other threads using this cluster connection since it will delay them getting woken up to serve the replies from the data nodes.

To ensure that the receive thread gets a higher priority we set the nice level of the receive thread to -20 if possible. As mentioned in the chapter on Installing MySQL Cluster in the section on adding a new mysql user, it is necessary to set the highest nice level that can be set by the user. To set this higher nice level the user mysql must have *CAP_SYS_NICE* capabilities as shown in the above chapter how to set.

Using a receive thread that is locked to a CPU and that gets activated as soon as more than one user thread is active is the most optimal solution for latency using the NDB API. But it requires that the mysql user can set the nice level higher and that it can lock CPUs in a safe way without interfering with user threads or other processes.

The default manner where the user threads takes care of everything has slightly worse latency, but it still scales very nicely.

53.5   NDB API CLUSTER MANAGER THREADS

There is a thread taking care of heartbeats, registering as a new node with the data node. This thread will wake up every 100 millisecond and send a heartbeat signal if needed.

53.6   BLOCKS IN API NODES

A block in the API node is simply an Ndb object. When referring to a block, it is referring to a pointer in an array that in turn points to an Ndb object.

CHAPTER 54

BLOCKS IN A DATA NODE

In order to understand the signalling diagrams that we will present in a later chapter on common use cases, it is necessary to at least understand the various blocks in NDB at a high level.

The code also documents some of the most important signalling flows in NDB. As an example the block Ndbcntr and in the code file NdbcntrMain.cpp contains a long description of a how a restart works. In the block Qmgr and in the file QmgrMain.cpp we have a signalling diagram for how the registration of new nodes into the cluster at startup happens and how this is the base for heartbeat signals sent later. In the block Dbdih and in the file DbdihMain.cpp there is a long description of how ALTER TABLE REORGANIZE PARTITIONS works with a detailed signalling flow. Hopefully with the aid of this explanation of the internals it will be easier to understand those descriptions in the code for anyone interested in understanding on a detailed level what goes on inside NDB to handle the complex online meta data changes.

54.1 LDM BLOCKS

LDM stands for Local Data Manager. It is a set of blocks that cooperate to deliver the local database service that is a very central part of NDB. In *ndbmtd* these blocks all operate inside the same thread in the *ldm* threads. It is not possible to break those blocks apart and execute them in different threads. It is however possible to have several instances of the *ldm* threads. Each *ldm* thread handles one instance of each of the below blocks, in addition it takes care of at least one log part of the REDO log.

54.1.1 DBLQH

DBLQH stands for DataBase Local Query Handler. This block is where most interactions with the LDM blocks starts. It does handle the REDO log, but its main responsibility is to interact with the other blocks operating the tuple storage, hash index, ordered index, page cache, restore operations, backup and local checkpoint services.

The most common signals DBLQH receives is LQHKEYREQ that is used for reading or writing a row using a primary key of a table (either a user table or a unique index table or a BLOB table). To serve this query it uses DBACC to lookup in the hash table and DBTUP that has the responsibility of the tuple storage and that performs the operation requested by the user.

Scan operations is the second most common operation and this is receiving a SCAN_FRAGREQ signal to order either a full table scan (implemented by either DBACC or DBTUP) or a range scan (implemented by DBTUX).

DBLQH also controls the execution of local checkpoints together with the BACKUP block.

One can say that DBLQH is the service provider for the LDM blocks that makes use of internal services delivered by the other blocks.

54.1.2 DBACC

DBACC has two main functions. It controls the local part of the distributed hash index that every primary key uses, and every table in NDB, including unique index tables and BLOB tables, have a primary key. Even tables without a primary key uses a hidden primary key.

The hash table in DBACC also acts as the locking data structure to ensure that rows are locked in the proper fashion by user operations.

DBACC stands for DataBase ACCess manager.

54.1.3 DBTUP

DBTUP means DataBase TUPle manager. DBTUP is where the actual in-memory rows are stored using the fixed row parts and the variable sized row parts. DBTUP has the ability to execute all sorts of operations requested by the higher levels of software in NDB. Thus this is where the actual reads and writes of data happens. DBTUP also contains a fairly simple interpreter that can execute a number of simple statements that can be used to push down condition evaluation to NDB. It also reads and writes the disk columns delivered by PGMAN.

54.1.4 DBTUX

DBTUX means DataBase TUple IndeX. It contains an implementation of a T-tree. The T-tree is an index specifically developed to support ordered indexes in main memory. Every update of a row involving an ordered index will perform changes of the T-tree and it is used heavily during restart when the T-trees are rebuilt using rows recovered.

The DBTUX software have been very stable for a long time. It does what it is supposed to do and there is very little reason to change it. Most new features developed are done at a higher service level in NDB and DBTUP has lots of capabilities that interact with higher service levels in NDB.

54.1.5 PGMAN

PGMAN stands for PaGe MANager and it handles the page cache for disk pages used for disk columns. Each *ldm* thread has a part of the page cache. It contains a state-of-the-art page caching algorithm that is explained in comments for the *get_page* function in this block.

54.1.6 BACKUP

The backup block is responsible to write local checkpoint and backup information to files. It does so by using a full table scan using the DBTUP block to ensure that all rows are analysed to see if they should be written into this local checkpoint or not.

54.1.7 RESTORE

The RESTORE block is only used during the early phases of a restart when it is used to restore a local checkpoint. The local checkpoint contains saved in-memory rows that are written back into DBTUP at recovery using more or less the same code path as a normal insert or write operation would use in NDB.

54.2 TC BLOCKS

TC stands for Transaction Coordinator. These blocks handle a small but important part of the NDB architecture. There are only two blocks here DBTC and DBSPJ. All transactions pass through the TC block and for pushdown joins the DBSPJ block is also used.

54.2.1 DBTC

The most common signalling interface to DBTC is TCKEYREQ and TCINDXREQ. The TCKEYREQ is used for primary key operations towards all tables. DBTC works intimately with the DBDIH block, DBDIH contains all distribution information. DBTC queries this information for all queries to ensure that we work with an up to date version of the distribution information. TCINDXREQ handles unique key requests.

DBTC uses the DBLQH service provider interface to implement transactional changes. DBTC ensures that transactional changes are executed in the correct order. This includes handling triggers fired when executing change operations. These triggers are fired to handle unique indexes, foreign keys and table reorganisations.

Scan operations and pushdown join operations are started through the SCAN_TABREQ signal.

DBTC handles timeouts to ensure that we get progress even in the presence of deadlocks.

If a data node fails, a lot of ongoing transactions will lose their transaction state. To be able to complete those transactions (by either aborting or committing them) DBTC can build up the state again by asking DBLQH for information about ongoing transactions from the failed node. It is the first *tc* thread in the master data node that will take care of this.

54.2.2 DBSPJ

DBSPJ stands for DataBase Select-Project-Join. SPJ is a popular phrase in discussing join queries in databases. The DBSPJ blocks implements the linked join operations that is used in NDB to implement a form of parallel query. DBSPJ has no function for anything apart from join queries.

54.3 MAIN THREAD BLOCKS

There are two threads used for various things, this is the *main* thread and the *rep* thread. Here we will first go through the blocks found in the *main* thread. These blocks all have only one instance. There are also a few proxy blocks. Proxy blocks is a special kind of block that was introduced to handle multiple block instances. The proxy blocks implements some functionalities such that it is possible to send a signal to a block and have it executed on all block instances of e.g. the DBLQH block. This was helpful in changing the code from the single-threaded version to the multi-threaded version.

54.3.1   DBDICT

DBDICT stands for DataBase DICTionary. It contains meta data about tables, columns, indexes, foreign keys, various internal meta data objects. It implements a framework for implementing any type of schema transactions. A schema transaction tracks the progress of a schema transaction. If a failure happens we will either roll the schema transaction backwards or forwards. If it has passed a point where it can no longer be rolled back, we will ensure that it will be completed even in the presence of node crashes and even in the presence of a cluster crash. Schema transactions cannot contain any normal user transactions.

DBDICT implements this by executing a careful stepwise change of each schema transaction. Thus the schema transaction is divided into many smaller steps, each of those steps are applied in all nodes in parallel. After completing the steps we record the information about the step we have completed in a file flushed to disk. This means that schema transactions in NDB are not so fast, but they can handle very complex changes. It is possible to use this framework for quite advanced schema changes. But introducing new types of schema changes still requires writing a few new functions and verifying that the new schema change variant is working well.

DBDICT has an important role in the startup of a node where it decides which tables to restore. It asks DBDIH to perform the actual recovery and will assist DBDIH in some of those recovery steps.

54.3.2   DBDIH

DBDIH stands for DataBase Distribution Handler. This is one of the most important parts of NDB. In DBDIH we maintain all the distribution information about all tables in the cluster. It contains algorithms to ensure that this information is synchronised with all other nodes in the cluster.

This distribution information is updated by schema changes and by node starts and by node failures. Thus for a specific table the information is very stable. Days and even years can pass without it being updated. To handle this we have used a mechanism similar to the RCU mechanism used in the Linux kernel. The idea is that when reading one performs the following, before starting to read we check if the data is currently being changed (checked by reading a flag on the table). If it isn't currently being changed we go on and read the information, but we record the flags we read before reading it. If it was currently being changed we will simply loop until the data isn't being updated. After reading the data we will check if the data have changed since we read (checked by again reading the table flags). If the data hadn't changed we're done, if it had changed, we restart the read once again.

This procedure is used to protect a number of variables regarding data distribution maintained by DBDIH. All the code to handle these protected regions are assembled together in DBDIH to make it easier to follow this part of the code.

DBDIH runs the global checkpoint protocol, global checkpoints was described in an earlier chapter and represents recoverable checkpoints on a cluster level. DBDIH also runs the local checkpoint protocol. DBDIH gathers information during the local checkpoint process that is used in restarts.

54.3.3 TRIX

TRIX stands for TRIgger eXecution. It is involved in handling online index builds, copying data during table reorganisations and online foreign key builds. It is a block that assists DBDICT by performing a number of important operations to move data around to implement complex online schema changes.

54.3.4 QMGR

QMGR stands for Cluster Manager with a little play on pronunciation. This block is responsible for the hearbeat protocol in NDB. It is the lowest level of the cluster management in NDB. It is involved in early start phases to register a new node into the cluster and maintains the order used to decide which node is the master node (it is the oldest node registered). Nodes are registered one at a time and all nodes are involved in this registration, thus all nodes agree on the age of a node. Next we decide that the oldest node is always choosen as the new master node whenever a master node fails.

54.3.5 NDBCNTR

NDBCNTR stands Network DataBase CoNTRoller. From the beginning this block was the block responsible for the database start of the data node. This is still true to a great extent.

54.3.6 CMVMI

CMVMI stands Cluster Manager Virtual Machine Interface. This block was originally a block that was used as a gateway between blocks implemented in PLEX and blocks implemented in C++. Nowadays and since 18 years all blocks are C++ blocks. It now implements a few support functions for other blocks.

54.3.7 DBUTIL

DBUTIL stands DataBase UTILity. This blocks implements a signal based API towards DBTC and DBLQH. It is a support block to other blocks like NDBCNTR, TRIX and so forth to execute database operations from the block code.

54.3.8 NDBFS

NDBFS stands for Network DataBase File System. It implements a file system API using signals. It was developed to ensure that file system accesses could use the normal signalling protocols. Given that all the rest of the code in the NDB data nodes is asynchronous and uses signals between blocks, it was important to move also the NDB file system accesses into this structure. Not every OS have an asynchronous API towards their filesystem, we implemented the interface to the file system through many small threads that each can do blocking file system calls. But they interact with the *main* thread whenever they are requested to perform a file operation and the threads send back information to the *main* thread when the file operation is completed.

The APIs implemented towards NDBFS supports a number of different models. The various uses of a file system is rather different for the functions in NDB. Some functions simply need to write a file of random size, others work with strict page sizes and so forth.

54.3.9 PROXY BLOCKS

The *main* thread handles the proxy blocks for DBTC and DBSPJ.

54.3.10 CONCLUSION

The *main* thread handles a variety of things. For the most part it is involved heavily in restarts and in meta data operations. NDBFS operations and checkpoint operations in DBDIH is the most common operation it does during normal traffic load.

54.4 REP BLOCKS

The blocks that execute in the *rep* thread are used for a variety of purposes. The name *rep* is short for replication and stems from that the SUMA block is used to distribute events from the data node to the MySQL replication servers.

54.4.1 SUMA

SUMA stands for SUbscribption MAnager. Events about changes on rows are sent from the SUMA block to the NDB API nodes that have subscribed to changes on the changed tables. This is mainly used for MySQL Cluster Replication, but can also be used for event processing such as in HopsFS where it is used to update ElasticSearch to enable generic searches in HopsFS for files.

54.4.2 LGMAN

LGMAN stands for LoG MANager. There is only one LGMAN block in the data node. But this block can be accessed from any *ldm* thread. In this case the *Logfile_client* class is used, when creating such an object a mutex is grabbed to ensure that only one thread at a time is accessing the UNDO log. These accesses from the *ldm* threads is only writing into the UNDO log buffer. The actual file writes are executed in the LGMAN block in the *rep* thread.

54.4.3 TSMAN

TSMAN stands for TableSpace MANager. The creation and opening of tablespace files happens in the TSMAN block. The actual writes to the tablespace files are however handled by the PGMAN blocks in the *ldm* threads and the extra PGMAN block described below.

Any writes to extent information is handled by TSMAN. These accesses are executed from the *ldm* threads. Before entering the TSMAN block these accesses have to create a *Tablespace_client* object. This object will grab a mutex to ensure that only one *ldm* thread at a time reads and writes into the extent information.

54.4.4 DBINFO

DBINFO is a block used to implement scans used to get information that is presented in the *ndbinfo* tables.

54.4.5 PROXY BLOCKS

The proxy blocks for DBLQH, DBACC, DBTUP, DBTUX, BACKUP, RESTORE and PGMAN are handled in the *rep* thread.

54.4.6 PGMAN EXTRA

The PGMAN block has one instance in each *ldm* thread. There is also an extra PGMAN instance. The main responsibility of this instance is to handle checkpointing the extent information in tablespaces. The tablespace data used by normal tables is handled by the PGMAN instances in the *ldm* threads.

The extent information is a few pages in each tablespace data file that are locked into the page cache. The checkpointing of those pages are handled by this extra PGMAN block instance. This block instance also executes in the *rep* thread.

54.5 THRMAN

THRMAN stands for THRead MANager. This block has one instance in each thread. It handles a few things such as tracking CPU usage in the thread and anything that requires access to a specific thread in the data node.

54.6 TRPMAN

TRPMAN stands for TRansPorter MANager. Transporters are used to implement communication between nodes in NDB. There is a TRPMAN block in each *recv* thread. This block can be used to open and close communication between nodes at request of other blocks.

CHAPTER 55

VIRTUAL MACHINE IN DATA NODES

In this chapter we will discuss a few more things regarding the virtual machines and its threads in *ndbmtd*.

55.1   THREAD TYPES IN *ndbmtd*

55.1.1   *ldm* THREADS

The *ldm* thread cannot communicate with any other *ldm* thread in the same node, it can communicate with all *tc* threads and with the *main* thread. It can communicate with itself as can every other thread. The first *ldm* thread is a bit special in that it controls backup execution and thus this first *ldm* thread can communicate with all the other *ldm* threads.

The *ldm* threads have an important characteristic regarding its CPU usage. It is extremely efficient in using the CPUs. The instructions per cycle (IPC) is as high as 1.2. This is one of the reasons why it doesn't pay off so much to use two *ldm* threads per CPU core. There isn't enough execution units in a CPU core to keep two threads moving in parallel. The thread has a branch prediction miss rate of less than 2% and also L1 cache misses are only about 2% of the accesses. Misses in the last level cache is however about 15%. This is where the actual accesses to the data parts come into play.

The *ldm* thread can benefit much if they stay at the same CPU all the time and their CPU caches are not influenced by other threads executed in the machine.

This is why CPU locking is an important method to improve performance of NDB data nodes.

55.1.2   *tc* THREADS

tc threads communicate with all other threads. *tc* threads have very different characteristics compared to *ldm* threads. The signals executed are very short and there is a lot of those small messages. So the *tc* threads are up and running for a short time and goes to sleep for a very short time.

tc threads benefit a lot from hyperthreading, we get 40% extra performance for each CPU core by using hyperthreading. The IPC for *tc* is also a lot lower around 0.4 per cycle.

tc threads play an important role in handling sends to other nodes, both when using *send* threads and without specific *send* threads. Thus you can see a lot of CPU usage by the OS kernel from this thread. The send assistance by *tc* threads is important to decrease the response time for requests towards NDB.

Having too many *tc* threads can easily lower total performance of the node. Most likely that we get to send too much small packets to the API node, this will have a negative impact on API node performance.

55.1.3 *main* THREADS

main threads are normally not very busy at all. They are mainly used for file system signals during normal operation. They can be fairly busy during ALTER TABLE commands that reorganize data, build indexes and build foreign keys. Most of the CPU resources for this thread type can be colocated with the *rep* thread, but in larger configurations it can be useful to separate those threads on their own CPUs.

55.1.4 *rep* THREADS

The *rep* thread is used to send event data to the NDB APIs that have subscribed to change events. It is also used for ALTER TABLE operations that build indexes, foreign keys and reorganise tables.

Other functions should have very small impact on CPU usage.

The main thing to consider for the *main* and *rep* thread is that they normally will use very little CPU resources, but at times they can spike when running a heavy ALTER TABLE operation.

Both *main* and *rep* threads can communicate with all other thread types.

55.1.5 *recv* THREADS

recv threads benefit greatly from hyperthreading. One important thing to consider for *recv* threads is that they benefit from not using a full CPU. Locking *recv* threads to a CPU, one should strive to not use the CPU to more than 60%. The reason is that it is very important for the *recv* thread to quickly wake up and take care of any actions and similarly to ensure that other threads can quickly wake up to to handle the received signals.

If the *recv* thread uses more CPU than 60%, it is a good idea to add more *recv* threads. The *ndb_top* tool is a good tool to check how much CPU a thread uses if the threads are not locked to their own CPUs, in this case the *top* tool can be used as well.

55.1.6 *send* THREADS

There are many other thread types that can assist *send* threads. Using a single *send* thread is mostly ok and having more than one might even have negative performance impact.

Still there are cases when more *send* threads are needed. Often performance can increase a bit by using all the way up to 4 *send* threads. HopsFS is a good example of an application that requires much CPU resources for sending.

send threads benefit from hyperthreading.

55.1.7 *io* THREADS

When using NDB is an in-memory engine without compressing backups and local checkpoints, the CPU usage in *io* threads is very small. Adding compression to backups and/or local checkpoints using the *CompressedBackup* and *CompressedLCP* configuration parameter quickly increases the CPU usage in the *io* threads significantly. Similarly using disk data means that *io* threads gets a lot more work.

The *io* threads can use many CPUs concurrently.

55.2   Communication between threads in *ndbmtd*

Communication between threads uses highly optimised code paths in NDB. We use lock-free communication where each communication buffer is only used for communication between two threads. This means that we can use a single-reader and single-writer optimisations that avoid using any locks when communicating, only memory reads and writes combined with memory barrier operations is sufficient. This part of the code is the main portability hurdle for NDB. This code is currently working on x86 servers and SPARC servers. Some attempts have been made to make it work on POWER servers, but it has not been completed.

To wake up other threads we use futexes on Linux that are combined with special x86 instructions. On other OSs we use normal mutexes and condition variables to wake up other threads.

In a configuration with many threads in the data node, there will be significant amount of memory allocated to the communication between threads.

55.3   Scheduler in *ndbmtd*

Each block thread (*ldm*, *tc*, *main*, *rep* and *recv* threads) have a scheduler that executes signals. It has settings that can be changed through the configuration parameters *SchedulerResponsiveness*. These settings define how often we will flush signals to other threads and nodes. Flushing often have a negative impact on throughput, but can have a positive impact on latency. Flushing seldomly means that latency increases and throughput can increase. The scheduler supports delayed signals through a special time queue.

What one always find when running various benchmarks is that NDB as a distributed system is a highly coupled system. So to get best performance and latency one has to find the right balance of resources.

The *MaxSendDelay* is a parameter that works well in very large clusters where we need to constrain the nodes from sending to often. Sending too often will use too much resources in other nodes. To get good performance it is important that a node isn't running so fast that it sends smaller packets that gives other nodes more work to do. This will have a negative impact on system performance.

55.4   Single-threaded Data Nodes, *ndbd*

The *ndbd* is the original data node program that was developed for NDB. In those days a large server had two CPUs and about 1 GByte of memory. Thus machines of today have a lot more CPUs. This means that a multithreaded approach was required.

At the same time the *ndbd* is extremely efficient and have optimal response time characteristics. Thus *ndbd* is helpful when employed for very small databases where the performance is not much of an issue.

Eventually *ndbd* will be fully replaced by *ndbmtd*. But there is still a reason to keep *ndbd* around a bit more.

The model for *ndbd* is very simple. It has one thread that does everything except the *io* threads. The *io* threads still exist there and you can also run multiple threads to build indexes during restart.

55.4.1 SCHEDULER IN *ndbd*

The scheduler for the *ndbd* program is a combination of a block thread scheduler, the *send* thread and the *recv* thread in *ndbmtd*.

It starts its scheduler loop by checking for delayed signals. Next it waits for inputs on the sockets. As soon as something arrives it starts executing it. After executing a number of signals it comes back to the scheduler. Next it will send signals to those nodes that we have addressed during the execution phase.

As can be seen in *ndbd* we are sharing one thread for everything, this is more efficient, but obviously isn't so scalable. Thus in low-end scenarios it can be useful. But the *ndbmtd* can scale to almost 50x higher performance.

CHAPTER 56

DETAILED NDB INTERNALS

This chapter mentions a few basic foundations for the software design in NDB. We have already touched upon that we use the fail fast model for software development. This is natural when you expect that your nodes are always setup in a replicated fashion. It is not so natural when you have downtime associated with each node failure.

56.1 INTERNAL TRIGGERS IN MySQL CLUSTER

When I did my Ph.D thesis I developed quite a few algorithms for node recovery, for online schema changes and so forth. Most of those algorithms are based on a trigger approach.

In NDB we make use of triggers for a wide range of topics. We use triggers to maintain our ordered indexes (T-trees). Thus every change on a column that is part of an ordered index will generate an insert trigger and a delete trigger on the ordered index.

We use triggers to maintain our unique indexes. We use triggers to maintain our foreign keys. We use triggers for various meta data operations such as when building an index as an online operation.

When adding nodes we dynamically add more partitions to parts of the table. This partitions are built as an online operation and we use triggers to maintain these new partitions. We use triggers to maintain fully replicated tables.

The nice thing about our triggers is that they are very well integrated with our transactional changes. NDB does almost every change in a transactional context. This means that using triggers makes it is easy for us to perform additional changes required by online meta data operations and maintaining indexes and so forth.

There are asynchronous triggers as well that are used to maintain our event reporting APIs that are used for replicating from one cluster to another.

56.2 TRANSPORTER MODEL

All our communication methods are located in a transporter. Transporters interact with the remaining parts of the virtual machine in the data nodes. The virtual machine need not worry about what technique we are using to transport the data.

Over the years we have implemented transporters for Dolphin SCI technology, shared memory, TCP/IP and a special transporter for OSE/Delta messages.

The SCI transporter is no longer needed since Dolphin technology can be used with Dolphin SuperSockets. These provide communication to another within less than a microsecond and is even better integrated with the Linux OS compared to using a native SCI transporter.

Shared memory transporter code still remains in the data node, it will be reintroduced in some later version, but so far it has been enough to provide a TCP/IP transporter.

NDB runs well on Infiniband as well, previously we used SDP in the same fashion as for Dolphin SuperSocket, but now it is more common to use IPoIB (IP over InfiniBand).

Since almost all technologies are available through the socket interface, we have focused most of our energy on the TCP/IP transporter.

56.3 MEMORY ALLOCATION PRINCIPLES

Historically memory allocation was a very expensive operation. Thus to get the optimal performance it was a good idea to avoid allocating small amounts of memory.

This reason for managing your own memory is gone with modern malloc implementations that scale very well and have little overhead.

Managing your own memory is however still a very good idea to ensure that you can get the best possible real-time experience. The preferred method for using NDB is to set the *LockInMainMemory* parameter to 1 such that the memory is locked once allocated. NDB data nodes allocate all its memory in the startup phase. Once it has allocated the memory it maintains the memory itself.

Allocating memory dynamically provides a more flexible environment. It is much harder to provide the highest availability in a flexible environment. Most every program in the world can get into hang situations when overallocating memory. Overallocation of memory leads to swapping that slows the process down to a grinding halt. So even if the process still is considered up and running, it is not delivering the expected service.

In contrast the NDB data nodes takes the pain at startup, once the node is up and running, it won't release its memory, thus ensuring continued operation. Our flexibility instead comes from that data nodes can be restarted with a new configuration without causing any downtime in the system.

The MySQL Server and the NDB API use a much more traditional memory allocation principle where memory is allocated and released as needs arise.

56.4 ANGEL PROCESS

Automated responses to failures is important in MySQL Cluster. Our approach to solving this problem is to ensure that any node failure is followed by a node restart. We implement this by using an angel process when starting a data node.

When starting the data node it is the angel process that is started. After reading the configuration from the management server the angel process will fork itself into an angel process that simply waits for the running data node process to fail. The actual work in the data node is executed by the forked process.

When the forked process stops, the angel process discovers it and restarts the process and thus a node restart is immediately started after the node failure.

It is possible to configure the cluster such that we don't get those automatic restarts, but I see very little reason to use this configuration option.

CHAPTER 57

SIGNAL FLOWS IN NDB

We will go through some of the most important signalling flows to give an idea about what happens when a query is executed against NDB.

For queries against the database there are three main flows that we use. The key lookup flow used to read and write data through primary keys or unique keys. The scan flow used to perform full table scans, range scans and pruned versions of these. We have pushdown join that is essentially linked key lookups and scan operations. Pushdown joins builds entirely on top of the key lookup and scan flows.

In addition there are a number of protocols implemented in NDB to handle all sorts of node failures, node restarts, schema changes and so forth. We will go through a few of those and in some cases simply point out where one can find descriptions of these in the source code.

To maintain various secondary data structures we use triggers and these are integrated into the key lookup protocol and we will describe how this happens.

57.1 KEY OPERATIONS

NDB was designed with efficient key lookup transactions in mind. Almost all applications that was analysed before implementing NDB had a major portion of key lookups. Most of them had a high percentage of writes as well.

One of the problems with DBMSs in the 90s was that the overhead of transactions was very high. This is still to a great extent true. For example in other MySQL clustering solutions there are limitations on how many transactions that can commit in parallel.

With NDB each row operation is committed in exactly the same fashion if it is a single row transaction or if it is a transaction with 1000 rows being updated. We have worked on streamlining this implementation and there is absolutely no limitation on how many transactions that can commit in parallel. The only limit is the CPU resources, memory resources, networking resources and disk resources.

57.1.1 BASIC WRITE TRANSACTION

We send one signal from the NDB API for each row to be read, updated, deleted, written or inserted. The same signal is used for all types of key operations.

The figure below shows the signal flow for a single row transaction.

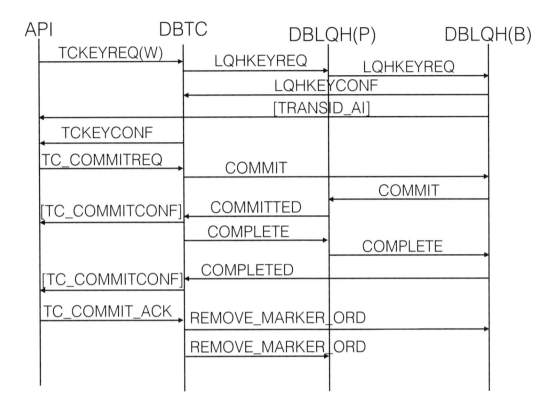

The signal used is called TCKEYREQ and this signal is sent to any *tc* thread based on some hinting techniques described in the chapter on the NDB API.

DBTC uses DBDIH to discover the placement of all the live replicas in the cluster of the row. Next it sends LQHKEYREQ to DBLQH in the node where the primary replica belongs. The signal is sent directly to the proper *ldm* thread owning the partition where this primary row resides.

The idea with sending it to the primary replica first is to avoid deadlocks which would easily happen if the writes are sent to replicas in any order.

There is no special signal to start a transaction. Start of a transaction is indicated by one bit in the TCKEYREQ signal.

There is a commit signal that can be used called TC_COMMITREQ. In the signal diagram above it is used. It is not necessary to use this signal. One can also send a TCKEYREQ with the commit bit set. In this case the transaction is committed immediately after completing the last operation and no more TCKEYREQs will be accepted in this transaction after receiving this bit in a TCKEYREQ signal.

The primary sends a signal to the backup replica, the first LQHKEYREQ contained the list of nodes to update. It sends a LQHKEYREQ, the code executed in the backup replica is almost exactly the same as executed in the primary replica, both replicas will update the row in the prepare phase. The new row will be stored in a copy row, the old row is kept until the commit point. This means that readers that want to see the latest committed row state can always proceed and perform the read.

When all replicas have been updated the last replica sends LQHKEYCONF back to the DBTC that handles the transaction. In this case the TCKEYREQ had both a start bit and a commit bit set, thus the transaction will immediately be committed. We will get the GCI (global checkpoint identifier) of the transaction from DBDIH and send COMMIT to the backup replica. Backup replicas will simply record the commit state and send COMMIT to the next replica in the chain until it reaches the primary replica.

At the primary replica it will release the lock and commit the row change by installing the copy row into the row state and by writing the commit message into the REDO log buffer. After this any reader will see the new row state. Next the primary replica will send COMMITTED to DBTC.

When receiving the COMMITTED signal in DBTC the behaviour depends on if the table is a READ BACKUP table or not. If it isn't (default table setting) DBTC will send an ack to the API using the TCKEYCONF signal. In parallel it will send the COMPLETE signal to the last backup replica. In the complete phase the backup replicas will release the locks and commit the row changes. It will also release operation records and any other memory attached to the operation.

The primary replica will send COMPLETED back to DBTC. At this point the READ BACKUP tables will send TCKEYCONF. After executing the COMPLETED in DBTC the transaction is committed and we have released all records belonging to the transaction.

A final part is happening in the background. The NDB API when receiving TCKEYCONF indicating transaction commit will send TC_COMMIT_ACK to the DBTC. This will generate a number of REMOVE_MARKER_ORD signals. These signals clear transaction state that we needed to keep around when for some reason the NDB API didn't receive the confirmation of the commit decision.

A final note is that most of these signals are sent as packed signals. This is true for LQHKEYCONF, COMMIT, COMMITTED, COMPLETE, COMPLETED and REMOVE_MARKER_ORD. This saves 12 bytes of overhead for each of those signals in the transporter part. Cost of sending data over TCP/IP sockets is a large part of the cost of executing distributed transactions.

One more important lesson that I learned through a master thesis project more than 20 years ago is the cost of flexible protocols. The original idea for the NDB protocol was to use a standard telecom protocol using BER encoding. This turned out to be much too expensive. Thus we invented a streamlined protocol where all parts of the protocol are 32 bits in size. Thus we don't have to process one byte at a time, rather we can process 4 bytes at a time which is using the most efficient CPU instructions.

Most signals are fairly static, thus the code that reads the signal data knows exactly where to find each item. This makes the code very efficient.

A special note on key writes is that they can also read data while updating it. For example it is possible to send a delete operation that reads the record while deleting it. These operations can read either the values before the update or after and it is even possible to send back calculated values.

57.1.2 BASIC READ TRANSACTION

The reads through a primary key uses TCKEYREQ as well. In this case the signal goes to DBTC and from there it is sent to one of the DBLQH blocks. For default tables it will always be sent to the DBLQH of the primary replica.

For READ BACKUP tables and fully replicated tables it depends on the type of the read. READ COMMITTED can be sent to any node with a replica. For reads using read locks or exclusive locks it is sent to the primary replica.

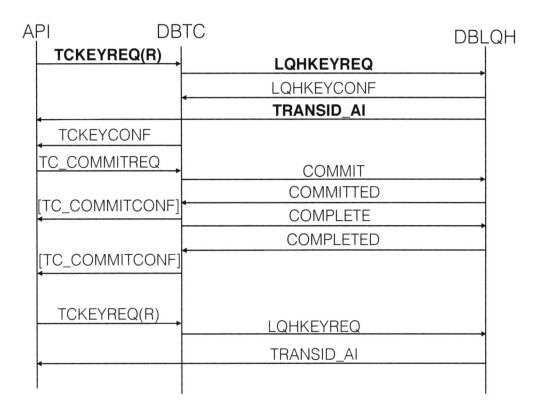

DBLQH sends the data immediately from the *ldm* thread back to the API using the signal TRANSID_AI. For READ COMMITTED there is no other signal sent to the API. I've highlighted the signals that are sent in this specific case in the figure above.

For all other reads there is a signal going back to DBTC called LQHKEYCONF to ensure that the read can be integrated in writing transactions, this signal will lead to a TCKEYCONF signal sent back to the API. TCKEYCONF can contain multiple responses in one message.

57.1.3 UPDATES IN FULLY REPLICATED TABLE

Now let's look at how updates happens in a fully replicated table. The protocol is the same as for a normal write transaction. The difference lies in that a trigger is fired on the primary replica when updating the row. This trigger sends a signal called FIRE_TRIG_REQ to

DBTC. The trigger contains the information to change in the rows. This information is packed into a number of LQHKEYREQ signals, one LQHKEYREQ signal per extra node group.

The updates in the base fragment and the replicated fragments will then proceed in parallel.

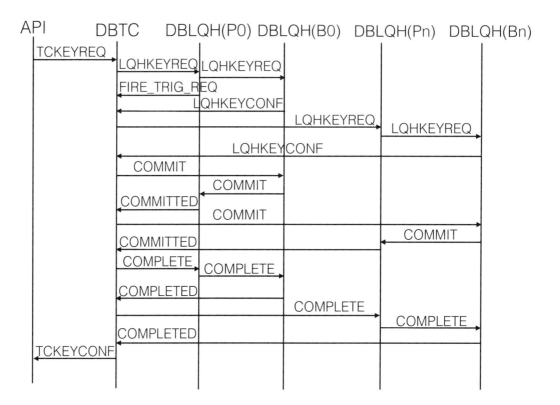

Using this trigger mechanism integrates the changes to the other fragments naturally into the transaction.

57.1.4 MAINTAINING A UNIQUE INDEX

Unique indexes are maintained using exactly the same technique as updates are performed in a fully replicated table. In this case there will be only one LQHKEYREQ to update the fragment where the unique key resides. A special case is a unique index in a fully replicated table, in this case the unique index trigger fires a transactions similar to the update in a fully replicated table.

57.1.5 BUILDING NEW PARTITIONS

When executing the SQL statement ALTER TABLE t1 REORGANIZE PARTITIONS we will reorganise the table to use the new nodes in the cluster.

While building the new partitions we will have triggers that ensure that operations on the table partitions that are reorganised will be sent to the new nodes. This follows the same type of protocol as for fully replicated tables. In this case only rows that are moved to the new nodes will execute those triggers.

57.1.6 ASYNCHRONOUS OPERATIONS

Asynchronous operations in the NDB API is not the standard method to use the NDB API. But it is a very efficient method that at times have been shown to outperform other methods by as much as 10x.

The reason for a higher efficiency can easily be seen in the below figure showing the protocol at a higher level.

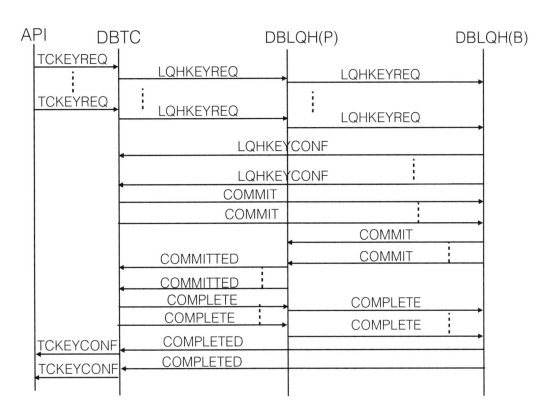

In this mode of operation we receive multiple operations on the table in a small number of TCP/IP packets. Next those processed signals send a batch of LQHKEYREQ signals. In principle the protocol is the same as before, but now everything is heavily parallelised. By sending 200 updates in a batch instead of 1-2 updates at a time, we can gain up to 10x higher throughput.

Asynchronous operations can only be key operations at the moment.

57.1.7 UNIQUE INDEX READ OPERATIONS

Unique indexes can be used for both updates and reads. As mentioned before they constitue a challenge since they can cause deadlocks since reads of the index and updates of the base table can interact with primary key updates of the base table in sequences that can cause a deadlock.

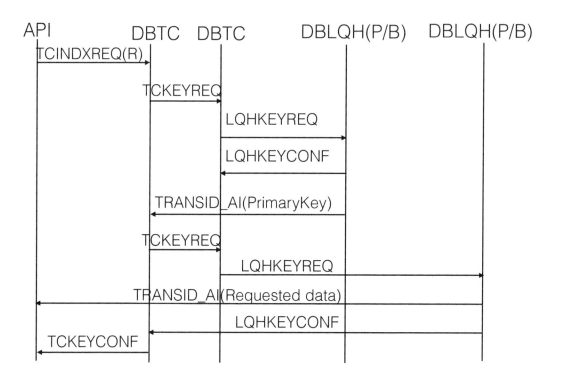

The signalling is easy, it uses a normal read of the unique index table to get the primary key. This key is read back to DBTC that will use the key to start up a normal TCKEYREQ to read/write the row.

57.2 TABLE SCAN OPERATIONS

The second class of query operations that NDB handles are scans of a table. Scans can use a full table scan if no indexes are present. Scans can use ordered indexes to get data in index order. There are three types of full table scans, one uses the hash index in DBACC, a second one scans in rowid order, a third one scans in disk order in DBTUP.

57.2.1 BASIC SCAN OPERATION

All scan operations use the same base protocol. It starts by sending SCAN_TABREQ from the API to the choosen DBTC. DBTC discovers where the partitions of the table reside. Next it sends SCAN_FRAGREQ in parallel to all table partitions. An exception is for pruned scans that only scan one partition. It is possible to limit the amount of parallelism using a parameter in the SCAN_TABREQ signal.

SCAN_FRAGREQs are sent in parallel to a set of DBLQHs that house the partitions. DBLQH has a local scan protocol to gather the data using DBACC, DBTUP, and DBTUX blocks. This protocol is local to one thread in the data node.

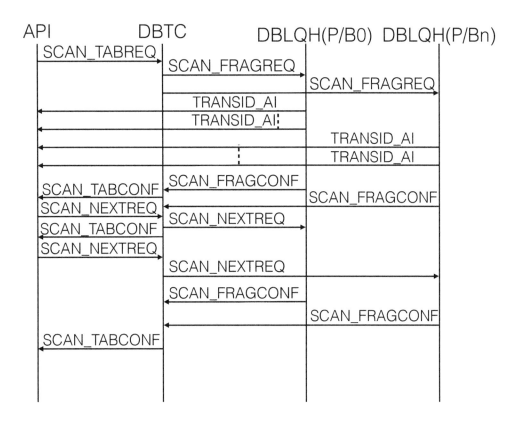

Each signal execution in DBLQH will gather up to five rows. This takes roughly from 2-3 microseconds to 20-30 microseconds or more. Thus even if a scan goes through 1 million rows, it will not cause real-time issues for other scans or key lookup operations. Such a scan will be divided up into hundreds of thousands of signal executions automatically. Thus millions of operations can execute on the same data in parallel with the scan operation even in this case.

DBTC serialises communication with the API. The communication between DBTC and the NDB API has one talker at a time. When one of the DBLQH blocks sends back SCAN_FRAGCONF to DBTC, two things can happen. If NDB API is still waiting for input from DBTC one sends a SCAN_TABCONF signal back to the API immediately. If we have sent SCAN_TABCONF and are waiting for the SCAN_NEXTREQ signal to proceed we will queue the scan results in DBTC. When SCAN_NEXTREQ arrives we will immediately send a new SCAN_TABCONF to the API if any results were queued up. At the same time we will send SCAN_NEXTREQ to the DBLQH blocks that already reported ack to the API.

SCAN_TABCONF will normally report back rows read from multiple DBLQHs at a time.

How many is completely dependent on current system load.

SCAN_TABREQ carries two signal parts. One part is the interpreted program to execute on each row scanned. The second is an index bound (only used by range scans).

The interpreted program carries out filtering and will report back whether the row read was sent back to the API or if it was skipped. The actual row data is sent directly from the *ldm* thread to the API using the TRANSID_AI signal.

The API can always send SCAN_NEXTREQ with a close flag if it decides that it has seen enough. This will start a close protocol of all the outstanding fragment scans.

57.2.2 RANGE SCANS

Range scans are by far the most common scan operations. It carries an index bound that can contain more than one range. All rows that lies within those index bounds will be scanned.

57.2.3 PRUNED SCAN OPERATIONS

Scans have two options, either they can scan all partitions of a table, or they can scan just one partition of the table. The scans that only scan a single partition are called pruned scans. The reason that they only need to scan one partition is that they have knowledge of the partition key.

This is similar to the design in sharded systems. In a sharded system it is necessary to know the sharding key to be able to query the data. Otherwise all shards must be queried.

This is exactly how NDB works as well. A shard in NDB is here a table partition and the sharding key is the partitioning key.

Designing a scalable solution with many data nodes and many *ldm* threads requires use of a carefully selected partition key on the tables.

57.2.4 FULL TABLE SCANS

Full table scans are necessary when no keys are present. Even in this case NDB can scan fast. Since scans are automatically parallelised we can easily scan many millions of rows per second if the query uses a filter that ignores most rows.

57.3 PUSHDOWN JOINS

Pushdown joins are implemented on top of the key lookup protocol and scan protocol. They use a linked join algorithm where keys for the tables down in the join are sent to the DBSPJ block for use with later scans and key lookups. Columns that are read are immediately sent to the NDB API for storage in memory there waiting for the rest of the queried parts that are fetched further down in the join processing.

I will not go into any more details on this implementation in this book.

57.4 FOREIGN KEYS

Foreign keys have two parts. The first part are the consistency checks that the foreign key defines. The checks are executed in a special prepare-to-commit phase executed when starting to commit. If this phase is successful the transaction will be committed, otherwise it will be aborted.

The second part is the cascading actions. These are executed exactly as the other triggering operations. One special thing to consider about foreign keys is however that triggers can fire recursively. One small change is capable of triggering very massive changes. This is not desirable, it is important to consider this when defining your foreign key relations.

57.5 TABLE REORGANISATION

In the block DBDIH in the file DbdihMain.cpp, there is a section called Transaction Handling module. This describes exactly how the global data in DBDIH used for query processing is maintained. In particular it describes how table reorganisations are executed in NDB. It contains a description of the signal flows for this algorithm.

57.6 META DATA OPERATIONS

Meta data operations starts with a phase where the meta data transaction is defined by using signals such as CREATE_TABLE_REQ, DROP_TABLE_REQ, ALTER_TABLE_REQ, CREATE_FILE_REQ and so forth. These signals are spread to all data nodes and are processed by the DBDICT block.

After defining the meta data transaction, there are a great many steps for each of those meta data parts where there is a number of different phases to step forward, there is also a set of steps defined to step backwards when the schema change didn't work.

These steps are implemented by a signal SCHEMA_TRANS_IMPL_REQ and its response SCHEMA_TRANS_IMPL_CONF. All the nodes steps forward in lockstep until all phases have been completed. If something goes wrong in a specific phase, there is a well defined set of phases defined to abort the schema transaction. Obviosuly aborting a meta data operation is a lot more complex than a normal transaction.

57.7 CLUSTER MANAGER OPERATIONS

The node registration protocol and the heartbeat protocol following it are described in some detail in the Qmgr block in the QmgrMain.cpp file in the NDB source code. It contains signal flows for this algorithm.

57.8 LOCAL CHECKPOINT PROTOCOL

The local checkpoint protocol is actually a number of protocols. The first step is a protocol using signals TC_GETOPSIZEREQ/CONF, TC_CLOPSIZEREQ/CONF. These are used to decide when to start a new LCP based on the amount of changes in the data nodes.

We have to acquire a schema lock also for a short time to decide on which nodes to integrate into the LCP. Only the tables defined at the start of the LCP will be checkpointed. New tables created after starting a local checkpoint will have to wait until the next local checkpoint.

One important part of the LCP protocol added in 7.4 is the pause LCP protocol. This ensures that we can pause the LCP execution when a node is starting up to copy the meta data in the cluster. There is a long description of this protocol and the LCP protocol itself in the block DBDIH, in the source code file DbdihMain.cpp. The aim of this protocol is to ensure that DBLQH stops sending LCP_FRAG_REP signals that will change the state of distribution information in DBDIH. This protocol is only required during restart of a node.

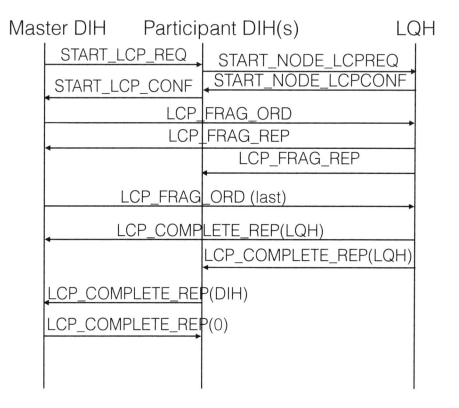

The above figure shows the execution phase protocol of a local checkpoint. It starts by sending START_LCP_REQ to all nodes. Before sending this signal we acquired a mutex on the distribution information in DBDIH. The aim of this signal is to set the flags on what table fragments that will perform this local checkpoint. Since we have locked the distribution information all nodes will calculate this locally. After completing this preparatory step of a local checkpoint each node will respond to the DBDIH block in the master node with the START_LCP_CONF signal.

After receiving this signal from all nodes we have finished the preparation of the local checkpoint. We can now release the mutex.

The next step is to start sending the signal LCP_FRAG_ORD to DBLQH. Each such signal asks DBLQH to checkpoint a specific table fragment. Many such signals can be outstanding at a time, they are queued up if DBLQH isn't ready to execute them.

Whenever DBLQH finishes execution of a local checkpoint for a table fragment it will send the signal LCP_FRAG_REP to report about the completed checkpoint. This signal is sent to all DBDIHs (one per node).

When the master DBDIH have completed sending all LCP_FRAG_ORD to all nodes, it will send a final LCP_FRAG_ORD with the last fragment flag set to true. This indicates to all DBLQHs that no more checkpoint requests will be sent. Thus when DBLQH finishes executing the last checkpoint in the queue and this signal have been received, it knows that its part of the local checkpoint execution is completed.

At completion of local checkpoint execution in a DBLQH it will send the signal LCP_COMPLETE_REP to all DBDIH blocks. This signal will first go to the DBLQH proxy block, only when all local DBLQH instances have sent this signal will the proxy block send this to the local DBDIH block, that in turn will broadcast it to all DBDIH blocks. This signal will be marked by DBLQH completing its part of the local checkpoint execution.

When a DBDIH block have heard this signal from all nodes and it has completed saving the changes to the distribution information from local checkpoint executions, it will send LCP_COMPLETE_REP to the master DBDIH block. This signal will be marked that DBDIH has completed its part of the local checkpoint execution.

When the master have received this signal from all DBDIH blocks, it will send LCP_COMPLETE_REP to all DBDIH blocks with a 0 indicating that now the entire local checkpoint execution is completed in all nodes.

PART XIII

CONFIGURING MySQL CLUSTER

Configuration of MySQL Cluster is important. Since MySQL Cluster was designed for predictable latency, highest performance and highest possible availability, it was important to not use a very dynamic memory allocation. NDB has strict control over all types of resources. At startup of a data node we set the limits on the various resources we are using.

This strict memory allocation behaviour makes it a bit more challenging to configure MySQL Cluster. There is work ongoing to make it easier to configure MySQL Cluster in many different aspects.

MySQL Cluster have developed a significant number of configuration parameters over the years. There are a few parameters that should be set in most clusters. There is a substantial number of configuration parameters that will only be used by a small percent of all users. Often these parameters were developed to solve a specific problem in some specific user setup.

I will explain shortly most of those configuration parameters. But for the most part, those parameters should be possible to ignore until you meet a specific problem where those parameters is the solution to your issue.

In the explanation of the configuration parameters I will define the areas of configuration and give an idea of how important it is to consider configuration parameters in each area.

CHAPTER 58

PROCEDURE TO DEFINE CONFIGURATION

The first choice for setting up MySQL Cluster is to select the number of replicas to use. By default and by far the most common is to use two replicas. The code supports 1 to 4 replicas, but only 1 and 2 replicas are supported features in MySQL Cluster 7.5.

Next one needs to define the set of data nodes, the set of management servers, the set of MySQL Servers and any additional API nodes to use.

Next it is important to set *NoOfFragmentLogParts*. This parameter specifies the number of log parts per node. It is a very important parameter in defining the number of partitions of the tables and how many *ldm* threads we can have in each data node.

Most of the data in NDB resides in memory, setting up the memory resources available for the database is the next important step.

All changes of the databases in NDB happens through transactions. Transaction resources can be configured.

Tables, indexes, foreign keys, disk data objects and so forth, all of them require schema resources. These schema resources can be configured.

NDB is a distributed DBMS, thus communication between nodes can be configured.

Recovery in NDB is an important part, it is also highly linked to the partitioning scheme in NDB and this in turn has a great impact on the thread configuration.

Setting up the optimal thread configuration requires a fair bit of understanding about what affects it, this is covered in a few special chapters. We cover configuration of disk data in NDB in a separate chapter and we cover configuration of MySQL Servers for use with MySQL Cluster in a separate chapter.

58.1 SETTING *NoOfReplicas* AND *NoOfFragmentLogParts*

Setting *NoOfReplicas* is a very important parameter, it can currently not be changed in any other manner than by initialising the cluster and restoring a backup. It cannot be changed without downtime. At the same time it is normally set to 2 and this is the only supported setting other than 1 which is not used for high availability setups.

The number of partitions in a table for a default partitioned table is number of replicas multiplied by number of node groups multiplied by number of *ldm* threads.

The number of *ldm* threads can never be set higher than *NoOfFragmentLogParts*. Thus it is a very important parameter influencing the number of *ldm* threads. In MySQL Cluster 7.5 it is expected that *NoOfFragmentLogParts* is equal to the number of *ldm* threads except that

NoOfFragmentLogParts is always set to at least 4.

Setting number of *ldm* threads can be done in two ways. By setting the configuration parameter *MaxNoOfExecutionThreads* we implicitly define the number *ldm* threads.

Setting *MaxNoOfExecutionThreads* between 0 and 3 gives 1 *ldm* thread. Between 4 and 6 gives 2 *ldm* threads. 7 through 11 gives 4 *ldm* threads, 12 through 15 gives 6 *ldm* threads. 16 through 19 gives 8 *ldm* threads, 20 through 23 means 10 *ldm* threads. 24 through 31 gives 12 *ldm* threads. 32 through 39 gives 16 *ldm* threads. 40 through 47 gives 20 *ldm* threads, 48 through 63 gives 24 *ldm* threads. 64 and up to 72 gives 32 *ldm* threads. The parameter cannot be set higher than 72.

The second method to set number of *ldm* threads is by using the *ThreadConfig* parameter. These parameters will be described in more detail in coming chapters on configuration of the threads in the data nodes.

It is possible to set the *NoOfFragmentLogParts* higher than the number of *ldm* threads. But there is no real gain from doing this. The best is to decide on the number of *ldm* threads you want to have and set *NoOfFragmentLogParts* to the same value. Changing the number of log parts can only be done using an initial node restart and old tables will have to be reorganised to use the new number of log parts. Tables can only be reorganised to increase number of partitions, the number of partitions in an existing table cannot be decreased other than through backup and restore.

Thus deciding on number of log parts and number of *ldm* threads is very important. The number of *ldm* threads should be set according to the amount of CPU resources available for the data node.

The preferred method of configuring thread resources is by using *ThreadConfig*. For production purposes this gives the ultimate control over your environment and the best chance to have a stable environment.

Setting *MaxNoOfExecutionThreads* is easier and can still be combined with CPU locking using *LockExecuteThreadToCPU*.

58.2 SETTING UP NODES

The cluster configuration must contain all nodes that will be part of the cluster. We have to define the data nodes, these are equal to the *ndbd* or *ndbmtd* processes we start in the cluster. Similarly the management server nodes is equal to the number of *ndb_mgmd* processes we start.

This is not true for MySQL Servers and other API nodes. In this case each MySQL Server can use a number of API node ids.

We strongly recommend to use node ids on all data nodes and on all management servers and on all static servers using the NDB API, such as the MySQL Server or any other program that is expected to be up all the time when the cluster is up.

One can also define a few API node slots for NDB tools, these need not have a node id.

Similarly we recommend strongly that data nodes, management servers and all static servers (MySQL Servers and others) set the hostname allowed to connect on each node id.

For security reasons it is a good idea to do the same also with the free API node slots to control from where API nodes can connect to the cluster.

58.2.1 SETTING UP DATA NODES

I recommend that data nodes are the only nodes set up to use node ids 1 through 48. This provides the possibility to grow the number of data nodes to the maximum size without any hassle with reconfiguration of API nodes and other nodes.

As mentioned we recommend to set node id and host name of each data node.

These parameters should be set in the section for each unique data node.

More or less all other parameters should be defined in the default section for data nodes ([NDBD DEFAULT]).

In addition each data node should set the parameter *ServerPort*. Not setting this means that the management server assigns dynamic ports to use in connecting to a data node.

More or less every modern IT environment have firewalls that makes it very hard to work in such a manner. Thus it is recommended to set the *ServerPort* for all data nodes. There is no IANA defined port for this purpose. I recommend using port 11860 for this, it is easy to remember since the management server by default uses 1186 and there is no conflicting IANA port for this port number.

By using this port there are 3 port numbers to consider for MySQL Cluster installations. The 3306 for MySQL Servers, 1186 for NDB management servers, 11860 for NDB data nodes. Using the X plugin and MySQL Document Store means adding 33060 to the set of ports to open in the firewalls to set up MySQL Cluster.

It is important to define at least *DataDir* to ensure that we have defined where the various files for a data node is stored, more on other configuration items for file set up will be described in the next chapter.

58.2.2 SETTING UP MANAGEMENT SERVER NODES

As mentioned one should set node id and host name of the management server.

Normally *PortNumber* use the default port number 1186 for NDB management servers, otherwise this needs to be set.

DataDir will default to */var/lib/mysql-cluster*, this variable should always be set.

58.2.3 SETTING UP MySQL SERVER NODES

Given that each MySQL Server requires one API node for each cluster connection it uses, it is important to set up the correct amount of MySQL Server nodes in the cluster configuration. For example if the MySQL Server uses 4 cluster connections it is necessary to set up 4 API nodes. As mentioned above it is recommended to set node id and host name of all those nodes. In this case all 4 of the API nodes must use the same host name but different node ids.

58.2.4 SETTING UP API NODES

Setting up API nodes for permanent servers follows the same principle as for MySQL servers. Setting up API nodes for use by the various NDB tools usually doesn't require any fancy setups. For security reason it could be a good idea to set the host name. There is no specific need to set the node id on those nodes.

58.3 EXAMPLE *config.ini*

Here is a basic configuration file for two data nodes and two MySQL servers that are colocated. It only sets up the number of replicas, the nodes themselves, the data directories, hostnames and node ids. More details will be covered in later chapters.

config.ini

```
[ndbd default]
NoOfReplicas=2
NoOfFragmentLogParts=4
DataDir=/usr/local/ndb_data
ServerPort=11860

[ndb_mgmd default]
DataDir=/usr/local/ndb_data

[ndb_mgmd]
NodeId=49
Hostname=192.168.1.102

[ndbd]
NodeId=1
Hostname=192.168.1.100

[ndbd]
NodeId=2
Hostname=192.168.1.101

[mysqld]
NodeId=51
Hostname=192.168.1.100

[mysqld]
NodeId=52
Hostname=192.168.1.101

[api]
```

CHAPTER 59

CONFIGURING DATA NODES

Configuring data nodes have quite a lot of configurable resources and parameters that affect various internal algorithms.

59.1 CONFIGURING MEMORY RESOURCES

59.1.1 *DataMemory* AND *IndexMemory*

The most important parameter for a data node is the amount of memory that can be used for data storage. Rows are stored in memory configured through *DataMemory*. *IndexMemory* is the memory used by the primary key hash index. Each row has one entry in such an index, this includes unique index rows. Each table use around 15 bytes of space in *IndexMemory* for each row, similarly each row in a unique index consumes about 15 bytes per row.

DataMemory is used by copy rows. Each row change (except insert row) creates a copy row that contains the data before the row change happened.

DataMemory is used by ordered indexes, expect that each row consumes about 10 bytes of memory per row per ordered index. If a table has 1 million rows and three ordered indexes, the indexes will consume around 30 MBytes of *DataMemory* space.

Personally I usually set *IndexMemory* to around 10% of *DataMemory*. This works fine with row sizes around 100-200 bytes. Larger rows means less *IndexMemory* and even smaller rows means more might be required.

We will always leave a bit of free space in *DataMemory*. The reason is that temporarily the database can grow during restart. To avoid running out of memory during recovery we won't allocate any more rows when we reach the limit on minimum free pages (except during restart when all memory is available). The default is that we save 5% of *DataMemory*. The default setting can be changed through the configuration parameter *MinFreePct*.

59.1.2 *DiskPageBufferMemory*

Another important memory resource parameter is the size allocated for the page cache. This is set in the configuration parameter *DiskPageBufferMemory*. By default this is set to 64 MBytes which is too small for almost every realistic use of disk columns. If disk data columns are used, it is important to set this parameter to a proper value.

Extent pages (there are 4 bits per extent in the extent pages) are permanently stored in memory. The memory allocated for the page cache should be substantially bigger than the memory required for storing the extent pages.

DiskPageBufferEntries is explained in the chapter on disk columns.

59.1.3 *SharedGlobalMemory*

This is a common resource that can be used for various purposes. If we run out of send buffers we can extend our send buffers up to 25% by using this memory.

If we haven't defined *InitialLogfileGroup* in our cluster configuration file we will take the memory for the UNDO log buffer from this memory.

Memory used by disk data file requests are taken from this memory pool as well.

All the operation resources that are specific to pushdown joins are directly using the memory in *SharedGlobalMemory*. The operation records used for meta data operations allocates 2 MByte of memory and if it needs to extend beyond this it starts to use memory in *SharedGlobalMemory*.

59.2 CONFIGURING TRANSACTION RESOURCES

This is another area that is often required to change for production usage or benchmarking. The default setting will work fine in many situations and even for production in some cases. This section describes the parameters and when it is required to change those. It describes the memory impact of increasing versus decreasing them.

Any record size provided in this chapter is from a specific 7.5 version and can change a few bytes up and down without any specific notice.

59.2.1 TRANSACTIONAL RESOURCES

When we execute any read or write of data we always use a transaction record in a *tc* thread. A transaction record is also used for every scan we execute in the cluster.

The maximum number of transaction records is set through the config parameter *MaxNoOfConcurrentTransactions*. By default it is 4096. The setting is per *tc* thread. With more *tc* threads we get more transaction records.

When using the MySQL Server to access NDB the number of transaction records in parallel is fairly limited. Using the asynchronous NDB API it is possible to execute many millions of parallel transactions. In this case it is good to increase this setting. The default setting is good for a fair amount of cases, but with highly concurrent applications it should be increased.

The size of the transaction record is 896 bytes, the real record size is 288 bytes. But we need one extra record to handle the complete phase for each transaction record and additionally we need one record to ensure that we can handle node failure handling. In addition we have 2 records of 16 bytes in DBDIH for each transaction thus giving 896 bytes in total.

59.2.2 PRIMARY KEY OPERATIONS

Every primary key operation uses one operation record in the transaction coordinator and one in the *ldm* thread. If it is a write operation there is one operation record for each replica. In addition each scan operation uses also one operation record in the transaction coordinator and one operation record in each of the scanned fragments in the *ldm* threads. This parameter is configured by setting *MaxNoOfConcurrentOperations*.

This parameter impacts allocation both in *tc* threads and in *ldm* threads. It defaults to

32768. This will allocate 32768 records in each *tc* thread. In addition we will allocate 32768 multiplied by 1.1 and divided by number of *ldm* threads to each *ldm* thread. With multiple *tc* threads it is a good idea to specifically set the number of operation records in the *ldm* threads.

The number of local operations in *ldm* threads can be set through the configuration parameter *MaxNoOfLocalOperations*. The above describes the default setting.

With 4 *ldm* threads it is a good idea to set this to around 150000 to ensure that full use of operation records in *tc* threads can happen without running out of operation records in *ldm* threads. If most of the operations are writes the number should be set higher since there is more operation records used in *ldm* thread per operation in a *tc* thread. As will be described later the local operation records are allocated also while performing a local scan operation.

The default setting of 32768 provides a bit of parallelism. In most of my benchmarks and experiments it is necessary to increase to at least a few hundred thousand. Setting this a bit higher can avoid issues with large transactions that are sometimes used by various tools, especially tools that load data. It is reasonable to use around 5% of the memory available for operation records given that it is such an essential part of any reads and writes issued in the database. Each GByte of memory assigned to operation records provides for a parallelism of about 1.25 million row operations.

The size of operation records in the *tc* threads is 304 bytes. The size is around 152 bytes, but we need two records per operation, one is required to handle node failure handling when we take over failed transactions.

The size of the local operation records in the *ldm* threads is 496 bytes. The record is actually split in one part in DBLQH, one in DBACC and one in DBTUP.

For a read the total operation record sizes used are 800 bytes and for an update with 2 replicas the operation record sizes used are around 1300 bytes.

59.2.3   SCAN OPERATIONS

Scans use a transaction record and a scan record in the *tc* thread. The scan record size is 120 bytes. The maximum number of parallel scans is set per *tc* thread. It is set by default to 256 and has a maximum number of 500. The reason that the number of scans is limited is due to the high parallelism we employ in the scan operations. It is necessary to limit the amount of parallel scans in the cluster to avoid various overload cases. Changing the default is through the parameter *MaxNoOfConcurrentScans*.

Each scan allocates a set of scan fragment records as well in the *tc* thread (currently 64 bytes in size). The number of scan fragment records is one if the scan is a pruned scan, otherwise it is equal to the maximum scan parallelism. The maximum parallelism is the number of partitions in the table. It is possible to limit the scan parallelism by using the SO_PARALLEL option in the NDB API. There is no specific setting in the MySQL Server to change this. Scans from the MySQL Server always uses a parallelism equal to the number of partitions in the table. For a default table the number of partitions is the number of nodes multiplied by the number of *ldm* threads. E.g. with 4 data nodes and 4 *ldm* threads there would be 16 partitions.

All the scan resources are released as soon as the scan has completed. Only operation records from key operations are kept until commit time. A delete that is using a scan have to execute a primary key operation that uses a special scan takeover request to ensure that the lock and the update is kept until commit time.

Given that scan resources are released after execution, the amount of scan records is more based on the amount of parallelism rather than the amount of data in the cluster. The default setting of 256 parallel scans per *tc* thread should work fine in most cases.

The number of scan frag records is the number of scan records multiplied by number of *tc* threads multipled by number of *ldm* threads multiplied by number of data nodes in the cluster. For example with 2 *tc* threads, 4 *ldm* threads and 4 data nodes and a maximum of 256 scans in parallel we will have 8192 scan fragment records in each *tc* thread.

The same amount of scan records exist in the *ldm* threads as there are in the scan fragment records in the *tc* threads.

For each scan we have a scan record that is in total 588 bytes, this record is divided into a 96 byte record in DBACC, a 112 byte record in DBTUP, a 136 byte record in DBTUX, a 232 byte record in DBLQH. Next we also allocate an operation record for each scan that is 496 bytes in size. In total we allocate records of size 1084 bytes per local scan in an *ldm* thread.

In addition for each scan record in the *ldm* threads we allocate a certain number of lock records. A lock record is 120 bytes in size (96 byte record in DBACC and a 12 byte record in DBTUP and DBTUX). We allocate as many lock records as our batch size per local scan. The default for this parameter is 256. Thus each scan record allocates 30 kBytes of lock records. In the above example we will have a total of 16384 scan records in the *ldm* threads that consumes around 500 MBytes of memory where most of it is the lock records.

Most scans are not using locking, the above allocation is on the safe side in an extreme manner. The above means that scans can lock up to 4 million records, 1 million records in each *ldm* thread. Remember that a normal scan from SQL uses READ COMMITTED mode, this uses no locks at all. Next if we use a lock on the scan we only hold the lock from when we scan it until the NDB API have signalled back that it has completed using the row. This time period is normally less than a millisecond. The risk of us using all the lock records is neglible.

To decrease the allocation of lock records one can set the *BatchSizePerLocalScan* to a lower value. Setting it to e.g. 64 should most likely suffice for almost all installations. Even lower values can most likely even be plausible if the number of scans using locks are low. Even setting it as low as 8 will provide the capability to handle 128k of concurrent scan locks in the above example.

It is possible to set the number of scan fragment records in *ldm* threads through the configuration parameter *MaxNoOfLocalScans* if the above default setting isn't ok. To increase the operation records also used by local scans it is the *MaxNoOfLocalOperations* that one needs to increase.

As can be seen the default setup for scans are configured to handle the worst case where no scans are pruned scans and where every scan is using locks and using a batch size of 256 on scans.

If the application is using a lot of pruned scans we can decrease the amount of local scan records by setting *MaxNoOfLocalScans* lower.

If the application is never using only locking scans or the batch size is smaller than 256, the *BatchSizePerLocalScan* can be set significantly lower and thus saving a lot of memory.

It is important to have the same configuration of these values in all nodes. These changes should always be set in the default section for data nodes in the cluster configuration file. Changing those values to smaller values can cause temporary issues with out of resources since one node that still have high values will consume resources in the nodes with a lower configuration.

The only problem with misconfiguration of scans are temporary errors. All scans in internal algorithms uses preallocated records.

59.2.4 UNIQUE INDEX OPERATIONS

Access to a record through a unique index uses two steps, the first step is a read of the unique index, the second step is a normal operation using the primary key read from the unique index.

The first phase uses a special record in the *tc* thread. This record is only kept until the first read of the unqiue index have completed. Immediately when the read has completed, the record is released. The record has a size of 160 bytes and the default is to have 8192 such records per *tc* thread.

To set this to a higher value to avoid concurrency issues or to save a bit of memory by setting it lower one can set the configuration parameter *MaxNoOfConcurrentIndexOperations*.

It should be very rare that anyone needs to change this variable.

59.2.5 TRIGGER RESOURCES

Similar to unique index operations we keep a record for triggered operation from that we receive them until we executed them. This record is 80 bytes in size and we have 4000 records per *tc* thread. It is a bit more common to run out of this resource when committing large transactions with many foreign key checks. It should be very rare to need to change this parameter, if required the parameter is *MaxNoOfFiredTriggers*.

When a trigger is fired, its values are sent to the *tc* thread exeuting the transaction. Until the resulting action is executed we keep the before value and after value sent in the trigger in a buffer. The size of this buffer is set through *TransactionBufferMemory*. By default this is set to 1 MByte per *tc* thread.

59.2.6 LIMITING MAXIMUM TRANSACTION SIZE

It is possible to limit the maximum size of a transaction. By default this option is off, to set it use the parameter *MaxDMLOperationsPerTransaction*.

59.2.7 FINAL WORDS

The configuration of transaction resources can be a bit daunting we understand. There is work ongoing to improve this significantly in future versions of MySQL Cluster to ensure that transaction resources can be configured with at most a single configuration variable. The *MaxNoOfConcurrentScans* parameter is likely to stay since this configuration parameter is also ensuring that we don't overload the cluster.

59.3 CONFIGURING SCHEMA RESOURCES

This section is required to consider for use of MySQL Cluster with a large number of tables, attributes, foreign keys, indexes and so forth. It describes the parameters and when to consider changing them, it describes the memory impact of those parameters.

59.3.1 *MaxNoOfAttributes*

MaxNoOfAttributes defines the maximum amount of columns that can be defined in the cluster.

There are two important records that are influenced by the number of columns. The first is in the block DBDICT where we have a record of 160 bytes that describe the column and its features. The second memory area is in DBTUP where we have a memory area with a great deal of pointers to methods used to read and write the columns. This area is 120 bytes per column in each *ldm* thread. Thus if we have a node with 4 *ldm* we will use 640 bytes per column. The default setting for *MaxNoOfAttributes* is 1000. This is a very low value, thus increasing it should probably be done for anything except very minimal cluster sizes. Even increasing it to 10000 should not be any concern. It is conceivable with large applications that the number of columns in the cluster is counted in millions even.

The maximum number of columns in the cluster will also affect the size of memory allocated for *StringMemory* as explained below. In the default setting it will use an additional 3533 bytes per column.

59.3.2 NUMBER OF TABLES

There are three types of objects that all use table objects. Normal tables is the obvious one, the unique indexes are stored as tables, these have to be counted as well. In most situations the ordered indexes are also treated as table objects although they are tightly connected to normal tables and their partitions.

When calculating memory used per table, the three values *MaxNoOfTables*,

MaxNoOfOrderedIndexes and *MaxNoOfUniqueHashIndexes* are added. The default value of those are 128, 128 and 64. The default number of table objects are 320. The maximum number of table objects is limited by DBDICT where at most 20320 table objects can be defined.

In most places the sum of those values are used. They are used to calculate the number of triggers in the system and here they are used individually. The number of ordered indexes have a special impact on the number of objects in DBTUX. DBTUX is only used by ordered indexes, thus this is natural.

There are many different records that are describing table objects. In DBDICT we have a table record of 280 bytes, we have a meta data object of 88 bytes and we have a global key descriptor of 520 bytes. In addition we have two hash tables on meta data object id and meta data object name. Hashes has at most an overhead of 8 bytes per table object. The table record in DBDIH is a bit bigger and consumes 3296 bytes. In addition we have around 24 bytes of memory per table object in each *tc* thread. In the *ldm* threads we have 76 bytes per table object in DBACC, 72 bytes in DBLQH, 144 bytes in DBTUX and 544 bytes in DBTUP. There is a total of 836 bytes per *ldm* thread.

In total for table records we have in the example with 2 *tc* threads and 4 *ldm* threads we use about 7700 bytes per table object.

Table objects is not the only memory consumer for meta data objects. The memory consumption also comes from the fragment records in various blocks.

The default number of fragments per *ldm* thread is equal to the number of replicas in the cluster set by *NoOfReplicas*. Thus normally equal to 2. Each fragment record is 496 bytes in DBLQH, 304 bytes in DBACC, 472 bytes in DBTUP and 96 bytes in DBTUX. DBTUX only stores fragment for ordered indexes, this record can almost be ignored in the calculations. Assuming that we have 2 replicas in the cluster, we have around 2600 bytes of fragment records per table object per *ldm* thread. With 4 *ldm* threads we consume about 10400 bytes per table object in the fragment records.

We have both fragment record and replica records in DBDIH. DBDIH stores one fragment record for each fragment in the cluster, the number of fragments per table by defaut is the number of nodes multiplied by the number of *ldm* threads. The number of replica records is this number multiplied by the number of replicas in the cluster. The fragment records are 48 bytes and the replica records are 148 bytes. With 2 nodes and 4 *ldm* threads and 2 replicas we use 2752 bytes per table object in DBDIH.

In the example case with 2 data nodes, 4 *ldm* threads, 2 *tc* threads and 2 replicas we consume a total of 20852 bytes per table object. Thus the table and fragment records in a default setup (a total of 322 table objects) uses around 6.5 MByte of meta data storage.

Thus even with the maximum amount of tables in this setup (20320 table objects) we consume no more than around 400 MBytes of metadata for table, fragment and replica records.

Scaling to a higher number of *ldm* increases most sizes linearly since more threads need table and fragment records while the number of fragments per *ldm* thread stays constant.

Increasing number of nodes influences the storage in DBDIH where more memory is needed since the number of fragments in a table increases linearly with the number of nodes. For example in the case with 48 data nodes with 4 *ldm* threads we get about 66 kBytes per table object instead in DBDIH.

59.3.3 *MaxNoOfTriggers*

The default setting of *MaxNoOfTriggers* is based on the amount of table objects that the cluster should handle. The default setting is set 768, but when the value set in the configuration or the default value is smaller than the calculated value, we will use the calculated value.

The cacluated values assumes that each unique index requires 3 triggers (one for insert, one for update and one for delete operations). 1 trigger is required for each ordered index. In addition we will take height for one set of 3 triggers for a metadata operation such as add partitions. Each normal table that is fully replicated will use 3 triggers as well. We take height for 100 table events. This number will be compared to the configured value and the higher value will win.

Thus the main reason to increase *MaxNoOfTriggers* is to ensure that we can add foreign keys, that we can add triggers for altering the amount of table partitions and when more events are added by users to the system.

The amount of memory used for triggers is fairly small. The DBDICT block consumes 116 bytes per trigger object, the DBTC blocks consumes 36 bytes per *tc* thread and the DBTUP block consumes 112 bytes per *ldm* thread. In our example with 2 *tc* threads and 4 *ldm* threads each trigger will use 636 bytes of memory.

We will have extra trigger records in DBTUP, these extra records are there to accomodate backups, backups do not use global triggers, they only use local trigger. We will add 3 extra trigger records for the number of tables defined by *MaxNoOfTables*.

Given that the memory consumption of triggers is low, it is a good idea to set this configuration parameter such that it is prepared for a set of foreign keys, add partitions and events on all tables through various resources.

59.3.4   *StringMemory*

StringMemory defines the amount of memory to allocate for column names, default values for columns, names of tables, indexes, and names of triggers and it is used to store the FRM files used by MySQL servers to store metadata.

In NDB the FRM file is stored inside NDB, thus when a MySQL Server connects to the cluster, it will receive the tables and their metadata from NDB and store it in the local file system of the MySQL Server.

The maximum size of a table name is 128 bytes, the maximum size of a column name is 192, the maximum size of the default values is equal to 14004 bytes (4 plus the maximum row size in NDB). The maximum size of an FRM file is 6000 words.

DBDICT will allocate memory to ensure that we can fit also very large table names and column names and so forth. The size is calculated based on maximum sizes and the maximum amount of columns and number of table objects and triggers.

Now this size is a bit overexaggerating to use for allocation. So *StringMemory* is defined in percentage. If the memory is calculated to be 20 MBytes and we use the default setting of 25, then the allocated size will 25% * 20 MBytes = 5 MBytes.

Even 25 is a bit large, for example most columns have a much smaller default value compared to the maximum size of 14000 bytes. Thus going down to 5% is mostly ok.

Assuming that we set this value to 10% each column will use 1420 bytes in *StringMemory* and each table object will consume roughly 620 bytes. Probably tables would in reality require a bit more whereas columns require a lot less.

The actual default value used in normal query processing is stored in DBTUP and it uses the *DataMemory* to store one such row per table per *ldm* thread. This size of this default row is limited by the maximum row size that is 14000 bytes currently.

59.4   Event configuration

Configuring events is ensuring that sufficient amount of records exist in the block SUMA where events are handled.

59.4.1   *MaxNoOfSubscriptions*

A subscription is 128 bytes in size, thus it doesn't take up a lot of resources. The most common use case for subscriptions is that it is used for MySQL Cluster replication.

Normally in this case there is one subscription per table that is replicated. The default value of this parameter is to set it to 0. In this case the value it is the sum of the *MaxNoOfTables*, *MaxNoOfUniqueHashIndexes* and *MaxNoOfOrderedIndexes*. Given that a subscriptions can only be set on normal tables it means that we get a bit more subscription records than what is required for normal MySQL Cluster Replication.

This is good since subscriptions are also used for online meta data operations such reorganising partitions, building indexes and building foreign key relations.

Normally there is only one subscription used even if there are multiple MySQL servers doing replication. They will subscribe to the same subscription. The handler has a specific name on the subscription to ensure that it knows how to find the subscription.

If the replication setup is different for the MySQL replication servers they will require different subscriptions, in this case the name of the subscription will differ. One case where this will happen is if the MySQL replication servers use a different setting of the *--ndb-log-updated-only* configuration option.

NDB API programs that defines events on tables are also likely to use their own subscriptions. It is possible to synchronize several NDB API nodes to use the same subscription by using the same name of the event.

The default setup will work just fine in most cases, but if the user has different MySQL replication server setups and/or is using the NDB Event API, it would be required to increase the setting of *MaxNoOfSubscriptions*.

59.4.2   *MaxNoOfSubscribers*

A subscriber is using a subscription, there needs to be more subscriber records compared to the number of subscriptions. Each NDB API node or MySQL Server node that listens to events from a table uses a subscriber record. The default number of subscriber records is twice the default number of subscriptions. Thus it is designed to use two MySQL replication servers in the cluster that listens to all table events without any issues and even handle a bit more than that.

The subscriber record is only 16 bytes, thus there is very little negative consequence in increasing this value to a higher setting.

59.4.3   *MaxNoOfConcurrentSubOperations*

Suboperation records are used during the creation phase of subscribers and subscriptions. It is set to 256 and should normally be ok. The record is only 32 bytes in size, no problem exists in increasing this setting even substantially.

59.4.4 *MaxBufferedEpochs*

Event operations was explained in some detail in the chapters on MySQL Cluster Replication and the API towards it in the chapter on the C++ NDB API.

Events are gathered one epoch at a time. One epoch is a group of transactions that are serialised towards other epochs.Thus all transactions in epoch n committed before any transaction in epoch *n+1* was committed.

The time between epochs defaults to 100 milliseconds and this value is configurable through the parameter *TimeBetweenEpochs*.

Now the SUMA block that maintain events grouped in epochs, must keep track of epochs. For this it uses a special epoch record, this is only 24 bytes in size. By default we have 100 such records. Thus the memory used for these records is completely ignorable. It is still important to set this parameter properly. The default setting of 100 together with the default setting of 100 milliseconds for *TimeBetweenEpochs* means that we can track epochs for up to 10 seconds. If any part of the event handling cannot keep up with epochs rapidly enough, subscribers will start losing events and this will lead to that we will close down the subscriber. The parameter is set in number of milliseconds.

Setting this a bit higher is not a problem. What can be problematic is whether we will have memory buffers enough to handle more epochs. This depends on the update rate in NDB and amount of memory buffers we have available for saving epochs.

The buffer space for epochs is controlled by the configuration parameter *MaxBufferedE-pochBytes*. This value defaults to around 25 MByte. In a high-performance environment it is quite likely that this buffer should be significantly increased.

The parameter *TimeBetweenEpochsTimeout* can be set to a a non-zero value, in this case we will crash the node if it takes longer than this value to complete the epoch.

59.4.5 *RestartSubscriberConnectTimeout*

The parameter *RestartSubscriberConnectTimeout* is an important timeout during node restart. If an API node or a MySQL server have subscribed to some table events, the starting node will wait for this API node or MySQL server to connect during the last phase (phase 101) of the node restart. Normally these nodes will connect very quickly and the restart will proceed. If a node subscribing to events are down, this is the time that we will wait for those nodes to connect again.

By default this timeout is set to 2 minutes (set to 120000, set in milliseconds).

59.5 BASIC THREAD CONFIGURATIONS

The preferred manner of setting up the thread configuration is to use the *ThreadConfig* variable. This is explained in detail in a coming chapter. A quick manner of configuring the threads is to set the *MaxNoOfExecutionThreads* variable.

The MySQL manual describes exactly how many threads of various sorts that we get when setting those from 0 to 72. As described in the previous chapter it is important to keep track of how many *ldm* threads the number generates (described in the previous chapter) and it is important to set *NoOfFragmentLogParts* to the number of *ldm* threads.

It is possible to use a simple method to lock threads to CPUs by using the configuration variable *LockExecuteThreadToCPU*. This variable expects a comma separated list of CPU ids. The number of CPUs must be at least as many as the threads defined (*ldm*, *tc*, *main*, *rep*, *send* and *recv* threads).

LockMaintThreadsToCPU can be combined with the above two variables to set the CPU to use for *io* threads. Only one CPU can be used in this configuration variable, if necessary to lock *io* threads to more than one CPU, it is necessary to use *ThreadConfig* to configure this.

The remainder of the thread configurations is considered advanced and will be explained in a coming chapter.

59.6   Restart configuration

There is a wide range of configuration items that affect restarts and when node fails.

59.6.1   Start logic

NDB is designed for automatic restart. The default behaviour of a data node is that it is executing two processes, the starting process is called the angel process and is responsible to restart the node automatically after a crash. There are three configuration parameters controlling this behaviour.

StopOnError

Setting *StopOnError* to 1 means that the data node process will stop at failures. Default is 0, thus the default is to automatically restart.

MaxStartFailRetries

If the node restart fails we will count this failure. The *MaxStartFailRetries* is how many attempts we will do before we stop the data node completely. As soon as the restart is successful the fail counter will be set to 0. By default this is set to 3.

StartFailRetryDelay

It is possible to invoke a delay before the node restart begins after a crash. This delay is set in *StartFailRetryDelay*, the unit is seconds. By default there is no delay.

59.6.2   Start timers

Whenever a node starts up there is a set of timers that affect for how long we will wait for more nodes to join before we proceed with the restart.

StartPartialTimeout

The *StartPartialTimeout* affects how long time we will wait for more nodes to join, in the case when the cluster is starting up. If we discover during the heartbeat registration that the cluster is up and running we will start immediately. During the wait we will print in the node log which nodes we are waiting and which that have connected and for how long we waited.

In the case of an initial start of the cluster we will always wait for all nodes to come up except when the user have provided a set of nodes to not wait for on the command line using the *--no-wait-nodes* option.

This parameter defaults to 30000, this means 30 seconds since the unit is millseconds. Setting it to 0 means waiting forever until all nodes are starting up.

StartPartitionedTimeout

This parameter provides a possibility to start a cluster even with a suspected network partititioning problem. Setting this parameter to 0 means that we will never start in a partitioned state. By default this is set to 60000, thus 60 seconds.

This parameter should always be set to 0, the default value is not a good choice. It is strongly recommended to not start up if it is suspected that the cluster is in a network partitioned state.

StartFailureTimeout

This parameter is by default set to 0, this means that restart will proceed until they are done.

If we know by experience that a restart should be completed in a certain time period, then we can set this parameter to a high value to ensure that we get a crash instead of an eternally hanging state of the node.

One should be very careful in setting this parameter (unit is milliseconds) given that restarts of large databases can take a substantial amount of time at times.

StartNoNodegroupTimeout

This parameter sets the time we will wait for nodes with no node group assigned while starting. A node has no node group if it is assigned *NodeGroup* equal to 65536. Nodes without node group contains no data, so they are not relevant for cluster operation, they are only relevant to extend the cluster size.

This parameter is set to 15000 (15 seconds) by default.

59.6.3 CONFIGURING HEARTBEAT

Heartbeat are mainly interesting to handle when a computer dies completely. When the data node process fails the OS will ensure that its TCP/IP sockets are closed and thus the neighbouring nodes will discover the failure. Heartbeats are also good to handle cases where a node is not making any progress.

For example in Mac OS X I have noticed that accessing a zero pointer leads to a hanging process. The heartbeat will discover this type of failures.

HeartbeatIntervalDbDb

This parameter specifies the heartbeat between data nodes. It was originally set to 1500 milliseconds. Thus the node will be considered as failed in at most 6 seconds, after 3 missed heartbeats. Every missed heartbeat is logged into the node log, if the node is often close to the limit, the node log and cluster log will show this.

To ensure that NDB works better for early users we changed the default to 5000 milliseconds, thus it can take up to 20 seconds before a node failure is discovered.

In a high availability setup with computers that are dedicated to NDB and its applications, it is possible to decrease this configuration parameter. How low it can be set depends on how much the OS can be trusted to provide continuos operation. Some OSs can leave a thread unscheduled for a second or two even in cases when there is no real resource shortage.

In a production environment it is recommended to use the old default 1500 milliseconds or even lower than this.

It is important to understand that when changing this value, one should never increase it by more than 100% and one should never decrease to less than half. Otherwise the sending of heartbeats will cause node failures with other neighbouring nodes that haven't updated it heartbeat interval yet. The heartbeat interval in different data nodes should only differ during a rolling restart to change the configuration.

HeartbeatIntervalDbApi

This parameter sets the heartbeat interval between an API node and a data node. The heartbeats are sent from the API node once every 100 milliseconds and it expects a return within three heartbeat periods. This parameter has a default of 1500 milliseconds.

The consequence of losing the connection to the data node is smaller than a data node losing its connection. If the API node is declared down, it will immediately reconnect again normally.

HeartbeatOrder

The heartbeat protocol assigns a dynamic id to each node when it starts. This id provides the order of starting nodes. Thus the node with the lowest id is the oldest node. The node with the lowest dynamic id is choosen as the master after a failure of the master node.

Heartbeats are sent to its right neighbour and received from its left neighbour. The definition of who is the right and left neighbour is defined by the order the nodes are starting up, thus through the dynamic id.

It is possible to specifically set the order of the nodes in the heartbeat protocol instead of using the default.

The manual contains some description of when it might be useful, but I am not convinced that it is a very useful feature.

ConnectCheckIntervalDelay

This is a boolean variable that adds two more heartbeat intervals before a node is declared dead. After three failed heartbeat intervals the node will be in a suspected state and in this state the node will be checked from more than one node during the last two heartbeat intervals.

This parameter makes it possible to improve the heartbeat handling in environments where the communication latency can vary.

This is a rather new feature that is an improvement compared to only using heartbeats between neighbours. If used one should adjust the heartbeat settings since with this extra check we will not fail until after missing 5 heartbeats.

59.6.4 CONFIGURING ARBITRATION IN DATA NODES

There are several ways to setup arbitration in the cluster. The default behaviour is that the arbitrator is asked for its opinion when we cannot be certain that no cluster split has occurred.

To ensure that it is possible to use clusterware to enable running the cluster even with only two computers, we have implemented a special mode where external clusterware makes the decision on arbitration.

ArbitrationTimeout

This parameter sets the timeout waiting for a response from the arbitrator. If no response comes within this time period the node will crash. The default for this period is 7500 milliseconds.

Arbitration

By default this string variable is set to Default. It can also be set to Disabled which means that no arbitration is performed and thus the cluster crashes if there is a risk of network partitioning.

There is a mode WaitExternal that was explained in the chapter on handling node crashes in NDB. This ensures that a message is written into the cluster log ensuring that some external clusterware can decide which part of the cluster to kill.

59.6.5 OPTIMISING RESTART EXECUTION

BuildIndexThreads

This parameter enables the use of extra threads during restart to build the ordered indexes. The number of threads used is limited by the amount of fragments of a table within one data node. Thus setting it to 128 is a simple method of ensuring that maximum possible parallelism is used for ordered index building.

By default this is not enabled. It is recommended to enable this feature, it has been used succesfully for many years by multiple users and has been extensively used in test suites for as long as I can remember. It is set as default in MySQL Cluster 7.6.4.

TwoPassInitialNodeRestartCopy

This parameter is a boolean that is not set by default. By setting it, an initial node restart will be executed in two phases, the first phase loads the data from another node. Next a fully parallelised ordered index build is performed. After this a second phase of copying data from live nodes is performed where only changes since the first phase is copied to the starting node.

It is recommended to set this parameter. It has been set in crash tests for many years. It was set to default in the MySQL Cluster 7.6.4 DMR.

MaxParallelCopyInstances

This parameter sets the parallelism used when copying data from the live node to the starting node. By default the parallelism is equal to the number of *ldm* threads. There should normally never be any reason to change this variable.

59.6.6   ___at_restart_skip_indexes

This configuration was probably invented to handle some support case where indexes were corrupt and thus no restart was possible. It should never be set unless as a last option to get the cluster up again to restore its data.

59.7   CONFIGURING DEADLOCK DETECTION

Deadlock can occur in a database using row locks to implement concurrency control. Our method of resolving deadlocks is based on timeouts. When an operation doesn't return from a read or a write we assume that it is in a lock queue and since we don't come back we assume that we're involved in a deadlock.

NDB is designed for applications using short transactions that complete in a number of milliseconds, when an operation doesn't return within seconds we assume that something is wrong. An operation would normally return in less than a millisecond and even in a highly loaded cluster would it take more than a few milliseconds to return for an operation.

This deadlock detection timeout is also used to ensure that transactions that rely on a node that have died will be aborted. The timeout here should not be materially larger than the time that it takes to detect a node failure using heartbeats. Normally it should be much smaller than this.

Short deadlock detection timeout means that we recover quickly from deadlocks. At the same time if it is too short we might get too many false indications of deadlocks in a highly concurrent application.

59.7.1   *TransactionDeadlockDetectionTimeout*

This parameter sets the deadlock detection timeout. The default deadlock detection timeout is 1200 milliseconds.

59.7.2   *TimeBetweenInactiveTransactionAbortCheck*

Deadlock detection timers are not constantly checked. A check of all running transactions is performed with some delay in between. This delay can be increased with this parameter, it defaults to once per second and should normally not need to be changed.

59.7.3   *TransactionInactiveTimeout*

This sets the time that a transaction is allowed to be inactive from the API. In this case we're not waiting for any nodes, rather we are waiting for the API to decide to proceed. By default this wait is almost forever.

Given that the transaction can have locks while waiting for API, it is a good idea to set this to a much lower value of say 1500 millisecond. This ensures that misbehaving APIs will not mess up the database.

59.8 CONFIGURING LOGGING

Logging in NDB for data nodes happens in a number of places. We have the cluster log that is generated in data nodes and sent to the management server to place it into the cluster log. It is possible to also direct these messages to the node log.

We have the node log, here comes various log messages that are only written locally, normal printouts end up here as well.

The cluster log levels are controlled by a number of configuration parameters. Each such parameter controls a specific part of the logging. Each message is active at a certain log level and not on lower log levels.

The log levels that are definable are the following:

LogLevelStartup, LogLevelShutdown, LogLevelStatistic, LogLevelCheckpoint, LogLevelNodeRestart, LogLevelConnection, LogLevelCongestion, LogLevelError, LogLevelInfo

These can be changed temporarily from the NDB management client.

59.8.1 *MaxNoOfSavedMessages*

Whenever a data node crashes we generate a set of trace files to describe the crash. The *MaxNoOfSavedMessages* controls the number of crashes that will be saved. By default this is set to 25. When the 26th crash occurs it will overwrite the information in the error log and the trace files generated by the first crash.

59.8.2 *EventLogBufferSize*

This is the buffer used to store log events in the data node until they are sent to the cluster log in a management server. It is by default 8 kBytes.

59.9 DISKLESS CONFIGURATION

The *Diskless* parameter is a useful parameter for testing when the servers don't have sufficient disk bandwidth to handle the load.

It can be useful when the application have no need of any recovery. For example a stock market application will have no use of database recovery since the stock market data have completely changed since the cluster failed. In this case one could use *Diskless* set to 1 to ensure that all writes to the file system are thrown away. It is similar to mounting the file system on /dev/null.

A better method of doing this is to create the tables with the NOLOGGING feature. This ensures that the tables are still around after a restart although the tables are empty.

59.10 WATCHDOG CHECKS

NDB data nodes is designed with a virtual machine that handles execution of signals and ensuring that we can communicate those signals within a thread, between threads and to other nodes.

The virtual machine is designed such that when a signal executes, it is up to the signal execution code to return control to the virtual machine layer. Thus as an example a run away signal that enters an eternal loop cannot be detected by the virtual machine.

Signals are supposed to execute only for a few microseconds at a time. This is by design, and so of course a bug can cause a signal to execute for much longer.

Now if a thread does execute for too long it is likely to be detected by other nodes in various ways through timers. But a deadlock in one thread could be undetected if the other threads keeps the other nodes happy.

To detect such run away threads we use a watchdog mechanism. Each thread registers with a watchdog thread. This watchdog thread wakes up every now and then and checks if the threads have moved since last time. If no movement has happened it will continue waiting. When the watchdog timer expires the node will crash.

59.10.1 *TimeBetweenWatchDogCheck*

This is the time between watchdog checks. When four such intervals have expired and no progress have been reported we will declare the node as dead. The default setting is 6000 milliseconds and thus we will detect watchdog failures after at most 24 seconds.

59.10.2 *TimeBetweenWatchDogCheckInitial*

During memory allocation it is more common to get stuck for a long time. Thus if 24 seconds isn't enough time to allocate memory we can increase this time here. When working with very large memories this can easily happen. In a large data node it would be fairly normal that one would have to increase this variable.

59.11 Configuring index statistics

Index statistics are maintained by the NDB data nodes, but are used by the MySQL server. The configuration of index statistics requires both a part in the data nodes and in the MySQL Server.

By default the data node will not generate any index statistics at all. It is still possible to generate index statistics by using the SQL command ANALYZE TABLE.

The actual index statistics is stored in a system NDB table. The index statistics is only based on one fragment in the table. The reason is two-fold, the first is that the only ordering is within one fragment. There is no ordering between two fragments. The second reason is that it simply is faster to work with one fragment instead of all. Given that the hash function is randomising the placement of rows, there should be very small differences between different fragments and thus it should be sufficient to analyse one fragment.

When using NDB as an SQL engine, it is recommended to activate those options. Running complex queries without analysing the index statistics can cause a query to execute thousands of times slower compared to when you have activated index statistics.

59.11.1 *IndexStatAutoCreate*

If this variable is set to on it will generate index statistics at create time of the index. Defaults to off.

59.11.2 *IndexStatAutoUpdate*

If this variable is set the data nodes will regularly update the index statistics automatically. Defaults to off.

59.11.3 *IndexStatUpdateDelay*

This parameter defines the minimum time between two updates of the index statistics. It is measured in seconds and defaults to 60 seconds.

59.11.4 *IndexStatSaveSize* AND *IndexStatSaveScale*

These two parameters define how much memory will be used in the index statistics table to store the samples from the index. The calculation is performed using a logarithmic scale.

By default *IndexStatSaveSize* is set to 32768 and *IndexStatSaveScale* is set to 100.

We calculate first the sample size as the sum of average key size and number of key columns plus one times 4. Assume that we have three columns that have average 16 bytes in size. In this case the sample size is 32 bytes = (16 + (1 + 3) * 4).

We multiply the sample size by the number of entries in the ordered index. Assume we have 1 million entries in the index. In this case the the total unfiltered index statistics would consume 32 MByte.

Instead we calculate size taking the two logarithm of 32 MByte. This is equal to 25. Now we multiply 25 by *IndexStatSaveScale* times 0.01 (thus treating *IndexStatSaveScale* as a percentage).

Next we multiply this number plus one with *IndexStatSaveSize*. In this case this means that we get 26 * 32768 = 851968 bytes. Next we divide this by sample size. This is 26624. This is the number of samples that we will try to get.

These numbers now apply to all indexes in the database. Using the logarithmic scale we ensure that very large indexes do not use too large memory sizes. The memory size must be small enough for us to store it and not only that, it has to be small enough to process the information as part of one query execution.

As can be seen here even with 1 billion entries in the table the two logarithm of 32 GByte only goes to 35. The index statistic size grows by about 38% with a 1000-fold increase in storage volume for the table. We can increase the scale by changing *IndexStatSaveScale* and we can move the start state by changing *IndexStatSaveSize*.

59.11.5 *IndexStatTriggerPct* AND *IndexStatTriggerScale*

Similarly we have two configuration parameters that use logarithmic scale to decide when to start the next index statistics update.

We get the number of entries in index first. We take the two logarithm of this number. In the case with 1 million entries in table, this number will be 20 in this case. This number is now multiplied by *IndexStatTriggerScale* times 0.01. By default this is 100, so scale down factor becomes 1+ (scale * 0.01 * 2log(number of index entries)). We keep track of number of index changes since last time we calculated the statistics. If this percentage of rows is higher than the percentage calculated. For example the defaults for a one million row table is that the calculated scale down factor is 21. Thus we start a new index statistics update when 100 / 21 = 4.76% of the index entries have changed.

By setting *IndexStatTriggerScale* to 0 we change to a completely linear scale. In this case *IndexStatTriggerPct* is used directly to decide when to activate a new index statistics update.

If *IndexStatTriggerPct* is set to 0 it means that there will be no index statistics updates issued. In this case the only way to get an index statistics update is to call the SQL command ANALYZE TABLE on the table.

Both *IndexStatTriggerScale* and *IndexStatTriggerPct* is by default set to 100.

59.12   Specialized configuration options

59.12.1   *LongMessageBuffer*

When a signal is sent with sections it uses a long message buffer to store the sections in. By default this buffer is 64 MBytes, this is sufficient for most scenarios, but in cases with large rows and many threads in the data node this might have to be increased.

Buffers are allocated from this pool when messages with sections arrive through the receive thread. These buffers are kept until the destination thread have consumed the signal.

Similarly when a new signal is created with one or more sections it will allocate buffer area from this pool. This buffer will be kept either until the signal destination within the same node have consumed the signal or if it is sent to another node it will happen when the signal is copied over to a send buffer.

Thus the long message buffer stores signals that have been received, but not yet consumed and signal created, but not yet sent or consumed.

Most of those signals will be waiting in a job buffer in one of the threads. There can be many thousands of signals in one of those job buffers and we can have up to a bit more than 50 such threads. We can theoretically have up to 40.000 signals in the queues. Not all these signals have sections, but there can definitely be tens of thousands of such signals executing in parallel. The size of the sections depends mostly on how much data we read and write from the database.

The long message buffer size has a limitation and 64 MByte should be enough to handle all but the most demanding situations. In those extremely demanding situations it should be sufficient to increase to a few hundred megabytes.

In smaller setups this buffer can even be decreased to at least half without running any real risk of running out of the buffer space.

If we run out of this buffer the node will crash.

59.12.2 *MaxSendDelay*

This configuration option was invented to handle a very large configuration with 30 data nodes and hundreds of API nodes running a heavy benchmark.

The logic behind this variable can be understood by considering traffic in a large city. If one highway in the city is very efficient and lots of cars can be delivered and those cars all come into a bottleneck, then a major queue happens and the queue will eventually reach the highway as well.

Now in a traffic situation this can be avoided by slowing down traffic on the highway. For example in some cities we have traffic lights when entering a highway, this limits the amount of cars that can pass. This limitation avoids the queues in the bottleneck since cars are flowing into this bottleneck at a sustainable rate.

Limiting the traffic in an area without any bottlenecks can actually increase the traffic throughput in a city.

Similarly in a large cluster it is important for nodes to not send too often. We want nodes to not send immediately when they have something to send. Rather we want the nodes to send when they have buffered data for a while.

The analogy is here that nodes that have no bottlenecks, slow down and wait with sending data. This ensures that bottleneck nodes do not slow down the entire cluster.

The above is the explanation of how this feature solves the problem in the large cluster. We saw 3x higher throughput on a cluster level and consistent throughput with this parameter set to 500 microseconds.

Without the parameter performance in the cluster went up and down in an unpredictable fashion.

What the feature does is that when a node is ready to send to another node, it checks if it has sent to this node the last microseconds. If the number of microseconds since last send exceeds the configured value we will send, if not we will wait with sending. If we have nothing more to do in the thread and wants to go to sleep, we will send anyways.

By default this feature isn't active, the unit is in microseconds. It can be set to a maximum of 11000 microseconds.

59.12.3 *Numa*

The default memory allocation behaviour is defined by the OS. Most OSs use a memory allocation that prefers memory from the same CPU socket. Now when NDB is used on a multi-socket server and where a data node spans more than CPU socket, it makes sense to spread memory allocation over all CPU sockets.

A data node often allocates a majority of the memory in a machine. In this case it makes sense to interleave memory allocation on all CPU sockets. By setting *Numa* to 1 on Linux where *libnuma* is available, this policy is ensured.

One consequence of setting *Numa* to 0 means that we might overload the memory bus on the CPU socket where the allocations were made. In a multi-socket server it makes sense to set *Numa* to 1. However if we have one data node per CPU socket it might work better to set

Numa to 0. *Numa* is set by default to 1.

59.12.4   *LateAlloc*

When we allocate memory we touch each memory page to ensure that the memory is truly allocated to our process and not that we only allocated swap space. This parameter delays touching parts of the memory until we have received the second start order from the management server.

To delay this touch of memory is default.

59.12.5   *CrashOnCorruptedTuple*

We protect the fixed part of tuples with a checksum, if this flag is true we will crash when encountering a checksum that is wrong. If the flag isn't set we will only report an error to the user trying to request this row.

59.12.6   *DefaultHashmapSize*

Only there to support downgrades. Should normally not be set to any other than the default value.

59.12.7   REPORT FREQUENCIES

Various reports can be produced with some frequency in the cluster log. By default none of these reports are produced. The unit is seconds.

MemReportFrequency

We can get a regular report on the usage of *DataMemory* and *IndexMemory*. If not we will still get a report when we reach a number of thresholds like 80%, 90% and so forth.

StartupStatusReportFrequency

During an initial restart we spend a long time initialising the REDO log. This report specifies how many REDO logs we have initialised and how much of the current file we have initialised.

BackupReportFrequency

This parameter ensures that we get backup status printed in the cluster log at regular intervals.

59.12.8   *MaxParallelScansPerFragment*

Currently we have a limit of a maximum of 256 scans per fragment. Each such scan gets an index between 0 and 255. Full table scans from MySQL uses scans through hash index. There can be at most 12 such scans in parallel. These always use index 0 through 11.

Range scans will by default use index 12 through 121, by default we can have at most 110 parallel range scans per fragment.

TUP scans are used by local checkpoints and some special operations. These use index 122 through 255, thus there can be up to 134 parallel TUP scans per fragment.

This parameter can be set to increase the number of parallel TUP scans.

This parameter should never ever need to be set.

In reality only locking scans require a scan index. Any scan using READ COMMITTED would not really require a scan index. At the same time the parallelism we support is quite sufficient. If more scans are trying to start up they will queue, thus no errors will happen due to the limited scan parallelism on a specific fragment.

The most common scans are range scans, 110 parallel such scans in parallel should suffice. It is possible to track the number of scans that are queued up through an *ndbinfo* table.

59.13 EXAMPLE *config.ini*

Here is a new *[ndbd default]* section based on the recommendations in this chapter.

```
config.ini

[ndbd default]
NoOfReplicas=2
NoOfFragmentLogParts=4
DataDir=/usr/local/ndb_data
ServerPort=11860
MaxNoOfAttributes=10000
TwoPassInitialNodeRestartCopy=1
BuildIndexThreads=128
StartPartitionedTimeout=0
BatchSizePerLocalScan=64
HeartbeatIntervalDbDb=1500
ConnectCheckIntervalDelay=1
IndexStatAutoCreate=1
IndexStatAutoUpdate=1
StringMemory=5
```

CHAPTER 60

CONFIGURATION OF API AND MGM NODES

Most of the configuration of MySQL Cluster is in the data nodes and in the MySQL Servers. There is a few things that is configured also through the API section in the cluster configuration. In the cluster configuration there is no difference between API and MYSQLD sections.

For MySQL Servers it is recommended to set the node id and hostname of each node used.

60.1 CONFIGURING SEND BUFFERS

These applies to both API and management server nodes. They will be covered in the next chapter on communication configurations.

60.2 CONFIGURING ARBITRATION

This applies to both API nodes and management server nodes.

60.2.1 *ArbitrationRank*

ArbitrationRank provides the priority for a a certain node to become arbitrator. 0 means that it will never become arbitrator. 1 means that it can become arbitrator. 2 means that it will be selected as arbitrator before all nodes with 1 set in arbitration rank.

The aim is to ensure that the arbitrator is placed on machines that can have an independent vote on which side of the cluster that should win. For example with 2 replicas and 3 computers we want to place the arbitrator on the third machine containing no data node.

We achieve this by setting *ArbitrationRank* to 2 on the management server on this third machine (or possibly an API node that is always up and running.

60.2.2 *ArbitrationDelay*

Delays the arbitration response by some amount of milliseconds. By default set to 0, no reason to change this that I can come up with.

60.3 CONFIGURING SCAN BATCHING

These applies only to API and MYSQLD nodes.

When performing a scan the data nodes will scan many partitions in parallel unless the scan is a pruned scan that only scans one partition. The NDB API must be prepared for all partitions to send back data.

We control the sizes each data node can send back by setting the batch size that the NDB

API can handle.

An NDB API user can override the configuration setting of batch size below by using the SO_BATCH option. The NDB API can also affect the execution of the scan by setting SO_PARALLEL to define the parallelism of a table scan (can not be used to influence of parallelism of sorted range scans, these will always use full scans).

60.3.1 *MaxScanBatchSize*

The maximum scan batch size is measured in bytes and defaults to 256 kBytes. This sets a limit to how much data will be transported from the data nodes in each batch. This is not an absolute limit, each partitioned scanned can send up to one extra row beyond this limit.

This setting is used to protect the API node from both send buffer overflow as well as using up too much memory. At the same time it is desirable to have the size not too small since this will have a negative impact on performance.

The send buffer sizes should take into account that multiple scans can happen in parallel from different threads, this limit only applies to one scan in one thread.

60.3.2 *BatchByteSize*

The *BatchByteSize* limits the amount of data sent from one partition scan. If the size of the data from one partition scan exceeds this limit, it will return to the NDB API with the rows scanned so far and wait until the NDB API have processed those rows before it proceeds with the next batch.

It defaults to 16 kBytes. The actual limit on the maximum scan batch byte size is the parallelism multiplied by this number. If this product is higher than *MaxScanBatchSize* we will decrease the batch byte size to ensure that the product is within the bounds set by *MaxScanBatchSize*.

60.3.3 *BatchSize*

We will never send more than *BatchSize* rows from a partition scan even if the rows are very small. This is an absolute limit, the NDB API must however be prepared to receive this amount of rows from each partition scan.

60.4 CONNECT CONFIGURATION

These applies only to API nodes.

There is a few configuration parameters controlling the connect phase when an API node is connecting to a data node.

These parameters controls the behaviour after the connection was lost and the timing of connect attempts after a number of failed attempts.

60.4.1 *AutoReconnect*

The NDB API was designed to handle failures transparently. When the connection to a node went down for a while, it will be immediately reused as soon as the connection is back up again. It is possible to disable this by setting *AutoReconnect* to 0.

60.4.2 *ConnectBackoffMaxTime*

When an API node have already connected to at least one data node in the cluster, this parameter specifies the maximum delay between new attempts to connect to another data node.

This parameter was introduced to avoid that hundreds of API nodes constantly attempt to connect to a few data nodes. The default is to make a new attempt after 100 millisecond. For small clusters this is not an issue, but in a large cluster this can cause serious overhead on the data nodes when too many nodes try to reconnect at the same time.

It defaults to 1500 milliseconds. The time between new attempts will increase with every failed attempt until it reaches this value. If set to 0 it will not back off at all, it will continue sending with a delay of 100 milliseconds.

Regardless of how big this is set to, we will never wait for more than 100 seconds and we will use an exponential backoff algorithm that will send first after 100 milliseconds, next after 200 milliseconds, next after 400 milliseconds and so forth until either we have reached 1024 intervals or we have reached the above set maximum delay between two attempts.

60.4.3 *StartConnectBackoffMaxTime*

When an API node isn't connected to the cluster at all, we can also use a back off timer. This defaults to not being used, it defaults to 0.

After connecting to the first data node, this configuration will be replaced by the *ConnectBackoffMaxTime*.

60.5 *HeartbeatThreadPriority*

By default the cluster manager thread and the arbitrator thread is perfectly normal threads. It is possible to configure them to run at a higher priority on Linux kernels. Only applies to API nodes.

This is done by setting the *HeartbeatThreadPriority* equal to a string with either fifo or rr where fifo means the SCHED_FIFO and rr stands for SCHED_RR and 50 is the priority level that will be set. If 50 is not considered one can also configure as fifo,60 to override the default priority level 50 by 60.

60.6 *DefaultOperationRedoProblemAction*

This parameter will be explained in the coming chapter on configuration of the REDO log. It controls what to do with operations that finds the REDO log buffer full. Only applies to API nodes.

60.7 *DefaultHashmapSize*

Only to be used for downgrades to older MySQL Cluster versions.

60.8   *ApiVerbose*

Setting this to 2 or higher means that we get printouts when we perform meta data operations. Only to be used in debugging the NDB API. Only applies to API nodes.

60.9   MANAGEMENT SERVER NODES

There is a few configuration options that apply only to management servers.

60.9.1   *DataDir*

Management servers have a special *DataDir* where the node log and cluster logs are placed. In addition we store the binary configuration files in this directory. It is recommended to always set this variable in the cluster configuration.

API nodes have no special node logs, the output is channeled to stdout. The MySQL server will redirect stderr to the error log and will skip output to stdout.

60.9.2   *LogDestination*

There are three values for *LogDestination*.

CONSOLE means that the cluster log is redirected to stdout from the management server. I've never used this and see very little need of ever using it.

FILE means that the cluster log is piped to a set of files stored in *DataDir*. This is the default behaviour and personally I never changed this default. The default name of the cluster log files are e.g. *ndb_49_cluster.log* where 49 is the node id of the management server.

The file is swapped to a file named *ndb_49_cluster.log.1* when the file reached its maximum size, the maximum size is 1000000 bytes. At once a new empty file is created when the first one becomes full. A maximum of 6 files are kept by default.

To set any other file name or maximum size or maximum number of files the syntax used is the following

```
FILE:filename:ndb_cluster.log,maxsize=10000000,maxfiles=25
```

There is also an option to redirect the cluster log to the syslog in the OS.

To do this use the following syntax:

```
SYSLOG:facility=syslog
```

There are numerous options for where to redirect the syslog, see the MySQL manual for details on possible options.

It is even possible to use multiple options, it is possible to redirect output to CONSOLE, a FILE and the SYSLOG at the same time.

60.9.3 *HeartbeatIntervalMgmdMgmd*

The management server uses the *HeartbeatIntervalMgmdMgmd* for heartbeats between two
management servers. This heartbeat is used when communication between the management
servers to keep track of when management servers are coming up and going down.

By default it is set to 1500 millseconds.

60.10 EXAMPLE CONFIGURATION

Here is a part of cluster configuration file focusing on how to setup arbitration in a correct
manner. First set it up with *ArbitrationRank* set to 2 in one of the management servers and
after that one more management server and MySQL server that set it to 1. The rest can set it
to 0.

```
config.ini

[ndb_mgmd]
NodeId=49
Hostname=192.168.1.100
ArbitrationRank=2

[ndb_mgmd]
NodeId=50
Hostname=192.168.1.101
ArbitrationRank=1

[mysqld]
NodeId=51
Hostname=192.168.1.102
ArbitrationRank=1
```

CHAPTER 61

COMMUNICATION CONFIGURATION

61.1 CONFIGURING SEND BUFFERS

The most important configuration parameter for communication is the send buffer sizes. This is configured partly through communication parameter and partly from node parameters.

61.1.1 *TotalSendBufferMemory* AND *ExtraSendBufferMemory*

In the past in NDB the memory per communication channel was allocated independent of others. Now the memory is allocated globally and all transporters share this memory. The memory size of this global buffer can be calculated in two different ways. The first is to add up all the *SendBufferMemory* settings.

The default option allocates memory to ensure that we can handle the worst case when all transporters are overloaded at the same time. This is rarely the case. With nodes that have many transporters it makes sense to allocate less memory to the global pool.

For example if we have 4 data nodes and 32 API nodes and the *SendBufferMemory* is set to 2 MByte, the default setting will be to allocate 70 MByte of send buffer globally. Now there is a very slim risk of us using this much memory at a single point in time. It would make sense to set *TotalSendBufferMemory* to e.g. 35 MByte.

ExtraSendBufferMemory is 0 and can stay that way. It is always the sum of *TotalSendBuffer-Memory* and *ExtraSendBufferMemory* that is used, so there is no need of using two parameters here.

The opposite could happen in rare cases if the user runs very large transactions. In this case the commit phase might generate signals that increase the send buffer beyond the *SendBufferMemory* limit although we abort both scans and key operations.

In this case we might decide to set *TotalSendBufferMemory* to more than 70 MByte instead.

In the API nodes the global memory allocated is all there is. In the data nodes we can overcommit up to 25% more memory than the global memory allocated. This memory will be taken from *SharedGlobalMemory* if available.

Setting *TotalSendBufferMemory* in a data node to 35 MByte means that the real limit is almost 44 MByte.

61.1.2 *SendBufferMemory*

The *SendBufferMemory* is normally set in TCP default section in the cluster configuration file. It defaults to 2MByte. It can be set per communication channel where both node ids must be set and the send buffer memory size is provided.

As described in this chapter, *SendBufferMemory* influences the global memory allocated unless *TotalSendBufferMemory* is set and influences the *OverloadLimit* unless this is set.

If both those parameters are set, the *SendBufferMemory* is ignored.

61.2 *Group*

Group sets the priority of one connection. This is used when selecting the transaction coordinator from the API nodes. It is handled by other configuration parameters, it is not expected that the user changes this parameter.

61.3 *SendSignalId*

This is mostly a debug option. By using this option each signal sent over the network is tagged with a signal id. This adds 4 bytes to each signal header. It makes the trace files a bit more descriptive since it becomes possible to connect on a distributed scale which signals that initiated signals executed in another node. Internally in a node all signals are tagged with a signal id, but by default we don't use this option for distributed signals.

61.4 *Checksum*

This feature can be useful to ensure that no software or hardware bugs corrupt the data in transit from one node to another. It adds a 4-byte checksum on each signal sent. This is not used by default. If a faulty checksum is found the connection between the nodes is broken and the signal is dropped with some descriptive error messages.

61.5 *OverloadLimit*

We have a few ways to decrease the pressure on a communication channel. The first level is to declare the channel as overloaded. When this happens any scans using this channel will automatically set the batch size to 1. Thus each scan will use the minimum amount of send buffer possible and still handle the scans in a correct manner.

This happens when the send buffer has used 60% of the *OverloadLimit* setting.

The default for the *OverloadLimit* is 80% of the *SendBufferMemory* setting of the communication channel (called transporter in NDB software).

When the overload limit is reached we start aborting key operations in the prepare phase. Operations in the commit phase will continue to execute as before.

This parameter makes it possible to set the *OverloadLimit* independent of the setting of *SendBufferMemory*.

61.6 *ReceiveBufferMemory*

Each transporter has a receive buffer. This buffer is used to receive into from the OS. Thus we can never run out of this buffer, we will ensure that we never receive more from the OS than there is buffer to receive into.

Before we receive more, we need to handle the signals we received.

The size of this buffer is set to ensure that we can receive data from the socket rapidly enough to meet the senders speed of writing. It is set to 2 MByte by default.

61.7 CONFIGURING OS PROPERTIES

The main reason why the possibility to change the send and receive buffer options and setting *TCP_MAXSEG* for the connections was to handle API nodes that was accessing NDB through a WAN (Wide Area Network) connection.

The default settings of TCP_SND_BUF_SIZE and TCP_RCV_BUF_SIZE are set to fit LAN settings where nodes are in the same building or at most a few hundred meters apart.

The number of outstanding IP messages that a socket can handle is controlled by these parameters together with TCP_MAXSEG.

The reason is that the sender must know that there is memory space in the receiver to avoid useless sending.

To handle API nodes that are longer apart these three parameters were added to the list of configurable options on each connection.

All of these default to 0 which is interpreted as using the defaults of the OS.

The normal OS send buffer size and OS receive buffer size is around 100 to 200 kBytes.

For long-haul connections one might need up to a few MBytes to ensure the parallelism is kept up.

By setting the configuration parameter WAN to 1 on the communication channel the *TCP_SND_BUF_SIZE* and *TCP_RCV_BUF_SIZE* is set to 4 MBytes instead and *TCP_MAXSEG_SIZE* is set to 61440 bytes.

61.7.1 *TCP_SND_BUF_SIZE*

Sets the send buffer size allocated by the OS for this socket.

61.7.2 *TCP_RCV_BUF_SIZE*

Sets the receive buffer size allocated by the OS for this socket.

61.7.3 *TCP_MAXSEG_SIZE*

Sets the TCP_MAXSEG parameter on the socket.

61.7.4 *TcpBind_INADDR_ANY*

By default the server part of the connection (the data node or the data node with the lowest node id) will bind the server part of the socket to the hostname provided in the config. By setting the *TcpBind_INADDR_ANY* parameter to 1, we skip binding the socket to a specific host. Thus we can connect from any network interface.

Chapter 62

Configuring MySQL Cluster file systems

In this chapter we will discuss how to setup file system related configuration parameters for both in-memory data and disk columns.

The following things need to be considered when configuring disks for MySQL Cluster. How MySQL Cluster disk data works was covered in an earlier chapter on *Disk Data columns* where we covered the potential configuration parameters. Here we will focus on recommended ways to use those parameters.

1. Decision on which disks to use for tablespaces

2. Decision on which disks to use for UNDO logs

3. Decision on size of DiskPageBufferMemory

4. Decision on size of Undo log buffer

5. Decision on which disks to use for REDO logs and local checkpoints

62.1 Directory placement

The default placement of disks are specified by the configuration parameter *DataDir*. This should always be set in the configuration file.

We can move all the disk usage except the node logs and trace files to another directory using the configuration parameter *FileSystemPath*.

Currently local checkpoint data and REDO logs cannot be separated on different disks. They are always written with sequential writes, so this should not present any issues.

A tough challenge is to provide predictable latency for MySQL Cluster using disk data. When NDB was designed this was simply not possible and thus early versions of MySQL Cluster had no support for disk data.

The main reason why it is now possible to overcome these challenges is the hardware development that have happened the last years. Nowadays we have access to SSD devices that can respond in less than hundreds of microseconds and NVMe devices that are even faster and even persistent memory devices that cut down latency to only a few microseconds.

An installation that uses a properly configured hardware and have setup the file systems in a good way can definitely use disk columns and still maintain predictable latency requirements where transactions with tens of round trips can be executed in tens of milliseconds even involving disk data.

The throughput of MySQL Cluster disk data is not equal to the throughput of in-memory data. The main difference is in writes where disk data columns uses one tablespace manager that manages extents of tablespaces and allocation of pages in extents and one log manager that handles the UNDO log. Thus there are a few bottlenecks in mutexes around these manager that limits the write throughput for disk data tables. It is still possible to perform hundreds of thousands of row writes per second of disk data rows for a cluster of NDB data nodes.

Reads on tables with disk columns are as scalable as in-memory tables and are only limited by the amount of reads from the file system that can be served. It is expected that millions of rows per second can be read per cluster even when the cache hit rate is low and with high cache hit rates tens of millions of reads per second and even hundreds of millions of reads per second is possible per cluster.

Most of the decision making here is about choosing the correct disk architecture for your application and the rest is about selecting proper buffer sizes.

It is recommended to avoid using the same disks for tablespaces as is used for local and global checkpointing and REDO logging. The reason is if the disks containing tablespaces are overloaded by the application it will affect the operation for checkpointing, REDO logging and so forth. This is not desirable. It is preferrable to ensure that logging and checkpointing always have dedicated disk resources, this will remove many overload problems.

As an example if we want to setup MySQL Cluster in the Oracle Bare Metal Cloud using the HighIO option we can do the following. This machine comes equipped with 512 GBytes of memory and a total of 12.8 TByte of space using 4 NVMe devices.

One way to use this setup is to use two devices for local checkpoint files, REDO log files and the backups in MySQL Cluster. Let's assume we set up this file system on */ndb_data*.

The other two devices are used for tablespaces and UNDO logs. This means setting up two file systems using a RAID 0 configuration on two devices in both cases. As an example we can use 1 TByte of disk space for the UNDO log and 5 TByte disk space for tablespaces. Let's assume that we set up this file system on */ndb_disk_data*.

Thus we will set the configuration variable *DataDir* to */ndb_data* and we set the configuration variable *FileSystemPathDD* to */ndb_disk_data*.

DataDir will also contain node logs, cluster logs, trace files and pid files generated by the data node. It could be useful to place these files on a separate device. Normally those files will not grow extensively, but if the data nodes hit some situation where information is written to the node logs a lot, it could be useful to also remove those from the same disks as checkpoint files and REDO log files. *DataDir* is always used for those files, but if *FileSystemPath* is also set then local checkpoint files, REDO logs and metadata and system files are moved to this directory.

It is possible to specifically set a directory for backups in *BackupDataDir*, for tablespaces in *FileSystemPathDataFiles* and a specific directory for UNDO log files in *FileSystemPathUndoFiles*.

62.2   COMPRESSED FILES

To ensure that we can fit at least one and possibly even two backups we should use compression on the backup files. This means setting *CompressedBackup* to 1 in the configuration.

It is possible to use compressed local checkpoints as well by setting *CompressedLCP*.

Compressing happens in *io* threads and uses a *zlib* for compression. Expect this library to use one second of CPU time for around 100-200 MBytes of checkpoint files or backup files.

62.3   CONFIGURING THE REDO LOG FILES AND LOCAL CHECKPOINTS

Local checkpoints and REDO logs are an important part of the configuration setup for MySQL Cluster.

We write the update information of all inserts, updates and deletes into the REDO log. It is important to be able to cut the REDO log tail every now and then. This happens when a local checkpoint have been completed. At recovery time we first install a local checkpoint and then we apply the REDO log to get the state we want to restore.

62.3.1   CONFIGURING REDO LOG

It is important to set the correct size of the REDO log before starting up a production cluster. It is possible to change the size, but it requires that the nodes are restarted using an initial node restart.

NoOfFragmentLogParts

We already described the reasoning behind the number of log parts. This should be set according to the number of *ldm* threads we want to use in the nodes or a minimum of 4.

NoOfFragmentLogFiles AND *FragmentLogFileSize*

The size of each log part is defined by the number of log files

(*NoOfFragmentLogFiles*) multiplied by the size of each log

file (*FragmentLogFileSize*).

The log file size isn't that important, but the default is too small. It is advisable to set the log file size to at least 256 MByte. Otherwise we might run into issues when writing to the REDO log at high speed if the file system cannot keep up with creating files at the speed required. The number of log files isn't very important either, but at least three files is a minimum and even 4 is advisable as a minimum.

It is a good idea to set the total size of the REDO log files to a size that is larger than the *DataMemory*. This will ensure that MySQL Cluster can handle the data load phase without running out of REDO log. After the data load phase the local checkpoints will move the data out to checkpoints and the REDO log can shrink back to a small size again.

For example with 8 Gbyte of *DataMemory* and 4 *ldm* threads we could use the following settings.

```
NoOfFragmentLogParts=4
NoOfFragmentLogFiles=8
FragmentLogFileSize=512M
```

InitFragmentLogFiles

At initial start of a node, the REDO log files will be initialised. This ensures that the REDO log space on disk is really allocated. Otherwise the OS might fake the allocation and we might run out of REDO log although not all of it was used.

In a testing environment it might be useful to speed up initial starts by skipping this initialisation phase. For this purpose it is possible to set *InitFragmentLogFiles* to sparse to avoid this initialisation phase. Thus there is a risk instead that we run out of REDO log although there is supposed to exist space in the REDO log. This will cause the data node to crash since we cannot write anymore to the REDO log.

RedoBuffer

At commit time the REDO log messages have to be written to the REDO log buffer. This is an in-memory buffer that will be written to disk at intervals prescribed by global checkpoints and we write to disk at certain intervals. If the disk cannot keep up the *RedoBuffer* usage will grow. This parameter sets the size of this buffer. When we run out of REDO buffer we can abort transactions in the prepare phase. The commit messages must be written into the REDO log buffer, so we ensure that there is always some space left in the buffer for this purpose. Thus running large transactions requires a large *RedoBuffer* setting.

The setting of *RedoBuffer* is per *ldm* thread. The total memory used for Redo buffers is *RedoBuffer* multiplied by the number of *ldm* threads.

DefaultOperationRedoProblemAction

When a transaction finds the REDO buffer full, it has two choices. It can either abort the transaction immediately, or it can queue up and hope that the REDO buffer situation improves.

The API node have a configuration option for this purpose called

DefaultOperationRedoProblemAction. This configuration parameter can be set to ABORT or QUEUE. It can be influenced by an option in the NDB API for NDB API applications.

RedoOverCommitLimit AND *RedoOverCommitCounter*

As long as we have IO bandwidth to write out the REDO log in the same rate as we write the REDO log, there are no problems.

If we write more to the file than what is acknowledged, we know that the disks are not able to keep up.

If the disks cannot keep up, we can calculate the disk IO rate through the acks of file writes. By measuring the amount of outstanding IO we have at any point in time, we can measure the IO lag.

The IO lag is measured in seconds. If the IO lag in seconds exceeds the *RedoOverCommitLimit*, we will increment a counter with the lag divided by *RedoOverCommitLimit*. If we have a lag also the next second exceeding the *RedoOverCommitLimit* we will add even more to this counter. When this counter reaches *RedoOverCommitCounter* we will start aborting transactions to gain control of the REDO log writes. The default setting of *RedoOverCommitLimit* is 20 and of *RedoOverCommitCounter* is 3.

Every second that we have a lag of the REDO log writes, we will write a message to the node log describing how much lag we are seeing.

62.3.2 CONFIGURING LOCAL CHECKPOINTS

There are three reasons why transactions can be aborted due to the REDO log. The first we saw above was that we run out of REDO buffer space, we simply can't write to the REDO log quick enough to move data from the buffer to the disk IO subsystem.

The second reason is that the disk IO subsystem cannot keep up with the REDO log writes as explained above.

The third reason is that we run out of REDO log space.

The only way to get REDO log space back is to ensure that the REDO logs are no longer needed. This happens through a local checkpoint.

Local checkpoint execution is controlled through a set of configuration parameters.

The first decision to make is when to start a local checkpoint again. We have one parameter that directly controls this, it is the *TimeBetweenLocalCheckpoints* parameter. In principle NDB is designed to execute local checkpoints continously. There is no real reason to change this parameter, it is also a bit complex to understand.

The second configuration parameter controlling when to start an LCP is the *MaxLCPStartDelay*. This parameter is effective during node restarts only. When the master decides that it is time to start an LCP, it will check if there are nodes that soon will need to wait to be part of an LCP. The reason for this is that any node restart is finalised by participating in a local checkpoint. The *MaxLCPStartDelay* sets the time we will wait for those nodes to be ready for an LCP before we start an LCP.

The next set of important parameters controlling LCP execution is a set of parameters controlling the speed that we perform the local checkpoints. This speed is controlled by an adaptive algorithm that have min and max values that depends a bit on the situation.

The execution of LCPs is controlled also by the buffer space available for local checkpoints and how much we write to disk at a time for an LCP.

We have a parameter that oversees that the LCP doesn't hang due to some software bug. This is a watchdog that watches over the LCP execution. If the LCP stops making progress for too long, this will cause a node crash with some log messages written describing the state of the LCP at crash time.

TimeBetweenLocalCheckpoints

The default setting of this parameter is 20. This parameter is logarithmic. Thus 20 means 2 raised to 20 words, thus 4 MBytes. We measure the amount of committed information since the last LCP was started. If it is bigger than 4 MBytes, we will start a new LCP.

Thus as soon as there is some level of write activity we will start an LCP. If NDB is used mainly for reading there will be no LCP activity.

The setting can at most be set to 31 which means that it will wait for 8 GBytes of write activity to occur in the cluster before an LCP is started.

It is recommended to not change this parameter, mainly because there is little value in changing it.

MaxLCPStartDelay

This parameter is set in seconds, defaults to 25 seconds. If an LCP is starting and we know that it is close to be ready to join an LCP we will wait for this long before starting the LCP.

MinDiskWriteSpeed

When an LCP is executing it will use an adaptive algorithm to set the desired disk write speed of the local checkpoint. By default this parameter is set to 10M (= 10 MBytes). Thus we will attempt to write 10 MByte per second in the node. Thus if there are 4 *ldm* threads, each of those threads will attempt to write 2.5 MBytes per second.

MinDiskWriteSpeed is the minimum speed that the adaptive algorithm will never go below.

The adaptive algorithm will choose normally the currently active max value. There are two reasons to decrease the disk write speed of a local checkpoint. The first reason is that the CPU is used quite a lot in the *ldm* thread. We measure CPU usage in *ldm* threads both by asking the OS how much CPU we used and by measuring how much time we spent being awake. If the time of awakeness is higher than the executed time, it means that the OS removed us from the CPU to execute other threads even when we were ready to execute on the CPU. This will impact the adaptive algorithm a bit as well.

We will start slowing down execution of LCPs when the CPU is becoming too much used. At 97% we will step down the disk write speed, we will move faster in decreasing disk write speed if we reach 99% and even more when reaching 100% CPU usage. If the CPU usage drops down below 90% we will start increasing disk write speed again.

If any REDO log part has an IO lag of 2 seconds or more as described above in the section on *RedoOverCommitLimit*, we will quickly decrease the disk write speed. Currently the REDO log and the local checkpoints are always placed on the same disk, if the REDO log cannot keep up, it can be a good idea to decrease the disk write speed of LCPs.

MaxDiskWriteSpeed

In normal operation the maximum disk write speed is set by *MaxDiskWriteSpeed*, this defaults to 20 MBytes per second. It is the total for all *ldm* threads.

MaxDiskWriteSpeedOtherNodeRestart

When another node is executing a node restart we increase the disk write speed since executing faster LCPs means that we can restart faster. In this case we have a higher max disk write speed. The same adaptive algorithm can still decrease the speed of the LCP.

This setting defaults to 50 Mbyte per second.

MaxDiskWriteSpeedOwnRestart

When we are restarting ourselves and in cluster restarts, we will use this setting as max disk write speed. This defaults to 200 MBytes per second. During a cluster restart there is no risk of the adaptive algorithm stopping activity since there is no transactions ongoing while running the LCP.

BackupWriteSize AND *BackupMaxWriteSize*

As soon as we have gathered up records to write *BackupWriteSize* of data to the checkpoint files we will initiate a write to the checkpoint disk. We will never write more than *BackupMaxWriteSize*.

BackupWriteSize defaults to 256 kBytes and *BackupMaxWriteSize* defaults to 1 MByte.

BackupDataBufferSize

The *BackupDataBufferSize* is the size of the data buffer where we gather records that are ready to be written to the checkpoint files.

The default of this parameter is 16 MBytes, there are very good reasons to set this parameter much lower. The reason is that it improves the predictable latency that we are aiming for. By setting the buffer size to 16 MBytes we spend a lot of CPU resources to fill up the buffer, after filling the buffer we will not do much for a while until we are ready to fill the buffer again.

The recommended settings for those settings are rather:

```
BackupWriteSize=256k
BackupMaxWriteSize=512k
BackupDataBufferSize=512k
```

These settings will improve the predictable latency and still give a good disk throughput. One can increase the settings to improve the disk throughput and decrease it a bit more to improve the predictable latency even more.

LCPScanProgressTimeout

This sets the watchdog timer for ensuring that there is progress of LCPs. It is set by default to 60 seconds and after a third of this time, after 20 seconds we will start writing warning messages to the node log.

62.4 CONFIGURING BACKUPS

To configure backups we need to configure an appropriately sized log buffer for backups and we need to handle the imbalance of backup execution.

Writing backups is controlled by the same parameters as the execution of LCPs. This means that if a backup is executing in parallel with an LCP, the LCP and the backup will share the disk write speed.

There is one problem with this approach, the backup is only written by the first *ldm* thread. There is an imbalance in the use of the disk write speed resources.

To accomodate this imbalanced behaviour the first *ldm* gets a percentage of the disk write speed of the node in addition to its fair share to execute LCPs.

62.4.1 *BackupDiskWriteSpeedPct*

The *BackupDiskWriteSpeedPct* sets the percentage that is reserved for the *ldm* thread executing the backup. It defaults to 50. So for example if the maximum speed is 20 MByte per second, 50% of this is allocated for backup, thus 10 MByte. Assuming we have 4 *ldm* threads, the *ldm* threads gets 2.5 MBytes each.

Thus the first *ldm* thread gets a total of 12.5 MBytes per second of disk write speed and the remaining three gets 2.5 MBytes each.

This only affects disk write speed while writing a backup.

62.4.2 *BackupLogBufferSize*

A backup must both write out all records (in-memory data and disk columns). In addition it must write all changes during the backup. The changes is a form of UNDO log or REDO log that we must write during backups in addition to all other logging and checkpointing that is going on in a data node.

By default it is set to 16 MByte. In a cluster with much write activity it is recommended to set the size of this buffer much larger, e.g. 256 MByte. This buffer is only allocated in the first *ldm* thread, thus only one instance of it is allocated.

62.5 CONFIGURING GLOBAL CHECKPOINTS

62.5.1 *TimeBetweenGlobalCheckpoints*

In NDB data durability at commit time is ensured by writing into the REDO buffer in several nodes as part of commit. Durability to survive cluster crashes happens when that data is committed to disk through a global checkpoint.

The default timer for global checkpoints is set to 2000 milliseconds.

If the data node runs on hard drives this number is quite ok, it might even in some cases be tough to sustain high loads at this number with hard drives.

With SSDs this value should be perfectly ok and should normally not be any issue unless the write load is very high.

With faster SSDs or NVMe drives one could even decrease this time since the IO bandwidth should be a lot higher than what NDB will be able to match with its updates.

62.5.2 *TimeBetweenGlobalCheckpointsTimeout*

When the disks gets severely overloaded the global checkpointing might slow down significantly. To ensure that we don't continue running when we are in an unsafe state we crash the node when the time between global checkpoints is more than *TimeBetweenGlobalCheckpointsTimeout*. This is also a watchdog ensuring that we don't continue if global checkpoint execution has stopped due to a software bug.

It is set by default to 120000 milliseconds (120 seconds or 2 minutes).

62.6 MEMORY BUFFERS FOR DISK COLUMNS

The DiskPageBufferMemory is a very important parameter, by default this will be set to 64 MBytes. This is not for production usage, only for trying out MySQL Cluster on a small computer.

It is a good idea to consider this parameter specifically. If it is set too low it will have a dramatic impact on latency and throughput and if set too high it will remove the possibility to store more data in the *DataMemory* (in memory data).

The size of the UNDO log buffer is set either in *InitialLogfileGroup* or in the command where the UNDO log buffer is created. It is not changeable after that, it is important to set it sufficiently high from the start. There is one log buffer per data node.

The Undo log buffer size should be sufficient to ensure that transactions can proceed without interruptions as often as possible. The pressure on the log buffer increases with large transactions when large amounts of change data is written quickly into the log buffer and it increases with large amount of parallel write transactions. If the buffer is overloaded it means that commits will have to wait until buffer content have been sent to the disk. Thus transaction latency can be heavily impacted by using disk data with a too small Undo log buffer and similarly by using a disk device for Undo logs that cannot keep up with the write speed.

62.7 NEW TABLESPACE AND UNDO LOG FILES

New undo log files can be added as an online operation as shown in the chapter on disk columns. Similarly for tablespaces. Tablespaces can also be added through the configuration parameter *InitialTablespace*.

62.8 FILE SYSTEM CONFIGURATIONS

62.8.1 *DiskIOThreadPool*

When writing to tablespace files we can have several file system threads writing to the same file in parallel. These threads are in a special pool of threads for this purpose. The number of threads in this pool is configurable, it defaults to 2, but can be set higher for higher write rates to tablespace files. The 2 here means that we have 2 dedicated threads available for writing to the tablespace files. If both of those threads are busy writing any writes will have to wait for one of them to complete its file operation. We can set the number of threads in the pool for writing to tablespace files higher through the configuration parameter *DiskIOThreadPool*.

62.8.2   *MaxNoOfOpenFiles*

It is possible to set a maximum limit to the number of open files (and thus file threads) in a data node. It is set by default to 0 which means that no limit exists. It is strongly recommended to not change this parameter other than to get an understanding of the system and see how many files it opens. There are no problems associated with having many open files in parallel and the algorithms in NDB are designed to limit the amount of open files in the data node.

62.8.3   *InitialNoOfOpenFiles*

InitialNoOfOpenFiles is the amount of file threads that are started in the early phases of the restart. It is not necessary to change this parameter. But setting it higher moves some work to create threads to an earlier point before the node has started up and is executing transactions. It defaults to 27. The number of open files required is very much dependent on the data node configuration.

File threads consume very small resources, it mainly uses a 128 kByte stack. There are no real issues associated with ignoring this thread creation and the memory associated with it. Modern operating systems can handle hundreds of thousands of concurrent threads and we normally use less than one hundred threads for file IO.

This is an area where we rarely, if ever, see any issues.

62.8.4   *ODirect*

ODirect is a special file system option that bypasses the page cache in the operating system. This option is always used on UNDO log files and tablespace files. For REDO log files, backup files and local checkpoint files it is configurable whether to use it or not.

It is recommended to set this parameter on Linux unless you are running on an ancient Linux kernel.

62.8.5   *DiskSyncSize*

This parameter ensures that we write out any buffers inside the OS frequent enough to avoid issues. It was added since in Linux you can buffer the entire memory in a machine before the writes start to happen. This led to a very unpleasant behaviour when too much buffering happened in the file system. This parameter ensures that we write out buffers frequently and defaults to 4 MByte. Setting *ODirect* means that this parameter is ignored. Setting *ODirect* is the preferred method on Linux.

62.9   FINAL WORDS

The above mentioned machines in the Oracle Bare Metal Cloud represents a very good example of a high-end machine that fit very well with the requirements MySQL Cluster have on the disk subsystem when using disk columns.

The two devices used for tablespace data and UNDO log data will be able to sustain millions of IO operations and thus reading and writing several GBytes of tablespace pages and writing of UNDO log files per second.

Thus it can sustain several hundred thousand updates per second of disk rows which is more than what one node currently can handle for disk data rows (for main memory rows it can handle millions of updates per second in specific setups). This setup is a safe setup for MySQL Cluster where there is very little risk that the disk subsystem becomes a bottleneck and a problem for MySQL Cluster.

Chapter 63

Configuring the MySQL Server

Now that we have covered everything except advanced thread configurations for the cluster configuration we will take a deeper look at what configurations that are useful when setting up a MySQL Server to use NDB as a storage engine.

Most of the configuration options to consider are NDB specific, but I will mention a few general MySQL options as well. I will not discuss any configuration options for InnoDB.

63.1 Basic MySQL server options

Basic options are required whenever you set up a MySQL server independent of what storage engine you use. These options specify where to find the files, which port to use, where to place socket files, where to log errors, how many connections we will be able to handle in parallel and so forth. Most of those options can be set either at command line or in the MySQL server configuration file. I will not discuss details on exactly where they can be placed, this information is available in the MySQL manual.

I will not discuss any performance schema options. The performance schema have few advantages when using the MySQL server with NDB as storage engine.

63.1.1 *--ndbcluster*

To use the NDB storage engine with the MySQL server it is required to use the *--ndbcluster* option when starting the MySQL Server. It is important to use a MySQL Server from a MySQL Cluster installation when using the NDB storage engine.

63.1.2 *--datadir*

--datadir specifies the data directory of the MySQL Server. This is where most files related to the MySQL Server will be stored. This includes error logs, data files, pid files and so forth.

In MySQL Cluster you will normally have many MySQL servers connected to the cluster. To make it easy to know which MySQL server you are examining it is a good idea to have the node id (or one of the node ids if there are multiple ones) as part of the directory name. This makes it easier to find your way about in the various logs produced by the nodes in the cluster.

63.1.3 *--basedir*

--basedir points to the installation directory of MySQL Cluster. It is used among other things to find the error messages for different languages.

63.1.4 *--log-error*

The *--log-error* option specifies that you want errors logged and where you want those errors to be written. A filename can be specified, the location of this file will be in the *datadir*. The default name of the error log is the hostname with .err as file extension.

63.1.5 *--pid-file*

A pid file contains the process id of the MySQL server process. This is a file located in the data directory. A filename is provided in the option.

63.1.6 *--port*

This parameter defaults to 3306. If another port is desired it should be provided in this option.

63.1.7 *--socket*

If the MySQL client is located on the same machine it can communicate to the MySQL server using Unix domain sockets. This is normally a bit faster compared to using a TCP/IP socket on the local machine. The default setting for this option is /tmp/mysql.sock. It can be set to point to a different socket file name in this option.

63.1.8 *--bind-address*

It is possible to specify the network interface that the MySQL server will accept connections from. This can be useful to avoid accepting connections from a public network and only accept connections from a specific private network.

One manner to specify the network interface is to provide the IP address of the desired network interface.

The default behaviour is to accept connections from any network interface.

63.1.9 QUERY LOGGING

The MySQL server can set query logging on all queries, the log output is specified using the *--log-output* option and by setting *--general-log* all queries are logged and by setting *--log-slow-queries* one can set logs on only queries that are slower than a certain time.

63.1.10 *--ndb-extra-logging*

The NDB handler will log more or less dependent on the setting of the *--ndb-extra-logging* option. This defaults to 1. Setting it to 0 means that most logging is disabled, setting it to 20 means that all possible messages are printed in the error log.

63.1.11 QUERY CACHE SETTINGS FOR NDB

The query cache works with NDB, but the query cache will limit the scalability of the MySQL server, it is not recommended to use it unless one is really sure that it pays off to use it. The query cache is disabled in MySQL 8.0.

It is highly recommended to ensure that the query cache is completely shut off when starting the MySQL server. If not properly shut off, it will limit the scalability of the MySQL server on systems with many CPUs.

To shut it off completely set *--query-cache-size=0* and *--query-cache-type=0*.

If the query cache is used with NDB one should consider setting the *--ndb-cache-check-time* option to a proper value.

63.2 CONNECTION OPTIONS

There are a few parameters that are important to configure properly when starting up a MySQL server to be part of an NDB Cluster. It is important to point the MySQL server to an NDB management server (or a set of them) such that it can get the cluster configuration. There are parameter settings to ensure that we can decide how to handle cases where it takes time to connect to the cluster (it might be starting up for example).

It is important to decide how many API node slots this MySQL server will use and it is important to set the node ids of those API node slots.

63.2.1 *--ndb-connectstring*

This option points to the management server from where the cluster configuration is fetched. It is possible to specify several management servers in which case the configuration is fetched from any of those management servers.

The default setting for this parameter is localhost:1186. If only a hostname is provided the port is 1186 by default.

63.2.2 *--ndb-cluster-connection-pool*

By default one cluster connection is used. In this case one can set the node id of the MySQL server using the option *--ndb-nodeid*. If more than one cluster connection it is still possible to set the node ids of those cluster connections (and recommended to do so in both cases). In this case one uses *--ndb-cluster-connection-pool-nodeids* to set the node ids.

This option specifies the number of cluster connections.

Normally one cluster connection scales to at least 8 CPUs and in many cases it can scale to around 16 CPUs. To scale to a higher number of CPUs for the MySQL server requires using more cluster connections.

In my experiments I have been able to scale the MySQL server to at least around 60 CPUs using 4 cluster connections.

63.2.3 *--ndb-nodeid*

With one cluster connection this option can be used to set the node id of the MySQL Server. It is recommended that MySQL server have specific node ids that are set in the cluster configuration with a node id and a host name.

63.2.4   --ndb-cluster-connection-pool-nodeids

This option accepts a comma separated list of node ids when using multiple cluster connections.

63.2.5   --ndb-wait-connected

If a MySQL server is started it will first connect to the NDB management server and then it will perform various synchronisations with the existing cluster to ensure that the MySQL server knows about the tables that are present in the cluster and that it gets informed of any new tables added or tables being dropped or altered.

   This parameter specifies the time that the MySQL server will wait for NDB to connect before it proceeds assuming that the NDB storage engine is unavailable. Defaults to 30 seconds.

63.2.6   --ndb-wait-setup

This option specifies the amount of time the MySQL server will wait for the NDB storage engine to perform its startup. Defaults to 30 seconds.

63.3   DEFAULTS FOR TABLE CREATION

Your MySQL server is up and running and you want to start creating the tables in your NDB Cluster. There is a number of options that have an effect on the tables that are created.

63.3.1   --ndb-read-backup

Before MySQL Cluster 7.5 NDB always read the primary replica. In 7.5 the option was introduced to create tables that can read any replica. See the chapter on table options for more descriptions of this.

   By default the tables are still created without the read backup feature. However if you are planning to use NDB mainly for SQL and use a lot of SELECT queries and in particular if you are planning to colocate the MySQL server with NDB data nodes, we recommend that you create all tables to use the read backup feature.

   A read backup table will have a slightly higher latency when updating the table to ensure that we can read our own updates.

63.3.2   --ndb-fully-replicated

If you are using NDB to build a cluster with read scaling, you want to connect up to hundreds of MySQL servers and many data nodes that all read the same data and still have the ability to update from anywhere such that all MySQL servers see your updates.

   In this case it might make sense to make all tables use the fully replicated feature explained in the chapter on table options. In this case all data is replicated in all data nodes.

   This option set to 1 will ensure that all tables are created as fully replicated tables.

63.3.3   --ndb-table-temporary

Setting this variable has no effect.

63.3.4 *--ndb-table-nologging*

Setting this option to 1 means that any table created will use the NOLOGGING feature explained in the chapter on table options.

NOLOGGING tables will be restored as empty tables after a cluster crash.

63.3.5 *--ndb-default-column-format*

By default column formats used are FIXED which means that they will use fixed size part of the row for fixed size columns and the variable sized part of the row for columns that are variable sized.

If set to DYNAMIC all columns will use the dynamic part of the row. Columns that are stored in the DYNAMIC section will use no memory to store a NULL value, but will use a bit more memory when not NULL.

All new fields added through an ALTER TABLE with algorithm set to inplace will be using the DYNAMIC part of the row.

63.3.6 *--ndb-distribution*

This option should no longer be used.

63.4 ALTER TABLE OPTIONS

There are options to provide control over ALTER TABLE as well.

63.4.1 *--ndb-allow-copying-alter-table*

If this option is set to 0 it means that copying ALTER TABLE isn't allowed. It is recommended to set this option to 0 since copying ALTER TABLE should be avoided and not be used by mistake. Setting this to 0 means that it must be explicitly enabled before a copying ALTER TABLE can be performed.

63.4.2 *--ndb-use-copying-alter-table*

This defaults to 0 and is recommended to stay that way.

63.5 EXECUTION OPTIONS

With some tables added into NDB, it is now time to start querying those tables. There is a fair amount of options that control execution behaviour.

63.5.1 *--max-connections*

The MySQL server caps the number of connections it will accept. By default it is set to 151 connections. In many applications it is desirable to use a lot more connections. In my benchmark runs I always set this variable to an appropriate value.

63.5.2   *--max-prepared-stmt-count*

The server caps the amount of prepared statements that a server will accept. It is set by default to 16382. A prepared statement is bound to a connection, so with many similar prepared statements the server can use more than 16382 prepared statements.

As an example running *sysbench* will prepare around 20 prepared statements per connection, running a benchmark with 1024 connections requires this parameter to be changed.

It is set a bit lower for security reasons. It cannot be set higher than 1048576.

63.5.3   *--sort-buffer-size*

The MySQL server limits the amount of memory a connection can use for sorting to 256 kBytes. To use more than that requires changing this configuration option.

63.5.4   *--autocommit*

autocommit is set to 1 by default. This means that every statement is a separate transaction and will be committed as part of the query execution. It is still possible to start a longer transaction using a BEGIN statement and end it with either COMMIT or ROLLBACK.

When this option is set to 0 every statement after a COMMIT or ROLLBACK will start a new transaction that have to be completed with a COMMIT or ROLLBACK.

There is not many reasons to change the default setting.

63.5.5   META DATA OPTIONS

The MySQL server caches table metadata to speed up queries. Each connection uses one table object from the table open cache for each table it queries, in addition it uses a table objects from the table definition cache. To retrieve such objects there is a number of parallel hash tables to ensure that many connections can access these hash tables in parallel.

--table-open-cache

Each query needs one table object from the table open cache for each table it uses. This option sets the amount of table objects that can be in the cache before we start deleting table objects. There can be many table objects referring to the same table since every connection needs its own table objects.

The default is to allow for up to 2000 table objects. Increasing this also increases the number of file descriptors that the MySQL server uses.

--table-definition-cache

Each table object is read from an *frm* file normally stored in the *datadir*. The table definition cache specifies how many *frm* files are stored in memory such that we don't have to open the *frm* file to get the meta data of the table.

The default value is calculated based on the setting of table open cache. If this is set to its default it will be set to 1400.

--table-open-cache-instances

This specifies how many hash tables are used to access table objects. It defaults to 16, this number makes the MySQL Server scale to a high number of CPUs. To improve scaling on very large servers one can increase this number, there is very little reason to decrease this number other than to save a bit of memory.

63.5.6 *--memlock*

By setting this option to 1 we ensure that the MySQL server locks all memory it uses, so it will fail allocating memory when there is no real memory available.

63.5.7 *--lc-messages-dir*

--lc-messages and *--lc-messages-dir* is used to set the error messages in a proper language. The default is english and a directory found through *basedir*.

63.5.8 *--ndb-use-exact-count*

--ndb-use-exact-count defaults to 0 and should always stay that way. The alternative is to use a full table scan to get the number of rows. This is less exact than the default method, thus there are no benefits in changing this option.

63.5.9 *--ndb-force-send*

When a connection is ready to communicate with the data nodes it can either use force send or adaptive send. Force send is the default and works ok in most situations. In a highly concurrent environment the adaptive send might have some benefit, the difference between the two methods is usually very small, should only be changed after testing with your application.

63.5.10 *--ndb-optimized-node-selection*

Should never be changed, was introduced for backwards compatibility.

63.5.11 *--ndb-data-node-neighbour*

In most cases the MySQL server will be able to deduce which data node is the closest neighbour by comparing the hostname of the MySQL server and the hostname of the data nodes.

If they are running on the same machine and using different hostnames one can tell the MySQL server explicitly which data node is the closest neighbour.

The proximity of a data node will be used to select transaction coordinator when no specific hint has been provided.

63.5.12 *--ndb-use-transactions*

This option has a weird name. It is set by default to 1.

The meaning of setting it to 1 is that large insert statements will be split into several transactions. If set to 0 also large insert statements will be executed using normal transaction boundaries.

63.5.13   --transaction-allow-batching

When NDB discovers a large insert, delete or a large update, it will normally use batching. Batching here means that multiple row writes will be sent in parallel to the data node. This is the default setting and should normally be kept.

The only reason I can think of when it could be interesting to not set it is when it is required to avoid overloading the data nodes.

63.5.14   --ndb-batch-size

During large write operations we keep a memory buffer for retrieved values. By default this buffer is 32 kBytes in size. Increasing this can lead to a higher batch size for large write operations and thus higher throughput at the expense of using more memory per connection.

63.5.15   --ndb-autoincrement-prefetch-sz

The default value of this parameter is 1. This means that auto increments will use steps of 1 between rows inserted in using an auto increment column.

Normally an autoincrement columns should use a BIGINT and thus have no problems that the autoincrement numbers have gaps and that they are not necessarily inserted in perfect order.

In this case this size should be set much higher, setting it to 1024 will make it fairly safe that the autoincrement column will not cause scaling issues.

The default setting will for sure cause scalability settings with many parallel inserts into the autoincrement table.

The maximum it can be set to is 65536.

63.5.16   --ndb-blob-read-batch-bytes AND --ndb-blob-write-batch-bytes

These two options control the behaviour of accesses to BLOB tables. When this option is set to a non-zero value, the MySQL server will send reads and writes to the BLOB tables in batches of this size. It defaults to 64 kBytes. If the MySQL server

By increasing this size we will perform more work in parallel when reading and updating BLOB tables. At the same time it increases the risk of overloading the cluster. The default setting is intended for a balanced setting.

63.5.17   --tmp-table-sizeAND --max-heap-table-size

The maximum size of temporary tables created during query execution is limited by the minimum of these two options. Both are set to 16 MByte by default.

63.5.18   --ndb-deferred-constraints

Is not intended to be changed. It delays the check of constraints to the end of the transaction.

63.5.19 *--ndbinfo-show-hidden*

By default the MySQL client only shows the documented ndbinfo tables. The base tables are not documented since they can change from release to release. If one wants to also see the base tables one should set the option *ndbinfo-show-hidden* to 1.

63.6 OPTIMIZER OPTIONS

There are a number of options that directly impact the query optimisation.

63.6.1 *--ndb-join-pushdown*

Pushdown of joins is a key feature of NDB. It means that many complex queries can execute various row conditions in parallel. It uses a form of linked joins.

It is possible to set this option to not be used. This might be useful in some cases when testing have shown that a certain query is more efficient when executed using a different algorithm present in the MySQL server.

There should be no reason to reset it when starting the MySQL server.

63.6.2 *--ndb-index-stat-enable*

Index statistics is enabled by default for NDB. Enabling index statistics can at times provide major improvements to query execution time through a much better query plan.

63.6.3 *--ndb-index-stat-option*

There is a great number of options that can be influenced through this option. It is beyond the scope of this book to go through all of those. The MySQL manual contains a list of the options and how to set them.

63.6.4 *--ndb-optimization-delay*

When executing OPTIMIZE TABLE we will have a delay between each batch of rows sent for optimisation. This delay defaults to 10 milliseconds.

63.6.5 *--optimizer-switch*

This variable is a massive switch that can be used to enable or disable 19 different algorithms.

63.6.6 *--optimizer-trace*

There is a set of options available to trace the workings of the optimizer. Many applications have problems in developing SQL queries that work well. The optimizer trace feature will give detailed information about what makes the query optimizer choose certain paths and avoid other paths.

During query development and query debugging this feature can be very useful. This option is only available in debug builds of the MySQL server.

63.7   Receive thread configuration

Each cluster connection have one receive thread. This thread or some execution thread that takes on the role of receiver executes all signals received from the data nodes. The behaviour of the receive logic is important to get optimal performance when running the MySQL server using NDB.

63.7.1   *--ndb-recv-thread-activation-threshold*

By default the user threads will take care of the receiver role of the cluster connection until at least 8 threads are active in waiting for response from the data node.

When more than 8 threads are waiting for response from the data nodes, the receive thread will take care of the receive role.

For optimal performance it is usually best to ensure that the receive thread takes care of the receive role in all situations except when there is a single thread executing.

To get optimal performance the receive thread must be able to execute on its own CPU.

For the receive thread to use its own CPU requires that we have locked the MySQL server (and other processes running on the same machine) to other CPUs, thus ensuring that no other thread is using the CPU assigned to the receive thread.

To lock the MySQL server to certain CPUs I use the *taskset* program or the *numactl* program.

For optimal behaviour the *--ndb-recv-thread-activation-threshold* should be set to 1.

63.7.2   *--ndb-recv-thread-cpu-mask*

By default this is not set and thus the receiver thread(s) can execute anywhere. When set, it should be a comma separated list of CPU ids. The number of CPUs in this list should be one for each cluster connection we use.

63.8   MySQL Cluster replication setup

There is a wide range of options to use for MySQL replication servers. Remember that in NDB these are normally specialized MySQL servers used primarily to be replication masters or replication slaves.

Most of these options were explained in their context in the chapters on MySQL Cluster Replication.

63.8.1   *--log-bin* AND *--ndb-log-bin*

In a replication master the *--log-bin* must be set to the basename of the binlog files. By default it is OFF. In addition the *--ndb-log-bin* must also be set (is ON by default).

In addition the *--ndb-log-bin-index* should always be set when setting up a MySQL replication server for NDB. This is ON by default, no action is required for this to happen.

63.8.2 *--server-id*

Each MySQL replication server must have a unique server id.

63.8.3 *--server-id-bits*

This option defines how many bits of the 32 bit server id to actually use. It defaults to 32, but can be set as low as 7. The idea with this is to provide room for NDB API applications to use special NDB API options to insert changes into the binlog using special server ids.

63.8.4 *--sync-binlog*

By default the binlog is synched once per transaction. NDB writes one epoch as a transaction into the binlog, synching this is what we want. So *sync-binlog* should be set to 1 when replicating from an NDB Cluster. There is about 10 epochs per second generated, so there will be no performance impact from this.

63.8.5 *--relay-log*

When the MySQL replication server is executing as a slave it will use relay logs to store the binlog information retrieved from the replication master before the logs are applied to the slave cluster. This option can be used to set a non-standard name of the relay logs.

63.8.6 *--slave-allow-batching*

To achieve the desirable speed of the slave, this option should be set to 1. It ensures that the slave applier uses batching to improve the speed of applying the replication logs in the slave cluster.

63.8.7 *--ndb-eventbuffer-max-alloc* AND *--ndbeventbuffer-free-percent*

The *--ndb-eventbuffer-max-alloc* option can be used to set a maximum on the memory available to use for event buffers in the NDB API. By default there is no limit. If this option is set and we reach the maximum allocated size, the free percent option indicates how much memory must be free before we start receiving new events again. By default that is set to 20%.

63.8.8 *--ndb-report-thresh-binlog-epoch-slip*

This option defaults to 10. It sets the number of epochs that the injector binlog thread will be behind before the MySQL server logs this lag to the error log.

The epochs are first received by the NDB API into a memory buffer. Next the injector thread injects them into the binlog. This reports when the injector thread cannot keep up with the NDB API.

63.8.9 *--ndb-report-thresh-binlog-mem-usage*

Sets the level when reports about memory usage are written in the error log.

63.8.10   *--ndb-log-updated-only*

By default this is set to ON. Thus only columns that are changed are logged and columns that are not changed are not part of the log records. This makes replication to other NDB Clusters more efficient.

It is required to set it to OFF also when using the conflict detection functions.

63.8.11   *--ndb-log-update-minimal*

This option is used to minimize the amount of binlogging required when using conflict detection functions *NDB$EPOCH2* and *NDB$EPOCH2_TRANS*. It should never be set in any other situation. It is OFF by default.

63.8.12   *--ndb-log-update-as-write*

By default NDB logs updates as writes, this ensures that no before value image is required and thus higher efficiency. When replicating to another storage engine and when using any of the conflict detection functions this option should be set to OFF.

63.8.13   *--log-slave-updates*

In a circular setup where the slave cluster will replicate to yet another cluster (or another storage engine) we must enable the *--log-slave-updates* in the MySQL replication servers that act as binlog servers.

63.8.14   *--ndb-log-orig*

This option is off by default, it needs to be set to enable circular replication. It is necessary to know the origin cluster of the log records such that we can stop replicating when we are back at the originating cluster. It should be set on all binlog servers in the circular replication.

63.8.15   *--ndb-log-empty-epochs*

It is possible to log also empty epochs, by default this is disabled. In the chapter on global failover architecture we discussed how this could be used as part of a failover script. With this feature we can use the *ndb_log_apply_status* table for updates to see if replication channel is up and running.

63.8.16   *--ndb-clear-apply-status*

By default the RESET SLAVE command will clear all entries from the *ndb_apply_status* table. By setting this option to OFF the table will not be cleared as the command RESET SLAVE is executed.

63.8.17   *--ndb-log-apply-status*

This option is OFF by default. When ON it ensures that updates to the *ndb_log_apply_status* table is replicated to the slave cluster.

It is used in chain replication and circular replication to ensure that the replication chain can be discovered.

63.8.18 *--ndb-log-transaction-id*

This option is required to be set to ON when using the *NDB_EPOCH2_TRANS* method for conflict resolution. By default this option is OFF.

63.8.19 *--ndb-log-exclusive-reads*

This option can be used for the *NDB_EPOCH2_TRANS* method for conflict resolution. By default this option is OFF. If it is set the option *--ndb-log-empty-update* must also be set to ON.

63.8.20 *--ndb-slave-conflict-role*

See the chapter on MySQL Cluster replication for a description of this. It is only related to replication with conflict detection functions.

63.9 *--ndb-show-foreign-key-mock-tables*

Shows some mock tables that are used by NDB to handle the foreign_key_checks equal to 0. Adds a bit more descriptive logging in the error log.

63.10 VERSION INFORMATION

It is possible to display information about the NDB version, the ndbinfo version and the NDB version in text format by using the following options *--ndb-version, --ndbinfo-version*, and *--ndb-version-string*.

63.11 *--core-file*

If it is desirable to get a core file when the MySQL server crashes this option should be set.

63.12 MySQL SERVER STATUS VARIABLES

There are many different status variables available in the MySQL Server, both for the NDB storage engine and for general MySQL Server usage. We will not go through them at all in this book, we will instead refer to the MySQL manual that contains a description of each and every one of those status variables. They can be helpful in examining a MySQL server in production.

Chapter 64

Analysis of hyperthreading performance

In this chapter we will look at the concept of hyperthreading specifically. It is important to understand when hyperthreading helps, how much it helps and in which situation to use it and when not to use it. We have one section for x86 servers that always have 2 CPUs per CPU core. We will also analyse things for the SPARC M7 servers that use 8 CPUs per CPU core. It is important to understand this to configure MySQL Cluster properly. Especially for advanced configurations where one wants to get the best performance using MySQL Cluster it is important to understand this. Some thread types benefit very much from hyperthreading and some almost not at all.

The analysis in this chapter is a direct input into the next chapter on advanced thread configuration options for MySQL Cluster.

We will analyse *ldm* threads, *tc* threads, *send* threads, *recv* (receive) threads in the data nodes. We will also analyse normal MySQL Server threads used to execute SQL queries and we will analyse the send and receive threads of the NDB API cluster connections.

Most of the analysis done was performed running Sysbench OLTP RW. On Linux the behaviour was analysed using *perf stat*, a command in the *perf* program suite that is used to among others calculate IPC (instructions per cycle executed). On SPARC/Solaris the method used was running benchmarks and ensuring that the thread type analysed becomes the bottleneck.

64.1   *x86* servers

The *ldm* threads is the thread type in the data node that dominates the CPU usage in the data nodes. This is especially true for Sysbench OLTP RW where a lot of scans for 100 rows are performed. *tc* threads gets more work when used with many small primary key lookups. *send* threads always have a fair amount of work to do and gets more when nodes to send to are on other machines.

64.1.1   *ldm* threads

In a Sysbench OLTP RW execution the *ldm* threads uses almost 75% of the CPU usage in data nodes. There are two things affecting usage of hyperthreading for *ldm* threads. The first is the efficiency of hyperthreading for the *ldm* threads and the second is the fact that increasing the number of *ldm* threads means more memory to communicate between threads and more partitions to handle.

The number of *ldm* is tied to the number of REDO log parts in the data nodes. Thus doubling the number of LDM threads means that the number of partitions in the tables doubles.

The consequence of doubling the number of partitions is the following. A bit more memory is used for storing information about the partitions and their fragment replicas. This doesn't have any immediate impact on performance. We can declare small tables to use only one partition per node or node group if we want to remove this problem.

However large tables and tables that are heavily used should be spread amongst the *ldm* thread instances as much as possible.

When a large table is used with unique key lookups and primary key lookups the queries will always go immediately to the correct partition, the number of partitions doesn't matter for performance in this case.

For scans that are using the partition key properly one can ensure that the scans only go to one partition, for these scans the number of partitions doesn't matter.

However all other scans, both full table scans and ordered index scans will perform the scans on all partitions. This means that if we are only looking for a small number of rows the overhead in starting up a scan one one partition will be noticable. At the same time the parallelism will increase with more *ldm* threads and thus latency at low load will decrease. For a generic application that haven't been optimised for partition pruning it generally means decreased scalability of the application to have an increase in the number of partitions.

The gain in performance of using one *ldm* thread per CPU rather than one *ldm* thread per CPU core is only 15%. Thus for generic applications it isn't really beneficial to use hyperthreading for LDM threads. It is better to use only one thread per CPU core for *ldm* threads.

There is also a third thing that affects latency and performance when the number of *ldm* threads increases. Doubling the number of *ldm* threads can have an impact on the number of application threads required to reach the top performance levels. This is more or less an effect of queueing mechanisms and that with more *ldm* there are more hardware paths that are used. It is also to some extent the effect of some internal mutexes that have some effect on things as the number of *ldm* threads increases.

Our advice for *ldm* threads is the following. If your application is perfectly scalable (all scan queries are directed towards only one partition) it might be ok to always use hyperthreading also for *ldm* threads. When running on very small number of *ldm* threads there is no specific reason to avoid it.

However for example when running on a computer or VM that have 16 CPU cores we would definitely argue against using 20 or 24 *ldm* threads on 10 or 12 CPU cores and instead go for using 10 or 12 *ldm* threads using the same CPU cores. Increasing the number of *ldm* threads beyond 16 gives a small performance loss due to mutex contention.

Up to 4 *ldm* threads it is ok to use hyperthreading more or less always, but from 6 *ldm* threads and up it is often a good idea to use one *ldm* thread per CPU core.

The maximum number of *ldm* threads are 32, thus one data node can at most scale to around 40-48 CPU cores. One can still have multiple data nodes in one computer if more cores need to be used for data nodes.

Exactly why the hyperthreading for *ldm* threads isn't so beneficial we don't exactly know, it is not uncommon for database engines to not benefit so much from hyperthreading. Our experiments shows that *ldm* threads have an IPC of 1.27, a likely cause is that with 2 threads per CPU core we run out of computing resources. But the cache levels definitely have an impact on the behaviour as well.

64.1.2 OTHER THREAD TYPES

For the remaining threads hyperthreading is beneficial although it is good to know to what level it is giving benefits.

For *tc* threads the benefit is at 40% increased performance. For *send* threads it increases performance by 40%. For *recv* (receive) threads the benefit is a lot higher, it is all the way up to 70% increase in performance. The reason is that the receive thread is doing a lot of work on preparing protocol headers for the other threads, it does a fair amount of CPU processing on each byte it receives on the wire. *ldm* threads work a lot on large memory segments and thus have a lot of cache misses that misses in all cache layers.

The MySQL Server threads that execute SQL queries benefits 60% in increased performance by using hyperthreading and a similar number we get for the receive threads of the NDB API cluster connections.

64.1.3 CONCLUSION FOR X86 SERVERS

The simplest rule to follow is to use hyperthreading for all thread types except for *ldm* threads. A more complex rule is to look in more detail on the application scalability, number of CPU cores to use to decide whether to use hyperthreading for *ldm* threads. However it is not likely to bring more than 15% more performance to use hyperthreading for *ldm* threads.

64.2 SPARC SERVERS

The analysis of SPARC servers is based on the SPARC M7 processor. This CPU has 32 cores per CPU socket and each CPU core have 8 CPUs. Thus a single CPU socket provides up to 256 CPUs to play around with.

64.2.1 ANALYSIS OF MySQL SERVER THREADS

We ran a Sysbench OLTP RW benchmark where we kept the number of *ldm* threads constant at 8 and ensured that the other thread types wasn't a bottleneck. We used 4 SPARC cores constantly and only varied the number of CPUs we made available to the MySQL Server (using the *pbind* command).

Using 1 CPU per core we got 1363 TPS, with 2 CPUs per core the result was 2183 TPS (+60%). Using 4 CPUs per core the performance increased to 3315 TPS (+143% compared to 1 CPU per core) and when making use of all 8 CPUs per core we got 3888 TPS (+185% compared to 1 CPU per core). Almost 1000 TPS per CPU core the SPARC M7 was able to crunch out on the MySQL Server side. The SPARC CPU is very well suited for the thread types used in a MySQL Server. The MySQL Server requires a bit more cluster connections compared to when used with x86 servers.

For MySQL Servers where often we have many threads running independent tasks that have a fairly large working set the SPARC CPU is very well equipped to achieve good use of the CPU resources and it pays off to use all 8 CPU threads in each CPU core.

64.2.2 ANALYSIS OF *ldm* THREADS

We made a similar experiment where we ensured that the MySQL Server wasn't the bottleneck. We kept the number of *ldm* threads stable here as well at 8. We tested using 1 *ldm* thread per core, 2 per core, 4 per core and 8 per core.

The result was that 1 thread per core delivered 740 TPS per core. With 2 threads per core the result was 1000 TPS per core (+35%). With 4 threads per core we scaled all the way to 1640 TPS per core (+122% compared to 1 thread per core). With 8 threads per core we scaled to almost 1800 TPS.

Here it is clear that we get a major advantage of using up to 4 CPUs per core. It seems that each additional CPU provides almost 30% extra performance up to 4 CPUs per core. However using more than 4 CPUs per core isn't a good idea. Doubling the amount of partitions in the tables for less than a 10% increase in performance is certainly not worth the extra overhead that the extra partitions provide for the same reasons as for x86 CPUs.

64.2.3 CONCLUSION FOR SPARC SERVERS

Using SPARC to execute MySQL Cluster seems like a good idea as a method of handling many smaller clusters. Given that even a very capable data node with 16 *ldm* threads can fit in 6 CPU cores and that a very capable MySQL Server can be handled within 8 CPU cores it means that a virtual machine using half of a CPU socket will be a very capable node in a cluster.

Chapter 65

Advanced Thread Configurations

Quite a few of the products currently using MySQL Cluster are building real-time applications. Examples are various types of network servers such as DNS servers, DHCP servers, HLR (used in 3G and 4G networks), LDAP servers and financial use cases with high requirements on response times.

To design a real-time service using MySQL Cluster one need to take special care in setting up the threads and how they are operated in the data node configuration. We will treat this here.

We will start by describing how to set up the single-threaded *ndbd* for real-time operation and next move on to how to set up the multi-threaded *ndbmtd* for real-time operation. The reason that we start with *ndbd* is that the solution for *ndbmtd* has evolved from the solutions used for *ndbd*. It is good to see how we solved the problem historically for *ndbd* before we move onto showing how we solved it in *ndbmtd*. Most of the solutions in *ndbmtd* have a direct mapping to how it works in *ndbd*. Sometimes the parameters used for *ndbd* still applies to *ndbtmd*.

Also the *ndbd* setup is much easier to understand, by explaining this first we build the foundation to make it possible to fully understand the thread configuration options for *ndbmtd*.

65.1 Setting up ndbd for real-time operation

When setting up a real-time service the optimal configuration is to use the old binary ndbd for data nodes. This binary only have a single thread executing both read from network, write to the network and performing database services. We have kept this configuration possibility since there are cases when response time is the overall target and the performance requirements are smaller.

In most environments one will set up data nodes to use ndbmtd, the multi-threaded data node given that the throughput of *ndbd* is very limited, *ndbmtd* can scale to more than 10x the performance of *ndbd*.

We will describe how to setup both of those environments for real-time use cases.

This setup is still used in production all over the world and it helps to understand the design ideas from here and how they later translate into similar concepts in the ndbmtd. *ndbd* is a very popular use case when you simply want a highly reliable data service and don't care so much about performance and you want a very cheap IT infrastructure.

One important feature to be able to control the execution environment is to lock the threads into specific CPUs. It is vital to ensure that these CPUs are shielded from both OS activity and interrupt activity.

The only OS that supports this shielding is Solaris that has the ability to exclusively lock CPUs to threads. In Linux, Windows and FreeBSD it is possible to lock threads to CPUs, but not to avoid having other threads executing there as well. In modern Linux one can use the *cgroup* concept to make lockings exclusive. Systems such as Docker makes extensive use of the *cgroup* concept to control resource usage.

Linux provides some means to control execution of OS threads and there are means to control interrupt execution.

In *ndbd* we have two important configuration parameters that control CPU locking. The first one is *LockExecuteThreadToCPU*. One sets this configuration parameter to the CPU id one wants the execution thread to be locked to. The other part is to set the *LockMaintThreadsToCPU*. This controls the locking of the file system threads to a CPU.

Thus *ndbd* will execute on one 1 CPU core or for the optimal use case one will use 2 CPU cores, one core for execution thread and the other core for file system threads.

It is important to remember here that when using the feature of locking to CPUs it is important to control other programs running on the same machine to not interfere by using the same CPUs. This can be done by using *taskset* or *numactl* to control placement of programs to CPUs. With the aid of those two parameters we have now gained control of the execution environment for *ndbd*.

This is still not sufficient to provide a real-time service environment making full use of the ndbd environment.

To achieve extremely low response times requires busy waiting. Thus the execution thread cannot go to sleep after completing its work. We control this through the *SchedulerSpinTimer* configuration parameter. This specifies for how many microseconds the execution thread will spin in the main loop waiting for external input before going to sleep.

In *ndbd* we have one more configuration parameter that can be used to control the execution thread. This is the *SchedulerExecutionTimer*. This controls the number of microseconds we will execute before we perform the send operation. For extreme real-time services we need to set this to a low value possibly even to 0. By default this is set to 50 to improve throughput.

Most OSs provide a real-time scheduling mode. This means that the thread cannot be interrupted, not even by the OS itself and not even by interrupts. MySQL Cluster contains protective measurements to ensure that we never execute for more than tens of milliseconds without going back to normal scheduler priority. Executing prolonged on real-time priority will completely freeze the OS. Setting this mode is done through the configuration parameter *RealtimeScheduler*.

There is a protective setting *LockPagesInMainMemory*. By setting this the parameter memory is locked such that no swapping can occur. In the normal case this will have no effect, but if there is an issue with not sufficient memory than swapping can occur and this can have very significant effect on response times. This feature is useful if the data node operates in a shared environment where for example a MySQL Server is executing in the same environment.

There is one more option that affects response times and this is the choice of transporter. MySQL Cluster have an architecture that supports different transporter types. We currently only use TCP/IP sockets.

Historically we've had experimental support for the shared memory transporter, this transporter was useful in running a benchmark on a 72-CPU SPARC machine in 2002. We managed to execute 1.5M reads per second already at that time using a 32-node cluster where each node used one of the 72 CPUs available and the communication was using the shared memory transporter.

There was a SCI transporter based on an API that Dolphin developed for the SCI communication card. This hasn't been used in many years since Dolphin developed a driver that makes it possible to use SCI through a normal socket protocol. I worked a lot with Dolphin a number of years ago to ensure that the Dolphin socket driver had the optimal configuration and had minimal response time issues. The Dolphin socket driver and Dolphin cards is still an interesting option to use for MySQL Cluster.

Dolphin still delivers cards, today they are based on PCI Express. The driver software is still the same, Dolphin SuperSockets. Using this driver one can get a very low-latency network drivers. To use this driver one uses normal TCP/IP sockets and ensure that one uses the IP addresses used by Dolphin SuperSockets.

The other low-latency approach is to use Infiniband. Currently this requires using IP over Infiniband (IPoIB). This will still use the normal TCP/IP transporter, we're only changing the underlying transport network. We have made benchmarks at Intel sites where we have connected 100s of computers using IPoIB and managed to handle to perform 205M reads per second of around 120 bytes of data per read. Thus transporting 25 GByte per second (200 Gb/s) in user data between the hosts.

In order to configure ndbd for a real-time environment it is necessary to consider the following options:

1. Configure *LockExecuteThreadToCPU*

2. Configure *LockMaintThreadsToCPU*

3. Configure *SchedulerSpinTimer*

4. Configure *RealtimeScheduler*

5. Configure *SchedulerExecutionTimer*

6. Configure *LockPagesInMainMemory*

7. Use a low-latency transport network (Dolphin or Infiniband)

This concludes the type of settings required to set up a real-time service using *ndbd*. It is required to handle locking threads to CPUs, it is required to have the option for threads to spin instead of immediately sleeping, it is required to run the thread as threads operating with real-time priority, it is required to ensure that memory is locked such that swapping cannot occur and it is required to control send processing.

65.2 Setting up ndbtmd for real-time operations

Setting up *ndbmtd* for real-time operations requires us to deal with the same set of challenges as with *ndbd*. We need to control CPU locking, we need to control if any spinning should be done while waiting for input. We need to control the thread priority. In ndbmtd all of those things are controlled by one complex configuration variable *ThreadConfig*. This variable defines the number of threads of various sorts that we use in ndbmtd.

The configuration parameter *SchedulerSpinTimer* is still used in ndbmtd, it is the default value for the spintime of threads. This value can be overridden by a value in *ThreadConfig*. *RealtimeScheduler* is handled in the same manner, thus the value in this variable is the default and can be overridden by values in the *ThreadConfig* variable.

LockPagesInMainMemory has the same meaning in ndbmtd as it have in *ndbd*. It can be set to 0 indicating no locking and it can be set to 1 to indicate that we ask the OS to lock the memory before the memory is allocated. Setting it to 2 means that we first allocate memory and then we ask the OS to lock it in memory thus avoiding any swapping.

The *ndbmtd* program have one more configuration variable that will impact its real-time operation. This is the *SchedulerResponsiveness* variable. By default it is set to 5. It can be set between 0 and 10. Setting it higher means that the scheduler will more often synch with other threads and send messages to other nodes. Thus we improve response time at the expense of throughput. Thus higher value means lower response times and lower values means higher throughput.

There is an undocumented variable ___*scheduler_scan_priority*. This variable can be used to decrease priority of scan operations and raise the priority of key operations. We don't expect this to be used other than in very special cases with very high requirements on response times. Setting it will decrease throughput significantly (up to 10%), so it is an option for extreme real-time applications, but for most applications it should not be used. Setting it to 1 means that 1 row per real-time break will be executed in scan operations. The default is 6 rows per real-time break (except first row which will be only 1 row during frst real-time break independent of configuration).

There is no correspondence to *SchedulerExecutionTimer* in *ndbmtd*. However the environment is very different in ndbmtd, some of the aspects on how often we send is handled by configuring *SchedulerResponsiveness*. We still have the option to hold onto sending to a node for some time. This is defined by the config variable *MaxSendDelay*.

When a signal is executed it can generate new signals sent to both the same thread, other threads in the same node and to other threads in other nodes. *SchedulerResponsiveness* controls scheduler parameters that control how many signals we will execute before we perform the actual delivery to other threads, it controls the the maximum number of signals executed before we deliver the signals to other nodes.

When a decision to send to a node has been done, we will send to nodes in FIFO order (First In First Out). We have always a bit more focus on sending to other data nodes in the same node group (to ensure that we have low response times on write transactions).

In order to get the highest throughput, this is especially true in large clusters, we might need to delay the sending of signals to ensure that signal buffers are as large as possible to get the highest possible throughput. *MaxSendDelay* sets the maximum time to delay signals in the ready to send state. It is provided in microseconds.

65.2.1 THREAD TYPES TO CONFIGURE IN *ThreadConfig*

ThreadConfig is by far the most complex configuration variable in MySQL Cluster. One can use a simple version of this by using *MaxNoOfExecutionThreads*. One can even specify the CPUs to lock those threads to by providing those in a CPU bitmap in the configuration variable *LockExecuteThreadToCPU* and IO threads can be specified in *LockMaintThreadsToCPU* as in ndbd. This possibility is mostly for simplicity, it doesn't necessarily provide a good configuration.

Using *ThreadConfig* is definitely the preferred manner of configuring the thread configuration and the characteristics of each thread in terms of CPU locking, thread priority and spin time to provide an optimal real-time service using *ndbmtd*.

ThreadConfig makes it possible to configure the following thread types, ldm, tc, send, recv, main, rep, io, wd. We will describe each thread type and how to configure it.

ldm THREADS

ldm is the most important thread type. This is the thread where the local database is located. In order to read any data in NDB one has to access the *ldm* thread. LDM stands for Local Data Manager. *ldm* contains a hash index, a T-tree ordered index, the tuple storage, handling of checkpoints, backups and various local trigger functions.

The number of *ldm* threads is very important since it defines how many partitions default tables will have. By increasing the number of *ldm* threads we increase the availability for reading and writing. Unfortunately increasing the number of *ldm* threads adds to the cost of range scans since they need to scan all partitions to find the data.

There is a very important correlation between the number of *ldm* threads and the number of fragment log parts. It is highly advisable to have this set to the same number. This is set by the config variable *NoOfFragmentLogParts*. Setting this variable lower than the number of *ldm* threads means that a number of *ldm* threads are unused and setting the number of log parts higher than the number of *ldm* threads means that we can get unabalanced load on the *ldm* threads.

Setting the number of *ldm* threads is the first thread type one starts with when designing the configuration.

tc THREADS

The next thread type to consider is the *tc* threads. How many *tc* threads one needs is very much dependent on the query types one uses. For most applications it is sufficient to have around 1 *tc* thread per 4 *ldm* thread. However if the application uses a high number of key operations the number of *tc* threads will be higher.

As a thumb of rule that will work for most applications one should have about half as many *tc* threads as *ldm* threads. *tc* threads will assist the send threads a lot, having a few extra *tc* threads will be useful and mean that we can have fewer number of *send* threads.

TC is used for all key operations, these make heavy use of *tc* threads. Scan operations makes less use of *tc* threads, even less for scans that perform much filter processing. *tc* threads are also used for pushdown joins.

The rule of thumb is to use half as many *tc* threads as *ldm* threads. But if your application is consistent in its work profile, it makes sense to perform some kind of benchmark that simulates your application profile and see how much it makes use of the *tc* threads.

The ndbinfo table *cpustat* can be used to get CPU statistics about the different threads in your data nodes.

recv AND *send* THREADS

The next important thread type to consider is the *recv* threads and *send* threads. The *recv* threads takes care of a subset of the sockets used to communicate to the data node. It is usually a good idea to avoid having the *recv* thread at overload levels since this will delay waking up the worker threads (mainly *ldm* and *tc* threads). Actually this is true for both *recv* and *tc* threads since if these are not fully loaded they will make sure that the *ldm* always stays fully active.

send can work well at a very high load. Usually if the load on the *send* threads goes way up the traffic patterns will change such that larger packets will be sent which will automatically offload the *send*.

In addition in MySQL Cluster 7.5 all worker threads (*ldm*, *tc*, *main* and *rep*) will assist *send* threads when the thread themselves aren't overloaded. The data node keeps track of the CPU load status of all the threads in the data node including the *send* threads and *recv* threads.

If a thread is loaded below 30% it will assist the *send* threads until there is no more data to send before it goes to sleep again. When the load goes up and is between 30% and 75% we will help the *send* threads at moments when we are ready to go to sleep since the thread has no work to do. At higher loads we will offload all send activity to other threads and not assist any other thread in executing sends.

It is usually sufficient to configure the data nodes with a single *recv* thread. For larger nodes with around 8 *ldm* threads and up it could be useful to increase the number of *recv* threads. In particular if the application uses the asynchronous API parts the *recv* can be quite loaded due to the high number of signals that needs to be put in internal data structures. The *recv* thread can handle a couple of million signals per second, thus this is quite unusual. But it does occur e.g. when I ran flexAsynch benchmarks where data nodes handle more than 10M key lookups per second.

There is usually a need of a few more *send* threads. However the design in MySQL Cluster 7.5 where worker threads share the burden of sending with the *send* threads means that fewer *send* threads are needed. It is in most smaller configurations quite ok to run with a single *send* thread. Using about 1 *send* thread for each 4 *ldm* threads is a conservative number.

main AND *rep* THREADS

main and *rep* threads are simple, there will always be one of each in an ndbmtd process.

The *main* thread is used mainly for schema transactions and various backgrounds activities like heartbeating. It is used quite heavily in the startup phases from time to time. In MySQL Cluster 7.4 it was heavily used in scan processing and could even in exceptional cases be a bottleneck where scan processing was very significant. The scan processing in MySQL Cluster 7.5 still uses data in the *main* thread, but it accesses it directly from the *tc* thread using RCU principles and mutex protected access. In large clusters the *main* thread could get a lot of work to handle at certain states of local checkpoint processing, especially when the number of small tables is high.

rep thread is taking care of MySQL Cluster Replication in order to get information about all updates in the MySQL Cluster to the MySQL servers in the cluster configuration responsible to handle MySQL replication from one cluster to another cluster or to any other MySQL storage engine. It handles some other activity related to multithreading and file activity. If there are much updating and one uses MySQL Cluster Replication than this thread can be heavily used.

Those threads are also heavily involved when we reorganize a table to a new table partitioning e.g. after adding a new set of nodes.

io THREADS

io threads can be configured although the count is here ignored. The actual number of IO threads is runtime dependent and can be controlled by the configuration variables *DiskIoThreadPool*, *InitialNoOpenFiles* and *MaxNoOfOpenFiles*. However as mentioned in the documentation it is more or less considered a bug if one has to change the **NoOpenFiles* variables. The interesting thing to control for *io* threads is their priority and the number of CPUs they are bound to.

Normally the *io* threads use very little CPU time, most of it is simply starting up OS kernel activity and this can as well happen on any other kernel thread defined by the OS configuration. There is a clear case for controlling *io* threads when one has set either *CompressedLCP* and/or *CompressedBackup*. Given that both local checkpoints and backups send a lot of data to disk, it makes a lot of sense to compress it if CPU capacity exists and disk storage is a scarce resource. It is likely that using this feature will compress the LCP and backup files to at least half its size or even less. The compression uses the *zlib* library to compress the data.

As mentioned it comes at the expense of using a fair amount of CPU capacity both to write the data to disk as well as to restore it from disk in a restart situation.

If one decides to use this feature it becomes important to control the placement of *io* threads on the CPUs of your servers.

wd THREADS

One can control the *wd* threads. This is the watchdog thread and a few other background threads used to for connection setup and other background activities. Normally it is not essential to handle these threads in any special manner. However if you run in a system with high CPU usage it can sometimes be useful to control CPU placement and thread priority of these threads. Obviously it isn't good if the watchdog is left completely without CPU capacity which can potentially happen in a seriously overloaded server.

65.2.2 THREAD SETTINGS IN *ThreadConfig*

For each thread there are 3 things that one can control.

1. Which CPUs to lock threads to

2. Which priority should threads execute at

3. Should threads be spinning when idle

Controlling CPU placement can be done using 4 different configuration variants. *cpubind*, *cpubind_exclusive*, *cpuset* and *cpuset_exclusive*. The exclusive variants are performing the same action as without exclusive except that they ensure that no other thread from any other program can use these CPUs. We get exclusive access to those CPUs, even the OS is not getting access to those CPUs. Although a nice feature it can unfortunately only be used on Solaris which is the only OS that has an API to control CPU placement at this level. We can use *cpubind* and *cpuset* on Linux, Windows, Solaris and FreeBSD. None of the settings can be used on Mac OS X since Mac OS X has no API to control CPU placement.

cpubind SETTINGS

When a thread or a set of threads is bound using *cpubind* it means that each thread is bound to exactly one CPU. If several threads are in the group they are assigned to CPUs in order. In this case it is necessary that the number of CPUs is at least the same as the amount of threads in the group (*io* are a bit special since they perform round-robin on the CPUs when they are started if several CPUs exist in the thread group).

Two thread groups can use the same set of CPUs in *cpubind*. This can be useful to have several light-weight threads not having a dedicated CPU resource. E.g. the *main*, *rep*, *io* and *wd* threads can share one CPU in many configurations.

The number of CPUs should be equal to the number of threads and cannot be smaller than the number of threads.

cpuset SETTINGS

The *cpuset* means that each thread is allowed to be on any of the CPUs in the CPU set. Here the number of CPUs in the CPU set doesn't have to be the same as the number of threads although it is usually a good idea to not oversubscribe your HW since it will have a bad effect on response time and throughput of MySQL Cluster.

One can define several thread groups to use the same CPU set, but it has to be exactly the same CPU set, one cannot define overlapping CPU sets in the configuration.

THREAD PRIORITY SETTINGS (*thread_prio*)

We have the ability to control the thread priority for the various thread types. This is done by using the *thread_prio* parameter. We can set it to any value between 0 and 10. Higher value means higher priority and the normal priority is 5.

On Linux and FreeBSD this parameter sets the nice value of the thread going from -20 for 10 down to 19 for 0. This uses the *setpriority* system call. Setting it to 10 gives a nice level of -20, 9 gives -16, 8 gives -12, 7 gives -8, 6 gives -4, 5 gives 0, 4 gives +4, 3 gives +8, 2 gives +12, 1 gives +16 and 0 gives +19.

On Windows we make use of the Windows API function *SetThreadPriority*. We use priorities from THREAD_PRIORITY_LOWEST at 0 and 1, THREAD_PRIORITY_BELOW_NORMAL at 2 and 3, THREAD_PRIORITY_NORMAL at 4 and 5, THREAD_PRIORITY_ABOVE_NORMAL at 6 and 7, THREAD_PRIORITY_HIGHEST at 8, 9 and 10.

Solaris has a wide variety of settings for thread priority. For a database engine that often executes for a long time we selected using the FX priority class which gives a fixed priority level that doesn't change with execution time. With increasing thread priority we increase the FX priority starting at 15 and going through 5-step increments up to 8 which is 55 and 9 is 58.

Using priority 10 on Solaris 11.3 and higher has a special meaning, this sets FX priority 60 and this has a very special meaning. It means that Solaris will attempt to ensure that the thread can execute alone on the CPU core it is assigned to. Thus the CPU thread will be undisturbed by any other threads running in the machine.

Mac OS X provides no APIs to control thread priority, the *thread_prio* parameter is not possible to set on Mac OS X.

realtime SETTINGS

Most OSs support some method of setting real-time priority of threads. On Windows we can use the *SetThreadPriority* call using the parameter

THREAD_PRIORITY_TIME_CRITICAL. On Linux we can use the call to

sched_setscheduler to set real-time priority. On Mac OS X, FreeBSD, Solaris we can use the *pthread_setschedparam* call.

These calls are very dangerous, they can even put the entire OS into a freeze state. We are providing a manner to avoid those freezes by downgrading from real-time priority to a normal priority level if we execute for more than 50 milliseconds without going to sleep. This means that using real-time priority is most effective when we don't have massive loads to handle but rather want very quick response times and very predictable response time in those situations.

There are two ways to configure real-time settings. The first is to set the configuration variable *RealtimeScheduler*. This parameter also works for *ndbd* processes. For *ndbmtd* processes it sets the default value for all threads. This default value can be overridden by the settings in the *ThreadConfig* parameter by setting *realtime* to 0 to not use real-time priority and setting it to 1 to enable real-time priority.

spintime SETTINGS

We can set the threads to spin for a while before going to sleep. Thus the thread is ready to go to sleep. It has no work to do, but we decide that we want to be awake to quickly service requests when they come in. If we can do this spinning without affecting other parts of the system in a negative way it could be a very important feature to improve response times. We've seen as much as 20% better response times at low loads through using the *spintime* parameter.

This feature is available on all OSs since it doesn't involve any OS calls. It simply means that we avoid calling the condition wait call until we've spun for the time configured. This time is configured in microseconds.

Setting spintime works the same way as when setting *realtime*. One can set a configuration parameter called *SchedulerSpinTimer*. This works also in *ndbd*. In *ndbmtd* it sets the default value for all threads in the process and can be overridden by settings per thread type in *ThreadConfig*.

spintime can be set to maximum 500 microseconds, if it is set higher it will be set to 500.

Chapter 66

Linux configuration

In order to get the optimal real-time experience it is necessary to setup the operating system infrastructure to ensure that MySQL Cluster is continuing to deliver in all circumstances.

The challenge comes primarily from two sources, the interrupt processing of the Linux network stack, the handling of CPU resources used to run the operating system which includes things such as error logging, handling IO interrupts, and various background maintenance activities. In addition we can be challenged by other applications that we install and run ourselves on the servers used to run MySQL Cluster nodes.

One example from early NDB history was a user that every night ran a backup of his machine, this backup process consumed most of the CPU and memory resources of the machine and caused the NDB data node process to stop every night at around 2am. It is important to confine such processes to not consume all the needed CPU and memory resources of the machine and thus endangering the health of the MySQL Cluster installation.

Running a MySQL Cluster installation means that there will be a lot of network traffic. Thus we need to understand how the OS handles interrupts from network devices and how it executes the network stack to ensure that it doesn't conflict with the NDB processing.

In addition the OS can contain many other processes that want access to CPU resources. These could be application processes, it can be operating system activities such as logging, it can be various management processes.

Setting up this infrastructure is very dependent on the application and the environment MySQL Cluster is running in.

We will describe ways to control placement of various important CPU activities in different OSs.

66.1 Linux infrastructure

We will start by describing the Linux infrastructure, Linux is a very capable OS, but configuring Linux for best real-time experience is not so straightforward. We will describe a few different methods used to control the use of CPU resources in Linux, we will start with the network interrupt handling, next we will look at an option to isolate CPUs from being used for anything else than the processes that bind themself to these CPUs. It isn't very straightforward to control CPU resource usage in Linux, this is one of the reasons why the use of frameworks like Docker have been so successful, they essentially make use of the cgroup infrastructure in an easy manner for applications to use.

The most important thing to understand is how Linux handles network interrupts. Execution starts with a hardware interrupt. There are two common defaults for interrupt handling, one is that all interrupts are running on one CPU, the other is that HW interrupts are spread on all CPUs. In both cases we want to ensure that interrupt processing isn't happening on any CPUs where we have significant CPU processing.

The *ldm* thread is normally the most important thread type to protect, it is usually a good idea to ensure that *ldm* is the bottleneck for the NDB data nodes. Sometimes the *tc* is a bottleneck, the *main* should never be a bottleneck, *rep* threads are seldom a bottleneck, but in cases where we have lot of NDB Event API handling it could happen (this is used for MySQL Cluster Replication among other things, but could also be used for other application defined services). *io* threads are normally not a bottleneck, but at the same time it is important to ensure that these threads are protected from massive overloads since if these threads are blocked from executing the checkpointing of MySQL Cluster is not going to work properly.

66.2 LINUX RECEIVE INTERRUPT HANDLING

In Linux the first step is to control the HW interrupt for network receive. Some devices only support one interrupt model where they wake up a specific CPU. The most common is that a modern network device can support many interrupt models. Most modern network device drivers employ a technique called Receive Side Scaling (RSS). This means that the network card will calculate a hash function based on local address, remote address, local port number and remote port number. Some devices support a configurable hash function and some devices support hash functions with less parts as inout to the hash function. The network device will for each packet place the packet into a receive queue, there will be several such queues and each will be placed onto at least one CPU. This CPU is the one receiving the HW interrupt when a packet arrives.

66.2.1 NAPI MECHANISM

Modern Linux systems uses the NAPI (New API) mechanism. Thus when a HW interrupt arrives the NAPI scheduler will issue a soft IRQ interrupt, when it has issued this soft IRQ it will disable the HW interrupts such that no more HW interrupts arrive until the interrupts are enabled again. When the soft IRQ have executed to completion for the receive queue, it will check the receive queue for more messages that have arrived. If no more messages have arrived it will enable interrupts again. This simple algorithm means that in a system with low load the interrupts will ensure low latency network operations. At high load when interrupt arrives faster than they are processed, then they are quickly put in the queue and we are using a poll-based mechanism instead which provides much higher throughput for a very busy networking infrastructure.

66.2.2 RECEIVE SIDE SCALING (RSS)

RSS is configured by default, the number of receive queues has a default setting which is often equal to the number of CPUs in the system. It is unlikely that we want to use all CPUs for interrupt processing and it hasn't been shown to be of any value to have more receive queues than the number of CPU cores in the machine. In addition we want to protect some of our cores from interrupt processing, thus we would benefit from even less number of receive queues. Setting the number of receive queues is done as part of configuring the network device driver. Check the device driver documentation and set the number of receive queues appropriately.

Even if the default settings are used for number of receive queues is used we can still ensure that the receive queues are handled by CPUs that don't disturb the NDB threads that we want to protect from network processing.

The hardware interrupts for each of those receive queues is handled by one interrupt number for each receive queue. Which CPU(s) this interrupt number will wake upon is controlled by the */proc/irq/70/smp_affinity* file where 70 should be replaced by the interrupt number. The interrupts number for the receive queues can be found by looking into the file *proc/interrupts*. If we have a machine using eth0 as the ethernet device, we should search all lines in this file for the *eth0* key. This line will start with the interrupt number followed by a *:*

Based on this information we will use the following command to set the CPUs that are allowed to execute the HW interrupt for a certain receive queue by writing the following command assuming that the interrupt number is 70 for the receive queue and assuming that we want to use CPU 4-11 for handling networking interrupts. This CPU mask defines both where the HW interrupt is executed as well as where the soft IRQ are handled.

```
echo ff0 > /proc/irq/70/smp_affinity
```

66.2.3 RECEIVE PACKET STEERING (RPS)

Now in older Linux versions (before version *2.6.35* this would be sufficient to control network receive processing. In newer versions it is still sufficient if Receive Packet Steering (RPS) is either not compiled into the Linux kernel (using CONFIG_RPS) or if the RPS isn't configured to be active in the Linux kernel. Default is that RPS is compiled in, whether it is used by default in the OS depends on the Linux distribution used.

If the network device supports RSS it isn't necessary to use RPS unless we also want to use Receive Flow Steering (RFS) which we will describe below.

When RPS is enabled it means that the soft IRQ has a very short execution, it will simply issue a call function interrupt to a CPU selected to the bottom half processing of the packets. This function call interrupt will perform the same functionality as the soft IRQ would have done otherwise. As is fairly obvious there is no benefit to RPS unless either of two things is present. The first is that the network device can only distribute HW interrupts to one CPU (this CPU might even be hard-wired to be CPU0). In this case it is a good idea that the HW interrupt is doing as little as possible and quickly starts up another kernel thread to do the bottom half processing. One popular example of such an environment is when you are running in a normal Amazon EC2 environment, in this case it is important to use RPS to distribute interrupt load on more than one CPU if you are using MySQL Cluster with high load.

The second case when RPS is beneficial is when RFS is used and the kernel can use some knowledge about where the recv system calls are processed. In this case it can issue the function call interrupt to execute on that particular CPU. If the recv is often called from the same CPU, this is very beneficial to CPU caching and thus improves throughput and latency of the system.

For NDB data nodes all recv processing is done by the *recv* thread for *ndbmtd* and by the execution thread for *ndbd*. Thus if the recv threads are bound to a CPU or several CPUs the recv execution will be very efficient for the NDB data nodes. The MySQL Server have a number of recv calls done by the NDB API. By setting *ndb_recv_thread_cpu* to the desired CPU to use AND setting *ndb_recv_thread_threshold* to 0 all recv execution for the NDB API will be handled by the CPU(s) set in this variable. If the MySQL Server uses several connections to the NDB data nodes then several CPUs are normally used. The MySQL Server connection threads are handled by each SQL thread in the MySQL Server.

For RPS to work well in combination with RFS it is important to control the CPU placement of the execution of the recv calls. For the absolute best real-time experience and absolute best performance of MySQL Cluster these are options that are worth conisdering and experimenting with. For the majority of users of MySQL Cluster this is likely not a good idea to consider.

Disabling and enabling of RPS can be done per receive queue. Disabling is done by the following command (with eth0 replaced with the device name and rx-0 replaced by the name of the receive queue).

```
echo 0 > /sys/class/net/eth0/queues/rx-0/rps_cpus
```

To enable it one uses the same command and replaces the 0 by a comma separated list of hexadecimal numbers (each hexadecimal number contain up to 64 bits, only in systems with more than 64 CPUs is it necessary to use a list rather than one hexadecimal number). E.g. to configure the rx-0 queue for eth0 to use CPU 1,2,3 and 5 we set it to the hexadecimal number 2e.

When not using RPS the network driver will first interrupt the CPU with a HW interrupt, then after processing the HW interrupt it will wake up the ksoftirqd/5 (where 5 is the number of the CPU where the HW interrupt was happening, this process always executes bound to CPU5. The ksoftirqd process will do the rest of the processing and will then wake up any threads waiting for data on the socket.

When using RPS the same execution will happen, but the major part of the Soft IRQ processing is handled through a function call interrupt. This interrupt wakes up one of the CPUs that was part of the bitmask for the receive queue as set above.

To control interrupt processing when using RPS we need to configure both the CPUs used to take care of the HW interrupts as well as the CPUs used to handle the function call interrupts for the larger part of handling the network receive stack.

It isn't necesary to use the same CPUs for HW interrupts as for function call interrupt processing.

66.2.4 RECEIVE FLOW STEERING (RFS)

As mentioned above it is possible to use RFS in conjunction with RPS. RFS means that the function call interrupt part of RPS has data structures setup to ensure that we can send the function call interrupt to a CPU that is close to the CPU or even the CPU that last called recv on the socket for which the packet arrived.

In order to set up those data structures Linux needs to know how many active sockets to work with, Linux will only keep track of active sockets and when they last used the recv system call. The intention of RFS is to ensure that the recv system call can start up immediately after the interrupt processing is done by the kernel thread. Since they execute on the same or a CPU close (from a CPU cache point of view), this means that the packet processing will be faster since we will have very good CPU cache behaviour.

For RFS to work well it is important that the recv calls on a socket are performed from CPUs that are not that far away from each other, the best case is if they are always executed on the same CPU or same CPU core. For NDB data nodes this means controlling the CPU placement of the recv thread such that this thread is either on the same CPU all the time or on a CPU set that is close to each other. For RFS to work it is necessary that the CPUs used by the RPS processing contains the CPUs used by the *recv* thread, or at least very close to those CPUs.

RFS is not configured by default and it requires setting CONFIG_RFS when compiling Linux (on by default). To configure RFS to be active one needs to set the number of active sockets to track. This is done by setting this value in the following manner:

```
echo 32768 > /proc/sys/net/core/rps_sock_flow_entries
```

The number 32768 have been found to be appropriate in medium-sized configurations. In a node that primarily runs a NDB data node and/or a MySQL Server this value should be sufficient.

In addition it is necessary to set the number of sockets tracked per receive queue. This is normally simply the total number divided by the number of receive queues. The below example shows an example of setting this for receive queue *rx-0* for the *eth0* device. Replace 0 by the receive queue id and replace *eth0* by the device name in the general case.

```
echo 4096 > /sys/class/net/eth0/queues/rx-0/rps_flow_cnt
```

Both values are rounded up to a value of the type 2^n. Both values need to be set for RFS to be active on a receive queue.

If the network device driver supports Accelerated RFS (ARFS), this will be automatically enabled provided two things. First the Linux kernel must have been compiled with CONFIG_RFS_ACCEL, second ntuple filtering must be activated using the *ethtool*. ARFS means that the network card will automatically send the interrupt to the correct CPU. This is implemented by a call to the device driver every time the call to recv is done from a new CPU for a socket. It is desirable that this CPU doesn't change so often.

66.3 Transmit Packet Steering (XPS)

In the same fashion that many network cards have multiple receive queues they will often have multiple transmit queues. In order to ensure that locking on those transmit queues isn't hurting scalability it is possible to specify which CPUs are able to use a certain transmit queue.

One complication in using the XPS feature is that when a stream of packets for one socket have selected a transmit queue, it isn't possible to change the transmit queue for this socket until an acknowledge have arrived for the outstanding packets. This introduces unnecessary delays when sending is done from any CPU in the system.

With MySQL Cluster we can send packets on any socket from many different places. For example an NDB data node needs to able to use the same set of transmit queues from all CPUs that is used by the NDB data node. However if we have several data nodes on the same machine, or if we have a MySQL Server on the same machine that uses different CPUs, then it is possible to use different sets of transmit queues for the different processes.

To configure XPS the Linux kernel must be compiled with CONFIG_XPS (default) and for each transmit queue one must set the CPUs that can use this transmit queue.

```
echo fff > /sys/class/net/eth0/queues/tx-0/xps_cpus
```

The above setting means that transmit queue *tx-0* can only be used from CPU 0-11 for the device eth0. Replace 0 by the transmit queue id and eth0 by the device name for the general case. Here a hexadecimal number representing a bitmap with a comma separated list of bitmaps when more than 64 cpus exist in the machine.

66.4 LINUX CPU ISOLATION

There is a boot option in Linux called isolcpus. This option makes it possible to remove a set of CPUs from normal scheduling, thus these CPUs are not considered when scheduling a thread to execute. There is one way to assign a thread to execute on those CPUs, this is by explicitly binding those threads to those CPUs. When using the *ThreadConfig* variable and setting *cpubind* or *cpuset* on a set of threads this happens, also when using the configuration variables *LockExecuteThreadToCpu* and *LockMaintThreadsToCpu*.

The *isolcpus* option could be used to isolate the NDB processes from other processes in the system. In this case one should ensure that all thread types have been locked to CPUs in the machine that are part of the *isolcpus* and when using the MySQL Server one should either bind the MySQL Server using *taskset* or *numactl*. Another option is to use the *isolcpus* to isolate the CPUs used for network interrupt handling to ensure that the most predictable latency can be ensured for the user of MySQL Cluster.

66.5 CONCLUSION

To setup the operating system properly for use by MySQL Cluster means that you should ask yourself a couple of questions.

The first obvious question is if you are willing to spend time to optimise the installation of MySQL Cluster at this level. If you are trying out MySQL Cluster for a simple application it is probably not worthwhile. If you are developing an application or an infrastructure component in your company used by thousands of people it is still fairly questionable if you would do this. A normal Linux installation will get you far and spending a few hours extra or days isn't likely to get you such benefits that makes this worthwhile.

If you are a student and you want to learn how MySQL Cluster works, how Linux works and build competence for this and other projects, for sure go ahead and try out all possible variants such that you have a good understanding of the Linux network stack and how MySQL Cluster operates in its context.

If you are developing an application that will be used by millions of users or even billions of users and you are living in a competetive environment where your solution is compared to other similar solutions, it is likely going to pay off to read this chapter and apply some of those in your production setup. If you are delivering 1000s of servers and this setup can improve performance by 10-20%, it is worthwhile to spend time optimising the installation.

A time when you need to read this chapter and apply it to your installation is when you hit specific bottlenecks that are required to overcome before your installation is considered complete.

One good example where you might hit specific bottlenecks is if you install MySQL Cluster in a cloud environment and you get hit by the fact that the single CPU used to handle networking interrupt is limiting your throughput.

This is the first technical question you should ask yourself if you decided to go through and the apply the techniques provided in this chapter.

The question is thus if your network card(s) only have one receive queue to handle networking interrupts. In this case you are limited to only one CPU that can handle the receive part of the networking. In this case you should go ahead and use RPS.

If your network devices already supports multiple receive queues more questions are needed before you decide if you should use RPS or not. The next question is if you have decided to setup a MySQL Cluster installation where you have decided to control the CPUs and ensure that you are in full control over where processes are executing. If this is the case you should go ahead and use RPS, but not only that you should take one more step further and also use RFS. Using RPS without RFS where RSS exists is simply extra overhead without any benefits. It will increase your response time to queries in MySQL Cluster without creating any benefits.

Next step is to decide whether to use XPS, this really only applies on large servers. It can provide benefits when you are colocating the MySQL Server and the NDB data node on the same machine or on the same virtual machine. In this case it is a good idea to consider to ensure that data nodes are placed on one set of CPUs and use its own set of transmit queues and the MySQL Server uses a different set of CPUs and transmit queues.

These are things that one should put into scripts and automate as part of process of setting up MySQL Cluster machines. The above description works both for bare metal machines as well as for virtual machines as well as for machines in a cloud environment.

Interrupt processing of the network stack requires a fair amount of CPUs, this is an important part of the MySQL Cluster infrastructure to consider. One should definitely expect to use around 20% of the available CPU resources for network interrupt processing in a distributed MySQL Cluster environment, counting both send and receive the cost of communication can often be half of the available CPU resources.

66.6 EXAMPLE CPU BUDGET

Let's consider setting up one MySQL Cluster Data Node using an OC5M instance on the Oracle Cloud. In this case we have a virtual machine that have 16 Intel Xeon v3 cores with 240 GByte of memory.

In this case we will allocate 8 cores to run 8 *ldm* threads, 3 cores to handle the *main* and *rep* threads and the *io* threads.

This setup assumes that one will use compressed backups and compressed LCPs. This means that a few CPUs can be used for compressing writes to files in the worst case. These 3 cores are also intended for use by the operating system.

Next we will use 3 cores for *send* and *recv* threads. We will use 3 CPUs for *send* threads and 3 CPUs for the *recv* threads.

Finally the last 2 cores are intended for 4 *tc* threads.

The *ThreadConfig* setting for these would be.

```
ThreadConfig=
ldm={count=8,cpubind=8-15,thread_prio=10,spintime=500},
tc={count=4,cpuset=6-7,22-23,spintime=100,thread_prio=10,spintime=100},
send={count=3,cpubind=4-5,21},
recv={count=3,cpubind=3,19,20},
main={count=1,cpuset=0-2,16-18},
rep={count=1,cpuset=0-2,16-18},
io={count=1,cpuset=0-2,16-18}
```

In this setup it would be a good idea to use all of RSS, RPS and RFS and ensure that all receive function handlers are handled by the same CPUs as the *recv* threads. It might be a good idea to move one CPU used by *send* threads to the *recv* threads. In this manner the OS can always route the interrupt processing to the same CPU where the actual application receive processing is done.

In this case we would thus use CPUs 3 and 19-20 for network interrupt processing, especially the RPS part, possibly also the RSS part. Thus we will ensure that the 3 CPUs used for the *recv* thread is part of the CPUs that can be used for the network interrupt function handlers.

This means that the CPU mask to use in this case would be 0x180008 (note that the CPU mask is always a hexadecimal number and so is this). This mask can be used both to set the CPU mask for HW interrupts as well as for RPS CPUs.

We could isolate the transmit interrupts. At first we disable sending from the *ldm* threads. Thus sending can happen from the CPU core where the send threads and from the core where the *main* and *rep* threads are, and from the two CPU cores used by the *tc* threads. Thus send interrupt will happen from 13 CPUs and we can thus setup XPS to use those 13 CPUs only and thus completely isolate the *ldm* threads from both receive and send activitites.

If we want to isolate the *ldm* threads from the rest of the activity in the OS as well we can set *isolcpus* as (not possible to do on Cloud instances as far as I am aware):

isolcpus=8-15,24-31

CHAPTER 67

BASIC CONFIGURATION SETUP

When you look at the forums it is quite obvious that the absolute majority of the NDB users are looking for a very basic high availability setup with one VM per node in the cluster.

We will look at setting up the configuration for such a basic cluster as an exercise now. The previous chapters have given us a lot of input on what parameters that matters the most. We want to setup a memory efficient setup that can handle some load, but not the very highest load. We are not aiming for the absolute highest performance here, it is enough to setup things for a basic user that wants a very basic HA setup.

The most basic HA setup has 5 VMs, one for the NDB management server, two VMs for the data nodes and two VMs for the MySQL servers. In addition we will add one API node for use by NDB tools.

We assume that the management server is using IP address 192.168.1.100, the data nodes are setup on 192.168.1.101 and 192.168.1.102 and the MySQL servers are using 192.168.1.103 and 192.168.1.104.

As preparation for setting up the cluster we assume that the VMs have opened up port 1186 to communicate to and from the NDB management server, 3306 to communicate to and from the MySQL servers and port 11860 to communicate to and from the data nodes. This is particularly important to consider when the OS by default closes down all ports.

When setting up things in the cloud it is very common that one can define the ports to open up, in a cloud setup almost all VMs open up port 22 for SSH access, but in addition we need port 1186, 3306 and 11860 opened up here for the VMs.

In /etc/my.cnf we store the configuration used to startup the MySQL server nodes. In this file we need to ensure that the MySQL server can use the NDB storage engine and we need to ensure that it can connect to the management server.

In the NDB configuration file we need to create 6 nodes, the management server with node id 49, the two data nodes with node id 1 and 2 and the two MySQL servers with node id 51 and 52. In addition we provide an API node that is using node id 231. This node is not bound to any specific host.

In this case we assume that the cluster is used to store a fairly small database of up to 200 MByte of data. It is enough to configure with 256 MByte of *DataMemory*. In addition we need a bit of *IndexMemory* to handle the hash index. 40 MByte is sufficient to store more than 2 million rows, so should be sufficient for a database size of 200 MByte.

```
config.ini

[ndbd default]
NoOfReplicas=2
NoOfFragmentLogParts=4
NoOfFragmentLogFiles=4
FragmentLogFileSize=64M
DataDir=/usr/local/ndb_data
DataMemory=256M
IndexMemory=40M
DiskPageBufferMemory=0
#DiskPageBufferMemory=256M
ServerPort=11860
MaxNoOfAttributes=10000
BatchSizePerLocalScan=64
StartPartitionedTimeout=0
TwoPassInitialNodeRestartCopy=1
BuildIndexThreads=128
ConnectCheckIntervalDelay=1
HeartbeatIntervalDbDb=1000
MinDiskWriteSpeed=1M
MaxDiskWriteSpeed=2M
BackupDataBufferSize=512k
BackupMaxWriteSize=512k
BackupWriteSize=256k
ODirect=1
IndexStatAutoCreate=1
IndexStatAutoUpdate=1
StringMemory=5

[ndb_mgmd default]
DataDir=/usr/local/ndb_data
[ndb_mgmd]
NodeId=49
Hostname=192.168.1.100

[ndbd]
NodeId=1
Hostname=192.168.1.101
[ndbd]
NodeId=2
Hostname=192.168.1.102

[mysqld]
NodeId=51
Hostname=192.168.1.103
[mysqld]
NodeId=52
Hostname=192.168.1.104
[api]
NodeId=231
```

We have commented out setting a higher value for DiskPageBufferMemory, instead we set it to 0. This means no disk columns are allowed in any table. If the user wants to use disk columns we create a properly sized page cache such that the user can have up to about 2 GByte of data in disk columns as well. If so, swap the *DiskPageBufferMemory* rows.

This configuration will allow us to create 320 table and index objects with up to 1000 columns in the tables. This should be sufficient for a small database.

We have changed the configuration parameters where it makes sense to change the default settings. These are as discussed in previous chapters *BatchSizePerLocalScan* to decrease memory usage for lock records. Setting *StartPartitionedTimeout* to 0 to avoid ever starting up in a partitioned state. Setting *NoOfFragmentLogParts*, *NoOfFragmentLogFiles* and *FragmentLogFileSize* to get a proper sized REDO log. In this case we have 4 parts with 4 files each and each file is 64 MByte, thus in total 1 GByte.

We have changed the defaults of local checkpoint buffers to avoid large buffers that are not needed and even increase latency of queries towards NDB. Given that the database is very small it is a good idea to decrease the checkpoint write speed to avoid wasting disk bandwidth on writing checkpoints very fast.

Setting *NoOfReplicas* to 2 isn't absolutely necessary since it is default, but it is good to be clear since this is a very basic configuration parameter.

We need to set *DataDir* to ensure that the placement of NDB files is set.

We use the *ConnectCheckIntervalDelay* parameter that provides a safer handling of heartbeat failures and we combine this with a shorter heartbeat timeout that should be long enough.

We use the most efficient algorithm to perform initial node restart by setting *BuildIndex-Threads* to 128 and *TwoPassInitialNodeRestartCopy* to 1.

Many of those defaults have changed in MySQL Cluster 7.6. It is a good idea to use those also in MySQL Cluster 7.5.

Using *ODirect* is preferrable in most file systems so we set it here.

```
my.cnf

[mysqld]
ndbcluster
ndb-cluster-connection-pool-nodeids=51
ndb-connectstring=192.168.1.100
query-cache-size=0
query-cache-type=0
ndb-read-backup=1
ndb-allow-copying-alter-table=0
ndb-autoincrement-prefetch-sz=1024

[ndbd]
connect-string=192.168.1.100

[ndb_mgmd]
connect-string=192.168.1.100
config-file=/usr/local/ndb_data/config.ini
nodeid=49

[ndb_mgm]
connect-string=192.168.1.100
```

In the *my.cnf* file it is important to ensure that the query cache is entirely disabled to ensure that it doesn't prevent the MySQL server from scaling to a large number of CPUs.

Using NDB for SQL applications means mostly that the focus is on read scaling. We set the flag that ensures that all tables use the Read Backup feature. To ensure good scalability of autoincrement tables we set the prefetch size to 1024 to avoid any scalability issues with inserting rows with autoincrement keys.

To ensure that the user doesn't use a copying ALTER TABLE by mistake, we set the flag that disallows using a copying ALTER TABLE.

Whether to set the node id of the MySQL server, data nodes and management server in the *my.cnf* is a matter of choice. Here I have done so, but this means that the file must be changed in each VM. Otherwise one can provide the node id in the startup command.

PART XIV

VARIOUS TOPICS

Chapter 68

Platform support

Platforms that MySQL Cluster supports gets regular testing, every change of the MySQL Cluster software triggers execution of tests on around 10 different platforms such as various Linux variants, Solaris on x86 and Solaris on SPARC, a few Windows variants and Mac OS X.

Even more platforms are tested in daily and weekly test runs.

68.1 MySQL Cluster on x86

MySQL Cluster have some special optimisations in *ndbmtd* to make use of the *x86* CPUs from Intel, AMD and other vendors. This is by far the most well tested platform.

68.2 MySQL Cluster on Linux

MySQL Cluster is designed to run on all Linux variants. It is most well tested on Oracle Linux, other OSs that gets a fair chunk of testing is Ubuntu, Debian, Red Hat, Fedora and Suse. There are Linux repos available on Oracle Linux, Red Hat, Ubuntu, Debian and Suse.

Linux is by far the most popular platform to run MySQL Cluster in production.

68.3 MySQL Cluster on Windows

MySQL Cluster is supported on Windows. There are a few production installations, but it is mostly intended as a development platform.

It is quite a popular operating system for downloads of NDB.

68.4 MySQL Cluster on Solaris

MySQL Cluster 7.x is supported on Solaris.

MySQL Cluster have a fair share of users still running on Solaris, both using *x86* and SPARC.

68.5 MySQL Cluster on Mac OS X

MySQL Cluster is supported on Mac OS X. I am personally developing on Mac OS X, but it is mostly intended as a development platform.

68.6 MySQL Cluster on Intel NUC

I am personally very fond of Intel NUCs as development platform for MySQL Cluster. It provides a cheap server that you can even have in your living room since it uses very little fans. I install some Linux variant on those and sometimes even some FreeBSD variant.

It is perfect for having your own development cluster with real machines close to you. 4 of those machines use less power than most desktops does.

68.7 MySQL Cluster on FreeBSD

MySQL Cluster is not supported on FreeBSD. I have tested running the autotest suite on FreeBSD. I had 3 failures that doesn't exist on Linux in a test run with about 500 tests. It isn't ready for production usage, but it is stable enough for demonstration purposes.

68.8 MySQL Cluster on ARM

MySQL Cluster is not supported on ARM processors. It works to get MySQL Cluster up and running on e.g. Raspberry Pi's for demonstration purposes. In this case one must use the *ndbd* process for the NDB data nodes. *ndbmtd* uses low level CPU operations such as memory barriers that haven't been fully ported to the ARM architecture yet.

68.9 MySQL Cluster on Power

MySQL Cluster isn't supported on Power. I haven't tested MySQL Cluster on Power myself, but Stewart Smith reported some experiments using MySQL Cluster on Power a few years ago. There were some issues with memory barriers and so forth in the *ndbmtd* binary. These problems were fixed. There are probably a few more things to fix. As usual the *ndbd* program is better to use on Power since it uses less things that require CPU support.

CHAPTER 69

MySQL Cluster in the Cloud

At the beginning the concept of the Cloud was as vague as the term sounds to be. Now with the development of the Amazon Cloud, Google Cloud, Microsoft Azure and the Oracle Cloud it has become a lot clearer what the concept entails.

The cloud offers a very rapid development environment, you can spin up a computer in the form of a virtual machine (VM) that you get access to within minutes. You can as well spin up many different VMs at the same time and the cloud is very flexible in how those computers look like.

Today many companies use the cloud to off-shore their IT department. Many companies want to avoid spending too much of their precious resources on IT personnel and rather have another company with specialised skills in IT to take care of their internal IT needs. Whether this process is a good or a bad idea and when it works and when it doesn't work is outside the scope of this book. In this book we will focus on how the cloud relates to MySQL Cluster.

69.1 General considerations

So is running MySQL Cluster in the Cloud a good idea?

As usual the answer is a mixed one. For test and development it is a great thing. You can easily setup a cluster with a high availability configuration at a very low cost. Without the cloud it was necessary to invest in a cluster of computers before you could do any Proof Of Concept, POC installations. Now you can use the cloud to do such a POC and you can also use the cloud in the development phase of your application.

For test and development the answer is a simple yes, it is a good idea in many cases. For production usage the answer is a lot more mixed.

MySQL Cluster is designed to be always up and running. It has been proven in the field to provide 99.9999% availability (Class 6). At the same time most of the public clouds do not offer more than 99.95% availability on their service. There are ways to improve this by using various availability solutions that we will discuss in this chapter. But for the very highest availability the public clouds is simply not the place for your application.

There are clouds designed for the highest availability. As an example telecom vendors such as Ericsson also provide cloud solutions. These cloud solutions are designed to run telecom networks and are designed with normal telecom requirements. These telecom requirements means hardened servers, servers that can handle earthquakes, predictable environments where each of the VMs will get a predictable amount of resources.

Thus in most cases it is possible to find a cloud provider that can give you sufficient availability to run your MySQL Cluster and its applications. But if you have the highest availability requirements it is important to to be careful in your choice of cloud provider.

69.2 CLOUD ARCHITECTURES

Most of the public cloud providers that we will look into with a bit more detail are built around the same typf of architecture. They can have 1-3 levels of dependability you can use.

At first they are divided into regions. These regions contain at least two data centers and most of the time three and sometimes even more. Most of the time the regions should be more or less independent failure units. They are far away from each other, the most important dependency between regions is that if one region falls over, the other regions in the area is likely to get a very much higher traffic due to fail over of various services. Also they have dependencies in that they are operated by the same company and have common strategies for how to maintain the region. Other than that a region should be more or less independent of the other regions of the cloud provider.

A region is implemented using a number of data centers called Availability Zones (AZ) in Amazon and Google, and Availability Domain (AD) in the Oracle Cloud.

Microsoft Azure for some reason doesn't have this concept in their architecture. They only support regions and don't let the user control placement within a region. They instead use a concept called Availability Set. An availability set contains a number of Update Domains (this is the same as Availability Zones) and Fault Domains (this is essentially a restart domain, all servers in one fault domain can be restarted by scheduled maintenance, but not more than one fault domain). By default there are 3 update domains in an availability set and 5 fault domains and servers are placed into those in round robin fashion.

Thus in Azure we can ensure that nodes are stored in different Availability Zones, but we have no knowledge in which zone we are currently residing in. Thus there is no concept of locality. Also it isn't possible to ensure that arbitrator is in a different zone than the data nodes are in.

A cluster setup within one availability domain/zone can have single failure units such as a switch and even two VMs being placed on the same computer. To get high availability in the cloud one should use several availability domains/zones.

Some cloud providers go further and make it possible to use a concept sometimes called anti-affinity. This means that a set of instances will NOT be placed onto the same host and will be placed in a different failure unit. IBM supports this feature for placing out container services.

The cloud services are clearly focused on various levels of ease of use and availability. Amazon is easy to use and well documented. But it lacks a lot of interesting availability features and have even deprecated some of the ones they already supported. IBM and Oracle are clearly more focused on High Availability and therefore have more features to control instance placement.

Supporting anti-affinity comes with a complexity cost in that it becomes a harder problem to choose where to place the instance.

Communicating between instances inside the same AZ/AD is measured in the range of hundreds of microseconds. Communicating between availability zones is measured in at most

1-2 milliseconds. Communicating between regions on the same continent is measured in a few tens of milliseconds. Regions in different continents can easily take a hundred millisecond to send a message from one region to another.

Bandwidth is available inside an AZ/AD, but also within a region there is a large amount of bandwidth available. Communicating between regions is however much more limited. Latency is one of the biggest problems to handle when running MySQL Cluster in the Cloud.

The cloud provider that has the best latency between availability domains/zones is Oracle. Their latency is several times better than the competition. Oracle has also built the network infrastructure inside an AD to avoid oversubscription, thus we will get the promised bandwidth even with noisy neighbours. This is obviously a very important feature for a high availability service in any cloud solution.

69.3   Cloud instances for MySQL Cluster

There are four different instances we can have in a MySQL Cluster. First we have the natural ones, the NDB management server, the NDB data node and the MySQL Server. The fourth is a combined instance where we have both a MySQL Server and an NDB data node (could also be one data node and a number of MySQL Servers in the same instance. The reason to have those together is that this improves the communication between the data node and the MySQL Server. Given that these nodes are very integrated it is a good idea to not have to communicate between data node and MySQL Server in some cases.

From a performance perspective it is a good idea to combine the MySQL Server and the data node in the same instance.

At the same time from a stability point of view it is safer to have the MySQL Server in a separate instance. The reason is that the data node have complete control over its memory and once you have ensured that the memory fits in the instance it will continue to fit. The MySQL Server consumes resources without any real boundaries, thus if someone queries MySQL in a way that allocates lots of memory in the MySQL Server the memory in the instance might be overcommitted and thus leading to swapping of the memory also in the data node. One manner to overcome this problem is to start the MySQL server inside a Docker container that is given limits on how much memory it is allowed to use, see the chapter on MySQL Cluster and Docker earlier in this book.

For production usage it is recommended to use instances that have local storage on the VMs. Interestingly using instances with block storage means that NDB (a shared nothing DBMS) relies on a shared nothing implementation of a file system. For testing using instances with block storage is mostly ok.

69.3.1   Cloud instances for the NDB management server

Now first looking at the management server this can be served by a very small instance, one core should be sufficient for the management server and it doesn't need much memory and it doesn't need much disk space either. To handle peaks it is a good to have a full core, but other than that there is no reason to use more than a minimum instance type with one core.

ndb_mgmd instances

VM

OC1 Oracle Cloud
c4.large Amazon Cloud
n1-standard-2 Google Cloud
Standard_D2 Azure Cloud

ndb_mgmd

69.3.2 CLOUD INSTANCES FOR THE NDB DATA NODE

The NDB data nodes are the instances that need a memory optimised instance. It needs as much memory as it can get. In addition it needs about 2.5 times its *DataMemory* to contain the local checkpoints, it needs a fair amount of REDO log to handle the worst case when somebody is inserting a lot of data. It needs space to fit at least one full backup as well.

It is a good idea to place backups on a block device, it isn't required for restarts and it is good to place it such that is separately available from the data node VM. To avoid using too much bandwidth towards the block devices it is a good idea to use compressed backups.

Thus it is enough to have room for LCPs and REDO logs on the local disks. Using compressed LCPs these would fit in around a bit more 3x the size of the *DataMemory* setting.

From a CPU perspective the data node is the bottleneck in the cluster and in particular the *ldm* threads are the key bottleneck. On the API side we can always add more API nodes and MySQL Server to increase the throughput of the cluster. For data node we will mostly use the memory optimised instance types. To avoid having to scale the cluster to more nodes than necessary one should choose the largest instances for data nodes.

There are also cases where the data size is fairly small and the activity is very high in which case it might be sufficient with an instance of normal size or even a compute-optimised instance.

<u>Data node instances</u>

VM

VM.Standard2.16 Oracle Cloud
r3.8xlarge/r4.8xlarge   Amazon Cloud
n1-highmem-32 Google Cloud
Standard_GS4 Azure Cloud

ndbmtd

We select here machines with 16 CPU cores and around 240 GByte of memory as good examples to run data node instances in the cloud on. These instance types all rely on block storage.

There are also instances with local disks, but these are seldom perfectly fitting a MySQL Cluster 7.5 installation.

69.3.3 CLOUD INSTANCES FOR THE MYSQL SERVER

The MySQL Server consumes a fair amount of CPU resources, it can consume a fair amount of memory resources although compared to the data node it is very small requirements. The MySQL Server should use compute intensive instance types. The MySQL Server in MySQL Cluster is a true stateless application. It can restart anywhere in the cloud as long as it doesn't move away too far from the data nodes.

The number of CPUs in MySQL server VMs should be roughly similar to the CPUs used in the data nodes.

Mysql server instance

VM

VM.Standard1.16 Oracle Cloud
c4.8xlarge   Amazon Cloud
n1-standard-32 Google Cloud
Standard_D5_v2 Azure Cloud

mysqld

69.3.4 CLOUD INSTANCES FOR COMBO MYSQL SERVER AND NDB DATA NODE

Moving towards the combined MySQL Server and NDB data node we should use the memory optimised instances. Given that the MySQL Server uses a lot of CPU resources and a smaller amount of memory whereas the data nodes use a lot of memory but not so much CPU resources we can conclude that we should be able to balance these two binaries in the same instance.

Most of the memory (around 80%) should be used by the data node and the MySQL Server should have most of the CPU resources. At the same time it is important that the data node CPUs aren't overloaded since this will have a negative impact on latency and throughput. A conservative approach is to essentially divide the CPU resources in two halfs, one for the data node and one for the MySQL Server. However it is likely that the MySQL Server can probably at least take 60-65% of the CPU resources in the instance in most cases.

Combined MySQL server and data node

VM

VM.Standard2.24 BareMetal Oracle Cloud
r4.16xlarge   Amazon Cloud
n1-highmem-32 Google Cloud
Standard_GS5 Azure Cloud

mysqld

ndbmtd

69.4 SIZE OF MYSQL SERVERS IN THE CLOUD

As we remember the MySQL Server is perfectly stateless, there is no real reason to create massively large MySQL Server nodes. The main bottleneck of the MySQL Servers is the cluster connection. We can have multiple cluster connections per MySQL Server, but there is no real reason for it since we might as well use multiple MySQL Servers (one reason to use larger MySQL Servers could be to minimise the number of MySQL Servers to manage).

It would be sufficient to use around 16 CPUs per MySQL Server instance. This would use one cluster connection, we can choose instances with 32 CPUs per MySQL Server instance using 2 cluster connections per server. Even 64 CPUs per MySQL Server instance can be used with 4 cluster connections although other MySQL Server bottlenecks will start to have an impact as well.

Thus the main choice is 8-core instances and larger (naturally for a small application one can choose something smaller).

Thus we can have literally hundreds of MySQL Server in one MySQL Cluster that act as full masters in the cluster, they can both read and write all the data in the cluster using strong consistency. Thus MySQL Cluster scales to a few thousand CPUs handling tens of millions of SQL queries.

69.5 AVAILABILITY DOMAINS/ZONES

In the figure below we show an example of how to build a highly available cluster setup using AZ/ADs. It is important to ensure that each node group has nodes located in different AZ/ADs.

Similarly the MySQL Servers should be in both AZ/ADs where there are data nodes. The third AZ/AD should be used for the management server that acts as the arbitrator. This makes it safe to handle even a complete outage of one AZ/AD.

The figure shows separate VMs for MySQL servers and data nodes, but this setup can be used with combined MySQL server and data node VMs as well.

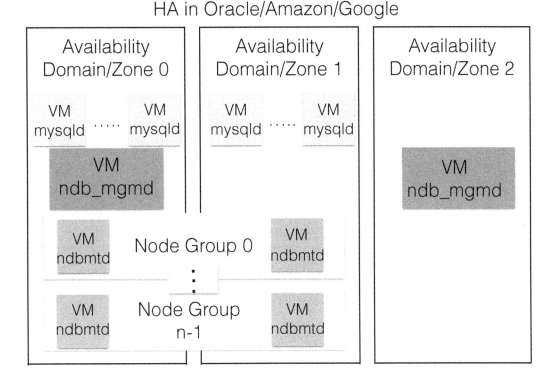

To achieve the absolutely highest availability this should be combined with MySQL Cluster Replication to a similar cluster setup in a different cloud region. This region could be in the same cloud provider or in the cloud of a different cloud provider.

69.6   AZURE CLOUD

A highly available setup in the Azure cloud requires creating at least 3 different availability sets (or two if using combined MySQL servers and data nodes). One for the management servers, one for each node group of the data nodes and one for the MySQL servers.

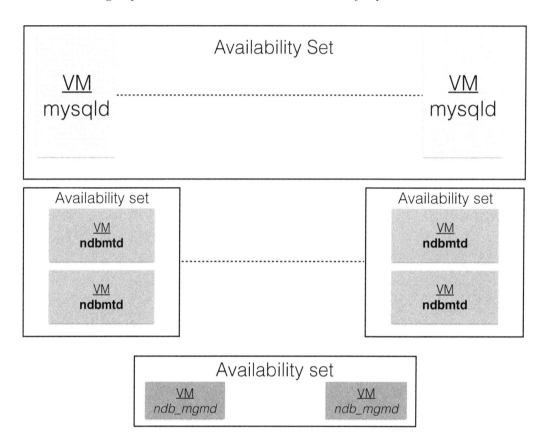

It is important here that data nodes belonging to the same availability set belongs to different node groups.

Chapter 70

Test framework

MySQL Cluster is used in extremely demanding applications. It has a great variety of features that are only used in failure modes, upgrade mode, meta data change modes. Thus a normal user will seldomly test the features in all manners possible. To ensure that we can guarantee that users don't get problems with unexpected failure modes we have an advanced battery of tests that is executed both on each push, on a daily basis, on a weekly basis and some extra tests of more manual nature that are executed at creation of a new release of the software.

70.1 MTR

MTR is the main test framework for testing MySQL. It runs mainly SQL queries against one or a few MySQL Servers and compares the result of running those queries against a result file. Each test run must generate exactly the same result each time, otherwise the test has failed. In addition no nodes are allowed to fail during the test run.

Tests are organised in test suites. For the NDB storage engine there is a general test suite called ndb, there is ndb_rpl test suite that focus on testing MySQL Cluster replication, there is another test suite rpl_ndb that tests a part of the MySQL replication tests against NDB (not all MySQL replication tests are applicable to NDB). Other test suites are ndb-big for tests with a bit bigger footprint. We have test suites focusing on DDL for MySQL Cluster in ndb_ddl. We have one test suite for testing the special memcached server using MySQL Cluster for storage which is called ndb_memcache. There is a test suite for testing specifically that NDB storage engine interacts well with the binlog which is called ndb_binlog. There is a test suite with some tests of autodiscovery of tables in a cluster and similar functions in ndb_team. There is a test suite called ndbcluster which is used when developing the latest version of the MySQL Server. MySQL Cluster uses a fork of a GA version of MySQL. This means that in developing MySQL Cluster we have some extra time to always ensure that we can guarantee the stability of MySQL Cluster based on all the changes made in the MySQL Server. The latest MySQL Cluster version is based on the MySQL 5.7 version. There is a new test suite called gcol_ndb that tests NDB support for generated columns.

The NDB test suites contains a fair amount of test code, the total number of test lines (not counting the result lines) is about 60k lines of tests and this counts only the tests for the NDB storage engine, there is an additional 850k lines of test code for the MySQL Server.

MTR is a functional test framework and it tests mainly the NDB storage engine and parts of MySQL Cluster used to perform metadata operations. It has very few tests that interact those things with restarts of various sorts. MTR is focused on functional testing. It is a very powerful tool for running functional tests. Given that SQL is a very expressive language it is fairly easy to generate complex functional tests that exercise very large parts of MySQL Cluster with fairly little effort in writing test cases.

70.1.1 QUICK WAY OF STARTING A CLUSTER USING MTR

It is very easy to start up MySQL Cluster using MTR. One simple command starts up a cluster that you can use to play around a bit with a cluster.

```
cd MYSQL_SOURCE_INSTALL_DIR/mysql-test
./mtr --start ndb.ndb_basic
```

The above commands will start up a cluster that will be up and running for about 30 minutes. The command will hang and when you press Ctrl-C the cluster and all its MySQL Servers and NDB nodes will automatically shut down. You can use *--start-and-exit* instead, this means the cluster will run until you stop it. You have to shut down the cluster yourself.

The cluster configuration is defined in the file

mysql-test/include/default_ndbd.cnf. This is the default configuration used by MTR test cases for NDB. Other test cases can use a test case specific cluster configuration.

70.2 AUTOTEST

MTR is not designed to handle the most important part of the testing of MySQL Cluster. This is restart testing. Given that MySQL Cluster is designed to survive failures in any type of operation in a distributed system the most important part in testing MySQL Cluster is testing it while crashes of various kinds are happening in the system.

To handle this testing we have built something we call autotest. This is a framework that has automated test runs such that one can run a test suite for almost a day automatically where a battery of up to 500 tests are executed one at a time. Each of those test cases can contain many different crashes. Given that crashes and failures usually don't occur in the most critical places these tests can inject errors in the code to ensure that we can test failures in all sorts of scenarios.

The test cases executed in autotest is to a great extent developed inside the Hugo framework.

Autotest is a functional test framework although it is focused on testing restart functions whereas MTR is more focused on functions used in normal operation.

Given that autotest is a generic framework testing using the NDB API and the Hugo API it is possible to run the autotest framework in many different configurations. We do have a fair amount of hardware resources that can be both used for manual testing and automated testing. Thus we have the ability to run tests in many different configurations to ensure that we can handle all sorts of configurations of MySQL Cluster.

70.3 HUGO

Hugo is a framework we developed for testing MySQL Cluster. It is very simple to setup a new test case, one describes what to do initially, what to do at the end and what to do in parallel in a number of steps. Each of those things is a function in the test program, those functions can have some simple parameters sent to them. Each of those test functions have access to a great set of Hugo functions that does things like fill a table with data, read a set of data, update a set of data, stop a node, start a node, wait for nodes to be started, run a backup, inject error codes into the data nodes and much more.

70.4 BATTERY OF TESTS

Each push we do in our testing sets off both MTR tests and autotest execution. Thus each time we push new code we are able to verify that our code changes do not introduce instabilities in the code.

70.5 UNIT TESTS

We have a set of unit tests for basic frameworks used by the MySQL Cluster code.

70.6 MANUAL TESTS

Our testers have developed their own set of frameworks to easily set up and run a bit more manual tests and do things that a user might do and see how MySQL Cluster survives those some times corrupting events.

Chapter 71

dbt2-0.37.50 Benchmark scripts

In my personal work I do a lot of work on optimising MySQL Cluster and historically I have done a lot of work on optimising MySQL/InnoDB. To be able to verify that MySQL Cluster behaves well under various load scenarios I have developed a test framework for system testing where we test MySQL Cluster under very heavy load scenarios.

This test framework grow out of the need to run the DBT2 test a bit more automated. This development started already in 2006 when I was working for a year and a half as an indepdent consultant doing various assignments around MySQL Cluster and related software.

The development was a fork of the dbt2-0.37 version. It added a set of shell scripts to automate benchmark execution. Later on in the process automated execution of sysbench and flexAsynch have been added. A few years ago we decided to make those scripts available to the public to ensure that our benchmark results can be verified. This framework has been used to run 205 million reads per second towards MySQL Cluster, to run several million SQL queries towards a cluster of MySQL Servers in MySQL Cluster using the DBT2 benchmark and to run many hundred of thousands of SQL queries on a single server using sysbench. It also works well to benchmark MySQL Cluster on tiny boxes like the Intel NUC.

When it was made public we got permission to release dbt2-0.37.50. So all new versions of this framework is called dbt2-0.37.50.X. X is currently at 15. Together with this framework we release a tarball for sysbench execution based on the sysbench-0.4.12 version. This is developed further a bit and is now in version sysbench-0.4.12.14.

In 2015 Tonci Grgin joined my performance team and as a way to get into MySQL Cluster he developed a set of benchmark scripts in PowerShell to run sysbench and DBT2 in a pure Windows environment. He developed a set of PowerShell scripts mimicking the top tool on Linux to ensure we can see what goes on in Windows when running MySQL Cluster on Windows.

These PowerShell scripts is part of the dbt2-0.37.50 tarball and likewise there is a set of perf scripts to assist in analysing performance on Linux and find bottlenecks.

The Unix shell scripts have been executed on various Solaris versions, various Linux versions and various Mac OS X versions and is likely to work well on FreeBSD versions.

71.1 How to setup benchmarks on Linux/Solaris/Mac OS X

We will describe how to prepare to run a benchmark using those scripts. At first you need to download the dbt2-0.37.50.15.tar.gz from

```
http://dev.mysql.com/why-mysql/benchmark.html
```

If you are going to run sysbench as well you need to download

sysbench-0.4.12.14.tar.gz from the same web page.

Next is that you need to download either a source tarball from dev.mysql.com or a binary tarball from the same place. It is possible to run the benchmarks against an existing MySQL Cluster installation. But here I am going to describe how to use a cluster that is used purely for benchmarking.

Next step is to create directory where you are going to run the benchmarks. In my Linux laptop that would be */home/mikael/bench*.

In this directory one needs to create a directory where the tarballs are placed. I normally call this directory *tarballs*. Next we need to have a directory to place the binary installation. I normally call this *mysql* and place it beside the *tarballs* directory. I need to have a data directory, I usually call this directory *ndb*. The *ndb* directory needs to be placed in a directory that has sufficient disk capacity and disk bandwidth to house the data files for the MySQL Server and the NDB data nodes.

If I use several machines in the benchmark I need to ensure that the benchmark machine can use SSH to log into the other computers, it needs to be setup such that one can use password-free log in between those machines using pre-installed SSH keys.

Normally all machines can use the build at the benchmark machine, in this chapter I will assume so. It is possible to use a Mac OS X computer as benchmark machine and then as part of the build do a remote build on one or more Linux machines.

When setting up a homogenous environment one needs to place the base directory (the *mysql* directory) and the data directory (the *ndb* directory) on the other machines in the same directory as on the benchmark machine.

Before starting any benchmarks ensure that the base directory and data directory can be created on all computers involved in the benchmark. The scripts will create those directories if it has permission to do so. It isn't necessary to create those directories before starting.

Now ensure that the DBT2 tarball, the sysbench tarball and the MySQL Cluster tarball is placed in the *tarballs* directory.

Next unpack the DBT2 tarball using *tar xfz dbt2-0.37.50.15.tar.gz*. Put the *bench_run.sh* script found in the *scripts* directory in the *bench* directory.

Now we need to create a directory for the benchmark run. Let's assume we are running a sysbench benchmark against MySQL Cluster 7.5.6, we could create a directory called *sysbench_756*.

In this directory we need to create a configuration file driving the benchmark. This file is always called *autobench.conf*.

A very minimal *autobench.conf* to run a sysbench benchmark needs to contain the following:

```
autobench.conf

#
# Software definition
#
TARBALL_DIR="/home/mikael/bench/tarballs"
BENCHMARK_TO_RUN="sysbench"
DBT2_VERSION="dbt2-0.37.50.15"
SYSBENCH_VERSION="sysbench-0.4.12.14"
MYSQL_VERSION="mysql-cluster-gpl-7.5.6"
MYSQL_BASE="5.7"
#
# Storage definition
#
MYSQL_BIN_INSTALL_DIR="/home/mikael/bench/mysql"
DATA_DIR_BASE="/home/mikael/bench/ndb"
#
# MySQL Server definition
#
SERVER_HOST="127.0.0.1"
SERVER_PORT="3316"
ENGINE="ndb"
#
# NDB node definitions
#
NDB_MGMD_NODES="127.0.0.1"
NDBD_NODES="127.0.0.1;127.0.0.1"
#
# Benchmark definition
#
SYSBENCH_TEST="oltp_rw"
THREAD_COUNTS_TO_RUN="1;8;32;128"
MAX_TIME="90"
```

There are example files for running DBT2, sysbench and flexAsynch benchmarks in the *examples* directory in the DBT2 tarball. In this directory there is also an *autobench.conf* that contains a fairly complete description of all the options you can place into *autobench.conf*. There is quite a lot of options that one can write into *autobench.conf*. This directory contains a few examples of larger benchmark runs done in the past. These aren't aligned with the latest version of the scripts.

The above simple benchmark will run a sysbench benchmark where each test run will run for 90 seconds, it will run 4 test runs, the first with 1 client thread, the second with 8 threads, the third with 32 threads and the last one with 128 threads.

The above definition only uses a single node of most sorts, it is possible to create multiple ones in the same variable by separating them with a semicolon (;) in the fashion used here by the NDB data nodes (NDBD_NODES). The same principle can be used also for the other nodes specified in SERVER_HOSTS and NDB_MGMD_NODES.

Important to remember is that *autobench.conf* is treated as shell script code with only variable assignments, thus no extra spaces is allowed and no empty lines and one always need to assign using quotation marks as seen in the example. Comments are allowed, comments needs to have a # in the first character on a new line and then the entire line is treated as a comment.

Now we have done all the preparations to run the benchmark by executing the *bench_run.sh* script.

The first time we execute a benchmark after installation is done we need to build both benchmark code and the mysql code. To run the first benchmark after installation we use the following command:

```
./bench_run.sh \
   --default-directory /home/mikael/bench/sysbench_756 --init
```

This script will first build MySQL (in the case of binary tarballs this means installing the binaries in the directory specified by MYSQL_BIN_INSTALL_DIR, next it will generate all the internal configurations and also the MySQL Cluster configuration file.

The next step is to start the cluster, this is done by first starting the NDB management server(s). Next the NDB data nodes are started. Next we wait for the cluster to be started. Next we start the MySQL Server(s) and wait for those to be started. This cluster start is normally only performed when the *--start* flag is set, but it is also done when the *--init* is specified.

Finally it will run the actual benchmark and produce the result files.

If we want to write our own NDB configuration file it is possible, we add *--skip-start* after *--init*, this means that we will not start a cluster and run a benchmark, we will stop after building and generating the various configuration files. Thus we can go in and edit the config_c1.ini file that contains the NDB configuration before starting the cluster. It is placed in the same directory as the *autobench.conf* file.

The MySQL Server is always started with only parameters from the command line. The reason is that the MySQL Server searches for configuration files in too many directories. I grew weary of this since there was always some config file that I missed that changed the behaviour of my benchmark and made it very difficult to analyse what was going on.

I decided to skip entirely the MySQL config files and instead set all MySQL Server parameters from the command line. Each parameter that I have needed in my benchmarks over the past 10 years have been added to the benchmark script and it is very easy to add another one. Since benchmarks are often executed on machines with other installations of MySQL it makes it a lot easier to manage benchmark executions on arbitrary machines.

The result of the benchmark is found in the *final_results.txt* file found in the *sysbench_756* directory. There will be many other files in this directory with more detailed logging of the benchmark run. The benchmark can produce a *jpeg* file with a graphical description of the benchmark run.

If you want to repeat the benchmark with exactly the same setup you can skip the *--init* flag and run again. This means we will skip the build phase, the generate phase and the start phase. The cluster will remain up and running after the first command since we didn't provide any *--stop* flag.

```
bench_run.sh --default-directory /home/mikael/bench/sysbench_756
```

If we only want to change some benchmark parameters we can go into the *autobench.conf* file and edit the parameters, for example we might want to change the *THREADS_TO_RUN* parameter to see how it goes with other thread counts.

If we now run again we need to add the *--generate* flag to ensure that we regenerate the internal config files used to drive the benchmark. Other than that the command is the same as seen here.

```
bench_run.sh --default-directory /home/mikael/bench/sysbench_756 \
   --generate
```

The *--init* command generates a file called *config_c1.ini* which is the config file for NDB. If you want to be in control of this file and edit it yourself you need to add the flag *--skip-generate-config-ini* after the *--generate* flag.

If you want to edit the configuration of the cluster we first need to stop the cluster. This can used by issuing the flags *--stop --skip-run*. This means that we skip running the benchmark but stop the cluster. Next we edit the file *autobench.conf* and after saving we now run the command with the flags *--generate --start*. This will regenerate the internal config files and the NDB config file and start the cluster using those new files and finally running the benchmark again.

```
bench_run.sh --default-directory /home/mikael/bench/sysbench_756 \
   --stop --skip-run
```

```
bench_run.sh --default-directory /home/mikael/bench/sysbench_756 \
   --generate --start
```

When starting the cluster we normally perform an initial start. This ensures that benchmark runs are done from an initial state. If we want to start and retain data from the cluster we use the flag *--start-no-initial* instead of *--start*.

Now we have all the knobs needed to run many different benchmark runs using MySQL Cluster and analyse its performance in various situations.

71.2 SYSBENCH BENCHMARK

The most common variants of Sysbench is to use the OLTP RW and OLTP RO tests. The table used in Sysbench is a very simple table with an integer primary key field, then an integer attribute and a payload CHAR(120) string.

When executing a sysbench benchmark one always starts by creating the table, filling the table with a set of rows as specified by a command parameter. Next the actual benchmark runs. After completion of the benchmark the table is dropped. A sysbench benchmark can run with several tables, we can define partitioning of the table to be a specific number of partitions using RANGE PARTITION. Another option is to use a secondary index on the integer field.

The transactions in sysbench will never change the number of rows in the table. An OLTP RW transaction starts by inserting a row, next it does 10 primary key select statements. Next it does 4 select statements that scans 100 rows in some way, the first does a simple range scan, next the scan is producing ordered result, next scan is producing distinct results and the final scan is producing a sum of the integer field on all rows. After those scans, two updating operations are done on some row and the original row inserted is deleted again.

OLTP RO is the same transaction where we skipped all inserts, updates and deletes. There are parameters when starting sysbench to decide how many primary key selects and how many scan operations of each sort we should do and how many indexed updates we should do in the transaction.

Sysbench is a very good tool to measure the most basic operations of a storage engine with very simple SQL queries. There is a lot of parallelism possible by using many threads in parallel running the benchmark. There is very little parallelism inside the individual transactions except that we scan 100 rows at a time in the scan queries which can be parallelised in a number of *ldm* threads in the NDB data nodes.

In our benchmark tool we set *SYSBENCH_TEST* to indicate which sysbench benchmark variant we want to run. The most popular variant to use is *oltp_rw* as described above. We use *oltp_ro* a lot too. We have 3 standard variants of the OLTP RW variant. These are *oltp_rw_less_read, oltp_rw_write_intensive* and *oltp_write*.

oltp_rw_less_read decreases the reads by only scanning 5 rows instead of 100 rows and only performing 1 primary key lookup instead of 10. *oltp_rw_write_intensive* changes *oltp_rw* by doing 10 indexed updates instead of 1. *oltp_write* removes all selects, both primary key lookups and scans and only performs the insert, 2 updates and a delete per transaction.

A special variant is *oltp_ro_ps*. This one only performs 1 primary key lookups per transaction. This is completely focused on the amount of very simple queries that we can perform.

There is one more set of benchmarks in the sysbench program. We run those by setting *SYSBENCH_TEST* to *oltp_nontrx*. These are used to test e.g. massive inserts into the database.

Sysbench was mainly designed for a single MySQL Server, we have however made it possible to run autonomous sysbench benchmark towards different MySQL Servers in the same cluster. Each of those tests will use its own database, thus there will be no interaction of data in one benchmark program to the other. But they will run against the same set of data nodes in MySQL Cluster.

Comparing MySQL Cluster with MySQL/InnoDB delivers better performance on OLTP RO for InnoDB since it will do the entire SQL query within one thread, in MySQL Cluster there will be many threads involved in the query since we employ a functional distribution of the various thread types.

In this benchmark it is easy to see that MySQL/InnoDB and MySQL Cluster has different design goals. MySQL Cluster has a good write scalability. Thus it can handle millions of writing transactions per second. Using the read backup feature and the fully replicated we can enhance greatly the read scalability.

MySQL Cluster really shines when you require a database engine that uses synchronous replication. You can have up to 48 data nodes that all have exactly the same data and any update from any MySQL Server will be synchronously updating all other nodes.

Sysbench is a good program to benchmark the basic access patterns for a MySQL storage engine. It can be used to check scalability, I have used it a lot to see how we can scale the MySQL Server when running with MySQL Cluster. Each MySQL Server can scale to use at least 60 CPUs. MySQL Cluster scales equally well with OLTP RO as it does with OLTP RW. This is more or less unique for a database engine. Most, if not all, other database engines scales much better when employed in read-only scenarios.

I have used sysbench to optimise in particular the scan access for MySQL Cluster. Sysbench puts some heavy requirements on the receive thread handling. In one MySQL Server running OLTP RO we have to handle more than 3 million messages arriving per second into each NDB API receive thread. Sysbench is an excellent tool to optimise the primary key access, the scheduler of the data nodes, the checkpointing and many more things.

One thing to note is that Sysbench in its original design for some reason gives a lot of deadlocks. To avoid the benchmark becoming a benchmark for handling deadlocks we implemented a flag to the sysbench program whereby deadlocks are avoided.

71.2.1   BENCHMARK PARAMETERS FOR SYSBENCH

There are a great deal of dimensions that one can use to change the behaviour of the Sysbench benchmark in these benchmark scripts. We will go through them one by one. Setting those parameters in the *autobench.conf* file will change the behaviour of the benchmark run when *BENCHMARK_TO_RUN* is set to sysbench.

MAX_TIME sets the time to execute the actual benchmark run for each thread specified. By default it is set to 60 seconds.

THREAD_COUNTS_TO_RUN is used to specify the number of threads to execute. Multiple thread counts can be tested in one test run. Separate the thread counts by using the semicolon character ;, e.g:

THREAD_COUNTS_TO_RUN="1;4;8"

By default this is set to run with 1 thread.

NUM_TEST_RUNS can be set to a number of times we want to repeat each test. By default it is set to 1.

SYSBENCH_INSTANCES is a very simple manner of parallelising the sysbench test. It will run this many number of sysbench instances in parallel using the prepare step first, then the run step and finally the cleanup step. This parameter is by default 1. If there are multiple MySQL Servers defined in the configuration the sysbench instances will spread out on those MySQL Server instances in a round robin fashion.

SYSBENCH_ROWS is used to set the number of rows per Sysbench table. The default value for this parameter is to have 1 million rows per table which means that each table will be around 130 MByte in size.

SB_NUM_TABLES can be used to use more than one sysbench table. It is set to the number of tables that are desired to be used. It defaults to 1 table.

SB_PARTITION_BALANCE can be used to set the table to use the proper partition balance. There are four options possible to set. *FOR_RA_BY_NODE* means that we will have one partition per node group, this is the absolutely minimal configuration we can use automatic settings for, it will give some imbalances in load between the threads. *FOR_RP_BY_NODE* will create one partition per node, thus we will get as many partitions per node as we have replicas. This is a good configuration for a table that is not heavily used but still can get a fair load. *FOR_RA_BY_LDM* gives us one partition per LDM per node group. This ensures that all LDMs use the table. It will not get perfect balance between threads since the primary role isn't spread among all *ldm* threads. *FOR_RP_BY_LDM* is the default table partitioning which gives us one partition per *ldm* per node. This will give perfect balance over all *ldm's*. It will give possibilities for improved restart times in the future. It is the default partition balance and should normally be used for all heavily used tables and all large tables.

SB_NUM_PARTITIONS can be used to set the number of partitions in each sysbench table. By default it is set to 0 which means a normal table for InnoDB and an automatically partitioned table for NDB. By setting it to e.g. 4 we create 4 partitions that will use RANGE partitioning on the NDB table. RANGE partitioning can be used on NDB but isn't a supported feature since it doesn't support online changes of number of partitions and it can only be used from the MySQL Server.

In a setup with only one MySQL Server and one data node this feature can still make sense since we are using NDB as a local storage engine for MySQL and this is essentially the benchmark type that Sysbench was originally designed for.

SB_AVOID_DEADLOCKS is by default set to yes. For some reason the Sysbench is designed such that deadlocks will frequently occur. To avoid that Sysbench becomes a test of deadlock handling we have changed access patterns in Sysbench such that we avoid deadlocks when running the benchmark.

SB_TX_RATE and *SB_TX_JITTER* can be used to specify the transaction rate instead of just starting the next transaction when one transaction is done. The transaction rate is provided in transactions per second and the jitter is given in microseconds of variation, by default it is 10% of the time between transactions (so the extra wait time can change from 0% to 20% of the time between transactions).

SB_DIST_TYPE can be used to change the distribution of queries in the table. This is by default set to uniform distribution. One can set a gaussian distribution and there is a very specialised version that can be used by setting it to special.

SB_USE_AUTO_INC can be set to yes to make the sysbench tables use autoincrement on the primary key of the table. By default this is not set.

SB_MAX_REQUESTS changes sysbench from running a specified time set by *MAX_TIME* to instead to run a certain number of requests specified by this parameter.

It is possible to change the behaviour of point selects. Setting

SB_USE_IN_STATEMENT to yes turns every point select into 10 point select queries by inserting a list of 10 keys instead of just one key into each point select.

SB_USE_MYSQL_HANDLER can be set to yes to make sysbench use a HANDLER query instead of a SELECT query for point selects.

SB_USE_SECONDARY_INDEX can be set to yes to create an extra ordered index on each sysbench table. This cannot be combined with an auto increment on the primary key.

CHANGING BEHAVIOUR OF *oltp_rw* AND *oltp_ro*

You can create your own version of *oltp_rw* and *oltp_ro* by changing the following parameters.

SB_POINT_SELECTS changes the number of primary key lookups from 10 to some other number (even 0 is allowed).

SB_RANGE_SIZE is used to change the number of rows in each range used by the scan queries. It defaults to 100 and can be set to any number smaller than the number of rows in the table and 0 is ok.

SB_SIMPLE_RANGES can be used to specify the number of simple range scan to perform per query, defaults to 1. Similarly *SB_SUM_RANGES* can be used to set the specific number of SUM range scans to perform per transaction. *SB_ORDER_RANGES* sets the number of order range scans and *SB_DISTINCT_RANGES* sets the number of distinct range scans.

71.3 DBT2 BENCHMARK

The DBT2 benchmark is based on the TPC-C benchmark which is a standard for benchmarking DBMSs. DBT2 does not claim to be standards compliant. For the most part when running DBT2 we skip the requirements of TPC-C in how many transactions are allowed per warehouse per time unit. DBT2 is mostly used to test open source DBMSs and those rarely can afford the millions of dollars of HW equipment to run a standards compliant TPC-C. But DBT2 is a good compromise that uses the same queries and same table distribution, but with more queries per warehouse per time unit.

DBT2 is a benchmark where each transaction is executed in the context of a warehouse. Thus as long as there is at most one transaction per warehouse executed at a time there is no risk of deadlocks. This means running with 1 terminal per warehouse in DBT2 language. A terminal is in practice implemented by one thread. Given that normal DBT2 execution runs a new query in a thread as soon as one is completed it means that using a lot of terminals per warehouse gives rise to a lot of deadlocks. We rarely go beyond 3 terminals per warehouse and usually stay at 1 or 2.

DBT2 is useful to demonstrate scalability of MySQL Cluster. Already in 2015 we were able to run more than 2 million SQL queries against a set of MySQL Servers in the same cluster.

DBT2 is useful to test real-time response time requirements. It was an important tool in developing an improved scheduling algorithm in 7.4.

DBT2 runs 5 different transaction types. The DBT2 transactions are fairly complex and use a fairly large number of SQL queries of which a large part is updating SQL queries. It is a somewhat realistic benchmark in that sense although most real applications probably do a lot more reading and less writing.

71.3.1 RUNNING A DBT2 BENCHMARK

To execute a DBT2 benchmark one uses exactly the same commands as to run sysbench using the *bench_run.sh* script. The only difference is the content of the *autobench.conf* file. To run DBT2 benchmarks we normally use another file placed in the same directory called *dbt2_run_1.conf*. This file contains the number of MySQL Servers, the number of warehouses and the number of terminals per warehouse used in each benchmark step.

```
autobench.conf

#
# Software definition
#
TARBALL_DIR="/home/mikael/bench/tarballs"
BENCHMARK_TO_RUN="dbt2"
DBT2_VERSION="dbt2-0.37.50.15"
MYSQL_VERSION="mysql-cluster-gpl-7.5.6"
MYSQL_BASE="5.7"
#
# Storage definition
#
MYSQL_BIN_INSTALL_DIR="/home/mikael/bench/mysql"
DATA_DIR_BASE="/home/mikael/bench/ndb"
#
# MySQL Server definition
#
SERVER_HOST="127.0.0.1;127.0.0.1"
SERVER_PORT="3316"
ENGINE="ndb"
#
# NDB node definitions
#
NDB_MGMD_NODES="127.0.0.1"
NDBD_NODES="127.0.0.1;127.0.0.1"
#
# Benchmark definition
#
DBT2_WAREHOUSES="128"
DBT2_DATA_DIR="/home/mikael/bench/dbt2"
DBT2_TIME="90"
```

One additional detail is that to run DBT2 one needs to define all the data to be loaded into the MySQL Server in the load phase. This is a set of CSV files that are loaded before the actual benchmark starts running. These files need to be generated before the benchmark can start running. This must be done as part of the build, when running the *--init* command one needs to add another parameter *--generate-dbt2-data*. When this parameter is set we will ensure that all CSV files for the warehouses used in the benchmark are created.

To run DBT2 one needs to define all the data to be loaded into the MySQL Server in the load phase. This is a set of CSV files that are loaded before the actual benchmark starts running. These files need to be generated before the benchmark can start running. It is important to set *DBT2_WAREHOUSES* to a number of warehouses which is as big is we will use in our benchmarking. This is the number of warehouses we will create CSV files for and the number of warehouses that we will load into the cluster. Each warehouse consumes a bit more than 100 MByte of data in each set of CSV files and that will be loaded into the database in the load phase.

One natural way of handling is to run with *--init --generate-dbt2-data* and *--skip-run --skip-start* at the first run of the benchmark. When we have built all CSV files we can use *--start* on the first benchmark run.

```
bench_run.sh --default-directory /home/mikael/bench/dbt2_test \
   --init --generate-dbt2-data
bench_run.sh --default-directory /home/mikael/bench/dbt2_test --start
```

Here is the content of *dbt2_run_1.conf* file:

```
dbt2_run_1.conf

#NUM_MYSQL_SERVERS NUM_WAREHOUSES NUM_TERMINALS
1                  1              1
1                  4              1
1                  16             1
1                  64             1
2                  1              1
2                  4              1
2                  16             1
2                  64             1
```

We show an example using two MySQL Servers since DBT2 is intended for testing clusters and not just single node installations. Two MySQL Servers used towards a cluster with two data nodes is the minimal test setup that the test is aiming at.

One additional thing is that if we have already loaded the data and makes another test run we might want to skip the loading phase. The loading phase is normally done in each DBT2 benchmark. But by setting the parameter *--skip-load-dbt2* we can skip the load phase. Important to remember here is that the database grows for each DBT2 run since all new order transactions generates new records. Thus results for later runs are not exactly reproducable compared to the first one although the difference is not likely to be very big.

Also for DBT2 we produce a file called *final_results.txt* that contains a summary of the test results. In the test directory we will have the following directories with more detailed information about the test runs. *dbt2_logs* contains a log of the load phase. *dbt2_output* contains many details about the actual test runs, it contains the output from both the client program and the driver program. The client program is the program interacting with the MySQL Server and the driver program controls benchmark execution by interacting with the client program. The directory *dbt2_results* contains summary results for the benchmark runs, these files are used as intermediate files to produce the final result file.

We produce intermediate results in a file called *intermediate.log* in the driver directory in the output directory of the benchmark run. This is useful to see how the benchmark results vary over time and also to follow the benchmark in real-time. The output from the sysbench program when running sysbench also have this feature of reporting results every 3 seconds.

71.3.2 BENCHMARK PARAMETERS FOR DBT2 TESTS

When running the DBT2 benchmark we can change the table definitions of the tables in various ways. We can either define the DBT2 tables using PARTITION BY KEY or PARTITION BY HASH. The default beahviour in MySQL Cluster is to use PARTITION BY KEY. We always ensure that all tables in the DBT2 benchmark partition using the warehouse id as the partition key and not the full primary key. PARTITION BY HASH isn't fully supported yet in MySQL Cluster. At the same time it delivers more predictable benchmark results since if I make a benchmark run with 12 warehouses then it is easy that the warehouses are not evenly divided among the *ldm* threads due to normal statistical variation. To get more predictable results I often use PARTITION BY HASH since that delivers a perfect distribution of warehouses to *ldm* threads.

The *DBT2_PARTITIONS_TYPE* is set to HASH for PARTITION BY HASH and to KEY to use PARTITION BY KEY, it is set to KEY by default. When using PARTITION BY HASH it is important to specify the number of partitions, this should be done in the parameter *DBT2_NUM_PARTITIONS*. It can be set when using PARTITION BY KEY, but here the defaults will work just fine. We will by default only create the hash indexes for the primary keys. If it is desirable to run the test with ordered indexes defined on the tables one should set the parameter *DBT2_PK_USING_HASH* to be empty.

By setting *DBT2_LOADERS* we define how many parallel loaders we will use to load up the warehouses. This is set to 8 by default.

DBT2_WAREHOUSES sets the number of warehouses to load before starting the benchmark. *DBT2_TIME* sets the time for each run of the DBT2 benchmark.

We have a complex parameter called *DBT2_SPREAD*. This parameter can be used to make DBT2 execution perfectly scalable. Normally each MySQL Server will run the benchmark against all warehouses. However using the parameter *DBT2_SPREAD* we can ensure that each MySQL Server only works with a subset of the partitions. E.g. if we have 4 node groups and set the spread to 4 it means that the first MySQL Server will only use warehouse with id 0,4,8 and so forth. Thus it will always work with the first node group of the data nodes if using PARTITION BY HASH. This is not used by default.

We can change the port numbers used by clients to listen to the driver. This is by default set to 30000. By setting *FIRST_CLIENT_PORT* we use a different range of port numbers.

71.4   FLEXASYNCH BENCHMARK

flexAsynch is a benchmark program that puts the NDB data nodes to the ultimate test. For a benchmark that runs SQL, the overhead of running the MySQL Server consumes most of the CPUs available. To get the data nodes to show their possibility the benchmark needs to use the NDB API directly.

The flexAsynch benchmark not only uses the NDB API directly, it even uses the NDB API in the most efficient manner possible by using the asynchronous NDB API.

The flexAsynch was the inspiration to designing the *ndb_import* program that is used to quickly load data into NDB. This program is introduced in 7.6.

```
autobench.conf

#
# Software definition
#
TARBALL_DIR="/home/mikael/bench/tarballs"
USE_BINARY_MYSQL_TARBALL="no"
BENCHMARK_TO_RUN="flexAsynch"
DBT2_VERSION="dbt2-0.37.50.15"
MYSQL_VERSION="mysql-cluster-gpl-7.5.6"
MYSQL_BASE="5.7"
#
# MySQL Server definition
#
SERVER_HOST="127.0.0.1"
SERVER_PORT="3316"
ENGINE="ndb"
#
# Storage definition
#
MYSQL_BIN_INSTALL_DIR="/home/mikael/bench/mysql"
DATA_DIR_BASE="/home/mikael/bench/ndb"
#
# NDB node definitions
#
NDB_MGMD_NODES="127.0.0.1"
NDBD_NODES="127.0.0.1;127.0.0.1"
#
# Benchmark definition}
#
FLEX_ASYNCH_API_NODES="127.0.0.1;127.0.0.1"
FLEX_ASYNCH_EXECUTION_TIMER="60"
FLEX_ASYNCH_NUM_THREADS="16"
```

The benchmark definition of a flexAsynch program is simple. The software definition needs the MySQL tarball and the scripts from the DBT2 tarball. It requires the storage definitions.

The only reason we need a MySQL Server is that the start of a cluster always starts the MySQL Servers, the MySQL Server isn't needed in the benchmark, but it is required when starting the cluster.

There is one important detail to consider, the tarball must be a source tarball since the flexAsynch program isn't part of the binary tarball delivered in MySQL Cluster tarballs. It is part of the MySQL Cluster source tarballs. One need to set the *USE_BINARY_MYSQL_TARBALL* set to no.

71.4.1 DESCRIPTION OF FLEXASYNCH PROGRAM

At first the flexAsynch program have a number of definer threads. These thread defines the operations to execute in the benchmark. In a real application they would be handling incoming requests to the application and setting them up to execute queries against NDB.

In flexAsynch they create an operation using a random generator. The next step is a crucial step to create scalability. In this step the random key is used to calculate the primary replica node of the record. This can be done by creating a transaction in the NDB API and using the key to get a transaction record on the proper node. Next the NDB API is used to ask for what node we got and immediately after this we close the transaction. In almost all cases this method can be applied without communication, only the first few calls will get a record from each data node. After that it is reused over and over again.

The node id is used to calculate which execution thread to take care of the request. The definer thread sends the operation to an executor thread.

The number of definer threads is by default 2, it can be changed with the parameter *FLEX_ASYNCH_DEF_THREADS*.

The number of execution threads must be a multiple of the number of data nodes in the cluster. This is for simplicity of writing flexAsynch. In a real application it might be done differently. If the number of nodes is 4, the execution threads should be 4,8,12 and so forth. The number of execution threads is set with the parameter *FLEX_ASYNCH_NUM_THREADS* used above.

Each group of threads handling all nodes in the cluster is called a thread group, with e.g. 16 threads and 4 nodes we will have 4 node groups. The number of thread groups must be a multiple of the number of definer thread. This particular case the number of definer threads must be either 1, 2 or 4.

Each executor thread becomes responsible for only one node, thus it will be very efficient in sending data to this node. It will use large sends and will receive large sends returned with data.

FLEX_ASYNCH_EXECUTION_TIMER is the time that the benchmark will run to gather statistics for the test run.

A benchmark using flexAsynch always goes through the following phases.

1. Create tables

2. Insert data into tables

3. Read data from tables

4. Update data in tables

5. Read data from tables

6. Delete data in tables

7. Drop tables

It is possible to change many of these steps, it is possible to insert other steps in the middle of the execution to test various forms of node restart handling.

There can be literally hundreds of flexAsynch programs running in parallel. flexAsynch have been used to demonstrate 205 million reads per second. In this benchmark there were about 70 large machines used to run flexAsynch programs and 32 data nodes used. The bottleneck was that the flexAsynch programs still could not get the data nodes to be fully loaded since we run out of API nodes to use for driving the benchmark. Each API node was capable of driving around 1 million reads per second.

71.4.2 PARAMETERS WHEN RUNNING FLEXASYNCH

flexAsynch is an asynchronous program that can run many transactions in parallel in each thread. The number of parallel transactions per thread is set by *FLEX_ASYNCH_NUM_PARALLELISM*. We can even have multiple operations per transaction with parallel transactions and the number of parallel operations per transaction is set by *FLEX_ASYNCH_NUM_OPS_PER_TRANS*.

Thus the total of key operations per round of execution is the multiplication of number of flexAsynch programs, the number of execution threads (default 16), the number of parallel transactions per thread (default is 32) and the number of operations per transaction (default is 1). In this case the number of operations per round is 1 * 16 * 32 * 1 = 512. But it is easy to set up a benchmark with 32 nodes, 256 parallel operations and 64 threads thus giving 512k operations in each round of execution.

In the parameter *FLEX_ASYNCH_EXECUTION_ROUNDS* we set the number of execution rounds to use.

With *FLEX_ASYNCH_USE_WRITE* we can change all inserts and updates to instead use writes.

CONTROLLING COMMUNICATION USED BY FLEXASYNCH

Each flexAsynch program is mainly limited by the number of cluster connections used. By setting *FLEX_ASYNCH_NUM_MULTI_CONNECTIONS* we can increase the throughput per flexAsynch program. By default it is set to 1. Each cluster connection uses one API node id and at most 255 nodes can exist in the cluster.

When *FLEX_ASYNCH_FORCE_FLAG* is set we ensure that we send the request immediately when a thread is sending.

CONTROLLING THREAD USAGE USED BY FLEXASYNCH

We can limit the number of threads used by the insert phase and the delete phase. It is not necessarily optimal to use the same amount of threads during insert and update as during read phases. This is set by *FLEX_ASYNCH_MAX_INSERTERS* which by default is to use the same number of execution threads as for all other phases.

CONTROLLING TABLES USED BY FLEXASYNCH

We can define both the number of attributes (*FLEX_ASYNCH_NUM_ATTRIBUTES*), the size of the attributes (*FLEX_ASYNCH_ATTRIBUTE_SIZE*), the number of tables used (*FLEX_ASYNCH_NUM_TABLES*), the number of ordered indexes used (*FLEX_ASYNCH_NUM_INDEXES*) and we can define whether to use restorable tables (*FLEX_ASYNCH_NO_LOGGING*).

CONTROLLING TIMING BY FLEXASYNCH

To ensure that all flexAsynch programs are running in parallel in the various phases some test phases have a warmup phase and a cooldown phase. This applies to the update phase and the read phases. These phases have a warmup timer (*FLEX_ASYNCH_WARMUP_TIMER*) attached to it and a cooldown timer (*FLEX_ASYNCH_COOLDOWN_TIMER*) attached to it.

CONTROLLING CPU USAGE BY FLEXASYNCH

We can control CPU usage by the flexAsynch program by setting *FLEX_ASYNCH_DEF_CPUS* for definer threads, *FLEX_ASYNCH_RECV_CPUS* for NDB API receive thread and *FLEX_ASYNCH_EXEC_CPUS* for execution threads.

A simpler variant is to simply use the *BENCH_TASKSET* also for flexAsynch.

In most cases where I have tested I have always used a full machine for running flexAsynch, this haven't been much used by myself.

CONTROLLING EXECUTION PARTS OF FLEXASYNCH

We can control which phases to skip and after which phase we should stop.

FLEX_ASYNCH_END_AFTER_CREATE set to yes means we are ending after creating the tables.

FLEX_ASYNCH_END_AFTER_INSERT set to yes means we are ending after the insert phase.

FLEX_ASYNCH_END_AFTER_UPDATE set to yes means we are ending after the update phase.

FLEX_ASYNCH_END_AFTER_READ set to yes means we are ending after the read phase.

FLEX_ASYNCH_END_AFTER_DELETE set to yes means we are ending after the delete phase.

FLEX_ASYNCH_NO_UPDATE set to yes means we are skipping the update phase.

FLEX_ASYNCH_NO_DELETE set to yes means we are skipping the delete phase.

FLEX_ASYNCH_NO_READ set to yes means we are skipping the read phase.

FLEX_ASYNCH_NO_DROP set to yes means we are skipping the drop table phase.

By default these are all set to no.

71.5 RESTART TESTS

We have used these benchmark suites to test restarts. So far the restart is not performed in these cases while doing traffic. But we have the ability to run any benchmark and after its execution we will restart a node or the entire cluster.

To enable restart tests set *NDB_RESTART_TEST* to yes and set to *NDB_RESTART_NODE* to the node id you want to restart or set it to all if you want to perform a cluster restart.

By setting *NDB_RESTART_TEST_INITIAL* to yes we get the node restart to be an initial node restart (it doesn't affect the cluster restart above).

This test has been mostly used in combination with the flexAsynch program where we can stop after any phase to test the restart performance.

71.6 ADVANCED CONFIGURATIONS

The advanced configuration settings are used to define where to store the files of the various nodes involved, to define the configuration used by the MySQL Server and the NDB data nodes and to define the hosts running the various nodes. We will show the config parameters that can be set in *autobench.conf*, in most cases those parameters have a one-to-one mapping to either MySQL Server parameters or NDB parameters.

71.6.1 SOFTWARE DEFINITIONS

Regarding software definitions it is mostly the build of source tarballs that we can change. We can set *COMPILER_FLAG* to the compiler we want to use (mostly gcc is used). We can set *WITH_PERFSCHEMA_FLAG* to compile without performance schema, by default we compile with performance schema. We can set *USE_FAST_MYSQL* to no to avoid compiling with the highest level of optimisation. We can even compile with feedback compilation where we make a test run with sysbench before recompiling with information gathered from this test run. Set *FEEDBACK_COMPILATION* to yes try this out (not very well tested and needs a MySQL source tarball).

To build with MySQL source tarball one needs to set the parameter

USE_BINARY_MYSQL_TARBALL to no, by default we will assume that the MySQL tarball is a binary tarball.

It is possible to set *CLIENT_MYSQL_VERSION* if a different MySQL version used for the client program. This variable should point to an already installed MySQL version.

Sysbench and DBT2 programs are always compiled as part of the build process.

Once upon a time it was even possible to run the benchmark from Linux towards a Windows server. This code haven't been used for many years but could probably be made to work again fairly quickly. Nowadays we use a special PowerShell program to run Sysbench and DBT2 on Windows.

By setting *BUILD_REMOTE* to yes and by setting *REMOTE_SRC_INSTALL_DIR* to the installation directory on the remote box it is possible to e.g. run benchmark from a Mac OS X machine and have some of the programs running on a set of Linux boxes. Probably mostly useful to myself.

71.6.2 STORAGE DEFINITIONS

No specific additions here are needed.

71.6.3 MySQL SERVER DEFINITIONS

As mentioned all the parameters for the MySQL Server is coming from the command line. Thus all these need to be added in the benchmark scripts and set in *autobench.conf*. If a parameter is missing it is straightforward to add it.

First add the default by declaring the new parameter in *bench_run.sh*. Next add the parameter in the method *write_iclaustron_conf* in *bench_run.sh*. Go into the benchmark script *start_ndb.sh* and look at the already existing code to add the new parameter in a similar fashion.

Here is a list of the parameter currently set for the MySQL Server.

At first we generate some code based on which version we are executing that points to the correct place of the MySQL Server binary. Secondly we have similar code to point to the correct place of the language files for error messages. We always use english as the language.

Next we always ensure that a core file can be produced. After that we start the MySQL Server possibly with some CPU locking directives and some *LD_PRELOAD* directives to use the proper malloc library.

Next we will always set the parameters *--no-defaults* and *--secure-file-priv=*. The first one ensures that we only accept command line parameters and that we don't read any MySQL configuration files from anywhere. The second one ensures that we can load data from a file as part of the DBT2 benchmark. This is deemed an insecure setup for production usage but for a benchmark it is ok.

Next follows a whole range of InnoDB options, these are only set if running with InnoDB as the storage engine. We will not document them here. Look into the scripts and the documentation of the DBT2 tarball for more details on these if you want to use these scripts to run benchmarks against InnoDB. I did that myself for a few years, but now my focus is on MySQL Cluster so I haven't updated those parts the last couple of years.

Next we skip the grant tables to ensure we don't have to work with passwords for the MySQL Servers at test.

We set *--max-tmp-tables* to 100, to change it set *MAX_TMP_TABLES*.

By default we run without activating the performance schema. To activate it set *PERFORMANCE_SCHEMA* to yes. It is possible to set *--transaction-isolation* by setting

TRANSACTION_ISOLATION. NDB only supports *READ_COMMITTED* so it only makes sense when running with InnoDB for the moment.

We always shut off the Query cache by setting *--query-cache-size=0* and *--query-cache-type=0*. We set *--temp-pool=0* always. To avoid running out of prepared statements we set *--max-prepared-stmt-count=1048576*. We always set *--bind-address* to the hostname of the MySQL Server. We set the socket file to file in the */tmp* directory named with mysql and the number of the node id of the MySQL Server.

We set *--sort-buffer-size* to 32768 and it can be changed with *SORT_BUFFER_SIZE*. No slow query log or general log is currently activated. The error log is simply called *error.log* and placed in the data directory of the MySQL Server.

--table-open-cache and *--table-definition-cache* are both set to 4000 by default, to run with very high number of threads this could be increased even further by setting *TABLE_CACHE_SIZE*. *--table-open-cache-instances* is set to 16 by default and for runs on very large servers set it to something on the order of number of cores used by the MySQL Server by setting *TABLE_CACHE_INSTANCES*.

To set *--memlock* set *LOCK_ALL* to yes. To set *--large-pages* set *USE_LARGE_PAGES* to yes. By default *--tmp-table-size* is set to 100M. To change this set *TMP_TABLE_SIZE* appropriately. Similarly *--max-heap-table-size* is set to 1000M and can be changed by setting *MAX_HEAP_TABLE_SIZE*. *--key-buffer-size* is set to 50M and can be changed with *KEY_BUFFER_SIZE*.

--server-id is automatically set to the node id of the MySQL Server.

It is possible to run the MySQL Server with a binlog activated. Set the *BINLOG* parameter to set the base name of the binlog files. *SYNC_BINLOG* is used to set *--sync-binlog* and is by default 1. Also a few more parameters are available for setting the binlog behaviour that are not documented here.

The *--join-buffer-size* is set to 1000000.

--ndb-autoincrement-prefetch-sz is set to 256 by default and can be changed with *NDB_AUTOINCREMENT_OPTION*. Join pushdown is activated by default using *ENGINE_CONDITION_PUSHDOWN_OPTION* set to yes. We always run with *--ndb-use-exact-count* set to 0.

--ndb-index-stat-enable is always set to 0. This feature is very useful in many cases, but not for these benchmarks where queries are ensured to always run with optimal query plans.

To run with the NDB Cluster storage engine we set *--ndbcluster*. We set *--ndb-extra-logging=0* and we set *--new* to enable the use of PARTITION BY HASH and similar unsupported features.

By setting *CORE_FILE_USED* to yes we ensure that core files are created when the MySQL Server fails.

We will set *--tmpdir* to */tmp*, *--datadir* will be set to the selected place of the MySQL Server based on the setting of *DATA_DIR_BASE*. Similarly we will set the *--basedir* parameter, the *--pid-file* parameter and the port number set through *SERVER_PORT*.

When running with a commercial version of MySQL Cluster we can decide to use the threadpool. The parameters *THREADPOOL_SIZE*, *THREADPOOL_ALGORITHM*, *THREADPOOL_STALL_LIMIT*, *THREADPOOL_PRIO_KICKUP_TIMER* are used to configure the thread pool.

IMPORTANT PARAMETERS

These are the parameters that are most likely to need change in your benchmark runs.

If you want to run any benchmarks with more than 1000 threads you need to set *MAX_CONNECTIONS* to an appropriate value, this sets *--max-connections*.

To create tables using the Read Backup feature set *NDB_READ_BACKUP* to yes. Similarly to create tables using the fully replicated feature (affects all tables) set *NDB_FULLY_REPLICATED* to yes. Neither of those are activated by default.

Force send can be effective sometimes and sometimes not. It can be set or unset using the parameter *NDB_FORCE_SEND*. By default it is set to yes.

Very important for scalability is the manner in which NDB API receive threads acts in the MySQL Server. By setting *NDB_MULTI_CONNECTION* to a number larger than 1 we can increase the scalability of the MySQL Server, each cluster connection will scale to around 8-16 CPUs dependent on workload. This sets the configuration option *--ndb-cluster-connection-pool*.

We can set the locking of these NDB API receive threads using the

NDB_RECV_THREAD_CPU_MASK parameter. This parameter can be set for several MySQL Servers by using the ; as separator. To e.g. bind 4 cluster connections to 4 CPUs one can set it to 4-7 or 0,1-3. This sets the parameter *--ndb-recv-thread-cpu-mask*.

We can set the activation threshold for when the receive thread starts taking over from user threads. This is set by setting *NDB_RECV_THREAD_ACTIVATION_THRESHOLD*. It sets *--ndb-recv-thread-activation-threshold* and is not set by default in which case it will be 8.

CPU LOCKING DIRECTIVES

It is very important to control CPU placement options when executing a benchmark. when running on the same machine this ensures that these programs runs on different CPUs. For the MySQL Servers we can control this using a number of benchmark parameters that can be used irrespective of which benchmark to run.

At first we need to set *TASKSET* to the program used for locking to CPUs. If we want to use the program *taskset* we set *TASKSET* equal to *taskset* and set the CPUs to be locked in the parameter *SERVER_CPUS*.

If we set *TASKSET* to *numactl* we use *SERVER_CPUS* to define the CPUs to lock the MySQL Server program to. With *numactl* we can set to which numa nodes the MySQL Server should bind its memory to by using *SERVER_BIND*. One can set the memory allocation policy to local or interleaved using *SERVER_MEM_POLICY*.

On Solaris we use *TASKSET* equal to *psrset* instead.

If these variables only have one definition it will be applied to all MySQL Servers. If we have e.g. 2 MySQL Servers defined we can provide one CPU locking directive for each MySQL Server. We use ; as separator.

Here is an example of setting definitions when using 2 MySQL Servers.

```
TASKSET="numactl"
SERVER_CPUS="1-3,61-63;4-6,64-66"
SERVER_BIND="0"
SERVER_MEM_POLICY="local"
```

71.6.4   NDB NODE DEFINITIONS

When we start the NDB data node we use the parameter *USE_NDBMTD* to decide if the binary *ndbmtd* will be used. It is set to yes by default. We ensure that we start the binary from the correct directory (the placement of the binary in MySQL installations have varied a bit in different releases). Other than that we set *--ndb-nodeid* to the node id decided for the data node. We set the flag to be *--initial* when we start from scratch. This is affected by how we start the benchmark.

We set the NDB connect string properly to point to the NDB management server. We can set core files to be used with *CORE_FILE_USED* set to yes. Most other NDB node definitions are inserted into the NDB configuration file that is called *config_c1.ini*.

If we decide to use realtime scheduler we need to start the data node using sudo. This happens if *NDB_REALTIME_SCHEDULER* is set to yes.

The following parameters are set unconditionally to change the defaults of the NDB configuration.

BatchSizePerLocalScan is set to 128, *MaxBufferedEpochs* is set to 500, *FragmentLogFileSize* is always set to 256M, *DiskSyncSize* is set to 32M, *BackupLogBufferSize* is set to 4M, *TransactionDeadlockDetectionTimeout* is set to 10000, *LongMessageBuffer* is set to 128M, *InitFragmentLogFiles* is set to full, *RedoOverCommitLimit* is set to 45, *DataDir* is set to *DATA_DIR_BASE*/ndb and *Numa* is set to 1.

The following parameters are changable but should normally not need changes. *NDB_MAX_NO_OF_CONCURRENT_TRANSACTIONS* sets *MaxNoOfConcurrentTransactions* and is by default set to 131072.

NDB_MAX_NO_OF_CONCURRENT_OPERATIONS sets *MaxNoOfConcurrentOperations* and is by default set to 131072.

NDB_MAX_NO_OF_CONCURRENT_SCANS sets *MaxNoOfConcurrentScans* and is by default set to 500.

NDB_MAX_NO_OF_CONCURRENT_LOCAL_SCANS sets *MaxNoOfConcurrentLocalScans* and is by default set to 8000.

NDB_BACKUP_WRITE_SIZE sets BackupWriteSize and is set by default to 1M. *NDB_BACKUP_MAX_WRITE_SIZE* sets BackupMaxWriteSize and it also sets

BackupDataBufferSize and it is set by default to 2M.

One can set *TimeBetweenLocalCheckpoints* by setting

NDB_TIME_BETWEEN_LOCAL_CHECKPOINTS.

Similarly one can set *MinDiskWriteSpeed*, *MaxDiskWriteSpeed*,

MaxDiskWriteSpeedOtherNodeRestart, *MaxDiskWriteSpeedOwnRestart* by setting

NDB_MIN_DISK_WRITE_SPEED, *NDB_MAX_DISK_WRITE_SPEED*,

NDB_MAX_DISK_WRITE_SPEED_OTHER_NODE_RESTART, and

NDB_MAX_DISK_WRITE_SPEED_OWN_RESTART.

It is possible to set NDB data nodes to compress LCPs by setting

NDB_COMPRESSED_LCP to 1.

One can set *SchedulerResponsiveness* and *___sched_scan_priority* can be set through *NDB_SCHEDULER_RESPONSIVENESS* and *NDB_SCHED_SCAN_PRIORITY*.

RedoBuffer is set to 64M by default and can be changed with *NDB_REDO_BUFFER*.

Log levels in NDB data nodes can be set through *NDB_LOG_LEVEL*.

One can set NDB to use *O_DIRECT* by setting *USE_NDB_O_DIRECT* to yes. One can set the parameter *DiskIoThreadPool* by setting *NDB_DISK_IO_THREADPOOL*. We can set *DiskPageBufferMemory* by setting *NDB_DISK_PAGE_BUFFER_MEMORY*.

We can set send buffer memory sizes by setting *TotalSendBufferMemory* through *NDB_TOTAL_SEND_BUFFER_MEMORY* and setting *SendBufferMemory* by setting *NDB_SEND_BUFFER_MEMORY*.

We can change *TimeBetweenWatchDogCheckInitial* from its setting of 180000 by setting *NDB_TIME_BETWEEN_WATCHDOG_CHECK_INITIAL*. We can set *SchedulerSpinTimer* by setting *NDB_SCHEDULER_SPIN_TIMER*.

IMPORTANT PARAMETERS FOR NDB

We need to ensure that *DataMemory* is set to be sufficiently large to run the benchmarks at hand. This is set to 3G by default.

IndexMemory is necessary to set on 7.5 and earlier versions. This is set by setting *NDB_INDEX_MEMORY*.

It is important to define the proper settings for *ThreadConfig* where we can define the proper settings for how to lock threads to CPUs and some other things. How to define this is properly walked through in the chapter on Advanced thread configuration in NDB. Setting this is done through *NDB_THREAD_CONFIG*. It can be set differently for the NDB nodes by using ; as separator.

Normally an advanced setting of *ThreadConfig* is the most important part of setting up the benchmark.

A simpler approach is to use the configuration parameter

MaxNoOfExecutionThreads set by *NDB_MAX_NO_OF_EXECUTION_THREADS*, this can be set differently using ; as separator. To lock to CPUs this variable uses *NDB_EXECUTION_CPUS* that sets the *LockExccuteThreadToCPU* configuration variable. The CPUs defined in this will be used to lock the threads defined by *MaxNoOfExecutionThreads*.

If this is set to 9 or higher the number of threads is the number set, thus the number of CPUs should be the same number. However for smaller numbers 0-3 uses 4 threads, 4-6 uses 5 threads and 7-8 uses 7 threads. To lock the IO CPUs use the *NDB_MAINT_CPUS* to set the *LockMaintThreadsToCPU* variable, if *ThreadConfig* is used this isn't used.

Hostname for each NDB data node comes from the *NDBD_NODES* parameter.

Setting up the REDO log parameters is usually important. This is set up through *NDB_NO_OF_FRAGMENT_LOG_FILES* that sets *NoOfFragmentLogFiles*. This is the number of log files of size 256 MBytes that is present in each log part. The number of log parts is set through *NDB_NO_OF_FRAGMENT_LOG_PARTS* that sets *NoOfFragmentLogParts*. Number of log files is 4 by default and so is number of log parts. The default REDO log file size is 4 * 4 * 256 MByte = 4 GByte.

IMPORTANT NOTE:

The number of log parts should always be set equal to the number of LDM threads in the data node. Otherwise the load becomes very unabalanced between the LDM threads.

NDB_REPLICAS can be set to use something other than 2 replicas (or 1 replica with one data node).

Often when one runs benchmarks for MySQL Cluster one gets access to very high-end machines with lots of CPUs but with insufficient disks to run MySQL Cluster the way they should be setup. To use these machines we have the ability to run *Diskless* and this can be set by setting *NDB_DISKLESS* to yes.

71.6.5   Malloc library settings

The default malloc library is usually the *libc* library. This library isn't very scalable on large servers. To benchmark on larger computers it is essential to use a proper malloc library.

To use a specific malloc library first set *USE_MALLOC_LIB* to yes. Next point to the malloc library using the parameter *MALLOC_LIB*. *MALLOC_LIB* should contain the full path to the malloc library to be used.

Personally I prefer using *jemalloc*. However in a recent version of *jemalloc* some scalability hogs was introduced. This scalability hog was used to ensure that memory that was free'd was made available to everyone again. To do this a *mmap* call is used. This call has a global mutex which puts a scalability limit on usage with *jemalloc*. To avoid this scalability hog in jemalloc use the parameter *PREPARE_JEMALLOC* and set it to yes. This will avoid returning memory from the program and thus avoid the *mmap* calls.

Another popular alternative is to use the library *tcmalloc*.

71.6.6   Generic benchmark settings

We have a number of generic benchmark parameters that define how the benchmarks are executed.

Both DBT2 and sysbench use a prepare phase followed by an execution phase. The prepare phase might affect the execution phase if they are too close in how checkpoints are executed (this is mostly used for InnoDB tests). To specify the time between prepare and execute phase use the parameter *BETWEEN_RUNS*, it is set to 1 second by default.

When we are starting up the cluster we will use a create database command to see if the MySQL Server is up and running. At first we wait for the number of seconds specified in the parameter *AFTER_SERVER_START* before we start checking if the MySQL Server is up and running. This is set to 10 seconds by default. Next we attempt to create a database, if successful we move on. If not successful we wait for the number of seconds defined in *BETWEEN_CREATE_DB_TEST* before we make another attempt, this is set to 5 seconds by default. We will perform the number of attempts specified in the parameter *NUM_CREATE_DB_ATTEMPTS* before we decide to give up. This is set to 40 by default.

After stopping the cluster we will wait for a few seconds before proceeding, this is mostly to ensure that the cluster stopped to ensure that a subsequent run that starts the cluster again will not fail. This delay is set in the parameter *AFTER_SERVER_STOP* and is set to 5 seconds by default.

We can set a parameter *TEST_DESCRIPTION* that is used to describe the graphs produced in the benchmark results in the *.jpeg* files.

CPU LOCKING DIRECTIVES

We can lock the benchmark programs to specific CPUs. This ensures that we can shield the CPU usage from the benchmark programs from the CPU usage of the programs we are testing. This uses exactly the same manner as when locking the MySQL Server CPUs except that we use the variables *BENCH_TASKSET*, *BENCHMARK_CPUS* and *BENCHMARK_BIND* instead.

CHAPTER 72

HISTORY OF MySQL CLUSTER

The history of MySQL Cluster started in 1989 when I received some personal inspiration to study for a Ph.D in mathematics and databases. At the time I had a bachelor's degree in Mathematics and Mathematical Statistics and was already signed up at the Stockholm University as a Ph.D student in the mathematical statistics department with Professor Anders Martin-Löf as my professor. At the time I was working at a small company, Tech Trade, developing a LAN product called MicroLink. There was no way to start the Ph.D studies immediately since I had already started a family and needed the income from working.

A year later I started working at Ericsson in the department providing courses on the Ericsson systems. Working at the course department of Ericsson was an excellent place to start my studies, I prepared classes in ISDN, object-oriented technology, testing telecom switches and a whole range of other topics.

After a bit less than a year working at Ericssson the opportunity to start working on databases emerged. The department was going to develop a course on a new DBMS for the AXE telecom switch, DBS (Database Subsystem). I volunteered to participate in this development and spent a few months developing a course on databases and as a start had some deep-dive courses on the relational database model provided by some experts in the field. At the same time I started taking some Ph.D courses at the Stockholm University on databases.

After developing this course for a few months I realised that I was more inclined to developing software rather than to teach about software. In the summer of 1991 I applied for a new job at the Ericsson systems department where I would focus on system studies around DBS and other technologies in the AXE systems architecture.

This was a perfect place to learn about developing software. AXE Systems contained several million lines of code, it had software that was developed in close cooperation with the department developing the APZ (the operating system and CPU of the AXE system). It had a unique architecture that both had very good development characteristics as well as very good performance.

During the first year in this department I spent my time learning about many different things and learnt how to manage projects and many other things.

I learnt one thing which I consider to be an important lesson of my life. I saw many people at Ericsson discussing software architectures using Power Point slides. I met a few people extremely skilled at describing systems using Power Point slides. I learnt a great deal of both presentational skills and Power Point development through those persons. These competencies came to very good usage later when I had innumerable meetings with various venture capital funds, large companies, early customers, Ericsson venture fund managers and many, many others.

The most important lesson I learned was that in Power Point development you can never convince anyone about the best architecture to use. I had many experiences where I tried to convince persons about the problems with various architectures. I noticed that on a Power Point slide you could easily make some penstrokes and all of a sudden you had solved the architecturial issue. The only problem was that many of those penstrokes would cost a million manhours to implement in real life and so wasn't really possible.

The lesson I took away from these years was that if I wanted to convince people about how to develop an architecture I had to do it by building it.

My first endeavour in this was in the area of the CPU of the AXE, the APZ. There was a lot of development going on in the industry where CPUs were developed to make use of pipelining to raise the CPU frequency in the 90s. I worked with some developers to suggest that the APZ would use similar concepts in the next version. My arguments was well received and it looked promising, but the direction was sent off in a different direction by a team that wanted to build upon the old APZ architecture.

I realised that the ideas I had developed was not going to win this battle. However I knew that in a few years yet another APZ project would start again. I decided to spend some time proving that the use of high-speed CPUs using lots of pipelining was better equipped to handle the ever increasing loads, compared to specialised CPUs that were expensive to develop and manufacture.

Since I was working on both APZ projects and at the same time dived deeply into working on databases it was natural for me to see how to make DBS, the database in AXE available in a set of SPARC computers. I got to buy a set of the most modern SPARC computers at the time, I got to buy SCI cards from Dolphin that made it possible to retrieve data from DBS in less than 100 microseconds even using very early versions of SCI and using a very slow APZ emulator running on the new SPARC machines.

I continued this work and built a more and more efficient APZ emulator and a more and more efficient communication framework based on SCI. At the same time I continued my studies on distributed databases. I had lots of contacts and discussions on cooperations with the team that developed ClustRa. It is another distributed database developed for telecom requirements, we joined forces with some of those developers again when MySQL was acquired by Sun 2008 since ClustRa had been acquired by Sun many years earlier. The original NDB API implementation is heavily inspired by the API used by ClustRa.

In 1996 this prototyping work and research work led to a point where it became clear that I needed to develop a new database engine. DBS was not possible to base the development on for various reasons, the APZ framework turned out to be an excellent environment to build a distributed database around since it had a message-oriented architecture.

Thus I could develop NDB and at the same develop AXE VM which was used as a base for developing APZ VM which is the engine that modern AXE switches runs on. At this point in time (1996) I had developed all the ideas on what NDB should contain, now everything was prepared to start developing NDB.

The two developments did go hand in hand for a few years and a first prototype of NDB was developed together with Telia and demo:ed in late 1998.

After this the development was handled as a "skunk" project in Ericsson for a year until it found a new home in Ericsson Business Innovation. A major reason for this to occur was an email sent to the CEO of Ericsson at the time Sven-Christer Nilsson that he forwarded to among others Ericsson Business Innovation. In Ericsson Business Innovation I met with Gunnar Tyrsing a very competent young manager that did a comet career in Ericsson. I had met him in one of my Ph.D courses and he immediately saw the potential for MySQL Cluster when we met and discussed what could be done of the work that I was doing. His approval of the idea was what it made it possible for it to find a new home in Ericsson Business Innovation.

After an evaluatory period in Ericsson Business Innovation an internal Ericsson venture was started at the 17th of June 2000 and we started building a bit bigger project and we started building a very strong development team where many of those original developers are still at MySQL in important positions.

In those days the IT boom was still ongoing so we started building NDB towards financial applications, particularly around the stock market and our first customer that tried it was a company that was active in swedish stock market. In 2001 we delivered the first 1.0 version to a customer, quickly followed by a 1.1 version. This version was completely focused on the real-time response requirements and NDBs ability to handle high write loads. This version still hadn't got any working node recovery, only complete cluster recovery.

The stock market boom came to an abrupt ending in 2001, so this market more or less disappeared. It was natural to find a new market to focus on. Given that NDB was designed for the telecom market we therefore decided to return to the telecom market. This started an intense development period where we added node recovery and the backup feature. We created a version 2.11 in 2002 that was a fairly good version.

We didn't get any market success in this year, most of the potential customers were asking for an SQL interface. Eventually we decided to implement an SQL interface. We built a complete SQL engine on top of the NDB API in a short time. We continued our development and we bumped up to version 3. This led to some first success with customers as well.

At the same time Ericsson was going through a lot of problems where they downsized from 110.000 employees to 47.000 employees in a few years. At the end of this downsizing the entire Ericsson Business Innovation company was downsized. In early summer of 2003 we got an assignment in our venture to find a new owner.

We were successful in finding a new owner quickly. We were particularly fond of the concept of joining MySQL. Joining MySQL meant immediately that we got access to a more complete SQL engine. It meant that the software would become open source which was interesting in itself. We joined MySQL at the 2nd of September 2003.

MySQL at the same time was in a growth period after receiving funding for going against the enterprise market. MySQL Cluster was a clustering solution that at the time wasn't available in MySQL.

When we joined MySQL we had gotten our first success in the market when we got Bredbandsbolaget as a customer. We developed the first production version of MySQL Cluster, version 3.4 in close collaboration with Bredbandsbolaget. We even had our office in the same place as Bredbandsbolaget, so their key developer could come into us and ask for help at any time and we could go into him and assist him at any time.

The first production version we provided was at the end of 2003 and it wasn't yet a

MySQL version, it was a standalone NDB Cluster using our internal SQL engine. But most of the application development of Bredbandsbolaget was made against the NDB API and they developed a quite sophisticated application for handling DNS, DHCP and other similar services. As far as I know this application is still used and I used it myself for a long time since I had Bredbandsbolaget as my internet provider for almost 10 years.

When we joined MySQL, we started working hard on the NDB storage engine. At the MySQL Users Conference in 2004, in Orlando, Florida, we presented the very first version of MySQL Cluster which was version 4.1.3.

We had some market success fairly early on and already in 2004 we had started working with some major telco vendors.

Most of the rest of the history of MySQL Cluster is pretty well known and can be found on the internet. Personally I spent a few years focusing on other aspects of MySQL such as MySQL Partitioning, scaling MySQL from 4 CPUs to 64 CPUs, and a few other scalability projects. The development of MySQL Cluster was done in very close cooperation with our biggest users. There is still a close cooperation with our biggest users, but at the same time we are focusing on requirements from more traditional SQL applications and have implemented a few such things in version 7.5.

A quick recap is that we added disk data support and a revamped node recovery algorithm in MySQL 5.1 which was presented at the VLDB conference in Trondheim in 2005.

Given that we needed to develop new versions at a higher speed than MySQL versions were provided we started delivering specific MySQL Cluster versions based on MySQL 5.1. We delivered 6.1, 6.2, 6.3, 7.0 and 7.1 based on MySQL 5.1. In 7.2 we upgraded to MySQL 5.5 and in 7.3 we upgraded to MySQL 5.6 and in 7.5 we upgraded to MySQL 5.7.

Until version 6.3 NDB data nodes had a single execution thread. This version was a great market success and is most likely still in active usage in many sites. I spent a lot of time ten years ago as a consultant working with MySQL, Intel and Dolphin to provide scalable benchmarks using version 6.3 of MySQL Cluster. I have continued this tradition in working with Intel together with MySQL to provide new benchmarks of our flexAsynch benchmarks delivering 205 million reads per second in 2013 using version 7.3.

With the introduction of multi-core CPUs it was obvious that we needed to scale up both the NDB data nodes and the NDB API. The first multi-threaded version of MySQL Cluster was 7.0, we added a lot more mult-threading in 7.2. In 7.3 we focused on scaling up the NDB API. 7.4 was focused on improvements of the restart times and on improving speed of scans.

In 7.5 we decided to make MySQL Cluster useful in more scenarios by adding more options for read optimisations. MySQL Cluster have always been very good at write speed, with MySQL Cluster 7.5 the ability to read at high speed was added by ensuring that we always read any local replica available.

CHAPTER 73

MySQL Cluster versions

We currently maintain 4 GA versions, 7.2, 7.3, 7.4 and 7.5. We constantly test and verify that all these versions can be both upgraded and downgraded to and from. In this chapter I will give a short summary of the key features and reasons behind the versions.

73.1   MySQL Cluster 7.5

MySQL Cluster 7.5 is the current GA version.

The focus on quality continued in 7.5. The 7.5 is most definitely the most stable MySQL Cluster version we have released.

73.1.1   Read Backup

A first step in focusing on SQL users meant that we provided a read backup feature that makes it possible to read any replica and not just the primary replica.

73.1.2   Fully replicated

Tables and even the entire cluster can now be fully replicated. This will improve query performance significantly for many applications.

73.1.3   New send thread design

Experiments in 7.4 showed that the send thread design could be improved to provide even better predictable latency. In 7.5 all threads can assist the send threads based on their current CPU usage levels.

This feature was an important feature to improve performance of HopsFS to reach millions of file operations per second.

73.1.4   Improved scalability of scans

Previously scans only scaled to a few hundred thousand scans per second, this is now removed and millions of scans per second can be executed per node.

This was very important to make HopsFS scale to millions of file operations per second.

73.1.5   Scheduler configuration

Even more work was put into predictable latency where the scheduler can be configured a bit more than before.

73.1.6 UPGRADE TO MYSQL 5.7

Upgrading to MySQL 5.7 meant among other things that we can now use JSON and that we have a bit more support for GIS features.

73.1.7 CPUSTAT AND MANY MORE NDBINFO TABLES

CPU tracking and many more ndbinfo tables were introduced in 7.5.

73.1.8 LINUX REPOS FOR INSTALLING MYSQL CLUSTER 7.5

A very important thing for making MySQL Cluster more adjusted for mass usage is the introduction of Linux repos for MySQL and now also for MySQL Cluster 7.5.

73.2 MYSQL CLUSTER 7.4

The focus in 7.4 was on quality improvements, improved restart times and improved scan performance. Quite a few new ndbinfo tables were added. There was some major efforts in developing the MySQL Cluster Replication solutions for conflict detection described in this book.

It is in very popular use by many users today.

73.3 MYSQL CLUSTER 7.3

MySQL added foreign key support that had been requested for a long time. It upgraded to MySQL 5.6 and the NDB API was redesigned to better handle machines with large number of CPUs. A Node.js connector (Database Jones) was introduced in this version.

73.4 MYSQL CLUSTER 7.2

MySQL Cluster 7.2 was and is still a successful release. There are still quite a lot of users on this version. It was a version that stabilised much of the development in MySQL Cluster 7.0 and 7.1. It upgraded to using the stable MySQL 5.5 release.

Pushdown joins was introduced in MySQL Cluster 7.2.

The ability to manage users in the cluster through distributing the privilege table was added in 7.2. It hasn't been described in this book, check the MySQL manual for a description of how to use it.

73.5 MYSQL CLUSTER 6.3

MySQL Cluster 6.3 was a very successful release. It was the last release where only the single threaded *ndbd* data node program was available.

CPSIA information can be obtained
at www.ICGtesting.com
Printed in the USA
LVHW102315141019
634227LV00014B/1811/P